MATTHEW BOURNE
and his Adventures in Dance

Alastair Macaulay has been chief dance critic of the *New York Times* since 2007, living in New York. Before that, he lived and worked in London. He served as chief theatre critic of the *Financial Times* (for which he also reviewed dance and music) between 1994 and 2007, as chief dance critic to the *Times Literary Supplement*, and as a leading examiner and lecturer in dance history at various academic institutions in Britain. In 1983, he was founding editor of the British quarterly *Dance Theatre Journal*. In 1988 and 1992, he served as guest dance critic to the *New Yorker*. In 1998, his biography of Margot Fonteyn was published by Sutton Books. He has contributed to books on the choreographers Frederick Ashton, Merce Cunningham, and Mark Morris.

MATTHEW BOURNE
and his Adventures in Dance

Conversations with Alastair Macaulay

faber and faber

First published in 2000

by Faber and Faber Ltd

Bloomsbury House
74–77 Great Russell Street
London WC1B 3DA

This revised edition first published in 2011

Typeset by RefineCatch Limited, Bungay, Suffolk
Printed and bound by CPI Group (UK) Ltd, Croydon, CR0 4YY

A CIP record for this book
is available from the British Library

ISBN 978–0–571–23588–9

6 8 10 9 7 5

In Memory
June and Jim Bourne and Simon Carter

Contents

List of Illustrations

Photographs courtesy of the generosity of AMP.

xiii

Introduction

In 1990, the choreography of Matthew Bourne was at British fringe-group status; and the dance company, Adventures in Motion Pictures, nearly folded, after four years of presenting dances by him and several other choreographers. As fringe-level companies go, it had enjoyed real success, giving several dozen performances per annum; and if it had closed operations then, it would have been remembered fondly.

Instead, however, in 1991 it became devoted solely to his choreography, at a time when very few British dance companies were vehicles for the work of one choreographer alone. The risk paid off. During the 1990s, Adventures in Motion Pictures went on to achieve major international success, running for months in London's West End, on New York's Broadway, and elsewhere. His *Swan Lake* – one of the dance sensations of the decade – became a set text for Dance A Level in Britain. This range of achievement was already phenomenal. In consequence, the enterprising Walter Donohue at Faber and Faber conceived the original edition of this book, *Matthew Bourne and his Adventures in Motion Pictures*, to meet the broad spectrum of interest in his work; it was published at the end of 1999. Neither a biography nor a critical study, it charted the story of how Bourne had risen to such eminence. It also allowed him to speak at length about his work and about aspects of the wider world it inhabits. At every point he answered questions with an openness and detail that I found unequalled among choreographers.

In the first decade of the new millennium, Bourne and his work went further, achieving levels of box-office popularity that have seldom if ever been matched in dance. In 2002, he reconstituted his company as New Adventures; the new name was justified by the success that followed. There were several seasons mid-decade in which two or three different Bourne dance productions were presented simultaneously – in large-scale theatres, seven or eight performances per week, for months on end – in separate international and national tours by his company. (In 2006, for example, his *Swan Lake* opened an extended season in Paris while his

Edward Scissorhands was touring the United States.) Few other dance companies can manage to present simultaneous different productions in different countries, fewer in big theatres, and no other company presents just one choreographer's work on this scale and with this frequency. Meanwhile Bourne's choreography for various musicals – notably *My Fair Lady* (2001), *Mary Poppins* (2004) and *Oliver!* (revised, 2008) – has run for years in the West End, on Broadway, and on major tours. BBC-TV screened his *Bourne to Dance* on Christmas Day 2001; his *Play Without Words* began life at London's National Theatre in 2002; in 2003, his *Nutcracker!* was the first stage dance production to be screened on BBC1 on Christmas Day in twenty years. He has received honours, prizes, and awards in several countries: not least, in 2003, the Shakespeare Prize in Hamburg, given each year to a leading British artist (he was the first dance person to have won it since Margot Fonteyn in 1977). In 2009, when watching his *Dorian Gray* (2008) at Sadler's Wells Theatre in London, I became aware that people around me in the audience were listing the various Bourne productions they had now seen in the way that London theatregoers used to follow the plays of Noel Coward or Alan Ayckbourn.

This would already be remarkable if Matthew Bourne were a playwright or director. What makes it extraordinary is that his productions – apart from the musicals – do not use words. He is now among the rare choreographers whose own genre of dance theatre has become an important form of drama.

Whether it will survive him cannot yet be said. The choreographer Salvatore Viganò (1769–1821) was known as 'the Shakespeare of the dance' in his lifetime, but, as Stendhal records, within twelve years of his death none of his ballets were to be seen. Bourne's work – like that of choreographers from George Balanchine to Pina Bausch – depends on dancers who know just what he wants. A number of prestigious companies have applied to present several of his productions without success because he insists that they cannot be relied upon to perform them with the right style. Dance is the art of the present tense: the triumph of one performance does not guarantee the success of the next. But it is worth recording that between 2000 and 2009 Bourne's triumphs (controversies, too) have occurred in many countries, on several continents, and in such historic cities as London, Los Angeles, Moscow, New York, Paris, Sydney, and Tokyo. The length of the 2006–7 tour of his *Edward Scissorhands* around North America – six months – surpassed the duration of even the longest tours by the Royal Ballet in the 1950s and 1960s. Soon after the 2000 premiere of *The Car Man*, Walter Donohue began to speak of a new edition of our book; the new chapters in it chart some of the developments in Bourne's work and his company's.

Matthew invited me to collaborate with him in 1998 on the first edition because we were friends and because I had watched most of his choreography since 1984. We first met each other in autumn 1982. I was twenty-seven, he twenty-two. He was starting his first term as a BA student in Dance Theatre at the Laban Centre for Movement and Dance; his classes there were the first formal study of dance he had ever undertaken. Today, when over a thousand students each year graduate in the UK with BA degrees in dance, it may be hard to imagine how things felt in 1982, when the Laban Centre's course was the only BA in dance in Britain and dance studies as an academic subject were an embattled area. I had begun teaching there in 1980. I doubt that any of my teaching colleagues felt confident at the time that the students of that era would make serious names for themselves in the world of dance. And yet the amalgam of students and teachers made the Laban Centre of that era fertile ground. Laban students who joined between 1980 and 1987 went on to make careers as professional dancers, dance critics, choreographers, dance teachers, dance scholars, and dance examiners. The Laban Centre has kept changing and growing; in 2001, it moved on to architecturally acclaimed new premises, and today's students would laugh in horror at the conditions with which Matthew and his contemporaries once coped.

Something in Matthew's mind made him particularly responsive to the subject I was teaching there: dance history. It is startling to recall now that in his very first October–December term we surveyed, as part of a course on nineteenth-century ballet, *La Sylphide*, *Swan Lake*, and *The Nutcracker*, all works that he went on to re-choreograph with great success in the following decade. I taught 'the two Freds' – Astaire and Ashton – with particular love; they already were Matthew's two favourite choreographers. For the second half of his degree, Matthew took dance history as his optional subject; his special subject in his final year was Astaire's choreography.

In those years, I was also working hard as a dance critic. I often encountered my students at London dance events and became involved in many passionate and analytical conversations. Several of the works we discussed then have turned out to be precursors of aspects of work Matthew went on to make in later years: Ian Spink's *Further and Further into Night* (1984), a remarkable work not seen on stage since 1985, seems to have been a particular influence upon Matthew's *Play Without Words* (2002), which was performed far and wide over three years.

When I was able to, I also watched performances of the students' own choreography. In spring 1984, when I for the first time watched choreography by Matthew and his contemporaries, his was the offering that impressed me most. The two pieces he showed during his third year more than confirmed my view. From that first piece, I still recall the unusual feeling for movement shown by one particular step; from the second, a wonderfully exuberant grasp of changing ensemble patterns and structures; from the third, ardently percussive and syncopated rhythm. As it happens, his choreography tutors did not think him the best of the bunch. I take pride in being first to single him out, responding to his work as a critic rather than as a teacher.

Perhaps a tutor can do nothing more important than encourage and help a student to find where his or her potential lies. Many students graduate with a still hazy idea of that potential. Of those that have begun to recognize it, some then fulfil it, others do not. I have encouraged other student choreographers or critics or historians who then made little headway; several have prospered long-term. More than any student of mine, Matthew has progressed – as this book records – to greater achievements. This speaks not of those of us who taught him but of Matthew himself. He has had an astonishing career because of the way he has remained true to himself, and because of the remarkable support (and never pressure) that his parents, June and Jim Bourne, gave him at every stage.

I am not Matthew's tame critic; he is not Trilby to my Svengali. It was always understood that, if the choice had to arise, I would set criticism above friendship. I took care not to review the early performances of Adventures in Motion Pictures; the company quickly attracted attention from critics and promoters without my help. *Greenfingers*, an early and short-lived work made by Matthew for AMP, was privately dedicated to me: I reviewed neither that nor most other AMP productions. When I spoke or wrote to Matthew about my reactions to his work, those were not all favourable. I don't recommend that artists read reviews of their own work, and I suspect that Matthew has never seen my most extensive published review of his choreography (in the *Times Literary Supplement* in 2005). In 1995, however, when I wrote a review of his *Highland Fling* (then a year old) for the *Financial Times*, he wrote to thank me, more for the particular reservations I expressed about the piece than for my overall enthusiasm for it. This review, he claims, strengthened his resolve about the line he was planning to take with his next work, *Swan Lake*. That's privately gratifying for me, but more important is that Matthew takes ideas from right, left or centre without seeking to please me or any other critic.

If you've marked somebody's dance-history essays, it's not hard for you to find fault in his or her choreography. Still, if you praise that choreography, other people may assume you're doing so just to promote your pal. (Or, in this case, to advance sales of this book.) When I began work as chief dance critic to the *New York Times* in 2007, I made it clear that in general I would avoid reviewing Matthew's work in its pages. Some promoters have told Matthew that they assume his work will now receive good reviews in the *New York Times*; he tells me he has replied, sometimes ruefully, 'That's not how it works!'

When Matthew invited me to join him in 1998 on the first edition of this book, I did not know how interesting the work would prove; I'm grateful both to him and to Walter Donohue. For that first edition, Matthew and I taped most of the interview material between May and July 1998, with a few additions prior to publication late in 1999. Thanks to Walter's encouragement and reminders, Matthew and I taped a series of further conversations between 2001 and 2009. We retain Chapters 1–10 of the earlier edition here, and have now added seven further chapters. I have re-ordered and edited the transcripts of those conversations to make them more direct for readers. Matthew and I have gone on tailoring them, often by email.

Matthew is remarkably undefensive and unguarded in discussing his work, but his memory is often faulty or weak. Mine, by contrast, is notoriously fussy and detailed. I have often found myself discovering things that it would have been more convenient if Matthew had remembered all along. For example, he always used to say that the first ballet he ever saw was Peter Darrell's production of *Swan Lake* for Scottish Ballet, as performed at Sadler's Wells in 1979. In 1998 I realized that he had seen another *Swan Lake* before that, and thought it might be a delicate moment when I had to point this out to him; Matthew was amazed, but laughed. Another tricky moment arose around the same time. After more than two months' hard work, I discovered, from a conversation over coffee with his colleague Etta Murfitt, that Matthew, before making his own *Swan Lake* with Adam Cooper as the Swan, had first choreographed a *Dying Swan* solo for Cooper; despite days of talking about *Swan Lake* and Cooper, Matthew had simply overlooked this. 'There's something you've forgotten to tell me,' I remember saying. Matthew listened, grinned, and said, 'Oh yes. You weren't asking the right questions.' If this new edition contains any other signs of my having omitted to ask the right questions, I apologize.

I was greatly assisted by many people at Adventures in Motion Pictures in the first edition of this book: notably the producer and co-director Katharine Dorè; the designer Lez Brotherston; the dancers and associate directors Etta Murfitt and Scott Ambler; and the dancers Adam Cooper, Will (William) Kemp, and Ben Wright. For this edition I have had help again from Katharine Dorè, Lez Brotherston, and Will Kemp. Robert Noble, Ben Chamberlain, and Simon Lacey at New Adventures, Thomas Schumacher at Disney, the composer Terry Davies, the director Richard Eyre, the press officers Lucinda Morrison and Mary Parker at the National Theatre, the producer Cameron Mackintosh, and the New Adventures dancers Gareth Charlton, Steve Kirkham, and Richard Winsor all checked parts of the book and provided further or revised material. Matthew Bourne, with whom I began interviews for this edition in 2001, has checked and revised each chapter many times; Walter Donohue and Katherine Armstrong have been kind, patient, encouraging, and thorough editors. To all of these, my thanks.

A.M.
April 2011

i Matthew Bourne. Photo courtesy of Matthew Bourne.

I

Early Life
1960–82

MATTHEW BOURNE: When I was young, I believed that you could be cured by music; that when I was ill, if I put on my favourite music, it would make me better. Not just make me happier; I actually thought it would cure me. And I still feel that music is therapeutic. I remember my mum telling me that I would pick up songs before I could put sentences together. And today I can still recite hundreds of song lyrics. Later, I used to sing along with records a lot – really loudly, not just humming away. I used to perform in the same way as years later I did in ballet classes: all feeling and no technique! But I used to feel it so much.

I think all those things contributed to what I'm doing now. It's about feeling music, which is the basis of what I do.

ALASTAIR MACAULAY: *What were your schooldays like?*
MB: I think I was leading some kind of double life. I just had no interest in what was going on at school at all. I wasn't made to enjoy literature, or art, or anything that I came to love later on.

My interests were very different from everyone else's there. I wasn't into the current trends, or the current music. I already had my own interests. At school my best friend was Simon Carter; he remains my closest friend. I got to know him when I was eleven. It was quite a rough comprehensive school, in Walthamstow. We were very much a pair there, quite gossipy. That probably made getting through the whole thing tolerable.

What we were doing – especially between the ages of fourteen and sixteen – was autograph-collecting. We would come straight from school on a 38 bus to first nights and hotels, stage doors and all that. That, I feel, was my education. Sometimes we'd get someone's

1 Bourne, aged about fifteen, in an amateur piece *Mr Bojangles* (*c.* 1974).

autograph without really being aware of whose it was, but once we had it in our collection, we would look up who they were and would find out everything about them. If there was a playwright we'd not heard of, we'd find out who he was and what he'd done, and we'd follow his work from that point onwards.

AM: *I have a friend who, aged forty-three, admits that she still does Oscar acceptance speeches to the bathroom mirror. Were you that kind of child?*

MB: Yes. Not exactly Oscar acceptance speeches, but the first time I ever did an acceptance speech for an award – even though you feel very naff and pretentious in saying the things you say on those occasions – it felt strangely like something that I'd always wanted to do; and I think the same now if someone asks me for my autograph. It's very strange to be on the other side of things.

AM: *Do you ever now get the urge to ask somebody for their autograph?*

MB: Yes, I do. In a roundabout way, though. When Adventures in Motion Pictures took *Swan Lake* to Los Angeles, we found that the celebrities there very much expected to come round and congratulate us after the show. So I kept a visitors' book in my dressing-room and asked if people would write in it before they left. That, in a sense, was still keeping up the old thing, but now at a more personal level. It's one of the lovely things that have happened to me. When someone's seen something you've done and admired it, then there is dialogue instantly; and often the admiration is mutual.

AM: *Your boyhood was in Greater London – in Walthamstow. How much of your childhood, and how much of your very gradual process of becoming a creative artist, was connected with being a Londoner?*

MB: A lot. I've recently seen documentaries on TV of Kenneth Williams and Noël Coward. In both cases it was mentioned that they spent an enormous part of their childhood or early teenage years on buses around London, taking in a whole variety of people and life. Well, I was like that. So was my mother, funnily enough. In her teenage years she was all over London, in queues for theatres and seeing various performers at the Palladium, and so on. She was always there in the queue, on her own. I think access to all that influenced me a lot.

I think now that I was very into self-education, without knowing it. In 1979, when I was nineteen, I saw my first ballet, *Swan Lake*. I wonder now: what made me go to Covent Garden, then to Sadler's Wells? I know that I went on my own. I think that I thought it was about time I saw a ballet, to see if I liked it; and the 38 bus went past Sadler's Wells and through the West End. Later I did the same with opera, which, to a lesser degree, I followed up for a while. Opera hasn't become the big thing for me that dance became, but I went because I felt that this was something to be discovered. With most things, no one encouraged me to do it; I did it myself. And I read books because I felt, 'I've not read that author – and I should do.'

AM: *Your parents obviously gave you terrific freedom to go out by yourself to the West End.*

MB: They did, but maybe because my mum knew that's what she had done. I don't think they had any idea of what I should be doing with my life. I don't even remember a conversation about 'what I was going to do'. I did A levels, and then I'd had enough of education, because I didn't feel I was gaining anything from it – even to the point where I did English Literature A level without actually reading the set books. I read Brodie's Notes; I just had so little interest in it.

So I applied for a job at the BBC. In a completely naive way, I thought that it would have some connection with entertainment. Quite soon afterwards I was offered a job in an office there, and I would get to watch all the radio shows. But it was an extremely naive approach; I can't even imagine what was going on in my head at the time.

AM: *Did the world seem either a frightening place or a strange place to you, the larger world beyond home?*
MB: I don't think it felt frightening. I had a happy home life with my parents and my brother Dan. I wasn't pressurized too much by them to be or do anything; and I was doing amateur theatricals all through those years.

AM: *I know you began to make shows for your own amateur company. How old were you when you started this?*
MB: The first production I staged was when I was five or six, I think. I did some fairy story that I've forgotten, something about the king's gold shoes. I remember the actual shoes – but not much about the rest of it.

But I was allowed to put on productions at school. Nothing with a script, but probably with music. I used to do productions of films that I'd seen, purely from memory, and I'd put them on with people in my class. Then it got to the point where I was allowed to pick from anyone in the school to do my shows. I did *Lady and the Tramp* and *Mary Poppins,* even *Cinderella.* I cast my brother as Cinderella; I was an ugly sister. All the men were women, all the women were men. It's very odd thinking that that's what I was doing then! I was probably about eight or nine at the time.

AM: *How much of these shows would have been dance? How much would have been speaking or singing?*
MB: It's difficult to remember completely, but I think it was a combination of songs and, certainly, some dancing and an improvised script of scenes. I don't remember writing anything or people having to learn words. I don't know what they were like, but they must have been reasonable, otherwise the authorities wouldn't have allowed me to do them. This wasn't part of what was going on at school; it was done outside of school. Then the school all piled in to watch.

So, at that point, I was seen to be someone who obviously wanted to act or work on stage; but then, when puberty hit, I became very introverted and quiet. At school, I never let that side come out again. I went on doing all my amateur shows, but only on the outskirts of school, not within school.

AM: *Using school friends?*
MB: Very rarely. I was almost embarrassed about it. At our school the girls were extremely rough, much more so than the boys. They used to beat you up. The fact that you liked to dance or sing wasn't the sort of thing you'd want known about yourself. So it was done with other people unconnected with school. My parents ran youth clubs, were youth workers for many years, and so had access to halls where I was able to have space to rehearse in the evenings. So it would be people who lived down the street, and friends of theirs – people at the youth clubs maybe – anyone interested who would be prepared to give up two evenings a week.

And I belonged to a Methodist church. One of the reasons I liked it so much was that there was a choir attached to it. We used to sing in the church every Sunday, rehearsing on a Tuesday evening; we also did shows, twice a year, of songs. I contributed numbers to those which involved dancing; and from that I formed another company, which was allowed to put on shows at the church hall and used guests from the choir. All this was when I was about fourteen or fifteen.

Then I had another company called Pumps when I was in my late teens – about seventeen, eighteen – which rehearsed and performed at youth clubs.

AM: *Would the numbers in these shows involve singing as well? Or would they be all dance?*
MB: The choir shows and the earlier shows had singing in, but that element gradually disappeared. By the time of the Pumps company, it was much more about dancing – and putting on a show.

I wasn't thinking in terms of myself as a choreographer, but I used to watch shows and films, and would want to imitate what I saw. People now would say I was inspired by what I saw; but I used to think purely in terms of: 'Let's steal that movement', and 'Let's try and do that thing that I remember'. I had no qualms about stealing, because I didn't feel I was in any kind of professional atmosphere.

AM: *During your childhood and adolescence, were you ever keen on the pop music of the day?*

MB: Not especially at the time, no. As an eighteen-year-old I started to go out and visit discos, around the time when disco was very big; but I wasn't buying a lot of the music. I enjoyed it, but I was listening to other things at home.

I was always into things from the past, really. The earliest things I was listening to were mostly shows, musicals.

AM: *Did you go endless times to* The Sound of Music?
MB: Yes, many times! You see, it was the first film that I saw at the cinema. I think I was taken to see it on my fifth birthday.

AM: *From that it was a mere skip to* Mary Poppins?
MB: Yes, very soon afterwards. After that, anything with Julie Andrews in it: *Star, Thoroughly Modern Millie . . .* But I was also very into *Funny Girl.* And plenty of other musicals, adaptations of stage shows that were made into films around that time. I remember seeing a lot of things on TV as well, a lot of MGM musicals – *Singin' in the Rain, The Band Wagon, Seven Brides for Seven Brothers, Kiss Me Kate,* all those things.

AM: *Were you a child of* West Side Story?
MB: Yes, very much. I regularly saw it at the cinema. It used to be on quite a lot then.

AM: *So now, having grown up through all of that, you find that, for pleasure, your musical taste is generally from Gershwin and Irving Berlin through to Rodgers and Hammerstein?*
MB: Yes. The sort of golden age of songwriters. I love the melody, and the wit of the lyrics. I love the way the words go into your memory without your having made any effort to learn them.

When I was using taped music for a lot of the pieces we were performing, I quite often incorporated these songs into what I was doing; and I could relate the movement to the lyrics – which is a very enjoyable way of working. You've got something to go on all the time; you can have fun with the way you go with or against the words. But ultimately I wouldn't be challenged in a theatrical way by that music, in the way I am by a score of Prokofiev or Tchaikovsky, where I feel the music's been designed to tell stories with movement.

AM: *Did your taste go back as far as ragtime?*
MB: Yes. In the 1970s Scott Joplin became popular with the film *The Sting*; and I liked that very much. That's how I got introduced to him,

6

and that's why one of the first ballets I ever saw was Kenneth MacMillan's *Elite Syncopations* – because it was set to Joplin music, and had been on TV.

AM: *In your mid-teens you came across two shows that were a revelation to you. One was* Gypsy, *the other was* A Chorus Line. *What was it about them that so impressed you?*
MB: *Gypsy* gave me a love of live theatre. I wanted to be in it; I wanted to be part of that world. It is the ultimate theatre piece in many ways. It was at the Piccadilly Theatre – where we've performed *Swan Lake* and *Cinderella,* over twenty years later! – and Angela Lansbury played Mama Rose.

The amazing thing about Mama Rose is that, if it's played by the right person, she is an ordinary woman with an ambition for living through her daughters; and whether or not it's true that she could have been a star herself, that is what she has eating away at her.

AM: *Does this dichotomy express anything of what you were talking about in yourself? You're an ordinary chap who's happy to be a Londoner – but would you say you had a driving ambition to make it in showbiz?*
MB: I've never thought about it before, but now you've said it, I suppose there is something there, yes. Because the autograph-collecting was a way of being involved on the sidelines. It's meeting people in a very superficial way, but it's a way of being close to that world; and I suppose Mama Rose is the same. The closest she can get is to make her children, who aren't actually very talented, into something. But she's got the drive to make them do it, even though they don't particularly want it.

I've always said that I haven't got drive or ambition. Other people say that I have, but I don't see it. Other people say that I'm a workaholic, but I feel as though I'm lazy. I do spend all my time doing work-related things, I suppose.

AM: *So it is ambition of a kind; and you've lived with it for so long.*
MB: Yes. I was desperately jealous of child stars when I was a child myself, desperately jealous. I absolutely hated Mark Lester, who was Oliver in the film; I really wanted to be him. And the children in *Chitty Chitty Bang Bang* . . . I remember thinking, 'How do you get to do that? How did they get those parts?'

7

AM: *Then you saw* A Chorus Line.

MB: I was sixteen. The difference is that it was more of a personal revelation to me. I saw it eleven times.

To hear people talking honestly about themselves – those monologues – revealing things about themselves and talking about their sexuality and family problems. Not that I was a problem person, but I did have my sexuality to deal with. I didn't come out to myself as gay until I was eighteen, but certainly I began to acknowledge that after seeing *A Chorus Line*. I think it was a great piece to have seen at that age. It was the beginning of me looking into myself, of being able to see who I was: turning the tables, and asking myself, 'What am I? What are my feelings and ambitions?'

AM: *Had you at any point found yourself in a milieu where you thought, 'This panics me. This is more than I can handle,' or just 'This is alien to me'?*

MB: Certainly there was one experience like that. I did try acting at one point, when I was fifteen, at Mountview theatre school. It was only an evening course that was supposed to lead to other things. I thought, because I was so into young film actors, such as Mark Lester and Jack Wild, that that was what I wanted to do. So I went there – and absolutely hated it. I didn't feel that I could be inventive in any way as an actor. There were acting games, which were like torture to me. I didn't enjoy the creative aspect of what I was being taught there at all; I hated speaking and felt that I was terrible at it. It didn't feel like the right form of expression for me.

AM: *Obviously you watched all kinds of musicals and popular entertainment. You've often spoken of your admiration of Fred Astaire. When did you first watch his films?*

MB: I used to watch Fred Astaire on TV as a child. I'm pretty convinced my parents used to make me watch his films, and that they told me he was a good thing. When I was five, six, seven – I don't remember a time when I wasn't aware of him or his films. Then I gradually singled him out as the one I liked the most.

AM: *Was there any particular point when you started to think, 'This isn't just adorable, it's also great choreography'?*

MB: I don't think I thought in terms of choreography in those days, even into my teens. I just got enormous pleasure from Astaire's dancing.

8

It was consistently interesting in a way that Gene Kelly wasn't. Not that I was consciously critical at the time. I always found the modesty of Astaire's personality more appealing, as well. I didn't go for the brashness and ego of Gene Kelly. The Fred and Ginger movies I had a particular love for – and then they disappeared for years. There was a whole period of time when they weren't shown on television. Then at the Everyman cinema in Hampstead, probably in the late 1970s, they showed all the Fred and Ginger numbers edited together from all the movies, in one day – something they've never done since. That had a big effect on me. It was so glorious to see all those numbers that I'd maybe only seen once before when I was seven or eight.

From that day onwards, I was absolutely convinced that this was what I wanted to do. I was so surprised at the variety and the seriousness of the work in the films. It was so rich.

AM: *Frederick Ashton often said that seeing Anna Pavlova for the first time, in his teens, was the revelation that changed his life. For you it was this Fred-and-Ginger-fest at Hampstead. How old were you at the time?*
MB: Maybe nineteen. I wanted at once to put something like those numbers into my shows. I've got videos of some of what I did then, which I've never shown. They're just cringe-making! One was a whole little fifteen-minute version of *On the Town*. I did a whole tango number; I can't remember what that was inspired by. We did an Adam and Eve ballet, which was based on the long Adam and Eve sequence that Shirley MacLaine does in the Cole Porter *Can Can* film.

AM: *When you did a can can or a tango, did you just pick up your idea of those dances from the films? Or did you make any formal study of what, for example, comprised a tango?*
MB: By the late 1970s, we had a video at home, and we used to tape everything musical from the TV. Some of these things I watched again and again, and knew them inside out. So I tended to borrow ideas or just copy them.

Inevitably, though, if you do try to use something you've seen, it turns into something else; and this, I suppose, was the beginning of me making choices as a choreographer.

AM: *Did you have any panic about the lack of direction in your life after leaving school? Was one part of you longing to get free of your humdrum existence?*

MB: I don't remember being panicked. I remember enjoying my life at that time so much – my social life, my theatre-going, lots of pubs and clubs. I was having a really good time. The jobs that I was doing were a bit boring; but when I worked for a while for the Keith Prowse theatre agency, I would get to go to the theatre every night for free. That was the reason for doing the job.

AM: *Did you leave home at this time?*
MB: No. I lived at home until I started my dance education at the Laban Centre, when I was twenty-two.

AM: *Did you have any particular feeling of freedom with all these pubs and clubs, the theatre life?*
MB: Yes. I felt very much that London was my playground; and I knew it very, very well. I spent a lot of time on the streets of London, and couldn't imagine myself anywhere else. I had no ambition to leave. Maybe that's what propels some people to go to university, or into career choices, more quickly than I did: they want to get away. I didn't have that sort of drive.

AM: *How important was sexual feeling to you from early boyhood until* A Chorus Line?
MB: I didn't have even a kiss till I was eighteen. At that age, I suppose, I realized it was time I did something.

It wasn't a very pressing thing, I must say; I was very involved in all the other things I was doing. In my teens, I never saw myself as physically involved in anything sexual. That's why I still have that distance in other aspects of my life. If I feel there's going to be any kind of contact, I'm off. I'm basically quite shy.

When I did have my first kiss with a man, and when I first had sex, I had no problems at all. It just seemed completely natural.

AM: *At the age of nineteen, you saw ballet for the first time. We'll talk about individual ballets and ballet choreographers in due course. But you recently mentioned that ballet itself, in general, you then found erotic.*
MB: I did. I don't mean it was the only appeal, or even the main appeal. What impressed me most was its seriousness as dance. I'd seen Fred and Ginger handling serious emotion in dance, I'd heard serious music in musicals too; but, until ballet, I hadn't encountered a whole genre that seemed to make dance, and dancing to music, something serious as a

matter of course. It was the impact of that which gave it an erotic quality, because it was seriously sexual and sensual. I had never found that kind of appeal in the stars and musicals and showbiz I'd been following up to that time.

AM: *To what degree was your erotic, or sensual, interest in ballet connected with the male performers? Or did you find that in the female performers too?*
MB: I definitely was sexually, or sensually, excited by a lot of male dancers. There's something about a male moving with feeling and beauty that I find very appealing. Dance movement can make someone appealing who wouldn't necessarily be appealing when just walking down the street.

On the other hand, I absolutely loved many of the women I saw dance – not in a desiring kind of way, but for the sexiness and the beauty of their dancing. So in some ways the appeal was the same, though I can't see it as a form of sexual desire. It's more a sense of eroticism coming out of the dancers' performance; it's an excitement in what they convey.

AM: *You're on record as saying that the two choreographers you most admire are the two Freds: Astaire and Ashton. Is that true?*
MB: Yes, it still is true.

AM: *I remember that you made a formal study of Astaire when you were a third-year BA student. But looking back now, can you see whether, or how, Astaire's style percolated into your work?*
MB: For one thing, I often incline towards a ballroomy style of partnering. One of the most important models for a great deal of what I do is the Astaire–Rogers format of starting a dance very simply, that then becomes more elaborate as it goes along. Likewise the device, in Astaire's own solos, of dancing on or around the furniture: the point being that dance can arise spontaneously in ordinary circumstances. With Astaire you so often see how he performs ordinary action, ordinary movement, and how that eventually flowers into dance. I've always tried to emulate that, but it's actually so difficult to do; and if you try to capture something of Astaire and Rogers themselves, it's virtually impossible, because their dances are so much about their own personalities.

Still, I often find that to take an Astaire idea and to elaborate on it is a good starting point for choreographic ideas of my own. Musically it's always so wonderful, and rhythmically it's so inspiring, to see how he plays with, or against, the music – quite amazingly off the music at times – then gets back on to it. Astaire isn't easy to watch for someone who's used to watching Gene Kelly, who's so on the music all the time and so easy to watch. Particularly in tap solos, what Astaire does at times is madness. Then, the more you see it, the more enjoyable it becomes. Repeat viewings seem to give completeness to things that you thought were unconnected before.

AM: *And the dance leads you deeper into the music somehow.*
MB: Yes. I'm not saying that I myself have got to that level of complexity in working with music; but I feel that Astaire's example is always there, nudging you on, to stop you being so simple, or so on the music – which is often the thing you have to remember most. When something's looking a bit boring, you think, 'Let's try to break it up a bit; let's work against or around the music.'

AM: *Fred Ashton put one obvious Astaire quotation – the 'Oom- pah Trot', which he had seen Fred Astaire doing on stage with his sister Adele, and which Astaire does with Gracie Allen in the movie* Damsel in Distress – *into his own 1948 ballet* Cinderella. *He and Robert Helpmann did it, as the two Ugly Sisters, in their duet with the oranges, hilariously; and it remains in the choreography for the two Ugly Sisters today. Do you find yourself consciously quoting Astaire movies when you choreograph?*
MB: Yes, many times! The pas de deux in Act Two of my *Cinderella* starts, absolutely, with the Astaire–Rogers idea I've been talking about: they just walk, they elaborate on the walk, and then that builds into a dance. The sort of things I tend to notice in Astaire, for possible use of my own, are certainly not his tap numbers: certainly not in terms of their steps; but I do take definite ideas from the duets. Not just Fred and Ginger actually, but also Fred with, for example, Cyd Charisse. 'Dancing in the Dark' from *The Band Wagon* is one that I watch again and again to remind me of something that's very simple but beautiful. It reminds you that you don't have to be complex and try working with lots of difficult lifts. If it's musical, and if it's felt, you can get by with something that's much simpler.

I've used Astaire exits a few times. I particularly love the exit at the end of *Let's Face the Music and Dance* – but, though I've tried more than once to put it into my work, it doesn't really work on stage! They arch right back while they're each on one leg; they each keep the other leg arched out in front; they start to fall forwards while still keeping that leg pointing forwards and while arching back. So you're left with this lovely image of them still in the air, in a sense. But in the film a curtain then comes across just as they're doing it. On stage, if you try to make dancers exit like that into the wings, half the audience can't see them properly anyway – because they're on the wrong side of the stage – and the other half is eventually going to see them plonking down on to the other leg. I know – I was still trying to bring that off at the end of the Spanish dance in *Swan Lake*! But in rehearsal it didn't work. So we changed it.

AM: *When did you first see Ashton choreography?*
MB: It must have been about 1980, when I was twenty. I think it was *La Fille mal gardée*. I just loved it. I suppose in some ways it was very close to the musicals I had been enjoying: it's got comedy, romance – a bit of everything. I saw it again and again; I took my mum to see it, and she loved it too. I also adored the pantomime aspect of it – the Widow Simone played by a man in such an un-drag way – and the sheer daring of having those dancing chickens at the very beginning. It all seemed very odd to me at the time; but I liked that. And it is also full of good choreography; it has dance interest throughout, even though it is a light piece. It's full of distinct characters, different kinds of dancing. I think that's why it's so rewarding.

After that, I just started to catch every Ashton I could. I still do. Naturally my Ashton knowledge is very dependent on what has been in repertory during the time I've been following it. Several of the other story ballets – *Cinderella, The Dream, A Month in the Country* – I've seen many, many times. But I had to wait years until I first saw *Symphonic Variations*.

I also began to watch the whole Royal Ballet repertory at that time: the classics, the MacMillan ballets, everything. Not just the Royal Ballet at Covent Garden: the Sadler's Wells Royal Ballet (now the Birmingham Royal Ballet) too. I saw a lot of new MacMillan ballets. One of the earliest pieces I saw, in 1980, made one of the strongest impressions: *Playground*. What I remember most is the way that he had adults within an institution playing children and children's games; and I liked the costumes that they wore in that piece. That was in my mind twelve years later when I did *Nutcracker*. I saw these evacuee *Nutcracker* children as being in shorts and little dresses, the way the dancers were in *Playground*.

AM: *I know that you're steeped in Walt Disney movies. Do you ever find that Disney is a natural influence on you?*
MB: It certainly is in terms of the way I work with stories. What Disney has done, very interestingly, and what I do, is to take old stories and retell them. You're taking a simple fairy story or a myth, and creating a version that will work for the modern audience. Most Disney films have now become the versions of those stories that we know. *Snow White and the Seven Dwarfs*: the Disney version is the most famous version of that story, even though it's quite different from the original. The same with all their works. That's an interesting phenomenon they've created.

I think in some ways that's the way I approach stories: How can I make this palatable? How can I make this work for a much bigger audience than it's already reaching? So that's what I have got from Disney. And the Disney people are quite daring at times, in how far they will go to tell a story.

AM: *Does Disney affect your movement?*
MB: No. I think it's all to do with story-telling.

AM: *Do you have in your video collection the* Silly Symphonies *or any early Mickey Mouse films?*
MB: They're very hard to get hold of, but I love watching them when I have the chance. They are very music-led; it's story-telling through music.

AM: *The subject of dancing to music leads me to the man I think of as the greatest of all choreographers: George Balanchine. New York City Ballet, which he founded in 1948, came here in 1979, when he was still very much its ballet-master-in-chief, and again in 1983, just months after his death, but still dancing a largely Balanchine repertory. How much of Balanchine did you see in those days? And to what degree were you interested in his work?*
MB: Well, I saw New York City Ballet in 1979. I went initially, mind you, more to see Baryshnikov than anything else. I thought of him as a film star, because he'd been in *The Turning Point*. I queued up to see him.

Balanchine choreography was a whole new world. A whole new world of choreography that seemed alien to me then. I probably enjoyed the music and the musicality of it.

Balanchine has never become my favourite choreographer. My body doesn't really respond to that style of ballet; and some of his pieces – such as his *Nutcracker* – I really don't buy; but I'd always try to see anything by him I hadn't seen before, and he can still surprise. On my last visit to New York, for example, I saw his *Walpurgisnacht* for the first time, where the girls all let down their hair halfway through. I really liked that. Just recently, I watched *Serenade* and *Western Symphony* on TV. I loved them both, and I realized how many ideas I've lifted from *Serenade* over the years – in pieces of mine from *Spitfire* (1988) to *Cinderella* (1997). I do see that he's a master. But in 1979, and again in 1983, the main impact was of a whole new bunch of exciting dancers I was seeing for the first time; and I was completely enamoured of ballet in general at that point as well: so I remember really having a great time.

AM: *Meanwhile you were also going to West End theatre. 1980 was the year of the Royal Shakespeare Company's epic production of* Nicholas Nickleby: *I presume you saw that?*

MB: Well, the way that piece told a story was very influential, not just for me, but for many other people. And later I worked twice with John Caird, who had co-directed *Nicholas Nickleby* with Trevor Nunn; I choreographed his productions of *As You Like It* (for the RSC, in 1989) and the West End musical *Children of Eden* (in 1991). I've always felt I learnt a lot from working with him. In particular, his open-mindedness towards ways of staging a story. Had I not had those experiences, I might not have done the sequence in Act Three of *Cinderella* with the screens; I just thought, 'I'll ask Lez Brotherston, the designer, for twelve screens, and I can do a whole series of scenes manoeuvring those around to make different worlds.' There was a bit in *Children of Eden* that I always loved, when the dove flew from the ark. John Caird pursued this idea – and in rehearsal I thought, 'I just can't see this working at all' – where all the cast would hold up a simple dove made of white tissue paper: they would turn around with it, it would disappear, they would pass it along, it would reappear; they were dotted all over the set, so that you saw stages of its flight. Frances Ruffelle, the girl who was singing the song at the time, just made a simple gesture as if to release the dove from her hands; and as she did, the first tissue came, and then you saw all these white flashes appear round the set. It really was brilliant. Such a lovely idea, and so simple. I thought, 'This is really great – you can create theatre from nothing, not just from spending a lot of money on big sets and special effects.' *Nicholas Nickleby* taught me that anything's up for grabs. You could build a carriage or a dormitory out of bits of set lying around, and create something out of nothing. The audience always loves pieces that manipulate simple means to make something wonderfully theatrical. I thought that we in AMP did that at times with *Deadly Serious* – we had a simple set that became lots of different things. We had a box that became a coffin, that became a table, that became a wardrobe. By turning it up on different ends, moving it around, we made it become different things. Audiences always respond to that.

I saw a lot of other West End productions then; I still do. I can see now that some of the ones I saw in the 1970s or 1980s have influenced my work with AMP. For example, the idea of Peter Shaffer's *Equus* was in my mind when I started to conceive *Swan Lake*. Probably there were others, whose influence I won't recognize until I find myself using them.

AM: *Up to these years, you'd been looking at theatre, films, ballet. Had you looked at any modern dance before the course?*
MB: Virtually at the same time that I started to go to ballet, I also started to see everything I could of all the bigger modern-dance companies. The first must have been Martha Graham, in 1979, in the season she did at Covent Garden with Liza Minnelli. That was actually just before I saw my first *Swan Lake*. Minnelli – who was playing the Narrator in Graham's *The Owl and the Pussycat* – was my reason for going; and my main memories now are of her and of Graham herself, who just spoke, at the side of the stage, with a microphone. I was nineteen, and I was fascinated to see Graham: she was a legendary figure, and she spoke for about half an hour. I don't remember not liking it, but I don't think it left any great impression.

In those days, there were very few small British modern-dance companies, whereas today there seem to be dozens. I started to go and see most of the dance companies that visited Sadler's Wells Theatre: the two leading British companies, Ballet Rambert (which later became Rambert Dance Company, but was already a modern-dance rather than a ballet troupe) and the much-missed London Contemporary Dance Theatre, and any that came from abroad.

One of the first modern-dance things I saw was Twyla Tharp's company, when it came for a fortnight to Sadler's Wells in 1981. I really took to that straightaway. I found it exciting because I felt that here was someone who was virtually doing whatever she wanted to do, expressing completely what she wanted to express at that time. I know now how formal her work really was, but that wasn't how it felt. It seemed so free. Having seen a fair bit of ballet by that point, I found it very unusual; but I was excited by it.

Her style as a whole made a big impact on me. I remember being at the bus stop afterwards – I'd just seen *Eight Jelly Rolls,* her 1971 piece to jazz music by Jelly Roll Morton – and I remember still moving around, imitating the amazingly fluid, slouchy, Tharp style of that era as I stood there, waiting for the bus.

AM: *One of my enduring memories of that season is of coming out of Sadler's Wells after one performance and seeing people still moving at the bus stop. It seemed absolutely the most natural response at the time; Tharp in those days had the strongest kinaesthetic effect on people that I have ever known in dance. Long after the show it made all of us just wriggle happily, as if it was still going on inside us; but I didn't know you were one of the wrigglers at the bus stop!*
MB: That's the main thing I can remember about it now: me at the bus stop afterwards, still moving.

(Conversations 1998–99)

2

Training
1982–86

ALASTAIR MACAULAY: *What made you change your life and take a three-year dance course?*

MATTHEW BOURNE: I had begun working as an usher at the National Theatre in 1980, and one of the ushers there, Dan O'Neill, was studying at the London Contemporary Dance School at The Place. (He later danced – as did I – for Lea Anderson as one of her Featherstonehaughs.) He told me about dance training, and about the Laban Centre, which had then started its BA course in Dance Theatre – the only British BA in dance in those days.

AM: *What degree of training of any kind did you have before you auditioned for the Laban Centre?*

MB: I had no formal training at all. I belonged to a dance group that was based at a church that I went to. This was called Mathews Dance Workshop: no relation! It was run by a woman called Hilda Rodl. It's been going for over fifty years. It was a performance group, basically around dance, that was available for anyone who had an interest. They used to do ballet classes, warm-ups and so forth, but I felt that was not what I wanted to be doing, which was probably a sort of paranoia about people thinking I was doing something a bit sissy. So I just turned up and did my stuff after the class.

So I hadn't done a dance class of any kind when I went to audition for Laban. I was self-taught until that point: watching performances, copying from videos, from other people. I never thought in terms of technique or even warming up: I just observed and did it.

Frankly, I wouldn't have got into anywhere except the Laban Centre in those days. It's interesting: I remember that three of the Laban Centre

2 Bourne and Emma Gladstone performing for Transitions Dance Company in
1986 in Ashley Page's *The Organizing Principle*.

students who went on to bigger things, Lea Anderson, Catherine White
(now Catherine Malone), and John Heath (later Jacob Marley), had all
been rejected by The Place, if not also by other dance centres. We all
knew, or came to know, that the technical standards at Laban auditions
were lower; and yet we wanted to prove ourselves. Later on, curiously,
things changed so much that, in the mid-1990s, the positions were almost
exactly reversed. The Laban Centre reached the stage of only accepting
girls with perfect bodies, while it was The Place who started to let in
people with less than perfect techniques who had some basic enthusiasm
driving them. Things have changed again since then; audition criteria
never remain fixed for long.

AM: *You passed the audition. Were you advised to do training before
you began the course?*
MB: No, nothing like that was said! There were only a few months
between doing the audition and starting the course. David Massingham
and I were the first people in our borough – Waltham Forest – to get a

grant to do dance: probably the last as well, I should imagine; but one of the reasons I got it was that, at that time, I was still putting on shows. The council got whoever was the most prominent in the borough in dance to adjudicate – she was a dancing teacher, and she'd come along to see one of my shows – and that's what I was judged on, and how I got the grant.

Particularly because it was Laban, I expressed a lot of interest in choreography when I auditioned. In the interview, I was asked what I'd seen most recently that I'd liked. Well, I just reeled off tons of things. So I think they were probably quite impressed by my interest. I don't think it was my marvellous dancing that got me in there! I can't imagine what I looked like.

AM: *The Laban Centre for Movement and Dance had moved to New Cross, in South East London, late in the 1970s, and has steadily expanded its premises and its scope since then. Certain crucial aspects of the work of its founder, Rudolf Laban, were maintained on all courses, but Dr Marion North, who had become its director during the 1970s, had developed the Centre in several new directions, and has continued to do so. There are former Laban students today who are still shocked by the fact that, under Marion North, the Centre began, in the 1970s, to embrace any teaching of dance technique or formal choreographic disciplines.*

Another new direction was North's establishment of the first British BA course in dance. It was, to be precise, a BA (Hons) course in Dance Theatre. I began to teach dance history there in 1980, a term before the first intake of BA students graduated. You began your course in September 1982, and yours was the fifth year of students to take it.

After graduating, you spent one further year in Transitions, the Centre's course for dance graduates preparing to become professional dancers. This, too, was a young course; yours was the third year of Transitions.

This was four years of intense study – yet you say that, hitherto, you'd never enjoyed schoolwork. What had changed?

MB: I enjoyed the course, first of all, because it was my choice to go there. I didn't feel any more that I was doing something I was obliged to do. And secondly, the subject – dance – just inspired me. Even when some of the teachers weren't inspiring, I was enthusiastic. I remember enjoying lectures: the guest lecturers, too. Do you remember Svetlana

Beriosova coming down to coach parts of *Swan Lake*? That was a major thrill.

AM: *Throughout that time, you were developing your technique as a choreographer. Looking back, to what degree do you now think that choreography can be taught? What do you think you learnt from a formal study of choreography? What do you wish you had learnt? What else do you wish might be taught to choreographers that might have been useful?*

MB: There are certain things I feel I did learn. Some just sparked off the imagination a bit; and I was fascinated by certain ideas we studied that other choreographers had formed, like Doris Humphrey's ideas about space and important areas of the stage. I still remember some of those things: where the strong points of the stage were, where the focal points were, and the travelling pathways that were the most prominent and registered the most. And the actual setting of choreographic tasks to do: obviously, I'd never done that before. To try to get to the essence of one idea by having a task set for you to do – you know, a solo that was purely using one idea – would concentrate my ideas and imagination. I think now that all those things help a student to find things that maybe are already there. What you can't teach is ideas; or imagination.

I don't think that you can teach choreography, but you can teach structures, and ideas, and ways of making movement: all the sorts of processes that you can go through to build the phrase. To me, all those kinds of things were very useful, and I still find myself using them. For example, reversing movement. Or, for another example, limiting what the body can do. Something I still use now is to isolate the upper and lower halves of the body; make one person work on the top half, another on the legs; then try to put those two separate products together, and see what happens. These processes sometimes come up with interesting results.

What is most valuable, I suppose, is enquiring about and developing movement. Of course, at Laban that went hand in hand with a lot of other things – ballet classes, modern-dance classes, movement study, history, music and other courses – but purely in terms of studying choreography, those are some of the things that I derived from it.

There was no one choreography teacher that influenced me in particular. The whole ethos was very much influenced by Bonnie Bird, and I do remember – indeed, have used during the 1990s – some of the things she'd say. Since she had danced with Martha Graham in the early 1930s and then had been Merce Cunningham's first 'proper' teacher in the late 1930s, it was exciting to come across her. But in my time she was moving into semi-retirement; she only spent six months of the year in Britain. No doubt as a result of her influence almost all my other choreography teachers at Laban were American; I would say that I learnt from all of them, or just from the whole discipline as it was being developed there. But I was hungry to learn. The whole idea of studying choreography – of studying dance – just fascinated me.

Still, I've always thought that I learnt more from watching choreography than from taking choreography classes. Studying choreography did lead me towards a certain amount of information; but I think that the more you watch great choreography, the more you learn from it. Even subconsciously: in fact, I always try to watch pieces for pleasure, rather than try to analyse them in any way.

I was lucky enough then to be seeing a fair number of works regularly in the theatre, seeing things again and again. And that's how they sink in. When I first see a piece, I tend to watch purely for enjoyment; even now. I'm not looking for things within; the first time I watch a dance, I just come away with an impression. But of course, the more you see a piece, the more you get from it. I wish I did that more now – watch a piece repeatedly – because I don't see works often enough for information or ideas to go in. It's always on second viewing that you really start to see; or so it is for me.

AM: *What about the degree to which you were required to keep notebooks on your own choreography and all that? Was that useful? Was that instructive?*
MB: Not always: because you felt sometimes that you couldn't – shouldn't – put a dance idea into words. That was the problem: trying to put into words something in movement. Sometimes it would spoil your idea: putting in black and white what you were trying to say in movement. It made it seem less interesting. At other times, however, that same requirement helped you really get to the essence of what it was you were doing.

But academically the Laban BA was an extremely taxing course at that time. Gruelling, too. I'm sure it's changed a lot now. When I hear of what other people have done at other colleges now to get a degree! . . . For us, the combination of practical and academic work was enormous, especially as we were rehearsing things as well. Often all of us would be up all night writing one essay assignment or another. We'd be just sitting there in our kitchen in Tanners Hill, with coffees, trying to finish these essays, because we'd been rehearsing till nine in the evening and we still had written work to do for some deadline in the morning. We would do it together, to try to help each other get through it. But that was very bonding; we were in the same boat.

Still, those were fairly early days for degree-course dance studies. There was a great deal of emphasis on the academic and written side – to justify dance as an academic subject, and to justify ours as an academic course.

AM: *Are there academic – non-practical – subjects that you think are useful in such a course? I don't mean ones that you enjoyed; I mean ones that are useful to a choreographer.*

MB: In theory, most of what we did could be useful. Certainly we had drama classes, which was good, because very few places will do that. I think the notation is not of great interest or use to a choreographer. No choreographer I know uses a formal notation system, either Laban's or any other. That's a specialist area that I think we could have done without.

Movement analysis – movement study, it was called – obviously can help you see what you've done. That was a core subject at Laban, because it was central to Rudolf Laban's own work with dance and movement. I regarded it as an extension of choreography, really. But I don't have much to say about it now; I'm not aware of applying it.

Music we studied, in a very small way really: about once a week during the first half of the course. But that certainly helped me to do what I do now in terms of counts: in terms of the little notation that I make – my own system! – when I'm working on a piece. I remember once having to set a rhythmic pattern from *The Rite of Spring*, having to choreograph to that series of counts: that made you listen to music in a different way. Very important.

AM: *Did you learn to read a musical score?*

MB: No. That was taught up to a point, but it didn't really go in. Certain things I've remembered from it and have used in my own little notation; but I've borrowed things from that – stresses and accelerations – so I did learn something there that I've gone on to use.

AM: *You were taught choreography; and you were taught music. But how important was dancing to music as a part of your choreographic course? I ask, because in the world of modern dance – certainly at that time – there has been such a strong tradition of dancing without music.*
MB: A lot of what we did early on in the course was entirely without music. Most of the 'studies' that we had to do were in silence. They were, I suppose, trying to get to the essence of movement; trying not to bring in any musical aspect until later on. I do remember doing some short solos to music, but I don't remember any serious discussion about musical values in choreography or about whether a dance worked for the music it was set to. And I still feel that a lot of the choreography I see is set to music that – it feels – you could do virtually anything to. Either the music has a steady rhythm that never changes; or it's atmosphere music that feels as if you could dance right over it perfectly easily.

I don't remember being taught how to fit movement to music.

AM: *Was that something you learnt for yourself?*
MB: Yes. Dance for me is – more and more – about the relationship between movement and music. I don't mind that modern-dance students are taught how to dance and choreograph without music; I do mind that they are taught little, if anything, about the connections between dance and music, between choreography and music. There are so many subtleties to be learnt, so many issues to be discussed: What music can or can't be choreographed to? What style of movement can suit which music? What sort of dance phrasing or dynamics will complement this or that musical phrasing or dynamics? Almost everyone in professional dance talks about this a great deal, and almost every choreographer concerns himself or herself with it all the time. But we weren't encouraged to think analytically about that at college; and I suspect that many – modern and ballet – students still aren't.

You know this already; but it's true that the most important thing, for me, was my interest in dance history. Learning more about that was very important to me. I feel that I've always involved dance history to some greater or lesser extent in what I've done on stage.

AM: *Were you interested in dance history before the course?*
MB: Yes. I'd started to be interested about two years before. I'd begun to read a lot of dance biographies: Buckle's *Nijinsky* and *Diaghilev*, Taper's *Balanchine* . . . And books about the early Royal Ballet – the Vic-Wells

Ballet, then the Sadler's Wells Ballet – and about Robert Helpmann and Margot Fonteyn. You see, whatever dance I'd be watching at the time would trigger me on to reading anything about it I could lay my hands on.

I also think that my musical education started when I started watching ballet. I had no knowledge of, or interest in, classical music before that point. I don't think I owned any recordings. I was into film music and into certain singers of jazz, swing, musicals: always a bit retro, never very current, just people I particularly liked – like Ella Fitzgerald. When I started to see ballets, I would grow to love the music, and I would go out and buy recordings of it. Then that would sometimes lead me to try listening to more works by the same composer. But most of my musical interest is led by ballet: not just music written for ballet, but concert music that ballet choreographers have used too. That's why I still don't have a great knowledge of some major composers that are not often used for dance – Bach, Haydn, Mozart, Beethoven – because not even Balanchine has choreographed much to their music.

So my musical taste is mostly formed by the Royal Ballet repertory, and by what has derived from that. Obviously my taste has gone on growing since that first exposure to the Royal; but that was my way into classical music. I do think that my interest in the past has always fed the work that I've done.

AM: *Do you think, though, that dance history is generally of use to a would-be choreographer? Would you recommend it?*
MB: I would think that some study of dance history is a necessity for a choreographer of classical ballet: in that genre, with such a tradition, such a legacy and such a repertory, to know where you're coming from is particularly important. But I also think that any choreographer should be interested in what's gone before. Plenty of modern-dance people feel that there's no point in learning about the long-distant past and, in particular, about the ballet past. No doubt dance history could be made to seem irrelevant to current dance practice. But to me it seemed very relevant.

I found that a formal study of history gave me a wider sense of dance practice. Even learning about long-dead ballerinas and long-extinct ballets interested me – because I was learning more about how dances and dancers had worked. As a choreographer, that knowledge can widen your options. It liberates you to hear how famous dances were

25

made; to look at the great choreographers not as icons but as artists-in-the-making, and at the great masterpieces not as shrines but as works-in-progress; to get deeper into their methods.

People are so busy being contemporary and being innovative that they don't see how the past can be useful. Yet it can be a revelation. It allows you to develop your own way.

AM: *Was dance history the only area where you were encouraged to consider narrative seriously? Particularly in modern dance, particularly in the early 1980s, narrative was very unfashionable. It was regarded as impure, outmoded.*

MB: In general, yes. I do remember that once, in our choreography course, we were asked to make short solos in the character of some historical figure or other. Of course, most of the women chose to be Joan of Arc! I chose to be Nijinsky in the asylum; it was a memory dance in which I worked in images from his dance past. All very short; it must have been a two-minute solo. But otherwise we were strongly encouraged to avoid narrative, and, while at Laban, I tried to proceed along the approved lines more or less. I realize now that I was always drawn to narrative, but it needed time. I needed to accept what were my own strengths.

Even so, I was always thinking along some historical lines or other. The group piece I choreographed in my second year – the first you saw of mine – was pure 1930s. Then, in the third year, our Christmas entertainment, 'BA IIIs on Broadway', which was largely but not entirely my work, came out of Busby Berkeley movies – I used his music – and took choreographic ideas from the repertory I knew, like the Chosen Maiden being passed along the heads of everyone in MacMillan's *Rite of Spring*.

Dance history would have been the only place in which I was encouraged to analyse narrative seriously. Probably that helped what I do now, but I wasn't thinking of using narrative then. History for me was just a very good way of learning more about dance qualities and about choreography.

AM: *One part of your course was also aesthetics. Was that in the least use to a choreographer?*

MB: We did dance aesthetics throughout the three years; and a sub-section of that course was the two-term course in dance criticism – which you taught. And I would say, looking back now, that that was the first time I began to think critically about why a dance might be good or bad:

Choreography   1   Matthew Bourne BA

5   June 1984.

FOR Dale and Bonnie

STIMULUS

I have long been fascinated by the few remaining photographs and draw-ings of Nijinsky's lost ballet "Jeux" (1913). I thought that I could use these groupings as a starting point for a choreographic study. The scenario of the original ballet is also a source of inspiration and could after certain changes be followed quite closely to its original form. It should be understood that I do not want to attempt to recreate the choreography of Nijinsky which has been completely lost, but to take the situation described in the scenario, and develop it in my own way, taking ideas from the few photographs that exist of the work and the six pastels by Valentine Gross, drawn at the time.

great

RESEARCH

The scenario, as described in Richard Buckle's book NIJINSKY, is very simple :-

3 From Bourne's BA course; choreographic coursework, 1984. The photograph, by Gerschel, is of Vaslav Nijinsky's ballet *Jeux* (1913). Nijinsky (centre) partners Tamara Karsavina and Ludmila Schollar.

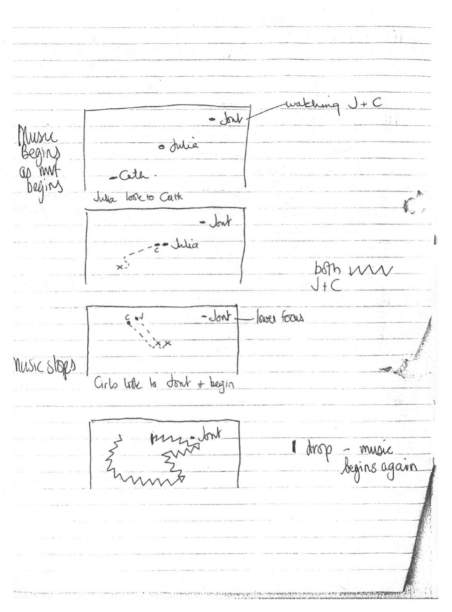

4 From Bourne's choreographic notebooks, 1984/85. *Ears to the Ground*, developed as an idea from Nijinsky's *Jeux*, was made for fellow BA students Catherine White, Julia Clarke and Jonathan Thrift.

to think about criteria. Until then, my instinct had been just to go to as many shows as possible, hoping that I would love most of them. That course encouraged us to look for pure-dance values in narrative works, for narrative values in plotless works, and to become more formally aware of our values. In my case, it did help me, in the long run, to look at my own work analytically. Also you showed us a variety of important dance works on video, as you did in history, and some of those made a lasting impression. So, for example, when I made *Spitfire* in 1988, I used one grouping idea from Balanchine's *Serenade*. Now that was a work I had only seen because you showed it to us.

Otherwise, no, I don't specially remember anything coming from all that aesthetics now. Yet I do remember at the time being interested in most of the things I was doing. I was just very interested in a subject – dance – that was so new to me, and that was taken so seriously. At the time I lapped it all up.

AM: *There was no particular area where you thought, 'This is a waste of my time'?*
MB: I never really took to 'Improv' – dance improvisation. There was a certain pretentious edge to the way we were encouraged to approach improvisatory movement that I didn't like. We would be set a task around which to improvise with movement. It could stem from a painting, for example; and I would find it futile to express this painting in movement. At the time I was watching a lot of very structured choreography in the theatre, so I just found this aimless.

I like intentional presentation of work. I've never been keen on chance things. That's why I've never been keen – as a general idea for dance theatre – on the Cunningham–Cage practice of making music and movement so independent of each other that they are only thrown together at the last minute. I recognize, of course, that sometimes, with Merce Cunningham himself, it has, in the event, worked beautifully. But by no means always; and I certainly think it's a very dodgy method for any other choreographer to use. Also I like an audience to be where it should be; I like the performance to be totally rehearsed, and nothing improvised. But the dance-theatre experiments of the 1960s and subsequent decades – all the experimental use of improvisation, of non-collaboration, of non-theatrical performance space, of making an audience move around or making a dance work impossible for the whole audience to see entirely – were held up in the early 1980s as exciting in modern-dance circles. And you know what? They still are. People still think it's so wonderful, and quite original, to work that way. A friend told me how exciting it had been the other night to see a piece that had been put on at King's Cross Station. You know: 'It's so much fun watching the public react to these dancers falling on the floor in the railway station.' But that kind of thing's been done a million times! Anyway, I just thought, 'Well, I can't think of anything worse.' I really do like to know the audience is there to watch, that there's a proscenium or some division between stage and audience, that this is the performance that has been rehearsed, and that this is what we intend to show the audience.

Obviously, you do use improvisation when you choreograph. You're improvising all the time when you're trying to come up with movement. You're trying to find things. But there's a specific goal there: you're aiming to end up with something concrete. That's why you're improvising. But in 'Improv' – as an area of study in itself – I felt that everything that had been created was lost straightaway. I didn't take to that.

AM: *What about dance vocabulary: how did your formal study at the Laban Centre enlarge, or change, your choice of movement?*
MB: I was studying lots of different techniques. That must have helped. The modern-dance techniques we studied included those developed by leading American choreographers: (Martha) Graham, (Merce) Cunningham, (Lester) Horton, (José) Limòn, (Alwin) Nikolais. Others, too. There was such a turnover of different teachers at Laban, that we had a lot of different dance styles going into our education. That was one of the very good things about the course. We never got to be great at any one particular technique; but at least we learnt to be adaptable and versatile. So, when you finally left the Centre, you could choose the technique that you knew felt best for you.

The ballet staff were varied as well. We were never really stuck with one ballet teacher for any long stretch. That, too, was a good thing.

AM: *Were there any particular styles that you found useful or congenial to your body?*
MB: I certainly didn't take to the Graham technique. It involves a particular amount of work on the floor. When I started it, I was twenty-two, and my body just couldn't handle those extremes – in particular, the second positions on the floor. My weight was always too far back. I could never get my weight forwards on to my legs in the second position on the floor – which a lot of the movement required. So I was in a

constant state of agony, trying to keep my weight forwards. And I think that that did permanent damage to my back. I've always had lower back problems since then.

I liked the drama of the Graham technique: the feeling. I admired its structure, too. But I couldn't do a lot of it successfully, and I really think it did me no good at all.

The one that I really enjoyed was the Cunningham technique. Partly because it had elements of ballet in it. Also because it had a formal structure – but one that I could do. I felt that I enjoyed both the look and the feel of it as well. I enjoyed its use of the back. The fact that it was upright, standing most of the time, was something that always appealed to me – because the fact that I wasn't very loose gave me problems on the floor. The Cunningham technique made me feel that I was a dancer. I liked what I saw in the mirror, when I was doing it. And it was a strong – strengthening – technique, whereas some other techniques felt a bit experimental, without building up any strength in you.

I also enjoyed the Limòn style. It gave you a greater sense of physical freedom, while also being grounded in a strong basis of technique.

What I now hate are classes where the movement is all about rolling around on the floor and getting in touch with your sacrum and all that waffle. There's a worrying stream of teachers and dancers, at the moment particularly, that have made all that very popular; and yet it's so wishy-washy. It's all about how it feels rather than how it looks. Nice to do – but dull to watch. I value those techniques – Cunningham, Limòn and Graham (if only it was better for my body) – where you can see the design, the form, in the movement. Where, in terms of pure movement, you can feel choreographic interest.

AM: *Twenty-two is pretty late to do your first ballet class. How did you find ballet suited your body?*
MB: I always felt that I had all the feeling but none of the technique! I used to enjoy doing it because I loved it musically; I responded to it. But I wasn't that brilliant at it, obviously, coming to it so late. I was always very disappointed in my assessments for it, the low marks I was given, because I always felt that I did have a feeling for it; but not, I recognize, enough technique. I also enjoyed it, of course, because I was watching a lot of it on stage. So I knew what I was aiming for.

AM: *Did you ever feel you were trying to be something you weren't?*
MB: At college, definitely; particularly on the choreography course.

I suppose, on any course, you try to please; and maybe I learnt from that. Still, at times I would try to do something for myself, and I was aware that some of my choices were frowned upon by certain choreography teachers. They wanted me to get more contemporary. That kind of reaction continued into the first years of Adventures in Motion Pictures. People – not least my former teachers – would say, 'Oh, when are you going to do something really new? When are you going to have something set in the present? When are you going to use new music?'

AM: *Now, your years at Laban were among the early years of Dance Umbrella. This festival of experimental dance, modern dance, postmodern dance, new dance, had had its first season in 1978; your first term at Laban coincided with the fourth Dance Umbrella. It's hard to explain now just how each Umbrella – occurring in such spaces as Riverside Studios, the ICA and The Place – opened British eyes in those years to new ideas of dance: to both the most radical local ideas and the most striking new work from abroad.*

But I very well remember that, for many Laban students, as for many other dance-goers, taking in some of the more way-out dance work was a difficult and sometimes infuriating part of their dance training. What are your memories?

MB: We used to have 'educational visits', as they were called; and I used to be our year's rep for them, which involved organizing the trips. I remember people creating such a fuss when we went to see Steve Paxton and Kei Takei. Certainly it made for a lot of discussion as to why we didn't like it, and whether this was dance. People were very angry and worked up about it.

AM: *What dance made you angry?*
MB: Steve Paxton I would still get angry about now. No, I don't get angry, but I just really have no interest in that kind of work. It may have involved some contact improvisation – that's what he was famous for – but what I remember is him working with a plank and a plastic carrier bag. No dance movement that I recall. That was the worst one, the one where half our group wanted to walk out; and some of them did, in the middle of it, in a very obvious way. Kei Takei had something going for her; but her work involved a lot of props – stones and pine cones and things – and that's all that I remember now. Those are the main two that I remember being a big problem for everyone.

It takes you a long time to identify satisfactorily the kind of work that you don't like, and the reasons why. Most people in our group found that – by their third year – they were enjoying work they would have loathed in their first year. For some of them, that included ballet at the one extreme, as well as radical work at the other.

For me, I came to realize that the reason for like or dislike in dance has mostly to do with music and the use of music.

AM: *Two important small British companies at that time – promoted by Dance Umbrella but also performing in London at other points during the year – were Extemporary Dance Theatre and Second Stride. I mention them with particular pieces in mind.*

Extemporary had been founded in the 1970s; it closed at the end of the 1980s. But in 1983 it enjoyed a certain peak, during which one of the pieces it performed was Fergus Early's Naples. *This was an ironic update of August Bournonville's nineteenth-century Romantic ballet* Napoli – *using much of its music and some of its choreography, while also comically giving us aspects of the scruffy Naples of today. I wonder if that example of taking material from a period-repertory ballet and looking at it from a modern ironic perspective made any impression upon you?*

MB: I'd forgotten that piece completely, but, now that you mention it, I remember enjoying it very much. I don't remember it being a version of *Napoli*. But the modernity of it seemed quite daring; and it was funny. It was costumed, it had a set, and the performers were all very much individuals with their own personalities. All that really stuck.

Extemporary was, for me at the time, the most exciting British company – along with Second Stride, which I think I discovered a little bit later on. I think that's the kind of company that we wanted to be when we started AMP in 1986. Extemporary was a model.

I remember them doing a residency at Laban, and creating solos that we were involved in watching and that they talked about. One of their dancers, Annelies Stoffel, had graduated from the Laban BA course in 1981, which was inspiring for all of us. In those days, nobody was sure if a BA graduate could make it as a professional dancer in Britain. Also, at that time, it was the whole idea of a rep company that we liked the idea of.

AM: *Second Stride had begun as a dance group in 1982 as another contemporary-dance repertory company, combining work by Richard Alston, Siobhan ('Sue') Davies, and Ian Spink. Since 1986, it has been entirely a group that reassembles for new projects by Spink.*[1] *But you began watching it in the period when Davies was still choreographing for it.*

There are two Second Stride pieces of that era that I would connect to your work, and one of them is her Carnival. *She made this first in 1982 to Saint-Saëns's* Carnival of the Animals; *and its most successful dance, to the music we always know now as the Dying Swan music, was a solo for a male swan – although it was a multi-layered solo, in which he also gestured at playing the cello (as in the music) and at being a human making 'swan' silhouettes with his hand and arm.*

MB: *Carnival* was quite influential for me. Simply in its use of a piece of mainstream classical music, and in just being animals but in a very inventive, witty and simple way.

I also remember her *Plainsong* from that time, a very pure piece to Satie music. I really enjoyed the purity of that. Sue was dancing in it as well, which made a powerful impression. Her work then had a sort of peaceful quality; and that work had almost the simplicity and peaceful beauty of Ashton's *Symphonic Variations*. There was a wonderful feeling of community in it, I felt, even though it wasn't really about anything. I've still got it on video, as I have *Carnival*, so I remember them both better than some other pieces that I may also have loved at the time but have since forgotten.

AM: *I also want to ask you about one piece by Ian Spink, which I remember you watching:* Further and Further into Night, *which was – I think it's safe to say – a deconstruction of the Hitchcock film* Notorious. *It didn't retell the story of* Notorious; *it just took incidents, atmosphere and values, from that film, and put them together in a highly ironic, non-narrative, very imaginative way. Nobody at that time had ever made a dance based on a film – certainly not on a thriller. But in 1992 you made your own non-narrative Hitchcock piece,* Deadly Serious. *I presume there's a connection.*

MB: I actually went to a performance in 1985 at the ICA where they showed *Further and Further* and then *Notorious*. But I think I'd already seen the piece once before, during Dance Umbrella 1984. I very much liked it; and I can't pretend that our own Hitchcock piece wasn't partly triggered by it, by wanting to do something like that.

---

1 Late in 1998, Second Stride folded. A.M.

I also think some of Spink's methods of choreography have influenced me. In that piece and others he used both repetition (repetition of individual movements, of short sub-phrases) and a particular way of working with character.

Second Stride was a great model for us as a company, because it too felt like a company of strong people: strongly individual, characterful dancers.

AM: *The mid-1980s was a period when you could see the work of certain British choreographers in the repertories of more than one British company. Sue Davies was choreographing not just for Second Stride (then later for her own dance company), but also for London Contemporary Dance Theatre. And Richard Alston, who'd been one of the founders of Second Stride, was the resident choreographer of the Rambert. The Rambert had three 'house' choreographers: Christopher Bruce, Robert North and Alston. There was also a wonderful period, in 1983, when it staged two pieces by Frederick Ashton: a revival of his 1930 'Capriol Suite' and a staging of his 1975–6* Five Brahms Waltzes in the Manner of Isadora Duncan.

MB: I loved all that period at Rambert. It felt that it was nodding to history. To see the mixture of very early Ashton work with Alston's current work was very exciting. You wished that there could be more companies like that, doing that variety of rep. And I just enjoyed a lot of the work that the Rambert was doing around that time.

AM: *What seemed more interesting to you about the Rambert than about London Contemporary Dance Theatre at that time?*
MB: Design. Variety of work. And the Rambert felt modern; London Contemporary somehow felt a little bit behind it, very conventionally 'modern-dance'.

AM: *At the Rambert in the early 1980s, were you interested in the work of Christopher Bruce? In 1993, he took charge of the Rambert again, whereas Alston and Davies now choreograph almost entirely for their own companies.*
MB: I did like Christopher Bruce at one point. I was into pieces like *Ghost Dances, Berlin Requiem* and *Cruel Garden*, because they're very theatrical. But then there's a folksy side to him that I don't like much.

Richard Alston's work I used to admire a lot. It felt like modern ballet to me. It felt like the future of the ballet – although it wasn't on pointe or anything – but it had a classical feeling to it. It also felt as if he was trying to emulate something that had been going on in early ballet, early British ballet anyway. That's why the Ashton–Alston connection was so interesting to observe, especially when Alston made a ballet in late 1983 for the Royal Ballet at Covent Garden too. His work also felt in the Diaghilev spirit too, because he commissioned designs from painters a lot and because he used new music. For me, admittedly, new music was a bit of a problem from time to time; but I understood that that was a great passion for him. I also thought, 'Someone's got to do it; to use new music', and he always showed that he was the one.

I was talking to friends the other night about this, saying that what you always saw with Alston, Davies and Bruce was that they really knew how to make dance, how to make phrases of movement that work; and you wholly admired the dance-making aspect of what they did. Nobody else has come along in Britain since then who has made pure dance with that kind of authority. They themselves are still working that way. In a way, their work has stayed where it was.

AM: *So when you see their work now, does it seem old-fashioned? Or does it seem a tonic?*
MB: Well, I wish I was more like that. You know, for Richard and for Sue, ultimately their love is movement; and movement invention; and creating movement. But I'm coming from somewhere else. The first thing that I have is all the other stuff – the ideas – and the last thing is the movement.

For Richard in particular, the movement just comes out of the movement of the music. I wish I could work that way – but put my ideas with it. Finding the movement is more of a struggle for me, whereas it seems to flow out of those people. And Sue has done interesting things with design in recent years. There's always interest in the way her works are staged. The lighting and the originality of the design, a lot of the time, have helped to keep her work looking very up to date. I also feel that she seems to have moved with something that is going on in dance at the moment. Whether you like it or not is another matter, but she has moved somewhere; I don't always feel that with Richard's work in the 1990s, although I've missed some of it. Sue's certainly does strike a chord with the way people enjoy moving now.

AM: *Another person who made a big impact on the British dance world in the 1980s was Michael Clark. Did you look at his work?*

MB: We were all very interested in Michael Clark, because he was big news at the time. He was a big dance star, and young. He was a discussion point for everyone. You either loved him or hated him.

AM: *Why would you have loved him or hated him?*
MB: Well, everyone loved his dancing and the look of him. His dancing was incredibly beautiful. I only started to watch him about 1983 or so, when he was an independent dancer, after his training with the Royal Ballet School and after his time with Ballet Rambert. And – the same has been said many times, I know – the reason to go to see his own choreography was to see the sections when he was dancing. I can't say all the stuff that surrounded it appealed to me at all: the punkish music, the dildos and bare bottoms, swallowing a goldfish – the shock values. I've never actually been into shock tactics in any way. I don't like being in an uncomfortable audience very much; I like the audience to be happy with what they're watching. And it didn't feel particularly shocking to me. It felt juvenile. I mean, I was older than other people at college. I know that I make use of some juvenile humour at times myself, but Clark's didn't really interest me. I found his work sexy, daring and exciting. But it didn't have any effect on me – and I hated the music.

AM: *During this period you carried on looking at the Royal Ballet.*
MB: Yes, and this was when I first saw Ashton's *Scènes de ballet*; and later, *Symphonic Variations*. I absolutely adored them. I think any young British choreographer would love looking at *Scènes de ballet* again and again: it's brilliantly made, and it's full of really surprising movement, even though it's a perfectly classical pure-dance ballet. I wished I could choreograph like that. But it shows such odd things! I love the entrance of the female corps de ballet when they come in, on pointe, but leaning right forwards from the waist, with their arms stretched behind them and upwards. They're in profile to the audience and the way they lean forwards – like chickens! – is so strange. If you see that when you're first learning to choreograph, as I was, it makes you want to try something that isn't the first thing that comes into your head, to go against the norm. It seemed a really daring piece to me, and very exciting. Not something that I could ever do myself, but something that I could take ideas from.

And *Symphonic* I loved as soon as I first saw it. I remember how David Massingham and other people that I was around at the time all had pictures of it on their walls. It was so perfect. The whole work has a wonderful tranquillity and peace about it. And there's a section of it, in the middle, that's so dreamlike: it's performed to a piano section, and it feels as if everyone's floating on air. Certainly I can't think of another piece that has the same sort of hold-your-breath perfection about it – where you feel you haven't taken a breath the whole way through it. Again, I can't see that it has had a direct influence on me, but I think there's something there that you want to try to emulate. Just the thought of it is inspiring.

Ashton was already in semi-retirement then, but there were a number of important revivals of his work. At the time it seemed like too few, though by current standards it seems as if we were seeing Ashton revivals all the time. I was very excited and interested in anything of his I could see in those days. The revival of his *Romeo* in 1985; later on, in 1988, the revival of his *Ondine*. And he was still making a few new pieces in those days: just small pieces, but I'd always rush along to see them. I particularly remember *Varii Capricci* in 1983, with Antoinette Sibley and Anthony Dowell dancing the leads, and with designs by David Hockney. I was in love with those two dancers at the time, and I liked the fact that it was a star vehicle for them. It was interesting that it was set in the modern world, although I remember thinking it was a little bit like an old man's view of a young world. The character Dowell played was a bit clichéd, with Elvis Presley hair and dark glasses. Maybe that would have worked better with younger dancers, but at that time they were both near the end of their careers.

AM: *Meanwhile, throughout this period, we were getting a fairly regular supply of ballets by Kenneth MacMillan, who was, I suppose, the dominant British choreographer of that time. And against whom a lot of people were reacting, because he was the story-telling, psychological, expressionist choreographer of the period. Many people found that there was just too little dance content in his work. Other people were excited by the fact that he was, at any rate, still trying to shake up the conventional ballet audience. How did all of that affect you? And which ballets made an impression?*

MB: Michael Clark was trying to shock through his dildos and things, whereas I thought Kenneth MacMillan's *Valley of Shadows* actually very shocking, but in the right way – because of its subject matter: depicting a concentration camp, and the gradual elimination of the Jews from their previously idyllic pre-war world. It was based on *The Garden of the Finzi Continis.* The ballet zigzagged between the garden and the concentration camp, with alternating music. Someone would be taken away from the garden, then you saw him or her in the concentration camp, and gradually the whole family ended up there. It was the destruction of a family. Well, when that was new, in 1982, it did show that MacMillan was still alive and kicking in no uncertain terms. I thought it was very powerful.

AM: *Did you see his full-length ballet* Isadora?

MB: *Isadora* was very, very influential for me. I must have seen it first around the time of its premiere in 1981, and I saw several performances of it. As soon as it was broadcast, I had it on video. What impressed me was that it felt like an original way of telling a story on the ballet stage – using words, which I've never done. I applauded MacMillan's right to do that. I loved certain sections of it; the sexiness of it really appealed to me then.

It was the first time I had ever seen Isadora Duncan depicted on stage. At that time, I hadn't seen the Isadora dances that Ashton had made, originally with Lynn Seymour. So I enjoyed the style of MacMillan's recreation of Isadora's movement very much. That way of moving to music, expressing music, which was the basis of her style of free dance . . . I've always found the idea of it – the idea of Isadora – exciting, and inspiring, and that was my first exposure to it.

AM: *Were you ever bothered by what people called the faults of these MacMillan ballets, their deficiencies?*

MB: Which were . . . ?

AM: *The thin movement. The constant, expressionistic effort to communicate a psychological or sociological point without giving you much to go by in terms of dance.*

MB: It's true that those pieces don't bear many viewings, but I don't think their weaknesses concerned me enormously at the time. I was very impressed by them as pieces of theatre. I can't fault MacMillan's desire to do what he was doing in choreography, and to look for psychological interest. What he was trying to do was very valid.

AM: *Now, towards the end of your BA course at Laban, I introduced you – at a Fred-and-Ginger film actually – to Ashley Page, who was moving also in an experimental direction. He was then a young Royal Ballet dancer who'd just started to grow up in a new way. He'd always danced in almost everybody else's new ballet, so he'd obviously been a very willing volunteer for everybody else's choreographic experiments there. Suddenly, like you, he was discovering all the other dance that was going in London. One would always see him in audiences – at Dance Umbrella, the Rambert, everywhere – at a time when it was extremely unusual to see any British ballet dancer at a non-ballet performance. Then, in 1984, he started to choreograph the Royal Ballet for the first time.*

When you two met, early in 1985, you straightaway became friends; and later that year he became interested in the work you and your colleagues were doing with Transitions. In fact, he choreographed for Transitions, which suddenly raised the national/international profile of that group.

MB: Actually, I got him that job. When we joined Transitions, one of the things we were asked was 'Who would you like to choreograph for you?' I said that I thought Ashley Page might be interested, if we asked him; and he was, because he hadn't done many professional pieces, and he was looking for more opportunities to choreograph. So we got the chance to work with him, which I was thrilled about. Emma Gladstone and I were the duet couple in his piece. He made a typically Ashley Page piece called *The Organizing Principle*. It was very mathematical – and organized in the way that only he can do. It also had within it many of the things that – when I look at it on video now – he's been doing ever since: taking classical movement and positions and putting them off on angles, for example. And the way he has the men manipulate the women in his pieces was, in essence, there, though in a very much simpler form. It's obviously gone through many stages of development and complexity now; but it was all there then, his way of wanting to present movement, and present women in particular. Mind you, in that piece he wanted Emma and me to resemble each other – we had to have the same boyish haircut, with gelled side parting!

AM: *Now, the two of you developed quite different choreographic styles and paths. He now choreographs maybe one piece per year for the Royal Ballet, usually a pure-dance non-narrative work in neo-classic style with some modern-dance elements. But you were good chums at that time, and took great interest in each other's work. Was that important for you?*

MB: Yes, it was. He was someone I'd liked very much as a dancer. I'd always found him very different from everyone else. He didn't smile, ever. And the Royal was a very smiley company, as most ballet companies are. He seemed like the odd one out. So when he started to choreograph for the Royal in 1984, I was already very interested in what he might do. And those first pieces he made I found very exciting. In his very first piece, *A Broken Set of Rules*, he used Michael Nyman music – which was very new and different at the time. Unfortunately, we've never stopped hearing it since! But at that time, to hear that sort of music at the Opera House, and to know that the orchestra was not happy about it – I thought it was exciting and bold on his part to do at all.

It was also exciting that he chose the younger members of the company to be in his work. So his work felt like the youth of the company expressing itself. And I did enjoy the piece very much. There was a purity about it, and it was obvious that he was doing something different with classical form.

Obviously we were doing very different things. But we were very supportive of each other's work – and still are to a certain degree. I don't see him a lot now, but fairly recently I watched a rehearsal for his new piece for an hour or so, and we talked about it a bit afterwards. And he enjoyed my *Cinderella*. I think that in some ways it's easy to have a friendly relationship with another choreographer who's doing very different work from yours, because there's no sense of any kind of competition – which does seem to affect a lot of people when they become successful in any way. Each of us can still appreciate what the other one's doing. He's quite provocative at times in what he says, quite funny.

AM: *While you were on the BA course for those three years, you were part of a large group of dance students who all got to know each other extremely well. Quite a number of them have stayed with dancing in one capacity or another. Some of them have gone on to be professional dancers, some of them professional choreographers, some of them dance teachers. How important was that group to you and to your own development?*
MB: Very important – partly just because we were helping each other to get through something so arduous. But also we were talking constantly about dance, about choreography, about the work we'd seen. It was easier, in some ways, to talk to your fellow students about what you felt than it was to express yourself to members of staff in an essay – because you didn't want to appear stupid in writing about what you felt. With the other students, you could suss things out, talk things through.

Particularly after the BA course, when we got into Transitions, that was very important. We were making work with other choreographers, like Ashley, and also on each other – which our group particularly made part of the course. So to talk about each other's work, and our own work, and the work that was being made on us, and all the dances that we were seeing elsewhere – that mattered a lot, and I have very happy memories of how intent and absorbed we all were.

It may have happened once or twice since then that Transitions dancers choreographed themselves. But we presented a whole show of our own work as well. We insisted that we did a programme of our own work, as well as the one we'd been given. I don't think that's ever happened since.

The Transitions course was the first time that I felt people had faith in me as a performer, that the Laban Centre thought I had some kind of stage talent. Until then, I would never have dared think that way.

Even now, I still have doubts about whether I can actually do the next thing; whether I can achieve what people think I should be doing. I have the same doubts about where to go next that I've always had – until I get the idea for the next piece. Once I get that, I take off with it.

(Conversations 1998–99)

3

First Adventures in Motion Pictures
1987–90

ALASTAIR MACAULAY: *How did you come to name your company Adventures in Motion Pictures?*

MATTHEW BOURNE: It's pure fluke that the name Adventures in Motion Pictures has become particularly attached to my work. People often say that it's a good name for the company's style and for what I do; and there's truth in that. Of all the people who founded AMP, I was the one with the greatest interest in films. But that is all coincidence.

The last date of our Transitions year was in Hong Kong. We had been dancing in a festival of dance academics from around the world, and were flying back home on China Airways. So this was the end of our course, we were about to form our own company, we were looking for a name, and the plastic bag that the headsets came in had written on them: 'Adventures in Motion Pictures'. It was some sort of translation that the airline thought made sense, but didn't quite; and Emma Gladstone said, 'Oh, let's call it that.'

'Adventures' was quite a nice word. It felt like *The Famous Five*; each new piece was an Adventure. And Motion Pictures: moving pictures, dance . . . People have put a lot of emphasis on the film connotation in recent years, but certainly we didn't set out to have any kind of filmic connection when we started.

Because Transitions toured a lot, some of us had begun to have the idea of forming a company together. We liked performing together, and we wanted to perform our own work; and the particular personalities in the group at that time were what helped to form AMP. From that start, Emma Gladstone was the one that got us thinking in a business way straightaway – which was very important. She really was the administrator of the company when we began, and was named as a fellow director.

43

There were seven of us in the original AMP: Catherine White (now Malone), Emma Gladstone, Susan Lewis, Carrollynne Antoun, David Massingham, Keith Brazil and I. Catherine, David and I had known each other for four years, having been on the BA course and then Transitions. Emma Gladstone and Susan Lewis had also joined Transitions after doing other courses at the Laban Centre. Then there were two other dancers who hadn't been with Transitions, but who had been students at Laban: Keith Brazil, who'd just finished the BA course the year after us, and Carrollynne Antoun, who'd done the three-year Dance Theatre course there. So we'd all known each other for some time.

AM: *You were following a year or two after the formation of the Cholmondeleys, a similarly Laban-originated company. Its founder-choreographer, Lea Anderson, had been a BA student a year ahead of you. Did you decide on any parameters to the company?*
MB: We all felt at the time that there wasn't a lot of work around for either dancers or choreographers. The example of the Cholmondeleys

5 Bourne as the Rt Hon. Remnant Blight in Jacob Marley's *Does Your Crimplene Go All Crusty When You Rub?* (1987).

gave us some courage and inspiration to continue doing our own work. Until then, we in Transitions had all been thinking, 'Well, what are the companies we can audition for?' Forming a company didn't occur to us for a long time – whereas nowadays it would occur quite quickly to people who are at college. The scene has changed so much in the last few years, thanks to the seasons at The Place and elsewhere. But in those days there wasn't that outlet, that hope.

We had a desire not just to work with ourselves, but with other choreographers as well. Basically it was a rep company that we were forming. There wasn't only one choreographer within the company. At least three of us wanted to choreograph: myself, David, Catherine expressed an interest in choreographing. Keith eventually choreographed; and both Emma and Susan did pieces during a workshop period we set up. Being a rep company would give us all the chance to make work if we wanted to, and also give us the chance to commission work from other choreographers. So the first AMP programme was made up of pieces by me, David, Julia Clarke (who'd been on our BA course, but hadn't joined Transitions) and John Heath (who performed under the name of Jacob Marley, and who had been a Laban student).

We formed the group in 1986, but the first performance was in July 1987. It began as an entirely Laban-originated group – more by accident than design – but that changed. Jo Chandler was the first dancer we took from elsewhere; and we started to use choreographers from elsewhere too. I remember approaching Russell Maliphant to ask him to consider making a piece on us. We did a piece by the French choreographer Brigitte Farges, chiefly memorable for the fact that Clement Crisp wrote in the *Financial Times* that we looked like 'the rugby team from Lesbos'. We also did a piece by Ben Craft, who had danced with the Rambert and was working as an independent.

AM: *How did you keep body and soul together in those days?*
MB: I had a part-time job at the National Theatre, where I'd worked for two years full-time before I started at Laban, and where I'd continued to work part-time while I was on the course – the odd evening – ushering and on the bookshop. Most of us were on something called the Enterprise Allowance Scheme, which was a government scheme by which, if you were working towards forming your own company, for a year you'd be paid £40 a week, as well as your rent and some money to live on.

That helped you achieve what you were aiming at, as long as you didn't earn a fortune during that time.

AM: *How did the company progress, in terms of success, between 1987 and 1990?*
MB: We were very lucky very early on, because we were involved in a couple of evenings which gave us great exposure to a lot of people in the dance world.

We had a piece by Jacob Marley called *Does Your Crimplene Go All Crusty When You Rub?*, which was extremely successful. It was actually the work that got us noticed as a company. A very odd piece, very much of his mind. All of us played characters based on people from his childhood, people he knew in the village where he grew up. He was an orphan, adopted, a black boy living in a West Country village; and we were all characters in the awful village-hall disco. It was misinterpreted quite a lot. Some people thought that we were making fun of old people with Parkinson's disease, and others thought it was about a mental institution; but there was never any intention that it should be like an old people's home. We were just all very odd characters – dancing to Mantovani, Abba and traditional Scottish music. It was very, very different from anything else around at that time.

We were all playing characters – for virtually the first time in any of the work any of us had ever danced. I loved doing that. I absolutely took to 'being' someone. You see, I had got to a point in dancing with Transitions where I never quite knew how to perform the pieces facially, because I was never given any indication as to what the mood was, or what I was supposed to be doing. I ended up being a version of myself, naturally, but I just felt uncomfortable, not really knowing how I was supposed to be projecting these pieces. So after I had to be a person in *Crimplene*, I never really wanted to do anything else!

The Laban Centre very kindly gave us the use of its studio theatre for our opening performance; they didn't charge us. For the first performance of this new company, we did a programme of rep. One was a piece by me called *Overlap Lovers*: a tango piece in three sections. One was a David Massingham piece – *Worlds Apart* I think it was called. One was a piece by Julia Clarke called *Grecian 2000* – Butoh-inspired, a quite odd, theatrical piece.

The *Crimplene* piece was noticed by a couple of people. As a result, we were asked to be in a one-off Dance Umbrella cabaret-style evening in October. The year before, Dance Umbrella had started a programme where they were able to show shorter works by several different performers or companies in a cabaret setting. That particular year, it was going to be the opening-night gala of Dance Umbrella 1987, a money-raising event. So, luckily for us, the audience was full of everybody in the British modern-dance world at the time. John Ashford, who ran seasons at The Place, a lot of the promoters from around the country, a lot of critics, a lot of dance bigwigs were there; and we went down very well. We were reviewed, briefly but quite favourably, by about three critics; and several promoters expressed interest in presenting us. So there we were! Very, very soon after starting our new company, we had people asking us to perform, rather than us trying to get dates – though we did that too, thanks largely to Emma.

Then, quite soon after that, in January 1988, we were asked again to do my *Overlap Lovers* piece in a gala at Sadler's Wells to mark ten years of Dance Umbrella – something to raise money for the next autumn's festival. It was very high-profile, and very nerve-racking for me. I remember standing at the back of Sadler's Wells stalls, next to Richard Alston, who was also standing there because his piece for the Rambert was on before mine. I remember being so nervous that, just before it started, I thought I was about to pass out through nerves: my legs were completely gone – Alston standing there, and this full house . . .

AM: *How did it go?*
MB: It went through without any disasters – that's all I knew at the time. But again, we got noticed. John Ashford expressed interest in presenting us at The Place, for example; and Clement Crisp gave me almost the only glowing review he's ever given me in the *Financial Times*: 'Very promising' – that sort of thing.

And so from then on we were reacting to offers, rather than trying to get dates – which, for so young a company, was a very enviable position to be in.

Lea Anderson had founded the Cholmondeleys (pronounced 'Chumleys'), her all-female group, a few years before. For one piece, she brought in a group of men as a chorus in one number; and she called them the Featherstonehaughs (pronounced 'Fanshaws'). Then she started to develop them as an independent group with a repertory of their own. Lea had never spoken to me while we'd overlapped as students at Laban; but in 1987 she came up to me, complimented me on my dancing, and asked me to be in this new group. So I became a founder Featherstone-haugh – all of which gives you some idea of the flexibility of the way that AMP worked at the time: the fact that I could be in two companies. The first two pieces she made for them – us, rather – were called *Clump* and *Slump*.

It may have been John Ashford who – maybe because I was in both groups at this time – had the idea of putting the Featherstonehaughs and AMP on together at the ICA for a two-week season in summer 1988. For AMP, the season was a landmark.

There were six pieces on this ICA programme. The Featherstone-haughs performed Lea's *Clump* and *Slump*. It was *Slump*'s premiere. And AMP did *Crimplene* again, a piece by David Massingham called *Mathematical Park*, and the first performances of my *Spitfire* (which was for four men, myself included), and *Buck and Wing*, a tap duet I'd made for Emma and Catherine. The whole programme was quite odd, quite different, but it went down very well. The season was sold out, and it got good reviews.

AM: *So how many performances per annum would AMP have been giving in that era?*
MB: In 1987, we probably hadn't performed more than about fifteen times; we gave almost that many performances at the ICA alone.

Still, I would think that, in the whole of the calendar year 1988, we can't have given more than thirty or forty performances – some in London, some on tour in England, maybe a date in Scotland. It's hard to explain to people outside that world, but, for a small modern-dance company, thirty performances per year is a lot! Then, it was amazing. Most modern-dance pieces are rehearsed for weeks on end – and then performed just once or twice. If you're lucky enough, you get a whole week of performances somewhere. Very few modern-dance pieces receive more than twelve performances, I would say. It may actually be harder now to get a tour together than it was then. Because we were lucky, my *Overlap Lovers* – which we didn't keep in rep very long – was probably performed about twenty times. My next piece, *Spitfire* – which I made for that ICA season that AMP shared with the Featherstonehaughs, and which has been revived over several years – has been done about forty times. And *Crimplene* had more performances than either.

That ICA season was the first in which we met Katharine Doré – no, not literally, because, the year before, when she'd been at Waterman's

Arts Centre in Middlesex, she'd booked us to perform there. But now she had been to the Arts Council with a view to becoming a dance-company administrator. So with this in mind, no doubt, she came along to one of those ICA performances; and, just a few weeks afterwards, she became AMP's administrator. She was assigned to us as part of a scheme from the Arts Council to give young companies administrative help. The Arts Council's idea was that small companies or solo performers would share an administrator. It was a good idea, actually, and several companies still work that way. She had a certain amount of choice in who she worked with; and so she also began administrating Rosemary Lee, who was working as a dance soloist (another Laban BA graduate, actually, though from just before my time there), and Pushkala Gopal, a British-based Indian dancer. We were lucky, because Katharine soon chose to concentrate full-time on us, and did so as soon as we were in a position to give her the work.

AM: *Was there any point where you felt any unpleasant resentment in the modern-dance world about the commercial appeal or comic emphasis of your work?*

MB: There were certainly some promoters who thought we were very lightweight – and possibly a little juvenile. Ours wasn't considered to be serious work. We certainly wouldn't have gone down very well at the Bagnolet New Choreography Festival – where all the other new British choreographers of that time were presenting work – or anything like that. We did try one tiny European tour once, late in 1988 I think, appearing in Amsterdam and Ghent. We did *Crimplene, Mathematical Park, Buck and Wing, Overlap Lovers* and *Spitfire*. It was a disaster. They just didn't find it funny. One review said, 'They performed five pieces, three of them unfortunately by Matthew Bourne.' I remember having to get that translated from the Dutch!

AM: Buck and Wing *I never saw.*

MB: I had been going through a Jessie Matthews phase just then, watching all her dance movies from the 1930s and listening to her songs. *Buck and Wing* was a female tap duet somewhat in her style. That was the idea, anyway. The problem for me was the music, which was commissioned from one of Lea Anderson's composers, Steve Blake; but, even though it was only six or seven minutes long, I wasn't ready for the rapid conditions of choreographing fast to music I didn't already know and love. That put me off working with composers, I must admit.

49

Jessie Matthews

'Head Over Heels'

Turn Turn (last) - end with back to audience

Crossed walks hands above head (Ondine style)
1,2,3.   4

Turn - chasing leg round in front
end

✓ Steps 1, 2, turn   Kick (head back, other arm pushes forward,

Tap   Jumping onto spot (overbalancing)
✓   fall back on heels

Cross legs to turn a corner
Then to turn on spot (false one to start)

6 *Buck and Wing*. From Bourne's notes. The diagrams refer to the 1930s dance films of Jessie Matthews and Eleanor Powell (to both of whom this work was dedicated) and to Frederick Ashton's 1958 ballet *Ondine*.

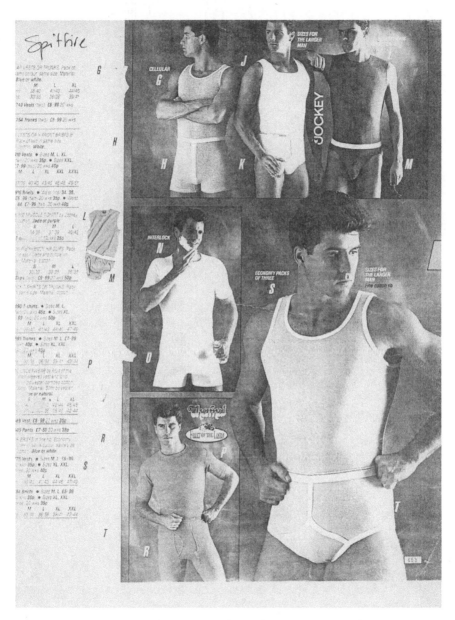

7 One of the pages of advertisements for male underwear used by Bourne as
source material for *Spitfire* (1988).

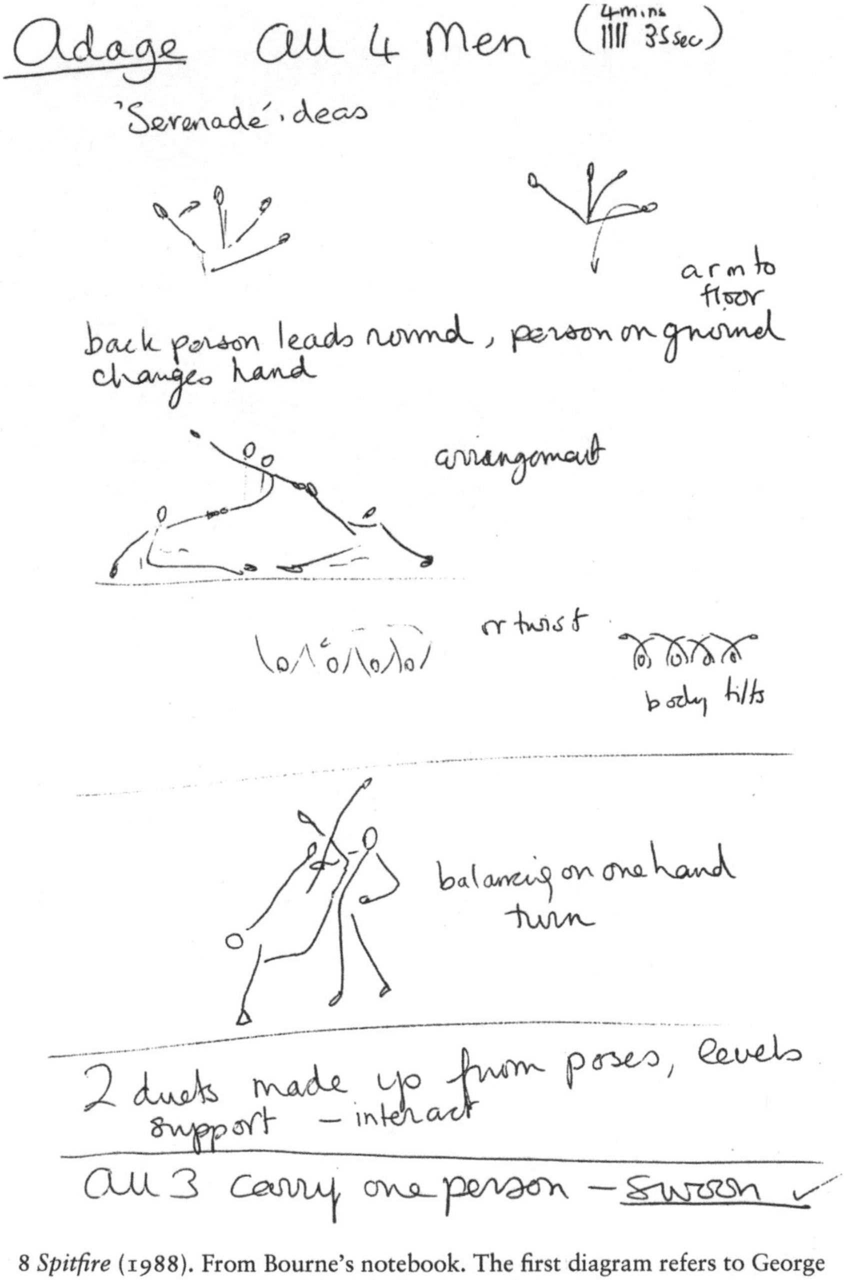

<u>Adage</u> All 4 Men (4mins IIII 35sec)

'Serenade'·ideas

arm to floor

back person leads round, person on ground changes hand

arrangement

or twist

\o/\o/\o/\o/

body tilts

balancing on one hand
turn

2 duets made up from poses, levels
support — interact

All 3 carry one person — Swoon ✓

8 *Spitfire* (1988). From Bourne's notebook. The first diagram refers to George Balanchine's ballet *Serenade* (1934).

Adage (cnt)

apollo ideas

4 heads in a row

take arm at begining and step over it
Same gesture as in solo —

run into it
pick some one
up along the
way

carry some one round to new position

also sit
on knee

tilt
(other
couple lift leg)

holding
arms

pivot on
knee leg

Horsey bit — change positions

hold onto
leg

9 *Spitfire*. From Bourne's notebook. The first diagram refers to
George Balanchine's ballet *Apollo* (1928).

10 *Spitfire*. Left to right: David Waring, Keith Brazil (kneeling), Joachim Chandler, Matthew Bourne (supported). This quadruple image of posing virility is a deliberate gender-reversal of all-female groupings in such historic ballets as Jules Perrot's *Pas de Quatre* (1845) and Balanchine's *Serenade*. Multiple images of virility would remain important, but would become less ironic, in Bourne's later choreography.

AM: Spitfire, *however, was the most popular piece you had made.*

MB: It was based on the idea of men posing. Partly it was about the poses men do in underwear adverts. When I was young, looking at those ads was about as near to an erotic experience as I was likely to get! Of course, they also look silly; I've still got some of them in my *Spitfire* folder. And it was also about the way dancers, especially male dancers, strike poses in ballet: sometimes they're poses at the end of a solo, but sometimes they're poses right in the middle of a dance. And they're audience-oriented in the way that the underwear ads are camera-oriented.

Then, because I had had the idea of making a dance like this for four men posing in underwear, I thought of the most famous dance for four women in nineteenth-century ballet, the 1845 *Pas de Quatre*. So the four men do groupings from the famous lithographs. But there are ideas taken from all kinds of other sources, too. One of the first groupings they do is taken straight out of Balanchine's *Serenade*. Balanchine had four groups of four women doing it, near the opening of the ballet; it just amused me to try it with four men. And I set the whole thing to standard nineteenth-century music for virtuoso classical ballet: solo variations by Minkus and Glazunov from *Don Quixote, La Bayadère* and *The Four Seasons* [or *Birthday Offering*] (some of it originally music written for female dancers).

There were separate ideas for each dance: one was a man rubbing himself in oil; one was a sort of striptease, undressing; one was sleeping . . .

Spitfire – like the pieces that followed – felt and, in fact, still feels to me like the great marriage of two things: what I had always been interested in, and what I'd learnt at Laban. Now I was able to take the craft I'd learnt and apply it to the interests I'd had all along.

Spitfire has stood up quite well over the years. We last did it at a fund-raising gala in 1995; Adam Cooper was one of the dancers, in the first performance he ever did with AMP.

AM: *AMP went on commissioning pieces from Jacob Marley during this era.*

MB: Yes, there were two others after *Crimplene*. One was *My Little Peasant Dance*, to traditional Slavic music; the other was *I Surrender, Dear*.

AM: *I remember that you were already fond of the Bing Crosby recording of 'I Surrender, Dear': so, as soon as I heard that recording accompanying Marley's piece, I presumed you had had some influence on it.*

MB: John (Jacob Marley) usually needed to be helped with ideas for music. As well as the Crosby, he used the Mozart Clarinet Quintet! But his imagination was absolutely his own, and somehow he always made his eventual choice of music work. *I Surrender, Dear* was a really strange piece, funny and haunting.

AM: *Your next piece was* The Infernal Galop. *This was inspired by Paris, and was designed by David Manners. David had been your partner for two years; and it was he who first took you to Paris.*

MB: David Manners influenced a lot of AMP work throughout those years, because he had so many interests. In 1992, he designed *Deadly Serious* and *The Percys of Fitzrovia*. He also wrote a piece of music for *Deadly Serious*. He gave me the idea to do *The Percys of Fitzrovia*, for example, because he was already interested in the Bloomsbury set. He was someone that I could definitely develop ideas with, that I could talk to about what I should do next. The relationship we had is the longest of my life to date: we were together six years.

I think I can live with someone. I've got friends who find it's not something that suits them, but I'm very adaptable. If I've been somewhere for a week, it's home. I'm adaptable with people as well. And I very much enjoy having someone there to share things with. I think any relationship I've had has influenced my work, to a certain extent, because, if you're very involved with your work, you're discussing it constantly. Certainly David was an important influence throughout those years.

AM: *In* The Infernal Galop, *the mood, and even the subject-matter, of the dance changes from one item to the next. Was this a new format for you? And what put it into your head?*

MB: I find it very difficult to pin down exactly what it is that I do, and where I might have been influenced. Once you make a piece that's successful, it's its own piece. It has an inner life that's more important than its sources.

But yes: *The Infernal Galop* was the first revue type of piece that I did. I thought that I could do a piece around one idea, and here the idea was Paris; but in the event *The Infernal Galop* had several things within it. I would say that the revue format – a series of separate sketches adding up to a whole piece – was something I had recently noticed Lea Anderson doing very well; but I also brought to it my own interest in musicals, vaudeville and all those other areas. Actually, I think that's why *The Infernal Galop* and some of the pieces that followed have – to me, at least – something of the feeling of some of Ashton's early pieces, like his *Capriol Suite* and *Façade*. When Ashton made those, he was working a lot in the West End, and that gives them their flavour.

When I brought what I'd learnt about popular entertainment to my AMP choreography, I started to realize that I didn't fit very comfortably into the world of British contemporary dance. A lot of the people I was surrounded by were interested in more contemporary issues, art and music. I always had a fear that everyone thought I was commercial because my interests had come from other areas; and my instincts were always historical, never very contemporary. For *The Infernal Galop*, my starting point was Charles Trenet's recording of *La Mer*; and then other old songs and recordings of popular music, all as French as possible.

AM: *The solo to* La Mer *is the most enduring image. This was for Keith Brazil, in a dressing-gown. He lay down with his back to the audience, and his heels together; and, as soon as the song started, he waggled his flexed feet like flippers. And the way he raised his head made you suddenly see a seal, or a sea-lion. The whole audience would recognize the illusion in the same moments, and laugh. It was an adorable dance.*
MB: I can't think what put it in my head to do that to that music.

AM: *I would say now – though I never made the connection then – that that* La Mer *solo was connected to the male Swan solo that Sue Davies had made in* Carnival: *the use of bits of animal and human mime on a lyrical dance current, in both cases for a male dancer.*

This sets off quite a train. The idea of feet as flippers you used more overtly in the film Late Flowering Lust; *and the idea of dancers lying on their sides with their feet seemingly bound together recurs for the sylphs in* Highland Fling.
MB: Yes, but where did I get the basic concept for *La Mer*? With him in a dressing-gown, green socks, shirt and tie!

AM: *Well, there's a connection to* Carnival – *where the dancers are in shirts and trousers, and where it's very clear that they're human beings representing animals.*
MB: Well, what I loved in *Carnival* was the very simple means whereby it created its images. I do remember Matthew Hawkins, for example, being a chicken or cockerel. He had red gloves, which he put in his mouth at one point. Things like that I enjoyed very much.

11 *The Infernal Galop*: Keith Brazil as the Merman in 'Fruits de Mer'.
The 'flipper' feet recurred in Bourne's choreography for *Late-
Flowering Lust* (1993), and the entire human/animal nexus is a
precursor of Bourne's swans in *Swan Lake* (1995).

Elsewhere in *The Infernal Galop*, I was taking ideas directly from the
famous Brassaï photographs of Paris in the 1920s; and, because I was
using a Trenet recording, I also took an idea from a picture of Trenet by
Jean Cocteau. The picture was on the cover of my Trenet album, and it
showed Trenet with wings sprouting from his back. We used that in the
finale of *The Infernal Galop*: the dancers leant forwards, one hand placed
in the small of their back, fingers splayed like spreading wings. Now that
led to all kinds of other things later on, by the way. There are winged
images in *Highland Fling* and *Cinderella*, but I particularly returned to
the Cocteau–Trenet image when I was making *Swan Lake*. The swans
splay their fingers behind their backs that same way; it becomes their
basic stationary position.

AM: *There's also a connection to Balanchine's* Apollo, *where the title character stands with one arm raised and one behind his back. In alternation,
one hand makes a fist, the other splays its fingers. The alternation occurs*

12 One of Brassaï's classic photographs of Paris used as source material for *The Infernal Galop*. Bourne reproduced this pose exactly in his choreography, with Brazil in the bare-chested role (left) and himself as the bare-legged man (right).

13 *The Infernal Galop* (1992 revival). Left to right: Scott Ambler, Ally Fitzpatrick, Matthew Bourne, Etta Murfitt, Andrew George, Simon Murphy. The splayed-hands motif was taken from Jean Cocteau's picture of the singer Charles Trenet: Bourne later recycled it in his swan choreography in *Swan Lake*.

like a metronome. But nothing's original: Balanchine said he was inspired for that by the neon lights flashing on and off in Piccadilly Circus.

MB: Well, I'd certainly seen *Apollo*. But the connection wasn't in my mind.

It was *The Infernal Galop*, by the way, that introduced me to John Caird. He and the composer Stephen Schwartz came to see it at a 1989 performance at Watermans. The place was half empty, but those two men just adored it; as it happens, we've got a video of this performance, and throughout you just hear them laughing their heads off. When I met them afterwards, I was so thrilled, because Schwartz had written *Pippin*, which was a show I'd loved in the 1970s; and Caird had co-directed *Nicholas Nickleby*, of which I was a huge fan. This led to the two productions I mentioned earlier: the RSC *As You Like It*, and *Children of Eden*, the West End musical.

AM: *Soon after this, in spring 1990, you went to Brussels to look at the American choreographer Mark Morris's work. He and his dance company were then resident at the Monnaie Theatre in Brussels.*

MB: Katharine Doré and I went over together and saw a programme of six pieces, some of them new; the whole programme was called *Loud Music*. One was a big piece, danced in silence, called *Behemoth*; but what I remember best was a lovely duet, to Bach music with bells in it, called *Beautiful Day*.

I'd seen Mark Morris on his first visits to London in 1984 and 1985, when he'd been performing with only a very few dancers. So it was very impressive to see how his work had grown. And he was always musical.

Around that time, I also saw a wonderful British TV documentary on his work, *The Hidden Soul of Harmony*, which was largely about his full-evening Handel work *L'Allegro, il Penseroso, ed il Moderato*.

Later that year Katharine went to New York to see the Morris company dance *L'Allegro*. I've never seen it live, unfortunately.

AM: *Katharine has said to me that Mark Morris gave her the courage of her convictions, that she saw that you can build a company around one person's vision. Was that so for you?*

MB: I think that she, in particular, felt that inspiration – especially after speaking to Barry Alterman, who was her counterpart in the Morris company. Obviously we weren't at the level that Mark and Barry were at that time; and Mark was achieving great things in different areas. But, after spending time watching their work, Katharine felt she could do the same for me. This happened just at the time, 1990, when we began to see that AMP would probably be re-formed as a vehicle for my work alone.

AM: *Yes, but, before AMP became the Matthew Bourne company it now is, you were hoping to have a Mark Morris piece.*

MB: That's right. We actually have a fax that says, 'You will be the first company in Britain to have a Mark Morris piece in your rep, never fear.' We thought it was a great idea at the time, because we felt that there was a similarity between our dancers and his; that his dancers were all very individual, and had a spirit that was similar to ours. And we felt, having seen what we'd seen of him – and he wasn't being seen here at the time – that it would be a great coup to get someone like him to work here with us.

In the event, none of that happened. I started to make all the choreography for AMP soon after that; and the first British company – still the only British company, I think – to dance a Mark Morris piece was London Contemporary Dance Theatre, a season or two later.

AM: *Later in 1990, you made a pastoral piece called* Greenfingers. *There are passages of that which strongly remind me of Morris's* L'Allegro.
MB: The spark of *Greenfingers* really – as with a lot of those early pieces – was a particular piece of music that I felt I wanted to work with. Somebody had given me a tape of Percy Grainger music. We were rehearsing somewhere out of town – we were working on workshop pieces – and I was playing a lot of this music as we were driving through the countryside. It seemed to go so perfectly hand in hand: the country and this music. I particularly liked *Handel in the Strand*, although I didn't actually choreograph any dance to it – just used it later as a musical introduction. But I also love *Country Garden* and the other more famous pieces of Grainger that were on this tape. At the time, this tape was virtually the only recording of any Grainger music that you could get. It's become very voguish since, and there are very many more Grainger pieces available now. At the time, he was someone to whom I really responded – and I certainly wanted to work with that music. I felt it was very cheeky and quirky, oddly and delightfully orchestrated, and moving. Very similar, I found, to the kind of work that I was trying to do at the time.

The TV documentary about Mark Morris's *L'Allegro* made a great impression. What was shown, and what I remember reading about it, was scenes of people forming landscapes: becoming trees and whatever was necessary for the piece. I loved that idea. So I used that idea in *Greenfingers*: those bits where people are trees, where they've got blossom and branches and bits and pieces like that.

The title of *Greenfingers*, and the whole approach, also felt very Lea Anderson to me – the use of the body, the gestural fingers, the short and sweet structure. I don't work that way any more, and nor does Lea, but I was happy to take some influence from her at that time. Again, there was plenty of early Ashton in my head while I made it.

Greenfingers was full of very quick, sharp images. It was the beginning of a style of choreography that I began to use a lot at the time: to have a blanket idea, list all the images that I could think of around that idea, cram as many of those images as I could into one piece of music, then go from one representational image to another, and try to create dance around all that.

AM: *Who were your dancers for* Greenfingers?

MB: Catherine White, Keith Brazil, Bill Eldridge, Susan Lewis. There is a bit where two of them become topiary, and the arms of the other two look like garden shears. The first two hit positions – like cherubs on one leg – and the others cut up their backs. It's a literal image, but the theory was always that, if you just show it very quickly and sharply, it's almost gone in a blink. It's all in the timing.

Another image is catching things in nets. There is also some tea-drinking. In the *Country Garden* music, the women hold their teacups and the men pour the tea. Actually, the women mime holding cups, very daintily; but the men actually mime being teapots, one hand on hip like a teapot handle, the other arm extended like the spout, and they tip sideways as if to pour tea. 'Teapot' became an AMP motif: we used it again in *Highland Fling*!

AM: *That's there deliberately as a comic reflection of domesticity?*
MB: Yes.

AM: *And you saw all this as being about England?*
MB: Yes. I'm very much a town person, I suppose. But driving through the country with this music made me love the idea of doing a piece about the English countryside. The combination of music with idea worked so well.

AM: *I want to ask you about dynamics. Today, when you talk about the dynamics you're looking for in dancers, you often emphasize in conversation the quality of flow, of legato. And you're always trying to get ballet-trained dancers to go for connections between positions rather than just holding static positions, as many of them are inclined to do. That makes sense to me from what I see of your work. Yet it also seems to me that quite a lot of your style actually has a hefty mixture of staccato. It goes from position to position to position. And it seems to me that this staccato quality – which you mix with legato – became very marked around the time of* Greenfingers. *Is that accidental? Or were you very definitely wanting that?*
MB: I was sometimes conscious that what we were doing was somewhere between dance and gesture, between dance and mime. But I thought that it needed to be sharper and cleaner to come across well. I've been watching myself in a couple of old AMP videos lately – and I'm so sharp and spot on! I was quite impressed by myself. Not in a dance way, I hasten to add, but just in the precision of timing and attack. Well, I think

that was part of our general desire to get things across: to be very clear and clean on what we were trying to show, which becomes a dynamic interest as well.

AM: *I never saw* Greenfingers *on stage. But you wrote to me at that time to tell me that you were dedicating it to me. Is there any particular reason why you dedicated that piece to me?*

MB: I felt that, within it, there were lots of nods to dance history, and to things that you'd drawn my attention to, and to discussions we'd had when we were watching pieces. I felt it showed a lot of the lessons I'd learnt. Also you were a farmer's son who became a dance critic, so I thought the country subject would appeal to you. You adore Ashton choreography, and I felt that *Greenfingers* was a very Fred type of piece.

AM: *At what stage of your career do you think you learnt most?*

MB: I'm still feeding off things I got excited about a long time ago. In those early AMP years, I felt both that I was learning a great deal and that I was putting to good use everything I'd already learnt.

I'll tell you what was very interesting to me: the other day, when we were looking through old photos of nineteenth-century and early twentieth-century dance history for this book, I thought, 'I must look at these more again now.' I remember being so inspired by mere pictures of older works, by seeing how highly designed a lot of the choreography seems to have been, in both ballet and contemporary work. I think that, earlier on, I was using many of those images in my mind. I could do with an influx of that again – to go back to looking at pieces that I loved and watched years ago. I feel that I learnt the most about choreography and theatre in those years when I was regularly watching a lot of other people's work, a lot of good and great choreography.

I've learnt other things along the way. Everything has fed into what I've done. I feel more experienced now and able to tackle more mature subject-matter. But in choreographic terms, that period of watching, learning and discussing work was very inspiring to me.

AM: *That stage of Adventures in Motion Pictures finally ended when the other founder members got work that took them in other directions. Were there hard feelings involved? Or was it just natural?*

MB: I remember Emma very tearfully telling me that she was going to join the Cholmondeleys. There was no hard feeling. It was just a hard decision to make. But she felt that's where her future lay. She had become quite bogged down with AMP administration. Until Katharine Doré took over, Emma had been doing all that, with my help to a certain extent; and she was very tempted by the chance to work with Lea Anderson as one of the Cholmondeleys. David Massingham felt the company was moving in a direction that wasn't very him – that is, the humorous aspect of what we were doing with Jacob Marley and me at times. We were known as 'the funny company', and that certainly didn't suit David. He was much more into pure dance, structure and movement invention. There were some painful conversations with him at that time; and eventually he formed his own company. Catherine White got an offer she couldn't refuse to go and tour with the Pet Shop Boys, choreographed by Jacob Marley, all around the world. And Keith was doing his own work. Carrollynne had already left. Emma and David were gone before I made *Greenfingers*.

AMP nearly folded. I wasn't sure I could keep it going as a Matthew Bourne company, or start over again with new dancers.

AM: *But you did.*

MB: Yes, and *Greensleeves*, the last piece I made on the old AMP, led directly to *Town & Country*, the first piece I made on the new AMP. And *Town & Country* is still, to me, one of the most important pieces I've ever made.

(Conversations 1998–99)

4

Further Adventures in Motion
Pictures, 1991–94

MATTHEW BOURNE: A lot of the Adventures in Motion Pictures dancers today find themselves in tears at the end of *Swan Lake*, when they see it from out front rather than actually dancing in it themselves. During the West End run, when we had more dancers, the first time they were able to go out and watch a performance they would always come backstage afterwards in floods of tears, saying, 'I never thought it was like that; I never believed when I was doing it that it looked like that.' This was lovely, and I've always wanted to react to it that way myself. But you know, I never have. (I felt with *Swan Lake* that I'm much more mature as a person; I knew what I was doing with it, and found the rehearsal process quite easy. I enjoyed it very much, and am very proud of the result. But I didn't feel that I was on a mission.) I'm always conscious of the effects that I was trying to create in *Swan Lake*, so I find it difficult to be moved by it.

Whereas, when I watch *Town & Country* – although it's very frivolous at times and I was much less mature when I made it – by the end I am much more moved. I feel very, very connected to all the things in that piece. I'm like that now when I watch it on video, and I was like that in 1991 when I was dancing in it. I wasn't on in the last section, and I would stand in the wings, and always shed a little tear. I love the music so much, as well.

Part of my emotion about *Town & Country* is about the time and the people and the making of it. But not all. I always felt that it was an affecting piece, but, because much of it was also light and humorous, often it was not taken very seriously. We were the company that people – even some critics – enjoyed watching, but didn't like to talk about in too serious a light. Only some critics, mind you; three

14 *Town & Country* (1991): Matthew Bourne and Scott Ambler in 'Dearest Love' in the 'Town' section.

critics wrote first-rate reviews of *Town & Country*, actually. You would see some senior British critics coming to the show and seemingly having a great night out and laughing away; and you would think, 'Oh, they're really enjoying this.' Then they would write awful things in the next day's newspaper. Yet you could tell, from the way they'd obviously enjoyed writing the reviews, that they'd responded to the elements within the piece more than they admitted. There is a peculiar embarrassment that affects some people who want to be taken as authoritative observers when they're faced with light, frivolous material: they don't want to take it seriously as art.

Anyway, to me *Town & Country* is very important. It has a special innocence about it; it's probably that that makes me cry at the end. And I'm proud of it because it was my first full-evening piece. I probably respond to it because it was made partly on my own body, when I was still one of the company's dancers. But I also value it – and this matters a lot – because I'd just discovered a new bunch of AMP dancers, whom

I loved working with, and three of whom are still with me. As I said about *Greenfingers*, it contains a lot of what I'd learnt from all kinds of different sources. With it, I'd begun a new way of working, which I still use. I love its music, and the whole English world it creates. People now talk of me as a recycler – as a choreographer who can only handle new-look versions of traditional full-length ballets. In any case, I don't think of *Swan Lake* or *Cinderella* as recycling; but when I look at *Town & Country*, it feels as if it unquestionably has a world of its own on stage.

ALASTAIR MACAULAY: *Yes, but it's a world we've known all our lives. We take one look at these English characters and English settings and we recognize them. That's a real gift – Ashton had it – but it's the kind of gift most critics undervalue. Tell me how you expanded* Greenfingers *into* Town & Country.
MB: To be honest, I can't exactly remember – apart from the fact that I lived down the road from the Town & Country Club. I passed that every day, so maybe that sparked off an idea.

Obviously, the original short piece, *Greenfingers*, had been very much to do with England and Englishness, the rural side. So now I thought, 'Let's show the two sides – town life and country life.' They do go hand in hand pretty much, the two sets of characteristics. I thought that the contrast would be nice for a full-evening work.

AM: Town *comes first. Much of this is a portrait of old upstairs-downstairs class values, yes? The housemaid, the toffs who dump their coats on her in a vast pile, the idea of arriving for a weekend party . . .*
MB: I always stated in the publicity that *Town & Country* was about an England that everyone supposedly remembers but probably never existed. It was very much about class. I think that, if I did it again, I'd go a lot further into all that. I'd probably do a whole evening of *Town* and a whole evening of *Country*. It was such a rich area for me to delve into that all the ideas came very easily. We could have done another complete show with other ideas of Englishness too.

At the time, we felt we were being quite daring in terms of structure. We started off with a group of people arriving in what looks like a hotel foyer, with coats and bags and sports equipment; and then we went into a sequence of people being washed – in the foyer! – in bath tubs and being dressed by their maid and their manservant. I was trying to set up a framework that I could then be very subversive with and eccentric about. Within this setting, anything was possible. It had a surreal feeling about it. Scott sits there quietly in the foyer – a privileged young English gentleman – and suddenly the maid and valet do a George Formby number to him, complete with ukulele. All this to Elgar's *Pomp and Circumstance*! Then, equally suddenly, when left alone, he produces some needlework. It's all utterly English, but utterly illogical.

AM: *And, amid this, you also suddenly had two men – Scott Ambler and yourself – dance together to Noël Coward's 'Dearest Love'. Was that the most clearly gay dance that you had yet made?*
MB: Definitely, yes.

AM: *How did that come about? And how would you describe the element of gayness in your choreography?*
MB: This is something that I've often spoken about in conjunction with *Swan Lake*. But the 'Dearest Love' duet – even more than *Swan Lake* – was a reaction against a lot of physical theatre that was around at the time. DV8, to be specific, had just been showing some very violent male duets. Well, I wanted to do something that was very simple and romantic. 'Dearest Love' is basically a Fred-and-Ginger number for two men – apart from the fact that they have trouble looking each other in the eyes and are obviously a slightly repressed pair. But they do end up pretty close, pretty much together.

AM: *Because of the initial repression, the ending is very touching. It's also the most serious emotion in the whole* Town *section.*
MB: Yes. One of the choreographic ideas was that we never looked at each other, but that all these little signals were going on. We may be putting our hands on each other, but are never actually making eye contact. When one of us even begins to look at the other, the other turns away quite quickly. But that was very much a representation of Coward himself. He seemed someone who hid his sexuality from the world.

Then we go into a whole, pocket-sized version of *Brief Encounter* in this same setting – which becomes a railway station. So the piece is also about changing a simple set into other things as well. We did have a lot of fun with that also in *Deadly Serious*, this idea of making many things out of simple sets, turning them into other things by lighting or by moving them around. In *Town & Country*, what we do is almost a précis of the *Brief Encounter* film: Celia Johnson getting something in her eye and Trevor Howard helping her, their second meeting in the

15 *Town & Country*. Left to right (Ally Fitzpatrick, Matthew Bourne, Ben Wright, Etta Murfitt, Scott Ambler, Jamie Watton). The choreography here provides a doubled version of David Lean's *Brief Encounter* film: Bourne would quote this same episode, although for peripheral characters, in Act Three of his *Cinderella* (1997).

park, their visit to the cinema, their bumping into his friend, back at the railway station.

AM: *The* Brief Encounter *scene is duplicated, with the same railway café episode happening at the same time on both right and left sides of the stage, quite close to each other in fact. Why the duplication? And what do you think the result is?*

MB: We had a theory at the time that if you were doing movement that was pretty naturalistic – mime or even just simple acting – it wouldn't look like choreography unless it was duetted in some way, that you wouldn't necessarily know that this was a thing set to counts – and all those moves, eye gestures: everything was on counts. So, because they weren't dance movements, having them doubled drew your attention to them as movements. It also enabled us to comment at the end – by having one end one way and the other another. With one couple, he comes back to her; with the other, he comes back just for a handkerchief that he's forgotten. It allows for a little punch-line gag at the end.

AM: *To me this recalls what Ian Spink had done in* Further and Further into Night *– taking sequences of movement from Hitchcock's film* Notorious, *duplicating them, repeating them. But we've spoken of that piece. This theory about duplication: is it one you've now dropped?*

MB: No, I still use it. In the underground station sequences in *Cinderella*, most of those people are in twos. You've got two male prostitutes, two female prostitutes. They're doing unison work, because what they're doing is not actually dance material, it's danced gesture and a certain amount of physical movement. If it was done individually, it would look less choreographed. So the duplication is to show that there is a choreographic form to it; and by showing that form, you are actually drawing attention to the specifics of the movement more than if only one person did it.

AM: *But, by making it look more choreographed, the danger is that you make it look less spontaneous. Two prostitutes don't do ordinary movements at precisely the same time. You're happy with taking that risk?*

MB: As long as there's enough combination of things going on at the same time, yes. I think that if you were doing a duet for two men alone on an underground station, you wouldn't want the whole thing to be a double solo in unison. You could develop the idea – to come in and out of unison maybe; but, in *Town & Country*, if we'd just had one couple (and one waiter) doing the café scene from *Brief Encounter*, audiences would wonder what's the point of just doing a mime version of the film. By giving them a split-focus doubling of the same episode, we're showing them a variation on the film.

Obviously, the film is a classic image of Englishness, so the duplication gives you some kind of 'There'll always be an England' idea – an idea that in England *Brief Encounter* is forever being repeated and relived. And it makes it funnier. In the railway café scene, Scott and I wait at the two tables simultaneously; and at one point, when the Noël Coward recording goes into a passage where Coward himself speaks sentimentally ('We may meet again . . .'), we lip-synch him. We were really playing waitresses, by the way, though we never had time to put on special waitresses' costumes! At the end, when the two girls playing Celia Johnson left their hats behind – what Clement Crisp in his review called 'that unforgivable hat' she wears in the film – both Scott and I took the hats and put them on our own heads.

AM: *The danger with that kind of choreographic device, when you're not going for comedy, is that movement can look contrived. This brings us on to general aspects of choreographic theory and practice. Duplication is one technique of bringing a gesture home. Repetition is another: not doing it twice at the same time, but twice in succession. Do you believe in using repetition as a device?*
MB: Yes.

AM: *But repetition is a very curious form of emphasis. You repeat in choreography a gesture that in life might well only be done once.*
MB: Sometimes you feel you may have hammered something home enough by doing it once, but I think that often for an audience it is not enough. An audience wants the chance to see and to take in what it is you're trying to get across. By repeating something a second or third time, you make an audience notice it. The first time people will have seen it, but won't necessarily remember it. The repetition is for the untrained eye. I think that something only becomes significant if it's done more than once or if it's held for a long period of time, so that you have time to take it in.

AM: *This kind of repetition and duplication of gesture often character-izes what ballet people, in lighter works, call* demi-caractère *choreog-raphy. It also marks the heavier kind of dance works – both ballet and modern-dance – that are often labelled as expressionistic. It's there in Leonide Massine's comedy ballets, in Kurt Jooss's* The Green Table, *in Ninette de Valois's story ballets – all mid-war choreography – and it carries through to some post-war choreography such as certain ballets by John Cranko and Kenneth MacMillan. The danger in most of these cases is that gestures are done twice to the left and twice to the right; and the emphasis is heavy. The audience isn't just being made to see the point, it's being bludgeoned. In* The Rake's Progress – *one of those famous ballets by de Valois that are actually a trial on the nerves to see more than once a year – the mother of the Betrayed Girl comes on doing the same sequence of bourrée, bourrée, stamp, shake the fist at the Rake; bourrée, bourrée, stamp, shake the fist at the Rake – eight times as she moves slowly across the stage. We got the point the first time; twice might just be all right. But eight times is insulting.*

71

16 *Town & Country*. Left to right: Scott Ambler, Ben Wright (bending),
Matthew Bourne, Ally Fitzpatrick. The 'milking' image is a deliberate
quotation from the Milkmaid dance in Frederick Ashton's 1931 ballet *Façade*.

MB: This repetition of gesture happens quite a lot in ballet, particularly
in narrative ballet. If you're going to repeat something, you should put
something else in between, so that the repetition doesn't immediately
follow. If, within several different movements, you repeat the same one
movement, it draws more attention to it. Just use the one movement as
a motif. But there are many options. Sometimes the cumulative effect of
something that builds and builds can, obviously, have a big emotional
impact.

AM: *For the* Country *part, you now expanded beyond what you'd
already choreographed in* Greenfingers.
MB: Yes. Because I delved further into Grainger, I tried to find more
music than had been on my original tape. The only other tape of Grainger
music available at the time was an album of songs put together by
Benjamin Britten and Peter Pears. A lot of pieces were sung by Peter
Pears; there was some choral singing too, and one piece was 'Shallow

Brown', sung by John Shirley-Quirk. It's been re-recorded now several times – once by a woman, last year – but I still think that's the best version, the most moving. I found it an overwhelming piece of music that just made me cry – not really knowing why. Obviously, there's something going on in the lyrics that is very moving, but it's not specific. It's about someone leaving someone. And it's got such a strange and haunting orchestration as well.

AM: *'Shallow Brown' makes me cry too. To me, your staging of it looks like an erotic nightmare – but very powerful and poetic. The change of mood is really extraordinary.*

The idea of the erotic dream, the vision in which the protagonist suddenly sees the full sensual allure of the other main person in her or his mind, this – I believe – from now on becomes an important theme in your works. It takes the dream, or vision, to overwhelm the hero or heroine and show them how smitten they are by the beauty, or the spell, of the other person.

MB: It's certainly a dream. The solo begins with Jamie Watton on the ground. It's like someone who's having a tormented dream. There are sections where he's feeling the ground next to him, like a person in bed who's missing something, like you might when you wake up in the morning. That was one of the ideas: that there was a missing person. Then struggling with the dream, and this dream becoming more of a reality. The dream is happening in the distance behind him.

It's got that idea of covering the eyes in it as well – which I later used in *Cinderella*. A sleepwalking idea: dream walking, dream dancing. And you know what? I've only recently realized that I took this idea from Balanchine's *Serenade*. With Balanchine, of course, the fateful figure who shields the hero's eyes is female. With me, at least in *Shallow Brown* and in *Cinderella*, it's male. At the end, there is a figure taken across the landscape at the back. It's actually Etta Murfitt on my shoulders, but the light is just on her face; it's a person in Jamie's mind. But it was my first attempt to do something that was a bit more serious in tone.

There's a bit where the chorus group come shuffling on with their hands wrapped over their heads. For me, this connects to the pictures of Nijinsky in *Narcisse* and *Spectre*; I like having the hands very relaxed, just hanging, and I like the hands and arms in contact with the face. But here it's part of tree imagery: blossom on trees.

73

Then there's a section which begins with the funeral of a hedgehog. We do a little walk across the back; and Scott holds the dead hedgehog. We take it very, very seriously: that's the thing. Then we do a dance at the end, which is another beautiful Grainger piece, called 'The Sussex Mummers' Christmas Carol'. It has a connection with the land; it's to do with Thanksgiving – we kiss the soil at one point. We were cringing a little to ourselves when we were first doing it! But that whole section became very important and meaningful; and it ends with us all just looking up into the sky. There was some special quality it had which came about through us making it and working as a team for the first time. You really remember those things, especially as a performer: those moments when you have the chance just to stop and feel something.

AM: Greenfingers *was already School of Ashton* – Fille mal gardée, *but also the young Ashton of* Capriol Suite *and* Façade. Country *is more so.*
MB: As I've said, I liked those early revue pieces because they seemed so open in structure and such a wonderful way of doing lots of short, sweet little numbers. I miss that way of working now, and, whenever I can use that format within a bigger piece, I try to do it.

You mentioned mood changes within *Town & Country*. It was wonderful to realize that you don't have to do a piece that's all along the same lines; and that, if you are using different ideas within it, they don't all have to be funny. The clog dance in the *Country* section used to go down like wildfire with audiences – gales of laughter. But the emotion of 'Shallow Brown' hit home too.

AM: *In* Town & Country, *the change of mood is drastic – and beautiful. Did you learn that from Ashton?*
MB: I think so. I always feel that, if you're laughing one minute and you're moved the next, you experience it more because of the difference in the way you felt. I've experimented in some pieces with trying to do it very quickly. We've had people laughing and suddenly taken aback by something, or moved by something.

That's just one method. The cumulative approach is also very effective: building steadily to one emotional climax, even when the audience can half-feel it coming.

AM: *You were still dancing in* Town & Country. *What would you say the difference has been between the works that you've danced in and the more recent works in which you haven't?*

MB: The positive thing about dancing in a piece yourself, when you actually have to create the movement for yourself as well as for everyone else, is that the movement tends to be more personal and works for your body. You know you're going to be doing it, and you approach movement in a different way. That's inevitable.

It also makes the pieces very personal to you. When I watch *Town & Country*, I see that a lot of the movement is very much from my own body, and is movement that I was happy doing. It would be nice to take a piece like that, now that I'm not going to dance in it any more, and develop it.

I also see that those pieces suffer from a lack of attention from me as a choreographer or a director. There's a point where they tend to stop – where I have to go into them, become one of the dancers, have a performance relationship with the people I'm doing it with and remember what I'm doing dance-wise.

AM: *You mean you would like to be giving more coaching to the others on the way they perform?*
MB: Certainly that, but also, more importantly, I can see the weaknesses choreographically. In fact, in the circumstances of my performing, I'm sometimes surprised the pieces are as interesting as they are. They've had virtually no attention from an outside eye for so long by the time they're put on stage, yet they are quite tightly choreographed in many ways. I suppose I left less to chance then. I was aware that I would be in the pieces and so wouldn't be watching them. I suppose we did use video then in rehearsal, but it's not the same.

AM: *The modern AMP really began with* Town & Country *in 1991, with the new nucleus of six dancers. Had any of them been with you before?*
MB: No. I found myself in the position of not having a company and wondering whether to continue. I said to Katharine, 'I'll try one more show and see if I can make it work with other people.' So I literally auditioned a new company.

A couple of people were highly recommended: they were Scott Ambler and Etta Murfitt. The people who'd recommended them thought they were right for the sort of thing I was doing. I don't think they came with any great sense of what we were doing at that time. We had just had a couple of successes with small works. There wasn't an AMP style. We had been working with different choreographers. This was the first attempt at a full evening of my work, and it was the point where it became solely my company as well. The other dancers I took on were Ally Fitzpatrick, Jamie Watton, and Ben Wright.

AM: *Ben Wright has gone and come back again since?*
MB: Yes. *Town & Country* was his very first job. Then he got offered a contract with London Contemporary Dance Theatre and went to join them. We always kept in touch, and he came back for *Swan Lake*, since when he's been in everything we've done.

Jamie Watton only did the one show with us. He went on to form his own company, and is now doing very well with it. Ally Fitzpatrick was with us until the rehearsals for *Highland Fling* in 1994. She doesn't dance any more, but she made a lasting impression on us all. We still refer to her a lot – very affectionately.

AM: *Scott Ambler and Etta Murfitt are the most important of this nucleus to you, I guess?*
MB: Yes. I think they definitely helped to develop the AMP style.

AM: *From now on, AMP becomes larger and tackles bigger pieces, narrative pieces, and then becomes a big West End company. But did the style itself, the movement, and the attitude to work, change?*
MB: I think it did, because I was very much the boss straightaway and wasn't answering to other choreographers in the company. All the people in the old AMP, don't forget, had been college friends, and there had been a lot of history between us. It had very much had a sort of co-op feeling. Now, because I was the only original member left, it established me as much more of a leader. I'd given these new dancers jobs, and there was no history. That was good, actually.

It was a strange situation to be in, but it was a fresh start. I began to form what I felt I wanted to do. And what made me love it was how quickly humour emerged between us. We had such fun making it. I remember laughing such a lot in rehearsals. We used to be hysterical, laughing. It's such a happy memory for all of us.

AM: *And it was now that you began the collaborative method, which has remained your formula.*
MB: One of the things that made the pieces so collaborative was that we premiered them out of London. We had an agreement with South West Arts that we premiered our shows in that region. And so most of those shows for the next few years – *Town & Country, Deadly Serious, Highland Fling, The Percys of Fitzrovia* – were made in Bristol for three

months each. We would be away from home all that time, spending the whole time together, evenings as well a lot of the time. There was twenty-four-hour involvement with people. You'd go out for a meal in the evening; inevitably, you'd talk about what you'd done during the day; and ideas would come up from that. And because we were away from home and all our other concerns, both the dancers and I tended to concentrate on the work a lot more.

I was trying things out a bit with people on *Town & Country*. Initially, I felt it was my job to lead. I wasn't asking much of them; and I had already made the *Greenfingers* section of the work. But, as it went along, we realized we were thinking along the same lines and laughing at the same things. So I asked them to contribute; and using dancers' contributions has been the way I've worked ever since.

AM: *Tradition has it that Balanchine told his dancers, 'Don't think, dear, just do.' This is often misinterpreted to imply that he wanted his dancers to be mindless robots. What Balanchine wanted was spontaneity rather than calculation: for dancers to be coolly stepping over the brink rather than dramatically signalling that they were stepping over the brink. When dancers show that they know their motivation, it can be a simply terrible spectacle.*
MB: Still, 'Don't think, just do' is something I'd never say.

AM: *There was a cartoon in a recent* New Yorker *of a dog being filmed by a whole camera set, sitting on a lawn with a bone. The dog is saying, 'OK, so I dig a hole, and put the bone in the hole. But what's my motivation for burying it?'*
MB: I am, I think, instinctive enough to know when a dancer should just get on and dance. And that's a good thing. But I think the reason I've had loyalty from people for a long time – and also the reason why a lot of people like working for me – is that I've never said 'Don't think' to anyone. I always listen – and I will always listen – to their ideas and to what they have to say. Sometimes I'll say, 'No, I don't think that's a good idea.'

AM: *Is that still true when you're working on coaching a later cast to do a show you've already made and had success with?*
MB: Yes, quite often. Again, there are things that I know I want within it: things that have been established as the choreography; but if they can't do some of it, or there's a problem with some of it, I'm happy to change

it. I'm always considering revisions anyway. No piece is ever finished. I have pushed people quite hard sometimes because of that.

AM: *I do remember going to one West End performance of your* Swan Lake *and Iain Webb, one of your rehearsal directors, turning up in the interval to tell you, 'Lynn Seymour has got another idea about her role!' – and you rolled your eyes.*

MB: Yes, but I'd always try to make time to listen to any new ideas Lynn or anyone else had about their role, even in the middle of a West End run. In fact, the role of the Queen is a nice example of how much I can adjust a role for a dancer. Fiona Chadwick was the original, and I still think she gave – gives – the definitive performance. Isabel Mortimer then did it, very well indeed, along lines very similar to Fiona's. But when Lynn joined the cast, she was an older dancer and several movements just didn't suit her at all. So it had to be rechoreographed. And Lynn was so intelligent and instinctive and canny that she then thought – couldn't help thinking – of all kinds of different accentuations. We'd discuss them, of course. Not every idea was perfect. But it was wonderful to work with someone who was so keen to put her own very original stamp on a role within a framework that had already been established.

AM: *Another example is that of Gelsey Kirkland. Her second book, all about dancing MacMillan's Juliet and Petipa's* Sleeping Beauty *with the Royal Ballet and finding the motivation for every little movement, becomes ludicrous; and, when she coached one English National Ballet dancer as Giselle, she took whole rehearsals before they even made the first entrance through the cottage door.*

MB: It's a delicate thing. Part of what gets these people on stage and doing what they do is that kind of enquiring mind, and that kind of involvement in their characters. You can't quash that; you mustn't. You have to give them their chance to go somewhere with it and bring it back.

AM: *You're right. When Bob Gottlieb was editing Margot Fonteyn's* Autobiography, *he asked her to expand on her roles. What, for example, did she feel about Giselle? 'Well, Bob,' she said, 'I just wait behind the cottage door until it's my cue, and when it is, I come out.' She was an intelligent woman, but she spoke as if 'Don't think, just do' was her motto too. In private, though, she would say to people, 'I have to have a reason for doing this step. I can't do this step unless I see its purpose.'*

But naming that purpose in words was something she avoided at all costs.

There are so many ways of working with dancers. I'm sure you're always inspired by the famous stories of Ashton walking into rehearsals and saying, 'Oh, I don't know what I'm going to do today. But last night I had a dream of a fountain. Hop around, become a fountain somehow.'

Would you ever do this to your dancers, though? Ashton walked into rehearsal without actually telling the young Anthony Dowell and Antoinette Sibley that they were dancing Oberon and Titania. All they knew was that they were being summoned for a pas de deux. Is that conceivable to you?

MB: I can't see me doing that at the moment. He certainly didn't always work that way, did he? I wonder why he did in that case. Perhaps he was waiting to see what they would be like to work with. You can't always be dealing with character. There are times when we experiment with the idea of flying, for example, and there are certainly no characters involved. It's a concept, or an image, or a feeling that's more abstract.

AM: *What collaboration, if any, had you done before* Town & Country?
MB: I had recently worked with the theatre director John Caird. I always say I learnt a lot about the working process from him. He has a way of making every member of the company feel very important, and of involving them on the level of character development. This is the way I work now, to get each ensemble dancer to give his or her role a character that they've worked on – a character that's not necessarily relevant to the plot, but which gives the show an interior life – and I learnt that from him. So I began to see myself more as a director, so that I could actually initiate some involvement from the performers, rather than me having to do everything.

AM: *A director isn't actually creating a play or a musical, he's simply shaping the production. But you are creating a new dance text. Therefore what you're doing also resembles the methods of a writer/director. Like Mike Leigh. It reminds me also of the dance group Second Stride. Did you know about that process? Or are these resemblances mere accident?*
MB: I didn't know about Second Stride's process, but they seemed to be a group of very intelligent individuals who – it would appear from watching the productions – had a great involvement in the conception of what they were doing.

I do think that the Mike Leigh connection is very interesting, because, having admired him for a long time before his talent was recognized, I found it an inspiration to hear then how he worked: how he made his actors become those characters before they even worked on the play as such. They would even go out as those characters into supermarkets and 'be' them, and improvise in that way. That inspired me to develop dancers' characters and their knowledge of the people that they were playing before we entered into any kind of movement.

The other thing about Mike Leigh is that people have said that his work is a caricature, an exaggeration, of people. And now people have said the same of mine. But I've never found his work exaggerated at all. I think you meet people like that all the time! You just don't notice how strange people are.

AM: *People say about Dickens that he's full of caricatures. But actually, when you meet certain people, you say, 'How Dickensian!'*
MB: I noticed that on holiday, just last week, watching people on beaches and thinking of Jacques Tati. People are just so funny, the way they walk into the sea and the way their bodies are. If you actually put a camera on that, it looks exaggerated. It looks as though you've taken it too far. But people are very, very strange!

AM: *The Adventures in Motion Pictures acting style: you've mentioned an emphasis on precise counts and timing, and there's a very precise focus that people on stage have to each other; but it also includes a large element of addressing things to the audience. Was that conscious or accidental? Where does it come from?*
MB: We've always likened our acting style to silent movies, especially in a larger theatre. We're trying to get something across.

AM: *You say 'always'. But you never thought of silent movies when you named your company Adventures in Motion Pictures. Nor would I say that the acting style involved in the Jacob Marley pieces was like silent movies. So at what point did your acting style become conscious?*
MB: *Town & Country*, and then *Deadly Serious*. *Spitfire* was certainly very frontal, but that's because it's about ballet performance.

The acting style is obviously to do with getting an idea across. Rather than playing it to each other, you have to be able to stage it, so that the audience can see it. In that respect, our style is very frontal. I've often had a problem with contemporary dancers, for most of whom it doesn't come very naturally to take in the audience, whereas I like to make a connection with the audience. Our mission is to be clear, and to engage. To me, the face and eyes, in particular, are very important.

AM: *You've been talking of* Town & Country *as if it was a major land-mark for you. But was it for your audience?*
MB: It was something that some people fell in love with. We had a week at the Royal Court that autumn, as part of its Barclays New Stages season in 1991. Jasper Conran, for example, came five times. He saw it on the first night and then came back every night afterwards to see it again.

Nicholas Payne and Martin Duncan came to see it then, which led to *Nutcracker* the following year. Yes, *Town & Country* was a real turning point for me and for AMP.

AM: *When had you begun work on it?*
MB: The very beginning of 1991. It premiered around March, April. We danced it maybe thirty times at most. The Royal Court must have been one of the last times we did it. You didn't revive a piece after its first year in those days, because all of us wanted to make new pieces, and there simply weren't enough performances yet to keep both old and new full-length pieces in repertory. I think the most performances we ever did of any piece prior to *Swan Lake* was *Deadly Serious*. That we did about forty-five times. We thought that was a very good tour: quite an achievement. Now we think an eight-week season of eight shows a week is a nice short season. It's odd.

AM: *You opened* Deadly Serious *in April 1992?*
MB: Yes; 1992 was a terrible year for me – a great year in some ways, but very hard – with three new pieces made in one year, two of them full-length. We made *Deadly Serious*, we opened in Bristol, toured it, did it in London. We went straight into *Nutcracker* rehearsals for five weeks, to premiere at the Edinburgh Festival in August. Everything went wrong at the dress rehearsal – chaotic, a nightmare, the set wasn't working – and we had all the pressure of all the national and international press coming to the first night, without any previews. I'd never do that now! Directly following that, we went into a three-month rehearsal period for *The Percys of Fitzrovia*. During the first three weeks of rehearsal, nothing happened; we still had nothing to show. It was the nearest that I've ever come to feeling that I was going mad. I remember coming in one morning and saying to Ally at breakfast, 'I think I'm going mad, I

think I'm having a breakdown.' We premiered *The Percys* for a week in Bristol, but then didn't tour it at that point. Instead, we went straight back into rehearsals for *Nutcracker* for the Opera North tour, which happened over Christmas, going into January 1993. Then we had to revive *The Percys* in two weeks, to open at the Lyric Hammersmith for a three-week season and tour it. Since *The Percys* wasn't a full-length work, we also revived *The Infernal Galop* as the other half of that programme. For a small company, this was colossal. We were all completely exhausted. There are parts of *The Percys* where we were all sitting down on chairs: that's because we were all shattered. I didn't dance in our original *Nutcracker* production (though I did later on), but I was dancing in *Deadly Serious* and *The Percys* and *The Infernal Galop*. My darkest time came when *The Percys* had its London opening at the Lyric Hammersmith. It was the day Nureyev died. A lot of people came quite depressed by that, so they weren't really in the mood for this Bloomsbury piece we had made. I think also that it was not rehearsed well enough. It needed confidence and full characterization to make it work. The reviews were terrible. You were the only critic who said anything nice about it – in a personal letter, at the end of the season, not in print.

Fortunately, *Deadly Serious* and *Nutcracker* were big successes, and a lot of 1993 was taken up by further performances of them. In Christmas 1993, we did *Nutcracker* as an independent production as the Christmas show at Sadler's Wells. That was a success, so we did it again there at Christmas 1994.

AM: Deadly Serious *was a Hitchcock piece, in two sections: black and white, then colour.*
MB: It was billed as a double feature; and it was presented like two films. Part One – based loosely on the black-and-white era of Hitchcock – is mainly ideas from *Rebecca*. Part Two – based on Hitchcock's colour movies – is partly *North by Northwest*, but quite a few other Hitchcocks thrown in. They had titles as well. The first half was called *Overwrought*, which is a word Mrs Danvers says in *Rebecca*: 'You're feeling overwrought, Madam.' The second half was called *Rear Entry*. These titles were in the programme. We billed it like two movie posters: 'Rear Entry, danced in glorious technicolor and not starring . . .' and then we'd list all the names of the Hitchcock stars we were, in effect, playing: Cary Grant, Doris Day . . . And it had a year: 1958. The first half was 1939.

AM: *We've already talked about Ian Spink's Second Stride piece about Hitchcock's* Notorious: Further and Further into Night *(1984). But why your own interest in Hitchcock?*

MB: Well, I'm always satisfied at the end of one of his films that I've had a complete piece of entertainment which has done everything I wanted it to. It's been exciting, it's usually been funny, it has star performances. It has a good story, and is very cinematic. Often the story is told through long sequences without dialogue, with strong set pieces of imagery that you remember long afterwards.

Hitchcock had quite a varied output as well. There are changing interests, over a very long career. And there are a lot of interestingly perverse sexual tensions and subcurrents going on in his films. Quite often there's a gay subtext, and strong characters.

And often, strangely, people give the best performances they've ever given in his films, although he didn't claim to direct anyone much. There must have been something about the atmosphere of the way he worked which made people give these great performances: people you didn't expect to give good performances, like Kim Novak, Doris Day. James Stewart revealed very different things about himself in Hitchcock's films. I think it was what Hitchcock could see in people that would make them work in a different way in his films.

AM: *Did you find you not only needed to see the movies but also to read around them?*

MB: Yes. Certainly we watched lots of Hitchcock movies at the start of rehearsals; the dancers just loved that! And I had read a lot around Hitchcock's ideas of movie-making. That was interesting for me, because I felt it was very visual. It's about the camera moving. Each shot was planned before, and story-boarded. I think that helped me to think about developing the plot of a dance piece. Previous to that, I would probably have thought everything would need to be developed in a studio with movement.

AM: *What sense do you think* Deadly Serious *made to people who don't know their Hitchcock? Did you intend the result to be comic, poetic, crazy – what?*

MB: We always thought that, even if you didn't specifically know those films, you would certainly know the general type of film we were dealing with. It was obviously more fun if you knew the films. But the intention in tone was similar to *Town & Country*: we were trying to go in and out of humour, and to change the mood quite rapidly from time to time.

I think most of it comes across as fairly comic. But there are some chilling moments. It ends that way in the second half, where we finish off with duets. That part is based on *Rear Window*, the section about voyeurism. The duets could be love duets. But it's the difference between violence and love-making, and how close they can be. It ends up with one partner in each duet dead at the end and one person walking away. So it's actually a murder you're watching and not a love duet – and you see the closeness of those things. The very end is a light bulb being hit, swinging from side to side across the stage. Quite chilling.

AM: *By calling it* Deadly Serious, *you make sure that everybody goes to it thinking, 'Oh good, I'm going to laugh at this one.' Especially with a company already known as the funny company of British modern dance.*
MB: We did have lots of little sub-titles or selling points: phrases like 'It's No Joke'. We were still well known for *Crimplene* and *Spitfire* and certain funny sections of *Town & Country*. The audience liked the humour of *Deadly Serious*, even if the serious ending also made its impact. It was a very popular piece, actually. We were asked to do it more than any other piece we'd done up to that point. I think it was because the idea was very clean and simple. The inspiration for it was clearer to many people than *Town & Country* probably was. It was specifically about one thing. On tour, a lot of people thought they were coming to see a film, because of the name of the company and because the poster is very much like a film poster. But we didn't get any complaints.

However, I was always worried about it as a piece. I felt there wasn't enough dancing in it. That didn't concern the company, mind you – just me.

AM: *What did your preparation for* Deadly Serious *involve?*
MB: Before rehearsals, there was already a great deal of involvement with David Manners on the design and ideas and the music.

AM: *You've mentioned that he wrote a bit of the score. But there's a lot of different music in this piece.*
MB: We used a few vocalists within it. There's Marlene Dietrich singing 'You Do Something To Me', which is the hypnosis dance – partly for the quality of her voice, which has a hypnotic quality. We had a bit of Dinah Washington at the end: a recording of the time, the late 1950s.

Also Peggy Lee's 'Mr Wonderful', which we make into a song about Cary Grant; and Etta Murfitt sang 'Que Sera Sera' live on stage. That was there as a joke. It's around someone who's supposedly been killed, but she goes on singing 'Whatever will be, will be' to it.

And two pieces of Sibelius. We used a very old recording of him conducting that lovely *Valse Triste*, from about 1907. It's ancient and slightly off-key at times, and it's got a weird crackly quality, which gives it the creepiness that works for the scene when Mrs Danvers comes down the staircase with her candle. The other Sibelius is a piece of incidental music from *The Tempest*, during a section we call 'Corridors', where Mrs Danvers is showing the second Mrs de Wynter round the house, with all the portraits and things, and she keeps coming across odd things in the house. It's a lovely piece of music.

The piece we use for the nightmare sequence at the end of the first half is Grofé, *Grand Canyon Suite*, again a historic recording, which gives it atmosphere. We used some actual Hitchcock music, some Bernard Herrmann, and the Hitchcock theme from his television series. It's the *Funeral March of a Marionette*, by Gounod. We used it for a dinner-party sequence: we eat dinner, then play charades, and all the charades we perform are the titles of Hitchcock films. That was quite a choreographic task! Mine was *Marnie*. 'Sounds like car'; and then 'knee'. You weren't supposed to get any of the charades really, and the second Mrs de Wynter has a terrible time too. They're all so into it, so good at playing charades and guessing them at top speed – and the second Mrs de Wynter is so out of her depth. Mrs Danvers's one is the easiest; she does *Rope*.

AM: *You don't get dafter than that.*
MB: But that was fun! It was just another way of coming up with movement. We all made up our own charade, developed it a bit, and fitted it into the time that we needed. Then we choreographed all the reactions. So that was a nice little process, because each person had a solo, and everyone's reactions to it were also choreographed to counts. Very difficult to remember, I must say – quite complicated.

AM: *I know that Scott Ambler insists that the action or mime bits of his roles – of all AMP roles – must be very precisely counted.*
MB: It annoys the hell out of me when people don't do that, and Scott more so. He feels that's AMP's style, the style we worked on a lot as

a small company. He thinks that our comic or dramatic timing is very much to do with how we organize the acting in terms of counts – where we all look at the same time, how we draw the audience's focus to things with group physicality. And he's right; but it's just more difficult nowadays with a larger group. At the time of *Deadly Serious*, we were very tightly choreographed indeed. There was nothing at all left to chance in it.

AM: *I think my favourite piece is the first part, the* Rebecca *part. But you're always taking each situation off into the daffiest dimensions, so that the second Mrs de Wynter is forever blithely going around her new fabulous ancestral home – and she's terribly, terribly in love – and meanwhile, whenever she's not looking, her husband is up to God knows what with the boy in the tennis shorts. Who is the boy in tennis shorts, by the way?*
MB: He's Guy Haines, from *Strangers on a Train*. That was a film that has always had quite strong gay connotations, with the relationship between Guy and Bruno, who obviously fancies this tennis hero. So I thought Guy the tennis hero was quite a good character to put in.

AM: *How far would you say the relationship between the second Mrs de Wynter and Mrs Danvers goes?*
MB: We try to bring that out a bit as well, but certainly no more than in the film. There is a lesbian angle there; just a suggestion. I have such affection for Ally Fitzpatrick, who played Mrs Danvers. She was always wonderful to perform with, so *into* her roles. She used to sit for at least half an hour before a performance just smoking, really getting into character. And she was great to be on stage with, because you completely believed her all the time. But the moment when she starts combing Mrs de Wynter's hair and suddenly starts unbuttoning her own long dress – to reveal a shorter dress underneath – always used to make me laugh.

Also we have Norman Bates in there, from *Psycho*, as played by Scott. He's Mrs Danvers's son, supposedly, and he's into women's clothes and dressing up. The whole household is into kinky things. He's very jealous of Mrs de Wynter's dress. He's also aware of what his mother is up to. There's a bit where she starts to take her gloves off – she's always taking bits of her clothes off – and he looks disapprovingly at her. It was fun to create our own story around familiar stories, to put separate Hitchcock stories together.

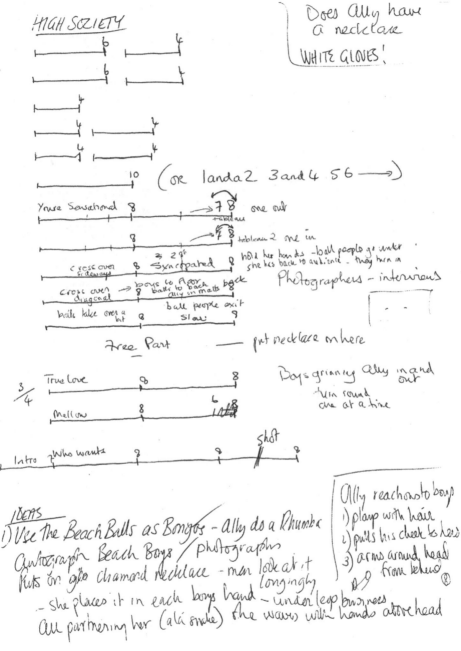

17 *Deadly Serious*. From Bourne's notes for the second half.

18 *Deadly Serious*. Left to right: Matthew Thomas (standing), Etta Murfitt (on floor) as the second Mrs de Wynter, Ally Fitzpatrick as Mrs Danvers, Scott Ambler as Norman Bates. From the work's first half. In the event, Matthew Thomas did not perform in *Deadly Serious*.

19 *Deadly Serious*. Matthew Bourne as Max de Wynter.

AM: *Describe* The Percys of Fitzrovia.

MB: It was suggested by David Manners. He was very into the Blooms-bury set and the different arts and characters involved. This seemed another chance to do something with an English side to it. And full of character.

Because we were doing it alongside *The Infernal Galop*, we felt we could do something a little bit more experimental. Rather than doing a dozen quick changes and playing lots of different characters and lots of different ideas, we were going to be the same characters and work purely through character, with different sections that featured each character in turn. So we had a section about listening to music; a section about a political activist (or someone who was trying to get his point across with a political pamphlet of some kind); a section about a poet having writer's block and trying to get ideas – which was very appropriate! There was a section about beauty – the thing of beauty – in which we had flowers. We cast Simon Murphy as an androgynous figure with a bit of Carrington in him: his role was called the Exquisite. Another section was artist-and-model: I was the artist, Duncan Grant; Ally Fitzpatrick was Vanessa Bell, the Mother Earth figure and sculptress, baking inedible buns all the time for everyone – which we actually included in the piece! Scott was a Lytton Strachey type of character. Etta was a more flamboyant character, like Nina Hamnett.

AM: *Am I right in thinking I saw an image from the famous Fokine/ Diaghilev ballet* Schéhérazade? *Somebody gets down on their knees before Etta; she's got egret's feathers erupting from her headdress; and she arches back glamorously with her arms in the air above her. Now, that's the classic pose for Nijinsky as the Golden Slave and Ida Rubenstein as Zobeide. Is that not conscious?*
MB: I don't think so. You see, you're full of these precedents I'm not aware of!

AM: *But, in the flower section for the Exquisite, you do put in a quote from the Rose Adagio of* The Sleeping Beauty, *yes?*
MB: Yes, that's there.

AM: *And the music was what?*
MB: There's a bit of Tchaikovsky in it, *Piano Concerto No. 1.* We mimed playing the famous chords at the beginning. There's a lot of salon music in it, actually: pieces that I found on a salon recording which I really liked.

I liked the piece very much. After three nightmare weeks in which we came up with no movement at all, we toned things down a bit, and got very specific about each section. The first piece that worked was all about reading a book; it was such a limiting, simple idea that it suddenly took off.

AM: *Then, in summer 1993, you made a TV film,* Late-Flowering Lust, *a Betjeman piece with the actor Nigel Hawthorne.*
MB: Yes. The only other one we've done for TV – also in 1993 – is a short film called *Drip.* That was a dance for the camera, character-based and set in a theatrical boarding house. It was around the theme of narcissism. We were all actors or singers or various fans or ballroom dancers. But it didn't quite work.

Late Flowering Lust is a very happy memory for all of us, though, and was a very good experience for me. It's about fifty minutes long. Because it had a quite reasonably sized budget, was filmed on location, and planned to last a reasonable length of time – to fill an hour slot on TV – it had a lot of possibilities for different kinds of ideas. Usually, when you get any TV opportunity, it's only for something brief. But this was a major piece. For me, it was a different way of choreographing, because it had to be arranged in terms of shots. It was like choreographing loads of little vignettes that were then put together in different places to complete the music. But when you see it put together, it's exciting.

It was Nicholas Hytner, the director, who set this project up. He had liked my work, and had worked with the actor Nigel Hawthorne on *The Madness of King George*. He was involved in the initial planning stages, then left us to get on with it. The director who made the film was David Hinton; and he, Nigel and I collaborated closely to plan the whole piece. The music is by Jim Parker. He had written it about twenty years before, to go with Betjeman reading a number of his own poems. I'm very fond of those recordings, but I have to say that our recording is better, because Betjeman himself wasn't musically very precise, whereas Nigel's timing is just wonderful. The three of us spent a lot of time choosing which Betjemania we would use, and the dramatic idea of the whole piece. We chose twelve poems – out of about fifty of the Parker recordings – and created a small story of some English country weekend, in which Nigel played a Betjemanesque figure: an older man who came, hopefully, for a quiet weekend away with friends in the country, and turned up to find that the daughter of the house had returned from finishing school and had invited a lot of her young friends over. It was about him observing these young people, particularly the women; and remembering; and feeling old – and trying to be young again. These women remind him of various women he used to like: the sporty girl; the schoolgirl . . . Different sorts of characters, all very Betjemanesque.

Basically, he is ignored by them. They never actually acknowledge his existence throughout the whole thing. He is very much on the sidelines. Even at the end, when he drives off and waves them goodbye, there's a 'Who's that?' feeling to their reaction. 'Who was he?' It's very poignant.

This was the piece, for the record, that converted Cameron Mackintosh to my work. He hadn't liked the musical *Children of Eden*, and that had put him off using me in any of his productions. But when he saw *Late Flowering Lust* in 1994, he adored it; gave copies of it to lots of people; and hired me to do the dances for the Palladium production of *Oliver!* later that year.

Making it was certainly difficult. We had five weeks in which to rehearse and then two weeks to film twelve poems. On the Friday of each of those weeks, we went to the location – a place in Stevenage called Bennington Lordship, which is absolutely beautiful. So that we could see where we were going to be dancing certain sections, we used the actual layout of the place: there were some steps, and two mounds in the grass, which we used for choreographic sequences. We used the location to create the movement; the movement wasn't just casually imposed on the location. But the difficult thing was to rehearse all twelve poems and then to record them on film individually. It was a twelve-day shoot. Day One was Poem One, and so forth . . . Well, by the time you got to Poem Twelve on Day Twelve, you hadn't rehearsed it for two weeks. Yet there was all the crew waiting to do it. Remembering all that work was very difficult. Still, we did it. And the whole thing is a very happy memory. When you see the film, it's very beautiful to look at. We all look gorgeous in it. We were so pampered! We would get in, and have our hair and make-up done; and the beautiful costumes . . . And it was lovely weather. Simon Murphy – our dancer who died three years ago – was in it, and so it's a lovely memory of him too.

I also found *Late Flowering Lust* very exciting in terms of discovering what you can do for film. It's rare that you can really work on something that's an hour long in dance for the screen.

AM: *During these years, the personnel and size of the company kept changing. For* Nutcracker, *in 1992, you took on twelve other trained dancers in addition to your current six; you also took on four non-dancing actors. Were any of these to be of lasting importance to AMP?*

MB: Some of the people that came then are still there now. Maxine Fone, for example, Sara Cook (Saranne Curtin, as she later became) and Barry Atkinson, who plays the Private Secretary in *Swan Lake* and the Father in *Cinderella*. There are some other people who have come and gone a bit, but several of them have come back. Teresa Barker was in *Nutcracker* originally. She'd been a founder Cholmondeley, and had been on the BA course at Laban the year ahead of me. She stayed with us for six years.

So AMP began with a nucleus of dancers, but *Nutcracker* gave us this wider pool of dancers that we could use or not use as well. So, although we went on still doing small works afterwards, when we did *Late Flowering Lust*, Maxine came and did it. With each show we've done, the possibilities of what dancers we might use have become wider.

AM: *Your next new stage show was* Highland Fling, *your full-length version of the Romantic ballet* La Sylphide, *in 1994. We're discussing that in a separate chapter. But fill me in now on the AMP chronology from then (1994) till now.*

MB: Yes. *Highland Fling* we premiered in Bristol, in the spring of the year, and then toured it. That production stayed around quite a long time. We first showed it in London at the Lilian Baylis Theatre; the next year, 1995, we brought it back to the Donmar Warehouse. In between, we took it to Italy. We revived *Nutcracker* a second time at Sadler's Wells for Christmas 1994.

The last half of 1995, most of 1996, and the beginning of 1997 were taken up by *Swan Lake*: first at Sadler's Wells, then on tour, then in the West End, then in Los Angeles. But in between the West End and LA seasons, to fulfil Arts Council funding requirements, we revived *Highland Fling* in London again, just for a week, this time at The Place. We even did a royal gala of it, to raise funds for The Place.

Then the last half of 1997 and the start of 1998 were taken up with *Cinderella*, the only show we've ever opened in the West End itself. Right now – summer 1998 – we're preparing to take *Swan Lake* to Broadway this autumn and *Cinderella* to Los Angeles early in 1999.

AM: *You have great love of – and pride in – this early work. But to what degree, if any, do you think there was any justification in the 'juvenile' tag that was sometimes applied to you? Would you adjust any of these pieces now if you were reviving them?*

MB: It is justified up to a point. But it's also something that certainly a large number of the audience really enjoyed about the company. People enjoyed the fact that they were laughing, that this was a form of entertainment that they didn't often get in a dance performance, and that the company was, in a way, quite charming.

Sometimes, you know, the old things are the best. And if you dare to be a bit obvious or frivolous or old-fashioned – and I do mean 'dare' when you bear in mind the highbrow tone so often adopted in the modern-dance world – then your more original and serious touches can be that much more effective.

Probably I would revise these pieces now, because I would be in the position of directing them without performing in them too. Maybe I would cut some ideas. Some I simply wouldn't revive: *Deadly Serious*, for instance. Certainly, however, I've thought about doing *Town &*

Country with young dancers, so as to make the innocence of that piece still work.

AM: *I think now that some people felt uneasy and unsure how to take your early work because, while the dancers were often showing innocence, youthfulness, lightness, they were also often looking out front at the same time. The mixture of calculation, or knowingness, in address with the innocent lightness of what was going on on stage left some people in the audience thinking, 'Is this serious? Is this light? What is it?'*

MB: Good point. My view now, with humorous things, is that, if you look as though you think you're funny, it's not funny. If you look to the audience as though you're asking for a response, it doesn't work. My lesson to performers is: Show what it is that you're trying to show, but don't be too obvious about it, and don't ask for laughs.

AM: *The 'juvenile' tag carried on into* The Nutcracker *somewhat and certainly into* Highland Fling. *Do you think it's fair there?*

MB: I certainly see it in *Nutcracker*; I see it to a lesser degree in *Highland Fling*. You yourself felt that there was some schoolboy humour in *Highland Fling* when you saw that.

AM: *Well, obviously* Highland Fling *starts with some schoolboy humour, but I enjoy that too. A larger reaction I have, though, to both* Nutcracker *and* Highland Fling *is the odd feeling that you might be embarrassed by the prospect of handling serious emotion: that you'd rather get through emotion by giving it an entirely comic emphasis. In* Swan Lake, *you refuted that totally. But I'm not sure that you ever did a complete refutation until* Swan Lake.

MB: Well, you wrote a basically complimentary review of *Highland Fling* when it came back to the Donmar Warehouse in 1995, but that was your chief adverse criticism. And reading your review probably went some way towards making me stick to my guns with *Swan Lake*.

AM: *What guns?*

MB: I always go into a piece with serious intent. And I certainly did with *Highland Fling*. But I get very pulled in the direction of humour, either by ideas of my own that make me laugh or by hilarious suggestions made by people within the company. Whenever that came up with *Swan Lake, I* pulled back and said, 'No, this isn't the place to do that. We're not going to do that here.' Often I would get quite a lot of opposition. People would say, 'Look, this is going to be really funny. This is really going to work.' Obviously *Swan Lake* does have its funny moments; but I was far more rigorous than before in deciding where humour could and couldn't occur.

(Conversations 1998–99)

5

Nutcracker

1992

Idea

MATTHEW BOURNE: I was initially shocked to be asked to do *Nutcracker*. It was something that I would never have considered. We had six dancers, myself included. For music like that you need a big production, more dancers, more money, more everything.

ALASTAIR MACAULAY: *Who came to you with the idea?*
MB: We were performing *Town & Country* at the Royal Court for a week, in 1991, because we were one of the Barclays New Stages award winners that year, and the Royal Court staged a season of the winners' work. A lot of work for us came out of that one week, no doubt because it was the first time we'd performed in a London performance space that wasn't specifically known as a dance venue. For that reason, we later looked into other spaces not specifically associated with dance, like the Lyric Hammersmith and the Donmar Warehouse.

One of the people who came to see us was Nicholas Payne, who was then artistic director of Opera North; I think he brought Martin Duncan with him. Martin had directed an opera or two for Opera North at that point, and the idea he had at first was to produce Offenbach's *Orpheus in the Underworld*, using Adventures in Motion Pictures. I didn't take to that idea at the time – I can't remember why – and later he produced it with another choreographer. But next Nicholas and he told me that they were planning to mount a centenary production of the 1892 St Petersburg Tchaikovsky double-bill of the opera *Yolanta* and the ballet *Nutcracker* – to re-create the original programme, but with new productions of both pieces. They had had the idea from the conductor David Lloyd-Jones, who is a great Tchaikovsky buff. Nobody had put these two Tchaikovsky

96

20 *Nutcracker* (1992): pre-production photograph. Above, left to right: orphan-age children played by Matthew Bourne, Etta Murfitt as Clara, Simon Murphy. Kneeling: Scott Ambler and Ally Fitzpatrick as the Dross children Fritz and Sugar. In the eventual production, Bourne did not play an orphan until the 1993 revival.

pieces on together since the premiere at the Maryinsky. Because there were so many classical versions of *Nutcracker* around, they thought, 'Well, if we're going to spend money on this, we'd like to do something different.' I think they had cast around quite a bit, even talking to the Rambert; and I believe that noses were put out of joint at Northern Ballet, who, naturally, felt that they were the rightful people to do a co-production with Opera North. Certainly I remember there was surprise when they offered it to us.

I can see now what they saw in us: the humour, the ironic acting style, the story-telling, the accessibility, the use of more traditional music. I think they thought those things would suit *The Nutcracker*, which is famously quite a light piece – but, once delved into, is not so light. But at the time we were such a small company! In addition to us six dancers, we had Katharine our administrator and one technician, Petrus Bertschinger. So the idea came as a shock. Then, very quickly, I thought, 'What a fantastic idea! That's what I'd love to do' – not that I saw it as a career move into the classics at the time. *The Nutcracker* seemed the right piece to do at the point we were at at that stage; I could see how it suited the sort of performers we had and the kind of work we were doing; and it was an exciting next step into doing full-length works of more substance. So I was happy to take it on at the time, and I consciously gave all the leading roles to people already in the AMP company. That may not have been the best idea in every case, but in most cases it worked really well.

By the way, whereas most productions are called *The Nutcracker*, we removed the definite article: so it's just *Nutcracker*.

AM: *Though* The Nutcracker *is staged all over the world, especially at Christmas time, most productions in the last forty years have had different choreography. Only a few keep sections of the original 1892 choreography by Lev Ivanov, and almost all of them have scenarios somewhat different from that. What previous* Nutcrackers *had you experienced? In London, it has, for almost five decades, been an annual institution with London Festival Ballet – or, as that company became in 1987, English National Ballet.*

MB: I may have seen one – the one staged by Ronald Hynd – at Festival Ballet. If so, it made virtually no impression.

The first one I really took in was Peter Wright's production for the Royal Ballet in 1984 – the one that the Royal still do (not to be confused with his later one for the Birmingham Royal Ballet, which is different in many ways). I remember that it hadn't been danced until then at Covent Garden for several years. I enjoyed the music so much, some of it familiar and all of it memorable. And the whole shape of the piece was a completely new experience for me. People often talk of *The Nutcracker* as a bore, but for me it was completely fresh. In those days, it still seemed that if the Royal Ballet did it, that was a seal of approval; this was the best version that you were going to get.

On the whole, that production was, I believe, the most complete return to the 1892 original I've ever encountered. It felt – mainly – very faithful.

AM: *That traditional* Nutcracker *tells the story of Clara Stahlbaum – an unusual heroine for a nineteenth-century ballet both because she's a child and because she's from a middle-class family – and of the Christmas family party where her present from the magician Drosselmayer is a Nutcracker. At night, the room changes size, the toys and Christmas tree attain huge proportions, and Clara and the Nutcracker and the toy soldiers fight a battle against human-size mice. They win, and he takes her on a journey, through the Kingdom of Snow, to the Kingdom of Sweets.*

There are several dichotomies in the traditional Nutcracker. *Act One is virtually all story and only occasional dance, Act Two is virtually all dance and only occasional story. Although Drosselmayer is the magician who has effected all the transformations in Act One – his nephew is the human Nutcracker who has been imprisoned in the toy Nutcracker – he never himself goes on the magic journey. By contrast, the ballerina of the piece, the Sugar Plum Fairy, is only seen in Act Two: she is the monarch of the Kingdom of Sweets, and the pas de deux she dances with her cavalier is the ultimate climax of the whole dance display that the Sweets put on for Clara and the Nutcracker. Clara and the Nutcracker are the heroine and hero of the story, but they scarcely dance at all.*

Peter Wright's staging makes a few changes – you see Drosselmayer and his nephew reunited at the end of the ballet, for example – but the basic gist of that original scenario is honoured in his Royal Ballet production. (His other production, for the Birmingham Royal Ballet, takes more liberties, as do most Nutcrackers.*)*

MB: Sometimes the Wright staging at Covent Garden went too far. There were bits that were probably very impressive if you were a historian, but that don't work any more. There's that silly bit when the Sugar Plum Fairy has to jump on a gossamer cloak – a butterfly's wing or something – and her cavalier pulls the cloak along the floor, with her on it. It's sort of fun, but only if you're aware that they're trying to do something as authentic as possible.

It's easy to say what I went against when I came to do *Nutcracker*. Often I enjoy a ballet in the theatre, but when I come to tackle it myself, I delve into it deeper and ask myself a lot of questions about it that I wouldn't ask if I was 'just watching' the ballet.

AM: *Had you any other* Nutcrackers *under your belt between the Royal Ballet one and your own?*
MB: I'd seen, on TV, *The Hard Nut* – Mark Morris's 1990 version in Brussels – which I was only partly happy with. It wasted some of the music. The fact that there was a new version around wasn't intimidating.

AM: *Your* Nutcracker *was your first story ballet?*
MB: First full-length story ballet, yes. The first half of *Deadly Serious* had a story; and there were individual sections of other pieces that told little stories. But this was our first to sustain one story across a whole evening.

AM: *So what non-*Nutcracker *works did you have in mind as models of how to make a dance story work over a full evening?*
MB: As in pieces I'd made before, I tended to take inspiration from other ballets for different sections of what I was doing. I wouldn't really use one previous ballet as an overall model for a whole piece of my own. I'd seen – was familiar with – most of the Frederick Ashton and Kenneth MacMillan full-length ballets, most of the surviving nineteenth-century ballets. I don't remember using any of those consciously as a model, though I'm sure they went into what I did.

AM: The Nutcracker *is usually done as a full-length evening by itself, albeit a short one. The same goes for* Yolanta, *which I've seen two Russian companies do as the only work of the evening. So – I well remember – the prospect of having both pieces on one programme seemed extremely daunting. But in fact the whole evening lasted three-and-a-half hours (which is less than, say, the four hours that* The Sleeping Beauty *still takes when danced without cuts at its home theatre). This was partly because you performed* Nutcracker *without an interval between its two acts, and partly because* Yolanta *has no interval anyway. The evening's sole interval occurred between the two works.*

And the evening worked very well as a tribute to Tchaikovsky himself, because the music and the stories of Yolanta *and* Nutcracker *are so very different. His sheer diversity really hit home.*

MB: Yes. In *Nutcracker* we didn't even bring down a curtain between the two acts. Later, when we did present it as an independent full-length work at Sadler's Wells, we changed that, and restored an interval.

AM: *With* Nutcracker, *you suddenly had a company of twenty-two dancers. What funding did you have?*

MB: I think the initial production was mainly funded by Opera North and the Kobler Trust. We may even have put a little money into it. Some money came from the Arts Council.

AM: *How long did it run with Opera North?*

MB: Just during the *Yolanta/Nutcracker* centenary year. First at the Edinburgh Festival in August. Then in Leeds, at Opera North's home theatre. Then a tour of about four venues. About fifteen performances at most, which is not very many for a new full-length work. We didn't get the chance to get into it really.

AM: *Then, when you realized that* Nutcracker *worked, you decided to present it as a separate project?*

MB: Yes. At Sadler's Wells Theatre, first for Christmas 1993, then again for Christmas 1994.

AM: *Did you look at the original Hoffmann story of* The Nutcracker *and/or the original scenario for the 1892 ballet?*

MB: The starting point would always be to do all those things, to read as much around the subject as possible, to read any source material for the original that you can get your hands on, so you know what you're going against or going with, so that you're knowledgeable about the piece as a whole. Often an idea from the original story or scenario will trigger you off to a parallel idea, and that re-states for you what the essence of the piece is about. Even if you don't use anything from the original, it will often have made its impression somewhere.

The Nutcracker, as a ballet, I felt to be quite confusing, actually. The story never made complete sense to me in any version that I read or saw. A lot was explained by pure magic, and I always found that rather annoying. Even in very detailed scenarios, important patches of the story would pass in a blur of magic, without explaining anything. It's always:

'Well, this man Drosselmayer is magic, so everything he does is fine, and it's the magical hour of midnight . . .' and so on. I wanted to make it more logical than that, if I could; but not take away from the fact that there are magical characters and magical occurrences in it. An important part of the story has to remain fantasy.

AM: *Is there any Hoffmann left in your* Nutcracker?

MB: I think there was a spirit of Hoffmann we tried to capture; Martin Duncan was particularly keen on that, and it's something I'd like to make yet more of, if and when I rework *Nutcracker*. The nastiness of the orphanage, and the way that its governors turn into rat-people: I think those show the spirit of Hoffmann without lifting anything specific from the Hoffmann story.

AM: *Why did you decide to set* Nutcracker – *at least its first scene and its ending – in an orphanage?*

MB: There were several things I knew I wanted to do at once. This is the same with most pieces I do: I need immediately to find a few particular things that I know I'm going to do, and then I can relax for a while before starting all the detailed work. As soon as I think, 'I'm going to do *Swan Lake* with male swans', that's fine. With *The Nutcracker*, several things came to mind.

The orphanage setting came about for practical reasons. We still had a small company: twenty-two performers, of whom four were non-dancers. So I thought, if we were going to involve children as characters at all – which you have to in *The Nutcracker* – we didn't have enough dancers to convey both parents and children at the same time. There-fore I thought, 'Why don't we have everyone as children? Make it all about children; about children without parents?' I also decided that the Christmas party in most traditional ballet versions was too sumptuous. For most children who are coming to see *The Nutcracker* – for anyone, for that matter – the party sections are almost as much a fantasy as the fantasy sections that come later. If you already start with this big fantasy Victorian Christmas with an enormous tree and presents, it doesn't seem serious if you go anywhere else fantastic after that. So I thought it would be good to have a real contrast. That's where the idea of the orphanage came in – to make it a very grim, really pathetic Christmas. For instance, a little twig for the Christmas tree.

AM: *Were you thinking of Dickens at all? The sadness of* A Christmas Carol?

MB: Absolutely – and the orphanage in *Oliver Twist* and Dotheboys Hall in *Nicholas Nickleby*. We wanted sadness, and, as well, a sort of bitter-sweet humour. The way the children were all dressed up for Christmas to impress the governors of the orphanage – and then it was all snatched away from them; all the presents were taken away. Having the two rich kids as well – the Drosses as we called them, the children of Dr and Mrs Dross – that was very nice to play with.

AM: *Had you used the idea of children in any previous choreography?*
MB: I think we'd been quite innocent in a way, innocent in approach, especially in parts of *Town & Country*. But we hadn't been children. I had devised a sketch, years ago, using Joyce Grenfell's nursery-school sketches.

A second decision I made was that the Nutcracker doll itself would be a ventriloquist's dummy, because I've always found those dummies

21 *Nutcracker*: pre-production photograph. Andrew George (left), Simon Murphy, and Leslie the dummy. Though George played the Nutcracker in the production, here he seems to take on the role of the magician Drosselmayer, the Nutcracker's uncle in E.T.A. Hoffmann's story.

103

frightening and creepy. They do have a life of their own. A dummy has a mouth that moves, like a Nutcracker doll – and it has a sinister quality, too. I still have our dummy upstairs – the one we rehearsed with, not the one we ended up using on stage. He's called Leslie.

AM: *Did you buy Leslie as preparation for* Nutcracker, *or did you happen to have him anyway?*
MB: No, I had him anyway. I bought him in the theatrical shop in Cecil Court.

AM: *So, having him anyway, you knew you'd got to work him into the show!*
MB: I think they probably designed those faces to look as though they had an indeterminate expression. In rehearsals, we used to think that his face changed. We used to come in each day, and we'd look at him, and we really felt that some days he looked happier than others.

AM: *It's like the masks worn by the* commedia dell'arte: *they're expressive, but what they express seems to change according to how they're worn and how they catch the light.*
MB: I think the dummy did bring a sinister edge with it. I love the film *Dead of Night*, which contains (along with several other short stories) the story with Michael Redgrave about a 'vent' taken over by his dummy. Also there's an Anthony Hopkins film called *Magic* with the same theme. I'm fascinated by the dummy–vent relationship – breathing life (and personality) into a piece of wood. It's an idea I'd like to investigate again.

AM: *Well, there is a whole lineage of doll and statue ballets:* Pygmalion, Coppélia, La Boutique fantasque, The Steadfast Tin Soldier . . . *You're in good company. But how did you fit this dummy into the* Nutcracker *story?*
MB: We decided that the governors of the orphanage – who visit once a year to check on conditions and things – come there on Christmas Eve. The people who run the orphanage, Dr and Mrs Dross, have organized a display for them of dances and physical fitness and so forth. These governors bring presents for the children, which are basically second-hand toys. These are given to the children, one at a time. And one of the toys is this old ventriloquist's dummy. Then, once the governors have left, the presents – including the dummy – are snatched back and thrown into a

big box. But whereas the Nutcracker doll really is something magic in the usual scenario, this dummy is only magic in Clara's imagination. Once the nightmare sequence starts, there are lights flashing from the box, and it eventually comes to life – but in a much larger form. The toy she loves comes to life; but only because it's in her dream.

Another initial idea I had for *Nutcracker* was that the snowflake scene was going to be on ice. I'd been watching lots of Sonja Henie films; and I just thought she was so perfect for the Sugar Plum Fairy – or Sugar, as she was in our version (Princess Sugar, as she becomes in Act Two). That sort of sickly sweet personality. I showed photos of Sonja Henie to Anthony Ward as my idea for the designs, because I wanted everyone to look like her.

AM: *Sonja Henie! Sometimes I blush when I talk to you.*
MB: Everyone thinks, of course, that I took the ice-skating idea from *Les Patineurs*, the Ashton ballet. Well, that was in my head as well – but only as an idea. I hadn't seen *Patineurs* for five years; I'd never watched it often, and I had almost no specific memories from it. All I consciously took from it was the basic fact that you could give the illusion of ice-skating on a dry stage. Of course, *Patineurs* brings that off better than we could hope to do.

AM: *Were there any important ideas you originally had for your* Nutcracker *that you then discarded?*
MB: Yes. The most important thing was about Dr Dross – which was, at the time, too nasty to deal with, I think. I had this idea – which Martin dissuaded me from – of Clara being Dr Dross's favourite. Drosselmayer is, after all, attracted to her in the original story and in the original ballet. I thought that Clara's whole fantasy could be triggered off by suggesting a child-abuse story. I had seen a documentary recently about child abuse; and I also knew someone who'd been abused as a child, who described the situation to me and what he felt and how sometimes the mind would completely block out the situation, would fix on to something else, and then would even forget that it had happened. I felt that we could suggest this sort of situation with Dr Dross.

One early version of our scenario says that he comes in at midnight, creeps into the dormitory, makes his way to Clara's bed, and tucks her in tenderly. I put it like that because I didn't want it to be too obvious what was happening. Then, in a later scenario, we wrote that, as Dross tucked her in, they sort of sunk into the bed together, that the bed swallowed them both up, and that then she emerged into this fantasy world. So no specific abuse was shown – but the idea was planted.

I think it was too strong an idea for Martin; and too strong, he may have thought, for Opera North.

AM: *Do you think he was right? Or would you reconsider it now?*
MB: I would reconsider it now, because I do still like it as an idea. And I think I have developed enough skill in presenting things so that they can be taken in different ways by different viewers. I think I could do it in a way subtle enough for those people who wanted to see that aspect, while not making it too frightening or off-putting for a family audience. And I think it gives some explanation as to why she goes off into a fantasy – the whole idea of her blocking out Dr Dross would be good.

AM: *I'm curious about several original details in your first published scenario, not all of which you used on stage. For example, you planned that the pillow feathers should become the snow. Where did that idea come from?*
MB: That was inspired by the Jean Vigo film *Zéro de conduite*, where there's an enormous pillow fight in a school and the fight actually fills the screen with feathers. I thought that would be a great way for going into the snow; it would create a snow world. We didn't do it in the end because feathers are an absolute nightmare to deal with. But the idea was still there: the orphanage dormitory has its white pillows and sheets, and there is a pillow fight, though not with feathers. A lot of pillows are thrown around.

AM: Zéro de conduite *is one of the classic screen treatments of childhood. Did you look at any other films about children?*
MB: Not that I remember. I do recall looking at lots of Victorian photographic portraits of children: books which contained pictures of very serious-looking children. We decided to use this in our development of the children's characters – quite disturbed, serious-minded kids, who have had difficult lives. Our research also took us to the Museum of Childhood and to a reproduction of a Victorian schoolroom in London's East End.

22 From Jean Vigo's film *Zéro de conduite* (1933). The snowstorm of flying feathers in this dormitory pillowfight scene was one of Bourne's initial inspirations for *Nutcracker*, connecting the orphanage dormitory scene to the later snow scene, even though the feathers/snow connection proved impossible to show in the theatre.

Preparation

ALASTAIR MACAULAY: *How did you start on this* Nutcracker? *Did you begin by working with Martin Duncan on the scenario?*
MATTHEW BOURNE: Yes. For me, that was the most successful aspect of our collaboration, the most rewarding. He was a director, he was also a composer, and he had been involved in writing scenarios for several successful anarchic pantomimes – such as *Cinderella and her Naughty, Naughty Sisters*, which had run at the Lyric Hammersmith. So in coming to *The Nutcracker*, his mind was quite subversive.

A lot of his original ideas we didn't end up using – the same goes for many of my own ideas – but the collaboration with him was very good inasmuch as it made me concentrate my mind at the story meetings that we had to develop the plot. This was the first time I'd had to do that. The production was so large that the set needed to be built prior to rehearsals. Therefore the whole piece had to be structured and designed before rehearsals began – and that is the pattern for work I've used ever since. At the time, though, this was a different discipline. In a small production, major things could change during rehearsals; you could be creating along the way and come up with new ideas at short notice. Whereas with this, you had to have at least your basic ideas ready for each scene; you had to fit your action into a set and costumes that had been already designed – which didn't allow for you to change very much beyond the details. So the basic idea had to be formed.

AM: *You worked on the scenario with him over a period of weeks? Months? How long did it take?*
MB: We had meetings regularly for several months. But not every week. He was busy. And I was making *Deadly Serious*.

AM: *During that period, I imagine you're having sessions alone with the music? Or do you go over the score with friends?*
MB: I usually work with the music on my own. I listen to it a lot on a Walkman, when I'm just walking down the street or on the tube and the music's playing, and suddenly it just strikes me in a different way. When I get an idea, I get so excited by it, because I know that that's another thing solved. Or I get excited because I just know it's going to work theatrically and I want people to see it.

Like many other directors that I've worked with, Martin helped me to learn how to become a director myself. I really wasn't a director at that point; but he was. And he helped me gain a different viewpoint on things, because, although I'm still a choreographer, I realize – the way I work – that I'm now a director too.

The problem for Martin was that, later, when we actually came to choreograph the piece, he was also directing the companion-piece opera, which took up a great deal of his time. Inevitably, decisions had to be made, and I couldn't keep passing them through him. So once we got going, his involvement wasn't as great as he may have wanted. There wasn't a lot he could do, because in essence the whole thing is choreographed, so he may have felt redundant at times, not having enough to do. He was certainly useful and helpful with the direction of individual performers.

AM: *When I spoke to him recently, he said that he entered into the entire* Nutcracker *project because he wanted to find what it would be like, as a theatre/opera director, to work with dancers, and I think he found it very exciting from that point of view. He very much enjoyed working on the character backgrounds with the dancers, especially for the orphanage, so that the orphans all had names and interior lives. He remembers asking each 'orphan' basic questions such as: 'How long have you been in this home? How did you arrive here?' Also he remembers working with them on how to react: showing them that some reactions can be very small on stage but can still make an impact.*

MB: All that's true. Even so, my impression is that it wasn't satisfying for him as a whole, though I think he was right to be pleased with all his considerable contributions to it. Really, I don't think it works when a director has to make a piece with a choreographer – simply because, in essence, if you're a choreographer, you need to direct also; you need to have that overall control.

AM: *What specific ideas did he bring to it?*
MB: When first we came up with our original scenario, he pushed it towards the fantastical direction that he liked. So the whole idea of Sweetie Land, and of Prince Bonbon, Queen Candy, King Sherbert and all those things – that was very him. I tend to like more realistic characters; my way wouldn't naturally have been to go so fantastical; and, inevitably, I found that quite difficult in terms of choreography, especially in the effect that that had on the costume designs for group dances. The shape of the costumes was such that you just couldn't see any form to a group dance. There were too many big pink blobs, or too many men with heavy boots on. It was all right when they were doing their individual dances.

But it was successful in many ways, and that's due to Martin. People love the look of those characters, and you gained as well as lost by having them. If it were redesigned now, I would like to make some of the costumes more danceable, but I would bear in mind how well the fantastical side went down.

Something we both wanted was to make all the characters that we saw in the orphanage turn into characters in Sweetie Land, as we called the fantasy land of Act Two. (The Kingdom of Sweets, it's usually called in the ballet. Or, originally, Confiturembourg.) Everyone reappears in a different guise, and everyone is recognizably a version of what they were as an orphan. That worked well for a piece with fewer dancers. The audience seemed to enjoy that process of recognition: that the child with glasses in the orphanage became the Gobstopper with the glasses in Act Two, and so forth. The twins in stripy pyjamas who were good to Clara in Act One became her attendant Cupids later on.

AM: *But were you also intending to make a point about the nature of dreams? That Clara populated her fantasy with people she knew from the orphanage – the orphanage being the only world she knew?*

MB: Yes, absolutely, because dreams have to develop out of some lived experience. This device also enabled us to have a narrative through-line with a childish love-story, without having to introduce characters half-way through – whereas in the ballet you only meet the Sugar Plum Fairy and all her realm for the first time in Act Two, all out of the blue.

AM: *How did you think of handling the love issue in* The Nutcracker?

MB: Because our *Nutcracker* was all about kids, it had to be a sort of schoolgirl crush on another boy in the class: the tallest boy, probably the most mature boy. That was Andrew George, who's very tall.

AM: *Like Julian in the* Famous Five *books, who's the most 'mature' and the most heroic of the children.*

MB: Yes. Clara has a crush on him in the orphanage, and has dreams about him. But he's also quite fancied by Sugar, the daughter of the Drosses who run the orphanage; she's the rich girl. So the competition is set up there: a conflict between the children being continued. Our *Nutcracker* is therefore also about a girl reaching maturity, and about that sort of love becoming more real as it goes along – at least in her dream.

AM: *And how do you introduce it into your story?*

MB: At one point during her dream, she's left alone, holding the coat that the giant Nutcracker has had on. He reappears – without the Nutcracker mask – as a man: basically as the grown-up boy she fancied in the orphanage; but now he's shirtless. They have this 'getting to know you' kind of duet. She tests his mouth with her finger to see if he's still the Nutcracker and if she can open his mouth; and he bites her. Basically, he's a big, sexy young man – and she's still a little girl looking at him in wonder. The whole scene is sexy, and it ends with him being joined by other similarly dressed men in a *Spitfire*-like dance that is all about male-ness and its overpowering effect on this little girl. I wanted some kind of sexual awakening there, in her dream, her private thoughts.

AM: *And the gesture of putting her fingers in the Nutcracker man's mouth is, of course, sexual.*

23 *Nutcracker*, Act One. Clara (Etta Murfitt) suddenly sees the Nutcracker (Andrew George) transformed as the leader of a group of 'beefcake' young men. Images of virile beauty as multiple objects of desire are important to Bourne's work, spanning from *Spitfire* (1988) to *Swan Lake* (1995).

MB: Yes. What they do there, especially the way she touches him, is all very tentative. It's about discovering somebody else's body.

AM: *What are his feelings for her?*
MB: It being her dream, he's a problematic character. He's a bit flighty in it, because, though at this point he's happy with her, he soon just as easily goes off with someone else. However, her dream could also turn into a nightmare, and it does when he goes off with Sugar during the skating sequence. Sugar flirts with him, she's very beautiful, she pretends to get an injury, he saves her. Basically he's gullible. He falls for the charms of Sonja Henie. But, when reality returns at the very end, he does go off with Clara – and that's all fine, and as it should be.

AM: *You make it sound like a Bette Davis movie, with Miriam Hopkins as her rival.*
MB: It is! Well, Sugar becomes a sort of spoilt brat character. We were looking for conflict; I remember that we talked a lot about that, and I

still do. When I come up with any idea, I always say, 'What's going on here? Where's the drama? Where's the conflict?'

We tried to keep the plot going through the snowflake scene. In most versions, Clara has just been journeying – you're never sure why – and then the snow scene happens and you're satisfied by the fact that this is the first decent bit of dancing, but that's all. I think it's nice to have a bit of a story left there, a 'What's going to happen next?' feeling. Ours is a skating party, but there's also a definite situation going on. Sugar now reappears as Princess Sugar; she entraps the Nutcracker and runs off with him. So the end of Act One has a cliff-hanger feel. He's gone off with another woman, with the rival; and Clara's left on her own once again.

AM: *How much of a pause was there in your original production between Acts One and Two?*

MB: None. It ended with her on stage, and then it kept going. The curtain didn't come down. Part of the initial challenge of this production was the continuation of the story and the sets. She stayed on stage at the end and was still distraught at the beginning of the Act Two music: which is when we introduced the two Cupid characters. They were the twins who'd helped her mend the Nutcracker doll in the first act, when it got broken by Sugar and Fritz.

When we redid the production, we did put an interval in, and we added a set change.

AM: *Are the Cupids the first people to introduce you to the fact that the characters are transformed in Act Two?*

MB: Yes. I'm not quite sure how the idea of them came about. They're still wearing the glasses that they were wearing previously, and they've now got wings – but I think we put them in the pyjamas because one of the original ideas we had had for the second half of the snow scene was that it was to do with sleep, sheets and bedding: she was dreaming, and the thing that suggested snow at the back of the stage was like a wavy sheet that was held in space. So the Cupids were part of that whole thing. They give her her dress, which came from above, from heaven, brought down by two doves. (That scene is called 'Help From Above'.) And the Cupids give her the courage to carry on, to go and fight to get her man back. They take her off in a Cupid-mobile!

AM: *There's definitely an angelic feeling to Tchaikovsky's music there.*

MB: I suppose I'm always drawn to things like that. I like angels and Cupidy, winged characters.

Another element is that Fritz becomes a character in the second half, called Prince Bonbon. He's still Sugar's brother, obviously working for her. So there's a constant battle all the way through: two girls fighting for the same man, one with a brother, one without. *The Nutcracker* is a light piece, and we weren't making it any great tragedy. We just gave it a bit more feeling, a bit more of an on-going plot; and we decided to make all those national dances in Act Two continue the plot in some way, however small. So the Spanish Dance, the Chinese Dance, all those dances became about guests getting into a wedding party and about Clara not being able to get in.

AM: *And you kept that plot tension going longer than in any other* Nutcracker, *because your hero is with the wrong woman from just before the end of Act One through to just before the end of Act Two. Usually, the story of* Nutcracker *has arrived at happy-ever-after – at Eden, as W. H. Auden once wrote in an essay about the Balanchine production – around the start of Act Two.*

MB: It's true, ours never really resolves until the very end. I always used to feel an enormous sense of relief on the audience's part at the end. When they finally got together, it used to get a round of applause, because by that point everyone so wanted it to happen.

AM: *Did you realize during the planning stage that there might be a problem between your narrative and the music? There isn't really any conflict in the music in Act Two, and virtually no narrative.*

MB: It was certainly harder to create 'drama' in Act Two. Where a problem arose, for many reasons, was in the Sugar Plum grand pas de deux. In our version, it ends up being danced by the Nutcracker and Sugar: which doesn't completely work, because she's not the person you want to see him dancing that music with. However, if we were going to go with that story, that was the only way we could do it, because it was the Sugar–Nutcracker wedding that Clara was gatecrashing. And this did work very well about two-thirds of the way through the music, when a certain amount of sadness can be heard in the orchestration. At that point, we had Clara appear at the top of the huge Busby Berkeley wedding cake; she looks down on to the dancers, the Nutcracker and Sugar, and the tragic tone in the music suddenly expresses her plight, her yearning, and her despair.

I must admit it was hard work to make a narrative from Act Two, both in planning and in rehearsal. That was the real challenge. Some plot points – trying to find reasons for these dances – were solved only in rehearsal, like the Mirlitons and the Sugar Plum Fairy variation. The score for Act One's no problem at all; it's all story-telling, with great scenes and with dances very clearly defined. Act Two's a series of dances, with very little music to go on that actually tells any story. We found reasons for all the dances in the end, but I remember it being an enormous struggle. When you get a simple idea – like the Mirlitons music occurring in Princess Sugar's bedroom, with a mirror and all her friends getting her ready for the wedding – it helps a lot, because then you've got something to work with. It doesn't have to be an idea with any great depth, just something that builds up some sense of continuity, without that feeling of just bringing on one dance after another in a parade.

AM: *Have you ever been able to get all the story of a piece fixed before you entered rehearsals?*
MB: No, no, definitely not.

AM: *You're still adjusting – determining – the story all the time.*
MB: Some pretty major solutions come about quite late on, through the sheer chemistry of rehearsals. In fact, I've never felt that I've solved every problem by the time of the first night.

I've just found the draft of an AMP announcement that was written some time before we choreographed *Nutcracker* that shows how the show was at an early stage of conception.[1] We wrote it to try to raise some money for the Opera North double-bill. The statement about our intentions reads:

> 'As AMP's choreographer, I was instantly thrilled at the prospect of radically re-interpreting this ballet classic, using a contemporary dance idiom, but more specifically AMP's particular style of dance theatre. Nicholas Payne has brought together an exciting team to collaborate on this project, including the internationally renowned artist, Howard Hodgkin'

– who, as we know, eventually didn't design it –

> 'and the director Martin Duncan, who will be devising the new Nutcracker scenario with me and also directing the opera. Howard, Martin and I have shared initial ideas and have found much common ground and a mutual excitement about the project. We are writing a

1 Document in Bourne's own collection.

narrative which can be understood whilst watching the production, rather than one that needs extensive programme notes explaining who has put a spell on whom before the ballet began.'

Bit of a nasty sentence there!

'Having researched into many previous and current productions of *Nutcracker*, we have decided to keep the basic structure, as dictated by the music, and indeed some of the characters, Clara, Fritz, Sugar Plum and Herr Drosselmeyer, who becomes Dr Dross. But to rethink many of the scenes and to give the piece a narrative that extends beyond the first act – where the plot normally ends and we get a series of divertissements.

'Artistic Treatment. At this stage, the treatment is not yet fully conceived, but initial ideas place Act I in a grim orphanage, run in rather Dickensian fashion by Dr Dross. Preparations are afoot for the annual Christmas visit by the school's Board of Governors. A play and a dance are being rehearsed by the children, all played by AMP dancers. Decorations are being put up to cover the usually dirty bare walls of the dormitory and the children are dressed up in party clothes. The Board arrives, the entertainment compèred by Dr Dross is presented, and gifts are handed to the children. Clara, Dr Dross's favourite, receives a Nutcracker doll'

– which changed. Actually, I think I already wanted to use Leslie, but didn't feel the need to explain our 'take' on the doll at this stage.

'Knowing that the gifts and Christmas finery are generally snatched away once the governors have left, Clara hides the doll behind the Christmas tree. After the party, later that night, when all the children have been put into their beds (several into each bed), Clara creeps out and retrieves her Nutcracker, bringing him back to her bed to sleep by her side. At midnight, Dr Dross, batlike, creeps into the dormitory and makes his way to Clara's bed; he tucks her in tenderly.'

This whole thing went.

'From this point, we enter into Clara's nightmare dream world and the scenario will evolve from ideas of a young girl's adolescent fantasies. The Nutcracker doll, having defended Clara from various horrors in the dormitory, such as rat people and flying children, turns into a handsome and gorgeous hunk, with whom Clara instantly falls in love. An enormous pillow fight turns the dormitory into a feather (snow) strewn landscape, where we find the glamorous and vain Sugar Plum Fairy, who enchants the gorgeous Nutcracker hunk and steals him away to the Land of Sweeties. Clara, now alone, decides to go off and search for her man. She journeys through many lands (various national dances) before arriving in the Kingdom of Sweeties to confront Sugar Plum and her attendants.'

You see, that was the original idea.

AM: *Why and when did Howard Hodgkin fall out of the production?*
MB: Howard started work on it, but I think ultimately had problems with the technical side of creating a narrative piece. He had worked quite successfully with Richard Alston at the Rambert on two or three pieces, especially *Pulcinella*, and also with Ashley Page. Very beautiful designs for those pieces. But I think my style – of wanting beds and props and all those things – was something that Howard had never had to achieve. It needed a simpler idea for Howard to come up with something. But very happily he agreed to become a patron of the company. So it wasn't a fall-out of any kind; it just wasn't something that we felt together was going to work. He's a big admirer of the company, and I'm certainly a great admirer of his work.

It was then that Anthony Ward was brought in. We gave him certain specific design ideas, and he brought others. We wanted all those beds for Act One, because they were quite important for giving the orphanage the right sense of place. We knew we were going to need quite a few props, and in rehearsal at AMP we always try to work with as many props as possible, to get a sense of the place and situation.

One big design idea we had had was that the Nutcracker kind of creates an earthquake or explosion in Act One. He magically cracks open the back wall of the orphanage – but at the same time this tree is growing at the back as well. It's the little twiggy tree the orphanage used by way of a Christmas tree; it's been thrown out the window, but now you can see it growing up behind the window.

AM: *Where did that idea come from?*
MB: We wanted to have a tree growing. We felt that it was one of the main things you have to deliver with *Nutcracker*. But, for the purposes of the plot, the Christmas tree we'd had in the first place was a little black twig virtually, with a little bit of tinsel on it. When it grew, it had a more evil, oppressive feel to it; and there's a big hand-like branch that

crashes into the room at one point. So the growth of the tree creates the break-up of the orphanage walls. It's like roots growing into the building, uprooting the foundations.

Anthony Ward also helped us to solve Act Two. That first scenario still says that Clara travels through various lands, with various national dances. We hadn't found what to do with them. All our ideas were centred around the action up to the snow, and everything seemed to work up to that point. Then the rest of it was something that had to be solved. When Anthony came in as the designer, many of his ideas went into creating that second act. He said, for example, 'Wouldn't it be fun to do some Marshmallow people? And some Liquorice people?' So then we tried to mix the feel of the music, like the Spanish music, to a Sweetie idea, which was Liquorice Allsorts. So their hair was made of liquorice.

But we were also trying to give a reason for the dances, and I honestly can't remember whose idea it was to have Clara trying to get in without an invitation.

AM: *Well, it's a way of keeping the plot's suspense.*
MB: Yes. We were very keen for that to happen.

AM: *It was a centenary production. Did you decide to use every scrap of music?*
MB: We didn't use the dance in Act Two that's often cut: 'Mère Gigogne', 'Mother Ginger'. We just didn't feel it was relevant. I sometimes thought, when we revived it, 'Should we find a way of putting it in?'

AM: *What's your musical expertise? Do you go back to the score itself? Can you read a score to any degree?*
MB: No, nothing at all. I have no musical training.

AM: *Do you have one recording? Do you find you buy more recordings than one to give yourself different ideas of tempi when you're preparing?*
MB: Yes. I usually get as many as I can.

AM: *Does that make a big difference, the difference between Bonynge and Lanchbery and Rozhdestvensky?*
MB: Yes, quite a lot. It definitely affects the story, because some recordings feel more dramatic. But also some recordings give you a different dance feeling when you start moving to them.

AM: *In a score like* Nutcracker, *do you have a clear idea which bits of music are dance music and which bits are action music?*

MB: Definitely.

AM: *There are some sections of* Nutcracker *where it's questionable whether the music is meant to support dance or action. For example, all the music after the battle in Act One before the snow scene Tchaikovsky wrote, following Petipa's guidelines, as action music; but quite a few choreographers have set a dance to it. You do too.*

MB: Well, I think that's dance music. There's a point where it goes into dance music. And it has so much feeling as well. It doesn't feel just like it's journeying music to me; it feel as if it's saying something. Then we move on.

It's usually quite clear to me – even when it's the other way round: when something is supposedly dance music and I don't feel it is. Like the end of *Cinderella:* I never felt that was dance music. As I say, I think it's very clear that most of *Nutcracker* Act One is story-telling music really. It does have these few dances within it – the children's march, the grandfather's dance – but relatively little dance music overall. Some music in the original is meant to accompany toy dances; in our version, Martin and I decided early on to have a school display. So we had an Isadora-Duncan-type dance and then a keep-fit dance. I remembered how, at the Laban Centre, Bonnie Bird told us how, in the 1930s, some American colleges required their girls to bring 'twelve yards of chiffon for self-expression'! And that gave me the idea of an institutionalized Isadorable dance. The keep-fit dance was an easy decision: we gave it skipping-ropes and dumb-bells and all that.

AM: *Do you have any ideas for specific actions or dance movements before you begin rehearsals?*

MB: As far as action goes, I'll usually have listened to the music quite a lot and will have imagined what will happen to it. There are certain bits where I know that people enter and that the music would be good for certain events to occur. Or there'll be music where I think, 'Oh God, there's something obviously happening here – what is it?' I've usually got those things pinpointed along the way.

In the days of doing *Nutcracker*, I used to choreograph a lot more before rehearsals. I wasn't as confident about doing things then. I always started off with a lot of ideas for steps – but never enough, because I can never store that much in my head! I don't worry about that so much now; I tend to do it on the spot much more. Or I'll work it out the night before with Scott and Etta or some other people that I pick. With

Nutcracker, because we were out on tour with *Deadly Serious*, when we had a free day, we did some rehearsal preparation for *Nutcracker*. That was when we worked out some of the school display dances and a lot of material for the skating sequence. Not much more than that, actually.

AM: *Have you already got an idea of the counts for each stretch of music before you come to rehearsals?*
MB: Yes. I'll have worked out all the counts for myself before we ever rehearse anything.

Development

MATTHEW BOURNE: Here are a few little notes I wrote for Act One. It's quite interesting to see what details changed or never got pursued:
'Preparations, First Section: paper chains, Christmas tree, party clothes, checked for nits and dirty hands, visit of Board.
'Inspections and Rehearsals: Board of Governors inspect kids and watch them dance, give them presents.
'Nutcracker doll. Sugar wants it, Fritz breaks it. Bandage. Hides it under tree.
'Performance of musical chairs.' In the event, we didn't do the musical chairs.
'Dr Dross compère. Matron does a turn. Play. Different dances. To bed.
'Presents taken away. Night clothes. Crowd into beds. Small rats are seen. Put out stockings for Christmas. Clara gets out of bed, gets Nut-cracker, puts him to bed.
'Dr Dross enters. Adolescent fantasies. Bat-like. Tampers with Clara. They sink into the bed. Tree shakes.' So, you see, it was still a very fright-ening idea at that stage.
'Christmas tree grows. Kids shake in beds. Nutcracker grows full size, still has bandages.' I think we imagine him quite frightening as well at this point. 'Comes out of bed.' So he was originally going to be in the bed with her and then appear somehow.
'The Battle. Flying kids in nightshirts.' Well, we obviously couldn't do that, because we couldn't fly anybody. 'Pillow fight. Feathers. Rat people.' I think the family were going to become rat versions of themselves. They were going to have snouts and be exaggerations of themselves. 'Nutcracker is knocked out defending Clara. After battle: is he dead?

Turns into hunk. They walk through the Christmas tree into snow. Iced-over pond (*Les Patineurs*).'

ALASTAIR MACAULAY: *So you see, you were thinking of* Patineurs *somewhat at that stage.*
MB: Yes, I'd forgotten that. Now Act Two.

'Clara is left alone.

'Vision. Two Cupids show her vision of Bohemian life in Sweetie Land (debauched). The Governors are there' – which they weren't.

'Journey. Each time Clara and the Cupids appear, they are more bedraggled.

'Land of the Sweeties. Waltz of the Flowers. Confrontation. Back in the dorm. She throws doll across room. The real Prince is in her bed.'

AM: *Are these ideas that you would have put down after initial discussions with Martin?*
MB: They may be the notes I was taking from our discussions. I think we may have been talking, and I was just writing down these quick ideas for things that we came up with, for each section.

AM: *What about your breakdown of the score?*
MB: It's just counts, more or less. It has some things written on it: 'Clara's solo, Etta enters.' 'The Isadora Dance.'

AM: *Let's look at these titles. You've got 'Overture'. What happens in the Overture?*
MB: The orphans enter during the Overture. They introduce themselves in front of a front cloth, and they stare at the audience – as children might, if they were pushed on to a stage.

AM: *Etta – as Clara – is the first. Then the others come on. Then we have the Orphanage Preparations.*
MB: This is the cleaning and the putting up of decorations, and the bringing in of the small Christmas tree in preparation for the Governors' visit. Then they are drilled.

AM: *Then you've got 'Clara's solo'. What kind of solo?*
MB: She does a very childlike, jumpy little solo for the boy in the orphanage that she fancies – who later becomes the Nutcracker character. Then she's made fun of by the others, and laughed at.

AM: *'Mrs Dross re-enters. Line up. Dr Dross enters.'*
MB: And he inspects them. They line up for him.

AM: *'Prepare for dance.'*

MB: They've rehearsed this dance to show to the Governors. The funny thing is they don't actually ever show it to them. But that's the idea: that they do the dance as a rehearsal. The 'Children's March' is very much made up of mock ballet partnering. Not classical, more like folksy ballet movements and childlike stampings. That goes into a 'Fritz and Sugar's Dance', which is a display from those two, who are supposedly trained dancers, because they've had classes and they do a little tap section in their dance. So they're showing how it's done. Then there's a scene where the kids rebel, once the Drosses have left, and they mess up Fritz's and Sugar's dance for them.

Next the Governors arrive. They're presented with bouquets by Sugar and Fritz, and there are various displays that the orphans put on for the Governors. They do a little bow and curtsey to them, then there's a 'Medical Dance', which was basically four eights, very fast inspections of each other. They were inspecting for nits, and in each other's ears – and that thing they used to do in schools, where you used to have to go behind a screen and lower your underpants and cough – those kind of things.

Then the Governors present two very big parcels. They pick two children to bring in these parcels, and the two think the presents are for them; but they're actually for Fritz and Sugar, who then open these presents, with everyone looking on rather jealously. Fritz gets a toy gun and some sweets. Sugar gets some sweets and a beautiful Victorian doll.

AM: *Sugar and Fritz: are these two based on the two dreadful Squeers children in* Nicholas Nickleby *– Fanny and Wackford Junior?*

MB: They are a bit, yes. They're the worst kind of spoilt brats. Great characters to play. They go away to eat all their sweets and make themselves sick. They used to have – inside their sweets boxes – some Nutella, so that it looked as though as they were eating the sweets, because they got chocolate all over their faces.

Meanwhile the kids do their exhibition dances. The Isadora Dance is basically a free-expression display with lengths of chiffon, which the girls and boys do. It's all based on Grecian-type dancing. Even at my school, I remember, we did this – when we went into the hall one afternoon a week, there was something on the radio, and you were asked to be a tree or something to the music, and pranced around in your plimsolls. At Laban it was always a joke. This little Isadora Dance is led

24 *Nutcracker*, Act One. Dr Dross (Barry Atkinson, centre) directing one of the orphans' display dances. Andrew George, playing the orphan who later becomes the Nutcracker, is seated on the extreme left.

by Mrs Dross. It's her little party piece, and she's very proud of herself. This is her way of showing herself off. She was once a dancer – a very long time ago.

Then we did the Eurhythmics, as it's called here. This again is something I got from Laban. There were several students who had studied Eurhythmics, and we learnt how it went back to Dalcroze. Here it's basically a keep-fit dance, and it's packed with lots of things: dumb-bells, skipping ropes. It's a highly designed little number. The end position of the Eurhythmics Dance is very complex: it's all skipping ropes; they intertwine, and open them out – like the ribbons in Ashton's *Fille mal gardée*.

The Governors bring in a basketful of presents. One at a time, the kids come forward and get their gifts. They can pick which one they want. This is where the sissy boy picks a doll. Mrs Dross snatches it back and gives him a football – which always got a very big laugh. The Nutcracker is the last one to be picked. It's hidden away in the basket somewhere. Clara picks him and dances a solo with him.

Then Fritz and Sugar re-enter, covered in chocolate, with the dolls. Sugar comes over to Clara, who shows off her doll – that his mouth moves. Sugar presses her doll's face and its mouth doesn't move. So she dumps her doll, gets Fritz to try to take the Nutcracker dummy, and both the Nutcracker's arms get pulled off as they pull him apart. Then we have a little Doctors and Nurses section, where the twins in the orphanage, who both wear glasses, help Clara. They play doctors and nurses, put on mock hospital masks and pass the instruments. They put him together again, and give him back to her. She thanks them; and thereafter they're her helpers.

The Governors have gone off into another room, by the way, while all this stuff's going on, for a drink. Now they re-enter and prepare for the Governors' Dance. The Dross couple are now a bit drunk and having quite a good time. There's a bit of flirting going on between Dr Dross and one of the Governors' wives. They do a dance. The kids snigger at it, and think the adults are ridiculous.

AM: *In the traditional ballet, you then get the departure of the guests, the beginning of the magic, the arrival of the mice, then the vast growth of the Christmas tree. But in your version?*

MB: An enormous amount happens in a short piece of music. The Governors of the orphanage, who are quite well-meaning people, leave – duly impressed by the way the orphans are treated, although we see that it is all a sham. The presents are snatched back – which happens just as the music goes rather sad. The orphans all undress for bed; all the presents and all the decorations are pulled down; the poor old Christmas tree is thrown out of the window of the orphanage. By the end of that piece of music, the orphans are all in bed, the lights are turned off, there's silence. It's the end of the day.

Then, to the change in the music where in most *Nutcrackers* you generally get the first mouse coming on, Sugar re-enters. (In my first plan, this is when Dr Dross was to come back and tuck Clara tenderly into bed. It's very furtive music.) Sugar is looking for the Nutcracker doll, the ventriloquist's dummy, which she quite likes the look of. She's jealous of it, because it can do things her doll can't: i.e. move its mouth and speak. So she comes to try and find it in the darkness of the dormitory, and hunts around all the beds. Eventually, she sees a flashing light coming from a big chest, in which all the presents and things have been put. He's been put in there.

But, halfway through that search, we get the midnight chime. At that point, Clara has seen her coming; she's hiding from Sugar behind the beds – and now you feel as though you've gone into another world. Actually, I feel it's really the least clever aspect of our plot, that we just go off into the dream world at that time. But it's hard to fight that in *Nutcracker*. The other world starts with the flashing light. Sugar opens up the box. A giant Nutcracker doll appears, like Frankenstein's monster. She runs off screaming to her family. Then we get the Christmas-tree music. The children are fearful of the Nutcracker, to begin with. He's a frightening figure – big and lumbering: scary. And he creates the earthquake or explosion I was just talking about before, magically cracking open the back wall of the orphanage, so that we can see the tree growing huge at the back. That music, with all its rising scales, is tremendous, and we made it a really alarming experience for the children: they're scared of what's happening to the tree, and they're quite frightened of the Nutcracker as well. Lots of sound effects were added to the Christmas-tree music, by the way: big explosions and thunder-cracks. They looked as if they were activated by the Nutcracker's arm movements; visually they were on specific parts of the score. But then, when the music reaches its climax – what I call the Philip Glass bit of music! – the orphans realize that the Nutcracker is there to help them and that, basically, he is giving them the means of escape from the orphanage. So suddenly they all look at him in a new light. They've got a new friend.

They hide him away just before the Drosses re-enter with Sugar. She's pointing to the box where he's been, and saying, 'There's a monster in there' or something similar. Dr Dross tries to shoot him, but he's not in there. All this goes on as the music starts for the battle with the mice; but our battle is between the family and the orphans.

It's just a big fight – and quite funny as well. The orphans tie Mrs Dross on to a bed. Someone gets the gun from Dr Dross. It's all about chasing – and a way of getting rid of the beds in the dormitory. Each of the Drosses gets dumped on to a bed, and hit with pillows, or shoved into a sack. Then that family are carted off on beds. Eventually the set is cleared of beds, there's great joy, all the orphans escape through a big crack in the wall to a better land, and Clara is left alone.

She's wondering where the Nutcracker's gone. After all, he's triumphed and saved the orphans from the Drosses and has finished off Dr Dross, as it were. So where is he now? She goes off stage, looking for him, and returns, carrying the coat he was wearing. He's disappeared; but suddenly now she is confronted by him – or rather, by the now handsome, hunky Nutcracker man he has become. The top half of his costume has been taken away and the head he had on – he had a sort of plastic head, which looked like a ventriloquist's dummy – has gone too. The reason you know it's him is that the socks he's wearing are quite significant, stripy socks, which are quite clearly visible because he's got quite high-cut trousers.

The first thing that he does is try to open his mouth and he bites her finger; we know she's making the same gesture she did with it earlier on. They do a duet, when she discovers his body and awakening sexual feelings. That vision is multiplied by all the other men in the company coming in bare-chested, giving an image of masculinity and sexuality. She almost passes out with glee. It does have quite an effect in the theatre.

He then directs her towards this new land, which is the Land of Snow – or 'The Frozen Lake', as we called it – and they encounter, first of all, the twins, who are now in beautiful Sonja Henie skating outfits. The women here are in little fur-edged skirts and the men in bobble hats and scarves and big winter jumpers. They all skate past them. It's a lovely, friendly world. Clara is cheering up slightly – but she then encounters the Drosses, who she runs away from. They wave at her in a friendly way – also in skating outfits. It's a world where everyone smiles and is happy to see each other. Eventually, all the orphans re-enter, now happily enjoying themselves.

'The Skating Party.' We tried to keep the drama going through even this big dance sequence, with the introduction of Princess Sugar – as she is now. She is Sugar Dross, and she is now the Sonja Henie figure, the Princess of Snow Land, of the Frozen Lake; and she obviously takes a liking to the Nutcracker character. She does a mock fall to the ground. He saves her, she thanks him, and thereafter she pretends to have an injured ankle. So she's a scheming little minx! And her brother, Fritz, is involved in this – Prince Bonbon, as he has become. He's her partner in crime. He enables Sugar to run off with the Nutcracker, who is enticed by her beauty. Clara, to be honest, does look a little drab next to Princess Sugar, because she's just in her nightdress and her bunches. Sugar is all beautiful, with fur and so forth. So that's how Act One finishes, with Clara left alone in the middle of the Frozen Pond, pretty distraught, obviously.

AM: *In the original Opera North production, you then carried straight on into Act Two.*

25 *Nutcracker*, Act One. Princess Sugar (Ally Fitzpatrick), lifted during the skating scene. This momentary lift, as frozen in this photograph, accidentally evokes a travelling tableau in Frederick Ashton's 'skating' ballet *Les Patineurs* (1937). This image became a poster and logo for Bourne's *Nutcracker*.

MB: This starts with a section called 'Help From Above'. Two Cupid characters enter – they're the twins from the orphanage who helped her put the Nutcracker together again! They say that she's not looking great; she needs to tart herself up a bit, win back her man. So they present her magically with a new dress. She looks a lot better now, and they take her off to the Land of the Sweeties.

Now we get the re-entry of Sugar with the Nutcracker. She's got her skating boots over her shoulder – real skating boots, with the blades on. They're followed by Fritz, who's sort of pissed off with them for being so lovey-dovey together. Then there are the mime scenes where we arrive at Sweetie Land. And the door to the castle has a sort of sexual look to it also. It's like a big mouth, but it has been likened to a vagina also. (I think that may have been intentional on Anthony's part.) Princess Sugar introduces the Nutcracker to the world of Sweetie Land, which is a delicious one, in that you can eat and taste the buildings and the people . . .

AM: *You make it sound very* Hansel and Gretel.

MB: Definitely. I know Martin was certainly into that aspect of fairy

26 *Nutcracker*, Act Two. The two pyjama-clad Cupids:
Maxine Fone, left, and Phil Hill, right.

stories. But the point was also about values. In Sweetie Land everyone is
judged on how they taste: surface values only.

Sugar shows the Nutcracker that you can lick the set, which he does.
Then she introduces him to her parents – who are the alter egos of Dr
and Mrs Dross. They are the monarchs here – King Sherbert and Queen
Candy – and they spend a bit of time judging whether he's appropriate
or not. (Sugar wastes no time in explaining that she means to marry
him.) The Queen tastes him quite a lot to see if he's up to scratch. They
decide that he is, and that they shall be married. Then, just as they're
entering the castle gates, Clara re-enters with the Cupids. She's just in
time to see the Nutcracker go in with Sugar and the Drosses. She tries to
follow, and the Cupids encourage her; but a Security Doorman comes
out, and stops her.

Clara wonders how to get in. This keeps her on tenterhooks for a
large part of Act Two. You need an invitation to enter; and so all the
dances that follow are about people who turn up with their invitations
to enter the castle – invitations to the wedding of Princess Sugar and

the Nutcracker. Just as Clara explains to the Security Doorman that she hasn't got an invitation, the Spanish Liquorice dancer arrives – she's got her invitation between her teeth, and she presents it – and then her two male Liquorice Allsorts (they've got shiny black hair) join her. They dance the Spanish Dance; Clara tries to copy the movement to try and get sexier. The Spaniard sweeties pass on into the castle.

The next person Clara encounters is the Knickerbocker Glory. He enters in a puff of smoke – he's smoking some sort of dope, he's very druggy. That's in the music: the Arabian Dance, with all that hypnotic feeling. The original idea was that he was dripping. He has ice-cream hair with the cherry on top, and it's all dripping down him – that greasy sort of feeling: slimy, yugh! Now, he happens to have two invitations, his own and a spare; and Clara is slightly taken in by what is coming from his cigarette, almost hypnotized, nearly enticed by him. But she doesn't like what she might have to do to get that invitation – he actually offers it to her and she declines – because he's a nasty bit of work. He enters the castle without her – in another puff of smoke.

Then you have the Marshmallow girls – which is the Chinese Dance. They're just flighty, Marilyn Monroe dumb-blonde-type girly-girly char-acters, pink and fluffy and chatty, all with their invites in their handbags. They all come in as a gossipy group. Clara tries to weave her way in amongst them, but she's found out at the last minute.

AM: *You mention Marilyn. Do you often have a movie idea behind your characters?*
MB: Quite often, really.

AM: *Is there one in the Arabian Dance?*
MB: Funnily enough, not originally. But later on, yes. Later on, I did it myself just for one season at Sadler's Wells; and I must admit I felt like Terry-Thomas – because of the cigarette all the time between my teeth. I felt very slimy. I know Terry-Thomas isn't really like that, but I did have him in mind a lot.

The last one was the Gobstoppers Dance – to the Cossack music. They're very rough, skinhead types, rude and lewd. They end up fight-ing each other at the end of their dance – and while the Doorman comes forward to break up the fight, Clara manages to creep into the castle behind him. This is the dance that people usually like the most, because the basic idea obviously feels as if it's taking liberties; it strikes people as outrageous to have these head-banging, punky types to

27 *Nutcracker*, Act Two. Two Gobstoppers: Phil Hill and Jason Lewis.

Tchaikovsky. I've achieved that effect a couple of times, where the reaction from the audience initially shows you that they feel it's wrong and then it feels right quite quickly afterwards. I think the same thing happens in *Swan Lake* in the Soho scene: at first it seems to have gone a bit too far – but then you realize that it's in the music somewhere, and that it works.

AM: *And you go straight from the Gobstoppers into the Mirlitons?*
MB: Yes, but that's a new scene.

AM: *So you have little silent passages in between dances to cover this action?*
MB: Not silence – we had applause!

AM: *And, instead of acknowledging applause, you fitted action to it?*
MB: Yes. After a while, you work out ways of getting applause. You can find ways of winning it without bowing after each dance. You just give each dance a finish that requires applause – and it generally happens.

AM: *But you yourselves, in* The Nutcracker, *just carry on.*
MB: Yes. It was aimed to be continuous.

AM: *So now you change scenes, you get into the castle . . .*
MB: All that happens is that a mirror comes down behind the doorway, so we're now in a room with a big mirror in it. Princess Sugar enters; it's her room. Then her friends – who are the Marshmallow girls, and are dressed in a similar colour to her – enter. It shows a sort of bitchiness between women: they do her hair, say how beautiful she looks, but also gossip about her behind her back.

AM: *It's a dance about conventional feminine vanity?*
MB: Yes, that kind of thing. Then, halfway through the Mirlitons, Clara manages to barge her way into the room. Sugar dismisses all the other girls, has a showdown with Clara, then calls in her brother Fritz to help get rid of Clara.

He manages to, and then leaves Sugar once again alone – she's already admiring herself in the mirror. At the end of the dance, Fritz rejoins her and pops a sweet into her mouth. She spins to the floor, and they both end up chewing, looking at each other in a self-satisfied manner. So, again, I'd decided to keep telling a story at that point.

Next is the long musical introduction to the Waltz of the Flowers, the harp solo, which was a transition into the wedding party. A huge invitation descends, quite far down stage, on an angle: 'You are invited to the wedding of Sugar and the Nutcracker.' The light goes on to it – and goes off the rest of the stage. Clara comes in, sees the invitation, reads it, and then runs off.

The invitation flies back up, and we reveal vast multi-tiered wedding cake, dripping with multi-coloured icing and candles, with all the Sweetie characters we've seen entering the castle all stuck to its various tiers like edible decorations! It's a real applause moment. This cake was Anthony Ward's idea, actually. It was one of the first things he said: 'I want a big cake and what can you do with that?' I liked the idea. It seemed relevant, in a nice way. This is Sweetie Land, and we've just been introduced to all its various characters – liquorice and marshmallows and things. Then to re-establish them all together – as though they were part of this huge delicious cake – was a really good idea. When the curtain goes up on the cake, it feels as if these characters are part of it, because they're still. If you screw your eyes a little bit, they almost look as if they're stuck on to it. All that was Anthony's idea, very much along Busby Berkeley lines.

Then we're into the Waltz of the Flowers, a long dance, which is all about tasting each other in a debauched way, referred to by the company as the 'Licking Dance', a big 'getting to know each other' company number. At the end of this, Sugar and the Nutcracker enter with long veils or capes attached to them, which are used in the choreography as a device for creating shapes and lines and arches. They're very long – about twelve, fifteen feet long – and made of silk. They're for people to jump over; or they billow up and people go under them. I think it's similar to the last act of Ashton's *Cinderella*, but taken further.

When the capes are removed and the stage is cleared, Sugar and the Nutcracker go into their duet. It has a certain amount of floor work, which was our way of making it not just your average pas de deux adagio. Still, this is the bit that, in some ways, made least sense. With everyone leaving the stage, the whole thing looks so set up. But one

28 *Nutcracker*, Act Two. Princess Sugar (Ally Fitzpatrick) and the Nutcracker (Andrew George), with Clara (Etta Murfitt) above. During the climactic pas de deux for Sugar and the Nutcracker, Clara suddenly appears at the top of the Sweetie Land wedding cake, adding a new tragic note to the nuptial jubilance. The cake, inspired by Busby Berkeley films, is designed by Anthony Ward.

particular point worked very well: the cake behind them lights up again, and at its top, you see Clara, looking down. It happens to a tragic piece of music, and it catches the idea that she's lost her man for ever. Then, as that adagio ends, there's a wedding ceremony. This is held with everybody else present, and King Sherbert proclaims them man and wife.

They all form in a social, ballroom-type setting around the stage for the Nutcracker's solo. This is basically a very brief, throwaway, bump-and-grind number. He just rolls his hips a bit. We were thinking of him as some Take That! boy-band idol. I'd certainly do something a bit different now, I think; but it was the right thing at that time for Andrew (George).

Next, the Sugar Plum solo starts off as a solo for Princess Sugar. This involves gestures of popping cherries into her mouth; she is obviously showing off, just as she did in the orphanage. But then, during the same musical item, Clara makes her way into the ballroom. Part of the reason for this is that it's a very long number, and – at least the way the AMP company was at the time – it didn't feel right to sustain a solo for that length of time. I wanted the story to come in again. So once again, Clara interrupts this scene; and to avoid the social embarrassment of this confrontation, the Nutcracker and Sugar's brother, Prince Fritz, come in and interrupt by dancing with them, so as to create a quartet. There are bits within the quartet where the partners swap. This involves various dramatic looks across to each other – a very similar device to what we do in *Swan Lake*, in the czardas, where the Prince and the Swan dance with different women, but look across to each other. The reason I've done this a couple of times is that it keeps some sort of story alive by having the central characters participate in a social dance in which other things are going on. So it's all dramatic, but it is still basically a dance; and it ends with Clara being carted off again by Fritz.

The coda music is the culmination of the wedding. Everyone dances with everyone, and, at the end, everyone chućks confetti in the air. There's a big wedding-photo-group finish. Clara has been chucked out for good! And then we go into the final celebratory waltz, which is a little history of social dance. This includes lots of social dance steps, including head-banging, pogo-ing, little Spanish movements, fashion-model moves, sixties dance, seventies dance . . .

At the end, when it's at its maddest, Clara re-enters. She's done a quick change; she's back in the night-dress that she fell asleep in. It's as if she's sleep-walking now: she walks across the front, very slowly, holding the Nutcracker dummy. Sugar and Nutcracker come toward her. As they pass her, she falls to the ground, just behind them. The stage clears. The palace turns into the orphanage. Then the dawn. She's asleep on the floor of the dormitory, back in the orphanage, alone. She wakes up, finds she's holding the Nutcracker dummy, and kicks him across the floor, because he's been a bastard to her, he's betrayed her. She makes to get back into bed, pulls the bed covers back – and he's there in her bed, the Nutcracker boy, without a shirt again, quite sexy. And it's not her dream any more.

AM: *Are they alone in the dormitory? Or are the other children asleep in their beds too?*
MB: We would have liked to have the full dormitory, actually. But there was no time. We could only get one bed on stage again. So – to suggest the rest of the dormitory – we put the bed in the middle.

When it turns out that he liked Clara all along, they plan, and decide to escape together from the orphanage. He opens the back window (they've tied sheets together from the beds); they climb down the sheets, and exit. The show ends with the twins running on in their nightclothes just as Clara's about to escape out of the window after him. They wave her on her way, wishing her good luck and goodbye. And that's the curtain.

Then we dance a sort of jolly musical bow, using the coda music again, which always got a great reaction. Years later, I tried to do the same musical bow again in *Cinderella*. It's OK in terms of a show like that, especially in a West End situation. Obviously with an ending like *Swan Lake* you couldn't do that.

Rehearsal

MATTHEW BOURNE: The fact that, for *Nutcracker*, we would have a sixty- or seventy-piece orchestra was already incredible; but also our conductor, David Lloyd-Jones, was so enthusiastic about the whole project. To have his seal of approval meant a great deal – basically because he absolutely adores Tchaikovsky; he conducts in Russia; he speaks Russian. And he was very encouraging. I remember him coming into a rehearsal and I was counting. Now I always count the way I hear rather than the way a musician would count. I count in melodic phrases, and I pinpoint certain sounds in the score and orchestration. The way I count the snowflakes is just ridiculous! David is quite imposing – he looks like a great man; he's very tall and actually very Russian-looking – and I said, 'Oh, I'm so embarrassed. I know this isn't the right way to count this music, but it's just the way I hear it.' I showed him the graphs that I do to counts, and he said, 'Absolutely, absolutely. Perfect way of doing it, because that's what the audience sees and hears. You're hitting all the right points in it; you're going with the flow of the music.' That made me feel good; I had been feeling vulnerable.

ALASTAIR MACAULAY: *You had your AMP nucleus of six dancers already. When you were auditioning the other twelve new performers, what were you looking for?*

MB: We were looking for a cross-section of looks. You know how kids in a group always look so odd and different? Some have shot up before the others and are much taller; they're like little adults. We wanted to catch that look. So at that point we were looking for a company of characters – and we ended up with some quite odd shapes and sizes. We didn't want them to look like a dance company. We were looking for people who had the potential to act a bit and show personality.

AM: *How do you test that in an audition?*

MB: We used to do things that showed us a bit of acting. In particular we used the 'Brief Encounter' sequence from *Town & Country*, where they go to the cinema, watch a film and change the mood according to counts. There were four counts of them laughing at something, four counts of them getting all upset, four counts for tears. It all helped to see if they had any potential for silent acting. You tend to be able to see whether people have an intelligence in the way they dance, the intelligence to develop an acting performance.

AM: *How do you judge this kind of intelligence?*

MB: It's to do with a naturalness in the way that they present movement – and a sincerity about the way the movement is done. It involves the entire person; it's not superficial, not bodily only. Some people draw you to them in that way. Also how they react when they're not dancing in the audition, what sort of questions they ask, how they are with people, whether they're comfortable with themselves: all those things I look at.

AM: *How did you start the rehearsals?*

MB: We started *Nutcracker* with a sort of homework. We told everyone that they were playing a child at an orphanage. I wanted them to go away and bring in, the next day, their little life history – how they got to the orphanage; have they got a special friend in the orphanage – that sort of thing. The next day they were to tell everyone about their character.

AM: *How did you arrive at this method? From theatre directors?*
MB: In *Children of Eden*, I remember us doing workshops, in little groups of five or six, on floods and on things for the Ark, rather than: 'You are the ensemble – you will run around screaming now.' So they all came up with their own flood story, and they were all characters. Very memorable sessions. I saw how well that went down with performers. They got so involved in their characters.

So in *Nutcracker* the dancers came in the next day, and they told us how old they were, their names, how they got there, and anything they knew about their past.

AM: *Had they all known that they were going to be children in an orphanage before Day One?*
MB: Not the newcomers to the company, no.

AM: *Was it a problem for any of them, having to invent a life that way?*
MB: No. It's odd, but I never encountered any kind of resistance to acting from anyone in the company. I found that, somewhere inside, they're all performers. They all want to be on stage, and acting is just an extension of that. Sometimes people are not that hot, or are too over the top, or too obvious; but then you steer them.

It helps if they've got something close to home to deal with, something that they've developed themselves. The reason I get them to do it that way – and not just say to them: 'You are this character' – is that they inevitably choose something they know they can achieve. Especially when they've not really had the acting experience to develop something that's not themselves, it usually happens that, when they stand up and talk about their characters, they're really talking about themselves a lot of the time.

Sometimes this becomes very interesting! We had an instance with one dancer in *Cinderella*. He had to tell us all about his character, who was the boyfriend of one of the sisters. It went on for about three-quarters of an hour; it was like a novel. It became quite funny; we were all laughing away. But we all knew that it was really him, so that it became quite sad, to hear all the stuff that was coming out.

AM: *Did he realize how much?*
MB: I don't think so, no.

AM: *Is that part of the trick of it? That they don't realize that they're playing themselves?*
MB: I think so, yes, sometimes. They develop a character that is never totally themselves; but when they're playing something close to home, you get an honesty, a kind of truth from them as performers. It does work well; and, with *Nutcracker*, it was a new thing for everyone.

The next stage is to put the characters that they've described into a situation with the other characters. They don't have to relate to each other, but they can if they want. So they improvise around, with some sort of guidelines. Maybe – as children in the *Nutcracker* orphanage – they've all got a toy. Then you see what happens. They tell us who their best friend is, and which ones they hate. Or one of them says: 'I haven't got any friends' – that sort of thing. It helped us start the scenes off.

AM: *How are you directing or advising on all this?*
MB: There are some things you know you're aiming for. I told two of them they were twins, for example. It was Maxine Fone and Simon Murphy: they had a similar way of performing, and they looked slightly alike. But it was quite open for the majority of people. With the principal characters, who were all played by the AMP nucleus of dancers, we'd already talked about it in greater detail. They knew the main story I wanted to construct; but a lot of the other stories were incidental to the main one, and could be flexible. And so, once I knew what their characters were, it enabled me to flesh out scenes I had only previously conceived in a general way. For example, I knew that there was a scene about children getting presents and what music it happens to; but I hadn't worked out precisely what happened in that scene. We would think, 'Which one did this? It's got to be that one, cos he doesn't like her.' Or, 'The little timid one, or the girly boy who picks the doll out of the bag – it would obviously be that one.'

It was great to have a room full of characters, rather than just a room full of people waiting to be told what to do. One thing led to another, especially as they thought of the wider situation – say, the matron coming in. Instantly, a lot of work's done for you. Each one knows how his or her character would probably react – whether he or she was the one that stood up to her, or the one who would hide. Some people get so involved with their character that they feel it's that character's show.

They have a whole story going on that's not relevant, and you have to pull them back from it. But you don't want to destroy them too much. They've got to be allowed to feel fully about what they're doing – but maybe you position it in a corner somewhere.

When everyone is involved, they've had their own input into the production, and they can all tell you which bit was theirs and which section was their idea – which creates in them a loyalty and commitment to the performance every night.

AM: *At what point do you start connecting the characterizations to the story and to the music?*
MB: With something that's not a dance, what we tended to do (and still do) was to map out some action. Sometimes – as we found with the family in *Cinderella* – they're all doing different things all the time, and it's very difficult to keep track. So you make sure each one knows that he or she has got something to do, and is getting on with it. Then we play the music to find the points. The more we play it, the more we find those things within it. And we'll hear something in the music that will give us new ideas that relate to that section. Then we'll go backwards and forwards like that for a while. Action and music feed each other, until we've set something. It's quite laborious, because I, obviously, always want it to relate to the music completely; I'll have counts as well and, if the dancers can't quite hear cues in the music, then I'll give them their counts.

AM: *This process of becoming orphanage children: did that prepare them for what they were going to do in Act Two?*
MB: Yes, because something of their original characters was supposed to be visible later on as well. So the aggressive Gobstopper boys in Act Two had been the tough, rough ones in the orphanage – one of them with a plaster on his head.

AM: *Do you ask everybody to come to all rehearsals?*
MB: It's funny you should ask that. Early on, I do quite a lot of preparation work with everyone; I talk a lot; I show them pictures, videos – whatever I want them to see. I make sure they've got an overview of the whole thing. I want them to know what it is they're working towards and I want everyone to be clear on the plot.

But I hate wasting people's time! Some directors that I've worked with will have people hanging around watching, or sometimes even waiting in the corridors, just in case. I don't do that. Also, I can't quite handle a

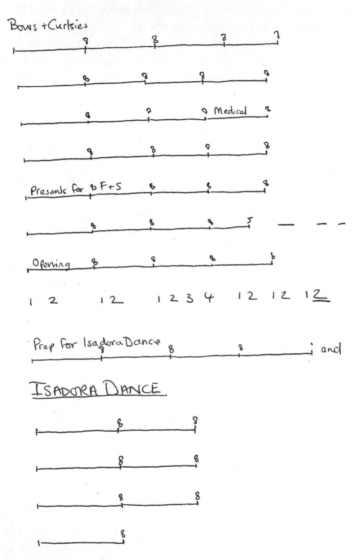

29 *Nutcracker.* From Bourne's notes on the music in the Christmas scene of Act One.

big group all the time. I need some times in a day when I'm just intimate with people. Sometimes I get more done if I just keep a couple of people behind – even if it is a group dance – and work on some stuff with them. Then, the next day, we just hand it over. It's easier than having everyone discuss everything.

I will say, 'Please, if you've got any ideas, I'd love to hear them.' Mind you, this can get out of hand. There are times when I just want everyone to stop. Some are more subtle than others, or more understanding. You don't want to rule out the fact that someone might have a great idea and that you might lose it. The good does outweigh the bad in this method of working. Still, at times, I've said, 'Right, I'm taking over now. This is what I want.' They take it quite well!

AM: *What kind of research into orphanages did you do?*
MB: We went to the Ragged School Museum of East End Life, which was a Victorian school for the poor. This suggested some of the ideas that we may have put into it.

AM: *The show starts with more or less three-dimensional orphans; and then you suddenly get this monster matron, Mrs Dross, a frightening cartoon. You really flesh out the cartoon. You understand her whole character, very vividly, the moment you see her.*
MB: I suppose I did conceive those two Drosses more as cartoony characters than the kids, because the kids are the ones that you need the sympathy for. Whereas she is symbolic in her nastiness. She's quite grotesque in a lot of ways.

AM: *Rosie Allen plays this role. How did you fix her whole performance style?*
MB: I can't remember basing her on anyone in particular. I suppose it comes very much from her, her manner, the way she holds herself. I knew that she should have a vanity about her, so that when she does her Isadora Dance, that's her chance to show off.

AM: *Somewhere between the rounded realism and pathos of the orphans and the cartoon grotesquerie of the Dross parents are Sugar and Fritz. How would you describe the mixture of caricature and realism in their characters?*
MB: A halfway house. They're quite caricatured brats to begin with. Spoilt. But I tried to give them moments of sympathy as well. There's a bit where no one wants to play with Fritz. His parents have gone off

with the Governors, and the kids have all got their toys. He hasn't got anyone to show off to, or anyone to play with. He goes to a couple of the children, puts his arm round their shoulders – and they run away. He's more or less alone.

The same with Sugar, really. She's so spoilt, but in her way she does want the friendship of the other children. She quite fancies the boy that Clara fancies and she tries to impress him. But when she doesn't get her way, she resorts to violence.

AM: *What is also uncanny in Sugar is that she is terribly demure much of the time and, of course, hideously perfect. Although she does become a much nastier character, she's not an instant brat.*

MB: No. She's not that caricatured really, is she? She's not like Violet-Elizabeth in the *William* books; she's not stamping her feet and screaming all the time. She is quite demure, yes, but Ally was good at suggesting that she was very two-faced. I remember there was one point in rehearsal where, just before the dance where the orphans are sitting around and she and Fritz are doing a little display, she had to circle round and look at everyone; and the whole company all reacted as one to her face: they all gasped, she had such a superior, evil look in her eye as she went round. That was Ally's big talent: a complete immersion in character, even in rehearsals, so that you were almost frightened by her at times.

AM: *She left AMP in 1994; Sugar was the last role she created. Andrew George, your Nutcracker, was in your next production,* Highland Fling, *but left before* Swan Lake.

MB: He choreographed a lot for operas – that was why he left – and he'd been the Nutcracker and didn't want to be merely a big swan in *Swan Lake*. The Nutcracker role had been geared closely for his talents.

If and when I stage *Nutcracker* again, I will adjust it for the technical level we have now achieved with our more recent dancers, but only to some degree. Etta, who was our Clara, was and is a beautiful dancer. She has great charm and a wonderful spirit when she dances. Ally had enormous acting talent, incredible preparation and great feeling for her characters. But – as she would probably admit herself – her technical level wouldn't work now in today's company.

There is now a danger, in doing pieces like this, of losing character when working with technically better-trained dancers. The odd characters that we had within the show originally helped to make it what it was. To try to hit that fine line is something I'm still concerned about. I often worry, 'Have I lost a lot of my characterful dancers?' I know that I've got some very good technical dancers, but I need those others to bring the scenes alive when necessary. *Nutcracker* was made up of a lot of interesting people. And I will be conscious of that when I do it again, to make sure it still has that element, which is an important part of the show.

AM: *Act One of Tchaikovsky's* Nutcracker *was, I think, unprecedented in ballet music, in the way that it has almost no breaks for applause. Three or four dances during the opening party can win just brief applause, but thereafter the music is absolutely continuous. And it keeps changing in the most astonishing way, from diminutive detail to colossal romance.*

MB: That's why it's a shame that Act Two is not similar. I always feel – if you're thinking of it as a piece for kids – that what kids most like is being told a story. But it's hard to tell a story in Act Two, and unless you find a way of doing so, then – despite what ballet people say – I really don't think *Nutcracker* is a great piece for kids. You can't just get by on lots of colour. The famous Balanchine version for New York City Ballet is not great for kids. After setting up some sort of story and an array of characters, it becomes just a series of dances. It stops making any attempt to make sense; and I think that, in some ways, it puts any child with intelligence off ballet. Children must wonder, 'What on earth is going on?'

AM: *In the dance when Clara discovers her hero Nutcracker bare-chested and then the whole of the male sex behind him, she actually walks down a male staircase. How did you suddenly dream up that?*

MB: I've often used that idea of using people as objects. I don't know whether I've seen it somewhere, but I like it. I used it again in Act One of *Swan Lake*, when the Young Prince walks down a human staircase from his bed.

AM: *Mark Morris has two women walking up parallel human staircases in* L'Allegro, *which you may have seen in the 1990 TV documentary on him. I think he, in turn, had lifted the idea from a Paul Taylor dance.*

MB: Actually, I think I must have taken it from something I'd seen earlier. But I can't remember what.

AM: *The Snow Dance: which bits come from Sonja Henie?*

MB: Quite a lot, actually; more than is necessary, in some ways. Sometimes, when we're making movement, we get very attached to one idea – as we still were with *Cinderella* at times – and then stick with it, where we could actually relax, open it out, and make more of possibly larger movement. That's probably what I would go back and consider revising now.

We watched a lot of Sonja Henie films; it was great fun. She had a very odd style. We used a lot of her affectation, and her personality as well, for the whole company: that sense of delight and wonder at everything we were doing. She has this way of running on her toes which I've never seen anyone do before or since. We used that for Sugar's first entrance. But it only looks strange when it's on ice; so it's actually a bit of a red herring on stage. If you're trying to create an ice effect on a stage without ice, it's slightly confusing to see someone running on tiptoes. However, we used it!

AM: *When you were a student in the early 1980s, Torvill and Dean were enjoying their great days: did the memory of that linger in your mind?*
MB: I suppose so. We did watch some Torvill and Dean, but the sort of invention that they did didn't work very well on stage.

We tried to do some death spirals, but they're very difficult to pull off, unless you are on ice. You want the stage to be more slippery than you would for other dancing, so that you can slide on it, to make the idea work.

AM: *You have a wonderful device of making people just strike a pose and then hold it on stage, as if they were sailing forwards on ice.*
MB: We tried to do some movement which had a sense of travelling but was actually on the spot. So we did it with our focus travelling somewhere. Or we had them balancing on the spot and shaking their own skirts, giving an effect of the wind on them. That used to work very well.

AM: *Another marvellous bit is when their male partners shake their skirts for them. Then there's also a wonderful moment where you really get the notion of the girls pushing off in the way that people do on ice. First you get Sugar, then another pair of girls, then another pair, each coming forwards and just holding the pose as if they're riding for yards. You get the sense of the push-off, and then – though they don't move – the sailing momentum on ice. They're virtually still. Just the stillness somehow gives you the feeling of momentum, although in fact there is no momentum.*
MB: That's quite a hard thing to pull off. It can become a bit static. You have to find a way of making it work. Later on, we divided it up more,

so that there were some people doing it and some people moving – so we got a sense of movement as well through that.

Another sequence, with the men and the women together, is where you get the woman pushed away by the man: i.e. she's the one who's supposed to be sent travelling back along the ice, as he pushes her away. But what we do is: he pushes her away, but it's him who moves backwards and she stays on the spot. That's a good idea which we almost didn't make enough of. It's brief, and it's disguised.

The idea behind the whole scene was that these orphans have been now released into a beautiful world. There they all are, in their bobble hats and scarves, having a fantastic time. I told everyone that what I wanted was a look of wonder on their faces; we had to rehearse this look, because some people had enormous trouble with trying to smile that way. So we tried looking upwards in wonder, and even opening our mouths when jumping – things like that. It made everybody laugh so much that we had to talk at length about those things – the smile, the open mouth – but it actually has an effect. It gets the idea across; and that idea, basically, was sheer joy and pleasure and fun and escapism. Because we'd seen the orphans all so regimented beforehand, this Snow scene had an extra feeling of happiness. They had escaped into a beautiful new world.

AM: *Your Act Two, in the theatre, has a complicated series of sets. How did you rehearse these scenes?*
MB: In this or other shows, we always try to get a sense of the physical aspect of the set by using larger props. The one thing we never had, when rehearsing *Nutcracker*, was the huge cake for the Waltz of the Flowers.

AM: *Act Two, musically, is almost all separate dances. On the one hand, you have to work up the applause that they require. On the other hand, you have to establish that there's a continuum that will make you want to see the next dance and the continuation of the story.*
MB: Yes. But no one takes a bow at any point in our *Nutcracker*.

AM: *And there are never any dances just for dance's sake alone. Everything's always plainly part of the story.*
MB: Yes.

AM: *Where did you do your homework for the Spanish Dance? You've now choreographed several; there's another in* Swan Lake.
MB: I feel as though that's not something I do have to do a lot of homework for. I've got books on Spanish dance forms; and sometimes we've

brought a book in, and looked at arm positions and maybe used those. But Spanish dance is a style that I really like and I feel happy playing around with it.

AM: *The Spanish Dance in* Nutcracker *is for one woman (Teresa Barker, later Isabel Mortimer) and two men. The Spanish Dance in* Swan Lake *is also for a single woman and a clutch of men. The other national dances in Act Three of* Swan Lake *are also each for one woman and multiple men. Is that idea – one girl with two or more men partnering her – a format you're fond of for these divertissements?*

MB: Yes. In *Swan Lake*, the task is to feature each woman, each Princess, in a different way. It's very MGM musicals: the female star with her chorus. I enjoy that.

But the other national dances in *Nutcracker* have different formats. I like them; they're all funny, light. Again, there's a juvenile side coming out in me here, but, in *Nutcracker* – which is about children – that works fine. The Gobstoppers used the idea of skate-boarding bovver boys: BMX-type thugs.

AM: *The next dance, the* 'Mirlitons', *has probably the most famous, or notorious, music in* Nutcracker – *at least, to those of us in Britain who remember the old Cadbury's Fruit and Nut(case) advert that used to employ it. What's it like, tackling that?*

MB: I'm always slightly nervous of tackling very famous pieces of music. At that point, using Sugar and her flighty friends in her room, I was thinking: 'We'll do a gestural dance with this.' It became too intimate a dance for a big stage, I felt, because there were a lot of tiny little ideas in it. If I was to do it again now, I would find more dancing in it.

AM: Nutcracker *has two big waltzes. We've spoken of the Waltz of the Snowflakes at the end of Act One. Now, over halfway through Act Two, you have the Waltz of the Flowers. I can't help feeling that this is the much harder to choreograph of the two. Is that true?*

MB: It shouldn't be; but yes. The Snowflakes Dance has dynamic changes within the music. There's a point where the storm picks up, which is great: it gives you another idea to work with. Then it goes back to something beautiful for a wonderful ending. That helps you a lot. The Waltz of the Flowers just goes on and on along the same vein. It just builds as it goes along, but without any strong variation. Therefore, trying to sustain one idea throughout it – it's a long dance – is quite difficult.

It actually took us a long time to determine what that dance was about. They're all Sweet characters, so the idea we came up with in the end was that it was all to do with taste. Because in Sweetie Land you are judged on how you taste, rather than how you look, this is a whole dance about people tasting each other, licking each other. And this helped to add a sexual connotation. But it was fun as well. Earlier in Act Two, when Sugar introduces the Nutcracker to her parents, the King and Queen of Sweetie Land, they almost take a bite to see what he tastes like. That's in the music, where there's traditionally the Nutcracker's long mime passage, telling the Sugar Plum Fairy on his arrival in the Kingdom of Sweets about his fight with the mice and Clara's help. When David Lloyd-Jones arrived, he was a bit thrown by it to begin with; but afterwards he was forever telling the orchestras we played with: 'You know why they're doing this, don't you? It's because that's how they judge each other in Sweetie Land.'

AM: *But wasn't it hard to sustain a licking idea throughout five minutes of waltz music?*
MB: Yes. Maybe I'd find other things to do with it now. There was too much repetition – not just of the basic idea, but of the steps as well. Some of it was really good, I think, but I don't think I made it all fully visible enough. And the dance level of the company, in a big dance number like this, was patchy at the time. This is the sort of number we would be able to sustain far better with the overall level of dancers we have today. Still, the charm of it certainly made it work for audiences, most of whom don't notice technical things much – or choreography as such. They just know whether they're enjoying it or not.

We finished it off with the ceremonial entrance of Sugar and the Nutcracker wearing long capes. I'm sure I took this from something I'd seen, but I can't remember what. Partly, I think, from the final scene of Ashton's ballet *Cinderella*, where Cinderella and the Prince come on with those very long trains behind them. We used the trains, with a lot of elaborate manoeuvring around: people running under them, people holding them up, people dancing under and around them.

AM: *Then the music for the big Sugar Plum pas de deux, opening with its colossal – sublime, virtually tragic – adagio.*
MB: Here, too, I would try to create more interesting duet work. This was always the low point of our *Nutcracker* for a lot of people. It's

one of the most overpowering pieces of music to dance to; it keeps climaxing again and again. It isn't possible to cut it, and you need the right two people to sustain so huge a number. At that point, it would have been wiser, with those dancers, not to build them up and expose them so much. We left the stage empty for them, as if they were going to deliver a virtuosic pas de deux. It was my fault, not theirs. In those days, I felt that that's what you were supposed to do – what *Nutcracker* called for.

I quite like some of it, but now I feel it just doesn't go far enough. It wasn't until *Swan Lake*, when I worked with Adam Cooper and Fiona Chadwick, and *Cinderella*, when I worked with Sarah Wildor and Adam, that I really attempted to develop partnering much further. Scott and Etta have also been a great help in the development of that aspect of my choreography.

At the time, though, this show was very much appreciated precisely because people felt relieved to see a *Nutcracker* that had a through line, was a lot of fun, and had very charming performers. A lot of its weaknesses were forgiven; people were won over in other ways. And we were still telling a story. We turned the very end of that adagio into their wedding – Sugar's and Nutcracker's – brought on the father to oversee it and to pronounce them married, with everyone else present. That helped; and the whole number improved each time we did it.

AM: *After the solo dances for the Nutcracker and Sugar, you then have a coda that is, as you've said, a medley of twentieth-century social dance. What actual kinds of dance?*

MB: There's the twist, there's punk pogo-ing, various sixties and seventies types of dance – all through the century actually. There's the tango, for example; there's some ballroomy, partnered stuff, which a couple of times goes down to the floor as well. It's all very modelly and posey.

We also tried to give it the whirlwind, falling-back-to-earth feeling of coming out of a dream. In particular, we thought of the whole pack of cards in *Alice* flying down through the air and back to reality.

There are points all along the way where – in *Nutcracker* or with other shows – we were still fixing details of the story as we went along in rehearsals. But at least in *Nutcracker* I knew what the end was going to be, and that it would work. That's always comforting. What was worrying in *Swan Lake* was that, for a very long time, I really didn't know how it was going to end.

However, endings give you different problems. I always get to a stage in rehearsals where there's what feels like an undo-able amount of music left to choreograph before the first night. In *Highland Fling*, there was a good eight-and-a-half minutes of music, with just one day left to choreograph it. I knew how it would end, but the problem, as often for me, was how to fill that music to get there. Curiously, the last act of *Swan Lake* just fell into place at short notice and gave me no grief, whereas the stress of finishing *Nutcracker, Highland Fling* and *Cinderella* was tremendous. *Swan Lake* was the only one where I felt I wasn't going mad. With *Cinderella*, I was waking up in the middle of the night with cold sweats, hearing all the music that I hadn't yet worked out how to solve.

Production

ALASTAIR MACAULAY: *Was* Nutcracker *the first time you worked with live music?*

MATTHEW BOURNE: Basically, yes. We had done one performance of *Town & Country* at the Queen Elizabeth Hall to mostly live music, which was great. But *Nutcracker* was the first production that was always accompanied by live music, and that's such a pleasure.

AM: *Did you have the offstage children's choir that Tchaikovsky asks for during the Waltz of the Snowflakes?*

MB: Maybe for the Edinburgh premiere, but never on tour or at Sadler's Wells. We just couldn't quite stretch to that expense. But it would have been nice; and very relevant.

AM: *You performed* Nutcracker *in the centenary double-bill with* Yolanta *for Opera North, throughout August and September 1992. Then what?*

MB: After the initial success at Edinburgh, in August 1992, Opera North revived the double-bill in Leeds on the actual centenary, on 18 December. That led to a tour – Nottingham, Birmingham, Manchester – that lasted up to early 1993. While that was going on, we decided to do *Nutcracker* by itself at Sadler's Wells, for Christmas 1993. I think we did it with sponsorship. Kobler Trust put money into both runs.

AM: *This meant that you were beginning to see some future for an enlarged AMP. Did that lead to extra AMP administration?*

MB: Yes. The company's steadily grown. By that point, we probably had an administrator as well as Katharine.

AM: *Once the original* Yolanta–Nutcracker *run ended in 1992, how large did the company remain? Were people just under contract for individual seasons or tours?*

MB: Yes. After the Opera North tour, we had no intention of continuing with a big company. We had talked about doing another full-length Tchaikovsky, i.e. *Swan Lake*. And Katharine got to work on that in advance. She talked to the Arts Council about what we wanted to do. So the plan was there to do it, if we could. But there was no plan to employ all those extra people again until we did *Nutcracker* the following Christmas. In the meantime, during 1993, we did a second tour of *Deadly Serious*. There was a lot of demand for that show. Then, in summer 1993, we made the TV film of the Betjeman *Late Flowering Lust*. We had been planning originally to do that as a stage production with Nigel Hawthorne, but it changed when the offer for the film came through from the BBC.

We then did *Nutcracker* at Sadler's Wells in Christmas 1993 and again Christmas 1994. But we had to deliver a new stage show quite quickly for 1994, because we had prior funding for that financial year. And, because I had enjoyed working with a theatrical score, *Highland Fling* came about, early in 1994. I hadn't intended to do those classics in a row like that, and yet I had already begun to plan *Swan Lake* (even though that took more than another year to come to fruition), and now I decided to re-do *La Sylphide* as *Highland Fling*.

Next, I worked on the West End production of *Oliver!*, which occupied me for most of the second half of 1994.

AM: *Was it with* Nutcracker *that the Friends of AMP started?*

MB: Yes, at first in a very small way. It's grown since then, especially with *Swan Lake*, and has about 700 members now. They're very loyal and generous, and we do events for them. They are just one of several big new dimensions to AMP's work that began with *Nutcracker*.

AM: *What changes did you make between the premiere of the production in August 1992 and its three revivals – the first with Opera North in winter 1992–3, the others at Sadler's Wells over Christmas 1993 and 1994?*

MB: A lot of work was done to make the choreography clearer. The thing about doing any new productions, especially with less experienced dancers, is that it actually takes a while for the choreography to reveal itself – because it's not got into their bodies yet in a good way, and it's not been analysed well enough. Once you've seen something in performance on stage, it becomes very easy to see where the problems, or the weaknesses, lie.

I anyway tend to try to improve any piece choreographically each time it's revived: I try to make it richer. If I see a weakness anywhere, or a lack of something, or something I can improve, then I work on that. Often it's just a detail of steps, but it's then that you can open yourself up more to working on the steps and the movement. It doesn't matter whether the piece is already a success. *Swan Lake* has been a very big success, but I'm still looking at small revisions.

AM: *It's interesting that you've constantly been mentioning ways in which you would consider revising your original* Nutcracker *if and when you do it again.*
MB: Well, I do want to do *Nutcracker* again, and whenever I revive a piece, I consider every way, small or large, in which we might improve it. There are elements within *Nutcracker* that I think I could make stronger. There are moments in Act Two within the Clara–Sugar relationship and within the relationship with Fritz, where I think it would be good to make it more of an adult drama, to show that Clara is on the point of becoming a woman. At the moment, it still feels as if they're children playing these roles.

We could certainly make it nastier at times. Even in the earlier scenes, I could probably think of a few more nasty things to happen to the children, before they got released into a wonderful world. I feel it is there in the music. The people of Sweetie Land could be more decadent characters in a decadent world. We did conceive it that way, but the costumes took it in a more sugary direction.

AM: *To do* Nutcracker *again, would you have it redesigned?*
MB: Only certain aspects. But yes. A lot of costumes would need to be redesigned.

AM: *What do you think you achieved with* Nutcracker *that you hadn't achieved before?*
MB: A completeness. A piece that felt like a whole, rather than an assembly of separate items. One of the interesting things about our full-length 'ballet' pieces – *Nutcracker, Highland Fling, Swan Lake* and *Cinderella* – is that there is very little you can lift from them as a set piece. When we're asked to do a gala or a TV appearance, there's very little that will

work on its own. You would need an explanation to show why these things are happening this way – which tells you how relevant the story is all the time. Whereas, before that, *The Infernal Galop*, *Town & Country*, *Deadly Serious* and others were all made up of short numbers, little set pieces, vignettes, that could be lifted out and performed on their own.

What I enjoyed doing most about *Nutcracker* was telling a complete story. And I was very proud to have worked with Tchaikovsky, quite honoured. Having worked with directors by that point, and found how rewarding it was to tell a story with sustained characters to a great score – it was the beginnings of feeling that there was something that we could do as a company that nobody else was doing. And this was accompanied by a certain amount of acceptance and wide encouragement from establishment people and press for what we were doing. Working with a complete piece of great music was perhaps the greatest pleasure of all.

AM: *I hate to say it, but I don't think you'll ever have the chance to work again with a score like Act One of* Nutcracker.
MB: No, there's nothing much else like it.

(Conversations 1998–99)

6

Highland Fling

1994

Idea

ALASTAIR MACAULAY: *You yourself nickname these four last full-length works 'classics'* – Nutcracker, Highland Fling, Swan Lake, Cinderella *– because they use the scores and (to some extent) the scenarios of ballet 'classics'. And I always feel that I should declare an interest here because, when teaching dance history to you and other students in the early 1980s, I paid considerable emphasis to these ballets, an emphasis unusual perhaps in modern-dance academe. In fact, in your very first term at the Laban Centre, we concentrated on Romanticism and the nineteenth-century ballet repertory.* La Sylphide *(the basis for your* Highland Fling), Swan Lake *and* The Nutcracker *were all discussed in some detail. The whole idea of Romanticism, in its full political and social context, was a wonderful way in which to make dance students see the excitement of history; and it was good to make them see how much there is to say about each of these old ballet warhorses when they're taken seriously.*

La Sylphide is, in most ways, the prototypical Romantic ballet; it was the first ballet that I used to ask students to consider, particularly its story.

MATTHEW BOURNE: Yes, and, in 1982, that was probably my first exposure to *La Sylphide*. The story really is a good one. That was what appealed to me when I was looking for the next full-length piece to make after *Nutcracker*. I had seen it on stage a few times, and I must admit I'd never found it very impressive. You know, I loved going to see *The Nutcracker* and *Swan Lake* and *Cinderella* before I ever thought of doing my own versions of them. But all that drew me to *La Sylphide*

30 *Highland Fling* (1994). Publicity handout. The two images of the Sylphide and James are of late nineteenth-century and early twentieth-century photographs of dancers in August Bournonville's version of *La Sylphide* (1836) above a Scottish tartan.
31 *La Sylphide* (1832): opening image. Marie Taglioni (kneeling) as the Sylphide in the original Paris Opéra production, with her brother Paul as the sleeping James. The Sylphide is appearing in James's dream. This production of *La Sylphide* (choreographed by Filippo Taglioni, father to Marie and Paul, to a scenario by the tenor Adolphe Nourrit) became the archetype of Romantic ballet throughout the nineteenth century – as well as the basis of Bourne's *Highland Fling*.

was its story. I re-read the scenario, I read a little bit about how the piece was the essence of Romanticism, I reminded myself – again, by reading – of what Romanticism was, and then I went out to buy a CD of the music.

AM: *So let's reconsider* La Sylphide. *Its premiere in 1832 changed the course of ballet history. It is about the love between a Scots farmer, James, and a winged female sprite from the glens, the Sylphide. It has all kinds of archetypal Romantic dualism. Act One is set in a Scottish farmhouse, in which only one character – the Sylphide herself – is super-natural: she alone shows the full language of classical ballet, dancing on pointe and in a soft romantic tutu. Act Two is set in the supernatural*

32 *Highland Fling*. Maxine Fone as the Sylph and Scott Ambler as James. In Bourne's variant of *La Sylphide*, James is stoned and the Sylph is a zombie-like drug-induced hallucination.
33 *Highland Fling*. Maxine Fone as the Sylph. The use of unpointed bare feet and angled knees is inspired here by accounts and pictures of the dancing of Isadora Duncan.

world of a Scottish forest, in which she is one of many sylphides, all female and all dancing classical ballet; James is the only human – and the only male – in their scenes there.

MB: The idea of two worlds is very appealing: two different worlds with the interval in between. It was a nice, neat contrast and structure, and it was a good length. I could see quite a lot of potential. But also a big challenge, because, after all, this was to be a small-scale touring show with only seven people in it. It was quite a decision to do a piece like this, to see if a small-scale full-length piece could work as well as a large-scale ballet. Very little change of set would be possible; this was a production made to tour to quite intimate venues.

AM: *The ballet's scenario is itself perfect Romanticism. James leaves his fiancée, Effie, to pursue the Sylphide – even though she is literally*

unattainable. He is impetuous, and offends the old witch Madge. How-
ever, when he later encounters Madge in the forest, he is tantalized by
the fact that he can never hold the Sylphide. Madge offers him a magic
scarf with which he can bind the Sylphide to him. He takes it, but it is
poisoned, and causes the Sylphide's death. (The moral about trying to
hold the unattainable is clear.) As he is grieving, Madge draws his atten-
tion to a wedding procession in the distance. Effie is now getting married
to another man, Gurn, who has loved her all along; and James has noth-
ing left, either in the real world or the supernatural one.

Were there other particular features that appealed to you in this?
MB: As I said before, I remember having to make a decision very quickly
as to what to do. I looked for a complete score, as I had done with
Nutcracker, to find one that I thought would work. I don't remember
looking at any other one ballet. As you know, *Swan Lake* was a project
we wanted to do, but later. And what took my fancy straightaway was
the idea of putting *Sylphide* into modern-day Scotland. Virtually everything I'd done had been set in the past, and people were always saying
to me, 'When are you going to do something that's set in the present?'
So it was fun to take what is virtually the oldest ballet in the repertory,
with its romantically Walter Scott notion of Scotland, and transfer it to
the present day.

AM: *Were you thinking of what Fergus Early had done in* Naples *(1983)*
to Bournonville's Napoli *by transposing it to modern-day Naples? Or*
of the I, Giselle *he and Jackie Lansley had made (1980) as a feminist*
version of Giselle?
MB: I'd seen and liked *Naples*, but – my memory being what it is – I'd
forgotten it. It may have influenced me, but subconsciously.

AM: *After* La Sylphide, *Romantic dualism – with the hero from the*
real world, the heroine from the supernatural one – became a standard
recipe for many ballet scenarios throughout the nineteenth century.
Ballet became largely a drama about the ethereal or exotic ballerina,
whose element was the air, and the mortal and earthbound hero, whose
love for her is doomed and tragic. And ballet dancing became something
essentially feminine. I'm generalizing, of course; there are important and
honourable exceptions to this rule.

The 1832 Paris version became world-famous, in particular, because
it was the perfect vehicle for the Romantic ballerina Marie Taglioni,
the dance sensation of the era. The music is by Schneitzhoeffer, and

this version – its original choreography was by Filippo Taglioni, Marie's
father and teacher – has been reconstructed a few times.

However, the version we usually see derives from 1836 and
Copenhagen. The Danish choreographer August Bournonville used the
original scenario, but changed its emphasis in certain ways. In particu-
lar, he gave much more dancing to the role of James. He commissioned
a new score by the Danish composer Løvensjkold – it is his Opus 1. Par-
ticularly since the Second World War, it is this version that has gained
international currency.

MB: I didn't know *La Sylphide* terribly well on stage. I'd seen Peter
Schaufuss's version for London Festival Ballet several years before, and
wasn't mad about it. I appreciated it on one level as a piece of history,
but I never got excited about it as a theatre piece.

Seeing it again recently, first with the Australian Ballet and then with
American Ballet Theatre, I have to say the Bournonville choreography
doesn't interest me very much. It also seems unmusical. It's not my
favourite piece in terms of dance, whereas *Giselle* completely works for
me still. In particular, I can't bear Madge the witch.

It took me time, curiously, to find much in the *Sylphide* music. Perhaps Løvenskjold sounded small fry after Tchaikovsky. I remember that
I went out and bought the CD with the idea of staging it already in my
mind as a possibility; and when I listened to it, I was slightly disappointed at first. It all sounded the same, I thought, and dated. I blush to
say that now, because actually it is a wonderful score, and bit by bit I
came to realize how theatrical it is.

AM: *What were your first ideas for the Sylph?*
MB: We decided that she should be not as pure as in the original; that
she should have a kind of evil side to her as well. That comes out in a
sort of naughtiness, a kind of daring to be different, daring him to be
different as well.

AM: *Well, Bournonville talks about her that way in his memoirs. He calls*
her a 'dark angel' and talks of her 'poisonous breath'.

You say, 'We decided.' I'm curious what you yourself decided before
it became 'we'.
MB: It's difficult to remember sometimes. But – this is interesting –
originally the Sylph was going to be a man. Then, when I decided that
that would be a better idea for *Swan Lake* – the two ideas were floating
around in my head at the same time – I quickly changed it.

AM: *Who did you have in mind to dance this male sylph?*

MB: Me – would you believe! And then – I think partly because I knew that *Oliver!* would prevent me from dancing in the piece anyway, partly when I had the *Swan Lake* idea of male swans – I just ruled it out.

AM: *How funny – because* La Sylphide *was already a gender-reversal. When Adolphe Nourrit created the scenario for* La Sylphide *in late 1831, he based it on Charles Nodier's story* Trilby, *which has a male spirit haunting and luring a female Scottish ferrywoman. But Nourrit, a tenor who had himself appeared on stage with Taglioni in certain operas, could see the potential in making the spirit a female role. Did you know about the* Trilby *original?*

MB: Again, if I did, I forgot. I was just interested in playing games with the conventional expectations of gender. *Spitfire* had been an all-male pas de quatre. In *Deadly Serious*, whenever we went into any kind of couplings, because there was a cast of four men and two women, there would always be one male couple, which sometimes had connotations and sometimes didn't. So we were always playing with sexual roles.

AM: *When did you think of putting drugs into it?*

MB: Very early on. That was the basis of doing the piece. It's the logic of why James sees her and why nobody else does. She's an hallucination. I knew that drugs occur in several later Romantic ballets – the most famous being in *La Bayadère*, where the whole scene of the Shades is an opium dream – and I wanted to connect that to the way people take drugs today. As *Trainspotting* shows, there's a big drug culture in Scotland, some of it very grim; but I also wanted plenty of comedy.

AM: *Your James is a junkie, and your version of the story makes it a 'Just Say No to Drugs' show. Did you know people who had taken too many drugs?*

MB: Not directly, no. I do now, actually, a few. But not then. I myself had had no personal experience whatsoever, and I don't think it's something I needed to have experienced to make this piece. But I certainly wasn't into making any great anti-drugs message. There seemed to be enough of that around. Drugs in general, however, just seemed very relevant.

The main message is that James is the kind of crass man who tries to impose his own possessive and destructive male desires upon his fantasies, as well as on his own disastrous real life. It is James's story.

AM: *Your Scotsmen are all lager louts?*

MB: Yes. I wanted them all to be rough and coarse. Then I thought, 'What's the most coarse? What's the worst place? What's the most we can make of this idea? What's the most unexpected beginning? Where would you find him?' Which is why it actually starts in a urinal – pretty startling for *La Sylphide* – with nasty graffiti on the walls. A urinal is a secret place, the place in clubs where people generally go to take drugs. So it would be the natural place for our James; and it's an unusual place for the Sylph to appear.

AM: *When we first see her, she comes up from the top of the urinal?*

MB: Yes.

AM: *I hate to say it, but isn't this the second urinal you've choreographed?*

MB: I'm afraid so, yes. There's history for you! Fame for no other reason: 'Incorporated two urinals into works, one French and one Scottish' – the other urinal being a cottaging scene in *Infernal Galop*.

AM: *Do the girls drink?*

MB: Yes. They're a pretty rough bunch, as a whole. So – as I was saying about the punk Gobstoppers in *Nutcracker* – the audience feels a kind of shock at the beginning of it, and then an added enjoyment when they realize that it will work. And the Sylph doesn't look the way you'd expect: not all beautiful. She looks a bit druggy herself, a sort of 'Say No to Drugs' victim.

Preparation

MATTHEW BOURNE: I purposely changed the title so as not to put off the kind of venues we were going to. We were performing in arts centres and the sort of venues that would normally have small contemporary dance companies. If we'd have been doing *La Sylphide*, it wouldn't necessarily have gone down as well.

ALASTAIR MACAULAY: *Do you remember where you did your homework?*

MB: I probably went through my old dance history notes! I tend to look into the *Balanchine Festival of Ballet* book. In the old edition, the scenarios are really excellent as stories. I looked at other dance history books (my notebooks have a Xerox from Lincoln Kirstein's *Movement and Metaphor*), and other views of Romantic iconography. I bought a book on the Romantic movement in art, and read around the wildness and the passion of all that. At once I thought that that went very well with the cliché of the Scottish character: hot-tempered, violent, abusive with drugs and drink.

And the music just kept growing on me; I ended up loving it. It's full of energy, variety, melody. We consciously made decisions to play up to the melodrama of the music, and not make our production too realistic. To that music, it had to be a very heightened form of drama; so the means by which we were telling the story had to be heightened as well. We decided – unlike in *Nutcracker* and *Swan Lake*, where we tried to tell the story through acting and dance – to use gesture and our own more literal form of ballet mime, to add to the melodrama. The more I listened to the music, the more the melodrama within it seemed to suggest lots of arguments and tempers flying about. It did seem to suit the characters and the setting, and it helped the story quite a lot. In Act One, though, we didn't completely follow the original music. We actually added a couple of musical items: the sort of tampering I wouldn't do in a larger-scale work. Because we were using recorded music anyway, it just seemed perfect to have *Brigadoon* playing on the TV when you first go into the flat. *Brigadoon*'s a piece that everyone loves to hate, really. And we also put the Wedding March in, just after the wedding reel, to show that they had actually got married.

I really like *Highland Fling* as a piece, actually. Whenever I come back to look at it again after a while, I see how everything gets tied up very neatly. Everything has its place, and it's very clear. I particularly like Act Two. We had completely our own story going on there, and I was working quite independently of how Bournonville uses the same music. Virtually the whole of the second half is a dance drama; it's danced from beginning to end, virtually the whole time.

AM: *That's interesting because – even though it's modern dress –* Highland Fling *seems less radical than your other shows. Am I wrong?*
MB: Well, it was my first real attempt to do something with a tragic ending. There's a lot of humour, and then, suddenly, when the Sylph's wings get cut off, very suddenly it has a change of mood.

I think it says something about a certain type of man. He appears to want something different. He's got this homely girl, Effie, who does the ironing and all the housework and is sweet, pretty, and seems the perfect wife; but he's excited by the Sylph, who's naughty, and sexy, and alluring, and strange. Then he quickly gets bored with her being different, cuts her wings off, and – basically – tries to turn her into a woman like Effie. He doesn't want her to be as she is; he wants her to stay at home and do the housework.

At the end of Act One, which is set in a high-rise, he jumps out of the window to follow the Sylph. Act Two takes place, logically speaking, in his mind while he's falling to his death. It's all over then. The sylphs kill him.

AM: *So the problem with James is not that he takes drugs, but that he has the crassest kind of male mentality in the first place.*

MB: Yes. And that kind of maleness is shown very much in the first scene: the disco scene at the pub. This is to additional music – or, rather, to Løvenskjold's overture. We thought there weren't enough dance possibilities in Act One, so we wanted to have an opening that had more movement and dance, and would introduce the characters. Well, they do all sorts of crass things in that. They're swearing, belching, throwing up, snogging in the toilets, peeing. It's all very much introducing that world.

As we went along with it, we talked about it a lot. When AMP was a smaller company, we would often sit around talking for hours about what a piece was saying and where it was going; and the more we delved into it, the more reasons we found for things and the richer it seemed.

AM: *You knew from the first that you were going to have male and female sylphs?*

MB: Yes. Out of necessity, but also because we'd already been challenging sexual roles in our smaller shows in various ways.

AM: *There's no difference between a male and female sylph?*

MB: No. Well, here and there, there are some slight differences with things that they do, but only at one point do they dance separately. And they are slightly differently dressed. All the sylphs have a costume like the one for Scottish country dancing, but all in white. They all wear sashes; the women have simple dresses, the men have kilts and belts and baggy shirts. (Clement Crisp wrote in the *Financial Times* that our sylphs looked 'like manic dirty laundry'.)

So they're like dead Scottish highland dancers. And they have these ties in their hair, which was inspired by Björk, who tied her hair in knots. I seem to remember that was my idea.

AM: *Do you think of your sylphs as having gender?*

MB: Yes.

AM: *And, having decided not to have a male Sylph, you decided to make the Sylph this rather wraith-like female.*

MB: Yes. What I didn't want was a conventional-feeling, romantic love-interest story. I didn't want it to be all pretty and dainty – that didn't feel right. I needed her to be touching at times, but she was more of an animal, a creature, dirtier, a bit more bedraggled, like someone that had lived in a forest, covered with grass stains. And she was destructive as well. Like Tinkerbell in *Peter Pan*. She's got a two-edged personality, which I like.

AM: *Your sylphs are barefoot. Taglioni danced in pointe shoes; but, curiously, a number of the Romantic lithographs depict her – like a Grecian statue – with bare feet. Were you thinking of those pictures?*

MB: We certainly looked at a lot of those pictures, in books of the Romantic Ballet. And we also decided to use ideas, not just from *La Sylphide*, but from the whole of Romantic ballet that followed. Certainly aspects of *Giselle* (1841) went into our version. In Act Two, our sylphs are much more like the demonic dead spirits of *Giselle*, the wilis of its Act Two, than they are like the ethereal, harmless sylphs of *La Sylphide*. The way they enter is very much like the way they do in *Giselle*, and the inspiration for the structure of the whole thing was much more *Giselle* than *La Sylphide*. In the beginning, we even had a queen of the sylphs, like the queen of the wilis in *Giselle*, though we cut her out when she proved just one character too many. And our Sylph throws flowers to James, which is very *Giselle*. (Usually in *Giselle* he doesn't attempt to catch them, but I once saw Wayne Eagling catch them very effectively at Covent Garden, and so I put that into our version.)

The other big influence on all the sylphs is Isadora Duncan, or the feeling of Isadora. I love that kind of movement. Of course, I don't really know exactly how Isadora moved – I never saw her dance – and yet I feel I know what this kind of movement is. It's a spiritual abandonment, a very centred kind of movement that spreads through the limbs from the centre of the torso, a very free way of interpreting music, and a floaty use of costumes. Our sylphs do a lot of jumping, and their arms keep moving while they're travelling through the air – not positional – because I wanted everything to come from some sort of impetus somewhere; and I feel that's very Isadora-ish. As are their bare feet.

I also had a book that's all about Fokine's *Les Sylphides*. It has many pictures, and we looked at it to get ideas for gestures, such as a 'listen' phrase we used. Whereas the 1832/36 *La Sylphide* didn't much inspire me in terms of its choreography – particularly in the dances for the sylphs themselves – the plotless 1908/9 *Les Sylphides* was a perfect thing to use.

AM: *When Fokine made it, he was probably more inspired by Isadora (whom he had seen dancing just a few years before, and whom he greatly admired) than he was by the Romantic ballet, which for him was mainly an idea of the past – largely, as for you too, shaped by* Giselle *– which he preferred to the more virtuoso ballet of more recent decades. Isadora danced to Romantic music, and her dancing had the simplicity and economy that he found poetic. So, even though she herself said she was the enemy of the ballet, she is not an inappropriate inspiration to a latterday Romantic ballet.*

At times in Act Two your sylphs become parts of the wood: trees, brambles, landscape.

MB: We felt that the sylphs were always watching, that they could be within a tree, that they could become a tree, that they could be anything they wanted to be. We knew we had a virtually empty stage and a backdrop. So our sylphs could become landscape. The stage becomes designed with people.

AM: *There are times when they also seem very sculptural – and, interestingly, like sculpture from just the neo-classical era from which Romanticism exploded. Is this accidental?*

MB: I certainly remember that we looked at lots of statues and paintings from the early nineteenth century.

AM: *I suspect that this connects to the way Taglioni danced; the classical and sculptural qualities of her dancing were especially praised, as well as the floating quality and lightness and pointe-work for which she is more renowned.*

When did the subtitle A Romantic Ballet *become* A Romantic Wee Ballet?

MB: Obviously a bit later on. Likewise, it was later that James changed from being a Scottish crofter to an unemployed Scottish welder.

AM: *In the original, the witch Madge has an important function in both Acts One and Two.*

MB: Yes. She's there in our first act. She's the ex-girlfriend of James; she's into tarot reading, seeing into the future and those sorts of things; she's a New Age kind of woman. So she makes the predictions, like Madge in the traditional *Sylphide*. She also supplies him with drugs, so she's responsible for his downfall there. Because they're ex-lovers, they've got an antagonistic relationship anyway; but she's still in love with him as well. She's jealous, basically – that's why she makes the prediction. But also he needs her, because she's the supplier. Unlike the traditional Madge, she's there throughout Act One; she's a fixed member of his social circle.

AM: *But she doesn't come back as Madge in your Act Two at all. This is the main change you made in the scenario.*
MB: In Act Two she is not relevant. That's why Act Two feels more like *Giselle*, because it's just him and the sylphs.

AM: *By removing Madge from Act Two, you remove some degree of plot. So that left you with music to fill in another way.*
MB: The strange thing is people always think – I suppose it's one of the questions you were hinting at earlier – that everything comes from story, feeling, and character in my work; but really, one of the things I'm looking for when I enter into doing something is the dance possibilities. 'Where can we get more dancing into this?' That was why, in *Highland Fling*, we also used Løvenskjold's overture. It feels like dance music and it builds up a great atmosphere. Likewise, the witches' dance at the beginning of Act Two. We even extended Act Two to put more dancing in: we used the beginning of the overture again, so that each act begins in the same way.

AM: *Do you distinguish between dance and acting, or between dance and what I would call physical theatre?*
MB: I've always found those definitions difficult to deal with. I'm never conscious of saying, 'All right, now we just dance.' But I know when I enter into doing a piece, there have to be good reasons for dance within the story that we're telling. People are always suggesting different books and plays and saying, 'Why don't you do . . . ?' I just think, 'But how does that turn into dance?'

By removing Madge from Act Two, we made it clear that the reason why the Sylph loses her wings is entirely to do with James's will. The whole show is based around him.

AM: *What about the music for her and other witches at the cauldron that opens Act Two?*
MB: It's such great music, the cauldron bit; it has that lovely witches'-brew, demonic feel to it. So it helps to introduce the world of the sylphs.

AM: *That makes it more* Giselle-*like, because you get the dark element?*
MB: Yes. And, as in *Giselle*, the beginning of the second act is about being introduced to the sylphs before the central characters re-enter. James only re-enters halfway into the music, and then we don't actually identify the Sylph. He's looking for her, but she's like all the others – until a particular point in the music, where they come face to face.

AM: *Later on, how does she lose her wings?*
MB: In one scene, the sylphs are all round him, and he's enjoying being in their world. They teach him how to fly, how to be a fairy; and it culminates in a big dance. Then they get too physical. They all want a piece of him, because he's a human. He brushes them all off and says, 'You have to choose between them or me. We're leaving together.' He's seen the way she is in the forest; he wants her to stop being what she is; he wants to turn her into a real woman. So she gets her little sylph bag and goes off with him. He takes her to another place in the woods, gets the shears out, and cuts her wings off – with garden shears. It's all very bloody – not pretty, but a real shock. It makes complete sense.

AM: *Then she dies?*
MB: She's around a bit longer. He's shocked at the whole thing that's happened. She comes back on and acts like someone who's had an arm cut off. She's shaking, and she does a version of some movement they've done earlier on. It's like the mad scene in *Giselle*, where she half does the steps she used to do but now in a broken way. The *Sylphide* music's lovely at this point as well. James begs forgiveness from her: he tries to get her to move again and to dance again; he helps her around the stage. She's nearly dead; she keeps on drooping and coming to life again.

It builds up again to the climax where she finally does die. Then the sylphs pick her up and take her away. It's done so that, as he lifts her up and they take her from him, it's as if she's disappeared. She's not there any more. And he's alone. He does a regretful solo. Her wings are left behind, and he puts them in the little bag that she's left, so that he's got them as a souvenir. It's ridiculous and very moving at the same time.

AM: *Did you know that Alicia Markova used to have a little bag for the wings she wore as Giselle? She wrote that she knew she had made* Giselle *famous when she left the bag in a taxi once and the driver said, 'Excuse me, madam, you've left your wings'!*

163

MB: And I thought we'd invented the wing-bag! I didn't know that story. Anyway, then the sylphs come back and have their revenge on him. They attack and kill him; but we don't see them actually do that. They do the death symbol; and then we have this little scene at the end to suggest his death, where Gurn and Effie are at home in front of the fire, drinking coffee. James appears at the window. He's now a sylph; he's got wings: he's haunting them.

AM: *This was your first collaboration with the designer Lez Brotherston.*
MB: We're much on the same wavelength in terms of the ideas that he comes up with. He listens; he'll talk things through; he'll get an idea of what we think we're going for, and then he will visualize them – very well, actually – in fully realized, painted drawings. When I first worked with him, I was always slightly embarrassed to say when I didn't like something, because it looked as if he'd put so much work into it. I said to him once, 'I don't know what to say sometimes.' He just said, 'Really, this is the best way to do it. I work very quickly like this, and this is the way I like to show you what the idea is. This is the best way.' So from that point onwards, it's always been fine. He does churn out beautifully realized drawings very quickly, and he works quickly in general with the sets later on. There's never any break, pondering on things for weeks on end; and he happily scraps ideas very quickly, which is great.

AM: *Diaghilev sent Picasso back six times to re-do the sketches for the set for* The Three-Cornered Hat. *So you're in good company.*
MB: It's a good working relationship Lez and I have. I think he particularly enjoys working for this company. We give him more freedom and the chance to have his own say in what goes on. He's very good at adapting costumes for dance, and very aware of what you can dance in and what you can't – aware of the way things should be cut, etc. He had already worked with Northern Ballet a lot, so he's used to dance floors and dancers' problems, and all those things you need to know about when working with a dance company. He's also very clever at making something look as if an enormous amount of money's been spent on it when it hasn't.

Rehearsals

MATTHEW BOURNE: Before the rehearsals began, I worked out all the counts for the music. I can do it quite quickly if the music's not too difficult. I can virtually do it while I'm listening to it one time through; but it would be something I'd come back to. I would do the counts first; then, once I'd got the counts sorted out, I'd listen to the music again, looking at my counts, which are in graph form; then I'd stop the tape where I thought something particular might happen and make a note above the particular column; and then I'd come back to it again and maybe write notes.

ALASTAIR MACAULAY: *When would you first have started doing this?*
MB: About a month before rehearsals; I would know the music very well by that time, and would already have an idea of what I'd do to it.

Having done just *Nutcracker*, I was very involved by this new way of working. It's because I could actually work with the score in advance in that way; and, having all this, I was very excited at entering the rehearsal period. Looking through my notes here, I can see all kinds of initial ideas: Cathy from *Wuthering Heights*, James as a crack addict, James having a seizure at the Highland Games. Then 'Madge injects him'. Oh yes, and everybody was going to bring toasters as wedding presents. These are some of my first thoughts.

Then, opposite, I've written counts: not how many beats there are in each bar, but the groups of counts I feel that the music falls into for my purposes. Very often I'm looking – if the music has two, four or eight beats in the bar – for counts of eight. If it's in three/four tempo, I'll adjust. But it's hard for me to know now which notes I wrote before rehearsal or during rehearsals. There are plenty of notes here that show ideas we had but never used. Some of them are ideas I brought to the first rehearsals; some of them are ideas we all came up with during rehearsals. Quite often the ideas that we never wrote down are the ideas that we ended up using.

A few things happened around the time of *Highland Fling* that connected with the piece. My friend James McCloskey – who had designed the first piece I did for AMP, *Overlap Lovers*, and all my amateur shows before I went to Laban – died from Aids two weeks before it premiered. Even the fact that his name was James seemed relevant. And within the show we had, as Gurn, Simon Murphy, who was also suffering from Aids at the time. There came a point where he couldn't continue with it; and although it was a humorous piece in many ways, that always made the end more touching in a way for those of us who were involved in it.

Highland Fling was also the first small-scale show I wasn't dancing in myself.

AM: *Does that change the physical style of a piece?*
MB: Yes, very much. I think that, when I was in the first performances of pieces, I got more physically involved, obviously, because I had to learn and develop the material and actually dance it as well. Sometimes that can lead you to develop material in a different way, to physically find more details and connections, which you don't do so much when you're not in it: you rely on other people a bit more to develop the movement. When you're not dancing, you watch more. The good thing is that, if you're working with good people, you get a lot of ideas you wouldn't have necessarily found if you relied only on your own physical or imaginative instincts. But it's wise to try to physicalize things if you still can, because otherwise you lose your own style of movement. Certainly I feel that there are particular things that I emphasize and that I like to do.

AM: *How long did you have to rehearse* Highland Fling?
MB: For small shows like that, we used to have eight weeks. For *Nutcracker*, we'd had five weeks, which was ridiculous – nothing. But we were all buoyed up by the success of *Nutcracker*, and we thought, 'This is what we're going to do – to retell these stories.' We felt we had a seal of approval for that, we felt braver; and I was now very into everything making sense, into giving references for everything.

We did the same character homework with these characters, but we talked about the story more first, to make sure the relationships were already sorted out. So I told them the general storyline, who they were, and what their relationships were with each other. Then they'd come back with more of a character and how they saw it. That would then help with fleshing out the individual scenes.

So here's the list of characters I wrote out during rehearsals after we'd all talked about them: 'James, or Jimmy, unemployed welder. Glasgow. Drink and hard drugs. Sympathetic.' I thought that, as he was the hero, he needed to have some sympathetic quality. The performers all chose their own jobs. Scott Ambler played James: it's the most central role I've ever given him, even more than the Prince in *Swan Lake*.

AM: *You had to cast all the roles among this small nucleus of AMP dancers. Were there any problems?*

MB: Simon Murphy had problems initially with Gurn. I wanted him to be a drip, and he didn't take to that. He solved it by making Gurn a born-again Christian, simple and nice, with a smily T-shirt with a 'Jesus Loves Me' slogan. He used to carry around a Bible when he did it, too. It worked really well. The notes just say, 'Gum, supervisor in furniture warehouse. Everything in moderation. Sympathetic. Born again.'

When Phil Hill took over that part, in 1985, he didn't like the born-again Christian thing, and he did his little strong-man act, which worked as well.

'Effie, clothes shop. Day-release business management. Slightly prudish. Unimaginative.' This was Emily Piercy, who went on to do the Prince's girlfriend in *Swan Lake* so well.

'Madge MacPherson, bar maid who organizes discos. Drug dealer small time.' This was Etta Murfitt; she just loved having a role that was so different from Clara in *Nutcracker*!

'Dorty, beauty therapist. Tough, common, materialistic, trashy, and has a sexual relationship with Robbie.' This was Rosie (Rosemary) Allen; again, quite a change from her role as Mrs Dross.

'Robbie's a red-head, oil rigger. Laddish, loutish, sexist.' This was Andrew George, who'd been the Nutcracker.

AM: *None of you were Scottish?*
MB: No. And, because I was worried about it being too clichéd, quite late on in rehearsals I went to my friend the actor Alan Cumming. I'd known him since he played Silvius in the RSC's 1989 *As You Like It*, for which I choreographed the dances.[1] He's Scottish, and I brought him in to watch, and asked him, 'Do you think it's OK?' He liked it a lot, thought it was fine, and helped us with a lot of Scottish graffiti in our toilets! – words that we wouldn't otherwise have known. Here are some notes I made during a meal with him. 'Haud yer wheest' means shut up; 'I've got the painters in' means having a period; 'Getting off at Paisley' means withdrawing(!). 'Lena Zavaroni gives me the dry boke'; 'Fur coat, nae knickers'; 'Taggart is a faggot'; 'I love Isla St Clair'. (Clement Crisp quoted some of these in his review and said, 'This is the level of humour in this piece.')

---

1 When Bourne won two Tony Awards for *Swan Lake* in New York in June 1999, one of them was presented to him by Alan Cumming – himself a Tony-winner the previous year for his performance on Broadway in *Cabaret*.

Then graffiti more related to the characters: 'Gurn is a dork. Madge is a les. James for Effie' (with a heart written round it). 'Dorty is a slag.' 'Jimmy is a fairy.'

As I've said elsewhere about any idea, I go for the most Scottish or the most French or the most whatever it is that you can do. The set was covered in any Scottish references we could find.

AM: *I remember laughing out loud at seeing those graffiti.*
MB: One of them was: 'Sit on my face, Jean Brodie.'

AM: *Your initial sketch for a poster says, 'Highland Fling – a romantic new ballet.' Then it adds in the corner, in your hand, 'As sweet as a Glasgow kiss.'*
MB: That's quite good, I should have used that. A 'Glasgow kiss' is a head butt, by the way. I learnt that from Alan.

Here are some notes I wrote, fairly early on, for the first scene: 'Smoochy dance. James corners Effie while Madge is in ladies. Four 8s, disco together, dance while talking. Then have a pee, go, freshen up.'

AM: *Is it clear what drugs James is taking?*
MB: I must have changed my mind about that. We had to decide whether he would inject or smoke or swallow. But I think we plumped for Ecstasy, partly because it seemed very popular at the time, partly because we wanted to show him taking pills.

AM: *Later on for this scene in the toilets, you've written down character ideas: 'Use sinks, adjust clothes, pose, apply make-up, argue, gossip, laugh, take drugs, drink, have a pee, revive James, Robbie has a nose-bleed, 2 people lean against each other, Dorty feeling a bit sick.' For the fight at the end, you've written: 'Three 8s plus . . . James going wild, Effie and Madge fighting. Centre it around this' – so that's a note about spacing – 'Girl intervenes, Dorty and Robbie get involved, free for all.'*

In your notes for the next scene, you've got plenty of eights counted out, with bits of scenario written where appropriate. At one point you've written: 'Syncopated altercation about partners.'
MB: That means I knew the movement would look good if syncopated against the music.

AM: *The Sylph actually makes her first appearance in this toilet scene, rising up from the urinal wall. And it is the Sylph – later, the other sylphs also – that suddenly lend a whole new astonishing dimension of seriousness to* Highland Fling. *How did you start off with your idea of the Sylph?*

MB: As always, much depends on casting. I'd already imagined the Sylph being like Tinkerbell, and I cast Maxine Fone in the role. She was just perfect. She's got a naughty side to her, she can look very beautiful, and she's not a woman that will accept playing a little pretty, nothingy sort of female character. She has to have a bit more spunk. And, while everyone else was researching their human characters, she did lots of research into sylphs and fairies. It was very much her thing: she loves anything Gothic; she loves horror movies; she reads constantly around the areas of fairies and goblins. She already had a lot of material, went and bought a lot more, and told us a lot about what fairies do: all the types of fairies there are, bits of information which were quite useful for coming up with movement material as well. So a great deal of our conception of the sylphs came from her.

AM: *Therefore, for Maxine and perhaps for you, a sylph is somebody with a life of her (or his) own: she's not just a figment of James's imagination?*

MB: In any kind of dream or hallucination situation, you have to create characters that have their own life. You believe in them. You have to believe that James did fly out of the window and go somewhere – and that, though this did happen in fantasy, it really happened. If you say, 'All you are is a figment of his imagination', then you haven't got much to go on.

I think that Maxine's body type really helped the piece as well. She's so petite; she's got a lovely little body. When the wings get cut off at the end, she seems so tiny and frail; her little hands were so shaky, you felt for her. I think that, by the end, you like her as a character. Yet she's quite destructive in the first act; she just causes havoc and smashes things. But her mischievousness is very appealing.

AM: *I do think you're on to something that was in the original* Sylphide. *Bournonville writes about the ballet in his memoirs, as if he rather regrets having tampered with something so tragic and dark and dangerous. He says, 'For me, the Sylphide has been what she was for James, a dark angel who tempered everything with her poisonous breath.'*

MB: I do feel that it's there in the music. That's probably why I find the Bournonville ballet – at least, as it is produced today – annoying; and

I don't find the witch frightening. Nothing really works for me in it well enough. It just seems pretty and period and harmless – unlike the score.

Here are some notes from research into sylphs: 'A middle nature between man and angels.' Known as sylphs in the highlands.' 'Evil fairies are strong and wicked in the highlands.' 'Fairies avenge wrong-doings with blights and illnesses or even death.' 'Especially handsome men are desired as lovers by fairies preparing princesses.'

AM: *One thing the sylphs have in common with the swans of* Swan Lake *is black-lined eyes, which gives a zombie impression. Is that the wrong word to use?*

MB: If 'zombie' means 'living dead', I think that's true. Less so in *Swan Lake*.

AM: *Now we're into your notes for the next scene. 'It is morning, James is asleep. TV on. "Brigadoon". Gurn turns it off. Hangover. Drug dance: Gurn and Robbie. They collapse or leave. Sylph enters (behind chair): solo. Sylph wakes up James . . . He sleepwalks. She leans on him. Balances her. Lifts her while he is asleep, tries to kiss her. She disappears, maybe later. He is shit scared.'*
Why the idea of sleepwalking?

MB: Because I wanted it to feel as if it was in stages, as if this was just the beginning of him being aware of her. I wanted to give the impression that he is actually asleep through all this. So that starts the scene. Then, suddenly, the development of the hallucination becomes a reality to him. I think sleepwalking does show a kind of sub-conscious need. It expresses something deeper within you.

AM: *From that we go back to trivial domestic matters. 'Effie enters with Madge and Dorty. They've been shopping for wedding things at Brides, wedding presents. The women clear up and do the housework: housework dance, feather duster dance, washing line, ironing. Men get in the way.'*

MB: Clichés abound!

AM: *'Effie, Gurn, Dorty emerge. Feather dusters. James gets in the way. Robbie hoovers.'*

MB: Robbie works on an oil rig and he's home for the weekend. So he's very randy. But they put a pinny on him and make him hoover.

AM: *'Gurn helps Effie with ironing. Lovesick.' It looks to me as if you've got an awful lot thoroughly conceived before you get to rehearsals. All this stuff about getting the performers to flesh out their roles is a fraud! You work out everything in advance.*

MB: But I'm prepared to change everything – and often do – during rehearsals.

AM: *Later, you have all Madge's predictions: 'Faster, strange rhythm, cards slower.' Then 'Robbie oil death.'*

MB: Death on his oil rig. We didn't mime that in the end. There's only enough music to do Dorty. You see, I also wrote, 'Gurn, he will sin', because Gurn is a born-again Christian; but we never did it.

AM: *Next, after James has taken more drugs, he sees the Sylph again. 'She seduces him with her abandoned sexuality (She is a tease. Uses length of chiffon to entrap him.) Finds butterfly. (She is a butterfly.) Feeling her face/body. Puts his hand through her. She intoxicates him. He begins to move like her . . .' Tell me about the Sylph's 'abandoned sexuality'.*

MB: She's freer with her movement, obviously, than anyone else is so far. And she has a kind of freedom in the way she's dressed; she's barelegged. She represents a sexuality to him that his prospective wife, Effie, doesn't. We were actively going against the image that one usually has of the Sylph, to make her more of a sexual being, as an alternative to Effie.

AM: *The Sylphide is really an adultery fantasy. But you're right. Taglioni's father trained her so that 'Women and children should be able to watch you dance without blushing.' And Gautier called her 'a Christian dancer', as opposed to Fanny Elssler (his favourite), a 'pagan dancer'.*

MB: 'Uses length of chiffon to entrap him.' We didn't do that in the end, but the idea was to reverse the traditional *Sylphide*, where he uses chiffon to try to entrap her.

As for 'butterfly', we had the idea that she was a real butterfly, that there was some sort of logic to his hallucination. Later on, he does bring on a real butterfly, at the end of the act, and he looks at her in the same way.

'Feeling her face/body. Puts his hand through her.' There's a bit where she runs towards him, and passes through him, and she comes out the other side. That's the effect we tried to give.

AM: *There's one lift in Act One, where she's on his chest, but she slowly moves her legs through a kind of scissor shape. It's wonderful, because you feel her progress forwards through the air even while she's leaning down on his body like some huge force.*

MB: Maxine saw herself very much as a vampire.

AM: *Then she has a wonderful movement when she bourrées back on half-toe in first position, writhing her shoulders up and down alternately in a figure-of-eight roll. What gave you that idea?*

MB: Goodness knows. But I'm very fond of using the shoulders. It always suggests something sexual and abandoned to me, and that's what I wanted from her at that point. It's very Ashton, as well. There's a movement I love in *Marguerite and Armand*, though I only know that ballet from film, when she's being kissed on the chest and she goes backwards, with her back to you; and the shoulders just give.

AM: *Am I right in thinking that there always has to be an impetus in or through the torso in your work?*

MB: Yes. I'm always looking for where the movement starts. Often dancers don't pick up on it. Like ripples through the arms, which we used a lot in *Swan Lake*. People start it around the biceps somehow. I always want it to start at the shoulder or in the back, but they're afraid of doing that, because it doesn't feel right. I say, 'Don't be afraid, because it's much more creature-like to do that, if you're a swan or whatever.' I always think of Ginger Rogers with her shoulders often so up; it's very interesting. And Lynn Seymour is actually rather like that. She completely distorts the upper torso and neckline when she wants; she'll hoist the whole of the shoulders up and around and put them into everything. Really inspiring.

AM: *And she ends up having immense repose around the shoulders too.*

MB: I've always enjoyed the use of the back in everything. That's what I always loved about watching Ashton's work. So whenever I see a possibility for that, I always get people to emphasize, or overemphasize, that.

AM: *Well, Ashton's two favourite words in rehearsal were 'Bend' and 'More'.*

MB: Right. You can see why; that's what dancing's all about. People who move that way – you just love watching them so much more than

34 *Highland Fling*. Scott Ambler as James, Maxine Fone as the Sylph. In this lift – inspired by Ashton choreography – the Sylph walks forwards through the air while pressing down upon James and pushing him backwards.

someone who's all prim and precise. It comes much more naturally to dancers with a contemporary background. They don't feel tied down by classical training; that freedom comes more easily.

AM: *At the end of this episode for the Sylph and James, you've written 'Soothes him. Faster. And she throws washing in the air.'*
MB: As he begins to want her, she shows the other side of her personality, which is naughty, wild. She wrecks the room: all the stuff that's just been tidied up, and the ironing that's just been done. She pulls pictures off the wall, and dumps the washing everywhere; so that when she disappears and he's left, it looks to all intents and purposes as if he's wrecked the room, when the others come in.

AM: *At one point here – so unlike a Romantic ballerina – she even walks on her heels around the room.*
MB: Yes, she stomps a bit. She becomes more like a naughty child.

AM: *Also here she sends up the whole Taglioni image. She's in a temper and she sarcastically does the classic Taglioni pose of resting her chin on the fingertip of one hand (with that elbow resting in turn on her other fingertip).*
MB: Yes, that's part of her naughty period. She starts off more serene and sexual, then she switches.

AM: *During the scene that follows, you wrote at one point, 'Bournonville phrase'.*
MB: We did allude to some Bournonville movement, in some jumps and some uses of the head. We also decided here to show that there was some sort of reality to the Sylph. Gurn returns to the house, alone, and hears the Sylph in the kitchen. He goes in – and comes out holding a white butterfly, stroking it. The idea is that that really is the Sylph. She may be an illusion in James's mind, but this butterfly is what he has projected the illusion on to.

AM: *Then we come to the reel. You've written, 'Bigger, swords'.*
MB: We did a dance with the men's legs being swords and the women dancing over them, crossing legs, and jumping.

AM: *Now it says 'teapot'. Is that the same 'teapot' dance idea of domesticity you used in* Town & Country?
MB: Yes. For the men. The left hand's on your hip, the right hand is the spout, and you tip from the waist like a teapot. The girls are like teacups,

and the men 'pour tea' into them. The music just seemed to have a little pretty feel about it here, which put the idea into my head.

AM: *When the curtain goes up on Act Two, we see the sylphs looking like so much nightmare scenery. They hold their arms like broken wings over their heads.*
MB: It's to create a sense of mystery. I wanted the idea that they were peering from behind things: that they were within the forest all the time, so that they were looking behind trees, between twigs. So rather than being wings, those arms are more like branches in our minds.

AM: *How do men feel being sylphs?*
MB: Quite happy. And there was a lot of nice dance material to do, which they enjoyed.

AM: *So how did your fairy research turn into movement in Act Two?*
MB: We began with various improvs. (The sylphs had names, by the way: Oona, Nuala, Taboo, Ethna, Mab and Nymphibia are the ones in my notes, but we came up with others for the men later.) One improv was using Romantic gestures. We had looked at the old lithographs and paintings of the Romantic ballet, looking particularly at the gesture of the position of the arms, and we used some of those gestures to develop movement, making phrases where you worked through these positions and made them transitional. A lot of the arm positions we studied and used – sometimes in a way that's ended up being quite disguised.

Another was about hunting and eating and killing. It was Maxine's idea that the sylphs should kill little animals, bring them on stage, and eat them. What did they eat? Worms, for example; mice. Fairies have to survive! So there is quite a savage feel to them.

Likewise we did one improv – it never really went into the piece, or a little bit maybe – where we experimented with flying. We tried lifts in which you lift a person as if they're in flight, for example.

From these various improvs and ideas, people came up with phrases. One example is the moon phrase, which the sylphs do when they first appear at the beginning of the act, when they're all opening towards the moon. They're moon worshippers, and it's a full moon. It's a directional phrase of movement. We had a big light that was like the moon as well.

We decided that the sylphs were all part of the Sylph. They felt what she felt. When she was in pain, they were in pain. When she was in love, they were in love. We also wanted the sylphs to be able to use the floor.

Their wings had to be rubberized, so that, if they rolled on their wings, they would come back into place. Above, all we wanted to be very free and wild. We took this from the meaning of Romanticism.

AM: *So, with your dancers, you develop all these phrases. You're using the music, and you're using ideas of character. Do you carry on until you've got enough phrases to fill the music? Or do you think 'Maybe seven different phrases is all I need for Act Two'? How do you get from individual phrases to the whole of a dance?*

MB: It is surprising how few you need to make a dance, because you can do so many variations on a phrase. You can divide it up, you can use separate elements of it – especially when it comes to working with a group – you can do variations on one movement in the phrase. So I do manipulate phrases a lot.

AM: *You say 'I' rather than 'we' for once. Is the manipulation of phrases your particular business?*

MB: That's mine.

AM: *Do you enjoy that aspect of it?*

MB: I do. The making of the phrase is less enjoyable for me, because it's finding something from nowhere, whereas, once you've got something to work with, it's much more fun. And I am always the one who sets it musically, who fits it to the counts.

AM: *Does all this make you see yourself as a craftsman?*

MB: In some respects, yes. If I'm given a phrase, the thing I will quite often do is change the counts. I will look at the movement, but then count it in a different way, re-emphasizing certain aspects.

AM: *By changing the counts, you're really trying to re-emphasize the dynamics?*

MB: Yes. I find that, when most dancers give you movement, the dynamic interest is the thing that's missing. They're more into trying to find some interesting movement, than making that movement interesting to watch. It's usually very even; dynamically flat.

AM: *When you put in a step like pas de chat, how strict are you about its execution? What quality are you looking for? Do you want the feet to meet in the air?*

MB: I personally like it when the legs are quite spread, so that it's not too neat.

AM: *And when they open out beyond the shoulder line.*

MB: Yes. I like the openness of Balanchine pas de chat, rather than the contained British ballet way of doing the step. In fact, in *Swan Lake* we call our *pas de chat* 'Merrill Ashley', because she used to do that step so brilliantly in Balanchine's choreography in New York City Ballet.

AM: *Did you get Lez to design around the dancers? Did they have any say in what they wore?*

MB: Yes: the women generally! I don't know why – it may be sexist to say this – but the women always have more to say about their costumes. There's a way of being seen, a way that they're happy looking. I'm not so sure that it's ever to do with the character they're playing. Some of the men, and perhaps some women, will say, 'I think my character should have this' and 'I need this to make this character work.' A lot of the women are quite particular about what they wear, how it's cut, and so on, but Lez won't be that pliable with them. If he's decided that this is what he wants, that's what he'll do.

AM: *Now, in Act Two, for the first scene between James and the Sylph, you've written, 'He wants to "have" her. He must become a sylph to do so. She feeds him with butterflies, etc.' Then, 'Animals? Birds'.*

MB: This was when we were working on how sylphs need to eat.

AM: *One thing I love in the* Highland Fling *choreography for all the sylphs – but especially for her – is the way that the line of the leg often continues straight up the angled line of the back.*

MB: I wanted that line through the body, but with the neck not continuing the line. Which is a very *Giselle* thing: with the head down, but with the arms in line with the body.

AM: *Particularly with Maxine Fone, there are moments where you give her a more fully outstretched ballet outline than you ever do with either the swans of* Swan Lake *or anyone in* Cinderella. *She really flies off into the wings with grands jetés like Giselle.*

MB: Yes. That's right for Maxine, and right for the Sylph – who's supernatural.

At the end of that first sequence, the sylphs become trees, like a landscape for James to walk through. By them passing him by – he comes from one direction, they're all going in the other – there's the illusion that there's a moving landscape. It feels like he's travelling somewhere through the forest, while he's looking for her.

AM: *You've written, 'Sylph diverts.' That presumably means divertisse-ment dances by the sylphs. The sylphs (plural) seduce him. Initiation ceremony. They carry her around. "La Bayadère" type entrance.'*

MB: I was probably thinking of a zigzag entrance, with a phrase that repeated, as in the famous entrance of the corps de ballet of Shades in the ballet *La Bayadère*. We didn't do it in the end. Or, rather, they do move in a zigzag column, but from the front of the stage to the back, the opposite direction to that in *Bayadère*. And it's a much more compli-cated phrase; it's not a repetition. It's a phrase that two people start, and as they're coming along this way, the next two start it across the back. So the phrases overlap. In fact, here in the notes, I've already written 'Echo canon' for what they do.

AM: *The idea of an ensemble zigzag entrance – which you use in the more traditional direction for the entry of the Swans in* Swan Lake *is, you know perfectly well, a favourite device of the nineteenth-century choreographer Marius Petipa. In both cases, you're aware of that precedent.*

MB: Yes, absolutely.

AM: *Later: 'He is taught how to fly.'*

MB: Yes. There's a little mime sequence where he asks questions and they say, 'Well, you can't be a sylph, because you haven't got wings', or 'You're not a fairy.' We were making up mime gestures here, which was a lot of fun. James wants to learn to fly, so they teach him how. They do movement; he copies them. So, by the end of that 'sylph diverts' sequence, he has become an honorary sylph.

The notes say: 'Teaching how to be a sylph. Queen presents him with wings after initiation. He tries them. They laugh. She gives him the hand of a sylph in marriage. A sylph is rampant. Orgy. He is spent, exhausted.' A lot of the detail here we dropped: for example, we didn't have a sylph queen in the end. The marriage – by 'a sylph', I think we always meant 'the Sylph' – was to parallel the human wedding in Act One; and the orgy was to show how much more liberated and voluptuous sylphs are.

AM: *And you've written 'ecstasy'. Erotic ecstasy, fantasy ecstasy, drug ecstasy?*

MB: It means that he found what he's looking for – for a while. This is where we move into Love Land, as we used to call it. Everyone is just having a wonderful time. Because the sylphs are a reflection of the Sylph, they feel what she feels. Everyone takes up the feeling of James and the Sylph, who are in love, temporarily anyway.

AM: *'Slow motion': does that happen?*
MB: Not literally. I often have those ideas of playing with time, with one couple slow and the others all going at top speed, for example. It's a Fred Astaire thing from *Easter Parade:* he dances in slow motion in front of a chorus of people who are dancing at the right speed, as it were.

AM: *Now, in the scene when he has had enough of all this bliss, you've put, 'He puts her in a pinny and gives her a feather duster.' That is the clearest example so far that he is a male chauvinist pig.*
MB: We didn't do that. But that was the idea. A lot of details fell into place while we were doing it. For example, the bit about James cutting off the Sylph's wings. That, with all the social/gender issues that we saw within it, occurred to us because we were always looking for answers and reasons.

AM: *On the right-hand page again, a particularly careful analysis of the counts here: '8, 9, 10, 8, 8, 8, 12'; then '1, 2 and 2 and 3 threatening. Corner him. She goes mad. She comes out. Blood on hands. Wings thrown out. They shake. They run when he runs out, avert their eyes. James blood on hands.' On the next left page, there's something you've written, then scrubbed out: 'Long death. She becomes ugly and distorted without her wings. They carry the dying body.'*
MB: We did all that.

AM: *In the right-hand column, you've written: 'She revives. Phrases 8s, tossing. 10s, tossing. 8s, first section. 8 moon phrase. Duet.' Then, beneath that, you've put: 'Blood appears. She is blind.' She does go blind in the original.*
   On the left-hand page: 'The sylphs attack James in revenge for the Sylph's death.' This looks like a prototype idea for what happens in Act Four of your Swan Lake.
MB: The feeling was the same; but I didn't intend any connection.

AM: *Then, in the final scene: 'Effie and Gurn are snuggled in an armchair in front of the fire. The figure of James, now a lonely sylph, is seen at the window (à la Wuthering Heights). Effie walks across and draws the curtain. Gurn crushes a butterfly.'*

MB: In the event, she doesn't actually get up to draw the curtain. But James remains in the window. And Gurn crushing the sylph butterfly I really liked as an image; but it was one image too many at the end. So, to keep it simple, we cut it. But, on the armchair they are sitting on, there is a butterfly. He just picks it up when Effie goes to sleep with him. He looks at it, crushes it in his hand, drops it on the floor.

AM: *You have here some pages written during rehearsals.*
MB: Yes, to help keep track of what phrases we'd got. 'Clap, listen', for example, is a phrase we developed from *Les Sylphides*. 'Catching butterflies' is a jumpy phrase. 'Picking berries' involves a certain amount of mime. 'Teaching flying' is a dance they all do. The phrase starts with a sissonne – a jump in which the feet scissor outwards from two feet to one – which they teach James.

And here is a floor plan of the set. We had an adaptable set, with pieces that were moved by the performers. So one side was the toilets, in the opening scene; and when the set turned around, it became the walls of the living room.

AM: *Were there any points where the music proved tricky?*
MB: There was one long section in Act Two, just after she's had the wings cut off and does a little solo, where there was lots more music even though it felt that the story was at an end. We really struggled with that part. But we found some quite simple ideas which worked well, about him trying to make her alive again, picking her up, putting her arm in his, as if they were getting married and walking forwards. Then she was lifted by the two male sylphs away from him, as if they were taking her away. Then he would walk forwards, but she wasn't there. He would go looking for her again, but as if everything else was invisible. Then he would get her again, and again the male sylphs would take her off somewhere. But it was one of those times, towards the end of the rehearsal period, when I was going a bit mad. There's always a point when I go a bit mad.

AM: *Is that visible to others?*
MB: I think so, yes! It's horrible. Funnily enough, I really don't enjoy the aspect of actually getting a piece finished. I like all the build-up to it, and there are certain parts of rehearsal that I really enjoy. But my favourite thing is creating ideas beforehand, and then working on it once it's finished. I find that it's like getting blood out of a stone sometimes,

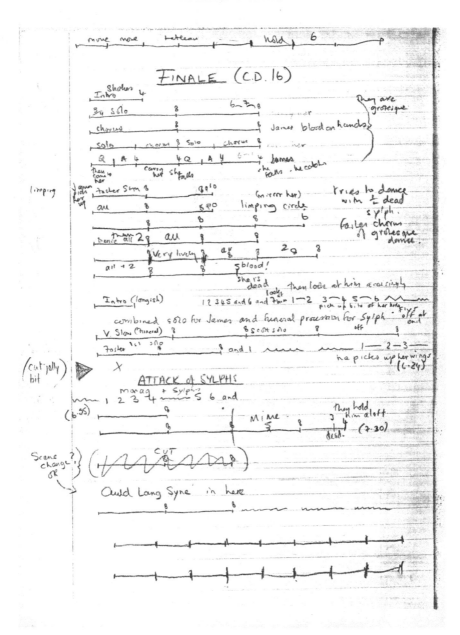

35 *Highland Fling*. Bourne's initial notes on the music for the end of Act Two, supplemented by notes made in rehearsal.

especially towards the end of a rehearsal period. I always feel that I just haven't got a single idea left. Your mind has been so much within the piece for so many weeks and nights. Curiously, the easiest one that I've done is *Swan Lake*. I didn't have any problem; I just loved every minute of doing that and got on with it and wasn't worried about it. With *Cinderella*, largely because I was ill in the middle of the rehearsal period, I was so short of time by the end that I was waking up in cold sweats in the middle of the night, remembering bits of music that we hadn't done yet and thinking, 'There's absolutely no way we can get this done.' But the company has always recognized the point where I get like that. And they're always very supportive, all of them. They buoy me up, and make me do more; and they'll help. That's when Scott and Etta come into their own. They agree to stay late every night; they'll put the show first before their families. That's why I worry about doing work for other companies: I know that, if I don't have those people around me, I couldn't get it finished. Choreography has to be made against the clock; and when you see the time ticking by, it's sometimes frightening.

Performance

MATTHEW BOURNE: We tended to rehearse and premiere everything in Bristol because we had funding from there. With *Highland Fling*, we did some touring, then we performed it in London at the Lilian Baylis Theatre, which was not ideal for it. But we've now done it at three different places in London: the others being the Donmar Warehouse in 1995 and the Place in 1997.

ALASTAIR MACAULAY: *What on earth was it like to do* Highland Fling *at the Donmar Warehouse with the audience on three sides?*
MB: I didn't feel it was the best, because of the limited stage space and the proximity of the audience. But the sort of audiences that were coming to it absolutely loved being that close to dancing. They had never seen anything like that so close up; and, because it was a theatre sort of audience, that was the comment I used to get: 'It was so great to see it so close up.' But also it helped the performers to get inside the characters a lot more. With no distance, you really felt involved and within the whole thing. It worked there – and it certainly increased our audience in a different direction. It helped us with that transition into the West End.

AM: *Did you ever do it in Scotland?*

MB: Yes, once. At the Edinburgh Festival, as part of a charity ball evening. There was a fashion show, and we did *Highland Fling*. It went down very well. I'd love to do it in Glasgow, of course, though that would be a bit nerve-racking.

(Conversations 1998–99)

7

Oliver! (1994) and other Musicals

ALASTAIR MACAULAY: *Before* Swan Lake, *something important came along, which was Cameron Mackintosh's 1994 West End production of the Lionel Bart musical* Oliver! *This was revived at the London Palladium; Sam Mendes directed, and you choreographed. The show was a big success, running in that three-thousand-seat theatre for three years. While we've been doing these interviews in summer 1998, you've just been preparing and launching a touring version of the production, which may run for several more years. At what point had Cameron Mackintosh become aware of your work?*

MATTHEW BOURNE: He had seen *Children of Eden*, which he didn't like very much, and that put him off me for quite a long while. The thing that really made him interested was *Late Flowering Lust*, which he absolutely loved. I hadn't met him at all, but when I was invited to his house to talk about *Oliver!*, he suggested that I meet with Sam to see if we would get along. The only person on the production with whom I'd worked before was Anthony Ward, our designer for *Nutcracker*.

Once Cameron decides he likes you, he can be very loyal to you.

AM: *Among other things, I believe* Oliver! *gave you the most secure income you'd ever had.*

MB: The first effect, though, was that it stopped me from performing. I had been planning on being in *Highland Fling*, but when I got the job in *Oliver!*, I couldn't. The tour of *Highland Fling* had to go ahead, which was fine. Choreographically, it actually had big benefits for that and later shows, because it obliged me to get a whole picture of each production. Personally, however, it was quite a big thing at the time, because I love performing so much.

It created a different feeling in me as a director of a company. Suddenly, I had that distance from the performers: I wasn't one of them. So it was a new way of working. That's developed over the last three years or so, especially as the company's got bigger.

Financially, obviously, *Oliver!* has helped me enormously. Because it is a success, that brings me in a secure income throughout its run. Such shows – when they are successes – are like gifts for any director or choreographer. I'm better known for *Swan Lake* and other AMP productions, but those to date have not brought in regular income by any means.

AM: *Did* Oliver! *involve the biggest company you'd ever worked with?*
MB: No. The biggest company had been back in 1991, when I choreographed *Show Boat* in Sweden. That had been for a state company – the Malmö Stadteater – which is made up of an acting company, an opera company and a ballet company, all sharing the same theatre. For any productions they did, they used people from all three companies; and the theatre's got the largest stage in Europe – the size of a football pitch! There must have been about eighty to eighty-five people in the production. About thirty of them were dancers.

That was a very odd production, because *Show Boat* is about blacks and whites in America, and there are no black performers in Sweden at all. So the Swedish performers were blacked up, like *The Black and White Minstrel Show.* Can you imagine that happening here? But it's somehow acceptable there. Still, I felt very uncomfortable about it, I must say.

I love *Show Boat* so much, and I enjoyed working on it. It was a good challenge at the time. A few of the principal dancers felt it was beneath them, and wouldn't appear. However, there was much more dancing in that production than there is in, say, the *Show Boat* that's just come to London from Broadway; and several numbers were on a very big scale. 'Can't Help Lovin' Dat Man' in the current production here feels quite minimal and naturalistic, whereas in our production it turned into a far more developed number.

AM: *Did you learn from doing it?*
MB: Yes, very much. Among other things, I had to deal with the estate of Oscar Hammerstein, which deals with *Show Boat.* There were arguments involved about which numbers you include or exclude – the entire text is on the John McGlinn EMI recording, but some items have to be cut in live performance – and I was involved in giving reasons why I thought certain numbers were relevant to our production. Because ours wasn't what the Hammerstein estate saw as a first-class production – it

wasn't in, say, New York or London, it was in Malmö – there was a lot of material that they weren't prepared to give me. So the negotiation, on a business level, and the subsequent change of plans meant that I learnt a lot about the adaptation of choreography to suit anyone other than myself: i.e. the composer's/lyricist's estate.

One of the director's ideas for the production – something that wouldn't happen in New York or London – was that Magnolia and Gay had dancing counterparts, principal dancers from the company. So when they sang 'Make Believe', it was also danced by this other couple; and so 'Make Believe' went off into a new direction. And the couple re-emerged at different times within the show.

AM: *How nice to have a director who's that dance-friendly.*
MB: Yes, he was, and he wanted a lot of dance in it. His name is Ronnie Danielson. He has an original approach, particularly with musicals – which he regularly did. He had seen my work in London – *Children of Eden* and some AMP stuff.

AM: *How many dancers did you use in* Oliver!*?*
MB: Two casts, each of twenty-four kids . . . and about another twenty-four or twenty-five adults. The majority of the dance work in *Oliver!*, though, is with the kids. (I put in some preparatory work on the 'Food' number and on 'Consider Yourself' with Etta Murfitt and Scott Ambler.)

Sam Mendes, who has since become a great friend, hadn't really worked with choreographers much before. And there was, from him and from Cameron, a certain amount of resistance to actually letting the show go off into anything experimental in terms of staging movement or dance. Cameron knew *Oliver!* inside out and was extremely proud of his association with it. (Lionel Bart was there as well, of course. He, actually, is quite open to experiment. He was always saying, 'Try it!')[1]

For example, 'Boy for Sale' is basically just a song for Mr Bumble on the street. With Geoff Garratt and Jonathan Butterell, who were my dance assistants on it, I worked out this whole number with the company, which was very stylized. We had people on the streets stopping and turning. It had an entire pattern to it, while the snow was coming down. Quite simple, but it looked very good, I thought. But that, at that stage, was just taking things too far for Sam and Cameron. They didn't

1 Lionel Bart died, after this interview, in April 1999.

want to be worried by something that looked like another style. But I felt, and still feel, that it would work.

I felt with *Oliver!* overall that I could have done more inventive things, if I could have done what I wanted to do. But I was dealing with Sam and Cameron and Lionel, all with very strong opinions. Often what would be put to me was: 'This doesn't look natural' or 'This doesn't look real.' (Dancing by its very nature is never a realistic or naturalistic way of telling a story, is it?) Or they'd say, 'This is too difficult' or 'The company can't do this.' But the people making the complaint didn't realize that dance – or any kind of movement – needs rehearsal. Performers don't just 'get' it instantly. This is especially true with people who aren't trained dancers. You need to give a company of performers the time to make something work; but when you're collaborating on a production, your colleagues are constantly asking you to simplify or cut sequences that could have been much more interesting, had there been time given to develop them. So you end up with something more conventional and predictable. That's a bit disappointing.

Working with the kids was great and a real pleasure. You either like working with kids or you don't. I had a great time with them. It was why I kept in contact with the show for quite a long time after it opened. I went in once a week or so to keep an eye on it; and I worked with each new cast, because it was always a pleasure to work with a new bunch of kids. Whatever you give them to do, it ends up looking charming. Kids do things in their own way, because they're not trained. You get an approximation of what you've given them, but, when it's done with enthusiasm and energy, it looks fantastic. And their characters come out through the way they move. That's such a joy; and each new cast kept it alive, because they were so different.

I think that, after a while of working on *Oliver!*, we realized you can't resist what it is. When Fagin comes in, it's like a musical turn. Fagin himself is a turn, a comic act, in the way that Lionel's structured the show. He comes in at a good point in the show, he does half an hour, and then he goes back to his dressing room. This allows for a certain amount of flexibility in the role – which can be awkward for choreography. We had five different men doing Fagin during the course of the run – Jonathan Pryce, Jim Dale, Robert Lindsay, Barry Humphries, Russ Abbott – and each one wanted to do something different from the last. But each one has to fit in with the kids, who have to be extremely drilled and to know exactly what they're doing. For the kids, everything's to counts. They know that they stand here; and, if they don't, they're told off. It's very much that kind of relationship. So there can be quite a conflict between the precision of the kids and the individuality of each Fagin.

It's funny with leading actors and actresses. As soon as you mention somebody else's name in their role, you have to be very careful about what you say. We would all say, 'That thing that Jim did' or 'That Jonathan thing'. But, as soon as you've said that, you've lost your current Fagin a bit. They don't want to know that they're being asked to do something that was someone else's idea. So we made changes, both with the Fagins and with what the kids did, but not always for the better. Ultimately, you should just be stronger and say, 'This version works best – we're doing this.' But it's not easy when they're star actors trying to put their individual stamp on the role.

Oliver! was the hardest job I've ever done. What I learnt most from it was the difference between how something feels in a studio and how it looks on stage, which has affected what I've done since. Apart from 'Food, Glorious Food', almost every number was completely changed when it reached the stage. A huge amount of rehearsal work was a complete waste of time; and the preview performances become more and more important. I wouldn't do a show now without a lot of previews. Preferably, I'd like to rehearse a show, get it on stage out of London for a couple of weeks, then have another two or three weeks' rehearsals before it opens in town and is reviewed. When you see a show on stage, you immediately see so many problems you've got to solve that you've never seen in a studio.

'Consider Yourself', for example. We did versions in the studio that were fantastic a lot of the time. So many ideas. We created waves of people, so that it felt as if you were walking down different streets and different pathways. In the studio it looked fantastic, because you could see everyone all the time. We had these hollow structures that represented part of the set, and they were like scaffolding. Even when people were in them, they were still visible, and the whole room looked busy. But on stage: 'Where is everyone?' Suddenly people seemed to be off stage as much as they were on, doing all these cross-overs, getting off to come to a new place, or climbing down ladders to get somewhere else. The effect in the studio was a lot of action, because you saw all these pathways and transitions; but on stage, you were wasting people a lot of the time. Some people who were at the top of a tower spent the whole middle of the number getting down a ladder and then coming on. You realized that you'd wasted them. So the whole thing was changed. And every number was changed. This involved working extremely quickly, at the last minute, on things that needed to go on stage that night: a nightmare to me and the cast.

Cameron was very demanding – quite kind to me; but if something doesn't work, though sometimes he hates to say it, he has to say it. And he's usually right as well. That was how I learnt to respect him as a producer. He doesn't always know how to solve a problem; he just says, 'It doesn't feel right, it doesn't make me feel the right things. I don't know what you need to do, but that's your job. I just know it doesn't work.' The other thing that I like about Cameron is that he is such an enthusiast. He has remained a fan with a childlike pleasure in his work. I can relate to that.

(Conversations 1998–99)

8

Swan Lake
1995

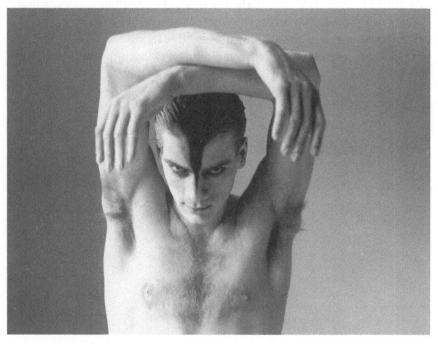

36 *Swan Lake*. Adam Cooper as the Swan: pre-production photograph. Dancers and choreographers often adopt different positions when modelling studio photographic images of their stage choreography. However, the pre-production images created by Bourne and his dancers in the photographer Hugo Glendinning's studio before actual rehearsals had begun are an important, perhaps unique, example of studio-created dance photographic images contributing to subsequent dance text. In particular, Bourne devised certain 'swan' motifs that entered the eventual choreography. The wreathing of arms above the head in this photograph is a motif inspired by Nijinsky photographs; and it came to characterize all the swans in Bourne's choreography. Another feature here, Cooper's direct stare under lowered brows into the camera, was later incorporated from this photograph as a central motif into publicity images for Bourne's production.

Idea

MATTHEW BOURNE: Like anyone, I saw swans in parks when I was a child. But had no special affinity with them. Actually, I rather disliked swans: found them frightening. It was only when I knew I wanted to do my own *Swan Lake* that I started to look at them a bit more and ask, 'What exactly are they? What exactly do they move like?' And my Swan was never just a swan. He was animal, pagan, in my mind. I was also thinking of *Equus*, you see; I'd seen both the West End production and the movie.

ALASTAIR MACAULAY: *There are large parts of your* Swan Lake *that aren't the Matthew Bourne story – but there are parts that are. I don't think any of its Oedipal mother–son anguish is your story; you yourself have a good relationship with both your parents. But there is something in the fascination with the beloved-dreamed Swan that comes out of you.*
MB: I don't need to have gone through things in my life to put them on the stage. But at that time, yes, this did seem a more personally 'felt' piece in some respects. When I was making it, I had had a lot of rejections; and I hadn't been in a relationship for a while – before which I'd gone through a difficult ending to a long-term relationship. So yes: I think all that must have affected it quite a lot. That may be what drove some of the Prince's emotional neediness in my mind – also the strange worship of a symbol, of a beautiful male creature-person. I suppose I have always had people like that in my life – people that you have a feeling for from a distance.

AM: *I've already pointed out, when we were talking of* Highland Fling, *that the 1832* La Sylphide – *the prototype for innumerable Romantic/ classical ballets that followed throughout the nineteenth and twentieth centuries – was itself a gender-reversal of Nodier's story* Trilby. *In the 1840s, the choreographer Jules Perrot made a ballet or two along* Trilby *rather than* La Sylphide *lines, in which he himself danced a male spirit who pursued or lured a mortal heroine.*
    Another French Romantic, Théophile Gautier, wrote the poem 'Le Spectre de la Rose'. In this the more-or-less male spirit of the rose addresses the girl whose breast he/it had adorned at her first ball. In 1910, as you well know, Fokine made a short ballet of 'Le Spectre de la Rose'. Its central idea was of the Girl – played by Tamara Karsavina – asleep in her armchair and visited in her dreams by the spirit of the rose,

37 *L'Après-midi d'un faune*. Vaslav Nijinsky as the Faun, with his sister
Bronislava Nijinska as a Nymph, in 1912. The many photographs of Nijinsky
(1888–1950) dancing have been a longstanding inspiration to Bourne's
choreography. Those taken of him as the Faune in his own radical 1912 ballet
were a particular stimulus to Bourne's conception of the Swan.

*danced by Nijinsky: which is a diametric gender-reversal of the premise
of* La Sylphide, *which begins with James asleep in his armchair and the
dancing female Sylph visiting him in his dreams.*

*The idea of the male dream object: how conscious were you of that
from Nijinsky's role in* Spectre?

MB: I don't think I was. You see, I was also thinking of other Nijinsky
roles, especially the Faun, who isn't a dream object – although that kind
of image can certainly fill your dreams.

Unconsciously, though, perhaps there is a connection. When I first
thought of doing *Swan Lake*, I wasn't thinking of Adam Cooper or of
anyone from the ballet world; but in due course, one part of my idea for
the male Swan became absolutely related to my excitement in working
with Adam. I certainly used to glorify – though I don't now – dancers
in his field, ballet. I would see them as little gods or goddesses. I found
that Adam had, certainly on stage, a mystery about him that could have

appealed to me because of my early enjoyment of those Nijinsky pictures. Mind you, this emerged gradually.

Before Adam, I had thought that Ashley Page was like Nijinsky in personality. The fact that he didn't smile much, that he was never flirting with the audience, that he had strange eyes, I found appealing, and quite unlike anyone else at the Royal. Adam – even though in build and dance style he's actually very different from Ashley – I felt had a similar persona on stage.

AM: *I think you're imagining both Ashley Page and Adam Cooper dancing Nijinsky's Faun. But are you imagining either of them dancing other Nijinsky roles? For example*, Spectre?
MB: No, not really. They're both more mortal, more masculine I suppose, than Nijinsky probably was.

AM: *Did you straightaway think of a male protagonist in the double role of* Swan Lake *– as both 'the White Swan' Odette and 'the Black Swan' Odile, as the roles are known in most versions?*
MB: I don't think that came straight away, no. My immediate idea was of a corps of male swans.

AM: *And a male Prince. So straightaway it becomes a sexual drama to some degree in your mind?*
MB: Yes. That was something that probably interested me from the first: the sexual issues within it. Because our production was so big and so much of a gamble (financially), I probably have played that down to some extent, in terms of the way I talk about it.[1] Certainly, early on, there were people saying, 'Don't play that aspect up.' The fear of a lot of investors was that it would get labelled 'The Gay *Swan Lake*'. But, yes, I think my initial impetus to do it was that sexual drama would be a strong part of it.

1 Certain points from a handwritten announcement of his *Swan Lake* production, dated June 1994, are of interest here. (AMP/Bourne archive)
  Bourne wrote (fourth paragraph) '*Swan Lake* is a great classical ballet, when performed with imagination and style, and AMP's version will be born of a great love and respect for the beauty and power of the original staging . . .' (Sixth paragraph.) 'AMP's previous interpretations of classics such as *Nutcracker* and *La Sylphide* (*Highland Fling*) have been radically different and yet faithful to their source material. The company has attempted to retell these stories by applying a modern-day logic, but without losing the essence of magic which is essential to these pieces. We have tried to look for contemporary messages within these stories whilst retaining the more universal themes of love and betrayal, good and evil. The

Still, the more I went along, the more I found other things in it. The Swan is free, in my version, and he's beautiful. Everyone's interested in him; everyone wants him. The Prince projects on to him. I found that it could be seen, and interpreted, in different ways; and, when we were making it, I made it a little more open for interpretation.

AM: *You made your* Swan Lake *in 1995. Before you started rehearsals in August that year, you drew up the scenario. Did you collaborate with anyone on this?*

MB: No, the scenario for this one's very much mine. I didn't really discuss it with anyone much to begin with. Before rehearsals began, Lez Brotherston, the designer, was the next biggest contributor.

The idea of doing it came to me soon after we had opened *Nutcracker* in Edinburgh in 1992. I had also been toying with the idea of dancing the role of the Sylph myself in what later became *Highland Fling*. And, the moment I dropped that idea, I thought of *Swan Lake* with male swans.

AM: *Is there any conscious effort on your part to make the Prince's drama in* Swan Lake *a reflection of Tchaikovsky's own life?*

MB: No. It has been mentioned, particularly by Jann Parry in the *Observer;* and I can see the reason why: the fact that he was a repressed homosexual. It isn't what I had in mind; but it's a valid point. He wrote the music, and that feeling is somehow there in the music.

AM: *So what else, after male swans, did you have in mind at first?*

MB: The second idea that made me know that *Swan Lake* was worth doing – and that it would work – was the Royal aspect to it. I could see the male swan in my mind, I never at any point doubted that it would work; but, when I started to think about the Royal aspect, then I saw how all the scandal surrounding the British Royal Family – and the introduction of young, new members of the Royal Family: Diana and Fergie and so on – could be applied to the story of *Swan Lake*. Because

same maxims will apply to our treatment of *Swan Lake*.' (Seventh paragraph.) 'AMP is renowned for its witty approach to dance, and humour often plays an important part in the success of our work. However, as proved in the company's most recent show, *Highland Fling*, that lightness of touch can also be switched into sequences of shocking cruelty and bitter tragedy, made all the more powerful by their easy juxtaposition. These elements are particularly important to *Swan Lake*, which has at its heart a tragic love story of unattainable desire.'

Only in the eighth paragraph does Bourne – after naming Anthony Ward (designer) and David Lloyd-Jones (conductor) as his colleagues on this production – announce 'a full corps de ballet of *male* swans'.

38 *Swan Lake*. Stuart Dawes as the young Prince, Isabel Mortimer as the Queen, Scott Ambler as the adult Prince. Pre-publicity photograph. Although no such scene occurs in the production, the Prince's phobia of press cameras became an element in due course. Only at the very end are the adult Prince and his younger self seen onstage at the same time.

of the way a prince can be hounded and can't have a relationship without intrusion – basically can't be the person that he wants to be, e.g. Charles and Camilla – I thought it was so relevant to the plot of *Swan Lake*. I thought that this was something that would work for an audience. Admittedly, the initial intention wasn't for it to look as specific as it ended up being. It was going to be a world that we'd created – a kingdom somewhere in Europe: Ruritania, Marchovia, wherever – with no particular historical period. We never intended to represent the current Royal Family. Several of its members gave us some of our ideas – the corgi is the most obvious example – but that's all.

I always felt that there was a certain amount of satire to be had from the Queen figure in *Swan Lake*. The private-public life was what I wanted to play with quite a lot. I've always liked characters that have two sides to them: two things going on. You think you know them; and then you don't. You can surprise the audience with character development.

AM: *Very few people in the last hundred years have made serious dramas about royalty. This has been the era for plays and operas and even ballets about middle- and working-class people. Still, when the central character is royal, you know that on his/her fate the destinies of many other people hang; and therefore you respond not just to private trouble but also to public implications. So a tragic dimension emerges. That's what happens in your* Swan Lake. *You restored the tragedy.*

MB: It's funny, isn't it? As soon as you call someone a prince, it all becomes very heroic and symbolic. Speaking in dance terms, ballet lends itself very naturally to royal characters. That's why the role of the Queen in our production is sought after now by quite a number of ex-ballerinas. A ballerina has what appears to the public to be a royal bearing, which works instantly for that role very well.

Obviously, ballet is full of princes and princesses; but we're saying that there is more to them than the more formal side that ballet usually shows. We're saying that royalty has another side: that there are real people beneath that ballet-like exterior.

AM: *In 1950, Ashton made* Illuminations *for New York City Ballet. At one point, the protagonist knocks the crowns off a royal, or mock-royal, couple. When this was brought to London later in 1950, Princess Marina, the Duchess of Kent, would hardly address Ashton at a gala performance, she so strongly disapproved. In 1977, MacMillan created a scandal of sorts by choreographing some* Gloriana *dances in which Elizabeth I (Lynn Seymour) was shown cavorting more or less sexually with a number of lovers. Since MacMillan made it for the Covent Garden gala marking Queen Elizabeth II's silver jubilee, it didn't go down too well.*

Something in the climate has changed since those days. Alan Bennett had a great success when he put the current Queen on stage in A Question of Attribution *in 1988; and he did so with a good deal of comedy. Did you see that?*

MB: I saw it on TV. The shock was that Prunella Scales was actually playing the Queen; but apparently the Royals liked that. It was done with such charm and affection that he got away with it. Actually, I think that the British Royals are no problem in this respect. The trouble starts with other people, who choose to get offended on their behalf when Royals are represented.

I was expecting more fuss about that aspect in the press. We had a lot of national press coverage, but all about the male swan issue. Lots of 'corps-blimey!' jokey items – using pictures side by side of Margot Fonteyn as Odette and Adam as our Swan. Really silly, awful pieces. The worst of them used a picture of Adam lifted on Scott's back; the caption read: 'Bum me up, Scotty'. Yet they didn't pick up on the Royal aspect at all – though the Prince's Girlfriend is so obviously like Fergie.

That awful costume she wears: very much like a short version of those terrible outfits Fergie used to wear. We always referred to her as a Fergie type – though Emily, who plays her, changed that somewhat. Lez Brotherston, in particular, made her look a little bit like Fergie: the long hair and bubbly personality and awful dresses. She may be a bit of a Sloaney type, but she's probably just a fun-loving girl, oblivious to the faux pas that she is creating, especially in the Royal Box. That's like Fergie; and even like Diana. Those two were often caught doing things that would have been quite normal behaviour for most young women; but because they were royal now, it was deemed to be unsuitable and wrong. So that side of the girlfriend's personality worked for that character.

I have a feeling a lot of the Royals might have watched our production on TV; to have come to see it might have been a bit close to home. Still, I think they would have loved the Royal Box sequence – especially Princess Margaret. When she came to see our *Cinderella*, I said, 'You must see *Swan Lake*.' She said, 'I've seen it.' I said, 'Where?' She said, 'On the television.' I said to her, 'It's much better live. You must see it some time.' She didn't comment after that. But, when we did the Royal Variety Show, we were told that we were one of about three personal requests from the Queen for what she wanted to see in that year's line-up. More recently, I was one of the people invited to the big Windsor Castle reception for British artists. So I don't think there's any sense of them being offended by *Swan Lake* at all.

AM: *Was it clear to you in conception that your production was going to be Oedipal?*
MB: Yes. I thought that one very clear aspect of royalty is its coldness between parents and children; and the idea of making the Queen a younger woman, who had younger lovers who were of similar age to the Prince, was another factor.

My friend Alan Cumming did *Hamlet* at the Donmar Warehouse in 1993; and I'd seen that production twice. I'd also seen Mark Rylance play it with the Royal Shakespeare Company in 1989; and the Zeffirelli film with Mel Gibson as well. So it was in my mind quite a lot. All those versions were very different, but obviously that relationship between Hamlet and his mother made a big impact in each of them – especially Hamlet's jealousy of her having another lover, another husband. I wanted to bring out the Prince's jealousy along those lines. Each time I saw *Hamlet*, I understood it more, and – because I was working on my

Swan Lake – I saw how that story could help mine. Eleanor Bron as the queen was great in the Alan Cumming *Hamlet;* they deepened the whole idea of the mother–son relationship for me. And Alan made Hamlet so tortured as a character. All that fed my *Swan Lake*, I can see that now.

AM: *Any inspiration from films in conceiving your* Swan Lake?
MB: I've learnt a lot from Hitchcock's films. Character structure; suspense; gradual revelation of surprising aspects of character. Even the look of Hitchcock films comes into it. I can't be specific about this. I've always loved Hitchcock, and we steeped ourselves in his movies when we made *Deadly Serious* in 1992, but I didn't go back to look at any of his movies when I was preparing *Swan Lake*. It's just that, in general, I feel there's a Hitchcock connection: in the character of the Prince and his paranoia and jealousy, in the way Rick Fisher lights it and uses shadow, in the strange mother–son relationship.

The one specific borrowing from Hitchcock in *Swan Lake* comes in Act Four. It's from *The Birds*, of course. No doubt my own childhood alarm about wild birds made me all the more attuned to that film. It only came to my mind suddenly, when we were doing Act Four, late in the rehearsal process. I didn't check out the film; I know it so well. Basically, we do the scene from *The Birds* where Tippi Hedren is sitting on a bench outside the school and there have already been several bird attacks. She's in the foreground: one bird swoops down and lands on a sort of playground climbing frame behind her; then another one comes; then two come. She's getting more nervous about the whole thing; she's lighting a cigarette, smoking it. She sees one bird flying past; she follows its path, and then suddenly she sees that there are hundreds of them there. You've seen a few arrive, and now suddenly you get this shock – that the whole frame is full of them. Next, she quietly tries to move away, to get the children away from the school, before they attack.

AM: *Your equivalent in* Swan Lake *is to do what?*
MB: The swans come on to the bed. We have the Prince and the Swan downstage – in a similar position to Tippi Hedren, in the foreground – and this build-up of swans. The bed is in centre-stage: they come on from the wings and jump on to it – some of them come from round it and hang on to it – they all have different ways of getting on to it. They jump, they slide across the bed. It's quite a powerful moment: a build-up of power and menace; the swans are obviously angry and about to attack – and I owe it to Hitchcock.

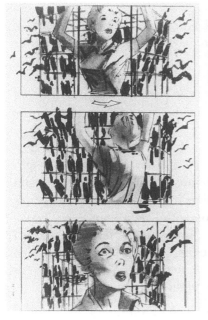 

39 Sketches of Tippi Hedren and the children's climbing-frame in Alfred Hitchcock's 1963 film *The Birds*. Bourne took this sequence as a direct model for the passage when the swans climb on to the Prince's bed in Act Four of *Swan Lake*.
40 *Swan Lake*, Act Four. The swans on the Prince's bed.

AM: *So what had* Swan Lake *been to you before you made your own? When was the first time you ever saw* Swan Lake *on stage?*
MB: The way I've remembered it for years is that I first saw the Scottish Ballet production, Peter Darrell's production. It was at Sadler's Wells in 1979, and I'm on record as saying it was not only my first *Swan Lake* but also the first ballet I ever saw. I've just discovered that it wasn't! But we'll come to that.

AM: *That Darrell production is a drug-dream retelling of* Swan Lake; *it has a fairly tormented, psychological drama. The swan scenes are opium-induced hallucinations in the Prince's mind.*
MB: Yes, but I thought this was *Swan Lake*; that all *Swan Lakes* would be along these lines. I didn't know then that Darrell's treatment of the story was something new.

AM: *Maybe it's also relevant that Darrell's production – unlike most* Swan Lakes – *uses the 1877 score that Tchaikovsky wrote for the original*

Moscow staging version. This 1877 score, in each of its four acts, is quite different from the version of the Swan Lake *score we usually hear in the theatre; and even that 1877 score, as you now know, has its alternative options within Act Three.*[2]

Your own Swan Lake *is almost entirely drawn from the 1877 score. And although it has several musical re-orderings, it has fewer of them than most* Swan Lakes. *In particular, your Act Four uses only the music that Tchaikovsky wrote for it.*

MB: As you can imagine, I knew none of that then; and my memory is that, because I loved the piece so much – I'd never seen a full-length dance piece before – I very quickly followed it up by seeing it again that summer, at Covent Garden. This time it was the National Ballet of Canada doing the Erik Bruhn production with Karen Kain.

During these conversations with you, however, I've discovered that I must have seen the Canadian production first! It came to Covent Garden early in August that year. The Scottish production came to Sadler's Wells about a fortnight later. This tells you something about my memory.

AM: *Bruhn's Canadian version is also a psycho-drama.*

MB: I don't remember it well. I just remember the swans, which made a greater impression with a bigger ballet company on a bigger stage than in the Scottish production. I was surprised at how fast they moved; I wasn't expecting that! The Darrell one certainly left a deeper impression on my mind. So much so that, for years, I've assumed it was the first I saw. I remember thinking, after the second *Swan Lake* in a fortnight, 'This is really different!' I had thought it would be the same. I had thought *Swan Lake* was *Swan Lake.*

AM: *And now, almost twenty years later, someone is probably thinking that your* Swan Lake *is the one and only* Swan Lake.

MB: That's literally true, I've discovered! Especially with young audiences.

AM: *1979 was a busy dance summer by London standards. In July 1979, the month before those two first* Swan Lakes, *you yourself had seen*

2 The Moscow production as a whole was choreographed by Julius Reisinger; but, when the second-cast Moscow ballerina tried to interpolate into Act III a new grand pas de deux that Marius Petipa had choreographed for her to music by Minkus, Tchaikovsky wrote music to fit it rather than have his score messed around further. So from the very beginning there were alternative versions, by Tchaikovsky himself, of the *Swan Lake* score.

Martha Graham's company at Covent Garden; in the month afterwards,
September, you saw New York City Ballet.

Later that year, the Royal Ballet staged a new/old production, very
traditional in outline and drawn from its own previous productions, at
Covent Garden. It was set in the medieval Age of Chivalry; which is –
you'll forgive my saying this – where Tchaikovsky intended it. It was full
of major classical choreography, albeit by five or more choreographers,
some of them then still alive.

The main text was the one arranged by Lev Ivanov and Marius Petipa
for the 1895 St Petersburg production (for which Tchaikovsky had
probably planned to revise his score, but died in 1893). Because the
Petipa–Ivanov choreography endured so well, the 1895 Swan Lake *has*
come down as 'the' traditional Swan Lake *– though every production of*
it makes large or small departures from it. We'll come to some of those
departures later.

I know that you saw that Royal Ballet staging, produced by its then
artistic director Norman Morrice, quite a number of times. How did it
strike you, after your first two Swan Lakes?

MB: Ballet is so strange and exciting when you first see it that you remember few specific details afterwards. Yes, those first two productions I'd
seen had been more psychological; yes, I do remember the Prince smoking opium in the Darrell production; and, yes, I was aware of differences
between each production. But I think I may also have made connections
between them that weren't intended. Because of the Darrell production,
I think I always saw the Prince in the Royal Ballet's *Swan Lake* as a
more complex figure than he actually was in that production. He always
intrigued me. I know in that particular production there wasn't a lot to
go on – I have the official 1980 video, with Makarova and Dowell in the
lead roles, so I can check out my memories – but, through the music, you
can feel more. To me that character was quite complex.

AM: *Perhaps that's because that production used, in Act One, a 'moody'*
adagio solo that Nureyev had added in 1963, to show the Prince in pen-
sive mood. As danced by Anthony Dowell and other Royal Ballet men
of that era, it usually made a poetic effect, and gave the Prince a period
of Romantic solitude early on in the drama.

MB: My memory of that solo is one of the things I take most strongly
from that production. I always liked that music; and even though I know
Tchaikovsky probably didn't write it for the Prince (it's part of the pas

de trois divertissement, I think), it sounds as if it's approaching the core of *Swan Lake*. Certainly I wanted to have that music, as a solo for the Prince, somewhere in my *Swan Lake*; and I use it just at the same point as Nureyev, just before he sees the swans at the end of Act One.

The Prince always interested me quite a lot in the traditional *Swan Lake* anyway. I suppose it was the possibilities of what was really going on. After all, he turns down one batch of women his mother puts before him in Act One; then he turns down another batch in Act Three, more emphatically. With some ballet dancers in the role, I couldn't help giggling.

I had no sense of disappointment in that production; I was excited by it. I may have projected on to it psychological ideas from the Darrell production; if so, they enriched it for me. I wasn't analysing things much; I just absorbed. And I was a balletomane: I saw virtually all the ballerinas at Covent Garden do it; I remember watching all the younger ones making their debuts as Odette-Odile. I used to like Bryony Brind in the role; and, of course, Fiona Chadwick – who later created the Queen in my production. I never saw Natalia Makarova on stage, but I watched the video of her performance a lot in those days.

AM: *Now, that Royal production, however traditional in appearance, had supplementary choreography by Frederick Ashton, by Ninette de Valois and by Nureyev. The whole fourth act was by Ashton.*

Then, in 1987, the Royal Ballet brought in a new production, which returned completely to the 1895 St Petersburg musical text and to a great degree to the 1895 choreographic text too – though there's always dispute about a great many details. On the other hand, this production – by the company's new artistic director Anthony Dowell and designed by Yolanda Sonnabend – updated the ballet to the nineteenth century.

MB: Yes; and, though it's interesting to see the original choreography, that production never made as strong an impression on me. The designs and the choreography aren't really in the same world as each other. So, by this time, I had learnt that *Swan Lake* was what a producer made it; that the structure is up there for grabs; and that the *Swan Lake* experience has to be as strong and poetic in drama as it is in dance.

There are ways of doing it well, and ways of messing it up. If you look at the video of the 1964 Nureyev production in Vienna, with Fonteyn dancing, it plays around with the music in a dreadful way. To me, that's unacceptable.

In the 1987 Royal Ballet *Swan Lake*, we lost a lot of the Ashton choreography, which I missed. I know that the music he used for Act Four includes one piece of music that Tchaikovsky had written for Act Three (in mine, I use it in Act One, for the Prince and the Queen); but it always felt like 'core' *Swan Lake* music – it felt right. Whereas I really didn't like the music for the swan dances in the 'traditional' Ivanov Act Four. Where does it come from?

AM: *Two of the pieces are actually Tchaikovsky piano music that he wrote in the last year of his life; he may have earmarked them for the St Petersburg* Swan Lake, *but it was Drigo who arranged them orchestrally and put them into the ballet after Tchaikovsky's death.*

MB: They never felt appropriate to me at all; and, you know, Act Four never felt to me, in any production, so substantial that it merited an intermission before it – the second, or even sometimes the third interval of the evening – not even with Ashton. So when it came to my production, I always knew I wanted it to run straight on from Act Three. In fact, when you go back to the music Tchaikovsky wrote for Act Four, it's an extremely short act anyway.

I was very much aware when we began to plan our *Swan Lake* that it would coincide with the centenary of the 1895 production.

AM: *The traditional* Swan Lake *has Rothbart the sorcerer presiding, in the guise of an owl, as an evil genius over the Swan scenes. (Usually he looks more like a giant bat.) Odette, the Swan Queen, is under his spell; and, when she seems likely to break free from his power with the help of Prince Siegfried's love, Rothbart then goes so far as to introduce Siegfried to his daughter Odile. Siegfried thinks that Odile is Odette and swears love to her. Because he has thereby broken his vow of love to her, Odette's doom is sealed – at least until, at the very end, she decides to commit suicide, in which Siegfried joins her. That love-death gesture at last breaks Rothbart's power.*

So Rothbart is very much at the core of the traditional Swan Lake. *The music's most famous theme is connected to his fateful power over Odette. Yet you cut him out. I like Rothbart in the traditional version; but the fact that you omit him strikes me as maybe the most brilliant feature of your production, because the element of magic and of fate that he represents, and the fatalism of that great theme in the music, now become shifted entirely to the Prince's mind. The central drama of the Swan scenes in the traditional version is about Odette being torn between*

Rothbart and her hopes of freedom and love. The other scenes are more about Siegfried. But in your version the drama is always focused on the Prince; and it is the conflict in his own mind that the story is all about. What led you to cut Rothbart out?

MB: I felt that he wasn't relevant to the story I was telling. I didn't want anything to be explained by magic, and I feel that that's what he was there for. So I decided simply to create the lesser role of the Private Secretary (originally he was the Press Secretary) as a sort of Rothbart substitute – someone manipulative at court who was just bad news for the Prince – but who didn't really affect the swan scenes in any way. Perhaps you could argue that the Prince has been under his thumb since childhood and that even the dream of the Swan had been controlled by this man. There is perhaps a connection; but not a magic one.

Above all, I didn't want that three-way relationship – Prince, Swan, Rothbart – in the swan scenes. I just wanted the simplicity of the Prince and the swans without something else controlling it. After all, it's in his mind. So it didn't seem appropriate to have anyone else involved.

AM: *So there is a romantic, unbridgeable gap between the Swan and the Prince in your* Swan Lake *as in the traditional one. But that gap isn't created by Rothbart's power in your version, it's created by the block, the repression, in the Prince's own mind. He can't fully grasp the Swan, be at one with it, for reasons that are entirely in his own mind.*

MB: Yes, that's right.

AM: *Do you remember any other* Swan Lakes *that made any impression, good or bad, before you set to work on your own?*

MB: I'd seen the Mats Ek one on video. I'd already seen his *Giselle*. The liberties that he took with those pieces must have given me a bit of a push as well to look at things – but, actually, his is a little too radical for me in some ways: the music is terribly cut and edited; and there are sounds within it, vocalizations, that I didn't like. Basically, though, I liked aspects of what he did; and I liked some of his movement style as well. He was the first new choreographer I'd seen for years whose work actually felt like something that I tuned into.

His *Swan Lake* is a very surreal world, for one thing, as opposed to the more literal world that I set it in. His is a world where everyone's got a bald head – but they seem to have a bun in there somewhere as well, I seem to remember! It's the Prince's story very much; but there is a strong mother-figure, a queen, and it's very nightmarish, I think. The White

Swan-Black Swan is danced by Ana Laguna – who's an amazing dancer, but quite mannish in a way. She's got a great face, but it's like Georgia Brown or someone like that: she's got a sort of rough-edged look to her. So the way the Swan was portrayed was very confrontational; and the Prince, though it's his story, was a bit of a puppet figure.

I liked the fluidity of his movement. It's actually also very exact in terms of gesture – but also full of dance. He's managed to combine the two very well, managed to combine interesting upper-body gestural movement with some more rhythmic lower-body dance interest. And it's very flighty as well, which is nice.

I'll tell you what I think I was most inspired by, when watching it. To see contemporary movements to that traditional music – both in *Giselle* and *Swan Lake* – suddenly makes you see familiar, or great, music in an entirely new light. I think this is the strength of a lot of modern choreography: if it uses good music in a musical way, it feels much more like real choreography. Too many of the traditional ballets – I say this, even though I've loved watching several of them – don't feel like living choreography any more.

AM: *But is this solely a dance response on your part? Or had you seen any theatre or opera productions that updated classic texts?*
MB: In the 1980s, I saw a lot of opera productions at English National Opera, and, yes, I was inspired by the liberties that the producers took. Some of them were updated, some were psychological, some were both: they seemed to be doing something very boldly which the ballet world wasn't. I remember reading the story of Dvořák's opera *Rusalka* beforehand and thinking, 'Well, this is the *Swan Lake* story' – but then, in that David Pountney staging at English National Opera, it became something quite different. The words told the more traditional story about a water-nymph and a prince; the production showed a very psychosexual, daughter-father-nursery interpretation of that story. That may have influenced my *Nutcracker* a little.

The famous Jonathan Miller *Rigoletto*, updated to gangster America, and – much more radically – the Pountney *Hansel and Gretel*, with its Freudian treatment of the Mother and Witch as the same person: all those were very exciting. And they were hits. Here were these producers changing the whole look and setting of a work, and people just loved it.

There are good reasons why these liberties aren't taken in the world of classical ballet: because it's the choreographic text, with all its stylistic tradition, which is being kept going as well as the music, whereas in opera only the music is being preserved from one production to the next. In ballet, if you try updating, it usually doesn't work. Look at Derek Deane's *Giselle* for English National Ballet. Why update it to the 1920s but keep the old choreography? They're wearing dresses they would do the charleston in, but they do the same ballet steps you see in other *Giselles*. It doesn't feel right.

I do think it's possible to make the traditional versions come alive in their original period settings, by the way; I really do. But that's for someone else to try; that isn't what I do.

AM: *As you know, you were by no means the first to choreograph a male Swan. I remember now – something I've tried to forget for years – a production by Roland Petit called* Ma Pavlova, *in which dozens of men all came on doing Pavlova's Dying Swan movements. Why they did, I neither understood nor cared.*

You had seen the Swan that Philippe Giraudeau (and, later, Jonathan Lunn) danced in Siobhan Davies's Carnival, *to the Saint-Saëns Swan music that, because of Anna Pavlova, everybody thinks of as the Dying Swan music. Was that an influence?*

MB: I had seen it – though really I remember it from watching it on video – and liked it very much as an idea. My vision of the Swan was different, because I saw it as more of an animal – even more than a bird, in some ways. I saw it as a pagan thing almost. As soon as I thought of doing *Swan Lake,* I thought of doing it with men; and it was always the wildness of swans that I wanted to show, that I felt would work – relating more to Act Four initially. Then the other thing that probably relates more to the Sue Davies Swan is that I also wanted to do something more lyrical for men – without emasculating them in any way. At the time there was a lot of violent male dancing around, European stuff – Eurotrash, Eurocrash, whatever it is – and all Lloyd Newson's physical theatre with his group DV8, with men hurling themselves against walls and on to the floor. I was reacting against that; I wanted to do something beautiful for men.

AM: *I wonder if – accidentally – your* Swan Lake *took ideas not only from* Hamlet *the play but also from Robert Helpmann's ballet* Hamlet. *That, too, is a psychodrama – Ophelia and the Queen become confused in the Prince's mind – set to Tchaikovsky. It had designs by Leslie Hurry, who was also responsible for the* Swan Lake *you often saw at*

Covent Garden. You saw that Hamlet *in 1980, with Anthony Dowell and Antoinette Sibley in the lead roles, and you've often looked at the photographs of the original production, with Helpmann himself and Fonteyn. I even have a dim memory that 'Bobby' (after Helpmann) was your nickname among some of your friends on the BA course at the Laban Centre, though you may have originated it.*

MB: Because of the amount of make-up I wore on stage!

1980 is a long time ago. But I certainly loved that *Hamlet* at the time; and I've always seen Scott as a latterday Helpmann in terms of acting. You know what? I even used to toy with the idea – years ago – of calling the company 'The Helpmanns'.

AM: *There are resemblances between your* Swan Lake *and Kenneth MacMillan's ballet* Mayerling. *That, too, is about the private lives of royalty: in particular the protagonist, Crown Prince Rudolf. In particular, both* Mayerling *and your* Swan Lake *have an Oedipal scene between royal mother and son, in which he strives to communicate and she is guarded and embarrassed.*

Needless to say, the British ballet press have made much of the parallels between Mayerling *and your* Swan Lake. *(Ironically – though people have now forgotten this – when* Mayerling *was new in 1978, some of the same critics discussed its parallels to the traditional* Swan Lake: *which has its Oedipal tensions too.) The fact that your first-cast Prince and Queen were Adam Cooper and Fiona Chadwick heightened the connection: he had danced Rudolf, she had danced more roles than one in* Mayerling. *Later, Lynn Seymour, MacMillan's most famous muse and one of the dancers of the original cast in* Mayerling, *played the role of the Queen in your production.*

You've seen Mayerling. *At what point did you think of any resemblance to that?*

MB: To be quite honest, I didn't even remember the Prince–Queen section of *Mayerling*. It had been a long time since I'd seen it, I'd never known it well, and I had grown confused – as *Mayerling* audiences often are – about which character is which: especially which is his mother, the Empress, and which is his ex-mistress, the Countess. What I liked most was the idea of the central character: a prince who was out of control, desperate. I think that aspects of that probably went into the overall feeling of my production.

I have seen *Mayerling* again since; I do see that a resemblance is there.

It came out of the fact that the Queen shows so much affection and love and sexual interest in all those other young men, but the one person she should be showing it to, her son, she can't even touch – probably because she was having this kind of relationship with other men. I'm sure that the MacMillan productions in general encouraged me to address different dramatic ideas; and I also think that, in the back of my mind, I thought it would be great to create a male role that was a great challenge for a male dancer – in the same way that Rudolf in *Mayerling* has become almost the one role that all male Royal Ballet dancers seem to want to play. In my case, of course, I was planning not one big male role but two. In films, the women are always complaining there aren't enough roles for women; but it's the opposite in ballet.

But that was only in the back of my mind. I didn't know if I could create a big male role. What I was initially interested in was to push male dancing. To show different kinds of male lyricism: that was what was in the forefront of my mind.

AM: *Would you say that you have a message to pass on in your* Swan Lake?

MB: When I'm asked to sum up what *Swan Lake* is all about, I say that it's about a very simple thing. It's about somebody who needs love: who needs, in the most basic and simple way, to be held.

I suppose you could say that *Cinderella* is the same story.

AM: *But it's not the story of* Highland Fling.

MB: No, it's not. It is of *Nutcracker*, though. *Highland Fling*, in some sense, is about wanting something but not knowing what you want. Which is what *Swan Lake*'s also about: not knowing what you want out of a person.

AM: *To what degree are all your shows about sexual longing? The 'Shallow Brown' dream in* Town & Country, *the emotion that Clara has for her Nutcracker hero, the adulterous desire that James has for one female after another (primarily the Sylph) in* Highland Fling, *the Prince's feeling for the Swan, and the longing that Cinderella and the Pilot have for each other: these are all striking stage visions of sexual desire.*

MB: I always see that as the basis of a good story. I'm very 'into' the dramatic structure of having sets of characters – as in the old-style traditions of drama: I like my central couple connected by love or desire, my comic character people on the sidelines, and a villain too. Very

Disney; but also very *EastEnders*. A lot of directors I know watch *East-Enders* with great pleasure, because it has all the essence of drama in it: your villains, your nice people, your young lovers, your comics – it's all there somehow, everything's catered for. But I suppose that I particularly need to feel something for the central person, or for the central relationship.

AM: *But beyond having a central relationship, you make an unusual emphasis on the huge longing of one central character for another. And unusual emphasis, too, on the distance between them.*
MB: I think that, once they're together, the drama's finished. The longing is the interesting thing. That, and the journey of getting together or not.

AM: *I would say that, very often in your work, it is also a longing for beauty. At several points in your shows, there is a moment of either the shock of beauty or the shock of sexual allure: in fact, a moment when the recognition of beauty becomes the recognition of sexual desire. For example, when Clara suddenly sees the bare-torsoed Nutcracker along with – by implication – the whole of the male sex.*
MB: I think that's true.[3] I think those feelings are something that I feel a lot of people share, so I'm aware of the impact they will have on a viewer. Yes, it's true; at that moment in *Nutcracker* and at the moment when the Swan first enters, I want the audience to feel the same impact as the character in the piece. I want them to be slightly overwhelmed by the beauty of what I'm showing, to feel its excitement.

AM: *Are you conscious that, along with all of that, jealousy is frequently an important element in your dance dramas?*
MB: I think it is, yes. Funnily enough, I myself am really not a jealous person; but I find it a very powerful emotion to play with, and the drama that ensues from it.

I like making my central character suffer quite a lot. Maybe they have a good ending, maybe they don't; but I like piling on the agony for the central character, and I've done it in several pieces. It started with all the things the second Mrs De Wynter goes through in *Deadly Serious*. And it happens to Clara in *Nutcracker*: lots of agony, lots of obstacles, before she gets what she wants. Likewise Cinderella.

3 Bourne headed an earlier rough version of the announcement quoted in note 1 with this: '"There is a swan whose name is extasy ..." Aleister Crowley.'

AM: *Your works put me in mind – not in their physicality, but in their ideas – of some of the sexual psychodramas that Martha Graham put on stage between the 1940s and 1960s.* Errand into the Maze *(1947) is a particularly strong example, and it made a huge impact here in 1979. It shows a woman's terror and fascination with a bare-chested male, part-animal, brutally sexual Creature of Fear. He's a phallic symbol of sorts, and shows plenty of naked flesh; she is much more fully clothed, and the drama is about the change in her perception of him.*

You saw Errand into the Maze *at the Graham gala you attended in July 1979. Do you have any memory of it?*

MB: No. I do like seeing early modern-dance works, and the photographs are all so interesting; but I don't remember seeing that one. I look forward to seeing it again one day!

AM: *These four 'classics', as you nickname them, aren't they also about your love of eccentricity and variety? In each piece, you seem determined to show us that characters don't have to conform to one ideal type. Do you always want to have short and tall, stocky and skinny dancers?*

MB: Yes. When we had a smaller company, we had a mixture of sizes. It was an odd group of people – going right up in height to Andrew George, who's six foot four – with quite a range of shapes. When we first tried to cast a bigger show, *Nutcracker*, we decided to keep that range of shapes and sizes. I know now that that's one of the reasons why our audiences are wider than a ballet audience. Sure, they love to see beautiful dancers; but they also love to see people with whom they feel they themselves have some connection. The same goes for the mixture of races in the company.

AM: *When you're casting the swans today, do you ever think, 'We haven't got a black dancer, we're running out of short boys'?*

MB: Ultimately, we always cast because of talent. We'd never cast anyone over someone else for any other reason. But, if we've got a choice between two people we're equally interested in, we'll go for the one who does most to widen the mix of people in the company.

Swan Lake divides itself up nicely that way. You have to have some small guys for cygnets, some big boys for big swans. When I talk to people at auditions, I tend to make a point of saying that. Sometimes they ask, 'Are you looking for one racial type? Are you looking for certain particular physical types?' No,' I say, 'we're looking for dancers.'

And you see these tiny little dancers, or very tall dancers, looking so relieved that they're not going to be discriminated against.

I know that a lot of our regular audience have favourites within the company who aren't necessarily in principal roles, whom they follow and watch and like to see doing different roles. It's because the company has such a mixture of people that they enjoy that.

AM: *So when did you think, 'I want Adam Cooper as the Swan'? And when did Adam Cooper indicate an interest in your work?*
MB: About a year and a half before the production. It was the first time we did *Highland Fling* in London, at the small Lilian Baylis Theatre that was part of the old Sadler's Wells, in spring 1994. Iain Webb, who is now one of our rehearsal directors, came to see it with his wife, Margaret Barbieri. He was then a Royal Ballet dancer; she, of course, had been a leading ballerina with the Sadler's Wells Royal Ballet. She then invited me to choreograph a piece (*Boutique*) on her students at London Studio Centre; and Iain came back to see *Highland Fling* a second time, this time bringing Adam and Sarah Wildor. Adam and Sarah were both rising stars of the Royal at Covent Garden, and I met them both briefly afterwards, because they wanted to say how much they'd enjoyed it. Then, a week or so later, Iain told me that he thought that they had expressed interest in working with me.

At the time I was having a problem anyway with the idea of casting this *Swan Lake*. I had mentioned the Swan role to one or two people, but I really hadn't decided. I certainly didn't feel then that I was in a position to approach just anyone in the whole dance world – which I do feel now. I would never have felt then that I had any kind of cachet to interest anyone from the Royal Ballet. So I was thinking, 'I'll find the right person from within our company', or 'We'll audition to find someone to do it.'

AM: *Ben Wright remembers that at one point you mentioned the role to him; and that he couldn't imagine himself in it, and asked to be considered for the Prince instead.*
MB: I must say I've completely forgotten that. As you know, Ben helped to create the role of the Prince, and – after Scott – has been dancing it, extremely well, ever since the initial Sadler's Wells season.

Anyway, when Iain said that, I thought instantly: 'Wouldn't he – Adam – be perfect for that role?' I had seen him dance plenty of roles; he appealed to me as a dancer. He's very manly. And I think, above all, that

41 *Swan Lake*. Adam Cooper as the Swan. Pre-publicity photograph. Here the entire body shape shows how far, in part, from traditional *Swan Lake* choreography Bourne was preparing to go.

42 *Swan Lake*. Adam Cooper as the Swan. Pre-publicity photograph. Although the swept-back 'wings' and bent-forward torso occur in some other productions of swan choreography, here the bare feet, bare calves, and bent knees show a new emphasis, while the Swan's direct stare into the camera shows the disturbing dream/nightmare psychological force with which Bourne was planning to invest the character.

it was the way he uses his arms that was the most appealing factor for this role. I could also see great intelligence in his work. Having met him briefly, I felt he was the sort of person that I could get on with – which is very important to me.

So I arranged to meet him, with Iain again. We went for a meal, and I said I had an idea for him. I didn't know anything about him at the time. I'd got an impression that he was an underdog Royal Ballet principal dancer, but someone who the Royal would mainly use for the more modern roles and in new choreography; which was good, I thought, for me. I think he'd danced some William Forsythe ballets with them by that point. Then, when I actually met him, I realized that he had a great love of the classics too: that, even though he wasn't doing the leading roles in them, he still loved the whole idea of them. That's why he enjoyed *Highland Fling*. And he loved the idea of working with those old scores and doing something different with them.

I think he was quite taken aback when I said it was the Swan that I wanted him to do. It obviously hadn't occurred to him that that would be the role he would be offered; and he probably pretended to be a little less shocked than he was. I think the whole experience of doing this role has changed him a lot; but at the time he would have been a bit worried. He's said to me since that, when he found that there was a Prince as well, he was taken aback; but you see, I never really talked to him in any depth about how we were going to approach it. I didn't say it was gay; I didn't say it wasn't. I just said, 'There's a Prince, and there's a Swan.' I told him the basic ideas for the story, and that the Swan was something in the Prince's imagination. That was all. I didn't really get specific with him about it.

AM: *Adam is heterosexual. But you didn't even tell him that his role was going to have – as the Stranger in Act Three – plenty of hetero activities?*
MB: Not at that stage, no. The next stage was to ask the artistic director of the Royal Ballet, Anthony Dowell, to give Adam leave of absence from the Royal Ballet. This was in summer 1994, about a year before we started rehearsals. Dowell talked to me about musicals quite a lot to begin with – they're his passion – but kept this very bemused approach to the whole project. The main thing I remember is just explaining what the part was and what we were doing, in wanting Adam to play the Swan. Then, when I said there would also be a male Prince, he just said 'Oh dear', with raised eyebrows.

Actually, I think Dowell found the idea of the project quite exciting. I'm sure the initial reason that he let Adam do it was that he knew that he himself would have wanted to do something like that at that point in his career. He knew how few opportunities there were for male dancers to do a big role in a full-length ballet, and I think that's the reason why he felt he couldn't say no. That was the dancer coming out in him.

Next, in spring 1995, when AMP did a fund-raising gala at the Donmar Warehouse, I made a swan solo for Adam. This was an important 'do' for us. Nigel Hawthorne, who's become a patron of our company, spoke at the dinner afterwards, and we certainly felt the honour of that because it was his first public engagement here after the Oscar ceremony and all the brouhaha he'd been through there.

The performance included items old and new. There was a section called 'On the Air', in which four numbers were danced to old music on the gramophone; that was an easy 'link', since all four of them had been made to old recordings (three of them, originally, on 78s). Two of these were revivals: the Lovers' Duet from *Infernal Galop* (Edith Piaf's 'Hymne à l'amour', and Scott Ambler and I danced 'Dearest Love' (Noël Coward singing) from *Town & Country*. Two of them were new, both to old recordings by Richard Tauber, whose recordings I had recently started to fall in love with. While Scott and I sat at the side in our *Town & Country* costumes, Etta Murfitt and Emily Piercy danced to his recording of 'Girls were Made to Love and Kiss'. Then, after we'd danced 'Dearest Love', Adam danced to Tauber's sung version of the Saint-Saëns 'Swan'. The *Infernal Galop* Lovers' Duet came last. Later, two dancers from London Studio Centre danced a duet from *Boutique*, the version of the Rossini–Respighi *Boutique fantasque* I'd made for Margaret Barbieri's students there. Finally, Adam danced in a revival of *Spitfire*, alongside Ben Wright, Phil Hill and Scott.

I didn't know what Adam wanted at that stage; I choreographed all the solo, and took him through it movement by movement. Possibly he found that difficult. He'd say, 'Oh, you look better than I do.' Possibly I used a few movements from earlier work I'd made. But we got used to working together – it was made, for nothing, in a week – and so it was an invaluable preparation for work later that year on *Swan Lake*. But it wasn't a try-out for actual Swan movement. Ironically, the solo wasn't about a swan at all. It was about dying, or illness. There were little catches in Tauber's voice that gave me the idea of someone with ailments, of things going wrong. Adam wore simple black trousers, a black cut-off T-shirt, and bare feet.

AM: *Was it an Aids dance?*
MB: Not at all. Really not. Nor did Adam 'die' at the end. It was more about someone coping with something that had gone wrong with him. I'd love to do it again.

AM: *Did you always plan the Prince as a role for Scott Ambler?*
MB: Yes.

AM: *When did he and Adam Cooper meet?*
MB: Probably quite soon after Adam agreed to do it. It's very much my way to cultivate friendship with people that I'm going to be working with – to make sure, actively, that we know each other well, and that we get on before the rehearsals begin. Adam and Scott hit it off very quickly. They're good friends now, work together very well, and have got certain similarities. They both smoke like chimneys. They're both quite calm about performing; they're very relaxed. You go into their dressing room before a show and it's a very relaxed atmosphere: they just sit there, staring into space and smoking. They laugh quite a lot – have a good relationship.

Highland Fling had been designed as a vehicle for Scott. In some ways the Prince naturally followed on from that, using the acting abilities that Scott has.

AM: *In what ways is Scott like yourself?*
MB: He is like me in that we have good ideas together, perform well together, and have similar ways of viewing performance. His knowledge of other forms of performance is similar to mine; and he sees the potential in the projects that I suggest – whereas a lot of other people don't. If I was to say to him, '*Giselle* – let's think about *Giselle*', he would say, 'Good, right', and he would read the scenario and come up with a whole series of ideas: 'You could do this, try this. If we put it in this setting . . .' He visualizes things in a similar way, so he's very good in that respect.

He is unlike me in many other ways. He's a hopeless case in terms of the way he lives: he smokes a lot, eats really badly, doesn't look after himself, is a workaholic, can't relax, has to be working all the time – performing, or, if he's not performing, doing something else in there. He flogs himself to death when he doesn't need to. I'm not really like that. It's easy to take advantage of someone like that when they're there all the time. My job mainly with him is to tell him to go home, to rest, to make sure he keeps fit, to be sure to look after himself. That said, he never misses a show – and, unlike me, he has the same body he had ten years ago!

AM: *Are there any ways in which you, consciously or accidentally, projected yourself into the role of the Prince?*
MB: Not as a character. I don't think the role has any characteristics of mine about it. I'm not that sad a person! I know that I visualized the Swan – but not in the way the Prince does. I was presenting a character – the Swan – that I felt was meaningful to me; but the Prince was someone else who was reacting to that character; and I was seeing the possibilities of that.

As it happens, all the dancers playing the Swan to date have been straight, and both the Princes gay. That may have added to the original shape of our production. Still, our next round of castings, for New York, could change that pattern.

AM: *Are there any ways in which you find any aspects of the Swan in you?*
MB: Strangely enough – if only I could dance it! – that would be the part that I would feel comfortable doing. Apart, that is, from the Queen, which is the role I'd love to do most. I have no great desire to get into drag, but I like playing characters that are in control of things. I don't mind a little bit of repression, but not to the point our Prince is at; and it's too emotional a role for me as well. I like to be the commanding presence.

AM: *Is that why you'd like to be the Queen?*
MB: No. The reason I like that role so much is that I love the revealing of the character as it goes along. I love being one thing and then another. There are little comic points in Act One where she's attracted to some of the young cadets; you have that really dramatic duet with the Prince, which is real tragic drama; you get to be sexy in Act Three, then tragic again at the end. It's just got everything in it, that part. You get to be funny, sexy – it's a great part for anyone who enjoys acting, dance acting. It's the part that I like directing the most.

AM: *At what point did Adam suggest Fiona Chadwick to do the Queen?*
MB: We were trying to find someone for that role, and I talked to a couple of people. Kate Coyne, from London Contemporary Dance

43 Anna Pavlova (1881–1931), famous for dancing *The Dying Swan*, with one of her famous and beloved swans at Ivy House, her London home.

44 *Swan Lake.* A publicity image of Scott Ambler as the Prince with a live swan. This Prince/swan photograph was one of a series taken before rehearsals, and was inspired by those of Anna Pavlova and by the famous obsession of King Ludwig of Bavaria with swans. Although photographs of nude men had become standard advertising ploys since the late 1980s, this connection of a naked man to a bird was sufficiently controversial to be dropped from publicity for the production's seasons in America.

Theatre, was one I talked to; and the Royal Ballet's Sandra Conley was the other person we were considering. Both Scott and I absolutely love Conley's performances in the Royal Ballet's character roles. She knows that we love her too, and she wanted to do something; but she was very concerned about just dancing at that time: she has had bad arthritis.

Then Adam Cooper suggested Fiona Chadwick. This was late 1994 or early 1995, and she'd recently lost her job at the Royal Ballet. Adam particularly liked working with her. He had danced with her a fair bit at Covent Garden – in *The Firebird*, for example, and in her farewell *Romeo and Juliet*, but also in other ballets – and thought she'd be very good. I think that they have a definite musicality that works together, and I think a rapport with each other.

I was, I suppose, a little bit nervous of her, to begin with. She had been a leading principal of the Royal Ballet for quite a number of years. I had seen her dance virtually every leading role in its repertory, she had worked with Kenneth MacMillan and several other important choreographers; but she was obviously a very good idea. Once she was on board, I organized a lunch with her, Adam, Scott and Etta – to make sure she would get on with everybody and they with her. Needless to say, we all ended up loving her.

AM: *I remember at one point you said, 'I can't really tell you the story of my own* Swan Lake.*'*
MB: I can't tell you the story of Act Four completely; I couldn't tell you exactly what was going on.

I consciously wanted to make *Swan Lake* about a man – very much a man, who happened to be a prince as well – who had trouble expressing himself and couldn't, for whatever reason, be who he wanted to be. He was also a needy person: that was the centre of it. And the swan was a symbol of what he needed – rather than some tragic figure who's been magically transformed into something else – I didn't feel it needed that. Once the decision was made that the Swan was in the imagination of the Prince and then projected on to a real person in Act Three, it made sense that other things were not relevant to our story.[4]

4 Performers are, however, allowed some freedom with this. In September 1998, after performing the Prince for nearly three years, Ben Wright decided that, in Act Two, his Prince does see the Swan in real life. Will Kemp, however, who has played the Swan to the Princes of both Ambler and Wright many times, said in the same period that he tried to adjust his Swan to each Prince and that he sees the Swan in Acts Two and Four as the projection solely of the Prince's mind.

So with no Rothbart and with everything in the Prince's imagination, Act Four is another kind of drama – I know that much – but I really don't want to specify exactly what it means as psychological narrative at every point. It means more if I leave it ambiguous, if I leave certain options open.

AM: *How much do you think of audiences when you're planning a work?*
MB: I've always thought about the audience completely at all times.

Perhaps that seems to be going a little too far, a little too populist; and certainly I do have to please myself as well. But when I say that I'm very audience-conscious, I mean that, all the time when I'm making a piece, my questions to myself are all about whether the audience will get this; whether this will be conveyed to the audience in the way I want it to be. 'Will the audience be lost at this point? Does the audience need signals as to how to react at this point? Do we need the audience to applaud at this point? Even for ourselves, do we need some response here from the audience? If so, how do we get it?' Particularly with humour in the pieces: that's an on-going process of trying to get the audience to react in the right way. 'Maybe it's timed wrong: so try it a different way' – until the audience does react. The relationship of a show with an audience works two ways.

I've always felt that I was audience-conscious while I was making work. Not necessarily at the outset. When I say, 'I'm going to do this piece or that', at that stage, maybe, to some people some of the choices I'm making don't seem very commercial or popular; but then I try to make them accessible – or understandable to anyone.

AM: *As you talk about individual works like* Swan Lake, *you're always trying to communicate – to get expressive ideas across – however ambiguous they may be.*

There is another attitude in some dance-makers' minds: that they make dances about dance, about movement – and here I include some very popular choreographers, such as Ashton and Balanchine. Is that any part of your thinking when you're making a dance show? Are there parts of Swan Lake, *for example, where dance – movement – becomes your subject matter?*
MB: I think that there are, but I suppose that, in my case, those are just parts of a larger show. In British dance today, that's the most obvious way in which I differ from, say, Richard Alston or Sue Davies; but I do look for those sections where we can just dance. Maybe, in some

of those sections, the dancing is based on a single dramatic idea – but basically it is about dancing. To have those passages in a dance show is obviously important.

AM: *In* Swan Lake, *I presume, you're talking particularly of Act Two, the first lakeside scene.*
MB: Yes. If it were true – as I sometimes claim! – that everything in it is story-led, I would have cut the dance for the four cygnets and the four big swans. But those are really there purely as the dance interest. They have character, and musicality; but they don't add to anything that's going on plotwise at all. The Prince and Swan aren't even on the stage. I do treasure those moments as well within a production. They're a sort of challenge for me too: I like to try to make those moments work. Pure-dance choreography is not my strongest point. So if I can make something like that work, I'm more pleased with it in the end than with something that comes more easily that everyone else thinks is very clever. It's the dance choreography, more often than not, that I'm trying to make richer or more interesting.

Preparation

ALASTAIR MACAULAY: *How did you prepare for the production itself?*
MATTHEW BOURNE: I had such a long time to think about *Swan Lake*. I played the music a lot, daily: first, to decide which music to use and to familiarize myself with the structure of the music.

AM: *I would assume, from having seen* Swan Lake *and much of your previous work, that, while you were preparing this show, you found yourself going deeper into the music than you ever had with music before: that you were giving rein to your own musical imagination or response.*
MB: Yes, I'd really listened to it a lot, but completely divorcing myself from images of the ballet. I am able to do that when I'm just listening to it. I wander around; I visualize situations; I shape a story in my head. When I've got a basic situation – the ball in Act Three, for example – and I've got the relationships between characters, I just go off into the story, listen to the music, see if the music does something with that story. Sometimes it leads to nothing, but it is a good way of working: just to let a scenario shape itself musically in your mind.

I had CDs and tapes of different recordings of the music; but all the versions that had ever been recorded up to that time were of the original

1877 version: which made it very difficult to get a feeling of the whole piece, because almost no stage version of *Swan Lake* uses that version of the score. I had grown familiar with the 1895 version in the theatre, and I wanted to keep some of the 1895 ordering of the music; but that involved a lot of dotting to and fro around the 1877 version, since there had never been a recording made of the 1895. In fact, when our recording came out in 1996, it was the first one based on a version that was being actually performed. Since then, one has at last appeared of the 1895 version; but I can't say that I take to all the Drigo emendations. I was very happy to get to know the 1877 score so well; although we re-order it at several points, I think that there are passages where it works very successfully in our production. I'm proud of those.

AM: *When you were researching it – thinking about the music – you read, or reread, Roland John Wiley's 1985 book* Tchaikovsky's Ballets?
MB: Yes, I read it.

AM: *One of the points he makes about the 1877 score is that there is an inner family (my word, not his) of* Swan Lake *music. Much of the music – by reason of either melody or orchestration or tonality – is connected to Odette, the swans, Rothbart or Prince Siegfried.*

In the lakeside acts, Acts Two and Four, this is hardly surprising. Some of the music in Acts One and Three, by contrast, has little or no connection with this family, and therefore was surely designed simply as divertissement music. But some of the other music in these non-lakeside acts is 'family' music – by which I mean that it belongs to the 'inner family' of Swan Lake *musical material – and (since documentation on the 1877 stage original is fairly thin) it's hard to say just what dramatic or narrative purpose Tchaikovsky and/or the original production team assigned to these individual parts. Maybe the musical connections are accidental, or were just part of Tchaikovsky's ambition to give his score more overall coherence than was required by the narrative. Two examples: the theme of the Waltz in Act One corresponds with that of Odette's recitative in Act Two; the Russian Dance in Act Three, which Wiley presumes was danced by the 'Black Swan' Odile by virtue of its solo violin (an instrument often assigned to the ballerina), may have been 'the dance that won Siegfried over to Odile'.[5] I would also say – though Wiley does*

---

5 Roland John Wiley, *Tchaikovsky's Ballets*, Oxford, 1985, p. 285 (n. 16). See also chapter 2, 'The Music of *Swan Lake*', passim, esp. pp. 68, 80–83, 88–90. Also pp. 43, 50.
  Bourne's own copy of this book is inscribed '1992' in his own handwriting, which suggests

not – that one of the other national dances in Act Three, the czardas, sounds as if it is somehow related to this Swan Lake musical family. By contrast, the Neapolitan Dance, Spanish Dance and mazurka never sound part of the story, part of the Swan Lake *inner world.*

I don't know whether you were inspired by Wiley, or if his book gave you confidence in your own instincts; but, as soon as I first saw your Swan Lake *in 1995, I was amazed to see that, in Acts One and Three, you distinguish dramatically between this 'family' and 'non-family' music.*

MB: I can't say that I consciously absorbed that point from him. He doesn't make that point forcefully; and I wasn't thinking hard of my textual decisions when I read his book. I would say that I made my choices from musical instinct. Still, it's possible that my instinct may have been subconsciously guided by having read Wiley; I don't know.

AM: *Who was the first person you brought on board to help you plan the production?*

MB: Lez Brotherston. Funnily enough, he hadn't been my first choice as designer, although we'd had a good working relationship on *Highland Fling*. The reason was that he'd recently done another *Swan Lake* for Northern Ballet Theatre, again, a modernish version. He had said to me, 'I think I could do it differently for you, but I understand. Still, if you are interested, I'm interested.' So instead I asked Anthony Ward to design it. He had done *Nutcracker* and *Oliver!* I told him the story of my *Swan Lake* but – I'm not sure what his reasons were; perhaps he felt it was not the right piece for him at that time – he decided not to. I was quite upset by that at the time. I then pursued Stephen Brinson-Lewis, but he wasn't available. So then I thought, 'Let's get Lez to do it', because we'd worked well before.

He was soon on board, and he was invaluable. He had an enormous amount to contribute in terms of ideas, and obviously in the way it looked. It plays with time so much all through Act One and then Act Three; it's a mixture of timeless costumes, 1950s and 1960s costumes, and very much modern-day costumes. All that was intentional. It wasn't the world that I initially had had in my mind, but it really worked. I had wanted something more abstract-looking, a strange world that had this kingdom

that he bought it while preparing his production of *Nutcracker*. There are several passages of chapters 1 and 2 that he (or, conceivably, a colleague) has underlined, but at no point do they particularly address the point under discussion here.

Press Secretary Act III

45 *Swan Lake.* Costume sketch by Lez Brotherston for the Private Secretary. Bourne, who has sometimes played this role, says that his interpretation is closer to this sketch.

within it, where he pushed it more towards something that was British-looking.

AM: *Did you draw up your idea of the musical text first and then your scenario? Or vice versa? Or both at the same time?*

MB: I would go from one to the other. I would have a dramatic idea, and then see if there was the music to support it. Or I would just find myself in love with some piece of *Swan Lake* music – maybe one that wasn't in most stage versions of *Swan Lake* – and wait till I knew how I could use it dramatically.

Eventually, I sat down with our then Musical Director, David Lloyd-Jones, and we worked through the music together. I knew David from our *Nutcracker*, and knew him to be an authority on Russian music, and on Tchaikovsky in particular. I would ask him where we could use, or could cut, repeats in the music. We would listen to it; and he would say, for example, 'Well, yes, this is just a repeat here, you can cut it perfectly all right.' Or I would ask if I could shift an item from this place in the score to that without violating the harmony. All that was very useful: to achieve the musical structure, and then to record an edition, a collage from various recordings, in the order that we wanted to do it.

Meanwhile I gave Scott specific research to do, mainly around the Prince character. He would read a lot of books – as I did myself, and so did others later on – and he would bring back what he thought was relevant information. That helped. We did a lot of reading around all the princes and monarchs of this century and last: virtually anything relevant that we could get our hands on. So the Prince in our *Swan Lake* is an amalgamation of characteristics of different kings and princes.[6] The one thing they all seemed to have in common – the royal men we chose to research – was that they all seemed very unsuitable for the job that they were born into; that they were not complete people. The actual job seemed to make them worse. We used the nervous twitches and the stammering of various kings. George VI was quite an inspiration: he was so unsuited to public life.[7]

AM: *Any foreign ones?*

MB: Ludwig of Bavaria, of course, because he was so obsessed with swans. In fact, he seemed too obvious a link. Still, we did read books about him, and a certain amount of him went into it.

AM: *Well, another book on your shelves that's extensively lined is* The Swan King (Ludwig II of Bavaria) *by Christopher McIntosh (1986). I can't begin to quote all the underlined passages to you, but let's pick one or two. There are areas of Ludwig's diaries that were destroyed decades after his death, and McIntosh asks why.*

> What was in the diaries that was incriminating? Why were there so many secrets about Ludwig? . . . The explanation, I decided, lay in one or more of the three areas of his life over which there had been intense speculation . . .

6 Relevant books on Bourne's shelves include: Craig Brown and Lesley Cunliffe, *The Book of Royal Lists*, Routledge and Kegan Paul, 1982; Desmond Chapman-Huston, *Ludwig II (the Mad King of Bavaria)*, Dorset, 1990; Vivian Green, *The Madness of Kings (Personal Trauma and the Fate of Nations)*, Alan Sutton, 1993; Paul James, *Prince Edward (A Life in the Spotlight)*, Piatkus, 1992; Christopher McIntosh, *The Swan King (Ludwig of Bavaria)*, Robin Clark, 1986; John van der Kiste, *Childhood at Court, 1819–1914*, Alan Sutton, 1995.
7 An undated three-side paper in Bourne's handwriting, presumably from this period, is called 'Royals and Madness'. (AMP/Bourne archive.)

The first of these problematic areas concerns his sexual life. It has long been known that Ludwig had homosexual leanings . . . The second sensitive point has to do with his death. The 'official' version is that on the day after his dethronement he drowned himself in Lake Starnberg near Munich . . . I believe, as I argue later, that though the cause of death was technically either suicide or manslaughter, the responsibility for it must ultimately rest with those who engineered his deposition . . . The third and most controversial area in Ludwig's life centres upon his supposed madness. Again, the official claim that he became insane is widely disputed. But there can be no denying that towards the end of his life, he developed very strange habits which were combined with a marked physical deterioration. (pp. 3–4)

So was it your study of Ludwig that decided you to make your Swan Lake *a study in madness or psychological distortion?*
MB: I think so, yes. Of all the princes and kings who we read about, he was closest to the character that we ended up portraying. But also he confirmed ideas that I had already had.

I think, initially, we were thinking that the Private Secretary, the Rothbart figure, was partly responsible for the Prince's madness, and created situations that would make his mental situation worse. The way a prince is constantly watched and followed and observed all the time: that could contribute to madness of some form. The original idea of the Private Secretary was to show him engineering situations that made the Prince feel he was going mad and eventually doing so. The Stranger was the son of the Private Secretary and was brought there in the knowledge that the Queen would go for him – and also maybe in the knowledge that the Prince might fancy him too. There was some kind of power-struggle there: a question of loyalty, trying to maintain the Queen's position.

All that was Ludwig-related, though probably not consciously. But the political sub-plot got too complicated after a while, and we simplified it.

AM: *Then McIntosh writes of Ludwig's childhood fascination with swans.*

Ludwig loved the swan not only because of its beauty and regal aloofness, but because it was associated in his mind with the other things that Hohenschwangau offered him . . . The murals that his father had commissioned the artist Moritz von Schwind to design . . . depicted scenes from stories and legends, such as those of Tannhäuser, the

Holy Grail and the Grail knight Lohengrin, who travelled in a boat drawn by a swan.[8] *Not surprisingly, Ludwig came in his fantasies to identify himself with Lohengrin. Part of him was the knight in shining armour. Another part was the swan itself, aloof, majestic and pure. He knew that one day, the swan in him would be able to take flight, but before it could do so, it was to spend frustrating years in a gilded cage. (pp. 15–16)*

This connects to your idea that the Prince in Swan Lake *starts to contain the Swan within his own mind.*

MB: Yes: the symbol of freedom. Another thing, in some descriptions of the symbolic associations of the swan, is that it's a sort of phallic symbol. The long neck: a sexual idea.

AM: *Then there's a whole chapter on Sophie, who I imagine is the nearest to a prototype for the Girlfriend in your* Swan Lake. *Among your underlinings here is: 'A natural reticence, even primness, in sexual matters was exacerbated by his cloistered upbringing . . . It could be said that fire and ice contended in his soul, with the ice usually winning.'*
Then he gets engaged to Sophie. Extreme confusion.

From the start there were hints that all was not as it should be . . . In the photographs of the pair standing arm in arm, Ludwig looks distant, awkward . . . As soon as he came to his senses and realized the full implications of the course he had embarked on, he began to draw back . . . Physical signs of passion were restricted to a few chaste kisses, which he placed on her brow. When she grew tired of this restraint and once kissed him on the mouth, he was so shocked that he nearly broke off the engagement there and then. (p. 85)

MB: Our Prince does kiss the Girlfriend, but it has the feeling of his trying to prove something. It's rather sudden: something he feels that he has to do, rather than something that comes out of passion.

AM: *Another volume here is* The Madness of Kings *by Vivian Green. Its subtitle is: 'Personal Trauma and the Fate of Nations'. There's one whole chapter here called 'The Swan King', about Ludwig. Lots of underlinings in your copy.*

8 In 1895 a St Petersburg critic remarked on the resemblance between the *Swan Lake* theme and Lohengrin's warning. See Wiley, op. cit., pp. 37, 282 (n. 35).

Certified as mad, he drowned himself or was drowned in June 1886 . . . His imagination was more especially gripped by the image of the swan, an emblem which was to haunt him throughout his life . . . Ludwig was very tall and radiated immense charm . . . He also had 'extra-ordinarily expressive eyes'. He was described as being 'mentally gifted in the highest degree, but the contents of his mind were stored in a totally disordered fashion'. (pp. 226–7) During his engagement, Ludwig wrote in his diary: 'I longed for, am athirst for, freedom.' (p. 228)

MB: There are so many parallels. The fact that he drowned, for example. He is quite a magical character. I remember seeing the Visconti film *Ludwig* in my late teens in London; it made a big impression.

AM: *And, in Ludwig's fascination with Wagner, isn't there a parallel to your Prince's longing for a soulmate?*
MB: Yes. But it was Wagner's music that was the passion, not the man. He didn't find Wagner a thing of beauty. If he found him a soulmate, it was because of the music he had made. He found it physically over-whelming; and it was the freedom he felt to listen to music that's the parallel to our Prince.

AM: *Wagner wrote about Ludwig: 'He is also so beautiful, spiritual, soulful and splendid that I fear his life must run away like a fleeting, heavenly dream in this common world.' (p. 230)*
MB: It was reciprocated quite strongly, wasn't it? It's very strange to read those letters now. Very romantic; they're like love letters. But Ludwig was also a prince; so there's a lot of flattery involved.

We really might have gone more for the Ludwig connection, but we were aware that he had been used as the Prince in some previous produc-tion of *Swan Lake*. Was it John Neumeier's? Not one I'd seen. But the idea had already been used.

Scott also read a lot about Prince Eddie, Queen Victoria's grandson, who has sometimes been thought to have been Jack the Ripper. And that whole period.

AM: *On to the actual planning of the structure and scenario: I imagine that the tricky act to work on was Act One. I remember seeing you in July 1995. You told me that you were working on the scenario for Act One, and you said with slight alarm, 'It's got seven changes of scenes so far!'*

MB: I wanted to tell the Prince's story as much as possible in Act One, to take it beyond the usual point of him just walking around, looking moody and a bit sad and dreamy. Before we got to the swan scene in Act Two, I wanted you to feel a lot for him and to know that he needed some sort of affection or love; and so I tried to fill Act One with two things. One was the life of duty and how he seemed unsuitable for that and bored by it. The other was his need for some sort of affection. So he's constantly being rejected or betrayed, one way or another, through Act One – by mother, by girlfriend, by society. So he's desperate. That's why he conjures up such a thing in his mind as the Swan. He also needs to have enough reasons to be veering towards a certain kind of madness. He can't just go mad. You have to know why. You have to think, 'This man is a desperate person.' So I wanted to show all those things in Act One as much as possible, so that we felt for him by the time we reached Act Two.

AM: *How early on did you conceive Act One beginning right back in the Prince's childhood?*
MB: Quite early on. It emerged from my concern that the hero should be more complex; that his feeling for the Swan should not be only something sexual. I wanted to show him in innocence early on as a child, with the vision of the swan – so that it was a vision that was there from childhood, but was also something that took on new meanings for him as he got older, something that he desired, wanted to emulate. Our first *Swan Lake* poster, or logo, made before we ever choreographed it, was of a naked young man (Scott) kneeling with a swan folding its neck around his – a young male version of the famous photos of Pavlova embracing her pet swan at Ivy House. But in our version it's altogether more intimate.

I think also it helped to show that he was a troubled child, having nightmares, alone in this great big bed – this tiny boy who's surrounded by adults all the time.

AM: *One of the main musical items of Act One is the waltz. Usually this is some kind of divertissement dance; Ashton choreographed it as such in more than one version for the Royal Ballet. In some other versions, such as the one choreographed by David Bintley for the 1987 Royal Ballet production, the Prince joins in the festivities. But you make the waltz an absolutely central part of the continuing narrative. How come?*
MB: It's terribly long. So I thought we should obviously employ some

kaleidoscopic story-telling procedure here, and I also thought that we could actually say a lot within it.

AM: *You say 'obviously'. It's not obvious usually. But I find your version musically satisfying because that waltz never sounds like a divertissement that's irrelevant to the plot; as I've said, its whole sound seems to make it part of the core 'family' of* Swan Lake *music.*

MB: By listening to the way it was musically structured, I just felt that it was episodic, with different themes coming into it. Also, because it repeats, I felt that it had a sense of time moving on as well. So there's a sense that you could repeat something and comment on it again later; which is what we do in the first section, in which the Queen remains age-less while time and routine move on.

I also think that the beginning shows very nicely the progression of the Prince's age, and also the boredom of royal duty. When he was a boy, they were going round, doing all these openings; then, when he's grown up, years on, there's a repeat sequence. It's as if years and years of royal duties have gone on.

AM: *You actually have scene changes during this one waltz.*

MB: This is the sort of area in which Lez's contribution as designer was terrific. The set develops. It starts off with the Prince's bed, which turns round to become the royal balcony; then that disappears. We decided that we wanted to do something very fluid. So that's why the idea of ropes came in. We used red ropes, which would rein back the crowds wherever these Royals – the Queen and Prince – were going; then the ropes would create gateways for the Royals to walk through. The ropes created places without loads of set moving around. So you get all the unveilings, the ship launch, the pulling of cordons, and the banners coming down. Then we go into a sequence where she's giving medals: a sort of military occasion with mothers and fathers watching. We're pleased with that rope device.

Next we get the introduction of the Girlfriend, and her first meeting with the Prince. When she drops her bag, it's obvious that she's done it on purpose to meet him; so that sets it up nicely. Then we keep moving on in time. The whole thing is like 'episodes in the life of the Royal Family'. Next we're into another occasion in the palace. We open up the back wall, the big crown comes down, the red carpet comes out. The Queen and Prince come in again . . . and it all ends with the Girlfriend re-entering his life at some later point, now having developed a relationship with him.

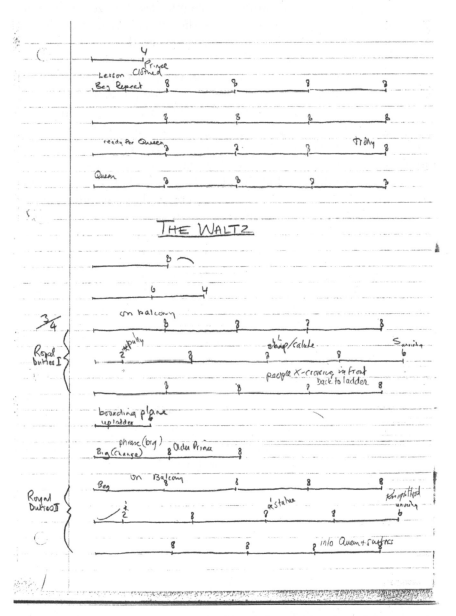

46 *Swan Lake*. From Bourne's annotated breakdown of Act One of the score: the beginning of the Waltz.

So it actually tells a lot of story in seven minutes. You get the growing up of the Prince. And you get plenty of the Queen's character: the fact that she does all her Royal duties, finds someone that she fancies, and has her little dance with the cadets, where she's obviously into all those younger men. We see the Prince's disapproval of that; and we get introduced to the character of the Private Secretary a bit more, the way that he seems to be involved in all these things. And the Girlfriend is introduced. The Queen disapproves of her, but the Private Secretary is very much behind her liaison with the Prince. So the Private Secretary has motives and plots of his own, not all of which we fathom – certainly not yet.

It does a lot of things – but the idea was always that there should be some kind of movement going on, to keep the feel of the waltz going all the way through. So there's background material going on, with various aristocrats or military people or court ladies or whatever. I saw the waltz as a really flexible thing that could do a lot and say a lot.

AM: *During Act One, you stage a very funny mock ballet, the Moth Ballet, to the divertissement music that is used, in the traditional* Swan Lake, *for the pas de trois. This Moth Ballet is in part a send-up of the corniest aspects of traditional – or just bad –* Swan Lakes. *The enchanted Moth heroine is very dolorous; she even attempts suicide (a direct quotation from the traditional Act Four of* Swan Lake *here); she finds love; but her lover has to combat the evil Troll who controls her destiny. How did you arrive at this little scenario?*

MB: I knew it was going to be one of those stories with good and evil, a hero, a heroine and a villain. I did want it to have some parallels to *Swan Lake*, but not in any way to be literally *Swan Lake* – just something that had parallels to some dreadful version of it. I was thinking that, in one way, our Prince goes to the ballet and later on re-imagines the ballet's events in his own mind. I even remember, early on, thinking of it being a beautiful ballet, one that made his mind go off into some sort of romantic reverie that led him into other things. But it went off in a different direction.

AM: *When was it that it turned into a joke?*

MB: By necessity. I felt that this was the way that we could make it work; largely for musical reasons: the music lends itself to comedy.

AM: *The coda is pretty brassy, as even the most devoted Tchaikovskians admit.*

MB: Yes: it's circusy. It's designed as an entertainment for the Prince, which is what it is in the original, except that here he's sitting in an actual theatre.

Originally, it was going to be like the early Sadler's Wells Ballet *Swan Lake*, with the Helpmann–Fonteyn look, tutus and tons of make-up and so on. But I decided that that was a bit too close to home; also, we didn't really have the people to do it. Another idea was to do a sea ballet like *Ondine*; I can't remember now why we chose not to. Eventually, she became a Moth; and the villain a Tree-Troll.

If we went further back, into pantomime-like Victorian ballet, and gave it those really awful Victorian stage effects – puffs of smoke and all that – then, I thought, we wouldn't be offending anyone. Even so, one critic did complain that we were sending up traditional ballet; but never mind. None of these dancers are supposed to be any good, and the characters on stage all think that they're marvellous: that was our idea. It's one of those awful, tacky ballets that probably played the London music halls: that was the feeling that I wanted from it. Once I knew the story we were telling, I found we needed one other short piece of music to help me tell it; and what we took was from the Act Three pas de six.

AM: *And you make a different sense of the pas de trois music. In this Moth Ballet, your hero enters to a very blithe and lah-di-dah piece of music; it's perfect for his silly, dancy, happiness.*[9] *The bit that you then interpolate from the Act Three pas de six is just a fifty-second dance, to express the lovers' conventional love-at-first-sight.*[10] *Then, to the music that the man usually has for his solo in the pas de trois, you bring on the villain – the Tree-Troll, which actually fits the brassy, rather martial nature of the music very well. (It's not far from the brassy martial music associated elsewhere in the ballet with Rothbart.)*

Now, another volume on your shelves is The Ballet Called Swan Lake *by Cyril Beaumont (1952).*[11] *Only two sections bear notes in pencil –*

9 The music is Variation III of the original *Swan Lake* Act I pas de trois. The information accompanying the Adventures in Motion Pictures CD recording of *Swan Lake* erroneously names it – Number 5 of the first half of the AMP score – as 'Tempo di valse'. It is, in fact, 'Allegro Semplice – Presto'.

Likewise the CD recording misdescribes its Number 7 as 'Allegro Semplice'. In fact, it (Variation V of the original pas de trois) is 'Moderato'.

10 Part IV of the Act III pas de six, also 'Moderato'.

11 Literature on *Swan Lake* on Bourne's shelves includes: Cyril Beaumont, *The Ballet Called Swan Lake*, C.W. Beaumont, London, 1952; Mark Helprin, Chris van Allsburg, *Swan Lake*, Ariel Books, Houghton Mifflin, Boston, 1989; Wilson Strutte, *Tchaikovsky – his Life and Times*, Paganiana, 1981; *Le Lac des Cygnes*, L'Avant-Scene Ballet/Danse, Paris, 1984; Maurice Moiseiwitsch and Eric Warman (editors), *The Royal Ballet on Stage and Screen – the book of the Royal Ballet film*, William Heinemann, London, 1960.

possibly not yours, since it's a second-hand copy. Still, these have to do with sets and costumes for the 1895 St Petersburg production. I wonder if you drew Lez's attention to them for the Moth Ballet.

> *Prince Siegfried, as interpreted by Pavel Gerdt, wears plumed cap, doublet and parti-coloured hose. The doublet is decorated with a quatrefoil design, and is scalloped at the lowest edge; on his breast is a small appliquéd shield decorated with a heraldic swan – perhaps an allusion to the Knight of the Swan – which seemed a little previous, since he has not yet encountered Odette. His waist is girded with a knightly belt, supporting on the left side a wallet, and on the right side a dagger. Note the long hair and beard and moustache, which hardly accords with a youth who has just attained his majority. (p. 61)*

MB: I may well have lent that to Lez. It was certainly him that had the idea of putting the hero into old-fashioned hose – a lederhosen version of the kind of costume that leading male dancers actually wore until Nijinsky. He certainly did his research into that.

AM: *Even the fact that the villain is a Tree-Troll connects to Rothbart, who – in the traditional* Swan Lake *– appears in the guise of a baleful owl.*

Immediately after this Moth Ballet, there occurs the biggest dramatic number of Act One: the bedroom scene between the Prince and Queen; based, I suppose, on the Closet scene in Hamlet. *Here you've brought a superb piece of music originally written for Act Three by Tchaikovsky and yet very seldom used there in any stage version. It's the second variation in the pas de six, the andante con moto.[12] Ashton used it in his version of Act Four, in 1963. He may have been the first to use it there; at any rate, since then, several other producers have followed suit. What Tchaikovsky meant by it is ambiguous. Certainly it is very momentous music, and again it seems to be central to the dramatic sound of* Swan Lake.

MB: This is where two separate ambitions of mine coincided. I wanted a duet for the Queen and Prince at that particular place. This was partly a desire to build up her role into a bigger dramatic figure and give her

12 One of the few *Swan Lake* productions to use this in its original Act Three location is Yuri Grigorovich's version for the Bolshoi Ballet. For other discussions of the usages of this music, see Arlene Croce, '*Swan Lake* and its Alternatives' (*Going to the Dance*, Knopf, 1982, pp. 182ff.) and Alastair Macaulay, 'Wiley's Tchaikovsky' (*Dancing Times*, March 1985).

a pas de deux, or something like one, in each half of *Swan Lake*, and partly for reasons of story-telling. You've seen the Queen and the Prince publicly; here you see them privately.

I also always wanted to use that music. In fact, there are two pieces of music in the 1877 score that I particularly liked and wanted to include but that were omitted from the 1895 version. The other one – the adagio for the alternative pas de deux he wrote for Act Three – I didn't manage to fit in.[13] This one I had always loved since I first heard it in the theatre. Moving it to Act One may have been our most radical musical decision, and David, naturally, wanted to check whether it would work there harmonically. It was my idea, but I wouldn't have made that kind of musical decision without his approval and help.

AM: *After that, the Prince – like Prince Rudolf at the start of Act Two in* Mayerling, *by the way – goes to some shady dive: a loud club.*

MB: He's in despair; he wants to drink; he's looking for his girlfriend – not because she's his soulmate but because he feels at least that she gives him some friendship. It's our parallel of the Peasants' Dance that usually occurs at this point in *Swan Lake:* same low-life idea (but taken further), same music. We call this scene 'Soho', and the club it's set in is meant to be a retro club – The Swank Bar, of course! – full of sixties characters: Sister George, Joe Orton, Cliff Richard, the Krays, Phyllis Dixie.

AM: *Who on earth was Phyllis Dixie?*

MB: She was the most famous British stripper of the 1950s and 1960s; the Gypsy Rose Lee of Britain. In our version, she becomes the fan dancer. The idea, you see, wasn't just retro; it was to create an idea of scandal. All these were scandalous figures from a certain period. Scandal entering the Prince's life: that's what that scene's about. The Prince doesn't know, though the audience has already seen hints of it, that the Girlfriend has been set up by the Private Secretary. The Private Secretary, you see, wants to discredit the Prince. The unsuitable girlfriend is one part of his plan; the Prince getting thrown out of the Soho club is another.

13 This is the four-section pas de deux composed by Tchaikovsky to accommodate the alternative choreography interpolated (originally to Minkus music and choreographed by Petipa) for his second-cast Odile (the ballerina Anna Sobeshanskaya) and Siegfried (see note 2). This music has no connection to the sound-world of *Swan Lake;* Roland John Wiley does not even deign to discuss it in his analysis of the score. However, the choreographer George Balanchine choreographed a virtuoso pas de deux to it in 1960, which has no connection to *Swan Lake* either in Balanchine's own one-act staging or in any other production, but which has been widely danced ever since. As a result, its music is known in the dance world under the name Balanchine gave to his version: the 'Tchaikovsky pas de deux'.

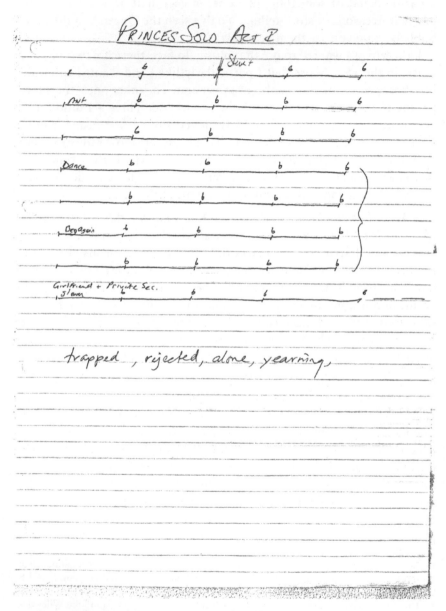

47 *Swan Lake.* From Bourne's annotated breakdown of the score for Act One: the Prince's solo.

AM: *Then you give your Prince an expressive adagio solo when he's thrown out of the club.*

MB: Yes. But I'm not claiming to be original. I put this solo there because it occurred there in the first Royal Ballet production I got to know.

AM: *Well, it works there musically. Tchaikovsky composed it in an earlier stage in the action, as part of Act One's main divertissement, the pas de trois. But, again, it is the one part of that section that doesn't sound like divertissement. In orchestration, melody, everything, it's absolutely part of the central* Swan Lake *sound-world.*

MB: It had always mattered to me. I knew I wanted it in my *Swan Lake*, and I had always associated it with the Prince's romantic loneliness and need for something beyond the world he knew.

AM: *Tell me about the lake in your* Swan Lake.

MB: At present, we're thinking of how to make it more visible for the New York production. Lez did design a layer at the back that sparkles, but so far the lighting or the staging has never made that show up well. We're using a curved mirror, which should pick up quite a lot of light and give an effect of water in the background.

It is really intended to be St James's Park. This is a good example of how Lez helped to give our *Swan Lake* a much more specific location than I had originally envisaged. Because of him, Scott and I went round St James's Park before we started rehearsing. We took a lot of photos. That's why there is a suggestion of gates there. St James's Park just seemed so perfect, because Buckingham Palace is there in view – and there are lots of swans there. I don't mean that it's a literal reproduction of that park, or that the audience should recognize it as such; but that was the idea in our minds. That's why the park bench is there and the sign – with the little royal crown on – that says, 'Please do not feed the swans'.

AM: *How did you and/or Lez devise the look of the swans?*

MB: Quite early on, I found a picture of an Indian dancer, leaping in the air. He had trousers that seemed to be made of fringing or something; they moved very well and looked good in mid-air. I took Lez this picture and said, 'I think it should be something like this, very simple.' I also said, 'Whatever we do, it's got to be very simple', because I didn't want it to be in any way comic: no beaks, not too much make-up – something that had a pagan feel about it. It ended up with a half-man, half-creature look. Years and years ago, I saw Roland Petit's *Hunchback of Notre Dame*, and the only piece of make-up that the Hunchback had was a black line across his eyebrows – just a straight thick black line, but it did do something to his face – and that was all. So I said to Lez, 'Why don't we just try a triangular beak-shaped dark line, from the hairline down to the tip of the nose?' We also decided very early on that the hair should be very, very short. The point was to get long, swan-like necks with the smooth lines of the head, neck and shoulders.

AM: *You always wanted the swans bare-chested and barefoot?*
MB: Yes. I would say that, of all the costumes, that was the one that I developed the most myself.

AM: *Do they powder their chests white?*
MB: They use a sort of water-based pancake make-up.

AM: *Did you ever ask them to shave their chests?*
MB: Never. I felt that one of the things we were trying to show was a masculine image anyway. We weren't pretending that they looked like swans. It was like creating a creature of our own that suggested swan in

48 *Swan Lake*. Costume sketch by Lez Brotherston for the male swans.

some way, but also very much suggested maleness. The same goes when we've had different skin tones among the swans: that just has never been really a problem or an issue.

AM: *Do you ever look at a finished work of yours and spot something you wanted to put in it all along? Is there in* Swan Lake *any moment when you've thought, 'I always wanted to put that in my version before rehearsals'?*

MB: There are always moments or movements I imagine or envisage. I don't ask for any help on them; I just put them in.

AM: *OK. What swan movements did you already have in mind?*

MB: I wanted that Nijinsky-type use of the arms crossed over the head – as in the photographs of *Spectre* or *Narcisse*. It has nothing to do with swans in particular. It just has a draping, hanging flow to it, that position. In *Town & Country*, during 'Shallow Brown', there's a bit where the chorus group comes on shuffling with their arms like that. There are some tree images that are a bit like that, like blossom on trees. I like having the hands very relaxed, just hanging. Either that or very cleanly straight, with fingers all together. I didn't like the spikily separated fingers you often see in ballet. I'm always getting people to close their fingers if they're taking a strong position: clean lines.

So the arms draped over the head does reappear quite a lot in my work. It feels sensual to me, and sexy as well, because it's about touching your own body, which is another thing that I like to use on stage. In *Swan Lake*, there's a bit where the swans wrap their bodies: like taking a T-shirt off – that type of movement.

A lot of those movements came about because Adam and I had to do a photo-shoot with Hugo Glendinning long before rehearsals and we hadn't any movement at that stage. All we had was a costume. It was easy to call upon some of those images, to play around with arms, looking through features, shielding the face. Having come up with these photographic images, we had a starting-point when we went into the rehearsal studio.

A lot of dancers, when we teach them *Swan Lake* material now, don't want to be having contact with their own bodies or heads. They're always leaving space between their arms and their head, or between their arms and their bodies. Constantly the shout from our end of the floor is: 'Arms on heads!' But it's an alien thing to a lot of dancers.

AM: *It also connects to a famous way that Pavlova had of wreathing her arms around her head and neck; which Ashton remembered and put into several of his ballets.*

MB: Movement works so much better if you actually make contact, rather than just keeping it in no man's land.

AM: *Did you also find yourself fascinated by the photographs of, say, Fonteyn in* The Firebird *and* Ondine, *where she is again wrapping the arms and hands around the head and torso in very picturesque ways?*

MB: I love those pictures; and I also think that *Firebird* was going through my mind in *Swan Lake*. I was probably thinking of several bird-like pieces that I'd seen. That *Firebird* image of shielding the face is in there somewhere.

AM: *Once you'd made the two major decisions about your lakeside scenes – that there would be no Rothbart and that the swans would be male – the general outline of Act Two seems to have fallen into place. A few of your choreographic motifs and patterns are adapted from Ivanov's choreography in the 1895 version, and in general you use the 1895 ordering of the score.*

MB: Actually, there were plenty of factors we had to reconceive from scratch. I talked about tempi quite a lot with David, about the tempo of virtually every item in *Swan Lake*. He said that a lot of the score had been slowed down far too much in modern times. We found some recordings that he felt were more appropriate as to how it should sound. The most interesting point was the pas de deux in Act Two, which he felt had been played slower and slower over the decades. We found a recording on Naxos, which played it rather fast, particularly the middle section. To begin with, it was a shock to hear it that way; but, after listening to it a couple of times, he said, 'Actually, this really is how it should be. This is how it's written and how it was intended.' The central section in particular, he said, was really quite lilty. Playful, even. Those aren't words people apply to any part of that pas de deux in the traditional *Swan Lake*, are they? But David drew us into hearing those qualities in the score. He said there's variety within that adagio that we should address. So that's how we choreographed it, with that central section as a jumpy section of movement.

That's often one of the challenges when someone who's conducted it a lot for the ballet comes to conduct it for us. They want to slow those parts down, and we have to say, 'This is the way we do it.'

That wasn't the only example, by the way. There were a lot of other changes of tempo to which he drew our attention and which shaped our idea of the show. So it was good to feel that we were doing something that was even more authentic musically than the traditional ballet.

AM: *Was it Lloyd-Jones who helped you solve the ending of the pas de deux? The 1877 version ends – very surprisingly – with a brisk allegro passage, which very few twentieth-century versions employ; Balanchine's one-act* Swan Lake *is one of those few. The 1895 version, arranged by Drigo, ends it on a beautifully prolonged diminuendo, and that version, as choreographed by Ivanov, is the ending we usually hear and see in the theatre.*

MB: We did try the allegro ending in rehearsals; but, whenever we got to that point, the music just made everyone laugh. The 1895 version wasn't on any recording – and that, too, just felt alien to me. So we ended up with the more straightforward diminuendo ending, which Tchaikovsky may have written. It's from his '*Swan Lake* Suite'. I liked its simplicity.

AM: *If he did indeed compose that version in his* Suite, *it suggests that he himself had come to the conclusion that it would be a better ending to the pas de deux that the original 1877 allegro.*

Another departure you make from the 1877 score is in the order of musical items. Tchaikovsky ordered the dances in 1877, after the entrance of the swans and the scene with the Prince and the huntsmen, as (i) tempo di valse (the waltz for all the corps de ballet of swans) (ii) moderato assai–molto più mosso (the solo dance for the Swan Queen) (iii) tempo di valse (a return to the waltz music, but now for the big swans) (iv) allegro moderato (the dance for the cygnets) (v) pas d'action (andante–andante non troppo–allegro) (the music for the pas de deux or – in dance terms – adagio for the Swan Queen and the Prince, often known as the White Swan adagio) (vi) tempo di valse (another return to the swan waltz material) (vii) coda (allegro vivace) (for all the swans).

However, in 1895 Ivanov and Drigo re-ordered these numbers as (i) (v) (iv) (vi) (ii) (vii). Your ordering is something along these lines, except that you put the solo dance for the Swan (ii) directly after the cygnets (iv) and before (vi), the dance for the big cygnets.

MB: The 1877 score uses that waltz music once too often, wonderful though it is; and it builds up to the pas de deux as an expressive climax, whereas in the theatre there's more contrast and sense of development if you let the other dances seem to develop from what the pas de deux has established.

AM: *Act Three of* Swan Lake *is often referred to as the 'black act', because the ballerina usually wears a black tutu here. Odile, Rothbart's daughter, looks so like Odette the Swan Queen – being danced by the same ballerina! – that the Prince takes her to be one and the same. He swears eternal love to her, and so breaks his vow of love to Odette; which is all part of Rothbart's evil plan.*

But this act is also a ball, given by the Queen to present her son with a number of potential brides. And there are a number of national dances, most of which – but perhaps not all – seem to have been designed as sheer divertissements.

Your Act Three is still a ball given by the Queen. It still has national dances. The principal dancer still reappears as a Black Swan, or as 'the Stranger', and, to the Prince at least, the identity of this new character is absolutely locked into that of the Swan. That said, your Act Three is a very different kind of drama; and it deepens the whole Swan Lake *experience considerably. How smoothly did your preparation of this act go? Were you able to get the scenario pretty clear?*

MB: A lot of it fell into place once I'd fixed the central idea, which is that – yes, it is a Royal ball; yes, the Prince is expected to pay his respects to these various women or princesses, though his heart is elsewhere. Then the Stranger arrives and attracts everybody: the Queen, the Prince, everybody. Originally, you see, I thought of the Stranger, or Black Swan, as the Private Secretary's son; and Act Three is where the Private Secretary's plot became more apparent. He wanted to discredit the Prince and to marry his own son off to the Queen.

There were certain problem numbers to address. Those show-piece national dances, for instance.

AM: *Yes. Most hair-raising of all, you start off the whole series with the Russian Dance: which is almost always omitted from twentieth-century stage productions of* Swan Lake, *despite its irresistible music. (Tchaikovsky added it to the 1877 production at a late stage.) Its use of the solo violin makes it very much the first soloist's dance; and Wiley shows that it was probably danced by Odile in the 1877 original. You give it to your Black Swan – or the Stranger – and a series of women.*
MB: I don't remember reading that in Wiley. As far as I knew, I was working from instinct. I certainly knew the Russian Dance, and I loved

it so much as music. It's certainly an extremely lengthy variation for one dancer to dance, if that's what happened in 1877. I have seen it done like that, but as a Russian character solo, in heeled shoes, out of the context of *Swan Lake*. Also in one production of *Swan Lake* – Northern Ballet Theatre's, I think – as a solo variation for the Russian Princess.

I felt that it had such a lot of feeling in it; but what I'm especially pleased with is that we use it straight after his entrance into the ball, rather than going from his entrance into the Spanish Dance; which is what often happens at that point, but which immediately takes you away from the situation.

There's a tremendously dramatic musical effect that happens when you put the Russian Dance straight after the Black Swan's entrance. I don't know whether it's ever been done before. When I heard it, it just felt that that's how it should be. It actually comments on the situation, because it's like a little exclamation mark just after his meeting the Queen. Then it brings in that violin solo, which creates this atmosphere of tension amongst everyone. I was really thrilled with that. It had been one of the suggestions that I wasn't sure that David would approve. But he did.

AM: *What about the other national dances?*
MB: I put them in this order: Russian; Spanish; Neapolitan; czardas.

AM: *You omit the mazurka.*
MB: There's always one national dance too many! I've always thought that in watching most *Swan Lakes* at that point: 'Get on with it.' But cutting musical items is difficult, just because they're all so good. I knew the Spanish Dance was going to be like a floor show, so that wasn't a problem.

AM: *The Spanish Dance, here as in* Nutcracker, *is for one woman and a clutch of men. Is that format – one girl and two or more men – one that you're fond of for this kind of divertissement? I think it's almost the rule in your* Swan Lake.
MB: Yes. The task there is to try to feature each Princess in some way or another.

AM: *It's also a touch of comedy, because it gives us a showbiz idea of the male chorus.*
MB: Yes. But I didn't want a whole series of different floor shows following on from that; I wanted some situations. With the Neapolitan Dance,

I had an idea for a very Italian sort of lover's quarrel: some embarrassing situation, triggered off by the man's jealousy. The czardas was quite difficult, because I wanted to make it part of the central story; we only solved that in rehearsals.

AM: *Again, I think that you reveal that the czardas somehow – because of its orchestration – belongs to the inner family of* Swan Lake *music.*

That leads, in your version, straight into what's usually known as the 'Black Swan' pas de deux. This raises some musical issues. Even in 1877, Tchaikovsky composed alternative versions of the main suite of dances for Odile and the Prince. The first was a very extensive and musically elaborate pas de six, which may have included dances for Rothbart and/ or his entourage, and which seems to deepen the mystery of Swan Lake *in fairly inscrutable ways. The second is a musically much more straightforward grand pas de deux which has virtually nothing to do with the sound-world of* Swan Lake.

Very few current versions use either. Tchaikovsky wrote another dramatic-virtuosic pas de deux in Act One – probably for the prince and some other female character, but we can't be sure – that, for a reason we no longer know, contains some very ominous pre-echoes of the later 'Swan' music. It was this music that, in 1895, the choreographer Petipa and composer Drigo inserted into Act Three as a grand pas de deux for the Prince and Odile. And this interpolation from Act One, this mysterious pas de deux, is the music you use here too.

MB: Yes, but what virtually nobody has ever mentioned is that we use the music as Tchaikovsky originally wrote it; and it's very interesting that way. In 1895, they not only reorchestrated it, they also chopped it up and cut out some of the most interesting passages. If you play it as written, as we do, there's only one point where the music really stops at all. In particular, the first section just continues right through, despite all kinds of very suggestive dramatic changes, for about seven minutes. The tension never lets up. We were talking about the difference of the two halves of *Nutcracker*: that in the second half there is almost nothing but a long series of separate numbers with definite finishes, whereas the first half runs almost continuously. Well, this sequence of music in *Swan Lake* has that kind of momentum you find in Act One of *Nutcracker*.

AM: *How clear were you just from listening what you wanted to do with this music?*

MB: Because it was drama-led, I had the whole thing mapped out in my head about what each piece of music was doing; and I was very clear on the ideas for each section – not necessarily on the actual steps, but the dramatic structure was very clear in my mind.

AM: *So was it clear, early on in your conception, that you were going to go in and out of reality? In and out of the Prince's mind? It seems to come out of the extraordinary changes in the music. But it's also helped by exceptional changes of lighting. Was that easy to achieve?*
MB: The lighting was not a problem. I did say to Rick Fisher, our lighting designer, that we would need a dramatic snap change of light to make it at least somewhat clear to the audience that we'd gone somewhere else. But there are still people who don't see that and who think it's reality. However, we know what we're trying to do! It all came out of the music. Nobody has really picked up on the fact that the music is different – and more authentic.

The first section happens in reality. It's for the Queen and the Stranger. I knew it wouldn't be a problem to do in rehearsal and it certainly wasn't; I'm sure we did it in about an hour or so, very quickly.

But when this first part of the music changes into its second section, that's when suddenly we switch into the Prince's mind. What I tried here – a filmic device – is to make the Prince put himself in the Queen's place. This dance is for the two men alone together, and it's where the music is suddenly at its most Black Swannish. I had a problem in my mind for a while about exactly what to do in this part. Then I saw one of those Argentinean tango shows that came to London: *Tango Argentino* or *Forever Tango* – it's all the same and it's all wonderful – where two men were dancing together. I thought their style of movement would work very well: that sort of dark intertwining of bodies. You've got a formal partnering style built in, which says something straightaway; and it allowed for us to develop something that got more violent and antagonistic between them after a simple start. It brought an older memory into my mind, of the film *Valentino*, where Nureyev as Valentino dances with Dowell as Nijinsky. They're just partnering each other in a ballroom in dark suits, observed by someone from a distance, and they do a whole tango.

There are two points where the music is really interesting and helpful. The first is at the end of an adagio section, in our version just as the Stranger leaves the Prince. The music continues – in the traditional ballet there's a dramatic break for applause here – into a kind of sarcastic rendition of the Swan music. It builds up; it has a definite edge that we tried to pick up on. For us, it's the business of taunting the Prince. It's a paranoia situation. It's just as the Stranger leaves the Prince; he walks out as everybody else walks in, all staring at the Prince, and the Prince acts as though the Stranger's still there. So it's as if it's going on in his mind, with his arm locked behind his back. He turns round and they're all looking at him, mockingly. He's been acting strangely; and they continue to look at, stare, and talk about him. His paranoia grows; and we're playing with what's reality and what isn't, and how much is in his mind and how much isn't.

The second is the fantastic violin solo that follows. In the ballet, it's all reorchestrated, and you don't get the incredible ending at all. In our version, they all laugh on stage there, and that came out of the amazing violin solo music that races over the orchestra. The company calls this the Sarcastic Dance; it's to do with taunting the Prince.

Then the Stranger re-enters with the Queen. Now, this situation is partly where we've left reality again, with the Prince's exaggerated view

49 *Swan Lake.* Left to right: Scott Ambler as the Prince, Adam Cooper as the Swan (or Stranger), Fiona Chadwick as the Queen, rehearsing Act Three, in 1998.

of his mother, the Queen, with the Stranger; but they probably are there together in reality too: we see that heightened through his eyes to the point where they are flaunting their affection for each other at him. It's a great piece of music, and yet it's generally not used.

As that long piece of music finally ends, the Prince runs out. There again we go into a very snap change of lighting, back into reality, with the Stranger downstage watching the Queen and princesses dance for him. We're back to the ball there; and this dance carries musically straight on into the coda (including the music usually associated with the ballerina's thirty-two fouetté turns on pointe), which we call the Competition Dance. This is a sort of male–female competitive affair: a *West Side Story* type of dance. Anything you can do, I can do better – that idea.

Then the dramatic denouement, in which the Prince goes hysterical and tries to fire a gun. Some of the details here took a while to fall into place, but the general gist fell into place in my mind out of the story so far and the music.

AM: *On to Act Four. What about the scene where the Queen and doctors officiate over whatever dreadful medical deeds are done to the Prince? When and how did that idea come to you?*
MB: Almost all of Act Four is the delirium of the Prince. After the incident at the ball in Act Three, he's been dragged off. That situation's partly real, but partly seen through his eyes. It's the Queen overseeing over all these awful treatments, but actually he's probably receiving some drug to calm him down. However, what we see is his horrific view of what's happening to him at that point.

AM: *And you've got multiple queens.*
MB: I remember that that was Lez's idea. It was the sort of idea I thought you couldn't pull off. I probably said, 'I want the mother to be officiating over this, and I want him to feel that she's doing him no good.' And he must have said, 'What about if they've all got the same face?' – a nightmarish thing – 'this face that keeps coming over you with all these different medical instruments and treatments is the same person'. He said that we definitely could do it using queen masks, so that they could all be the mother. I thought it was a great idea. They're all white, as well. That makes them some sort of halfway house between the swans and the court. They're also part of the second white act. So is the Queen. She's dressed in white, and so is the Private Secretary. That leads into a nightmare version of the swan world and of the swans

themselves. They, when they reappear, are more sinister than they were before.

AM: *There were several 'white' opera stagings at English National Opera in the 1980s, I seem to remember.*
MB: Yes, the Pountney *Hansel and Gretel* was like that. I do remember those.

AM: *And, of course, that* Hansel and Gretel *had the horror witch-mother.*
  Who decided to make the drama of Act Four largely a bedroom drama?
MB: One of my design ideas early on was that I wanted outsize, larger-than-life objects. I could see the Prince's room as enormous, with just two enormous things in it – like an enormous bed and a very big chair – so that they made him look very small. The idea was also to emphasize this with perspective, since the stage wasn't enormous. Eventually, it ended up just being the bed; and there's a big mirror-cum-window at the beginning as well.

AM: *The extraordinary entrance of the swans from under the bed . . .*
MB: Again, that was part of my whole idea for Act Four. The Prince having been in their world in Act Two, I now wanted them to enter his world in Act Four; but I wanted to feel that they were coming out of the walls. If I was to do a film of it, they would just walk through the walls, and through the bed.

  It just seemed to make sense – something of the imagination – because he's asleep on the bed at the time. It's a way of showing the sort of world he's gone off into, but also showing that it's now confined to his world. He can't escape.

  In the middle of the act, it actually goes into a sort of halfway house sort of world, where the bed seems to be suspended in mid-air almost, because the back wall disappears when the swan appears, and there's a starry background and a black floor. If you squint a little in the theatre, it appears that the bed is just suspended in a starry sky. It's as if the swans have come to get him, rather than him going to them.

Rehearsals for Act Two

ALASTAIR MACAULAY: *How did you structure the order of rehearsals?*
MATTHEW BOURNE: A funny order, actually, but practical. We began

with the swans. Before the rehearsal period, we had already choreographed quite a lot of the basic ideas and phrases for swan movement. I worked with Etta and Scott; and Adam was involved too, to a lesser degree. We watched swans in a park; and we watched a fair amount of documentary video material of swans, showing the differences of behaviour – flying, coming into land, attacking fishing boats – and we identified where we thought those kinds of movements would work. For example, we used the kind of movement that swans have when they're coming down on to the water, with the weight very much backwards, to slow themselves down. We wanted to put some ungainly things in, you see: we didn't want it to look all beautiful and serene; because, when swans are out of the water, they're very awkward, and slightly turned-in. So within the swan choreography, there are two contrasting elements. Sometimes they scrunch up, sometimes they open out again.

To a certain extent we were remembering the traditional ballet, but we were trying to get away from flapping wings all the time. Obviously you can't get entirely away from that in *Swan Lake*, but we wanted to find some variations on that: with birdlike head movements and twitches.

There also came a point when we decided to make the swans creature-like, at times, as well as bird-like. Also semi-human.

AM: *In your notebooks for* Swan Lake, *there's a section just called 'Ideas', in which – before rehearsals, I think – you've put down your conceptions for each of the four acts. But you've also added other ideas – especially movement ideas – during the early rehearsals. Here are some notes for Act Two. 'Notes for swan motifs. Head nestling.'*
MB: That's very much out of the traditional *Swan Lake*, isn't it – but then it's also what real swans do.

AM: *'Clean into luxurious.'*
MB: That means type of movement. A good example of it from Ashton's choreography would be in *The Dream*, where Titania strikes a firm arabesque in Oberon's arms and then melts throughout all her limbs.

AM: *'A gesture carried through the torso creating a curved shape. Dying swan position. Folded right over.'*
MB: There are quite a lot of passages where they lean right forwards while crossing their arms at the wrist – the 'wings folded' position.

AM: *'Hands framing head à la Adam.'*

50 *Swan Lake*, Act Four. Arthur Pita leading one row of swans. The arm position is taken from the Nijinsky-inspired motif created by Bourne for Cooper in their pre-production photographic session. (See illustration 36 and pp. 239, 249.)

MB: At the photo-shoot with Adam we had come up with some basic swan motifs that I decided would become part of the choreography. In particular, the Nijinsky-like motif of crossing the arms around and above the head.

AM: *'Feeding, flying, swimming, gliding.'*
MB: We didn't use all that in the end; I don't remember them feeding.

AM: *Then there are extensive notes for the entrance of the swans: notes about structure, basic movement ideas ('Beak', 'Low to high', 'Abandoned', 'Clap', 'Round wings', 'Canon'), floor-patterns, and so forth. 'Scott's material, reworked. Canon. Etta's, Matt's canon.'*
MB: Another thing these notes show is that we were thinking of all the elements. Water and air in particular, of course. 'Grass blowing.' 'Trees, changes of position, blown.' This was about being blown from one position to another. 'Rocks.'

AM: *'Waves.'*

51 *Swan Lake*, Act Two. The corps of swans. The zig-zag pattern entrance.

MB: That's a water idea, which we use at the end. Perhaps nobody's ever noticed this, but at the very end of Act Two, the Swan and the Prince turn around and run into the water; then the other swans all start to do pas de chat and to cross the stage with wave-like arm movements – first one line of swans, then the next. The image is of them running into the water.

We worked out the zigzag swan entrance beforehand, with about four of us doing it. Adam was involved, though he never danced that bit on stage. The formations were based on those from the ballet; I think I always wanted that entrance to have that zigzag pattern; but we used different steps.

AM: *You've mentioned the traditional* Swan Lake. *What other choreography was in your mind at this period?*
MB: Nijinsky's *Faune*. The general look of the costume, the intensity of the eyes, the two-dimensional feel to a lot of the movement. Particularly earlier on, when we started, I had the pictures of *Faune* in my mind for the atmosphere of what we were trying to create.

Also I felt an early modern dance influence. At this stage, José Limòn was in my mind. I had done a lot of Limòn classes at one time, and I took class for a few weeks with the Limòn company in New York in about 1988, 1989. What I remember is the feeling of the movement. Those classes are very long, about two hours, starting with barrework and

52 *Swan Lake*, Act Two. Scott Ambler as the Prince, Adam Cooper as the Swan, and corps of male swans.

53 *L'Après-midi d'un faune*. Lydia Nelidova and Vaslav Nijinsky in Nijinsky's ballet. The contact of arms, the distance between the bodies, the profiled angle of the head, and the Faune's headdress all influenced Bourne's *Swan Lake*.

centrework, and then with movement based in Limòn repertory. I enjoyed that style very much. Also for *Swan Lake,* I was looking through all the photos of Denishawn group pieces from the 1920s, trying to get ideas about group designs.

When we started company rehearsals, we had a week or two just for the male swans first, working entirely on Act Two. Again, we started with the zigzag entrance of the swans, and we encouraged them to reshape the material, to characterize it from within, to contribute to it. We worked in bare feet, with an approximation of the look they would have in costume, with rolled-up trouser-legs. So we had plenty of swan style going before Day One of official rehearsals. The challenge for Act Two is that the story doesn't continue non-stop. So several dances have to be entirely character-based and dance-based. Within the overall group of swans, we worked on making each one feel the character of his particular swan.

AM: *'Phrases. All do an upper-body phrase, two eights. All do a lower-body phrase, two eights, jumps, one of each, then swan.'*
MB: This was a way of getting to work in rehearsal.

AM: *You've got further suggestions here. '(1) Quite nippy, more curves and changes. (2) Adage, four eights longer than each movement. (3) Jumping, look at adage phrase from audition.'*
MB: All these things meant something to me at the time! I wonder what. We especially worked to give specific characters for the four big swans and the four cygnets. The cygnets were to be young and wild. For that rehearsal, we put the music on, and I just said, 'Start moving around.' There were certain types of movement I wanted from them: a shunty movement, a picking up of the feet. And I wanted them to be the most gauche, the ungainly fledgelings of the group. So I said, 'Let's all make up a couple of eights of movement using those few ideas and see what we come up with.' We would learn each other's phrases; then there'd be something to play with, and I would start manipulating it. We developed little partnering ideas, making connections between the four; and then I structured it.

AM: *Here are some more notes. 'Entrances and Exits and Wings in Groups.'*
MB: I'm not sure what that specifically refers to, but I always like playing with ways of coming on and going off, to make entrances and exits more

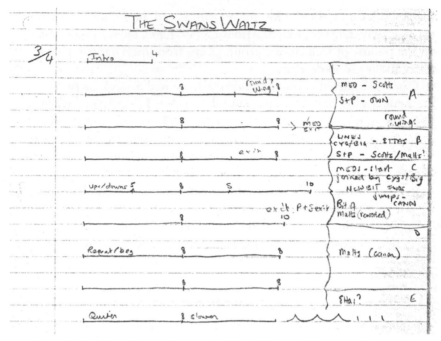

54 *Swan Lake*. From Bourne's annotated breakdown of the score for Act Two: the Swans' Waltz.

interesting. Because the set has pillars, we decided to use a lot of false entrances from them and exits into them.

AM: *'First waltz phrases all have up and down, swingy quality, flat-footed walk.'*
MB: That was an idea of how swans are when just out of the water. We played with it in rehearsal, and it's there on stage in the dance of the cygnets.

AM: *'Infernal Galop: wings beating.'*
MB: That was from the idea that I had had in *The Infernal Galop*, from the Cocteau painting where he drew Charles Trenet with wings. We had the dancers hold a splayed hand at the small of their backs, like wings; and we use that again in *Swan Lake*, but in Act Four only, as their basic still position.

AM: *So you have your swans fold their wings both before and behind. When they're behind, they turn out the wrists and slightly flex the elbows, creating a new shape. When the wings are folded in front, the wrists and elbows are left in calm lines.*

254

SWANS WALTZ

A
1,4
4,8'
S+P — OWN MAT.
MED — SCOTTS
CYGS+BIG — round wings (material)?

round wing — End of Ettas?

B
2,8'
BIG
S+P — Scotts?
CYGS+BIG — LINES — Ettas
CYG.

C
8,10
8,10
MEDS. start new phrase (1st 3)
Otherside in canon (2nd 3) (1 count)
CYGS+BIG — take over.
S+P — join with CYGS+BIG +
then carried off birds.

D
4,8'
MEDS begin MATTS. Canon?
round wings again? (CYGS+BIG)

55 *Swan Lake*. From Bourne's choreographic notes for floor-patterns and phrases in the Swans' Waltz. 'S + P' = Swan and Prince; 'mat' = material; 'Meds' = medium-sized swans; 'Scotts' = Scott Ambler's phrases; 'Cygs and Big' = 'Cygnets and Big swans'; 'Ettas' = Etta Murfitt's phrases; 'Matts' = Matthew Bourne's phrases.

In your notes during the waltz for all the swans, where there's a brief duet for the Swan and the Prince, you've written, 'Duet and Relationship in General. Searching, wanting, imitating, following, journeying towards yearning, waltz. Duet in waltz about physical reactions to each other.' Then, 'Lifted off in different directions at the end of the swans' waltz, (dream ideas), facing each other as contact is about to be made.'
MB: A lot of these things changed. Certainly not the lifting off. I'm not sure now what 'the dream ideas' were.

AM: *'End of entrance of swans. Runs involve lifts of Prince and Swan until they are face to face.'*

MB: That doesn't happen. What happens instead of that is that there's an attack of the swans on the Prince. They lift him in the air. The Swan isn't involved; he has exited. Then the Prince is saved by the Swan's re-entrance. They do end up face to face, but it's initiated by the Swan.

AM: *One of the four big swans in your original rehearsals was Will (William) Kemp. Within two or three months, you had him dancing the Swan. Was he the only dancer in the original company – apart from Adam Cooper and Fiona Chadwick – to emerge from ballet school?*

MB: Yes, and he was the only Royal Ballet School product to audition, too. At that point, we couldn't get anyone from the ballet world at all. It certainly wasn't considered a viable option at that point for anyone at the Royal Ballet School. It was entirely Will's initiative that led him to audition for us; he was still just seventeen. Since then, we have had many trained ballet students and many professional ballet dancers audition for us, probably owing to his example; but a high proportion of them aren't right for us. They're too 'ballet' – too precious and refined – and they don't use their torsos enough, or their weight. Those we take into the company tend to be the exceptions in those respects. As a dancer, Will fitted right in from the first.

AM: *Did the presence of Adam and Fiona have an effect on the class-work the company did? Did any of them start to take ballet classes? Or just to work harder in the classes they did?*

MB: I don't think so. In Britain, the contemporary dancers refuse to be intimidated by anyone who's a classical dancer. They take pride in the fact that they're contemporary dancers. In America, the worlds of ballet and modern dancers collide more. Here, there's much more resistance. It was more of a problem for Fiona and Adam and Will, coming from the ballet background; they were the ones that had to show everyone else that they belonged; and they did, of course.

But the entire level of technical accomplishment rose considerably with *Swan Lake*. After its premiere, one dancer, who had done leading roles with AMP years before, re-auditioned for us, and he honestly didn't have the technique to be one of the swan corps.

AM: *At what stage did you bring in second-cast performers?*

MB: They were there all the time in rehearsals. It was made very clear who was second-cast; most performances in the Sadler's Wells season would be first-cast. The second-cast were to have two matinées and two evenings in the initial run of two and a half weeks; and, once the tour began the following year, they would have many more performances. But they were learning it along with the first cast. Credit has to be given to them: they were equally involved in the creation of a lot of the movement and the ideas. David Hughes was the second-cast Swan; Ben Wright was the second-cast Prince. David Hughes left us after the tour, on which he performed the majority of first nights. He couldn't handle the situation of being second-cast to Adam, especially after the amount of press and praise that Adam received. He felt – rightly – that he'd brought a lot to the role and that he had influenced the way the role developed; and it was hard for him that his creative contribution received little acknowledgement. I have to say that Adam had been an important part of my conception of the ballet. I spent a few rehearsals with Adam alone, and I found that Adam was a very good member of the AMP company. But, to do David justice, when the show was in rehearsal, he was more animal-like, with greater fluidity; the movement came through the whole of his body more; he was down into the ground more. All this in turn influenced the way Adam did the role.

AM: *Ben Wright, however, has stayed with AMP, and performed the Prince frequently in the West End, in LA, and on Broadway.*
MB: Yes, and it's difficult to create the role along with Scott – who, because of his position in the company, tends to feel, of his own way with a role, 'This is exactly how it's done.' But Ben handled that very well; and he helped the whole show by developing a very different way of telling the story. He is a more vulnerable, younger-seeming Prince. Both interpretations are very valid. I think Ben feels that Scott's Prince isn't emotional enough; and Scott feels that Ben's Prince is a cry-baby character. That's fine. I'm sure it'll be done another way when somebody else does it.

A great deal of the relationship between the Swan and the Prince became clear only through rehearsal. There's a certain amount of fear to begin with on the Prince's part. The Swan has been quite frightening at the beginning of the piece, behind the window or the mirror; and he retains a bit of that as well. You're not quite sure which way he's going to go at any point; but I didn't start out with a really clear idea of where to go with it. I knew that would come from working on it, and I wasn't worried. I knew Act Two was all movement, so I knew the drama would clarify in rehearsal with the dancers.

AM: *Here you've divided the Swan–Prince duet into five sections. (B) is called 'Lyrical'; in brackets, you've put 'Swan Solo'. (C) is 'Nippy; in brackets, you've put 'Jumpy duet'. (D) is 'Very slow,' and (E) is 'Very upbeat'.*

MB: At this stage, I was still trying to use the upbeat 1877 ending – (E) – to the pas de deux. One solution I thought of was to bring in all the swans again; but, because of the way the duet developed, this felt completely wrong. The dancers kept laughing!

AM: *In more than one section of the pas de deux, Tchaikovsky is using some of his most long-phrased adagio composition. Did you have to work to find dance phrases that long?*

MB: It wasn't something that came automatically. But I had a feeling for this music; I did respond to it. It was a challenge to try to make it work. Although it wasn't so easy to organize the movement, I was helped by the fact that there was already a very strong idea about swan movement, about being something other than human. So the possibilities of what you could do with that seemed endless. I was certainly helped by having Adam to work with, because he is very musical, and because he was more used to moving like that to that kind of music.

There were certain problems we had to work through to make the Prince–Swan adagio work. All the lifts seemed odd, awkward, wrong, between two men. We were very concerned about that for a while. Then, very late on, we suddenly remembered that this is a dance between a human and a bird, or a human and a non-human creature. So it was about two different ways of moving, one more palpable than the other. Once we went back to thinking: 'What is this actually about?', to remembering that we weren't trying to create some great pas de deux, everything fell into place. We decided, for example, that the Swan couldn't hold with his hands, because they were wings: he had to lift the Prince up under the arms, with his hands still free so that there was a feeling of flight about it as well; and we decided also that at times the Prince must feel like a small child, vulnerable, as small as he can. But Adam found it difficult to give his weight to another dancer when the Swan is lifted or supported: he wasn't used to that at all.

The jumpy sequence during the pas de deux was particularly influenced by David Hughes and Ben Wright, the second-cast Swan and Prince.

AM: *During this adagio – in the musically very intimate moment when the cello and violin come closest together – the Royal Ballet version of the Ivanov (unlike the Kirov) has an especially affecting passage of choreography, when the Swan Queen is rocked in the Prince's arms. You have something both similar and different: it's the Swan who approaches the Prince from behind.*

MB: He wraps him in his wings, and lifts him up. It's like, 'No, you've got to accept me.' It's to bring the Prince back to his true nature. He literally clings to the Prince, leans back, and so can lift one leg up while the Prince lifts both his legs off the floor.

AM: *Is it an accident that this lift is related to a lift that the Queen does in the Stranger's arms in Act Three?*

MB: No accident. We were, in the Act Three duet, trying to find a few parallels, for jealousy's sake. At that point in Act Two, we had spent a lot of time wondering how far to go physically with the two men. Every time we came to that point, it felt awkward, too literal; but I think we hit it right in the end by keeping it quite ambiguous. The height of the physical relationship is the Swan's wrapping up the Prince with his wings and cradling him, which is quite moving. It's just what has never happened to the Prince before. He's been trying to get attention from his mother; you can feel that that's what he wants, and it's what he gets from the Swan. That's all he needs at that point: affection of some kind.

AM: *The feeling is literally an ambiguous feeling, because it is the Prince's longing for something unattainable, for a wild winged creature, but at the same time he wants to be held by it. There's an active–passive feeling.*

MB: Because the whole act is seen through the Prince's eyes, you have to make the audience feel the same as the Prince. That's why the role is quite difficult to cast. You want the audience to feel that they would be drawn by this Swan person as well – that they want to be in the Prince's shoes, basically.

AM: *You keep the Prince on stage during the Swan's solo.*

MB: Originally, we weren't going to; but, it made sense that the Swan was performing for the Prince. The Swan's a bit of a peacock here! Suddenly the solo worked, because you're seeing it through the Prince's eyes, which you need to.

With the dance for the four big swans, we started off by using some phrases from the swans' waltz. In their rehearsal, Will Kemp and Mark Mitchell suggested that we just jumped these phrases, and they got very carried away. It was a great rehearsal; I loved it, and laughed so much, they were working so hard. But they made it difficult for themselves! – to the point where the big swans' dance is not much liked by people who do it now: it's exhausting. So much so that, recently, we've taken out some of the jumps.

AM: *You've noted, 'Swan re-entry, big Swan solo'. Then, interestingly, 'Pleading.'*
MB: That was a feeling in the music at that point.

AM: *At the end: 'Swan lifted up by big swans, followed by Prince.'*
MB: That has happened in the production, or has been cut from it, at different stages. It depends whether the swans feel they're into lifting. We decided to do away with it last time, because it was such a hassle.

AM: *Did you do all of Act Two before moving on to the other three acts?*
MB: I think so, yes. It took the longest, and it was hard to get going.

Rehearsals for Acts Three, One and Four

ALASTAIR MACAULAY: *With which bits of* Swan Lake *did you already know how you wanted the movement to look?*
MATTHEW BOURNE: Quite a lot of it really, but there are some specific choreographic things, like the part of Act One when the dancers are all under the balcony at the beginning. I knew I wanted a sequence that looked like a crowd waving and that there was dance. Because I was so clear in the simplicity of what I wanted, I just did it, before the rehearsal – worked it out, taught it to people and then staged it which developed it a bit. That was a clear idea that I could just get on with, which is best when there's a lot of people involved; but the cygnets' dance, for example – I really didn't have any ideas at all about it until we got into the rehearsal room.

AM: *At what point did you give your dancers things to research?*
MB: Quite early on. They would know their role, or their line-up of roles, and I gave them different things to study or watch. Fiona Chadwick went away and read some books about the Queen and said, 'I'm more Princess Margaret – Princess Margaret as she would have been if she had become Queen.' Since Princess Margaret is patron of the Royal Ballet, she had probably met her many times, and Fiona requested the tumbler for the gin, or whatever it is she drinks – not an elegant glass, but a tumbler like the Princess's. Saranne – who played the Italian princess – I sent away to watch Anita Ekberg in *La Dolce Vita*. I said, 'I want that business of kicking the shoes off – an Italian woman getting

56 *Swan Lake*, Act One. Left to right: Fiona Chadwick as the Queen, Barry Atkinson as the Private Secretary, Emily Piercy as the Prince's Girlfriend. The programme clutched by the Girlfriend shows that they are about to attend the gala performance of the *Moth Ballet*.

up on a table and getting a bit of sexual energy going – that sort of feel.' So she went away and watched that. The Princess of Monaco (Kirsty Tapp) went away and watched a documentary on Grace Kelly. In the Soho scene, Will Kemp was the Pop Idol. Because it was British retro, I asked him to play Cliff Richard. That foxed him; he would rather have been Elvis Presley. He enjoyed playing the Italian Princess's lover in Act Three, because he had been having a relationship with an Italian girl in the Royal Ballet and had visited Italy, so he knew the way of life and enjoyed the Mediterranean jealousy of the character. Each had their thing. Maxine Fone, who was going to be the ballerina in the little Moth Ballet, watched the oldest choreography we could find on video.

AM: *Which was the Kirov Ballet dancing* La Vivandière.
MB: Yes, we used a bit of that. She has a great sense of humour – we laughed a lot doing that – affectionately – and she really understood what she was doing there.

AM: *The Prince's Girlfriend: did she continue to be modelled along Fergie lines?*
MB: No. Although Lez and I had very much seen her as Fergie, Emily Mortimer researched her and made her Texan. She's called Terri-Belle Pratt! Emily wanted to create her own person.

The next act we made in rehearsal was Act Three.

AM: *You begin it with the autograph-collectors. Is that a reference to your own past?*
MB: I suppose so.

AM: *Then the scene changes to the ballroom. After the first dance in which we see the assembled royalty and guests, you have the Swan or Stranger enter in black leather trousers. And the music goes straight into the Russian Dance.*
MB: Yes: as soon I heard the introduction to the Russian Dance in rehearsal, I just knew he had to sweep forward and kiss the Queen's hand in an outrageous way.

AM: *Then – more outrageous – he produces the riding-crop.*
MB: That was Adam's idea: one of several first-rate ideas he had for his role. Where he got it from, I don't know! It suggests at once that the Stranger is into kinky things, that anything goes with him. As for the leather trousers: Lez and I had instantly thought that black leather was a good idea for the Black Swan. People think Adam's like that character. That's what they expect him to be like when they meet him: so that either there's an almost visible disappointment that he's not like that, or they're scared to say much because they assume he's going to behave in that way. There's a side of Adam that is like that, or that certainly enjoys acting that way on stage.

AM: *The whole set-up for the Stranger's entrance and the Russian Dance, however, reminds me of one of Ashton's last ballets,* Varii Capricci – *which you and I both saw during its first British performances in 1983 and which was led by Antoinette Sibley and Anthony Dowell. She played a glamorous older woman, La Capricciosa; he played a sexy stranger, Lo Straniero, who has quite an effect on her, and then departs as mysteriously as he came. At one point, she stands closely in front of him, and puts her hand back right on to his thigh. His response is ambiguous. Much the same happens during your Russian Dance, when he launches into a steamy duet with the Hungarian Princess.*
MB: That's just the kind of reference that I can't discuss usefully, I'm afraid. I saw *Varii Capricci* several times; and, when you describe it, I remember it. But if it went into my unconscious memory and has influenced my *Swan Lake*, I can't say. It's interesting you bringing these references up; it's not that I'm denying the influence of other choreography

on me or claiming that everything in mine is original; but sometimes I'm conscious of my sources and sometimes I'm not. And sometimes, when I see a piece again myself, I suddenly realize that it has had an influence on me.

AM: *You've said that the czardas was a problem to choreograph.*
MB: Yes, because I wanted to keep some story going on there. Eventually we came up with an idea to do with partnering, where the Prince and the Black Swan are partnering different women, but looking at each other all the way through. This would lead up to the Stranger's flirtation with the queen as well. So the dance became all about looking, and about various lusty situations. The whole stage feels that way during that dance. It leads up to sexual things.

AM: *How was it working with the dancers on the role of the Queen?*
MB: Fiona just came and got on with the work; she enjoyed being in a more relaxed atmosphere. To begin with, people took her to be quite aloof – which they soon found wasn't the case. Her approach to the second cast was that it was rude even to watch someone else, let alone to comment. (Sarah Wildor was the same when she came from the Royal to rehearse *Cinderella.*) Fiona had her head in a book – which some people thought was rude – but it was her way of not interfering. She had her own very clear idea of what she was doing in the part, which she didn't want to impose on others or to have interfered with. She was so calm, and such good company during the run of the show, that she fitted in very well. She's a very intelligent dancer, and a much more remarkable actress than she probably realizes; every time she comes back to rehearse the role, she slips right back into it at once. When the show was performed and friends came to watch her, she was always telling them how nice it was to be around relaxed people – the fact that we'd all go for drinks after the shows, that we all spent time talking to each other.

AM: *Your second-cast queen was Isabel Mortimer.*
MB: Isabel was the easiest person to deal with in many ways. She knew that the role would be a completely new challenge for her and that she would have to learn a whole new regal way of behaviour. She learnt a lot from watching Fiona, and showed no ego. She never minded picking up from what other people did. Her relationship with Fiona was good, as it was later with Lynn Seymour. They talked about the role together, and sometimes she would come to me and say, 'I saw Fiona or Lynn doing this in the part. Would you like me to do it?' Sometimes I

would say, 'No, do what you're doing, that's fine', and sometimes, 'Yes, I think that is a good idea.' More than any other dancer – even more than Adam, who's very open in this respect – she's learnt from watching others: which, I feel, is a valuable thing for all dancers.

AM: *We've spoken of how you planned the 'Black Swan' dances: the Stranger's duet with the Queen, his tango duet with the Prince, the women's dance for the Swan, the 'sarcastic dance'. How much of that just evolved in rehearsal?*

MB: Because it was story-led, I had the whole thing mapped out in my head musically. I was very clear on the ideas of what each piece of music was doing, and the kind of dance style I wanted. The first section, the Stranger's duet with the Queen, I knew wouldn't be a problem to do. To have Fiona and Adam just letting rip, doing all these things, was a shock to the second-cast dancers at first; but the more permanent members are very good in that they don't kick up much of a fuss about it. They watch and learn from other people, and find new ways of working and moving; but that process works two ways. I know that Adam certainly picked up a new way of moving from contemporary dancers, a great fluidity. The second section was the two men, but once I had the Argentinean tango idea – that sort of dark intertwining of bodies – I thought that would work for the music and provide a formal partnering device; it says something straightaway and allowed us from a simple start to develop something that grew more violent and antagonistic between them. It seems to be a form that's almost open to anything.

AM: *I know that you were influenced by Hitchcock's* The Birds *in Act Four, but the whole drama of jealousy and alarm that builds up in Act Three also seems very Hitchcock to me.* Vertigo *comes to mind, and other films of his.*

MB: Yes, Hitchcock is definitely there, in the Prince's character and in the way we light the scene. A lot of Hitchcock's characters are in situations where they don't quite understand why they're wrongly accused; or where they have some reason to be paranoid about the way people treat them. Hitchcock also had a lot of strange mother–son relationships, didn't he?

One of Adam's most brilliant contributions came during the duet for the Stranger and the Prince. He had the idea of the Stranger walking to one side, dipping his thumb in the Private Secretary's ashtray, and tracing down the centre of his forehead the dark line the Swan has.

So – this is the Prince's fantasy, remember – the Stranger is saying, 'Yes, I am the Swan.' But in a taunting, sinister way. It's the Prince's dream, touched with nightmare.

AM: *In the coda, you capture the music's competitive spirit. In the traditional* Swan Lake, *the way in which the ballerina does her thirty-two fouetté turns over a drastic change in the music is always horridly unmusical.*

MB: I definitely stole one thing there. The way the Swan lifts the Queen over his hoisted leg over a series of tables; Fred and Ginger do that in the 'Yam', in *Carefree*. I'd always wanted to put that in somewhere! I think we tried to do something similar in *The Percys*, but it's quite difficult to achieve. However, when Fiona and Adam tried it, they just did it straightaway – it was great – and that helped other people to do it in turn. It's just a shame that we don't have as many tables as they had!

The interesting thing about all Act Three was that it felt dreadful in the studio. It never felt that it had any life to it whatsoever. I thought it was a disaster. It was only the first time we did it on stage, with the lighting, that it actually ever worked.

The next act we rehearsed was Act One.

AM: *Here are your notes for the prologue:*

'Boy (Prince) writing in bed having a bad dream. Awakes in a sweat on big chord; at same time, the Swan appears in large mirror above bed (it quickly fades) as the Queen enters the room (as if disturbed in the night). She comforts the young Prince. The Private Secretary appears at the doorway.'

So straightaway you've got that idea of a boy dreaming of a swan; it's the idea you used in the original poster image. But what kind of a dream does this boy Prince have of a swan?

MB: It's frightening when he's young. He's not yet worked out what the Swan is. We also ended up having the Queen a lot colder than that description; and the Private Secretary didn't appear there.

AM: *'Act One, Scene One. (The Private Secretary is directing all of this.) It is morning. Lines of footmen and maids are going about their business as if along corridors. They're regimented, almost clockwork. They carry things: towels, a basin, aerosols, a screen?, etc. How high bed? . . . Six or so servants prepare the Prince for his day of royal duties. They form staircase for him to walk down out of bed, they wash him, dress*

him, etc. He uses their bodies for seats, support, etc., eats breakfast?
He is given a lesson in royal protocol with blackboard: how to 1) walk,
2) wave, 3) posture, 4) salute (use trolley maybe as substitute coach).
Show Prince's rebellious/creative/imaginative side . . . '
   Did you show that aspect of the Prince?
MB: We got in as much detail as we could. Sometimes there wasn't
enough music. He doesn't eat breakfast, for example.

AM: '. . . *Perhaps the Queen interrupts his fun, takes his hand, and leads*
him into or through a doorway with flashlights. He resists . . . '
MB: That didn't quite happen there, but the feeling is true to what we
did.

AM: *Next you've put 'Toy swan?'*
MB: This was an *Equus* idea, really. In the play *Equus*, the horse image
was triggered off by a picture of a horse in his room that was staring
down on him from above the bed. So we were wondering whether, if our
Prince had a toy swan, that might, from a very early age, have started
all the nightmares.

AM: *'Act One, Scene Two, The Great Hall: waltz. Dancing lesson for*
young Prince? Maybe with Queen. Appearance on balcony.' Note in the
margin: 'How does all this work? Balcony/bed . . . '
MB: On stage the bed reverses to become the balcony. We didn't have
the dancing lesson.

AM: *'Line ups, walkabouts, unveilings, investiture, ropes to form*
barriers, red carpet, cutting ribbons, smashing a bottle to launch a ship
. . . ' Pretty much all of that happens on stage.
   'Transformation of young Prince to the Prince, using flash bulbs . . . '
MB: We did that, but not so literally.

AM: *'Note: dance possibilities (sections). Quintet, the Queen and four*
young admirers. Group dance, seven couples led by Prince and the
Queen. Two solos, the young Prince and the Prince . . . '
MB: We had the quintet, but the rest we either never tried, or changed.
Originally the Prince did a solo; then we changed it to have him meeting
the Girlfriend instead.

AM: *'Mixed group of dignitaries. Stiff, snobby, elegant . . . ' That's*
attached now to another note down the page: 'Girlfriend arrives on her

own looking (common) and different from everyone else . . .' Between that, you've got: 'Duet for Prince and Girlfriend. Somewhere in here we need to show Prince's personality/rebellion/fear, etc.'

MB: We did away with the rebellion. We showed his fear of people and cameras. He flinches every time there's a camera flash. He looks a bit out of it most of the time.

AM: *'Act One, Scene Three, continuation: the scene following the waltz . . .' You've got a note in the margin: 'How long do women need to get ready for ballet?' Main text: 'Prince tries to introduce his new Girlfriend to the Queen. This she avoids at first (she has some men with her). She exits (first fanfare) to prepare for evening engagement. Duet, Prince and Girlfriend interrupted by Private Secretary.' In the right-hand margin, in capital letters: 'NO MIME.'*

MB: I meant, in general for the whole scene, that we weren't going to have any kind of formal ballet mime as such. We were going to act it in a naturalistic style.

AM: *And you've got a note about the duets: 'Does Girlfriend have a wrap. Can she move?' Next thing: 'Queen returns ready for Evening Out, with her escort. Prince introduces her, "She's not good enough." Prince: "But you've got that toyboy." She gives in.'*

MB: Because we didn't use mime, we couldn't be that specific. But we did give the dancers some motivation.

AM: *'They arrive in Royal Box and stand as if for the National Anthem. As they sit, curtain opens . . .' You've got a note: 'Do we need a curtain?' Then:*

'Act One, Scene Four: The Ballet.' (You've got a note saying: 'Use lots of mime and bows to box.') Then 'First Section. Introduction to Idyll: first two butterflies, then other two. Two twos. Finally that Ballerina.

'Second Section, Hunter's Entrance and Solo. Chases butterflies, falls in love with the white one when she appears, and chases her.

'Third Section. Declares his love. She says she's held captive by evil forest ogre/troll, and cannot leave the forest. He vows to release her, etc.

'Fourth Section: ogre appears. Big fight. Hunter, dizzy spell in middle. He defeats the ogre.

'Fifth Section: they all celebrate. She dies at end?'

Then you've put 'Twist needed.'

MB: She collapses at the last minute. She withers away with excitement.

AM: '*Act One, Scene Five: Private, a room in the palace. Starts solos in 2 rooms. Could be with valet (boy) a maid (cover) . . .*'

MB: The idea was to have one room on each side of the stage, with the Queen in one and the Prince in the other, being undressed after the night at the theatre. Eventually, she was going to go into his room, but the beginning of the music was going to be them both thinking their private thoughts.

AM: '*She can sense him in his room. They're both distressed. He needs a bit of sympathy. His girlfriend has walked out . . .*'

MB: She storms out of the theatre. After this duet with his mother, he goes off looking for her.

AM: '*Queen becomes too intimate. He pulls away. She becomes angry. "Be a man." "I'm sorry," he says, "I just want a mother." She is incapable of that kind of love. She leaves. He feels betrayed and lonely, dons a disguise, and leaves . . .*' Needless to say, in the margin you've written, 'Psychology.'

MB: I'd forgotten the Queen getting intimate; we never used that. What we eventually felt was best was what we did on stage: to do with her not being able to touch him, and him trying to make her touch him, to bring her arms around him – things like that. If there's any sexual element to it, I don't think it works so well. It could work, but we didn't go for that.

AM: *Well, in a different ink, you've written, 'She is cold . . .' Take us through the action for this scene. What's the Prince doing here?*

MB: He's got a bottle; he's drinking in his mirror in his room, and she enters, but not seen by him, because he has his head down. All this is straight after the incident in the Royal Box during the Moth Ballet; the Girlfriend has gone off in a huff. Now the Queen has come in to try to talk to him. She sees that he's in a fairly desperate state. It looks at first as if she's going to try to be a bit more human about the state of things with him. She tries to touch him, but doesn't feel very comfortable about it. As soon as his eyes meet hers, he turns round and looks at her. She can't meet his look. There's something about him and her that doesn't work, doesn't connect in that way. Then he tries to explain, saying that all he wants is a bit of love in his life, that that's why he had the girlfriend. But it gets out of hand. The thing that changes her way of looking at things is that she suddenly sees the bottle, and she starts to bring up something that she's obviously brought up before: 'You're drinking again.' Whereas she was going to try to be tactful and sweet and human about everything, now she starts ranting again at him. So it's the same old story, and he, in turn, gets more violent with her. But for him it is more desperate. He tries to make her be physical with him. That's the idea of the duet; that was how we talked about the movement. It's all about him trying to bring her to him, trying to get her to hold him, and about her resisting that and getting upset by it. But there is also the sense at the end – once they end up on the floor together and she gets up – that this is not the first time this sort of thing has happened. He crawls over to the mirror. She's about to leave; she sees him slumped there; she just looks at him. She goes over to him, brings his shoulders up, makes him look at himself in the mirror, and meet her eyes – in the mirror. What she's saying is: 'Be a man. This is your job.'

AM: *Was all this in your scenario before rehearsals?*
MB: In the scenario, it's just one line about the Prince needing affection from his mother; but it's one of the ideas you knew would take care of itself once you got going on it. It was a simple idea that then became, as we knew it would all along, more complex. Of course, working with all four of them on that, with Fiona and Scott and Isabel and Ben, was very good. They all think very much from an acting point of view and were very uninhibited in the way they approached the whole thing. I remember asking Fiona to turn and look back at the Prince in three different ways. She did them all brilliantly, and it was the one she devised that worked best. I wish it was a bit longer, actually. It comes at a point in the show where you've had quite a lot of humour, and to get into this new mood takes a while. Although it can be very powerful, it's over before you really have a chance to get into this separate scene musically. Then you're into Soho. But it went down particularly well in America, that duo. It always got applause there.

AM: *Your notes for the end of this scene: 'The Private Secretary enters. Has seen the whole thing and contacts someone on his mobile phone. (Fade).'*
MB: The idea was that there was never any privacy. Even at home in his own room, the Prince was always watched.

AM: *'Act One, Scene Six: Soho Club. Several situations going on at once, Girlfriend is with the sailors. Fan dancer puts on a show. Little repeated group dances. Prince works his way around club trying to win back*

57 *Swan Lake*, Act One. The 'Soho' scene, set in a 'retro club' and peopled by figures of scandal from the 1960s. Eddie Nixon as the Club Owner, and William Kemp as the Pop Idol. Bourne told Kemp to base this character on the young Cliff Richard. Kemp, who only knew Richard as a much older performer, incorporated aspects of Elvis Presley: such as the knee-wobbles shown here.

Girlfriend. Sailor makes a pass at him. Fight ensues. Bit of jiving. Not necessarily all period dance. Go through relationships and groups.'
MB: Details like 'The sailor makes a pass at him' are there so as not to make the whole situation too sexually clear-cut for some members of the audience. I wanted to show that the Prince can't handle an advance from a man.

AM: *He wants the Swan/Stranger in his mind, but he doesn't actually want the sex. But could it be played either way? As I think Scott perceives it, the Prince is straight at this point, and then the Swan hits him as a sexual revelation in his own mind. But could the Prince be actually a closet gay who won't admit his sexuality to himself?*
MB: I don't think he should be consciously seen to be comfortable with flirting with men in a Soho club.

AM: *So it becomes a drama about repression of some kind.*
The next page is all counts. Eights and fours, mainly eights. Do you reduce all music to eights?
MB: No. But dancers are happier with eights than with any other counts. Obviously, if something is definitely in sixes, then you have to go with it. Later on, we've got tens, twelves, all kinds of other counts.

AM: *Here we've got floor patterns for your idea of the waltz; and you've worked on the casting here in some precision.*

MB: The floor-patterns we probably used. It's a case of sometimes dealing with the number of people you've got, and working out what shapes you can actually make with that many people; what your options are really in terms of formations.

AM: *We've got notes here for Soho material. 'Wobbly legs, head to head, jive, v. close.'*

MB: 'Wobbly legs' are Elvis Presley knee-trembles. Will Kemp did those as the Pop Idol.

AM: *'Prince's Solo, Act One . . .' Lots of sixes here. 'The Private Secretary. Trapped, rejected, alone, yearning.'*

MB: My idea for the Prince's solo was partly the solo the hero of Ashton's *The Two Pigeons* does when he's at his lowest ebb. Like our Prince here, his solo is in front of the drop-curtain; he's been thrown out of one milieu and he feels that he's lost. I know that it seems a lot of work to divide Act One into seven scenes. But I think that it's easier to do that than to have one great long Prince's birthday scene as usually happens in the traditional *Swan Lake*. There's much more music for Act One than for Act Two, and yet usually it has less plot. Once we knew what we were doing for each scene, it was more straightforward. In fact, it was the least problematic act to create.

AM: *What about Act Four?*

MB: To be honest, the scenario was very, very weak in that area, when we went into choreographing it. We were trying to get Act One finished and had little time left to do Act Four. In some ways, I thought, 'The basic idea is there.' It didn't need very specific organizing in the sense of this scene being about one thing and that scene being about another. The whole thing had one overall feeling, and it was driven by the music. So I thought that, once we got going on it, it would create itself. Still, I was getting worried time-wise. So, while we were doing Act One, I used to send Adam and David (Hughes) up into a studio, because they weren't needed in Act One. I told them, 'Just listen to the music and see what ideas you have. Just think it through.' I knew that there were things I wanted to pinpoint; but the problem was that the music had so many climaxes. Just when you think it's all over, it starts up again. And your first thought is, 'What on earth can we do with this next climax?'

AM: *You solve the climaxes. You've got more plot than most Act Fours ever have. What moments do you think you pinpointed in advance?*

MB: The Swan coming out of the bed (I love that; I think it's very significant); the reconciliation of the two of them; the regret. Then the point where the swans turn on them: there seemed to be a real change in the music that made that clear. It was definitely going to be the swans turning on their leader; but, until rehearsal, I thought that they might be attacking the Prince as well at that point.

One theme in Act Four is betrayal. The Prince must feel the Swan has betrayed him in Act Three. The Swan has to win him back by saying, 'I am the true one.'

AM: *Were you changing any of the musical text once you got into rehearsals?*

MB: We use the original 1877 Act Four, without any supplements, which virtually no production does. When I was worried about finishing it in time, I think I went to David Lloyd-Jones in desperation and said, 'Are there any cuts we can make in the first dance, without it sounding as if there are cuts?' The answer was yes: there were repeats that we could take out. That helped quite a lot.

AM: *The whole act is the climax to your whole conception of* Swan Lake *as psychodrama, and it has several turns of the screw. The first hair-raising moment is when the first swans appear from under the bed. As you've said, this came from your idea that Act Four was Act Two in reverse: the Prince had entered the swans' world, now they enter his. He had stretched his mind to include them, but now they invade his mind and his privacy.*

MB: There's the section where the swans are all attacking the Prince – they turn on him because he has turned against nature (going with a Swan – or with a man) – and leave him for dead. Then the Swan interrupts them, on that fantastic climax in the music. The swans all leave, and the Swan is left with what he at first thinks is the dead body of the Prince, and he's griefstricken.

AM: *At first, the way that the Swan seems to be left destitute by the corpse of his companion evokes Act One of the Peter Wright Royal Ballet production of* The Nutcracker: *little Clara thinks the Nutcracker is dead, and she's desolate; but when your Swan grieves, he opens his mouth in a howl. Were you thinking of 'swan song'?*

MB: Absolutely. Then, as he realizes there is life left in the Prince, he picks him up. Here we repeat the wrapping-of-the-wings motif from Act Two; at which point I remember thinking in rehearsal, 'Now here comes another whole piece of music that leads up to the end. Where do we go from here?' Then I remembered the idea I had had of the swans re-entering to destroy their leader. So their first attack really was on the Prince, to get rid of him. They don't quite succeed; and now, since he's still alive and since the Swan's obviously sticking with him, they turn on the Swan – because he has betrayed them – and attack him. At an initial stage we hadn't quite separated the two out. I had been thinking that they would attack the two of them; but, because of those two separate climaxes in the music, we divided it into, first, the attack on the Prince – whom the Swan saves, somewhat like *Giselle* reversed – and, next, the attack on their own Swan leader. Now, the way they attack him, the image that we had was from Tennessee Williams's *Suddenly Last Summer*. I only knew the film, in which the young Elizabeth Taylor gives a vivid, painful description of how the hero was ripped apart. It is very over the top, but I remember seeing it when I was in my teens and being terrified by the idea of someone being torn apart; I found that very shocking. I haven't seen it since, though I think I've seen clips from it. I don't think I even saw the sexual connotations that were slightly hidden in the film at the time; what I remember was the horrible image, even in verbal description; and also – as I've said earlier – I was thinking of Hitchcock's film *The Birds*. The bed is centre stage. The swans come on from the wings, and they jump on it. Some of them come from round it and hang on to it; they all have a different way of getting on to it. They jump, they slide across the bed. It's quite a powerful moment: a build-up of power and menace, in which the swans are obviously angry and about to attack.

AM: *Then comes the heroic big dive by the Swan into their midst. This connects exactly to the Swan Queen's suicide in the traditional* Swan Lake, *which occurs at the same point in the score, and it catches the note of Romantic despair in the music. But how did this Swan's dive emerge?*
MB: It was Adam's idea. I was a bit suspicious of it, to be honest; at first I thought, 'It feels a bit clichéd.' But I liked the fact that we saw the Prince downstage, blocked by all the swans, and the way this let them reach out to each other before the Swan was devoured. Anyway, it was one of those ideas Adam had devised upstairs while we were doing Act

58 *Swan Lake*, Act Four. Adam Cooper as the Swan, throwing himself from the bed into the chorus of swans. This self-sacrificial leap on the part of the Swan into the arms of the now cannibalistic and frenzied swans was one of Cooper's own original ideas. It occurs on the last great climax in the score.

One, and he wanted to do it. Once I saw how very well it worked, I left well alone!

It was amazing how quickly Act Four fell into place. We really had very little time left, but everything solved itself fast. I think that says a lot about the whole rehearsal process; by that stage everyone was deeply committed to what the show was all about. Normally, the final stages of completing a show are absolutely desperate for me; but in this case, despite the rush, I remember no panic. We had had a wonderful rehearsal period, and there was a lot of trust and devotion about.

Changing Casts

ALASTAIR MACAULAY: *We've spoken of the casts with whom you created* Swan Lake *in 1995. During these following three years, in fact, the role of the Prince has always been played by one or other of the same*

59 *Swan Lake*, Act Two. Will Kemp as the Swan; Ben Wright as the Prince.

two dancers: Scott Ambler or Ben Wright. However, there have been a few other interpreters of the roles of the Swan and the Queen. Of these, perhaps the two most important were Will Kemp as the Swan and Lynn Seymour as the Queen.

MATTHEW BOURNE: Will was around from the beginning, and was in the background for a lot of rehearsals involving the Swan, though not participating. He injured himself just before *Swan Lake* opened at Sadler's Wells, and was devastated by not being able to participate in the production he'd worked so hard on; but he watched every performance from the wings, and just lapped it up.

At the start of 1996, he then learnt the role fully from Adam; they had a very good relationship, and still do. Will was eighteen, and, as a recent graduate of the Royal Ballet School, he felt very much the excitement of learning this big role from Adam, who was still then a principal of the Royal Ballet, and who had received great acclaim for his performance in *Swan Lake*. Will also recognized Adam's generosity and practical good sense; but, even at that age, he found it natural to start doing things his own way. By the time he did his first performance, during the British tour in spring 1996, he seemed to have worked out for himself how he wanted to do it and what he wanted to bring out in it. Obviously, the differences in their techniques and in their styles of dancing make the role feel different anyway; but there were individual inflections and strokes of interpretation in Will which I found very impressive; it never felt like a copycat performance. We didn't change anything choreographically at all for him; he worked within the existing framework of the role.

AM: *Can you say what the difference in quality and movement was?*
MB: Adam is more over-powering and more dominant and has a much more powerful presence than Will does overall. His dancing has more strength and power and, therefore, seems to dominate the Prince much more easily, much more casually. Just by his presence, he can dominate the whole stage; and he actually looks much taller on stage than he is. When he walks on, in both Acts Two and Three, he looks enormous – and yet off stage he's the same height as me – not even six foot. I don't understand that at all.

AM: *This is what the critic James Monahan used to call 'the gift of tallness'. He was particularly fascinated by how the dancing of very petite ballerinas such as Fonteyn and Makarova registered colossally in huge theatres. It's something that a few people – actors and singers, for example – have naturally. But I think that ballet training – ballet is all about large-scale projection, after all – helps several people (though a minority) to acquire these heightened dimensions on stage.*
MB: Will, by contrast, is slight and boyish, a very different presence. He's only half an inch shorter than Adam, but that's not how it feels on stage. His presence is something he has to work at. His style is more gentle and fluid, and his intensity is something he worked on – whereas Adam's is natural. Adam has an incredible sexual magnetism for people, because it appears that he's not trying very hard – and probably he isn't – in terms of projecting the image that he does. What Will has is a quite different kind of mystery. It is perhaps a different kind of erotic appeal, but Will's is projected with greater innocence and a certain spiritual quality that's really remarkable.

AM: *I also think that they use the music differently.*
MB: Yes. Adam has a great way of playing with music. The music's really inside him, in the sense that he knows what he's doing, so that he goes for one chord or beat or sound in the music, or holds back from one.

He's in control of it, because he's got great resources of technique, and he brings some very strong dynamic qualities to individual phrases. Will's technique isn't such that he can exert that freedom; but he has a physical response to the music that feels more emotional; I think his style has a basic grace and fluency that complements the whole current of a phrase.

It's important to remember that Will has learnt all his professional skill and artistry with AMP, whereas Adam was already an established actor-dancer when he came to us. Adam is one of the world's great partners; women have complete trust in his hands. I'm sure that's the virtue of his they must miss most now at the Royal Ballet, where ballerinas so often feel terribly exposed unless they have an absolutely strong and reliable partner. Will has learnt a vast amount through sheer experience. There was at least one week in the West End when, because of injury to other swans, he had to dance all eight performances. And this is a role that Adam says is more exhausting than anything except Prince Rudolf in *Mayerling*. Will was just nineteen, but he always sustained the role.

As for Lynn Seymour, the thrill for me was that she saw *Swan Lake* at Sadler's Wells three times and asked me if she could be in it. I would never have dreamt of approaching her.[14] To be truthful, I missed almost all her career as a ballerina – though I knew much about her and I remember how often, as our teacher at Laban, you yourself would talk of her individuality and power. Certainly I had seen many of the ballets that Ashton and MacMillan had choreographed on her: *The Two Pigeons, Romeo and Juliet, Concerto, Five Brahms Waltzes in the Manner of Isadora Duncan, A Month in the Country, Mayerling*.

Once we decided to use Lynn for several performances during the West End run – Fiona, Isabel and she shared the majority of performances of the Queen – she was a brilliant colleague. I regard Fiona's performance as definitive, but Lynn did more than any other AMP performer to show how a newcomer to the cast of a show can stamp her own way on a role; and she had a very good relationship with Isabel. Certain passages – particularly the Act One duet with the Prince – had to be rechoreographed on her anyway, because there were certain things that were simply designed on a younger dancer, but it was great working with her in rehearsal; she's absolutely committed. Even though she's a

14 It is true that Bourne had never approached her. None the less, in an early note on *Swan Lake* casting (dated probably 1994), Seymour's name is one of the ten women Bourne lists as possible for the Queen.

60 *Swan Lake*. Act Three. Adam Cooper as the Swan (or Stranger); Lynn Seymour as the Queen.
61 *Swan Lake*, Act Four. Final tableau, with Isabel Mortimer as the Queen holding the body of the dead Prince (Scott Ambler), while Adam Cooper as the Swan (above) holds the young Prince (Andrew Walkinshaw).

great star, I really think she's happiest in rehearsal. She loves being part of a team, she laughs about herself, is very unpretentious, and the whole company loved having her around. She loved the AMP way of working, which draws extensively on the performer's own idea of a role. But she's also amazing during a run of a show. She's extremely inventive, and at almost every performance she'd have some new idea; usually she'd ask me what I thought, but occasionally she'd suddenly try something out-rageous on stage without having told anybody else that she was going to. She wrote me a letter to say that she felt like the Sleeping Beauty awakened – which made me feel very proud.

During the West End run we launched two other performers in the role of the Swan: Floyd Hendricks and Adam Cooper's brother Simon. They were both really good – and it was interesting to see how all of them quickly won a number of devoted admirers. Just now we're pre-paring Keith Roberts, from American Ballet Theatre, to dance the role during the Broadway run. On a purely technical level, he's very beautiful to watch. Finding people who can dance both the White and the Black Swan is not easy. Dancers are usually good at one or the other!

(Conversations 1998–99)

278

9

The West End, Los Angeles
and Broadway

ALASTAIR MACAULAY: *In autumn 1996 your* Swan Lake *was transferred to a West End theatre. There it ran for 120 performances: the longest run ever known in London for any production of a full-length dance classic. Of course, certain plays or musicals enjoy unbroken runs for years on end. But dance shows seldom command that kind of drawing power, and their expenditure of physical energy is, of course, infinitely larger. Your West End run of* Swan Lake *broke various precedents established by productions of Tchaikovsky's* The Sleeping Beauty *(or* The Sleeping Princess*) such as the Diaghilev staging at the Alhambra Theatre in 1921, the Sadler's Wells Ballet's opening production at the Royal Opera House, Covent Garden, in 1946, and the London Festival Ballet production which launched the first Nureyev Festival at the London Coliseum in 1976.*

You brought in a new audience to dance, and did it in part by appealing to the audience that might usually go to musicals. Since then, AMP has produced shows much along Cameron Mackintosh or Andrew Lloyd Webber lines. Like them, an AMP show has a logo for mass publicity; it has merchandise; it has a story that the audience more or less knows already; it has an album they can buy and play at home. What do you feel about this?

MATTHEW BOURNE: Selling a show as we do is something quite deliberate. It wasn't brought to us by the Cameron Mackintosh organization. I remember us saying, very early on in the original planning stage for *Swan Lake*, 'We need a Cameron Mackintosh-type logo for this piece', something that very much stamps an image on the production. In fact, that logo's changed a fair amount as we've gone to different places.

AM: *You began, in 1995, with a naked man (Scott Ambler) embracing a swan. Ballet people may connect that with famous photographs of Anna Pavlova in her garden embracing one of her pet swans; but this image very obviously had intimate psychosexual suggestions.*

MB: Yes. When it went into the West End, there was a lot of nervousness about a naked man. I don't know why! Naked men are used in advertising an enormous amount these days; and, as far as I'm concerned, ours was a quite innocent image.

Still, that became fainter for the West End publicity. He became less obviously a naked man; he sank more into the water-like background. In the foreground, however, we put the eyes – Adam's eyes – staring out at the camera from under his brow like a swan. Next, for Los Angeles, he disappeared altogether. They were nervous of it looking like a ballet; to make it look like a musical, they wanted Adam Cooper in the black leather trousers as their main image, set against a red background. And now, as we're going on to Broadway, I've insisted on going back to the eyes. The naked man holding a swan has disappeared altogether. The lettering of *Swan Lake* is similar to the original lettering, but now with water beneath it.

AM: *Did you ever think of logos before* Swan Lake?

MB: Yes, I think we always tried to stamp our pieces with a kind of single image: either a logo or a very strong poster. (See *Deadly Serious*, for example.) The lettering for the name Adventures in Motion Pictures was itself a logo, and we've retained that more or less the same over the years. So we were always very image-conscious.

As you know, the logo's only one of many things that go towards making a production more commercial. You mentioned subject-matter, stories people feel they already know. There obviously is a nod to commercialism there. There are certain titles you feel you can sell. What you actually do with that title can be any number of things: you can be creative within that structure. But if we'd retitled *Swan Lake* or *Cinderella*, it probably wouldn't have sold so well. That's a problem for a lot of ballet companies and for people presenting musicals. I'm sure *Phantom of the Opera* sells well partly because it's got an exciting title: it sounds great before you even buy your ticket, and it's a story you're vaguely familiar with.

I think that, if you're presenting a completely new story, that shouldn't put you off. But you have to consider that it should be a less expensive production, something that's less risky and maybe at a smaller venue. You can still make a success of a more experimental production, but you have to bear in mind that maybe you won't get the bigger audiences that you might with a well-known title. Recently I've been having conversations with Katharine about possible future projects, and at one point she remarked, 'I don't think I could sell, in the West End, a production called *Giselle*, for example.' If we were to do a version of *Giselle*, either it would be retitled, or we would do it in a smaller venue or in a repertory house.

AM: *Is this why you re-titled* La Sylphide *as* Highland Fling?
MB: We'd always invented our own titles. Because that was designed to be a small-scale or middle-scale touring production, it seemed to go along the same lines as our previous work; and so I didn't feel nervous about it. *La Sylphide* wouldn't have been a title that would have sold very easily to a general audience. *Highland Fling* sounds more colloquial, accessible, and has a nice double meaning.

AM: *Ashton found that his 1961 ballet* Les Deux Pigeons *did a lot better business when he anglicized the name to* The Two Pigeons.
Tell me: when you're planning a new show for AMP, how much do you think, 'I want to go back to the old story' and how much do you think, 'I've got to do a completely different take on it'?
MB: I don't really see the point in re-creating things that have gone before. We're not a ballet company, choosing to do a new production of *Giselle* or *La Bayadère*, because in that context you have the choreographic text. You can dress it up in different costumes and sets, but basically you're producing *Giselle* – whereas our mission and our job as a company is not to do that. We're not maintaining any kind of tradition. I would never feel that anything we do had any boundaries as to what we could do with it. We would choose something simply because it had a good story, structure, music, whatever – and then we'd work with that.

I'm consciously trying to appeal to an audience that doesn't have background knowledge about what they're seeing. You may feel, 'When I go and see *Les Misérables*, I know the book', but most people who go and see it don't know the book. There isn't the assumption there that we're all going to see that favourite old story of ours.

In some ways, with our shows, the problem is getting people to actually buy their ticket, come and sit down and watch it. Once they're there –

though I don't feel I've got to make it easy for an audience, necessarily – I do want to make it clear enough for them to feel comfortable watching it. I don't want something that mystifies them in any way. Obviously, a more sophisticated dance audience will accept a lot more in terms of abstraction than your average West End musical audience; but you can satisfy both of those sets of people, if you're clever and careful about what you do. I'm conscious of that.

AM: *What you do to* Cinderella *could, I suppose, be compared to a show like* Miss Saigon. *That's a reworking and updating of* Madam Butterfly; *your* Cinderella *is taken out of fairyland and put into the 1940s.*
MB: I think it is a similar approach, yes. But, when I saw *Miss Saigon,* I didn't know it was based on *Madam Butterfly.* I only realized that towards the end – and only because I'd seen *Butterfly.* It just seemed an original story to me at first, as I'm sure it does to many people; and that has new music, whereas we are using an established score.

AM: *But I and many people have certain qualms about big commercial West End shows. To me, a Lloyd Webber or Boublil–Schönberg musical doesn't just tell me a story I'm likely to know beforehand; it's also going to make me feel things that I've felt before. It sets out to press feel-good triggers in me: which I resent. It feels synthetic.*
Now that is not my reaction to Swan Lake *or* Cinderella, *or to musicals of the 1920s, 1930s, and 1940s. Am I being unfair to Lloyd Webber and Cameron Mackintosh? Do you like their shows more than I do?*
MB: It's difficult for me to say, because I admire so many of the people who have created them. I think you yourself would except certain Cameron Mackintosh shows from that 'synthetic' label. I'm interested in what draws a big audience, and I can see why these big musicals do. If you let yourself go with them, they can be highly entertaining and emotional. But yes, I find several of them manipulative in many ways. I call them 'push-button shows'. It feels as if there's no human involvement, because the technical wizardry going on is on such a scale that the human aspect of the show disappears. You've got these enormous sets and these miked voices and great sound; you can kill a show through doing that. *Martin Guerre,* for example, was actually a small-scale show, with some very fine music at times; but it was overblown into a big West End production, with enormous moving pieces of scenery. It's really very folksy, and probably would have worked better in somewhere like the Cottesloe. A

Théâtre de Complicité type of production could have worked equally well for that.

One of the charms of an AMP show, I think, is that we don't have that enormous amount of money to spend. We don't make things overblown; we don't lose the charm of Lez Brotherston's designs. His work does make you feel that you're going places, and he allows for us to do a lot, but actually it's done quite cheaply – and, inevitably, more inventively, because he has to make the most of limited means. Eventually, I think that's more theatrical: making something out of nothing, or making something spectacular out of limited means and limited possibilities.

AM: *Elsewhere we've been talking of dancers as mainly drawn from two trainings – ballet or modern. But there is almost a third genre: showbiz dance. Dancers who work in this category may be chiefly trained in jazz dance style. Some dancers work entirely in musicals, with a probably more hybrid training that will help them get through the varied requirements of this genre. Do you get any of those dancers coming to your AMP auditions?*

MB: We have had, but we've never yet accepted anyone whose prime experience is in West End musicals. This may change on Broadway, where the crossover of dancers is much wider. There you get dancers with very good dance training, ballet and/or modern, who've just moved into that area.

What do I admire in those dancers is their doing eight shows a week and giving it their full professional attention at every performance. This is something we've had to learn to do, and it's been a hard slog, actually. You go and see a West End show, it's some way into the run, and you're amazed at the enthusiasm and energy that's coming from the stage. Yet these people have been doing this for months and months, eight shows a week. At AMP meetings many times, I've said: 'I realize you're all here with various talents and for various reasons; but what you have to ask yourself, having done the West End, is: do you personally want to be doing eight shows a week? Is that something that suits you as a performer?' Because we have experienced a lot of problems with people getting tired and depressed, never having done a show that many times. It's a special skill that needs to be learned. In ballet companies, maybe you do a role three times in a year if you're lucky, and it always feels like a special occasion when you dance a particular role. To do it many times requires a different skill – that's what those commercial dancers have got.

They also have a performance ability that is very useful for certain aspects of what we do. So I don't rule out that kind of dancer at all; but they need the appropriate training to do the kind of work we're doing. It can't just be a jazz training; it needs to have covered other things.

AM: *Do you find that you've now got a company that has developed a West End style, a commercial-theatrical style?*
MB: I don't feel we're especially West End in style; I don't feel that we've changed in that respect. The performers have changed and have learnt how to project and how to maintain a long run. They know that they have to find ways of making the roles work for them, time and time again, and the dancing as well. They're mentally more prepared for it and are happy to find new things in what they're doing.

At times, I must admit I do wish for more presentation and style in the movement. There are things like the blue couples in *Cinderella* where I've often felt, 'I wish it was danced for the audience a little more; I wish it wasn't so internalized.' That's purely about just grabbing the audience. We talk about this quite a lot, but it's not something that comes very naturally to a number of the dancers. Early on, when doing *Swan Lake* in the theatres bigger than most dancers were used to performing in, we had to keep reminding them that there were people sitting way up there in 'the gods'. Often in *Swan Lake* it was 'the gods' that was sold out at every performance, because a lot of our audience were quite young and bought the cheapest tickets in the Upper Circle; so we had to acknowledge them. But you forget when you're used to performing in small theatres with people all in front of you on one level.

AM: *We've been talking largely of your appearances in Britain. What appearances did AMP make abroad before it took* Swan Lake *to Los Angeles and Broadway?*
MB: Very few. I've told you about our unsuccessful trip to Holland back in 1988! And that was the only foreign appearance in our first five years.

Unlike several British modern-dance groups of the same kind of size and experience, AMP never used to appeal to the producers who put on modern dance around the European continent. This was to do with our emphasis on humour. We were seen by the Europeans to be lightweight, entertaining: therefore not good. One exception was in 1995 when we took *Highland Fling* to Italy; that went down moderately well there. But anyone who ever came to see us, from France in particular, invariably hated our work.

AM: *The Channel can still be wider than the Atlantic.*

MB: But that situation – of European presenters not being interested in us – has all changed since *Swan Lake*. We've had quite a number of invitations, including several from France, to take the production there; and in 2000 we plan to tour it around Europe. I'll be interested to see how it goes down there!

We always felt, mind you, that we were likely to be more appreciated outside Europe. In 1993, we took *Deadly Serious* to the Hong Kong Festival, where it had quite a success.

AM: *How did your association with Los Angeles come about?*

MB: Soon after *Swan Lake* opened at Sadler's Wells, Gordon Davidson, the artistic director of the Center Theater Group at the Ahmanson in LA, came to see it; and we began to develop what has proved a brilliant relationship with him. He felt a great affinity for our work straight away. Because of his enthusiasm for our production, LA was the first place that *Swan Lake* visited, straight after its season in 1996–97 in the West End. We had a wonderful season there in spring 1997. Then, early in 1998, Gordon came to see *Cinderella* during its final week in the West End. We told him straight away how we wanted to work further on the production; and he worked with Katharine Doré to enable us to do just that – to spend six weeks early in 1999 rehearsing it afresh, and to spend money on revising the sets and costumes.

Cinderella in LA – here we're speaking in June 1999 – was a very happy experience for us. The dancers really began to love doing the show for its own sake; they also really enjoyed the accommodation they had there; and, once it opened, they felt very appreciated there too. Currently, we're hoping to present our *Nutcracker* in LA over Christmas 2000; and, as with *Cinderella*, we hope to be able to reconsider the whole production this time and revise it as we see fit. To have people like Gordon and Katharine who'll work this way is the best news.

AM: *Before* Cinderella *in LA, you took* Swan Lake *to Broadway. Then, after* Cinderella *in LA, you won a whole series of New York awards for* Swan Lake. *But what did New York mean to you in advance?*

MB: You know, New York and Los Angeles were the first two cities I visited in America, in 1979, when I was nineteen. I went to theatres in one and to movie studios in the other. I especially remember the things I saw in New York: Angela Lansbury in *Sweeney Todd*, Patti LuPone in *Evita*, Bob Fosse's *Dancin'*, and the opening night of *Sugar Babies*, with Ann Miller and Mickey Rooney (the first-night audience included Andy Warhol, Shirley MacLaine, Eartha Kitt, and – rarest of all – Rita Hayworth).

When I began training as a dancer, New York took on another meaning for me – because it's known as the dance capital of the world. In 1986, when *Transitions* appeared in Hong Kong, we made friends with dance students from the Juilliard School, who were also performing there. In February 1987, I went over to stay in New York for four weeks with one of them, Kirk Ryder, who's still a good friend today. That was when I began to sample the dance life of New York. I took class with the Limòn company; I went to as many dance performances – ballet and modern – as I could; and I even performed in a new piece (choreographed by another Juilliard graduate friend, Torbjorn Stenberg) at Dance Theatre Workshop.

Since then, I've made several visits to New York, and today it's both a theatre city and a dance city for me. Early in 1997, I went there with Sam Mendes and Scott Ambler for auditions for *Cabaret*. I hadn't choreographed Sam's original London production of *Cabaret* at the Donmar Warehouse, but now, after working together on *Oliver!*, we were hoping to work together on the New York production. In the event, because of making *Cinderella*, I just wasn't able to do *Cabaret* as well, but, a year later, Etta Murfitt and Iain Webb and I were able to attend the first night of *Cabaret* on Broadway; we were in New York at the time to do auditions for *Swan Lake* on Broadway.

So I had quite a sense of New York by the time we took *Swan Lake* there in September 1998 – but I'd never presented any work of my own there.

AM: *Do you think there is a difference between the West End and Broadway? Between theatre in America and in Britain?*
MB: The gap between British performers in the West End and American performers on Broadway has narrowed a lot in recent years, owing to the growth of the large-scale Mackintosh–Lloyd Webber musical. The standard of singing is certainly much higher. Because the shows are so long-running, there is a variety of shows for people to perform in. You can make a very good living from just show-hopping. People will do a

year in *Cats*, then a year in *Saigon*. So there's work there, and the training and performers have come up to scratch.

The interesting thing in America – having auditioned a lot of people – is that the community of dancers in New York is much more integrated than here. Here it's very much the three camps – contemporary, ballet and commercial – and there's very little mixing between them. In New York there seems to be a mutual respect between dancers. There is a greater respect for dancers all round; ballet dancers there have respect for contemporary and commercial dancers, and contemporary dancers are interested in watching ballet. We don't have that here.

AM: *That's partly because the two leading ballet choreographers, Balanchine and Robbins, had both worked extensively on Broadway. Agnes de Mille is actually more famous for her work on Broadway shows than on her ballets for American Ballet Theatre. The leading modern-dance choreographers – Martha Graham, Merce Cunningham, Paul Taylor, Twyla Tharp, Mark Morris – all have shown immense respect for Balanchine's work and for some other areas of ballet; and some have worked on Broadway: Tharp, Morris, Lar Lubovitch, for example. So there is a long tradition of crossover there. Many of the leading modern dancers take class with the ballet teacher Maggie Black – and are proud to say so in their programme biographies.*

MB: Yes; that's another thing. A lot of American contemporary dancers, if they're going to do a class, would rather do a ballet class. Here, there's a lot of discussion about where you can find a good contemporary class, which is very difficult to find. You do all this contemporary dance training in college – and then suddenly you're out and you find it's actually a lot easier to find a ballet class. To keep your training going is very difficult if you're a purely contemporary dancer.

AM: *That about Los Angeles? Did you find that LA audiences reacted to* Swan Lake *differently?*

MB: They did. The LA audiences had no preconceptions about us; they had no preconception of what we would be like at all. Our big fear was that the humour wouldn't work, but actually it worked better than it had done in London. I think they find the Royal satire aspect of it very funny. The little ballet in Act One they found hilarious; it went down much better there than it's ever gone here in London. Of course, they're very happy to react vocally, and they're very emotionally easy with things, in the sense that they're quite happy to cry at the end and not be ashamed. I think we also get more applause breaks there, because they're more readily reactive. As soon as any lights are lowered or something finishes, there will be applause.

AM: *Many Royal Ballet dancers remember that, particularly on the big tours of America in the 1960s and 1970s, there were passages of choreography which won applause – right through the music – that never would at home. (One was the 'cow-hops' in* Giselle; *another was the concentric rings revolving in opposite directions in Ashton's old garland dance in* The Sleeping Beauty.) *The roar of applause always made the dancers much more proud of the choreography.*

MB: That has happened to us too. In the West End there was always an 'eggy' moment after the Act One duet for the Queen and the Prince: no applause, though we'd have liked it, to cover the scene change. But in LA they'll fill any gap for you with applause, and that keeps the show flowing. However, applause for particular steps, which is common in New York dance performances, I find a little crass, particularly in more profound or serious work.

A lot of the audience in Los Angeles came as part of a subscription system, and hadn't specifically booked to see our *Swan Lake*. They can be quite conservative as well, but we found them very open-minded.

At this point, I'm still viewed in this country very much as a choreographer; in America I'm viewed as a director. Here I get offered choreography on shows where they've already got a director on board; but I'm really not interested in that any more, despite my pleasure in working on *Oliver!*. I need the whole vision, the whole piece, to come from me. This isn't a vanity thing. It's just because, otherwise, I know I can't do the choreography I'd like to do.

AM: *So what was your feeling about being on Broadway?*
MB: New York doesn't have London's variety of theatre. And theatres there are less characterized, less individual. There's a generalized theme-park feeling about New York theatres that I don't enjoy.

On the other hand, New York audiences can be very warm. To have a hit there is just as exciting as you might hope. I have to say that, for those of us involved in administration, there were some terrible technical problems backstage that at first spoilt our pleasure in working in New York. We presented the show with a mixed British and American cast, and the British dancers had a very good time there. And in due course, we all did.

Adam Cooper, Will Kemp and Floyd Hendricks all had great successes as the Swan – as did Scott and Ben Wright as the Prince, and Fiona Chadwick and Isabel Mortimer as the Queen. Some company dancers took leading roles for the first time: Ewan Wardrop and Tom Ward as the Prince, Detlev Alexander as the Swan. We'd hoped, during the run, also to present both Lynn Seymour and Natalia Makarova as the Queen, but both of them were injured. So Marguerite Porter, whom I'd often seen in her career with the Royal Ballet, joined us at quite short notice and ended up staying with us throughout most of our run: she was great to work with, and made the role her own.

AM: *Unlike the theatre world, the dance world in New York is larger and livelier than London's. Less so, however, than it used to be. I don't mean that smugly; London's dance world has not generally grown in scale or consequence, though it has become less narrow-spirited. New York used to be a Mecca that gave added vitality to the whole dance world. The deaths of the choreographers George Balanchine, Antony Tudor, Martha Graham and Jerome Robbins during the 1980s and 1990s have cast a pall.*

Meanwhile, largely for economic reasons, it becomes no easier to put on a dance production in New York: so that even the choreographers who live and work there can only present their work in New York very occasionally – often after presenting it a good many times on tour. What is it like being a foreign choreographer bringing a big dance production to New York?

MB: In *Swan Lake*, our experience was simply that the production – wherever we've done it – just got better each time we did it. The Moth ballet, the duet for the Prince and the Queen, the Soho scene: these went down better than ever in New York. This was partly to do with the audiences, but partly also because we'd kept learning how to get reactions.

At first, during previews, there was something of a 'Come on, show us' feeling in the audience. We felt we had more to prove. But that changed.

It was wonderful to be in New York for months on end. Several former Balanchine ballerinas – Allegra Kent, Merrill Ashley, Lourdes Lopez – were very enthusiastic about the production, and expressed a lot of interest in performing the role of the Queen. And Mikhail Baryshnikov was very supportive. He threw two parties for us: one during our period of previews and one on closing night. He'd already loved *Swan Lake* when he'd seen it in the West End. To have him – one of the greatest dancers of the century, and an inspiration to all dancers – behaving as a friend to the company in New York from the first meant a huge amount.

AM: *How did the American dancers in the company prove in performance?*

MB: Most of them were terribly professional in approach, and most or all of them loved doing it. They were a real mixture. One man had been in the Martha Graham company, and another, Krissy Richmond, got leave from the US touring production of *Chicago* to perform with us. (She played the Queen at the end of our run, and we nicknamed her 'The Fosse Queen'.) Keith Roberts, who played the Swan, was much more animal in his interpretation than we had anticipated – we had been awed by the purity of his dancing in audition – and I have the feeling that he surprised himself.

But I learned just how unusual, for all of them, our style was. Not just its acting demands; its dance style too. They were used to attack, to projecting the movement with lots of bite. And they found it hard to pace it, and to catch some of its fluidity.

Mind you, I wonder: could anyone else spot the difference between our British and our American dancers? If so, I never heard people talking of it.

AM: *Let's talk about all the New York awards you ended up winning. You won the Best Choreographer and Best Director of a Musical awards from three different bodies: the Outer Critics Circle, the Drama Desk, and the Tonys. That's six; and the Drama Desk also gave* Swan Lake *a Unique Theatre Experience Award. Also, for his contribution to* Swan Lake, *Lez Brotherston won an Outer Critics' Circle Award for Best Costumes, two Drama Desk Awards, for Best Costumes and Best Set, and a Tony Award for Best Costumes. Did any awards mean more to you than others?*

MB: Yes: the Astaire Award, for Concept, Direction and Choreography. I was thrilled to win it, and I had really wanted to win it. What a lovely thing to happen! Obviously Fred Astaire has always meant a lot to me. His widow was there for the award ceremony, and it was presented to me by Shirley MacLaine, who'd made a special trip to New York for the event. Of all the awards ceremonies, it was the most modest and the most pleasant. And I was very touched that Shirley said that my choreography represented the past, the present and the future. Adam won an Astaire Award too.

Obviously, the Tony Awards receive the most attention of all, and, coming last, there's a special sense of climax about them. The Tony committee, however, had deemed *Swan Lake* ineligible to win an award as a musical, or as a special event, or as a revival. So we were in an odd position. That was why, when I won Best Director of a Musical prize, I said in my speech, 'I'm astonished to win the award for Best Director of a Musical that's not a musical!' and then I made a face. I just meant it with gentle sarcasm; I meant that *Swan Lake* is musical theatre in the same way that dance shows like *Fosse!* are. The audience got my point, but I was reported in the press – in New York and London – as if I was simply astonished to have broken a category.

There was so much surprise that I'd won the Tonys that I almost felt I had to defend myself. If that makes me sound arrogant, please remember I'd just won the Best Director and Best Choreographer prizes at two other ceremonies. So I couldn't be *that* surprised to win the Tonys. I was, however, very proud.

(Conversations 1998–99)

10

Cinderella
1997

Idea

ALASTAIR MACAULAY: *You had choreographed* Cinderella *at the age of eight or thereabouts. What would* Cinderella *have been to you then? Had you seen a pantomime of it? Or the Disney film?*

MATTHEW BOURNE: At that point, the Disney film. *Cinderella,* as a pantomime, I remember seeing later: one, in the late 1970s – at what is now the Prince Edward Theatre – with Twiggy as Cinderella, Steptoe and Son as the ugly sisters, and Christopher Gable as the Prince.

AM: *As a stage dance work,* Cinderella *must have entered your life with Ashton's 1948 version for the Royal Ballet? It's still in repertory today.*

MB: Yes: around 1980. I saw it many times in that decade. The performances of Antoinette Sibley and Anthony Dowell – both then in their forties, and both glorious – were particular events. One of the things that was rewarding about seeing it again and again was getting to know the music, because at first the Prokofiev score seemed very difficult to me. It didn't seem like the kind of music I'd been used to in other ballets, but it grew on me. I loved Ashton's daring in having male performers as the Ugly Sisters; it was a surprise to see that in ballet at the Opera House, especially in a work otherwise along the lines of a fairytale classic.

But I was also very taken by Ashton's dance choreography in his *Cinderella.* I was fascinated by the changing patterns and intricate construction in the Star section; and I loved the Seasons solos, which seemed to express the four seasons so well. That, in a way, was an inspiration: expressing the essence of an idea – Spring, for example – in short pure-dance solos. I also loved the little theatrical strokes, such as Fairy

Autumn throwing leaves at the beginning of her solo. Particularly in *Cinderella*, I loved Ashton's use of the upper body and the back. In Cinderella's solo, there are little tips or arches backwards on pointe that are like nothing else in ballet. I thought that was so odd; I took great pleasure in things like that. He also made amazing theatrical effects by pure dance means. When Cinderella entered the ballroom coming down the staircase on pointe, looking straight into the air ahead of her – that made a big impression on me, as did the way, at midnight, that the whole population of the ballroom seemed to become like the mechanism of some chiming clock, with her trapped in the middle. I think now that getting to know that music was a big reason – maybe the main reason, as I go over it in my head now – for going back again and again. There's some sort of mystery, there's a dark side, to that music – which I tried to capture when I did eventually do it myself. I think it brought to Ashton's version a depth that made you want to see that again. There's a seriousness in the music that makes the choreography more alluring and mysterious.

AM: *In the meantime, during the 1980s or 1990s, had you seen any opera or theatre versions of* Cinderella?
MB: I saw the National Theatre pantomime during the mid-1980s, with Robert Stephens. During the last five years I've seen, on video, the Rodgers and Hammerstein musical. But nothing very inspirational.

The story itself has all you need. When you're looking for ideas, you just have to go back to the story, to make parts of it touching, parts of it magical: the transformation of Cinderella, her leaving for the ball.

AM: *Did the idea of choreographing* Cinderella *yourself – after your childhood version – only come to you after the success of* Swan Lake?
MB: Because I love it as a story, it's something I certainly would have decided to do sooner or later. I think the fact of the Ashton version being around always put me off doing it. It took the success of *Swan Lake* to give me the confidence, to feel that I could make any impression in a work that had already been done so well. In some ways, *Swan Lake* gave us a big problem: how could we follow a success like that? I wanted a production that would take us back to the old company way of working, with everyone intimately involved in their characters at the rehearsal stage, and I felt *Cinderella* would be good in that respect.

62 *Cinderella*. Publicity poster. Two famous photographs of the 1941 Blitz in London show St Paul's Cathedral silhouetted, as here, against the surrounding destruction, and the empty ballroom shoes outside the bombed Café de Paris.

All of us felt a great pressure on us after *Swan Lake*. There was a sense that we should do something on the same scale and should try to equal or surpass its success; people had already forgotten that our previous most successful productions, *Deadly Serious*, *Nutcracker* and *Highland Fling*, had been much smaller-scale, with far fewer performances. Once I thought of *Cinderella* as our next production, the idea of setting it in London during the War came quickly; and then a lot fell into place. The 1940s setting would make it just different enough, would make it my own. The story included plenty of different characters, which would be good for the company; and I would just use the music to inspire me.

AM: *Where did the wartime setting come from?*
MB: I read a book on Prokofiev and started reading anything I could find on *Cinderella* itself. What stood out was the time when it was written – that made me listen to the score again. Now I heard it very much as a 1940s piece, a wartime piece, and very filmic too. Prokofiev wrote famous film music, and loved films; you yourself have argued that some of his ballet music is really the best film music ever written. There were some bits that quite strongly put into my mind the idea of air-raids and bombings, especially just before she goes off to the ball. There's a section that sounds very much to me like lights flashing on and off, a feel of sirens. When I listened again to the end of the music for the nightmare chimes at midnight, I could feel, in the music, things crashing down, as if after a bomb. I thought, 'If we've got those strong points within the score that can say those things, then I think certainly we could build the rest of it around the idea.' Our *Cinderella* is still a story of romantic love, but it's romantic love set against a dark period in history, against all kinds of twentieth-century adversity; and it's not a story of Miss Perfect meeting Prince Perfect.

It also helped me that Ashton hadn't used all the music, especially in Act Three; I became very interested in the ideas that I got from the music he hadn't used. The deeper I went into it, the less I heard Ashton's version in the music. Now there are several sections in which I really can't remember what exactly he did with the music.

Apart from the music, I got more and more ideas just by thinking about and researching the War. I knew quite suddenly that my *Cinderella* would occur during the London Blitz, and I thought more and more about that. My parents were young then, so I'd heard about it from them; and I'd seen films. Certain images became very important, like the famous photograph taken after a bomb had dropped on the Café de Paris and, on top of the rubble, you see a pair of ballroom shoes. When you're working on a version of *Cinderella,* you have to think carefully about all kinds of crucial plot details: the shoes, the strokes of midnight, and so on. The more I reconceived these in the context of the Blitz, the more of an inner life and momentum my *Cinderella* began to have in my own mind.

AM: *I can think of one other Ashton ballet that connects to* Cinderella: *namely,* La Valse. *In 1996, I remember coming across you at a ballet evening at Covent Garden that ended with that 1958 Ashton ballet to Ravel's score; and you said to me, 'Yes, I love it so much, and I'm going to come back and bring Lez Brotherston to see it because I want part of my* Cinderella *to look like that.' This really surprised me, because many people complain about André Levasseur's costumes for Ashton's ballet – very old-style* Come Dancing, *they say; not many people find it, choreographically, one of Ashton's top-drawer ballets. Yet Anthony Dowell must share your taste, because it has been revived a surprising number of times during his regime as artistic director of the Royal Ballet.*
MB: It's a glorious piece. Very MGM, I find! It uses so many people and it's such a spectacle. But I also love anything waltzy. I don't think it's great choreography. I know people think it's a bit throwaway, but I do think it's a wonderful, glorious experience, and I feel that the atmosphere it creates is something quite special, especially the smoky atmosphere at the beginning.

AM: *It's not throwaway at all. It's very tightly choreographed.*
MB: It always feels like the best thing in the evening for me when I see it. There's an extraordinary doom-laden feeling amid all its jubilation, and that was what I had in my mind with *Cinderella* in the ballroom scene. I wanted it to look somewhat like a 1940s ballet in costumes, to look Beatonesque.

AM: *You eventually cast three dancers in the role of Cinderella, since the show ran for eight performances a week, but most publicity went to the first-cast Cinderella, who was Adam Cooper's partner, the Royal Ballet's young soloist, Sarah Wildor. At what point did you decide to use her?*
MB: Quite early on. I had liked her dancing very much in a lot of pieces at the Royal Ballet, and she stood out in a lot of minor roles, with an

individual approach to movement. I always felt she was a star, and had seen her do leading roles in several ballets: MacMillan's *Manon,* where it was good to see her handle the sexuality so well; MacMillan's *The Invitation,* which she danced so well with Adam. And I loved the quality of movement she showed in Ashton roles: Titania in *The Dream,* the ballerina in *Rhapsody.* Having met her, I felt that she was not your average ballerina type. She's from Southend; she can be quite plain-speaking and down-to-earth. Things like that impressed me about her.

AM: *So, as you're starting to cast your production, you decide to use Sarah Wildor and Adam Cooper from the Royal Ballet, the Royal Ballet School-trained Will Kemp – whom you liked so much doing the Swan that you decided to give him the role of the Angel – and the famous dramatic ballerina Lynn Seymour, who had worked so well in your company in* Swan Lake. *That means that the four leading roles in your work, in the first cast, are taken by dancers from the Royal Ballet or Royal Ballet School stable. This is quite a change of dance material for you.*

MB: I can't say I was ever conscious of trying to get more ballet people, let alone more Royal Ballet people, into the company. It has been misinterpreted quite a lot, both in and outside the company. 'What is this company then?' people have said. 'I thought that we were building up something to do with a certain type of dancer doing the kind of work that we do; but then we bring in all these guests. Why can't you build up people from within and create your own stars?'

I can understand this feeling, but I didn't see it like that. For one thing, I think I have always built up people within the company, where it seems appropriate: Scott Ambler, Etta Murfitt, Maxine Fone, Ben Wright are just the leading examples. Will Kemp may have come from the Royal Ballet School, but the Royal Ballet wasn't going to give him a job. He took the risk of joining our company – nobody there encouraged him, quite the opposite – and now he has achieved greater fame and larger roles with us than any of his contemporaries whom the Royal Ballet School favoured more. Probably, he wouldn't have been right for the Royal; and almost certainly none of his contemporaries would be right for Adventures in Motion Pictures. As I've said before, most of the ballet people – Royal or otherwise – who now audition for us are just wrong for my work, whatever their strengths may be in other directions.

I remain very interested in ballet and hope there will be other ballets to follow; but the heart of my work for the foreseeable future is with

63 *Cinderella*. Sarah Wildor as Cinderella; Lynn Seymour as her Stepmother.
Pre-production photograph.

Adventures in Motion Pictures, and I'm quite clear that there is a strong
distinction between what it does and what ballet companies do. My
work with Adam, Sarah and Lynn came about because they expressed
an interest in my work. They happen to be the kind of exceptional artist
who can commute between the two genres.

Lynn, after all, is the prime example – being the foremost dance
actress of the last forty years. I always think she's one of those few
dancers who's completely accepted by the whole world of dance, like
Baryshnikov. Whereas a lot of contemporary dancers don't get the point
of such ballerinas as Antoinette Sibley or Darcey Bussell, they do with
Lynn Seymour. They completely respect and admire her, and it seems
to me that her home now is in this kind of work. If any company can
assure further life on stage for Lynn now, I hope ours is the one. Likewise, Adam and Sarah are known as the up-and-coming dancer-actors
of their generation.

Sarah apart, much of my policy in casting *Cinderella* was to give roles – find roles, invent roles, in some cases – for performers who had made an impression with *Swan Lake* or other AMP works. I knew I was going to have the character of the Pilot (the hero) played by Adam and Will, just as they had worked on the same role in *Swan Lake*. I also tried to have Simon Cooper in that role: we needed three casts, and he had worked very well as the Swan. He had had real rapport with Saranne Curtin as the Queen in *Swan Lake*; he's very tall and would have been, temperamentally, a good partner for her; but I think he didn't want to work on a production alongside his brother Adam and endure the inevitable sibling comparisons from the very beginning of the production.

Then, because Will had had particular success in *Swan Lake,* and because Emily (Pearcy) had become very popular with audiences as the Prince's Girlfriend, I wanted to give them roles in the first cast of *Cinderella*. We had won a new public, who had favourite performers, and I wanted to make a show that would give them a reason to come back and see it with multiple casts. So I purposely put Will in that first cast, with his own role; likewise Emily as a sister, and Scott Ambler, Ben Wright and Andrew Walkinshaw (who's not really a dancer, but had been such a good performer as the young Prince in *Swan Lake*) as brothers. Whether or not everybody noticed, *Cinderella* was to do, not with me moving in the direction of the Royal Ballet, but with returning Adventures in Motion Pictures to a more intimate, ensemble way of working.

AM: *At what point did you decide you were going to have a male angel?*
MB: Oh, quite early on. I knew I wanted something a bit different, and I was conscious of everyone expecting, after *Swan Lake,* some kind of gender-reversal. I can't tell you how often I heard the question 'Is Cinderella going to be a woman?' when we first said we were doing it. Well, I wanted the heroine female and the hero male. But when I realized that I didn't like the idea of a fairy godmother as a character, I thought of changing the gender there. I knew I did like the idea of a guardian angel.

AM: *Well, you're in good company. Rossini's Cinderella opera,* La Cenerentola, *has a male guardian angel too: a bass role.*
MB: I also wanted to create something that was, in a way, asexual. I didn't want the audience to feel that there was any kind of competition between this other man in her life and the man she falls in love with. So we tried not to make him of sexual interest to her. But there is in him a

sort of a caring, guiding force that's ambiguous: it could be for good or ill, but it's fateful. He saves her from the bombing, but then he is also around when the bomb does happen; and he enables her to find out new things about herself.

We thought of having him turn up in several different guises. That proved too hard to manage throughout; but in Act Three he also appears in the guise of the psychiatrist. I also wanted to give the sense, at the beginning of Act Three, that he's like the Angel of Death, and, at the end of Act Two, that his dance is bringing down the buildings all around. So there are two sides to the Angel, and that's what we worked on when we first started to do the movement for him.

The first time he appears, in Act One, is when Cinderella is being tormented by the family. The scene turns into a sort of nightmare, where they've all got invites that they're waving at her and pretending to give to her only to snatch them away. So she screams. I said to the three girls playing Cinderella, 'It's as if you're crying for help', and the Angel appears, suddenly, at the top of the fireplace.

AM: *Does it occur to you that – as you describe it – that's rather like what happens in some traditional* Nutcrackers? *Clara has been pursued by the mice, she screams for help, and then Drosselmayer appears – in some productions (including the 1892 original) at the top of the clock.*
MB: I hadn't thought of that. But it's true.

He then hypnotizes her, in a way, and leads her to the door – whereupon the Pilot enters and breaks the spell. We return to real time, and Cinderella looks after the Pilot; but we sense that it's the Angel who's brought him to her.

AM: *Cinderella always has stepsisters, but you chose to make a big role for her stepmother, who is not in all, or even most, versions of the story. You also gave her stepbrothers. How come?*
MB: One of the reasons behind the casting of the show was to go back to what I'd done in AMP's smaller shows, by having more intimate, family scenes. At the same time, I wanted in other scenes – the ballroom, for example – to use the larger scale and big dance impact we'd shown in *Swan Lake*. So I wanted, in the family scenes, more roles than just the usual two stepsisters. I had a lot of people to cast, and I thought it'd be good to surround Cinderella with a bigger family than usual. It would give us more characters and more ideas to play with, and would provide the chance for more people – with two or three casts in each

role – to have a go at creating and playing a character; and a large, noisy family would create a context in which Cinderella would keep being submerged.

AM: *When did you decide on such wartime details as the fact that the hero is a pilot?*

MB: At one point, we thought of making the Angel look like a pilot – because of the connotations of the air, the sky, from which he comes and through which he travels. But then, as we thought of the various armed forces in the war, we decided to make the hero a pilot because the Air Force was the most glamorous. Think how many World War Two movies are to do with the Air Force. We were looking for who would be Cinderella's dream man, and we thought a pilot would be the sort of person she might idolize. The Nureyev version of *Cinderella* is all about film history and film stars; and I think that, if that version hadn't existed, I – with my interest in film – might well have made Cinderella's hero/ boyfriend a film star. It's a logical idea, which Nureyev – although I don't enjoy his actual choreography – pursued intelligently as a producer.

64 *Cinderella*. Adam Cooper as the Pilot. Pre-production photograph.

I was also inspired by the film, *A Matter of Life and Death,* which furnished my *Cinderella* with quite a lot of ideas. David Niven was the model, costume-wise and look-wise. The Pilot's moustache and whole persona come from Niven.

AM: *You mention Nureyev's version. Tell me what other versions of the Prokofiev ballet* Cinderella *you studied.*
MB: I saw Nureyev's version on TV or video. Likewise Maguy Marin's version, which I thought was so beautiful. There's not a great deal of dancing of any kind in it. It's like a doll's house come to life. The whole thing's done with masks. It's terribly endearing. The characters become like children in a way, and the whole production has a wonderful child-like quality to it; but the Prokofiev music is edited a great deal, and an echo is put in at times. I'm not keen on the Nureyev version; I think it's overblown, and there are whole sections I really dislike. There's an incredibly long pas de deux in Act Three – when Cinderella and the hero have met again – that's just waffle; and the story doesn't make complete sense either.

AM: Cinderella *was originally a Soviet ballet. Did you do any homework on any Soviet productions?*
MB: I had a video of one odd little version. It was quite fun, but I didn't really get much from it. What I haven't been able to see is the original Lavrovsky production. Prokofiev composed his music with Galina Ulanova in mind, and – even though no Soviet version of *Cinderella* has had the impact the Lavrovsky–Ulanova version of *Romeo and Juliet* has had – I'm sure many features of the music would fall into place if one could see the original production.

AM: *Still, your production is often most successful when it hears something quite new in the score. Perhaps the individual biggest hit dance of your production occurs in Act One. It's a dance conceived by Prokofiev for Cinderella alone in the kitchen: it's always known in British ballet circles as 'the broom dance' because Ashton has her dancing with a broom as if it were her imaginary partner. You, however, have her dance with a tailor's dummy – who suddenly comes to life as the Pilot. Now he's as stiff and immobile as a dummy, now he's partnering her as a dream lover. It's nicely ambiguous, and it goes like a dream in the theatre. Did you conceive that beforehand? Or did it just emerge that way through rehearsals?*

MB: The Dummy Dance, as we call it, emerged out of a conscious decision to build up the part of the Pilot. Adam was cast in the role, and he was, with Lynn, our big star. He didn't demand anything, but I was conscious that he needed more to do. So we thought: 'Well, how can we introduce his character into Act One – when it normally appears only in Acts Two and Three? And how can we give them a duet early on, when they shouldn't really even meet until Act Two?' So we came up with that idea of an image that was in her mind – the image of the man that she's dancing with rather than him himself.

The logic of it is that she's already met him briefly, when he took shelter in the house, earlier in the act. He has obviously been injured, comes to the house, and knocks on the door. She shelters him in a side room. Meanwhile the family come back, put on the gramophone, have the dancing lesson and all that business; and then the stepmother finds him in the house. She's suspicious of Cinderella and realizes something's going on. So the Pilot comes out and introduces himself.

The stepmother throws him out of the house; she's livid that Cinderella has been harbouring some injured member of the armed forces; and that's when she's left on her own. She sees him in the dummy, does the Dummy Dance; and the dummy comes to life. Now, when Cinderella's alone, she dreams of him, not as a sick man but as a romantic hero. This dream image of him will return throughout Act Two. Only in Act Three do we again see the Pilot as he really is.

AM: *You never thought of having a Buttons in your* Cinderella?
MB: Cinderella's friend? Well, one of my original ideas was that she had imaginary friends. She was a lonely child whom everybody ignored, but she had imaginary friends that she would conjure up. Maybe they were friends from long ago who were now evacuated to the country or to other countries. They would have been in white and grey, dressed as wartime children; and they would have appeared in the room from time to time and would have played with her, or danced with her. I really liked the idea, but it would have been one, possibly confusing, element too many on stage.

AM: *As you describe it, it sounds rather like another MacMillan ballet –* Solitaire *– in which the heroine has these companions, who may be dream figures but who always leave her alone in the final resort.*

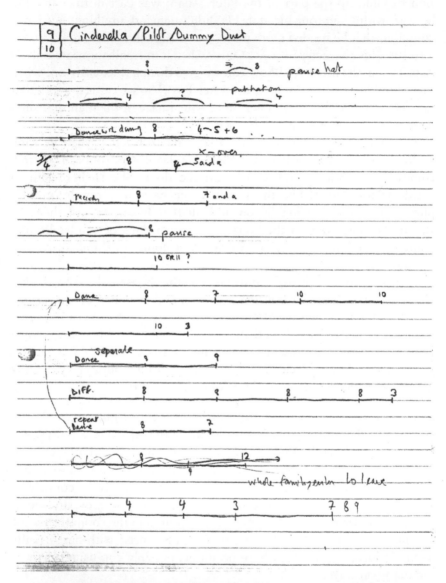

65 *Cinderella.* From Bourne's annotated breakdown of the score for Act One. The 'Cinderella/Pilot/Dummy' duet takes place to what is often known as Cinderella's 'broom dance' in more traditional versions of the ballet, notably Frederick Ashton's.

66 *Cinderella*. Adam Cooper and Sarah Wildor in the Act One 'Dummy' duet.
Rehearsal photograph.

MB: I haven't seen that, but another piece of his that has grown-ups
playing children, *Playground,* was one of the earliest pieces I saw, and
I very much enjoyed it. I loved all the psychology of it, and it was brilliantly performed; but, in particular, it made me interested in adults
playing children. It had a definite influence on my *Nutcracker*; and in
Cinderella I saw these evacuee children a bit like that – in shorts and
little dresses.

It's really the Angel who brings the fantasy into her life. Once I'd
given her the dance with the dummy, I thought, 'Well, we can't have
another thing that happens in her fantasy life before she goes to the ball,'
which is then followed by the family, having dressed to go to the ball
or New Year's Eve party that they're invited to, all leaving the house –
leaving her alone again. Now the Angel returns and entices her to follow
him outside into the street; but at some point within the dummy duet she
has lost her glasses. She doesn't see so well.

AM: *Had you always conceived her as bespectacled?*
MB: Yes – we wanted her to be quite frumpy.

AM: *The ballroom in which she – transformed into a glamorous dream image herself – dances with this dreamy war hero in Act Two gets bombed.*

In Act Three, she's had a breakdown; and the Pilot, who has a breakdown himself while looking for her, finds her when they're both in hospital. You make a lot of the hospital scenes, in which Cinderella is isolated from all her former life. Somehow, as we're talking about it, this connects to the third act of another ballet, one that Sarah Wildor has danced at Covent Garden: MacMillan's Anastasia. *The girl, who is the child of an important family – in this case, the Romanov dynasty – is seen in hospital. She's lost her home, everyone questions her identity, she's in torment. Was MacMillan's final hospital act anywhere in your mind?*

MB: I think it was, a bit. Especially since I'd seen Sarah in it fairly recently beforehand; but I'm always drawn to hospital and medical scenes with doctors and nurses, and I think MacMillan has been as well. We've got a bit of that in *Swan Lake* – the Prince having sinister treatments at the beginning of Act Four – which I choreographed before I ever saw *Anastasia*.

I do hate hospitals. I'm very frightened of going to the doctor or the dentist – anything like that. So probably that's why they keep reappearing in my work.

AM: *The words* film noir *were often bandied around in the publicity and reviews of your production. Did you really mean that genre as an inspiration for your* Cinderella?

MB: No. I'm not an enormous fan of *film noir* as a genre – though I'm not sure precisely what I understand by the term. I know a few, like *Double Indemnity*; and, if this qualifies, *Mildred Pearce*. I like them – but they're not an area I'm particularly drawn to. Usually *film noir* has a sort of dark, murderous or sinister storyline. I know my *Cinderella* has bleak elements, and certainly it has strong cinematic elements, but I don't think they're what real film buffs would call *noir*.

Several war movies did shape my idea of *Cinderella*. I've mentioned *A Matter of Life and Death*; there were others. Another idea I wanted to make at the end of the show is that Cinderella and the Pilot become part of the bigger story of the War. Their story begins to fade, and what takes over is lots of other little stories of other similar couples on the same railway platform. Well, this was a cue – as in *Town & Country* –

67 *Brief Encounter.* Celia Johnson and Trevor Howard in David Lean's wartime film (written by Noël Coward). The railway-station setting recurrent in the film helped to inspire the final scene of Bourne's third act, and near the end two minor characters are briefly seen to be re-enacting Johnson's and Howard's last farewell.

for a replay of *Brief Encounter,* of course! Celia Johnson and Trevor Howard, or the characters they play in that film, are just another couple on the same platform as Cinderella and the Pilot.

The whole feeling of the War – as I've understood it, partly from movies – led me to stress the intense, fleeting, dreamlike quality of wartime romance and fantasy, but also to show that these people were not really glamorous. They were ordinary mortals under stress in difficult circumstances. At the end, Cinderella and her Pilot – married – go off on the train together; but, though we've seen them be glamorous in their dream lives, they really aren't starry people now. They're just people at the station with a lot of other people. Cinderella's final scene with her father is emotional, but not a big demonstrative number. The feeling should be that she and the Pilot are perfect for each other. Nothing heroic about either of them. He's pleasant, but dressed quite drably; and so is she. They don't have to be a prince and a princess to have a happy-ending feel to it. It's more touching, in a way.

Then the Angel returns. She more or less thanks him, and he is happy to have brought them together; as happy as a not-quite-human Angel can be. Whereupon he promptly sees his next charge – the next girl he's going to look after – a similar-looking girl. Hopefully, you haven't noticed her until that point. She's been downstage, reading a book very quietly, for ages. She's quite sad-looking – and the Angel is advancing towards her. The train bearing Cinderella and her Pilot is just departing, as the curtain falls.

Scenario

ALASTAIR MACAULAY: *When did you start to prepare the production?*
MATTHEW BOURNE: I was working on it over the 1996–7 Christmas period while *Swan Lake* was still in the West End, and then when we took it to LA. But I think the initial meetings with Lez Brotherston – whom I always knew I wanted to design it – had begun in the summer of 1996. There were four of us involved in planning this production, and I had regular meetings with the other three: Scott Ambler, Adam Cooper and Lez.

I think that at first Lez thought it was odd to have Adam around. He thought of him only as a dancer; but I had several reasons. One: Adam had quietly had some very good ideas on *Swan Lake,* ideas that played very important roles in the eventual production. Two: he really seemed to enjoy that aspect of it. Three: since he was making a decision, at the time, about whether to leave the Royal Ballet or not, I thought that this – because it would give him something he could get his teeth into – would help him discover whether there was some kind of life outside the Royal that he could enjoy.

Meanwhile, I spent an equal amount of time working on the production myself. I would then present the ideas that I had to the other three, and see what they felt. Sometimes what I gave them, in fact, was not my ideas but my problems: 'I don't know what to do with this piece of music.' Again, that's where Adam can be very helpful. Whereas Scott and Lez had to get to know the score before they could be equally helpful in that area, I had only to say, 'What are we going to do with the Seasons music?' for Adam to understand completely what was concerning me. Largely because of the Ashton production, he knew the music well already. In the case of the Seasons, for example, he knew straightaway that they were a suite of four variations composed for solo dancers, he knew the nature of each piece of music. So he understood – because we weren't going to bring on a divertissement of Season fairies, and because we were going to keep the story going through this music that was essentially plotless – all the specific problems. Straightaway he would discuss the tempo and character of each piece of music with me and start to come up with ideas, or with further questions.

AM: *Take me through the basic narrative structure that you arrived at.*
MB: Act One is divided up a lot, because the music demands it. So we started with a Prologue. Then 'Meet the Family': a basic introduction to each character. A first solo for Cinderella follows, when she dances with one of the sister's fur jackets. Cinderella tries to get her father, who is wheelchair-bound, to recognize her and to give her some attention for the problems she has. Then comes the nightmarish sequence when the Stepmother and stepsisters and stepbrothers all torment her with their invitations to the ball. When Cinderella cries for help, the Angel appears. He brings the Pilot into the house.

Now all the various sisters' and brothers' boyfriends and girlfriends arrive. There's a whole scene using those characters. The mother puts on the gramophone, and gets them to dance her way. (We don't use recorded music here, of course – it goes on being played by the orchestra in the pit – but the characters on stage behave as if it was coming from the wind-up 78 record-player. All this is to the 'dancing lesson' scene that Prokofiev wrote for Cinderella's stepsisters.) The Stepmother finds the Pilot and throws him out. When Cinderella is alone again, she has a fantasy duet with a dummy. The family leave for the party.

The Angel reappears. The sequence which follows – which we call 'the blackout' – includes gas-mask dogs, as we called them (characters with snout-like gas masks on); a dance for airmen and planes that becomes more aggressive and turns into a dance of bombers; various imagery of the Blitz; then the air-raid itself, which goes into the 'departure waltz', in which Cinderella finally leaves with the Angel in the sidecar of his motor-bike.

Act Two starts with a 'back to life' dance. A bomb has dropped, and now the bodies are coming back to life. They're couples who've been in the ballroom. Then the family makes its entrance; the Stepmother's drunk. Several dances emerge from this situation. The Pilot, now glamorous and confident, enters with two colleagues; they do a 'heroes' dance. The Stepmother is very keen on him now, and makes him dance with her, in which everyone else follows. Cinderella arrives with the Angel: the grand waltz. Because it's all a dream scene, Cinderella's father now appears; he too is upright, composed and dignified. The ballroom couples – the blue couples, as we call them – dance, and Cinderella dances with the 'blue' men. There's a 'Refreshments' episode – which is basically the drunk dance of the family.

Now, outside the club, Cinderella and the Pilot have their big duet; and finally, back in the ballroom, the famous waltz comes in again. This leads up to midnight and the falling of the bomb. The Pilot finds Cinderella's shoe by the wrecked entrance to her house.

Act Three starts with the Angel of Death's dance. The people of London are living in fear, and the Angel passes amongst them, signalling their deaths. Most of the company are in the scene. As the Angel touches or passes these people in the street, they leave the stage. It suggests that, when he's touched them, they're dead.

We see the Pilot on the street with Cinderella's shoe, looking for her. There's an underground scene in which he's accosted by a prostitute. Up on the Embankment, he gets into trouble; then to the hospital. Cinderella has a memory solo, and the family comes to visit her. The Pilot is brought into the room next door. They find each other.

Finally, the Railway Station. You see various individual stories, then the family farewell, particularly between Cinderella and her father. She and the Pilot (newly-weds) depart on the train as the curtain falls.

AM: *You mentioned the idea you had of the Angel appearing in the Prologue. This wasn't the only idea you dropped, was it?*
MB: There was quite a big sub-plot at first, which we rehearsed and took into the preview performances before scrapping it. It was mainly a red herring. According to this sub-plot, beginning several years before the piece starts on stage, Cinderella, as a young girl, had seen or suspected that the Stepmother had killed her mother at a New Year's Eve party in her house; and that the Stepmother had got away with it, and had married Cinderella's father. The shock of this incident had made Cinderella lose her voice. She'd then blotted it out of her memory. This created a relationship of serious antagonism between Cinderella and her Stepmother; but we also thought that it could explain why the Stepmother

kept Cinderella away from society and wanted to hide her away when guests came round.

So we had a different prologue originally, which was great – except that nobody understood it! It opened with a gun-shot. Then through the gauze you saw the Stepmother (Lynn Seymour), standing halfway down the stairs in a fur coat. The picture you had was of her on the steps with a sort of smoking gun – while the mother was dead on the floor, by the fireplace. The clock was at midnight. Then the midnight chimes really rang out, and you saw Cinderella, as a little girl in a nightdress, in the background. Obviously, she had run in and seen this. It was a very tight scenario, which explained all kinds of details throughout the story. We'll talk about how and why we changed it later on.[1]

There were several other details that I wasn't always sure about. Having the father come to the ball in Act Two, for example: I thought that might be confusing, and I considered cutting it at one point. I kept it, largely for the reason that I wanted things to keep happening to Cinderella in the ballroom. I didn't want it just to be a scene of dancing without story; in my version, events have to keep occurring, even in the ballroom. In the event, it works well and helps to clinch the dreamlike nature of the whole scene.

Something else that I want to make clearer when I stage *Cinderella* again in 1999 is the whole blackout sequence outside the house towards the end of Act One. The idea of it was that she is following the Angel through the streets of London. We see it through her eyes – but her eyesight is bad. She hasn't got her glasses on, and we're in the blackout. So things that she would normally see on the street now become frightening. They take on different meanings to her. She feels threatened, that she's being attacked, perhaps. But we didn't make that clear enough in the London production, and I think it could be done a lot more clearly. We had people with torches to begin with. They were like wardens – that's fairly straightforward – but at the next stage, in which the people in gas masks appear to her like dogs with snouts, we need her to see their transformation. I think that can be done. We'll see. The whole blackout sequence should be more frightening.

AM: *Now, here you were working in opposition to, or despite, Prokofiev's intentions for this music.*

1 See pp. 345–7.

MB: Very much so. There are passages when I think *Cinderella* is hard to choreograph even when you are following Prokofiev's intentions; but this is the passage when it was at first hard to proceed because we were going against them.

AM: *It can't help that Prokofiev has anyway a peculiar conception of Spring and Autumn in particular: both quite aggressive and harsh.*
MB: But what I began to hear in the music was his emphasis on time. Those two Seasons have a quality of hectic speed; and since the whole ballet attends to the importance of time, leading up to the huge chimes of midnight at the end of Act Two, I began to hear how these scenes could have a different meaning. I also heard the qualities of flight and aggression in certain parts of the Seasons' music, and I began to see how I could use those.

I'm still not satisfied with what we achieved there. During previews, people kept saying to me, 'Cut it! If it doesn't work, cut it!' But, stubbornly, I was determined not to cut anything.

AM: *Instead, you not only use all four Season variations, you also use all the intervening music that Prokofiev wrote which is often cut in stage productions of the ballet.*
MB: Actually, those sections were quite helpful for moving the story on. I found it easier to hear them as action music rather than as clean-cut dances.

At the end, in the coda music, the Angel takes her on to another level, to a beautiful place, perhaps somewhere in the sky. They're journeying; but then reality breaks through again. We have an air-raid, a realistic situation with people running for shelter as she tries to get back to her house. As the street clears, she's at her front door again, but she can't get in. You have a sense of the planes coming towards her house, and she can see them in the sky. Just as she gets into the house, a bomb hits it. We have an explosion with lights flashing. Just as the doorway in the house moves away, you're left with the image of the Angel having caught her, having saved her from death.

The idea – as in *A Matter of Life and Death* – is that she's suspended between living and dying as Act One ends. The music continues, and we've gone into some kind of half-life world in a starry place, with the moon in the background. She has been knocked senseless and we're suddenly going off into her unconscious world; but the Angel has saved her, and then we go into the final waltz sequence. This again involves the

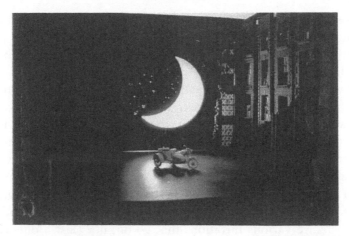

68 *Cinderella*. Set design by Lez Brotherston for the end of Act One. The Angel drives the motorbike, with Cinderella radiant in his sidecar, around the stage and off as the curtain falls.

airmen, who are part of the Angel's world – they could be dead pilots – and she ends up, in her fantasy, being driven off in the sidecar of the Angel's motorbike. I thought it was important to have some kind of vehicle; for me, it wouldn't be *Cinderella* unless she was driven offstage magically into a new world.

AM: *Act Two starts with the noise of a great bomb going off.*
MB: Yes. A snap blackout and a very big, surprise explosion, which makes people jump quite considerably – they're not expecting that. It's a very effective start to the act.

The Angel is soon visible. He's seemingly in control of all these goings-on. We did ask ourselves, 'If all this act is Cinderella's dream, why isn't she there at the beginning? Or why isn't she there with the Angel?' The answer was that, when you're in a dream, you're not necessarily in it yourself. You don't see yourself in a dream; you are within it.

Now the couples, who, seemingly dead, are lying on the floor and up against benches – come back to life. The sense here is that these blue couples are the spirits of dead lovers who have been killed in the war. The men are dressed like soldiers and the women have versions of 1940s ballroom dresses – which also look rather like 1940s ballet costume, with lots of tulle. I didn't at first want them to seem grotesque, but actually people liked that aspect of the production, and we gave them a more grotesque make-up. When we do it again, we may break down

313

their costumes even more, to make them seem more dusty and to hint more at the bombing.

Then the family enters. Originally, they entered wrapped in blankets and holding little mugs. In her mind, they had been on their way to the New Year's Eve party but had been ushered into this ballroom for shelter from the bombing on the streets. It was a nice image, but, after a while, we realized we didn't need it. It seemed to make more sense, in a dream, that they'd turned up to this ball, which they had an invitation to; but there was no one there, it was all destroyed. So they're wondering whether they've come to the right place, but they decide to make the most of it. The Stepmother's had a few drinks and she encourages them to get to know everyone – 'Since we're here, we'll have a good time!' – and there are various flirtations that go on, not least a one-way one between her and the Pilot. There's a feeling that another bomb might be about to drop at one point and there's a lot of frightened running around. Especially for the people who are already dead, there's quite a lot of fear; or rather a memory of their deaths. The fear came out of the music. One piece of the score begins with a sort of rumble, which leads into a series of false entries. So all the blue couples keep running up to the stairs – waiting for the entry of the Prince, the Pilot – but there's no one there, at least the first time, so they come back and go into a dance. Then they run to the stairs again, but – cheap joke! – it's just one of the family coming in, doing up his flies. The third time they run to the stairs, the Pilot finally does enter, with two other heroes, one from the Navy and one from the Army. Everyone applauds. The Stepmother and the sisters take a liking to them, the stepmother particularly to the Pilot. So then we get a duet – to a mazurka – for the Stepmother and the Pilot.

The Angel enters, and this previously ugly place becomes magical, with lots of twinkly fairy lights – and now Cinderella enters. The blue couples elaborate on the feeling of this situation by doing a series of partnered moves to do with covering the eyes and then having things revealed to you. What's revealed to Cinderella at the end of this is the Pilot. There's a fade from the Angel into the Pilot: the Angel backs away into the Pilot; they turn around, back to back, and then she's looking at the Pilot. The idea is that the Angel can become, or conjure up, the Pilot: that he can provide Cinderella with what she really wants. This leads into the waltz and back to a form of reality within all the non-reality; and, for Cinderella and the Pilot, a 'getting to know you' kind of dance. We wanted to have quite a realistic relationship, some real sexual chemistry between them, but starting off formally. He's smoking at the beginning, to make it fairly casual.

Then the father enters. He is in his wheelchair, as he has been all through Act One. We characterized him as someone who'd been a hero himself in World War One – and was injured in that war or had mental and physical problems resulting from it. In Act One, he'd stopped recognizing Cinderella any more. He becomes lost to her in many ways; but now, in the fantasy world of Act Two, the Angel brings him on, back to his former self as a dashing father-figure in full uniform; and he dances with her. It's all as if her dream has come true: a wish-fulfilment fantasy within a fantasy. As I said, I did worry that this didn't forward the plot – in fact, it interrupted it, since she and the Pilot had only just met – but in the end, this scene stayed because otherwise she and the Pilot would leave the ball too soon.

AM: *There's a subliminal psychological connection of all the male elements in her life falling into place at the same time: father and lover; which all works because of having a male guardian angel.*

MB: Yes; and, during her dance with her father, the family re-enter and start to wonder, 'Who is she? Who is he? Do we recognize her? Or him?' But they've all drunk a lot by that point, so they're not thinking clearly, and it's all: 'Oh no, it can't be him. Or is it?' She eventually flaunts her relationship in their face and exits with the Pilot, to which the family do a drunken 'reaction' dance – to the galumphing music that Ashton uses as the 'runaround' music for the two Ugly Sisters in his version. In our version, it's a drunken kind of jive, led by the Stepmother. Basically, when she's had a few, she's nicer than she is normally! She lets her hair down and has a good time.

That gives us another 'wipe', because we have to do a scene change there. They come downstage, then move across; and, as they leave, we're somewhere else. The set has moved, and a few things have gone: the piano and the side benches. A sign that was outside the ballroom has come down inside, in front of the stairway. Cinderella and the Pilot are seen coming down the stairs – with fewer clothes on now. We did originally have her dress coming off in the ballroom – which was interesting because, in the dance before she leaves the ballroom, she was surrounded by blue couples, and when they disappeared again, she walked out of the dress, left it behind, and made her exit. The top half was obviously the same. But it didn't quite work: it didn't feel in character.

AM: *Is that true in general? That, even if a theatrical effect you've tested works on stage, you will jettison it if it doesn't have emotional or psychological truth?*

MB: Yes, absolutely. So then there's the pas de deux outside the ballroom. The idea here always was that this was something intimate that happens in a private place. It becomes sexual; they end up on the ground, with signs of a post-coital feeling. He was even going to light a cigarette at the end, originally, though we dropped that when we found it looked a bit crass. Instead, they both start to go to sleep. One of my original ideas for the set here included an old bed with springs hanging out of it. The idea was that they were going to go back to this place; but it just wasn't possible to design a set like that.

Then the Angel re-enters, looking more menacing, as if to say: 'This isn't the right time for this.' He brings her back to some form of reality about her situation. She tries to wake up the Pilot, but she can't wake him up: it's the beginning of some sort of nightmare. She's asking for help but, instead, the Angel lets her relive bad memories: originally these included the shooting of her mother; her father being pushed back into his wheelchair, feeble again; and all the family showing their invitations and snatching them away. The Angel even shows her an image of the Pilot with one of her sisters. 'It was all a joke, and not true.' At the same time, there's a macabre business going on with the blue couples: lots of killing gestures, and bodies hanging on things and being carried: all Blitz-type imagery.

Actually, that material was one of the things in the production I'm very pleased with, but in the London production we never lit it well enough to show all the images that are going on. There's a bit where they all become wheelchairs, for example. Eventually, after all this nightmare, the Angel brings down the set. The buildings start crashing in. Smoke and bombs are going off. At the very end, where we really have gone back to reality, the Pilot is back looking the way he did in Act One – rather than the cleaned-up version. His uniform is dirty, he's injured again, and he's coming back to the house where he met her – only to find that it's been bombed. He finds her shoe in the rubble of her front door: the place she was when we last left her in reality. He's left wondering, as we were at the end of Act One: is she dead?

But you do see a body being carried away on a stretcher behind him. It is her, and she has got the other shoe on. Again, this could be better lit, but at some performances it caught the light perfectly. Meanwhile, in the background there's a homeless woman in hysterics (Etta Murfitt giving an Oscar-winning performance – worth the price of a ticket alone).

Images of mother with gun, brother with toy gun, Pilot with other woman, father in wheelchair, family with invites – those were all ideas.

AM: *Ideas you used?*
MB: Yes, we used all of them; they were all there.

AM: *Right at the end of Act Two?*
MB: Yes, but this will change now.

AM: *You used the music for the chimes of midnight for all of the Blitz scene. Is there any emphasis on midnight in your production?*
MB: Yes, though there could be more. Our original plan was that it wasn't just any midnight; it was New Year's Eve. Part of the set for the ball was a very big 'Happy New Year' sign, but it was so dominant and ugly that we cut it. The programme says that it's New Year's Eve. Originally, we wanted to establish that her mother had been killed on New Year's Eve, at midnight, years ago.

We have clocks throughout, including the face of Big Ben: I love how that looks, and it feels all the more wonderful to have achieved it on a limited budget; but there's no sense of 'You must be home by midnight', or any of that sort of thing. The sense that time is limited for her is expressed in other ways in our production: because this is the Blitz, because life itself could end any moment, there's the constant possibility that 'Your time is up'.

At the end of Act Three, the clock in the railway station is just past midnight. We've moved on.

AM: *As I think you know, there are a few anachronisms and errors in your account of the War. I'm no expert on these matters, but it's amazing how many people, even of my generation, know very precise details of the life of those years.*
MB: Yes. With some of these, I suppose I knew I was taking a slight historical liberty. For example, I wanted to have one stepsister involved with an American GI even though the Americans weren't actually over here at this period of the War. *Cinderella* is set during the height of the Blitz, which was 1941 – though the Blitz returned in 1944 for a while when there were GIs around, and you could claim it is set in that year.

In general, though, I try to be correct. However, we had a huge post-bag from people – even old generals – correcting us about insignia and things on hats. Actually, what we heard most about was the railway carriage. It has 'Second Class' written on it, but, during the War, there were only First and Third. I just passed them all on to Lez: 'You've done this wrong.'

AM: *You begin Act Three with several musical items which Ashton cut from his version.*
MB: Act Three of Ashton's *Cinderella* has always felt too short to me, especially as the story resolves itself fairly early on. So it was good to use all the music he didn't tackle but that Prokofiev composed for the Prince's journey around the world in quest of Cinderella – I really liked all that music as well. I thought it had such a lot of drive and energy. We had to spend some time, obviously, on how to adapt the music to our London version, since one part of the music describes the Prince's oriental journey and another part his trip to Spain.

Ours starts with a dance for the Angel and the people on the streets of London: the image of him as the Angel of Death. There's a 'Who's next?' feel to it: 'Who will he touch next?' At the end of that section, the Pilot reappears with the shoe. He's obviously a bit disturbed. There's a dance on the street – originally it was going to involve passers-by also – as if he is some madman getting strange reactions from other people; but, to be honest, we ran out of time, so that it ended up being a solo. That worked well too, because it suggested that he was addressing imaginary people in his mind, like someone talking to himself out loud. (Rick Fisher did some very nice lighting effects to heighten that effect. All the windows that surround the stage had a suggestion of fire in them – like flashing lights. So it was all a bit oppressive. The rain was coming down too, so it had a nice atmosphere at the beginning. Actually, the visual atmosphere throughout this act worked very well.)

Then the Pilot runs down into a tube station. This is to the Spanish music – which has a castanet effect that we ignored. We turned it into a kind of London Wartime underworld, with lots of prostitution and cheap sex. It's interesting how the castanets stop sounding relevant when you take away anything that looks Spanish from the stage picture! They just merge into the general orchestration. The scene is basically about his temptation by other women. There's also a sequence – *Guys and Dolls* thrown in, for no good reason except that it's a good joke – where the Salvation Army come down and try to save the souls. Now, we had a great deal of discussion, as to whether he should have sex with one of the women down there, or whether he should stay true to Cinderella. The thing that made us agree to it was our sense that he is only human – part of him thinks she's dead anyway – and that it doesn't give him any serious fulfilment. A similar thing happens in *Waterloo Bridge,* actually, but the other way round. (That's a fantastic film, with wonderful music.) When Vivien Leigh is told that Robert Taylor is dead, she becomes a prostitute. When he does return, she's at the station. She's there to pick up the new soldiers off the train, but he thinks she's there to meet him. She's now a prostitute, with a tarty beret on and a low-cut blouse.

Anyway, the Pilot does the business; but just before doing that, he looks at Cinderella's shoe and hides it – as if she shouldn't see what he's about to do. Afterwards he runs out, disgusted with himself, to the Embankment. (Lez does a nice scene change there, very simply.) He throws up into the river; and then, to the oriental music, he has a solo. The original idea was that this was going to be set in a Lyons Corner House. It was going to be about a misunderstanding between an oriental woman and her lover that ended up being a similar situation. The idea came from a Fred Astaire movie (*Ziegfeld Follies*) – but it wasn't relevant. As with the Spanish music, we realized that it would work perfectly well without having to illustrate some foreign colour. So in this solo on the Embankment, he imagines Cinderella in the shoes and tries to kiss her. He's watched by a woman – the Woman from the Savoy,

69 *Cinderella*. Set design by Lez Brotherston for the London Underground scene in Act Three, in which the Pilot searches for Cinderella.

according to our cast list. She's been at a party at the Savoy, she's had an argument with her husband, and she's come to have a coffee and calm down on the Embankment. She sees him and comforts him. There's a misunderstanding when her husband comes looking for her. A couple of thugs join in for the fun of it, beat him up and taunt him with the shoe. He's left a desperate man. He crawls off stage.

We 'wipe' that by bringing on the hospital screens – which is a nice filmic effect. It overlaps one world into another, without doing a scene change. The screens are moved around, the lights come up, and the whole sequence of the hospital scene is created through screens – forming rooms, corridors and doors. This is the re-introduction to Cinderella. We haven't seen her since the end of Act Two. Now she's here in hospital recovering, but having psychiatric treatment; and she has one shoe on: the other shoe. She's talking to her psychiatrist – played by the Angel in a white coat and glasses – and obviously the shoe is connected with her obsession. So she does a solo, telling her story and how she is. Finally, she throws the shoe to the ground. He comforts her and takes her back to her room. The screens re-form to another part of the hospital. The family – processing through the hospital – are coming to visit her! Basically, the Stepmother is trying to butter up Cinderella in case she spills the beans – or actually to do away with her. This is confusing in our current version, since the murder of the mother has been excised. Why would Cinderella's family even come to visit her? But we will resolve this before staging it in America in 1999. Anyway, here the Stepmother is. She has brought the others along – they're very reluctant – with gifts and flowers and chocolates. She says she doesn't want to see them, but they barge their way into her room. For once, she stands up to them and to the Stepmother and tells them to get out. So she has moved on and is changing as a person. They are thrown out. However, the Stepmother somehow gets back into her room again – Cinderella's asleep – and tries to smother her with her pillow.

The Stepmother is caught. Cinderella is saved, and points to her, accusingly. She could be saying, 'She tried to kill me!' or 'She killed my mother!' Then comes another wipe with the screens – and, along another corridor, by complete Dickensian coincidence, we see the Pilot. He's ended up in the same hospital, and has also been brought there for psychiatric help. He's got his suitcase and he's coming in, with a nurse. We see him, but Cinderella doesn't.

There's another quick change of scene with the screens. Now we have the Stepmother carted off by a couple of men in white coats, and the family rejecting her or feeling guilty. Then we're back to two parallel hospital rooms, with Cinderella in one and the Pilot in another – stage right and stage left. He is brought into his room to have some electric-shock treatment: some device that's put on his head and by which he's given this frightening treatment to the very violent banging music to which, in the traditional *Cinderellas,* one of the stepsisters tries on the shoe as hard as she can. Cinderella wakes up to the screams of someone in agony from the room next door; she rushes from her room to see what's happening, and arrives just as the doctors have left. She recognizes him, and wakes him up; but just as you're expecting the big recognition scene of true love, you have a little hiccup. He doesn't recognize her, initially, because he doesn't have his glasses on – we haven't found out till this point that he wears them. So they turn around: he's put his glasses on to see her, but she's taken hers off, so he still doesn't recognize her. Then they turn around again; she puts her glasses on this time, and now he knows her and she him – finally.

AM: *Some critics have said that your frumpy Cinderella who only becomes beautiful when she takes her glasses off in Act Two is just a rehash of the corny old 'Why, Miss Jones, you're beautiful without your glasses' situation. But this pay-off (non-)recognition scene is really the reverse of that. They may have dreamed of being glamorous, but in real life what they're looking for is an unglamorous fellow spirit.*
MB: Yes. The whole point of our conception was that these characters were ultimately very ordinary people: Mr and Mrs Ordinary; but with so much distorted reality and nightmare earlier on, it's only in the third act that you find out who the real Pilot is, and that Cinderella is more than happy with the way he really is. It's amazing how well this all fits into the music; or, rather, how easily it seemed to take shape from the music.

And then the final scene on the railway platform.

Film ideas easily floated into mind, like the quotation from *Brief Encounter.* I know I've already quoted from that in *Town & Country,* but here I couldn't resist. A railway scene seemed a perfect solution for all the leave-takings we had in mind; the music just called, emotionally, for one tear-jerking moment after another, and so *Brief Encounter* was just begging to be used again. But I decided to lift the whole energy of the act by putting in a sort of dance bow at the end. We use the big Waltz of the Stars, but in the version with extra repeats that Prokofiev arranged in his *Waltzes Suite*. All the dancers come on and dance, taking their bows at the end of their dances; and it's a Victory dance, with Victory-V salutes.

Preparation

ALASTAIR MACAULAY: *You've not only referred to several films (A Mat-*ter of Life and Death, Waterloo Bridge, Brief Encounter, *and others); you've also used the word 'filmic'. Do you find, in envisaging a ballet, when you're going through the music and imagining a show, that you're seeing it as a film as much as a stage work?*
MATTHEW BOURNE: At times. What excites me, however, is the theatrical aspect. I never see it overall as a film; but, yes, I see sections of it coming from film and I gain inspiration from film.

AM: *Both in* Swan Lake *and* Cinderella, *you've touched on moments that could almost belong more easily in a movie.*
MB: I suppose I often think in terms of movie techniques – like 'fades' and 'close-ups' and 'wipes'; but my instinct is theatrical, and musical.

AM: *To me, what you often bring out is a filmic quality in the music. Tchaikovsky is one of several nineteenth-century composers who sometimes seem to be composing music for film before film had been invented. Berlioz is another. Their music has long-shots and close-ups and travelling sequences: they are picturing poetically a view more complex than any nineteenth-century theatre could have staged, and they sometimes do it in their works for the concert-hall – writing music that is meant to conjure up a kaleidoscope of images. Arlene Croce called* Swan Lake *'the greatest unstageable ballet ever written', and part of the reason is that, in 1877, Tchaikovsky's vision far outpaced what any theatre could realize. Even later, when Tchaikovsky was working for the most sophisticated opera house in Russia and with a highly skilled team of theatre professionals, there are passages in his scores that must have taxed them to the limit and that still tax any theatrical producer. The second half of Act Two of* The Sleeping Beauty, *with the journey to, and arrival at, the sleeping palace is one example; as is the latter half of Act One of* The Nutcracker, *with all its transformations of the Party scene into the Mice* scene and then again into the Snow scene. The same goes, at times, for Berlioz's Damnation of Faust, and Wagner's Ring Cycle. These composers were composing as if they could already see what film directors would be achieving in a few decades' time. Virtually no stage then or now could provide the changing series of visions, landscapes and close-ups that they were assembling in their scores. This is also true for such concert-hall pieces as Tchaikovsky's Manfred Symphony.

I even believe that you bring to the surface a buried filmic quality in Act Four of Swan Lake. As for Prokofiev, he really did write movie music. Often enough in Cinderella, he really is writing very definitely for dance; but I always say most of Romeo and Juliet – his most popular score – is the best film music written in the twentieth century.

I, however, say all this from the perspective of one who sits in the auditorium. Does it ever feel like film music as you're trying to make it work in the theatre?

MB: Yes, it does: the more scenic music particularly feels as if it's written to accompany action and lend atmosphere. There are sections when it's very hard to find any real dance impulse in the music.

AM: *Which sections of* Cinderella *feel that way to you?*
MB: Act Two is where it feels most like a ballet – with both dance and theatre on its mind. Much of Act One and parts of Act Three feel very filmic. The music for the underground sequence in our piece changes a lot, as film music does, to accompany different action and quick changes of scene, place and character.

AM: *To me, one of the hardest bits to stage in* Cinderella *is the ending of* Act Three, *because there's very little rhythmic vitality.*
MB: It's not hard to stage, but it is hard to dance. I solved it by deciding not to dance it! The music has such enormous feeling in it, but it's difficult to choreograph to. As you say, there's nothing to hang the movement on, beyond the feeling of the music. It was a conscious decision early on – rather than a desperate 'haven't got much time left' decision – to dare not to dance through that long piece of music. Actually, we suddenly give the Angel a tiny dance around Cinderella and the Pilot as he's completing his mission.

AM: *One canny thing you did was to time your big emotional moments surprisingly. Following your* Cinderella *the first time round as an Ashton fan, I was more or less waiting to see what you did with certain*

cues in the music. There's one cue where I thought, with sudden disap-
pointment, 'Oh, he's not playing on our emotions at the moment when
Ashton's Cinderella makes her very touching farewell to her sisters.' I
had thought you would do a fond leave-taking between Cinderella and
her father there, but no. Then, however, when, from an Ashton point of
view, you're not expecting it, but on the next little spurt of emotion in the
music, you suddenly give us the last big recognition scene between father
and daughter. It affected me all the more because the timing took me by
surprise.

MB: But that really didn't come out of my trying to differ from Ashton.
By that point, I didn't remember precisely what he did to all that music;
and, meanwhile, the music just told me what should happen where.

AM: *You have here some of your preparatory notes.*
MB: Yes, for the Act Two pas de deux. Interestingly, in the light of what
you've just been saying, I got lots of ideas from watching videos. 'Roberta', my notes say. As you know, that film contains the classic example
of Fred and Ginger starting a dance duet by just walking. I was also
thinking of aspects of the 'I'm Old-Fashioned' duet that Fred dances with
Rita Hayworth in *You Were Never Lovelier*. ('Holding both hands, face
to face and shuffle backwards and forwards with turn,' say my notes.)
Then 'Let's Face' – that's the Fred and Ginger duet 'Let's Face the Music
and Dance' from *Follow the Fleet*. 'Pass from hand to hand at waist as
she turns,' I've written. Then, for the Angel and Cinders, I've written
'Hypnosis Dance' – that's 'Change Partners and Dance' in *Carefree*.

Lots of notes on film dance duets, actually! The last dance in *The
Barkleys of Broadway*. 'Between You and Me': that's a number from
Broadway Melody of 1940 with Eleanor Powell and George Murphy,
which I've always liked. Some of these things we used, some we didn't.
The only one I'm sure we used is the walking side by side from *Roberta*.

If I'm at a loss in a duet rehearsal for what to do, we might look
at some of my favourite musical numbers on video. Then we'll try out
something like that, and it will lead us on to the next thing. It's something to fall back on if we get a bit lost. I keep trying to add to my
stock of knowledge – I've been buying a lot of videos of less-well-known
musicals. There are some Debbie Reynolds and Donald O'Connor films,
Esther Williams films, and films with Gower Champion or early Bob
Fosse choreography that have fantastic numbers, absolute treasures
of choreography, but that haven't passed down into the established

pantheon of 'Great Moments from the Musicals' – *Give A Girl A Break* and *I Love Melvyn,* to name only two. Not to mention more famous dances that I often go back to, such as 'All Of You', which Cyd Charisse and Fred Astaire dance in *Silk Stockings;* or their big duet in *The Band Wagon,* 'Dancing in the Dark'.

It's easy to see what my notes mean when they refer to films. Elsewhere, even I can't tell what my notes mean: 'Use victims phrases', for example, later in Act Two. Here I've got 'Use *Late Flowering Lust* dance here.' That's the actual dance of the poem 'Late Flowering Lust' on our 1994 video, in which women are thrown over men's shoulders, and look grotesque and fall to the floor. This is part of what the blue couples were doing late in *Cinderella* Act Two, when the men were carrying them as if they were carrying bodies from rubble.

AM: *How much does it actually re-use your choreography from* Late Flowering Lust?
MB: I don't think it does at all, but we used the idea behind it. That dance in *Late Flowering Lust* looks like marathon dancing, with people collapsing in each other's arms, but still trying to dance. In my notes for Act Three, I've got a section called 'People living in fear'. This is the Angel of Death section near the start of the act. I was looking for ideas for dance phrases that I would then give to different members of the company, ideas for them to make movement. 'These are the people of London – on the streets of London – watching something or several things in the sky – possibly a plane or planes – suspicious of other people – hiding in shop windows – things dropping from the sky (avoiding them) – hearing things – lights in face – torches – car lights – not daring to look up – confronting things because of this' (I don't know what that means) 'Protective of each other keeping out of danger – looking for cover – rain – can hold umbrella.' There was an idea that a lot of people were going to have umbrellas at one point in that sequence, because the stage picture has it raining. But, obviously, they get in the way. 'Angel – look at whole group at end. And all look back at him.' Yes, we do do that. There's a little phone box at the back of the stage and at the end of the number he disappears. He opens the door of the phone box, looks back at them all, they look at him, and then he goes into the phone box. A bit like *Dr Who* – as if he lives in this phone box.

Here's a brief outline of one little scene – the family visit to the hospital. A lot is to do with nurses. '1, nurse on another journey. 2, nurse into room. Other nurse outside. 3, Cinderella says "No". 4, nurse says "No". 5, they barge in.' (That's the family.) '6, all smiles, because nurse is there. Give gifts, get bored. 7, nurse says "Time is up."' This is just to give me guidelines for what to do before going into rehearsal.

The scene with the hospital screens – because it was so complicated in terms of where those screens went – was done on the spot, because it was impossible on paper to keep track of where the screens were going.

Here I just have a breakdown of casting for the railway station: 'Maxine, Cinderella look-alike, sitting on suitcase.' She's the one the Angel ends up going to at the end of the piece. 'Etta and Ben, *Brief Encounter*. Just a series of couples, woman with baby, husband injured.' And then notes for the final 'Victory' dance. 'Knees up, conga . . .' Actually, what we ended up doing is a lot better than these notes. We did this dance quickly, and that proved a good idea. 'People running in and around phrases, chasing people for a kiss or a lift.' You know that famous picture of the sailor kissing the woman in Times Square, where she's really twisted over? I wanted that sort of impetuous feeling – of just grabbing anyone and kissing them with joy.

Rehearsals

ALASTAIR MACAULAY: *For how long did you rehearse* Cinderella *in the studio?*

MATTHEW BOURNE: For about ten weeks with everyone, and more time with individual people beforehand. However, I was ill for more than a week during this rehearsal process, and that led to a few problems we could have done without. It took about a week setting it up in the theatre. However, because I'd been ill, we had to cancel a couple of previews – when we went into 'tech-ing' the production, there were still bits of the show that hadn't been choreographed. So there was a lot of catching up to do.

AM: *I want to compare the way you work to the ways used by other choreographers. Can you understand how Frederick Ashton could make his* Cinderella *in six weeks? Or his* Fille mal gardée *in four weeks?*

MB: I don't know, no. I suppose that, if that's all the time you have, then that's what you do. We made *Nutcracker* in five weeks. It helps, obviously, if you are working with a company of people who are very used to the way you work, because they do half of it for you – they give you the performance straightaway. Strangely, the bits that need adjusting most in *Cinderella* now are the bits that we spent most time on.

AM: *Let's talk about choreographic method. As you know, some choreographers turn up to the studio and have worked out every movement beforehand. You yourself tended to work that way early on in your career. Other choreographers, like Ashton or Balanchine, certainly give everyone the impression that they have no movement ideas when they walk into the studio. They get the rehearsal pianist to play the music, they say, 'Now, let's see', and then they set to work.*

When Ashton was younger, he would sometimes rush around the studio in response to the music, and then ask his dancers to copy what he'd just improvised; but he had more methods than one even then. Once he turned up with a hangover and sat there with his hand over his eyes. 'Move around, keep warm,' he said to his dancers, but he didn't look. He was due that day to create a pas de trois – in Valentine's Eve, *his first choreographic version of Ravel's* Valses Nobles et Sentimentales *– and one of his three dancers, Peggy van Praagh, kept herself warm by doing particular exercises from the Cecchetti ballet syllabus. Suddenly Ashton, still with his hand over his eyes, said, 'That'll do, we'll use that.' Van Praagh said, 'But you weren't even looking.' Ashton said, 'Can you do it again?' She could; so Ashton took those movements, fitted them to the music, changed the rhythm and the angles, and set them for all three dancers as the pas de trois! Later he would sometimes say, 'I had a dream last night of a fountain,' and his dancers – in that case, Antoinette Sibley and Anthony Dowell, working as Titania and Oberon on their pas de deux in* The Dream *– would say, 'A fountain?' and had to try to 'make' a fountain in dance. In making* Cinderella, *he had the music for* Fairy Spring *played, and said to the dancer Nadia Nerina, 'What do you hear in it?' She said, 'Bursting of buds', and that image was what propelled the whole solo. Now, it may well be that Ashton had a more definite idea of what he wanted – at least its highlights and its overall shape – than he ever let the dancers know; and certainly, when he made* Rhapsody, *Lesley Collier said that all the movement for the ballerina role came out of him and that she – not feeling inspired that way – told him he'd have to invent all her movement himself. She claims she contributed no ideas or movement herself at all to what is an elaborate and extremely virtuoso role: Ashton was seventy-five at the time.*

Still, in general, his method was to invite the dancers to contribute to the creative process. But what you're talking about seems to go further, because, before the movement, you're asking them to help conceive the characterization and even details of the plot.

MB: Of course I do plenty of work before going into the studio. But it's often to do with structure or sense. Or music. When I go home in the evenings, often what I spend time trying to solve is how to make a piece of music work. It's usually not to do with the specifics of steps – it's to do with the ideas that are going to help create the steps. 'OK – we've got a piece of music. Maybe we've got a solo that needs to happen here. Now, I have not a single idea about why this solo is happening.' So, out of the studio, what I dwell on is all the whys and wherefores of that solo being there. 'What things are going to get us motivated into making the movement?'

It's taken a lot of confidence to get to that stage, but it seems to work for everyone, because it gives everyone an involvement. They know they're going to have to work and use their own minds when they get there; and the majority of performers relish that side of working with us.

I think that what I can do now is react quickly to movement that's given me. Even if I'm given the most awful phrase of movement by someone, I've got a way now of changing it without it seeming as if I've said, 'That's dreadful!' I can start from the beginning and make it into something else. I work best by making one thing into another rather than having to make something out of nothing; but I don't want to leave too much up to chance. With ensembles in particular, and curiously often with dances for women, I find I have a clearer idea of what I want to do. There are sequences like the underground scene in *Cinderella* where I made most of the movement just because I knew so surely what I wanted. Solos you can leave more to chance, and you can mould the material that emerges in the studio without too much problem.

AM: *As you say, your gift is in shaping the material into something of your own. That being so, can you say what your dance style is? What movement do you accept or reject? How do you shape the material you're given?*

MB: The first contribution I make is in rhythm and dynamics. The material you get tends to be even.

I also try to make it more full-bodied, to get the dancers to go further with each move. Often, I will add something more fluid in connecting one movement with another – to make things more sensual.

What else? I just look to see if there's a phrase of movement. I look to see what I feel's missing from it. Often it's a sexiness, and that's to do with the way the back is used; also the shoulders and the head.

AM: *And you're looking for a current that will connect the movement?*
MB: Yes. Occasionally it's good to surprise with a connection that doesn't seem to make sense, but it needs to be musical and as full-bodied as it can be; and dancers often pull away from that, you know. It's lovely to see dancers who go for everything, but by no means all of them do. So I'm usually pointing out how it could go further, lower, higher, deeper, whatever.

Sometimes I will add more gestural interests to movement that looks a bit ordinary. I'll say, 'Try it with a different arm', for example. Another thing that works really well is to tell people to go away and give it focus – but take their focus to the most unorganic, the most unexpected place – because everyone naturally falls into certain patterns. As soon as you take the head in another direction, as soon as you look the opposite way or are looking down when it feels that you should be looking up, it takes on different meanings. We start to see the human aspect of the movement. A great deal is to do with the use of eyes – but as the focus of the whole body, not just as a set of facial expressions, and not look-ing conventionally in the direction you're going in. It always works, that device, to give something more interest.

Unadorned classroom-type movement – which is often the first thing in the mind of the dancer – is often what I most readily reject. I also reject humour that's thrown in your face. Some ideas we work on do have humour, and I try and make them more subtle by disguising it. I don't like things that seem to say, 'Aren't we funny!' or 'Aren't we clever!'

AM: *Dance people often talk of a dancer 'creating' a role. How do you feel about this?*
MB: I wouldn't want anyone to believe that, in a show like *Cinderella*, first-cast people created a role without any contributing influence from other second- or third-cast performers.

When AMP began, there weren't two interpretations of an idea being presented to me at any one time. It was always the individual, and I worked with that person. He or she created that role with me, and there was no question that it was anything other than theirs. Later on, when we started to re-do shows, sometimes a dancer wasn't available and, for the first time, we encountered a new interpreter of the role. That was when we started to allow a certain amount of re-interpretation. Basically, the choreography already existed, and there was an idea of character obviously in that, but it made sense to allow the new dancers to bring a bit of themselves to the role.

In each case, I had to work out how flexible I was going to be. This is quite an issue. Certain things – you feel very firmly – work the way they already are. It's not always easy to work out whether this is to do with what you think the character should do, or whether you just want to impose on the next person the quality you loved so much in the original dancer.

In the shows we do now, however, we start off with two, three or four individuals preparing each role, working in the studio together to create movement. They must all understand that they can bring something of themselves to it.

When someone says that Sarah Wildor 'created' the role of Cinderella, in many senses this is true, because she was the chosen person to do the first performance. She was obviously there at all the rehearsals, a lot of her thought went into the role, and she interpreted the role in the way that she felt was right for it. But alongside her were two other people, Maxine Fone and Saranne Curtin, who were also dancing the role, feeding into the movement and ideas, bringing their own slightly different interpretations of those ideas and movements. So it's wrong to say flatly now that any one person creates an AMP role. Each role is an ensemble creation involving more people than me and one dancer.

AM: *So you start rehearsals. You take everyone through the story and the main ideas. Then you give everyone their character or characters, and then set them their homework.*

MB: At the beginnings of the *Cinderella* rehearsals, we watched a lot of videos together. We had at least a couple of days' worth of videos, with me showing Pathé newsreels with general background, so that people knew the specific historical world that we were going to be in. This method is used by directors in plays and musicals, and I have used something like it on most of my work with AMP for several years. We show the set, the costumes, the background material. On the second day of

Cinderella rehearsals, we had a class in authentic swing dance from the 1940s, taught us by a Lindy Hop expert, Louise Richards. It was fascinating to see who, of our dancers, was good at it and who wasn't – and often surprising. (You feel some of the ballet people might be a little stiff with it, but not at all – whereas people who are more into jazz dance look terribly awkward.)

We then did more specific character development: getting people to do their own research. I had a big video library in the rehearsal rooms and lots of books that people borrowed, like a library. Obviously, the Stepmothers were watching Joan Crawford movies! – *Mildred Pearce, Possessed, Harriet Craig* – but Lynn decided that she wanted to be Bette Davis as well: that suited her more. I could see what she meant – she wanted to be more animated than Joan is. Isabel Mortimer was much more true to Joan's stiffness: the broad shoulders, and the 'hardly-moving-at-times' quality of her acting. Lynn wanted to move more, which she found with Davis rather than with Crawford.

70 *Cinderella*: rehearsal for Act One. 'The Dummy Duet': Will Kemp as the Pilot; Maxine Fone as Cinderella.

AM: *How did Sarah, Maxine and Saranne develop their Cinderellas?*

MB: They talked to each other quite a lot; but I think the essence of their chats was to do with their decision that they would all have different ways of doing it. It was important to them to acknowledge amongst themselves that they would do that. Maxine's way was to make her character more in control, someone who was active in doing things, who would fight back. She doesn't like playing a wimp; she would never be meek or frightened. So she was more of a troubled person, disturbed rather than timid. Saranne probably gave in more to being put upon and being a victim – which was so interesting, quite a challenge, because she is brilliant at playing very alluring, sexy women. She had been very good as the Queen in *Swan Lake,* especially in Act Three. She has a very good sense of glamour and deviousness and sexuality. So this part was not something she'd done before; but she's a very intelligent actress – quietly gets on and does her own thing. Whereas Sarah Wildor, I think, probably fell somewhere in between. She was very enquiring, constantly – lots of questions, lots of new ideas all the time about the character, sometimes even working too much on the logic of the role, needing too many reasons for why she was doing things. Sometimes, however, she wouldn't ask – would just find solutions by herself. I'd say, 'Why aren't you doing that?' She'd reply, 'Oh, because she wouldn't do this because of . . .' Eventually, we talked about a lot of things, some of which the audience didn't need to know; but these things really mattered to her, to give everything complete logical sense. She was never hard to work with, but things would often stop because of that need to know. Obviously, logic is of major importance to me, and so are explanations of why a character is doing something. Still, she cottoned on to the way I worked – and was, ultimately, very creative to work with. They are actually all three very creative people in terms of developing character.

AM: *In the event, the performance Sarah Wildor gave had more heart-catching star quality than anything I'd seen her do at Covent Garden. Are you able to explain the radiance she had in the role? Was it just a smaller theatre?*

MB: Well, she really believed in what she was doing. She'd had the chance to study, create and work with the character for ten weeks of rehearsal, which she never gets at the Royal. She used to talk about it at home all the time, so she was obviously living this person. I think she also felt very

71 *Cinderella*. Rehearsal for Act One, with Saranne Curtin as the bespectacled Cinderella and Ewan Wardrop as the Pilot, as the Pilot is about to be thrown out of the house.

confident in terms of working with Adam – who is famous as a rock-solid partner and stops his partners from worrying about any insecurity.

I think maybe the smaller theatre did help. I know what you mean about the radiance that she had, but what surprised me was how far she went to de-glamorize herself. I expected that of Maxine, for example, because she's used to acting all kinds of characters; but Sarah even hunched her back over. I had said I wanted it to be a bit like that, but I hadn't expected how much she really took to it. It took her time: during previews, we didn't see just how strong her performance was going to be; but she, along with a lot of great dancers, has complete and utter trust in the choreographer. If you say something, they'll really go for it.

AM: *The bleak, unglamorous side of Cinderella is what astonished people when Fonteyn danced the role. When she'd been injured, Ashton had made it on Moira Shearer; but Fonteyn, coming to the role a few months later, made the fireside scenes more bleak and hopeless, and thereby the ballroom scenes all the more radiant.*

MB: I think it's one of those roles where you can save yourself for that. Our Cinderella is certainly gorgeous at the ball. I don't know how much of that we talked about.

AM: *How did they find dancing (a) in heels (b) in bare feet?*
MB: I remember the first movement I ever asked Sarah to do, she said, 'Is any of it on pointe?' I said, 'No.' She said, 'Oh, thank God!' For Sarah, bare feet weren't a problem at all. The heels were a problem, simply because they weren't the easiest of shoes: a bit big, with all those jewels on.

AM: *Did the three Cinderellas learn from each other?*
MB: That's certainly not something anyone will admit to! I feel there is much to be gained from watching fellow performers in your role. There is always something to learn. Maxine and Saranne would have seen Sarah's performance, because they were on stage in other roles most nights. Why I made them do that, I don't know. As well as learning Cinderella and helping to create her, they were learning other roles in the piece as well for other nights. They had a lot on their plates. But they were all very good – and Maxine and Saranne should have won more attention and recognition for their performances than they did. They're really remarkable performers.

AM: *How did the two contemporary-trained dancers take to the more ballet-related material? And vice versa?*
MB: I think it's harder for a ballerina, once she's off pointe, to get into the ground at all, to feel grounded in that way. Ballet dancers, especially the women, take all the emphasis upwards. And so there are certain types of movement that Sarah found quite difficult to do; or, when she did them, they looked like something else.

Another funny thing – I really don't know why this is – is that, when I'm working with male dancers, I can get quite a lot from the material they're giving me; but, when I'm working with female dancers from whatever background, I tend to choreograph it completely from scratch myself.

AM: *Do you have any character sketches for Cinderella, the Pilot and the Angel?*
MB: Not written down, but we'd discussed their characters in some depth. It was fun to ask Adam, after all his heroic roles, to play the Pilot as if he were really a bit of an accountant. The first rehearsal that we

did with Cinderella and the Pilot was the beginnings of the dummy duet. This happened very early on, because Sarah had to go off on tour.

We spent a lot of time on the Angel with several people who were going to be playing the role. We tried to come up with less of a character, more of a way of moving, a feeling as to what that character was capable of, some parameters: Who was he visible to? Could he make himself visible at times and other times not? Could he become other people? Was he a friendly presence or a mysterious presence? Was he always for Cinderella's good? Maybe he was just her fate and wasn't necessarily always a good thing, but was there to see her through her life.

AM: *It occurs to me that the Angel may be the most curiously and perhaps successfully hybrid role you've made. Adam Cooper was recently laughing and saying, 'I was very much aware four or five men contributed to the making of that role' – you being one of them. Its movement has ballet and it has contemporary and it has sheer AMP eccentricity. How did all this emerge and then merge in rehearsal?*
MB: Will Kemp, Arthur Pita, Adam Cooper, and Theo Clinkard – all the people who danced it – were equally involved, and they all contributed material to it.

We tried to find a way of moving that was like floating, hovering; and we watched the film with Alec Guinness as Jacob Marley in *Scrooge,* when he appears to hover, all covered in chains. A very odd way of moving – bits of his body float away at times – but it didn't feel right to keep that up the whole time. Then we had an idea that he was a bit Fred Astairish, or that he had a Cary Grant type of angel's presence. There's a film we watched called *The Bishop's Wife,* where Cary Grant plays an angel who does good for the bishop's wife, who's married to a clergyman played by David Niven. Our Angel wasn't going to have wings; he would be like an ordinary man. But maybe he would need to look different for the stage. So we identified him as a bit odd, but nothing outlandish. And we had books of angel paintings that we looked at: gestures from medieval paintings and from sculptures. We used quite a lot of those within the Angel's solos and developed movement from them.

Then we worked on the two sides of the Angel. One side was the caring guardian figure. The other side was the Angel of Death. The midnight section should, we thought, have a different vocabulary of movement. Will and Adam have ballet training, Arthur and Theo have contemporary training, and you can see aspects of both kinds within

72, 73, *Cinderella*. Will Kemp as the Angel, showing the character's various characteristic movement motifs in a studio photo session.

the material. There are some strong positions and jumps from ballet; and there is also some fluid movement. There are some almost body-popping moves – which came from that Alec Guinness example of initiating movement from one place and carrying it through the body. Men are good at working together in my experience; and these four did. We not only took material from all the dancers, we also spliced it: adding the upper-body movements of one dancer's phrase to the lower-body movements of another.

If two dancers played a role, they discussed it and then gave us a little talk on their character. The Stepmother was played by Lynn Seymour and Isabel Mortimer. Lynn really amazed everybody by the detail she brought in, and how logical it was straightaway, how much it helped the story. Hers was a very elaborate story – of her life with her various husbands. She had five children, and she explained which children were by which father, why they were like they were, and why she'd moved on to the next husband each time. What I remember being impressed by at the time was that it very logically made sense of the story that she already knew we were telling.

AM: *She was always revealingly logical in her career as a ballerina at the Royal Ballet. She made all kinds of new sense of MacMillan's Manon when she stepped into that role, making new decisions that explained all kinds of things about the character and gave new impetus to the story.*

MB: My notes from the Stepmother don't include everything Lynn came up with, but here goes. She's called Sybil, in her late forties. She's an ex-hooker. Four previous husbands. The first was a customer. The second was a tycoon, by whom she had the two sons. She was married to a politician, by whom she had the girls; and then to a spiv, with whom she had the younger brother. She is dangerous, stealthy, plotting, selfish, greedy, unpredictable, ritualistic, jealous of daughters.

I love people who bring that kind of logic to what they do. I'm forever asking: 'Well, why did they do that? What was the point of that?' and I really love it when someone has the initiative to make the whole piece more logical through their thought process. People who don't do that tend to annoy me after a while, in their acting choices. Sometimes, when we're into a run, you can really get someone who bugs you, because their performances show that they're not really thinking about it properly.

Cinderella's father is called Robert. 'He's fifty. Ex-public school, Cambridge, First World War officer, hero of trenches. Drafted early in War, Dunkirk. He was injured in some way, on a war pension; at one point he had a lot of money, which is why she went for him. Dashing, brave at one point, loving parent, now distant, periodic displays of interest, confused by other kids, her family.'

The dancer is Barry Atkinson, who came to dance extremely late. He's had an odd life – he's a world-renowned expert on earthquakes and has written books on them. He decided he wanted to learn to dance in his thirties, went to The Place and trained. He was never really a technical dancer, but he performed in some people's work. He choreographs operas as well. Yet he still has this earthquake expertise on the sidelines and is often contacted internationally about certain issues. He's now in his late forties and he does full company class every day. He entered AMP as Dr Dross in *Nutcracker;* then he was the Private Secretary in *Swan Lake.*

Brother One is called Malcolm, and is played by Scott Ambler and Colin Ross-Waterson. He's mid-to-late twenties, prissy, obsessive, cold, resentful, creepy, decorous, unfit for military service, claustrophobic. Wants to know everyone's business, obsessed with cleaning, appearance. Into knitting and sewing. Has a fear of the blackout.

The second brother is Vernon. Ben Wright and Theo Clinkard played him. He's lazy, calculating, still, slow, intellectual. He has a death obsession and a sick sexual relationship with Cinderella. Politically he's

74 *Cinderella.* Rehearsal for Act One. Lynn Seymour, as the Stepmother, approaching Sarah Wildor, as Cinderella.

75 *Cinderella.* Rehearsal. Lynn Seymour and Andrew Walkinshaw as Elliott, her youngest child.

ambiguous, possibly a spy or wants to be a spy. Everything is an experiment for him. Appears suddenly without warning.

Sister One, Vivien, is played by Heather Habens or Michela Meazza. She's twenty-one to twenty-two. She's into fashion magazines, she copies poses from magazines, does facial exercises, uses Cinderella as masseuse. (I tried to get them all to find things that Cinderella could do for them – but we didn't really do much of that.) She's self-centred, pretentious, into trends, house-proud. The war is an inconvenience. She draws lines on legs to look like stockings; in fact, that's one of Cinderella's duties.

Sister Two is Irene. Emily Piercy and Vicky Evans play her. She's in her mid-twenties, stroppy, moody, a martyr, bitter, neurotic, depressed, disappointed with her life, irritated by family. She resents not having a father. She's an ex-tomboy, wanted to be a racing-car driver, she hates chores, takes Valium, despises mother, dominates Stan, her boyfriend, flicks ash in Cinderella's hand, sends her out for pills.

Young Brother, Elliott – played by Andrew Walkinshaw – is fourteen. He hero-worships the GI. He's got a toy plane, picks his nose, is spiteful, vicious, a mummy's boy, hypochondriac, has tantrums.

Girlfriend One, Maggie – Etta Murfitt or Teresa Barker – is twenty-seven or twenty-eight. She's socially adept. She holds court, lets hair down from time to time, she's uninhibited, middle class, has brains, is active, upwardly mobile. Possibly she's protective of Cinderella, a little like Judy Garland in *Me and My Gal*.

Girlfriend Two, Betty, is played by Jacqui Anderson and Valentina Formenti. Her husband has died in the War. She's embarrassed by her appearance, wears glasses, was once active, is now getting over her loss.

The GI, called Buster, is played by Neil Penlington. He's twenty-three or twenty-four, well-hung, a womanizer, well-groomed, charming, arrogant, flirtatious, sexist, good background, has an easy life, is a jock. He uses chewing gum, has a constant beat going in his body all the time, like he's listening to music, checks his appearance in the mirror, has a high sex drive. He has a shallow relationship with the Stepmother, and no time for Irene. He makes advances on Cinderella.

Boyfriend Two, Stan, played by Phil Hill, has done it all. He tells lies, he's working class, he used to run market stall, met Irene in an air-raid shelter, is a Jack of all trades, clumsy. He bangs into things, is not well hung, slouches, doesn't understand his girlfriend. The Stepmother disapproves of him, but tolerates him, he supplies her with things on the black market. He uses the betting office, is a slob, a wheeler-dealer, absent-minded, leaves things behind, a dreamer, scruffy, not socially adept.

AM: *What a crew! Some of these aspects you dropped, of course, because you couldn't portray them within your show's narrative. Were there features, however, when you said, 'I'm sorry, that just won't work, it's wrong'?*

MB: That has happened – for example, with Ben Wright's brother. The character that he began to develop for it was obsessive, and what was coming across was that it wasn't physicalizing itself enough. He got stuck at one point and decided he wanted to change the emphasis of the character. He didn't really get into it the way he would have liked until some way into performing it, when he really found a way of doing things with it that worked for him.

I was trying to help. My problem was that it was too much in the head, with not enough coming out in movement. One task was to try to make the two sisters and the two brothers different from each other. Ben's character originally was going to be very bookish and intellectual, but there wasn't much you could do with that. In the end, we made him much creepier and a bit deviant sexually. He has nasty thoughts about Cinderella; he molests her – which is a serious moment, because you assume that he has done this before and that she just puts up with it.

AM: *What you're describing is a method of working adored by actors; but actors are generically an articulate lot. Many dancers, however, are far less articulate, and would be shy of contributing to an original conception of character.*

MB: This is why I'm so careful about people I pick to be in the company. Even then, maybe between ten and twenty per cent of them find it difficult; but often you can't predict who will take to it. Most of them do take to it very enthusiastically. They get carried away, and sometimes provide much unnecessary information; but you have to let them go with it, because it's giving them so much. It's time well spent. Mostly they are quite happy to talk to the whole group about what they've found – it's easier in groups. If it was left to the individual, I think each one would feel much more nervous about saying, 'This is who I am', but, having discussed it in a group, one of them will represent the others. It gives an initiative to people, which most people like.

AM: *I'm curious about the sources of movement for certain dances. For example, the big pas de deux in Act Two – where did those movements*

come from? It goes down well with ballet-goers – you've had it performed at a gala or two – and various observers are convinced that Sarah
and Adam contributed all the moves from their own Royal Ballet repertory. Some older AMP members or followers have felt that this pas de
deux is where you show strongest – to them, alarming – signs of moving towards real ballet choreography and away from AMP character-
based and narrative-based style. Adam, however, has remarked to me
that there are numerous absolutely contemporary-dance features to it
that both he and Sarah had to work hard on. Still, there is one lift, when
Cinderella is scrunched up around him, that does remind me strongly of
MacMillan's Mayerling; and I had to smile when I saw it, because, when
Mayerling was new, in 1978, we had seen nothing like several of its most
strenuously acrobatic/erotic/morbid lifts before – but now here they are
recurring in, of all things, Cinderella.

MB: Actually, in a number like that, I do get the dancers to contribute,
but in a different way. I'll have a strong overall idea of what I want, and
I'll say to them, 'I want something like this where . . .' I just explain it
very vaguely, and they all have a go at doing something like what I've
said. When I've got all these options to inspect, I can choose what feels
right. In the case of the pas de deux, the problems were solved very
democratically between the three couples that were doing it a lot of the
time. At times, you're aware that one couple is pulling in one direction
and others in another.

It looks different when Sarah and Adam do it, yes, and it looks like
something only they could do; but that's simply their emphasis in performance. And yes, they contributed movements, though I don't think I
could identify their sources, whether from Mayerling or elsewhere. Certainly when I look at the pas de deux now, I can still see just how many
of its problems were solved by Saranne Curtin and Ewan Wardrop. I am
also reminded just how much of it was material that I myself had given
them.

Looking at my notes, I remember that one thing Sarah and Adam
changed was the way I had organized the counts. As usual, I had counted
out the music in the way I heard it, often an irregular sequence – here a
3, a 3, a 12, an 11, a 4, a 6, a 12, an 11, etc. Adam and Sarah studied
these, listening to the music, and said, 'Could we just count this in 6s?'
And here are my revised counts – all 6s and the odd 3. It was the first
time, I suppose, that I'd been contradicted in my way of counting – and
it was a lot easier for everyone once we'd counted it their way.

I learnt a lot, of course, while making the pas de deux. I wasn't sure sometimes how high a lift could go; or where one lift could go once it was in motion. But I always had an idea in mind, an image that I was aiming towards – though sometimes it would go off at a tangent. Those rehearsals for the duet work were what I loved the most, actually; they felt the most creative. The solo work, and the ensembles, involved a different kind of contribution, in which I was often getting up and helping them do it. I always knew that I wanted the duet to be both intimate and sexually passionate. We were always talking about it from an acting point of view while we made it. I'm sure we'll fiddle around with it further, but I was always happy with it. What I would work towards now is to make it more natural-looking in its passion, rather than hitting spectacular positions.[2]

A lot of my work later on is to do with directing the action, and this is what my rehearsal notes show. They look like a director's notes for rehearsing a play. 'Sarah – more horror at gun.' 'Lynn – too much reaction to shoes, don't show it to audience.' Pages and pages of notes like that. Here are some notes for the third version of the Prologue: 'Lynn stays on. Sarah comes from party, sees her, gets father. Father distraught, holds body. Lynn comforts, Sarah drops teddy, Lynn and Sarah look at each other, Sarah accusingly, Lynn half smile.' As I've said, we ended up not using any of that.

AM: *During this rehearsal process, you got to know this large group of dancers well, and a number of them were new to the company. When you'd made* Swan Lake, *Will Kemp was the only Royal Ballet School-trained dancer to audition (some other ballet dancers auditioned). With* Cinderella, *however, you had had scores of ballet dancers to choose from; and likewise from contemporary backgrounds. How do you feel about the dancers you chose? And those you rejected?*

MB: The best dancers to work with, certainly in audition, are those who have a way of looking at the movement and just doing it, without bringing any in-built affectations or stylistic tricks to it. What happens with a lot of classical-ballet dancers that come to auditions – even dancers who, you think, should be able to do anything, dancers you've seen in many productions of different ballets by different choreographers – is that they can't actually string the movement together or make any sense of it. It's

2 Bourne did indeed alter this pas de deux in 1999 for the Los Angeles production, having Cinderella and the Pilot alone in a bedroom, evidently after sex. The beginning and end of the pas de deux in particular were revised.

too alien to what they know, and you just know you're not going to get anywhere. With student dancers from some of the ballet schools, it's certainly no better. Even at that stage, they're not open-minded enough to be able to take on something new.

That's a big problem with dance schools at the moment – not ballet schools alone. We've recently been round all the British schools, both ballet and contemporary, and there's something missing from the training. Dance students are set in the way they move, so that it's very difficult to get them to do anything else.

AM: *Is that partly to do with your strong emphasis on the torso and upper body?*
MB: Yes, but the main problem is to do with connecting movement together and not just hitting positions; they want to hit positions constantly. Dance, as far as I'm concerned, is going through positions, but to them it's about stopping in them. I know that Ashton and Balanchine would tell their dancers to hit positions – but they would also make a strong emphasis on a through impetus and on connective phrasing. Today's student dancers, to an alarming extent, are making no real phrases.

I wish, too, that there were drama classes within dance colleges and that there was more opportunity for dance students to create characters through movement. This isn't just because colleges are now very technically orientated. When I was a dance student, we did lots of non-technical things, but I think that only once in all our many choreographic sessions was I set a task that was anything to do with character.

Another problem is: Where does a movement start? You try to explain that, in anything that involves the back more, the shoulders always need to be kept down. The impulse should come from lower in the spine and torso, but they find it hard. As a result, they find it very difficult to live in the movement, to become something beyond themselves.

AM: *How has the feel or direction of your company changed?*
MB: I certainly try to improve the technical standards. The big difference is that a lot of them now are doing things beyond anything I could ever have done myself as a dancer. Whereas once I could always show the choreography and it all came from my body, that's no longer the case. When I look at some of my old works on video now, they seem so grounded; I'd make the dancers jump more if I was working on them now.

Something that's still an issue for us is partnering. A lot of the men in the company don't have a great deal of partnering experience or strength.

There's some resistance – 'Not another lift!' – amongst a lot of the male dancers. But there are now about ten boys from a ballet background, who don't seem to have a problem with it – it's part of what they've come from. For some of the contemporary dancers, lifts are a problem. It's always 'These lifts hurt the back' – which I'm afraid becomes boring after a while. This is an area where I could get more creative in time to come; I'm not making monstrous demands in that direction, and dancers really can train themselves to acquire the strength to cope with what demands I do make in this direction.

I've tried to get better dancers generally, both ballet- and contemporary-trained: by 'better', I refer less to technique, I think, than to spirit. Certainly someone like Adam has brought a certain integrity to the playing of a role that people have admired and learnt from. When we were rehearsing *Swan Lake,* he always gave the full performance, so that I could see what was going on. He acted full-out at people, so that they had to react and act back. Scott is similar. And Fiona also had this commitment to performance, to showing in the studio what her full performance would be like. Very inspiring. Elsewhere in the company, I had been getting a lot of, 'Oh well, we'll see it on the night' – especially for reactions. That's why Act Three in *Swan Lake* felt a bit dead in the studio.

Lynn is Lynn and she does what she does, but what people admire in her is her total involvement in character on stage. You have to rise to the occasion to work with her; but hers is a different form of acting. She doesn't connect so much as you might expect in terms of the eyes. Her style comes from a certain era of dance acting, which is much more operatic and larger than life. Some of our performers probably think more of it as film acting, but Lynn takes naturally to playing to large houses. Her much more out-front style took some adjusting to, even by seasoned performers like Scott – who in due course became devoted to her; but her commitment to performance is always an inspiration. As a result, both Saranne Curtin and Maxine Fone in *Cinderella* gave fuller and fuller performances in rehearsal – so that I could actually see what they were going to do.

Previews

MATTHEW BOURNE: I learnt from *Cinderella* just how invaluable the whole process of preview performances can be, and the danger of opening a big production in the West End straightaway. So many of our old shows opened in Bristol, and I missed that this time around. We weren't even opening at Sadler's Wells, as we had with *Swan Lake* – we went straight into the Piccadilly Theatre. Many musicals have been performed there, but most of them would have opened out of town first.

ALASTAIR MACAULAY: *How many previews had* Swan Lake *had at Sadler's Wells?*

MB: Just two performances before we allowed critics in. At the time, that seemed like a lot! Most dance productions open to all the press on their first night, but my whole experience with *Oliver!* was so much about previewing that – fortunately – I had that model in my mind when I was doing *Cinderella*. I had learnt that previews were a form of rehearsal, and I made sure the company of *Cinderella* knew that as well – that these were rehearsal days until a couple of shows before the first night. Partly because I was ill for more than a week during the official rehearsal period, we had to cancel two previews and were rehearsing and revising things right up to the first night. The pressure was intense.

One thing that happens during previews is that – for two or three weeks before the first night – all kinds of people feel the need to tell you how to fix the show. Sometimes this is useful, and sometimes it's dreadful. What was most useful and interesting to me was what Sam Mendes did. He came to the very first preview performance, we had dinner afterwards, and he simply told me what he thought he'd seen – told me the story as he'd understood it on stage. And that's what you want to hear – not 'This bit was good, that bit wasn't very good.' I'll say, 'What do you think you saw there?' and that's how I find out what's coming across.

You start to hear some odd things! I suddenly realized that the original Prologue, with its big emphasis on the mother and Stepmother, confused people. Many of them thought at first that one or other of them was Cinderella. Then, when Cinderella did appear, they weren't sure, until some way in, that this actually was Cinderella. So I listened to this, realizing that I needed to make Cinderella more central right from the beginning. She originally started at the side of the stage, just reading a magazine, completely anonymous, with all the brothers' and sisters' business going on. I had thought she would emerge from the group eventually and that we'd all know that that was Cinderella; but you've got to be more obvious with an audience sometimes. So we placed her centre stage – so that everything reacted around her – and then we all knew that she was Cinderella.

345

Another problem was that, even for those people who realized which character was the Stepmother and which was Cinderella, the point of the Prologue – Cinderella's real mother being killed, with Cinderella a witness of sorts – just didn't fall into place until well into Act Two, if then. 'Why have we seen this murder?' they'd say. 'What's it got to do with the main story?' Some of them thought that the main story was, in fact, a flashback to the past rather than the opposite. One detail whereby we managed to confuse people was to do with shoes. We wanted Cinderella to attach so much significance to this one pair of shoes because they had been her mother's; but the audience, seeing her mother die in those shoes, began to wonder if she too was Cinderella.

I realized that we all understood the story as if we knew the words they were speaking; but the audience doesn't know which character is which, or how each one feels about any of the others, until you make it clear. This sounds obvious as I say it, and most of our *Cinderella* was perfectly clear. I'm actually very proud that we made such a completely new version of the old story clear in so many respects to so many people. We didn't give them the Cinderella narrative they knew; we gave them one they'd never imagined. But there were features, especially to do with the Prologue, that didn't make sense to an audience at first. In fact, there still are, although only minor ones. I'll go on working on this production until I feel I've got it right.

Then there were people like Cameron Mackintosh. He had put some money into the production, and he had ideas, and – because he's such an enthusiast – he has to tell you all of them. He does it in a good way – but it's a hard time. You must listen to people's opinions, but when people, even people like Cameron, tell you, 'This doesn't work – cut it', you have to stick to your vision for the piece yourself and you mustn't lose sight of it. I've been told to cut things quite a lot, but I was determined to do the complete score. I felt I would be letting myself down if I didn't.[3]

Katharine (Doré) wrote me a letter after some of the first previews to make some suggestions. She didn't really know the show – she was just reacting as an audience member. She knew just how to handle the situation.

Likewise, certain members of the company who were not performing every night would go out and watch – and I would listen to some of

3 None the less, Bourne later cut two short musical terms from the Seasons suite in Act One when reproducing *Cinderella* for Los Angeles.

them. Ben Wright was very useful in this respect after an early preview –
mainly to do with passing on what people actually were or were not
seeing from the story.

Still, I discovered that an audience will accept certain things without
needing to make full narrative sense of them. Even when we reduced
the Stepmother's pre-history, the audience was just happy to accept that
Cinderella contained a bad character. People didn't need to know why
she had taken against her stepdaughter; that's merely what they expected
when they came to *Cinderella*.

AM: *So what changes did you make?*
MB: It was very hard when we decided to simplify the whole Prologue. We were removing things that, for some members of the cast,
were the entire reason for what they then did throughout the rest of
the show. Lynn, Barry, all three Cinderellas – to explain to them at this
late stage that the old Prologue wasn't important and that it would be
better just to introduce the characters at the beginning was really
painful. We did show Cinderella's real mother, but just briefly, and
showed the Stepmother taking her place; and at the same time we
showed how Cinderella's place in the family declined. Extremely simple,
and clear.

Achievement

ALASTAIR MACAULAY: *It impresses me that, while I've been doing these
interviews with you and talking to Lez Brotherston, Etta Murfitt, Scott
Ambler and Adam Cooper, all of you have calmly and openly talked
about the various things in* Cinderella *you'd still like to 'fix'. Some
choreographers refuse ever to make changes to a work.*
MATTHEW BOURNE: We're still making changes in *Swan Lake*! And I
don't just mean the changes that most choreographers make as they
adjust details to suit different dancers. There are still dances in *Swan
Lake* that I think can be clearer or more entertaining. I know it's considered a big 'hit' – but, for us, it's always a work in progress.

The same goes for *Cinderella* – only more so, because there are still
important details we want to adjust. The important thing will be to agree
on which direction to revise it. One option could bring back the old Prologue but focus it and integrate it better. Another is to re-accentuate the
role of Cinderella. The blackout scene needs revision, but we haven't
decided just what we will make of it. These things are best discussed by

a whole group of us: Lez Brotherston, Scott Ambler, Etta Murfitt, and, if he's available, Adam Cooper.

One very good suggestion that I'll consider came from Sam Mendes, after that first preview he saw. He felt that the whole thing should start with Cinderella in a hospital bed, having been in the bombing, and being on one of those sort of life-support machines with a beep going; there should be an enormous clock in the background; the Angel should come in, and the clock should stop just before midnight. Then the piece would start, like a flashback, but with this 'Will she die? Won't she die?' tension behind it all. Then we would get to that point again in Act Three, where she's back in the hospital. I loved it when he told me – very *Matter of Life and Death,* too – but it was so different from the story that we'd been pursuing at that point. We may not use it, but it's a terrific new angle on the whole story, isn't it? Few suggestions are that imaginative.

Another good idea – which we may well use when we revise it in 1999 – came from Adam. This would involve framing the whole show in the midnight section at the end of Act Two. The bomb goes off, the dream turns to nightmare, and the nightmare is Cinderella's recurrent memory of the Stepmother murdering her mother. This will explain why the Stepmother comes to the hospital in Act Three – to try and get rid of her.

AM: *Would you say there's any message to your* Cinderella?
MB: I'm not into messages.

AM: *I didn't think you were, but you spoke earlier of the message of* Highland Fling.
MB: But we didn't make *Highland Fling* to deliver a message. We simply found that, as we made the piece, it was saying something anyway. We were asking there, 'Why does James cut the Sylph's wings off?' The answer is that he wants to turn her into an ordinary woman. So the message is about a certain kind of accidentally destructive man who wants to possess and contain the thing he loves.

You could say that the message of this *Cinderella* is that each of us may have a guardian angel, that each of us may find love and fulfilment in surprising circumstances, that romantic love and glamorous fantasy can occur in very ordinary, unglamorous, or grim circumstances.

AM: Cinderella *is the fourth of your so-called 'classics'. As you look at the series –* Nutcracker, Highland Fling, Swan Lake, Cinderella – *do you think that you've got deeper into your music each time? It occurs to me that part of what makes your* Nutcracker *fun is that, from the over-ture on, there is an irony between what we see and what we hear. We hear wonderful innocence in the music, but we see these stock-still lost orphans. And that irony is there at one level in our minds right through your* Nutcracker. *In* Highland Fling, *that irony isn't so strong – but it's there from time to time. After all, it begins in a gents' toilet! Right in the middle of things, there are brief moments that look as if the dancers happen to be sending up* La Sylphide. *(Maxine Fone, in the middle of a dance, suddenly sends up a Taglioni pose; and, in Act Two, you do some of your most absurdly earnest mime to the music that, in the Bournon-ville version, accompanies the most tragic/heroic dance for James.)*

But with Swan Lake, *though it has plenty of irony, there's no point when you're seriously ironic about the idea of* Swan Lake *itself – except, early on in the Moth Ballet, which isn't really about* Swan Lake *but about bad old ballet. Likewise in* Cinderella, *you may do a completely new take on the old story, but it comes out of the music. You may some-times go completely against Prokofiev's deliberate intention, but you're not making some ironic comment on his score or its scenario; you are responding to numerous aspects of the music.*

MB: I hope you're absolutely right to see that, because I think my approach has indeed changed quite a lot. I've steadily tried for a more generally serious approach to the score and to the subject-matter – the seriousness doesn't preclude humour – and I have tired of needing to comment on a piece in the way I used to. I try now to get to the heart of the piece emotionally – rather than show how clever I am. Some people find, particularly with *Cinderella*, that there are whole sections that don't seem like the older AMP. Yet, funnily enough, one of my intentions with *Cinderella* was to return to the old smaller-scale AMP style in the family scenes.

If I was to do *Giselle* now as a piece, it wouldn't be anything like *Highland Fling*. I've done my ironic comment on the Romantic era in that one. I would approach my *Giselle* through the music much more.

AM: *We may well find it ironic just to conceive that anybody might make a 'classic' anyway in our time. But – this is a favourite theme of mine, and was a point I made when teaching dance history all those years ago – the word 'classical' in its wider sense (or senses) can be applied to such non-ballet dancers as Fred Astaire, and even Isadora Duncan;*

and it can be applied to the work of such modern-dance choreographers as Merce Cunningham, Paul Taylor, Twyla Tharp or Mark Morris. So, when you call these four works 'classics', do you think of yourself as a 'classical' artist?

MB: I was put into a 'Best of British' issue of *Vogue* last month. They'd grouped together various artists from different areas, and I was in a photo with a gardener, an artist, a clothes designer, a writer . . . We didn't know why we'd all been brought together, but apparently they'd put us under the banner of 'classicists'. It took several of us by surprise. I said at the time, 'I hope it doesn't look as if I'm calling myself this, because I think there'll be a lot of people that'll argue against that.' You being one of them!

AM: *I would, but I don't need to impose my views on you or on this book.*

MB: I don't feel as though I am. I do, as you know, acknowledge the past a lot; but it's for other people to say. I feel as though my approach is structurally quite similar to a lot of classical ballets in the way I approach work; but the actual movement, and the attitude to movement, is coming from somewhere else. Do you see this issue of dance classicism as something larger than the style of the steps?

AM: *Yes, I do. A dance classicist makes dances that are about dance itself, in a way that is as formally coherent as a piece of classical music. And dance classicism expresses a certain attitude to human energy and to artistic form, to the world and to connectedness of life.*

MB: As I've acknowledged before, dances about dance are not my foremost skill, though I try for that at times.

AM: *What surprises me in looking at your work – and particularly at* Cinderella *– is that it belongs to a genre almost now defunct, a genre formed in the eighteenth century: the 'ballet d'action', which is primarily about narrative and character and situation – about representation – and only incidentally or occasionally about pure dance values. In Act Three of* Cinderella, *you have virtually a whole act of mime – something that has hardly been attempted since the nineteenth century.*

MB: There are a couple of dance solos, but the emphasis is mainly gestural. It was instantly the most popular act, the act that completely worked for audiences and that needed least revision. It works straightaway for an audience that isn't used to looking at dance.

AM: *Are you proud of being able to make an entirely mimed act?*
MB: I feel it's part of the company's style, a style that we've developed for a long time now. In that sense, yes, I feel proud of that, because I know that very few people are choreographing this way today.

Performance

ALASTAIR MACAULAY: *When your company is performing in the West End, your leading dancers are commanding higher fees than they would if they were with the Royal Ballet – is that true?*
MATTHEW BOURNE: Probably, yes – some of them.

AM: *And the general ensemble members of your company are earning West End fees way above what they would in any contemporary dance company – and possibly more than if they were in the corps de ballet at Covent Garden.*
MB: Yes, that's true.

AM: *When their run is over, however, they go back on the dole queue?*
MB: Yes. They also have to take the risk – as many actors do as a way of life – that a West End or a Broadway run can close with two weeks' notice.

AM: *Taking that risk has worked very well for some of your company. It led Adam Cooper to choose between a secure contract at Covent Garden and an insecure but exciting independent career. Have there been other people who've chosen not to go into secure salaried dance jobs?*
MB: Yes, some of them from contemporary dance. People have chosen to work with us rather than going to Rambert Dance Company, for example, where they would have a secure job, probably for years. It doesn't always work to our advantage, mind you. There are dancers I'd like to attract who find that they need the secure job tenure that I can't offer them.

AM: *Although I missed all the brouhaha of the previews and the first night, I saw the production three times during its four-month run at the Piccadilly Theatre. I straightaway thought it told its completely different story very clearly (with one or two blips on the way). There were individual performances and dances that I loved more on each viewing. And I found that it cohered more each time. Was this growing coherence due*

*to the company getting it under its belt? Or were you able to rehearse it
and fine-tune it further during the run?*
MB: A bit of both. The more you perform any new choreography, the
more you can get on and do the movement – which is in the body – and
then give a performance on top of that; but also, they had time to talk
about their roles a lot in note sessions and in some smaller rehearsals.

AM: *How often do you do note sessions?*
MB: We have the possibility of doing it every day, after class and, if it's
needed, we use that slot. We don't use it every day during a long run, but
we do several times a week.

AM: *We've talked of how some performers developed during rehearsals
and previews. In the three performances I saw, I was especially struck
by the difference between Adam Cooper and William Kemp as the
Pilot.*
MB: I was surprised at how logically Will had thought through the whole
thing – he hadn't shown in rehearsal that he would be quite that thorough. I know now that he had thought it through with detail and feeling,
but the naturalness of it was a very happy surprise to me in the theatre.
Some dancers don't look as if they know why they're doing what they're
doing. It looks like: 'Now I move here – and I look here – and I do this',
which drives me mad. So, when I see someone who makes their performance work in that way, it's very exciting.

As with *Swan Lake,* there were several details that Adam just did
naturally to perfection. Will had to work harder. At first, he made some
of the English-smoothie character of the Pilot in Act Two funny in a
way I hadn't intended. He got real laughs; it was witty. But I wanted to
preserve the romance of the character, the real emotion behind it. He
had understood the whole shape of the role, however, and he caught
the nervous breakdown in Act Three with an intensity that was all his
own. Adam has a relaxation on stage that works uniquely well at several
moments: when he lights a cigarette and looks at Cinderella, he's so calm
that it's a powerful moment.

They're both very good in the role, and for them it was good to be
dancing the role of the Angel as well.

AM: *Etta Murfitt – dancing several roles, none of which took much of
the limelight – has said to me that the fun of the run for her lies in doing
three different roles each week.*

MB: Yes, it works for some people, and all Etta's performances were terrific. But it's much bigger sweat for other members of the company. The eight-show-a-week routine puts great pressure on everyone.

AM: *So tell me, what is the structure of a working week for a member of Adventures in Motion Pictures?*
MB: In the West End, there are six evening performances from Monday to Saturday, and matinées on Wednesday and Saturday as well. We try to give people one show off a week, if we can – but when some dancers get injured this often isn't possible. The dancers are contractually required to take a minimum of four classes each week out of six. Company class lasts an hour and a half; if they take class elsewhere, they have to clear that with us, the day before. We try to make classes as near to the show as possible – mid- to late-afternoon. Then, after that class, we put in a forty-five-minute 'emergency call' every day, in case we need last-minute rejiggings to cover things like changes of partner. This session is also when we give notes. When a larger rehearsal is needed, then the class may be shifted to midday or late morning. The rehearsal will take place after that. But if the rehearsal is smaller or less demanding, then we'll call in a few people before class and do a rehearsal from about midday onwards.

AM: *Tell me about company class. What range of teachers and range of styles do you draw from?*
MB: We try to vary it between classical and contemporary classes each week. We employ guest teachers for a week at a time.

AM: *Any particular kinds of ballet? Any particular kinds of contemporary?*
MB: In ballet, the dancers like a ballet class that's very dancy, that really moves: not one too tied to individual virtuoso steps. Much depends on the teacher, and we have found several good ones – such as Laura Connor – who are popular with the dancers. Also a few people within the company teach class sometimes: Iain Webb, Etta, Isabel Mortimer, Ben Wright, Vicky Evans.

The dancers who've been professional ballet dancers – Adam and Sarah, for example – do a few contemporary classes, but generally go to ballet class. There was some fuss made in the ballet press that Sarah was required by the Royal Ballet to keep up half-an-hour special pointe-work every day while she was with us. Maybe she was, but she didn't tell us about it. Lynn, of course, will only do ballet class, but she is very specific about what she likes. She has taught a few classes for us, but though they're good classes, the features that are, to her, articles of faith – the crossed-over fifth positions that she learnt in Stanley Williams's class in New York – really aren't useful to most of our dancers.

The contemporary classes tend to be more Cunningham-based. Whatever style of contemporary it is, it needs to be quite technical and strengthening – not the kind of contemporary that's more to do with finding your body, and rolling around on the floor, and release. Those just wouldn't be useful to us.

Revisions

ALASTAIR MACAULAY: *Tell me about the revised version of* Cinderella *you took to Los Angeles.*
MATTHEW BOURNE: The whole experience of the Los Angeles production of *Cinderella* was great. I loved the collaboration involved in planning revisions – we really got back to the things we valued most in our work. The whole production had much more of a company feeling; the dancers enjoyed doing it and took pride in it.

AM: *So how did you change it?*
MB: Lez Brotherston, Scott Ambler, Etta Murfitt and I spent several days discussing what we wanted to change, and why.

As a result, we made the whole family household in Act One more domestic in scale. There was a large drape to separate the hallway from the living-room, and there were lighting fittings hanging down to stop the room seeming palatial in height. We kept the simple Prologue in which the Stepmother and her brood of kids replace Cinderella's mother and demote Cinderella. And we began the family scene by giving the audience what it expects to see in any *Cinderella*: the heroine busy doing the housework centre-stage, her sisters lolling about. Then we introduced the other members of the family. We also made the Stepmother less of a star role and a more completely integrated member of her family.

And we gave the Pilot much more to do in this act – or, rather, we made him much more of a fleshed-out character at this stage of the show. The blackout scene involved not just Cinderella's search but also his.

In Act Two, we made the ballroom less dreamlike and more specific: a club, a place where a World War Two story really might happen, with a waitress and a *maître d'*. It had a much more realized bandstand, with a piano, a double bass, and a mike; and (instead of banquettes) it had chairs and tables, to make it more social.

At the same time, we made the whole ballroom look much more wrecked. At the beginning, we had Cinderella (still dressed as she had been in Act One) and the Angel, taking in the bomb-wreckage to the ballroom; and then we made much more of the Angel bringing the ballroom back to life. We approached the 'blue' couples as individual characters. Each had a different hairstyle; and they all looked much less like the dancers in Ashton's *La Valse* than they had before and much more like real people in the 1940s. Two of the five 'blue' men were no longer in uniform: one was a bandleader wearing a tux, another a *maître d'* in tails. They were still mainly 'blue' couples (with red accessories), and the fact that they were dead couples who come back to life for the duration of this act was made more emphatic.

It was still a 'dream' act, but we located the dream in reality much better this time. And we introduced Cinderella's mother here, with her father, both alive and well. They're a vision, a part of Cinderella's dream. She can't communicate with them, but they're part of the sense that this is a ballroom where dreams seem to come true. Actually, Cinderella's mother here is the one area in which we still confused audiences. She was in a white dress, and the production had used publicity showing Cinderella wearing a similar white dress in the London production. Cinderella no longer wore that white dress in Los Angeles, but a few people in the LA audience had already connected her with the white dress and so confused mother and daughter.

Just about everything for the 'blue' couples was rechoreographed. We gave them more of a flavour of 1940s social dance: not so much as to re-create those dances literally, but just enough to place them in a period and an atmosphere. The Stepmother no longer had a separate entrance; she entered with her family. That made a big difference. Cinderella now was more clearly her own fantasy: a sexy woman, like a film star. And not goody two-shoes. When the Pilot chooses her in front of all her family, she shows just a hint of malicious satisfaction.

We changed the pas de deux considerably. It was now more plainly a separate scene in another place, with a bed in which the Pilot was lying, plainly after they'd had sex. And the beginning, the ending, and parts of the middle were entirely changed.

The strokes of midnight worked much better largely because we lit the scene far better this time, but also because we clarified: the audience can see Angel warning Cinderella about the time, and there's a sense of his unrelenting control of events. When midnight starts, Cinderella sees one layer of nightmare after another. First, her family taunting her with the invitation to the party and leaving her out. Second, the shooting of her mother by her stepmother. (Whether or not this had actually happened in the past is deliberately left unclear; this is a nightmare.) Third, the family joins the Stepmother around the body of Cinderella's mother. (It would be almost the same group-portrait scene as we saw in the prologue to Act One, but for the mother's corpse.) Cinderella tries to shake her father and get him to react, but he doesn't respond. Fourth, he's pushed into a wheelchair. Fifth, Cinderella sees the Pilot with one of her sisters. Sixth, she – in hysterics – runs offstage (actually to do a quick change). Seventh, the Angel initiates the destruction of the buildings. Eighth, the 'blue' couples start to die again, in stylized movements, with images of bodies being carried like corpses and other people screaming. Ninth, on the final stroke of midnight, Cinderella reappears – dressed in her old drab clothes – and falls down lifeless amid all the bombing. Tenth, her body is picked up by air-raid wardens and carried off on a stretcher.

The whole show had much more logic.

AM: *How much logic does an audience need, though? We know this is a dance show; we know the hero and heroine will have a dance duet. Do we need to see the specific state they've reached in their sexual relationship?*

MB: I believe the audience does need it. Even when an audience comes expecting to see this situation or that in a well-known story like *Cinderella,* it helps if you give the world onstage such detail and motivation that each situation becomes unusually real.

Certainly it helps the performers. If you're going to do a long run of a show, you need to know why you're doing each and every movement if you're going to find satisfaction from performance night after night. In Act Three, for example, the West End audience may not have been bothered by the fact that Cinderella's family all went to visit her in hospital – but the performers were. They've never liked her, so why do they visit her? Now in LA we could make much clearer what we'd always meant to show – that all the members of the step-family have abused

Cinderella in some way and that they're frightened, now that she's undergoing psychiatric treatment after being traumatized by the bomb, that she'll tell on them. They want to shut her up, the Stepmother above all. In the scene when she returns to Cinderella, she used to try smothering Cinderella in her sleep. Now she confronts her, threatens her. There's a struggle. Possibly the Stepmother tries strangling Cinderella; it's not entirely clear, because at that moment other people arrive. That was our main change in Act Three; otherwise it was the act we could leave much as it had been.

AM: *I testify how much better the show was in LA; I was able to see it there three times. Among other things, I could see many more filmic resonances now. In Act Three, after we've seen (to one side) the* Brief Encounter *couple at their railway-café table, there's an amazingly moving little moment when she (Philippa Gordon in the Celia Johnson role) is briefly centre stage. She's alone now, and she turns and gazes at the table where they said goodbye. It's just a look, and it's absolutely laden with feeling.*

In Act Two, Cinderella now arrives in the ballroom with her hair flowing over her shoulders, in a sexy coloured dress rather than in debutante white. Sarah Wildor (blonde) looks like Veronica Lake; Saranne Curtin (redhead) looks like Rita Hayworth. Was that deliberate?

MB: No, that was just happy accident. We knew the look we wanted. Only when the dancers put those costumes on did we realize that they looked like individual film stars.

But there were other consciously film-related ideas we were able to bring off better this time. In Act One, we'd always had the idea that Cinderella tries to touch the Angel, but finds that she puts her hand through him, but we weren't able to put it into practice. This time, we really brought it off, entirely in movement terms. She gestures towards him. First, his body arches back before her hand in a concave arch, and then it suddenly snaps back into an upright position – with her hand sticking out now behind his back, and with her looking at it in alarm.

AM: *I met you in London just after you'd finished rehearsals, a few days before you flew to LA. You told me how pleased you were with how they'd gone, and you said, 'I think it's only the second time around that you do the real choreography!'*

MB: What's interesting is that, this time, I did much more of the creative work. The first time around, I encouraged the dancers to come up with much of the material for the movement. This time I had a much more precise idea of what I wanted. I've talked about 'we' as usual, and I don't think I would have been so clear in rehearsals if I had not been through those very productive discussions with Lez, Scott and Etta. They focused my mind.

There is no one sure formula in choreography. I'm lucky in that I work with like-minded people who help me to clarify what's in my mind; or to see the sense of what's in theirs. When work goes well, you just get deeper – it seems – into your own instinct. And into the music. I knew what I'd heard in Prokofiev's score all along, but this time I was able to bring much more of it to life.

(Conversations 1998–99)

11

The Car Man

2000

Idea

ALASTAIR MACAULAY: *Several things are going on at once in* The Car Man. *It's a movie-like story that partly resembles* The Postman Always Rings Twice – *but partly not. It's a new treatment of Bizet's score for the opera* Carmen – *but the music has been not only rearranged but also reordered. And the Carmen role – in the opera, Carmen is the working-class femme fatale who changes lives and who passes through more than one lover – is here perhaps both a male and a female role. Which idea came first?*

MATTHEW BOURNE: After spending five years with *Swan Lake* and *Cinderella*, my desire was to do something more earthy and real. I wanted to make a dance story without using any dream scenes. (Actually, even here there is one tiny dream. And a flashback. But dreams and memories aren't central to *The Car Man*, whereas in my *Swan Lake* and *Cinderella* they are.) So that was one task I was setting myself from the outset.

Another objective was to make something more contemporary in style; and to create characters who were more working-class. My company had spent the years 1995 to 1999 playing princes, princesses, period drama, with ballroom scenes, having to learn the social manners of other eras. That suited some performers, but not others. Some of my dancers are very good dance-actors, but it's just not natural to them to learn high-society manners. I thought, 'Wouldn't it be good to do something with them that's nearer to them as people: very young, very sexy?' After all the repression in *Swan Lake*, I wanted to let rip with real lust and sex. [*Laughs.*] And I wanted something where, if we were going to kiss, we were really going to kiss – not just touch lips!

359

I wanted a show for a smaller cast, but that would have two good roles for men. Adam Cooper and Will Kemp had both been so important in *Swan Lake* and *Cinderella*, so I was looking for something where I could contrast them on stage.

And I wanted two leading roles for women. I'd promised a role to Sara Curtin (aka Saranne Curtin), because she'd been a leading company member since *Nutcracker* days, and because I admire her so much. She goes back a long way with us, and has played the female lead in virtually every show I have done since *Cinderella*. When you look at the range of roles she's done, her list is quite astounding. My company is probably known for its male dancers, but we do have some wonderful women. I don't know many people who are better dancer-actresses than Sara is. The skill she brought to performances of the Queen in my *Swan Lake* in Paris in December 2005 was incredible. The detail and nuances she manages to get into every moment: she's very clever. Yet she's not really appreciated as much as she should be. I wanted also to make a role for Etta Murfitt, whose association with the company goes back yet further. She hadn't been in the original *Swan Lake* because of having a baby, and she had played only supporting roles in *Cinderella*. Etta is another great actress-dancer who needed and deserved a meaty role.

I mentioned Adam Cooper. I find it all too easy to forget now how central he was to my initial conception of this show because, in the event, Alan Vincent made it so much his own. I really began planning it with Adam in mind; the title role grew out of the Stranger character in *Swan Lake*. I thought, 'Well, he's so good at that, he could do this.' And I had asked him to do it. But we just couldn't make it happen. About two months before rehearsals started, I knew I had to recast the role. Recently I was going through my old letters, and I found a fax from him saying how gutted he was, how upset that he wasn't doing it. Perhaps these things are all for the best – I can't imagine any Car Man better than Alan Vincent proved to be, he's just perfect – but I'm sorry that those years of working with Adam came to an end. We've tried to work again several times since then, but he's never been able to make it for any new project.

I wanted, too, to choreograph a thriller – a show with suspense, where the audience would really want to know what was going to happen next.

I didn't know I had material for a show until several ideas came together. I'd known the opera *Carmen* since the 1980s, and I was thinking about adapting the story of *The Postman Always Rings Twice*. But those two ideas weren't enough by themselves. It was bringing the two together that made the show happen in my mind.

What interested me as a choreographer was not Bizet's opera but Rodion Schedrin's rearrangement of it. Bizet wasn't fresh in my head, so I wasn't aware just how free the Schedrin adaptation was: just strings and percussion. It was the first version of Bizet's music I'd heard that grabbed my interest as a choreographer. Though I think I'd heard it years before, now it excited me at once. It had the raunchiness I was looking for. And a lot began to fall into place around it.

AM: *You'd been looking into the* Carmen *story?*
MB: Yes. I had once had an idea of a sort of Almodóvar *Carmen*, with kinky Spanish sex;[1] and that led me to look for a small-scale orchestration of the Bizet music. The opera's Carmen works in a cigarette factory, and so my original idea was of a meat factory. I wanted the action dirty, raw, with meat and carcasses. I was thinking of Peter Greenaway's film *The Cook, the Thief, His Wife & Her Lover* (1989), especially the scene where Helen Mirren and Alan Howard have sex in the back of a butcher's delivery van full of swinging, bloody meat carcasses.

But that felt too gory at the time. So I changed it to a garage.

AM: *Did you see David Pountney's 1986 staging of* Carmen *for English National Opera? That was set in a car dump in a banana republic, and the critics drew attention to the 'car men' pun in the title.*
MB: I certainly saw that. I remember the cars, in enormous piles. I'm sure all that must have influenced me – though it was never at the top of my mind.

But at some point I rejected *Carmen* as a story. I didn't find it satisfying. For opera, of course. For dance, no. Though there certainly are connections. (For example, the character of Rita is based on the character of Micaëla in the opera.) By that point, I had discovered the Schedrin version of *Carmen*, but I started listening to it with ideas for adapting the *Postman* story to it.

AM: *Tell me about your interest in* The Postman Always Rings Twice.
MB: I knew the two Hollywood movies: the first with Lana Turner and John Garfield, directed by Tay Garnett in black and white (1946), the second with Jessica Lange and Jack Nicholson, script by David Mamet, directed by Bob Rafelson in colour (1981). I loved the premise of a

[1] See original edition, p. 370. ·

drifter arriving in a small town which had a 'Man Wanted' sign displayed outside the diner: I thought that was great. But when I got interested in making a stage show from it, I also saw the earlier Visconti film of the same story, *Ossessione* (1943). I loved its realism, much more pronounced than either Hollywood version.

AM: *Have you read the James M. Cain novel (1934) on which both versions are based?*
MB: Oh yes.

AM: *So the Stranger in* Swan Lake *led you to this drifter/car-man hero. And he, as an outsider arriving in a small town in America, points the way to Edward Scissorhands, another hero you'd also begun to consider in the late 1990s.[2] Might one also link these 'outsider' figures to those of Kenneth MacMillan?*
MB: On the whole, I'd guess my outsiders are psychologically different from his. I'd say that he's interested in people within communities who are spiritually or temperamentally different, rebellious, whereas in these pieces I'm interested in men who are literally outsiders, strangers who turn up and disrupt the community. If there's something similar about MacMillan and myself, then it's probably that he was always looking for a good story. He wanted a story good enough to excite him and interest him enough to make a ballet, a story about strong characters, a story that has something to say and somewhere to go, with some sort of arc to its journey. I have that instinct too, so we're sometimes drawn to similar material. Beyond that, I just don't know.

AM: *Reviewing this* Car Man *in the* Financial Times, *Clement Crisp wrote that you were selling other people's wares – that you were making your works by adapting other stage works. How do you respond to that?*
MB: What other stage works? He likes what Kenneth MacMillan did with *Manon* – telling the old Prévost story to different Massenet music than the opera – doesn't he? And what Ashton does with *La Fille mal gardée* and *The Dream*: that's just telling the old stories to more or less the same old music as other choreographers. Now, if you want to say that I'm doing the same thing as them but less well, that's another matter. But don't complain that I'm following a third-rate practice when

[2] See Chapter 16 on *Edward Scissorhands*.

actually you praise other choreographers for doing precisely the same thing.

To update old stories, to give them fresh twists: isn't that what a lot of modern theatre has been doing for decades? In my case, I'm going a bit further because I'm changing the stories too. I'm particularly pleased with that aspect of *The Car Man*, actually. We heard from so many people who loved the fact that they just didn't know where the story would take them. They'd recognize the *Carmen* music, they'd recognize part of the *Postman* story – and then they'd realize that they still didn't know what to expect next.

I now think that *The Car Man* started a new direction in my work. As far as I'm concerned, it wasn't one of my 'classics' – it wasn't based on an old ballet.

AM: *Schedrin wrote that* Carmen *suite for the Bolshoi Ballet. It was a great vehicle for his wife, the prima ballerina Maya Plisetskaya. How did you approach him with your different treatment of the score?*
MB: I wrote to him. He's living in Germany much of the time these days. My point was that I was very enthusiastic about his arrangement, but that it wasn't long enough for my purposes. I asked him: Did he have any ideas? I was hoping he'd have another hour of *Carmen* arrangements up his sleeve!

He was very generous when he replied. But really he wasn't particularly concerned what we did with his music, and he couldn't help with any extra material. He even suggested: 'If you're using a recording, why not play it backwards?' He'd evidently moved on! So that certainly gave me carte blanche.

Preparation

MATTHEW BOURNE: Now I contacted the composer Terry Davies to arrange more *Carmen* music, using the same instrumentation as Schedrin. He was perfect. More scrupulous than Schedrin in his treatment of Bizet, actually.

ALASTAIR MACAULAY: *One part of your score actually comes not from* Carmen *but from Bizet's* L'Arlésienne, *the Farandole. It's been changed so much that it took me quite a while to recognize it.*
MB: Yes, but that's a section that Schedrin put in. Strange – when you consider how much *Carmen* he left out! Terry, by contrast,

76 Matthew Bourne and Terry Davies in rehearsal.

would only use *Carmen* material. And even there, he didn't like to be as free as Schedrin sometimes was. Working with Terry on the Bizet score was a very good experience for me. I could get excited by aspects of Schedrin, and could discuss with Terry how he thought it might support my story. Or I could get excited by new aspects of the story I was planning, and could come to Terry to ask what music could support that.

For example, we needed a lot of music for the second female character, Rita. It was natural here to use Micaëla's music in the opera – but it was fascinating to work with Terry on finding which bits to use where and in what settings. The *idea* of Rita didn't come from Micaëla, even though each of them is the innocent second woman. Rita's function in the plot is not at all like Micaëla's. But her character is comparable. And so Micaëla's music was a good resource. All those sweet melodies, some of which Rita shares with her would-be boyfriend Angelo just as Micaëla shares them with Don José, *her* would-be boyfriend in the opera.

AM: *Just how much did you analyse the original* Carmen *music? For example, it has a very striking fate motif, which Bizet brings round in many guises – slow and legato and soft, fast and staccato and loud. It's so subtly used that many people aren't aware of it in the opera, though actually it's as much a leitmotif as anything in Wagner. Listening to it and watching* The Car Man, *I thought you were using it as a fate motif. But again, it wasn't obvious.*

MB: Oh, yes, Terry and I certainly planned that as a fate motif!

AM: *And to what extent did you devise your Car Man, Luca, as a male dance counterpart to Bizet's Carmen? In the opera, she announces herself with the Habañera. Here you give that music to him.*

MB: We weren't schematic about that. Yes, I gave Luca the Habañera. But that's not necessarily female music, is it? Not exclusively female, I'd say. It's raunchy. Cheeky.

Luca has aspects of Carmen to him, yes. And he is – among other things – a symbol of fate. He arrives, and everyone's life changes. But Lana, our heroine, has aspects of Carmen to her too. That's why we gave her Carmen's Chanson Bohème to dance later on.

In the opera, the Carmen–José affair is what's central. But what's central in *The Car Man* is a triangle: Lana, Luca and Angelo. And as I developed the story, I did find that I was able to connect Angelo to Don José a good deal. He's an innocent who discovers sex and violence, who goes to prison, who finds he's capable of killing.

Throughout all this, I felt that, with Terry, I was working with a composer – rather than with an arranger. I could be quite free, and ask him for big new structural aspects or tiny details. And he'd always oblige. At the same time, I knew that he had his own set of rules. In particular, he wanted to be true to Bizet. Often I'd start with quite a rough idea. Sometimes Terry gave me so much in response that I didn't need any more. Sometimes he'd give me choices, and that would make me more specific.

One passage was so complex that it was easier to stage first, before knowing just what music there would be. That was the ending of Act One, from the murder on, which was about ten minutes long. Here I really felt that I was making filmlike action and that I needed Terry to respond to it like a film composer. Then he supplied the music, and we went on to restage the action to it, setting it out in greater detail, finding cues within the music, and so pinning sight to sound.

AM: *There are passages of real dance-as-dance interest in* The Car Man, *but they occur early in each act. The murder that ends Act One, the fight that ends Act Two: these aren't dances at all, even though they're very precisely choreographed as musical stage action. How do you feel about this?*

MB: I was aware of that. I'm certainly not anti-dance! – and I knew where I wanted dance opportunities. But I knew that this story would move into realistic action at the end of each act, and that it would only weaken it if I tried to add any dance to those crucial scenes. I now see that this method – starting each act with dance, then paring away into suspenseful action – is something I've also employed in subsequent works: it certainly applies to my latest, *Dorian Gray*.

So the first twelve minutes of *The Car Man* is solid dance. I thought 'Let's give them a lot up front.' It shows the world of this stage community – it's about character and situation – but it's all in dance terms. In fact, even when the plot has started to move, the dance carries on. It's pretty solid for the first twenty minutes. The same goes in Act Two. Then you get the audiences hooked on the story.

AM: *But didn't you feel any need to give more dance?*

MB: Not in this show. What's important here is realism. If the fights had been too dancey – though, as you say, they are very choreographed

77 'Fight Night'. Alan Vincent (Luca) and members of the original cast. This dance, near the end of Act Two, is inspired by the contemporary film *Fight Club*.

(more so than most people in the audience ever guess) – it just wouldn't work. Wouldn't work for the audience – and that's who I'm choreographing for.

I'm aware that there are people who want more dance. But they shouldn't be wanting it of *The Car Man*, or of me. Why expect me to fit into other choreographic moulds? I've made other shows that had more room for pure dance, but that's never been my first objective. And there are other choreographers who make pure-dance work that I'm very happy to applaud.

AM: *But what about your dancers?*
MB: *The Car Man* was absolutely geared for dancers I knew. This was the kind of movement they wanted to do – and if you asked most of them what is their favourite show to perform, this would be the one.

I often meet other dancers who say to me that they want to dance in my company. But I look at them and really I doubt it. Neither Adventures in Motion Pictures as it was when I made *The Car Man* nor New Adventures, the company I have today, is the place to show off your technique alone. It's about so much more than just steps – whereas you can often tell from meeting some dancers that technique is what's foremost in their minds.

AM: *The story of* The Car Man *is violent. There are two extended fights, and two male characters die on stage. At some point while watching it, I remembered how you, in the 1980s, had objected to all the violence choreographed for DV8, and how you'd said that your lyrical choreography for men – from the Mer Man in* The Infernal Galop *to the Swan in* Swan Lake *and the Angel in* Cinderella *– was a reaction against all that. Haven't you now contradicted yourself with all this violence in* The Car Man?
MB: No. DV8 (in those days) felt violent to dancers. You'd see people bruising themselves on stage. And I don't mean DV8 alone. In those days, you'd see a lot of what dancers called the Eurocrash (even though I'm told it began with the Canadian troupe La La La Human Steps and its choreographer Edouard Lock): that masochistic way of throwing themselves into the air and then crashing hard onto the floor. Now, that's not how I work.

The Car Man, it's true, has very little lyricism for men. And its characters are not instantly likeable. But though the dancers are playing violent roles, the choreography is not about punishing them as dancers. In fact, it's there to release them – to give them those moments of release that actors love in roles, here in physical terms. I will try to show off dancers' skill and talents, but I'm not into destroying them physically either.

AM: *The narrative has its sources in* The Postman Always Rings Twice *and in* Carmen. *How did you develop it? Did you bring in others to help you?*
MB: I wrote it on my own. Over some months. On the computer! I could keep adjusting it. It was there, to be fiddled around with, on the screen.[3]

AM: *The title role of* The Car Man *is Luca. However, following the story in the theatre, I feel that his story is told from the outside, whereas Angelo's is told from inside.*
MB: Luca begins strong. Then, when he and Lana have murdered her husband, he becomes plagued by guilt. All that I took from *The Postman*. Mutual guilt keeps him and her together: guilt and fear. So that's interesting. He's set up as Mr Cool. He turns up, he seduces her: all quite conventional. You think, 'Oh, I know this story.' Then you think: 'Oh, is he seducing Angelo as well?' Next, you realize that he is far more affected by the murder than Lana is. He feels bad; he's plagued by hallucinations; he becomes weak and impotent.

Angelo certainly is seen from inside, yes. He has more of the audience's sympathy than anyone else. He has sweeter music than Luca, and more 'feeling' music too. His story creeps up on you. He's the victim – and, as you may remember, I always like to have one of those in a story: the sufferer. The second Mrs de Wynter in *Deadly Serious*, the Prince in *Swan Lake*, Cinderella. When you're telling the story, you make it as bad for that character as you can. Pile on the agony!

AM: *Luca is a bit of rough? that both Lana and Angelo find attractive?*
MB: Yes. But he's not an evil character. Everything that happens is circumstantial and unplanned. He is shown to have great regret: to be troubled by what he has done.

The issue of sympathy is interesting. I tried to make Lana not too much of a villain. She's caged; she's sophisticated; she's bored in a small town. Again, with her, you're subverting audience expectation. She turns out to be the strongest character. She's quite cold, in fact. When they've

3 See Appendix A.

368

killed her husband, she enjoys her freedom. But she doesn't like what's Luca's become. A drunken, weak slob! Not glamorous, not vital. She has no problem with guilt, even though that's what binds her to him now. But even she has some redemption at the end with her murder of Luca.

AM: *Both the male characters are complex. The two leading women are relatively simple.*
MB: I've attempted to make the women more complex, but I guess they change less than the men, who both reverse your initial perception of them.

AM: *Tell me how you see Rita's feelings for Angelo.*
MB: Kind of motherly, protective. He's the natural person for her to be drawn to. Deep down, she cares for him more than he knows, and she hopes for love between them, but she knows it's not happening. That's what their first duet's about.

AM: *And Lana's for Angelo?*
MB: She barely notices he's around. She's not interested. He just happens to be the wrong person in the wrong place at the wrong time. At the end, yes, she takes in that he's had a relationship with Luca, and she saves his life when she shoots Luca. And they're sitting next to each other when Luca's body is carried away. But they still don't relate. They're two shattered lives who have loved the same man.

The start of *The Car Man* is very *Postman*. The younger wife; the older husband, who's gone to seed. There's a 'Man Wanted' sign: that says it all! The stranger arrives, gets a job, is a friend to the husband (we don't show that too much). In the second Hollywood *Postman* film, Jessica Lange and Jack Nicholson have sex on the kitchen table; I always wanted that.

But that's all. (At the start of *The Car Man*, both Lana and Angelo sit beneath the 'Man Wanted' sign; Luca comes in; he looks at the sign; they look at him . . . The whole germ of the plot's been established.) In *Postman*, they plan the murder twice. And in the late 1940s version Lana Turner (even though we used her name!) looks very glossy, with a white turban and beautiful make-up. I generally preferred the feeling of the older Italian treatment of the same story, Visconti's *Ossessione*, from the early 1940s. It's so much more realistic. The Luca character even has a hairy back.

78 Saranne Curtin (Lana) and Will Kemp (Angelo), Prologue. *The Car Man* also ends with the same two, again waiting. The 'Man Wanted' sign is taken from *The Postman Always Rings Twice*.

79 Lana Turner (as Cora Smith) in *The Postman Always Rings Twice*.

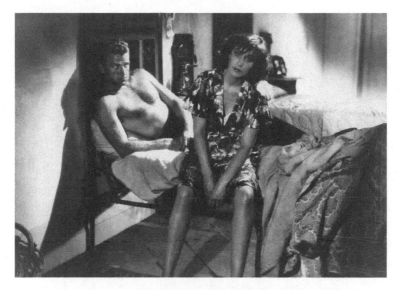

80 Luchino Visconti's *Ossessione* (1943). Massimo Girotti (Gino)
and Clara Calamai (Giovanna).

There are roles – even the Swan in *Swan Lake* – where I'm aware of
the individual qualities that at least three different dancers have brought
to the role. In *The Car Man*, however, I find Alan Vincent absolutely
definitive. He's just got the look. He looks so *not* like a dancer. People in the audience always comment on this, too: 'You don't expect
to find him in a dance show', 'He doesn't look as if he's going to be
able to dance.' So when he dances with such masculine grace it's dou-
bly exciting. Maybe that doesn't appeal to the conventional ballet audience, I dare say. But it's absolutely right for this role. For many ordinary
theatregoers it's absolutely part of what they like in the show . . . They
want real people. Alan does have this handsome ruggedness. And that
rugged quality is just what I took from the Visconti.

AM: *Any other film influences?*
MB: Plenty. *Rocco and His Brothers* (1960), another Visconti. The look,
the Italian feeling. I made them into Italian Americans; I didn't want to
lay on the Mediterranean detail too much. Luca and Angelo in my production are based in part upon the two brothers in *Rocco*: one tough,
and one (Alain Delon) angelic. They have a memorable, bloody, almost
operatic fight over a woman: I used that.

371

81 Rocco's elder brother Simone (Renato Salvatori) and Rocco (Alain Delon).
Rocco and His Brothers (1960).

82 Alan Vincent (Luca) and Will Kemp (Angelo),
2001 film of *The Car Man*, Act Two

Fight Club (1999), the Brad Pitt movie. People fighting for pleasure, getting their feelings out through organized violence. *My Own Private Idaho* (1991), with River Phoenix and Keanu Reeves. Angelo is influenced by the River Phoenix role: the neediness, the way he's in love with Keanu Reeves. There's a very touching scene when River wants to kiss Keanu . . . But it's not to be. There's a similar relationship between James Dean and Sal Mineo in *Rebel Without a Cause* (1955). Mineo, the younger man there, is also a model for Angelo.

Blood Simple (1985). That has a gory death, with the woman getting her husband killed. He seems to come back. They have to bury him alive. All that affected the killing of Dino at the end of my Act One, and the dream sequence in Act Two. The prison sequence was influenced by *Midnight Express* (1978).

Before we entered rehearsals, I knew which films I wanted individual dancers to study – the same method we'd used in *Cinderella*. The women playing Lana were to look not at just both the *Postman* movies and the Visconti movies, they were also to look at certain movies with Sophia Loren, Brigitte Bardot, Ellen Barkin (in *The Big Easy*, 1987), Kathleen Turner. The men playing Luca were certainly to look at Marlon Brando in *Streetcar Named Desire* (above all), Mickey Rourke, Ray Liotta, Jean-Paul Belmondo. The Ritas were to look at Natalie Wood, Susan Sarandon, Shirley MacLaine. The Dinos were to look at Dennis Hopper, Jack Nicholson, Orson Welles, Peter Falk. And so on through all the smaller roles, too.

AM: *Tell me about your preparatory work with Lez Brotherston.*
MB: My whole approach was that we wanted something more viable financially. *Swan Lake* had a large cast and orchestra and changes of set and costume. It's a big success, but it had always been on the edge financially. (That's changed. We'll come to this later.) So I wanted something with a smaller cast, a smaller orchestra. I wanted no wigs (though we ended up getting them!). The point with the set was not that I wanted it cheaper, but I wanted it tourable and free-standing.

Lez is great when it comes to restrictions. So he designed a set with its own flying system attached. The show can happen in the stripped-down stage space of any particular venue. The set has one central structure, with two side movable flats. We didn't want any stage wings. We wanted it raw, simple, with people on stage all the time, changing costumes in the immediate offstage areas.

83 Marlon Brando as Stanley Kowalski in *A Streetcar Named Desire* (1951).

AM: *When is it set?*
MB: 1960 – the year I was born. That's the year of *Rocco* and of some other films we were looking at. Lez likes to have a specific time. And place. This is the Midwest. An Italian-American community. It could almost be a Mediterranean community. The women are barefoot, free, in off-shoulder dresses, with skirts that ride up, buttons open.

AM: *Looking at your scenario, I see a few scenic/visual elements that got eliminated before the stage version. For example, in the opening scene, you originally planned one of the mechanics to be working on a motorcycle.*
MB: Yes, I always think big-budget at first! The motorcycles were some of the first things to go.

AM: *Did you always call it* The Car Man?
MB: We called it *Car Men* first. Obviously that's a pun on *Carmen*, and yes, that pun had been made when English National Opera had Pountney's production with used cars. Katharine Doré wanted *Car Men* very badly. She used to question it: 'What is a car man?' But I soon felt it was important to call it *The Car Man*. That's Luca. He's the title character; he must be. Everyone in the AMP office resisted. In fact, the

84 Saranne Curtin (Lana) and Alan Vincent (Luca). This publicity shot, taken on the stage set, is from the Act One sex duet on the kitchen table.

marketing people resisted so long that the original announcements went out for *Car Men – the musical dance sensation*. However, I insisted on *The Car Man*. Luca is the title character. He is a car mechanic. He is also a fate symbol. He gets the fate theme.

As for a subtitle, I added 'An Auto-Erotic Thriller' (an invention of my late friend Simon Carter). I liked calling it a 'thriller'. Obviously, the 'auto' was partly to keep the 'car' pun going into the subtitle. (This subtitle was dropped when the piece was revived in 2007.)

AM: *When you knew you couldn't use Adam Cooper, you chose Alan Vincent as the Car Man. To most of us, he was an unknown.*
MB: Alan hadn't really done a leading part with us at that point. But he had been one of my favourite members of the corps of swans in New York, in terms of being very true to the movement, very musical, very exact with the choreography. And he still is, as The Swan. He's the only person who does the choreography faithfully. The others all stray from it quite considerably. I always appreciate his accuracy. Also I just thought, 'Well, he does suit the character that we've written.' He just seemed ideal for it: bigger, rougher and very masculine. He also has great integrity as an actor.

AM: *There's an Incredible Hulk quality to him.*
MB: Yes, but only on stage. Off stage, you don't think, 'Oh, what an enormous guy he is.' He does stand out a little bit on stage because of his frame. Dancers tend to be such skinny people! And our audiences have got to know him better, now that, after *The Car Man*, we revived *Nutcracker* with him in the title role. And then *Play Without Words*, of course.

Rehearsal

ALASTAIR MACAULAY: *I was talking to Pip (Philippa) Gordon, the former Royal Ballet dancer, who has appeared in both your* Swan Lake *(as the Queen, among other roles) and* Cinderella. *She was having a baby when you made* The Car Man. *But as soon as she saw it, she loved it, and she wanted to play Rita. I was surprised; I hadn't imagined that being a tempting role.*
MATTHEW BOURNE: Well, she does get three great dramatic duets with Angelo! Pip's quite right: she'd be a very good Rita indeed.

When I was casting, I could see that several men – Will Kemp, Ewan Wardrop, and others – could play both Luca and Angelo. With women, however, I see them as either Lana or Rita. I haven't yet seen a woman whom I can imagine playing both roles.

The dancers playing Rita felt, at first, that they didn't like not having a sexual allure for Angelo. They related her to themselves, and they didn't like being rejected: they took that personally. They wanted to know why Angelo rejects her. I would have preferred Rita more frumpy, more homely. In 2000, our dancers didn't want that: and their version ended up working very effectively. But I did revise this character in 2007.

AM: *I have here the notes you gave the dancers on their characters on the first day of rehearsals. Rita: 'Late 20s . . . Angelo's sometimes girl-friend, genuine but sassy, devoted to her younger sister, Lana. Works as a waitress as Dino's Diner. Wise to Luca from the beginning, the only character who can see the trouble ahead.' Sassy?*
MB: Oh yes: I certainly thought that Etta made her sassy.

The men playing Angelo were also quite keen to push that character into a real relationship with Rita – a relationship which Luca, when he arrives, interrupts. I never said this to them, but I always felt that Angelo

85 Richard Winsor (Angelo) and Alan Vincent (Luca), with Michela Meazza (Lana) in the background on the extreme left. Rehearsal for 2007 revival.

hadn't found himself – that he was homosexual but hadn't thought it through or found the right guy. However, I'm fairly sure that Will Kemp felt his Angelo was going to end up with Rita.

AM: *Did any of this aspect of the story change in rehearsal?*
MB: Yes. While I was planning the Luca role for Adam Cooper, the Angelo–Luca relationship was just going to be Angelo's hero-worship of Luca. In my head, that worked better. I was planning twin solos for the two men, both in love, Angelo with Luca, Luca with Lana.

But just before rehearsals I realized that I wanted a kiss. I knew it would work. Why pussyfoot around sexuality here? I didn't want to imply it, I wanted to show it. Alan (Luca) was fine about it. But I had to persuade Will (Angelo): he didn't understand it at first. Etta and he were already working on troubled male–female relationships.

AM: *And Luca: you think he's naturally bisexual?*
MB: I've never used that word about him.

AM: *That's not true. Here are your rehearsal notes: 'Late 20s . . . Rough, intense, ruggedly handsome, dirty, ambiguous, bisexual, car-mechanic, violent edge, nervy, on the edge. A fatalistic symbol . . . his arrival affects all the other characters. Works out, part-time boxer/street-fighter.'*
MB: Well, I stand corrected. But I don't think it came up during the rehearsal process. It's not a good idea to use 'bisexual' as a label for actors. When you talk about sexuality, you have to approach it from different angles. In rehearsal, it wouldn't work with those men. You have to find a way to make them feel him from within. 'He's a horny guy – he can go in any direction – he likes two different challenges, two difficult challenges – the wife of his boss and the local outcast.' I don't apply labels to characters if I can help it. People are more complex than that.

The dancers, as usual with the Adventures dancers, gave him a whole history. Alan described him in detail, giving valid reasons for everything he did, explaining what his character was, and justifying that.

In theatre and in dance, we're constantly asking gay men to play straight. Here I wanted straight men to play the opposite, even if only part-time, and it had to be done seriously, from within.

AM: *Did you encounter any resistance?*
MB: I'd say that they were worried about losing sympathy. But that wasn't a serious problem, and it didn't last. Certainly now all my male dancers aspire to these roles.

86 Alan Vincent (Luca) and Will Kemp (Angelo), Act One, 2001 film.
Luca teaches Angelo how to defend himself.

The key was to make them understand Luca's attraction to Angelo.
He likes Angelo's hero-worship of him – likes having someone take that
much interest in him. But also Luca saves Angelo from the mob. So
Luca does have a nice, protective sympathetic side. Angelo is gentle, and
maybe that's what Luca likes.

Alan would say of Angelo: 'He's available – and he wanted it. I gave
it to him.' For him, it was just another fling on the journey. And his sex
with Lana gets interrupted – he's still horny – Angelo's there.

Luca has an attachment to Angelo, however: an affection for him.
That makes it hard for him in Act Two, especially when Angelo returns
and confronts him, but also earlier, when Angelo's jail sentence weighs
on his own conscience.

AM: *Your rehearsal notes for the narrative start with a group of photographs of Marlon Brando in* Streetcar.
MB: Brando was one of the types for Luca, and Alan has a similar body
shape to Brando.

AM: *You laid out a ten-minute period before the performance starts.
'Performers begin to gather onstage around ten minutes before the performance begins, going about their work in character. We hear work
sounds both mechanical and natural. Near to the beginning of the performance, the characters gather at the front of the stage, possibly staring
out at the audience (setting up the notion of the company as observers*

and witnesses as well as protagonists in the drama). As they do, the sound-effects get louder and reach a crescendo as the lights come down, and the company disappears into the darkness . . .'

MB: This was related to earlier AMP productions. The characters appear before the start of *Does Your Crimplene Go All Crusty When You Rub?*, and the way all the orphans came out during the *Nutcracker* overture and stared at the audience, introducing all the characters who are going to tell you this story. I'd enjoyed those, and I thought it would be good here. The audience really gets a sense of the community and the small town before the show starts. (We do the same in *Mary Poppins*.)

AM: *Then you planned a large cinema screen with film-style credits: 'ADVENTURES IN MOTION PICTURES presents THE CAR MAN'.*
MB: We didn't do that. Instead, the sign said 'WELCOME TO HARMONY, Population 374. Please drive carefully.'

AM: *You encouraged all the dancers to look at movies. How did they use that?*
MB: Among other things, it gave a range of choices to individual dancers. For example, Sara Curtin very much took Jessica Lange, rather than Lana Turner, as a role model for her Lana, whereas Michela Meazza was scrupulous about the quite different elements she wanted to integrate into her interpretation. Many people found her very Sophia Loren.

AM: *Any other changes to the scenario in rehearsal?*
MB: Yes. Originally it was Rita – not Lana – who shot Luca.

AM: *Blimey. I know you said that earlier. But it's still hard to imagine.*
MB: She seemed the most obvious. She never liked him. Her only feeling for him was disdain. He had – in her eyes – defiled and betrayed 'her' Angelo, and now he was on the point of killing him. So she shoots him. That was the idea.

But then I realized that it would add one more layer of suspense to have *Lana* kill him. She watches the two men fighting. She realizes her own disappointment with Luca: since the killing of her husband, he's never been the same man again. And she discovers that, even in the good days of their relationship, he had been double-timing her with Angelo. That's the last straw. In her eyes, she's redeeming herself by shooting Luca, because she's saving Angelo from death. Enough is enough, no more violence(!), no more disruption of the community: that's how she sees it. And Luca was the only person who could have incriminated her in Dino's death. But the main reason is that she was already disenchanted with Luca and now she feels he's betrayed her. Hence her timing.

The Ritas were not very happy when they were told they weren't to shoot Luca. They wanted to! So I said, 'Why do you want to shoot him?' They said, 'Well, it feels right.' I said, 'It's actually a little too obvious.' With Lana, it makes complete sense, but it's also the most surprising.

AM: *Your rehearsal notes for Lana say: 'Mid-20s . . . Works in diner attached to her husband's gas station/garage. Highly sexual in a very earthy way, a caged animal, bored, unsatisfied, passionate (raw), knows what she wants . . . ruthless, trapped in loveless marriage to an older man.'*

What about the character of her husband Dino? The rehearsal notes say: 'Mid-40s . . . Owns garage/gas station/diner. Employer of 10 to 15 men and women. Has let himself go, beer gut, chain smokes, greasy, dirty, heavy drinker, fairly oblivious to wife's flirtations. Violent?'

MB: Early on, I realised that this was the role for Scott Ambler. I wanted Dino greasy and unattractive. But Scott needs to make a character his own, and there were parts of my conception he resisted. I didn't want Dino unlikeable; he didn't want him gross. I wanted the audience to feel for Lana, not for him. Not for jolly old Dino (despite *The Postman*, where he *is* jolly). I never envisaged him as comic. Performers usually want their characters to be very sympathetic and attractive! Scott's feeling was 'Dino used to be handsome – now their relationship's gone sour.' I thought there was a chance to do something nastier. Anyway, the Dino we produced was a buffoon who's gone to seed. Flatulence, smoking, a beer gut . . . to make him unattractive. Dino and Lana have to look like an unlikely couple.

AM: *You mentioned the fact that even the minor characters were encouraged to consider movie precedents.*

MB: All of them are individual characters.

AM: *They've all got names in your rehearsal notes, and your descriptions vary quite a bit. 'Hot' Rod: 'Rugged, scary guy with plasters on his face and bruises, tattoos. (Types: Liam Neeson, Oliver Reed, Burt Reynolds, Gérard Depardieu.)' Chad: 'Youngest guy (18) – Joker, general help around place (trainee). Mascot to other workers. Has a crush on Lana. (Types: Leonardo di Caprio (Gilbert Grape), River Phoenix (My Own Private Idaho).)'*

MB: Those notes are pointers; I gave them all a range of options. I asked each to write his or her own life story. They had to fill in a form: 'What is your family history? How did you come to this town? How would you describe your sexuality? Who do you know?' Et cetera. So all of them had very rounded characters. They don't affect the main narrative too much, and so they're free to create their own stories.

AM: *Angelo and Luca aren't the only two men in town who've had sex together. There's a hot-night scene when we see all sorts of couples in the small town. One of them is male–male. What gave you the idea of them?*
MB: We talked a lot about this. It's a small town. Everyone's had several relationships, everyone knows who's been with whom. It stands to reason there'd be some gay activity. These two men – they're called Vito and Marco – aren't accepted by all the community. Hot Rod and the more bigoted garage workers won't stand for it. And they're both mechanics. So they're straight-acting as characters. Certainly not comic relief!

AM: *We see them together, sexually, just this one hot night. Are they just gay in the summertime?*
MB: They're gay for life! They're a couple. The rehearsal notes say: 'A gay couple. Non-camp, integrated and as physical with each other as the other straight couples.'

AM: *Well, you were way ahead of* Brokeback Mountain *(2005) in your reading of small-town America.*
What goes on between Angelo and Rita? Any nookies?
MB: They try it. But it's unsuccessful. The duet shows that. It suggests they're in bed together at one point. But he moves away. She looks up, as if he's left the bed. He 'says' (in movement), 'I can't.'
 Angelo's always on the outskirts of the community. He's taunted, and their relationship is made fun of.

AM: *The rehearsal notes for him say: 'Early 20s . . . Petrol-pump attendant, seemingly naive and inexperienced, unlike others, a loner, bookish (reads – has glasses), polite, hard-working, corruptible, attracted to Luca – hero-worship, has hidden depths, sympathetic. Made fun of by the other workers.'*
MB: In early rehearsals, Angelo had a pet mouse – his 'furry friend'. It crawled up his body. We dropped that, however. (Those Ritas didn't want him to be too weird! They wanted him 'misunderstood', but not the village oddity.) Likewise, originally you'd have seen him reading a book and wearing glasses, but all that went.

AM: *There's some nudity. A shower scene.*

MB: Which is completely gratuitous. It's there for fun. No dancer is made to strip, and no one cares. How much they want to show is optional, and I've been quite surprised at some performances just how much that is in some cases! The shower scene makes sense within the show, and the nudity occurs within that. It's a great image so early on in the show.

AM: *How did the supporting women feel about their roles? The rehearsal notes say of them all: 'Sexy, knowing, seen it all before, not particularly ladylike but not common. Uninhibited and physically free.' Then you go on to describe each one individually. Sandra, for example, is 'Mannish type in jeans – female mechanic. (Types: k.d. lang, Marianne Faithfull, Jodie Foster.)' And Dolores is 'Untouchable, more sophisticated type, always applying make-up, a tease. (Types: Cybill Shepherd, Faye Dunaway, Diana Dors.)'*

MB: They were all very happy playing roles more contemporary than usual. They loved being barefoot; they loved feeling the floor with their feet. And they really felt under the skin of their roles – they were happier than in any other AMP shows. The roles are all sexy, and they love that. Lots of flirtation: they're all at that age!

I can't emphasize enough that being a princess in *Swan Lake* and wearing high heels is not what comes naturally to women today, least of all women who've chosen to work in contemporary dance. These ones felt really free in the *Car Man* costumes, in the characters, in the movement.

AM: *We've been talking as if you rehearsed the whole thing with your whole company from the start. But I know that you usually start rehearsals with a small nucleus of dancers.*

MB: And that's what we did here. Scott Ambler, Etta Murfitt, Arthur Pita, Vicky Evans, Alan Vincent, and me. A lot of the movement came from them. For example, Lana's solo: we all contributed to that. Or Luca's Habañera solo. We'd play the music, we'd talk through the character and the situation, we'd listen to the music again. We had the idea of Luca smashing down a plate with a huge gesture, and leaning on the table with his elbow. Slouching movement, relaxed, not 'dancerly'. Lana, we realized, had to be free throughout her body, mustn't care where her clothes go, is happily open-legged. Luca is the same, very relaxed through his body, very full of open sexuality. Angelo, by contrast, is enclosed, caught up, covered, with never a conventionally big-stretched movement. That needed some exploring in rehearsal – to find a characterful way of moving that wasn't natural to these dancers, that was inhibited.

All that led to a workshop method. Each of us worked on specific dance phrases. I'd give them the idea for each phrase, and I worked on making phrases myself. Then they'd learn each other's phrases. And so on – till we came up with eighty phrases. A lot of the Mechanics' tool dance, the Heat scene, the Club scene, the Prison cell solo, the Jukebox dance were sketched in that way. We had one week with me, Scott and Etta leading these workshops. Then two weeks with the full group – and sometimes Will Kemp. Next, eight weeks with the whole company. One of the first things we worked on with the whole company was fights. And all the dancers were invited to contribute movement – which they did.

AM: *You've already indicated how some parts of your written scenario changed in the event. What about the situations that you'd left open anyway?*

MB: A good example is in the party in Act One, Scene Four. The scenario says that Lana, after all Dino's confrontations and suspicions, 'has had enough' and drags Luca away for what I simply wrote in the scenario as 'Duet'. This 'duet' turned out, as we rehearsed it, to have quite a lot of story. Now it's *Luca* who's had enough. The whole situation's getting awkward for him. It's really him who leaves the party. He goes back (I really like this touch) to pack his bags in the locker room. He's done what he wanted – seduced the two most challenging conquests in town. She finds him and confronts him. How can you leave? Now? She uses all her charms. The lust between them resurfaces, and she persuades him to have sex there in the garage. Dino finds them. And the Bizet fate motif – as if to remind us that Luca would otherwise have gone – as they wield the spanner.

And the spanner is something that emerged during rehearsals. I'd taken the gun from the movies I'd been watching. But in the context of our story it seemed right to kill Dino with a tool from the garage.

AM: *This scene reminds me of the aspect of* The Car Man *in which I think your craft became more sophisticated than ever before: that is, your ability to stage more than one thing at the same time. Earlier on,*

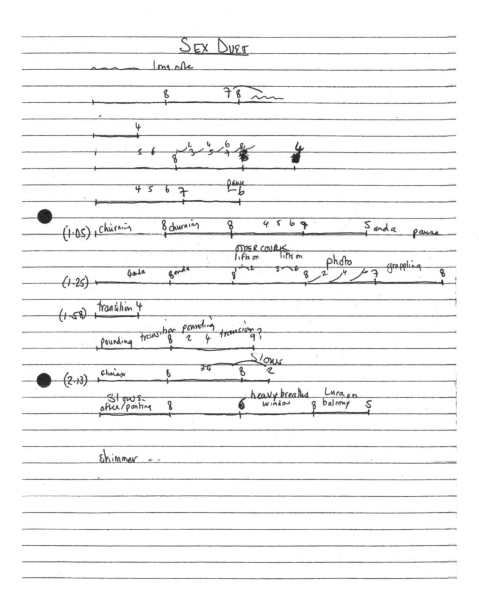

87 From Bourne's plans for Act One. The 'Sex Duet' sketched here is for Lana and Luca, but is then multiplied by other members of the cast into a 'dance orgy'.

the multiple sex scenes are one very clear example of this. So, in a differ-
ent way, is the double solo for Lana and Angelo, both in love. But now
you have two different layers of plot occurring in different parts of the
stage. This scene involves Lana, Luca, Dino, Angelo, Rita, and the other
partygoers.

MB: I always wanted some overlap between the scenes. The murder
wouldn't be so dramatic if we had forgotten how the party was still
going on. And so I brought in Rita to make a phone call to the cops
about Dino's earlier threats. (That's why the cops turn up so quickly, by
the way, after the murder – she's already called them.) Luca runs from
the garage with the murder weapon in his hand. Rita, not knowing yet
there's been a murder, asks him, 'Have you seen Lana?' She's suspicious,
but she doesn't know of what. Luca pacifies her: 'It's nothing.' Then
Angelo goes to the garage. Here I wanted to show how hard it is to kill
someone. Dino's still alive – crawling across the stage, and all bloody.
Angelo doesn't realize what's up until it's too late. Rita, outside, sees
the cops and says, 'Come to the garage.' When they do, Lana is ready
and has started feigning rape. Angelo is covered in Dino's blood. Rita is
appalled, and her immediate instinct is to believe her sister Lana's story.
Luca, meanwhile, doesn't know what's been going on in the garage.
He's gone to hide the murder weapon. When he sees how Lana's framed
Angelo, he's taken by surprise. And it's now that he realizes that she's
the clever controlling one, and that he's lost all control of the original
situation. He's stuck, and she's got him, through murder and guilt. Rita
runs to Angelo, as the police hold him; she sees the blood on his T-shirt,
and recoils. Angelo and Luca come face to face; Luca rejects him. Lana
looks up at Luca, with a flash of triumph.

So yes, there are a lot of different things going on at the same time.
But here they arose simply out of our interest in being true to our story
and all our characters. *The Car Man* is full of flashback and split-screen
methods; foreground and background action being quite different. It felt
experimental for me in terms of story-telling.

AM: *The club scene in Act Two includes a cabaret-act dance. It's quite*
surprising to see that your rehearsal notes say, 'Ultra-cool Lounge/
Song-and-dance act . . . Las Vegas style. Two men, one woman. (Types:
Ann-Margret, Harry Connick, Dean Martin.)'
MB: Well, we couldn't find any lounge-act music. So we tried it another
way. The club has become a beatnik club, therefore 'into' modern art,

88 Alan Vincent (Luca). This 'trailer trash' dance occurs at the beatnik club (named 'Le Beat Route'), which Lana and Luca, flaunting their money, visit early in Act Two. Luca's stetson and snakeskin-patterned jacket were inspired by Nicolas Cage in David Lynch's *Wild at Heart* (1990).

therefore 'into' modern dance. The dance is not supposed to be an out-and-out Martha Graham pastiche (though people have assumed that). It's meant to be a diva Martha Graham imitator trying to be 'artistic' in a performance-art-style performance. I was thinking of Danny Kaye's 'Choreography' number in *White Christmas* (1954) and Audrey Hepburn's beatnik number in *Funny Face* (1957). The three dance characters are called Virginia, Erick (after Erick Hawkins) and José (after José Limón). The music is meant to sound like 'difficult' modern music – by 1960s Midwest standards. At first, it's just plinky-plonky arty stuff; then it becomes more recognizably related to Bizet.

The success of this number varies from one audience to another. In 2007 I tightened the choreography and Lez gave it new designs: it now works more consistently. But it still requires some knowledge of Graham choreography, however small, to come across. Graham's fame was enough for Danny Kaye to parody her in *White Christmas*, and I'm impressed by how many people still react to our idea of it. But fewer of them do so when our production goes on regional tours.

AM: *In 2000 every British ballet-goer bar none spotted that the duet between Angelo and his Gaoler ended with a foot-fetish gesture straight out of Kenneth MacMillan's* Manon, *where it occurs for Manon and her Gaoler.*

MB: I can't deny it. Obviously, the simple difference is that here it's two men. But it's just a moment, isn't it? I was thinking much more of *Midnight Express* throughout this scene, where Brad Davis is sexually abused by the prison warder – who becomes lax on security, and allows his eventual escape. It's not there in our 2007 revival.

AM: *Yes, but British ballet-goers haven't been looking at cast changes in* Midnight Express *over the last thirty years. In* Manon, *they have.*

MB: I'm not so sure that 'British ballet-goers' make up a very large percentage of our audience these days.

But the whole scene is typical of me. I want my heroes to suffer as much as possible.

AM: *I know that the prison scene originally had several multi-layered ideas that you pared away. But it remains quite complex. Rita's story, which is so obviously – to us – a heightened and distorted version of the*

89 Kerry Biggin (Rita) and Richard Winsor (Angelo), Act Two duet, 2007. Angelo, having broken out of jail, terrifies Rita with his deranged behaviour. The company nicknames this 'the creepy duet'.

actual murder scene we saw in Act One, is one kind of complexity. Then there is the presence of the other prisoners.

MB: Yes, and I certainly used them to amplify Angelo's frustration at being imprisoned. When he attacks Rita, they all rattle the bars of their cells, as Bizet's fate motif returns. At another point, they echo his movements.

AM: *The Rita narrative feels like a dream scene – it's not quite realistic – and the next scene has another dream scene. This is where Luca, drunk, sees Dino's ghost.*

MB: Yes, it's certainly an unreal scene. The whole thing happens legato, which I like, as if it were underwater. Terry's setting of the music is strange, echoey, beautiful, odd. And all the Lucas play this scene so well. Shirley rejects Luca, you see, and it's one further sign that he's lost his touch, which virtually leads into his hallucination about Dino coming to life. The Rita scene is not a dream but a flashback told from her point of view. As she relates it to Angelo, we see the action unfold around her. It's brilliantly lit by Chris Davey, to suggest two overlapping scenes.

AM: *Did the final scene change in rehearsal?*

MB: In small and big ways, yes. At the start, for example, we only had one person at the diner at closing time for Rita to get rid of, before she is left alone. She is much more vulnerable and alone when she hears a plate smash in the diner . . . It builds tension for Angelo's return.

AM: *It's Angelo who wrote 'MURDERER'?*

MB: Yes. He's been there a while, biding his time, and he may have written it some time before.

And now it's not Rita, as I had originally thought, but Lana who pulls down the shutter and reads that word 'MURDERER'. Simpler that way. Luca is still guilt-ridden, and now he makes Lana face up to what she did. For the first time, the guilt does hit her. She runs to her room where we know Angelo is waiting for her with a gun. Luca lets out his guilt and anger in the 'Fight Club' sequence which follows.

Angelo re-enters, now holding *Lana* at gunpoint, a lot of detail is different or clearer. Angelo pulls down the shutter again, only this time in front of the whole town. He looks at Luca and Lana as if to say 'They – not me – are the murderers.'

AM: *This whole crowd mime scene is reminiscent of various crowd scenes going back to the Mad Scene in* Giselle.

MB: Yes, obviously. The final scene of *West Side Story*, too. It's classic – this kind of public confrontation. The challenge is not to make the melodrama become comic.

So then Angelo walks across to Luca. He caresses him. And then looks at Lana. 'He's mine,' he's saying to her. Luca has to accept this (Angelo's got the gun). But for Lana, it is one twist she'd never anticipated, and one loss of control. She feels betrayed and runs off hysterical.

Luca manages to get Angelo to put down the gun, and he challenges him to fight. Yes, he taught Angelo how to fight. (Nice bit of irony there.) But Angelo in prison has learnt how to fight better, and can turn that against him. Angelo is a new man here: scary, passionate, and even dangerous. Luca, despite his natural brute force, is a broken man.

Next comes the Judas kiss. Angelo kisses Luca before everyone. 'This is what we were,' he tells the crowd. 'Look at what we could have had together,' he tells Luca. (The fate motif occurs here. It makes the kiss work marvellously.) We cut the laughter I originally gave Angelo here. When Luca wields the gun on Angelo, there's a great emphasis here on eye contact between them. So Luca, looking Angelo in the eye, just can't shoot.

AM: *You've already said that you gave the eventual shooting to Lana rather than Rita – one more twist. But then you added a finale that wasn't in your original scenario.*

MB: Yes, and fitted it to Schedrin's music! It occurred to me that it would be another good twist to end the story as it began. Luca entered stage right on his way into town at the top of the show. In the Epilogue, he's carried off stage right – to be buried. Lana and Angelo just sit there, shattered. Rita starts to wash off the 'MURDERER' graffito from the diner shutter. Town life will carry on.

AM: *We've been talking largely about plot. I see how character and narrative are crucial for you. Can we now, in that context, talk of movement?*

MB: For me, the more you work out the character, the feeling, the motive and the action, then more and more of the movement falls into place. For the group dances, I drew from social dances of the late 1950s, the spirit of the jukebox era, and I wanted dance movement that was stamping, flirtatious, grounded. The whole intention was free and sexy from the outset. The solos and duets come much more from an emotional

90 Richard Winsor (Angelo), prison solo, Act Two, 2007. Bourne here was
inspired by the Act Two solo for the Young Man in Frederick Ashton's *The Two
Pigeons* (1961), who also danced with wrists bound.

and narrative place. They're expressions of the psyches of the leading characters.

AM: *I've mentioned ballets like* Giselle *and* Manon *as precedents for some of your choreography here.*
MB: I'm sure MacMillan in particular was a model. But we all draw from each other, generation after generation, don't we? If you look at Mercutio's death scene in MacMillan's *Romeo*, it draws obviously – and very well – from the Mad Scene in *Giselle*.

As so often, I thought of Ashton – in this case, for Angelo's solo in prison. I wanted to show Angelo restricted in some way. Obviously it wouldn't work theatrically to put him in a small cell and make him dance there, so I had to show the restriction some other way. I had his wrists bound with a leather strap, and the solo was inspired – in part – out of my memory of the way the young hero of Ashton's *The Two Pigeons* dances when his wrists are bound by a rope. I'm always happier with a prop or some furniture to dance over. This is where the 'other' Fred comes in, too!

AM: *You've often said how you've fallen ill at some stage during the rehearsal period for each of your shows.*
MB: This time I didn't. The whole rehearsal process went smoothly. Having so detailed a scenario really helped: all the performers really felt they knew and understood what they were doing. And they were committed to yet further detail as I always let it be known that my scenario was not set in stone. Both Sara and Michela, for example – the two original Lanas – were exemplary this way. They're performers who need to know every aspect of their motivation. Everything must have a meaning for them. And each came up with different decisions for various scenes.

In fact, illness during rehearsals seems to be a problem I've left behind me since the 1990s. My last two rehearsal periods for new productions have been blighted by the illness of my mum (*Edward Scissorhands*) and the death of my oldest friend Simon Carter (*Dorian Gray*). Because those put other things on my mind, the work, rather than being stressful, has been a release.

We also have much shorter rehearsal time now (five weeks for both *Edward* and *Dorian*), so a mid-rehearsal illness would result in an unfinished show! I'm not saying you can control when you get ill, but I do think that I look after myself better and possibly am a little less stressed these days.

91 Michela Meazza as Lana, 2007. Act One solo.

AM: *Two of your leading men, Will Kemp and Ewan Wardrop, played both Luca and Angelo.*

MB: Luca is the most difficult role, I think, and both Will and Ewan were very different, physically, from Alan. He's bigger and tougher, and a lot of the character and movement came naturally to him. But I didn't want them to clone him, and they both found different ways of releasing various movement features of the character to suit them. Will found a lot of 'swagger' to his Luca; and Ewan, being a natural comic, was cheekier to begin with.

Angelo may have more undancerly qualities in conception – the inhibited side of his character makes him very 'caught up' and internal to begin with. But Will, Ewan and Arthur Pita responded fervently to the intensity, the complexity and danger, of him. They saw that his character has the biggest arc. And the volcano eventually erupts.

I would say, though, that Lana is the hardest role to cast. I can't say I've spotted many potential Lanas around, whereas there are several people I can imagine bringing something particular to Rita or Luca or Angelo. Lana must be a diva performer. She must have presence, and a very pronounced acting ability – in particular, she must have the courage to play the unpleasant, unflinching side of the character without hamming it up.

Performance

ALASTAIR MACAULAY: *It opened in Plymouth?*

MATTHEW BOURNE: Yes, then it toured Britain before reaching London. It must have been a twelve-week tour.

AM: *Your rehearsal notes also include a character called Shirley. 'Lonely woman at bar (Act Two Scene Two). Dumped by partner in a previous scene. Drowning her sorrows, needs comfort and company. Finds it with drunken Luca. They dance (casual sex). She leaves. (Types: Jeanne Moreau, Simone Signoret.)'*

MB: She changed after the show opened in Plymouth. People there kept asking me, 'Who's that woman in black? Does she represent death?' They wanted to know her story. So she later became the woman who runs the club, rather than a sad barfly.

AM: *Am I right that* The Car Man *had your longest West End run since the 1995–6 run of* Swan Lake?

MB: Yes, nineteen weeks. Previews started in the week commencing 4 September; the final performance was 13 January. With the preliminary tour, it had 250 British performances in all. The Old Vic, where *The Car Man* played, was like the Piccadilly, where we had done *Swan Lake* in '95–6, in one respect. They had no passing trade. But we had the good fortune that *The Car Man* came within months of our second West End run of *Swan Lake*, early in 2000 at the Dominion Theatre. A good many from the Dominion followed us to the Old Vic.

It was a theatre audience. I felt, at the time, that I was coming to the end of my appeal for a lot of dance critics. They wanted, it seemed to me, a 'pure dance' approach. We were in transition away from that. So we were certainly delighted when the show won the *Evening Standard* Award for 'Musical Event of the Year'. That certainly gave a boost to the show.

All in all, we gained a new audience. *The Car Man* appeals to a young audience, whose members can identify with these characters. It also appeals to a general theatre audience. Actors love it in particular. Jonathan Pryce was blown away, Dennis Waterman was really excited. Harrison Ford, Michael Caine, Morgan Freeman all came.

AM: *Then in summer 2001 you took it to the States, where it toured.*
MB: *The Car Man* toured on and off for two to three years. It did the States, it did some European dates, it did Tokyo. We were playing it in Los Angeles, but the opening night was the night after 9/11. There had been such a buzz before we opened, but then this awful thing happened and people understandably stopped going out. The night afterwards, we gave a free performance for anyone who wanted to come: we made a speech about what had happened the previous day. It was a wonderful and memorable performance that made us remember how art and entertainment are so important to us all. Sharing that performance with the Los Angeles audience was very special – cathartic. We did our eight-week LA season, and it went well enough. (Another standing ovation from my beloved Ann Miller!) But the rest of the American tour was cancelled. People round America just stopped going out.

Back here, however, we took it to cities from Amsterdam to Tel Aviv. Then it was the first work we ever performed in Japan. The Japanese had been wanting *Swan Lake*, but this was what we were doing at the time. So we said, 'You'll have to have this first. Then you can have *Swan Lake*.' And we've been going back ever since. A lot of the individual

395

guys were worshipped out there: fan clubs, websites, etc. Quite right too!

Conclusion

ALASTAIR MACAULAY: *It seems to me that* The Car Man *was your most suspenseful show to date. Was that conscious on your part?*
MATTHEW BOURNE: Definitely. I didn't subtitle it a thriller for nothing! Back in *Deadly Serious*, I looked into the closeness of sex and violence. Sex and murder, in fact. So *The Car Man* is a return to that terrain.

It's a piece that has grown in popularity. And certainly the performers learnt an enormous amount through being in it, because that's where they honed their acting skills quite considerably: all of them, not just the leads.

AM: *Perhaps as a result, it also made your company look better than ever before as dancers – just as committed through-the-body performers.*
MB: Well, my intention had always been to give them a show in which they could feel natural, in which they could dance characters with total confidence.

AM: *The show ends with Lana and Angelo sitting side by side. The community life seems to be carrying on. What's going to happen next?*
MB: I think all the townsfolk make a collective decision to deal with the situation. To bury him. To forget he ever came. To rebuild their shattered lives.

Obviously there's a Part Two there somewhere – a *Son of Car Man* sequel! Angelo is a fugitive from jail. There would have to be another court case, and so on, wouldn't there? But what I like is the way that the ending shows the return to the community. Luca exits where he came on – but carried off this time. The community – remember it's called Harmony – has come together again, in a grim way. And the sign above them tells you: 'You're leaving Harmony. Come back soon.'

I've sometimes dreamed up how *Son of Car Man* would go. Lana goes to jail. Angelo gets off. Lana has Luca's baby in jail. Rita and Angelo bring up Luca's baby . . . Et cetera, et cetera.

AM: *Well, one of your sources is* A Streetcar Named Desire. *Did you know that in an early version of that, Tennessee Williams had Blanche and Stanley talking together the morning after they had sex? He's in awe of her – he's released a sexual violence and power in her, the like of which he's never encountered. He's going to go to the hospital, where Stella has had her child – but later he'll go off in search of Blanche: 'Wherever you go in the world, I will follow, and I will find you.' And Blanche says, 'Yes, and I will bear you a son – a child that will be more beast than human . . . to destroy, to build something immense . . . a new world where nobody is ungrateful.'*

MB: You see? There's always another great story waiting to happen after the final curtain.

The 2007 Revival

ALASTAIR MACAULAY: *For the 2007 revival, you dropped the subtitle 'an auto-erotic thriller'. Why?*

MATTHEW BOURNE: For several reasons. I think we overemphasized the sexual aspects of the show the first time around. I was keen for the piece to be taken more seriously as drama – as a thriller. This seemed to work. The revival was greeted as the return of some old classic by some of the same writers who almost seven years before had expressed distinct reservations. That's gratifying!

AM: *I wasn't able to see this revival. Were you able to keep any of the original cast?*

MB: I'm sad that you didn't see it. I was extremely proud of this revival, and felt that the piece had grown in every respect. Yes, several members of the original cast were still here, seven years on: Alan Vincent as Luca, Scott Ambler as Dino, Michela Meazza as Lana. Meanwhile such dancers as James Leece and Adam Galbraith, who had both been in the original cast, now took on the role of Luca as well. The newcomers in the principal roles were Richard Winsor and Sam Archer as Angelo, Gemma Payne and Ebony Molina as Lana, and Kerry Biggin, Hannah Vassallo and Shelby Williams as Rita. With all these dancers, I feel that this show (as had happened in the original production too) brought out of them some of the best performances they had ever given in any of my shows. As actor-dancers, they all rose to the challenge. Some performances were quite overwhelming, for audience and for the cast!

AM: *I remember your saying in 2006 that Sam Archer and Richard Winsor had their eye on Luca and Angelo while they were touring in* Edward Scissorhands.

MB: Yes, those parts have become the most prized male roles in our repertory with the Prince and the Swan in *Swan Lake*. I remember Richard and Sam hinting that they would like to play Luca (Richard) and Angelo (Sam), which I thought was very sweet at the time, since the characters become lovers in the piece and these two performers had become such good friends creating Edward Scissorhands together. I'm not sure they saw it quite that way, though. It's true that Richard (Dickie, as I always call him) could have played Luca or Angelo. But we did have the brilliant creator of the role returning. So I ended up casting them both as Angelo. Sam is a natural Angelo, being quite introverted and very touching in his acting choices. Richard just loved the acting challenges of making himself 'nerdy' and ineffectual, going against his normal stage presence, and transforming himself into the psychotic avenging Angelo of Act Two.

AM: *What changes did you make to the characterizations?*
MB: The biggest changes were made to Angelo and Rita, and they were quite considerable. They were clearly outsiders right from the beginning, both in their appearance and in their movement. For example, these characters used to dance together as part of the big jukebox dance at the diner at the top of Act Two. This seemed to me completely out of character when I looked at it again. Now we have a lovely moment when, during the wild dancing of the others, Angelo crosses the stage, straightening his hair, to ask Rita to join him in a dance. When they do actually start dancing together, the group movement looks awkward on them. The others all stop, stare, and laugh them off the dance floor. It's a small moment, but it tells us so much about the characters and the others' attitude towards them. When Rita and Angelo finally are left alone to dance together – I greatly improved the choreography in 2007 for this scene – their eloquent outpouring of emotion through the movement is all the more touching. We also changed their appearance quite considerably. Gone was Rita's bold red dress and glamorous wig. She now looks very out of place among the other more assertive, abandoned women. She is, after all, working as a waitress throughout the first scene! We lost Angelo's leather jacket in favour of work overalls, though he does don a cardigan and combs his hair to ask Rita to dance at the end of his working day. Unfortunately, Dickie still looked like a public-school boy with his scruffy blond hair and good looks. So we darkened his hair, made it more greasy, and gave him a monobrow. This seemed to work!

AM: *Were you looking to change those aspects of the characterizations anyway? Or did this emerge out of your new interpreters?*

MB: I knew that I wanted to look at those characters in particular, and I knew that I had the performers to do that. Don't get me wrong. Will Kemp and Etta Murfitt were terrific, and they created the roles; other Angelos and Ritas were also first-rate. But with the passage of time I could view the whole more clearly while seeing the parts in a new light. This new breed of performers love to get inside a character, and they're not afraid to look frumpy or nerdy or awkward if the role requires it.

AM: *How much did that change the choreography, and if so where and how?*

MB: Well, the whole show had a choreographic overhaul. We had taken a good look at all the movement the year before in a week-long workshop involving several of the new cast members. We had all learnt a lot in those seven years, and there was much more sophistication to the movement, richer characters and yet more truthful performances. The whole show came up several notches; it became a very solid piece of theatre that really worked at every performance. That was through tightening and changing some aspects of the choreography. I was particularly proud of the duets in this piece. I think they are the best I have ever done: I feel they're equally good as choreography, drama and characterization.

AM: *I know you go on reworking every piece with every revival, but I also believe that some aspects of each work eventually take on a fixed form. Do you feel any of these 2007 changes may prove definitive that way?*

MB: Absolutely. I have never been happier with a piece. I wouldn't dare to say that my work on *The Car Man* is finished, but it's certainly as close to definitive as anything of mine gets!

AM: *Any changes to the score? Or designs?*

MB: No. Those had always been more definitive than my choreography. The show now has a reputation as something people want to see again; and we look forward to reviving it in due course. It's not one of what we used to call our 'classics', in the sense of adapting a pre-existing ballet. But it has certainly become one of our classics.

(Conversations 2000–9)

12

New Adventures

ALASTAIR MACAULAY: *During the international tour of* The Car Man *came the surprise announcement that Adventures in Motion Pictures was to be no more. Your company in future was to be known as New Adventures. Katharine Doré had been central to the previous company since the late 1980s; she was not to be a part of the new company. Please tell me what you can about this change and this break-up.*

MATTHEW BOURNE: I remain extremely grateful to Katharine for everything she did for me and the company in the early years. Happy memories remain.

If it was *Swan Lake* that suddenly made Adventures in Motion Pictures famous in the West End and abroad in 1995, maybe it was *Swan Lake* that also helped to break the company apart. Katharine and I had both been excited by observing the Mark Morris Dance Group in 1990, and for Katharine it was wonderful to meet Barry Alterman, its general director. At that time, the Morris troupe had a scale and conditions that any British modern-dance company, and most anywhere, might envy. But the success of *Swan Lake*, and our new contact with Cameron Mackintosh Productions, suddenly meant that we were being encouraged to operate on a different, yet larger, scale.

I love Cameron and he's been an important part of my career for over fourteen years now, whereas I never knew Barry so well, and he's no longer working for Mark Morris. Still, here's what I mean. When Katharine and I first watched the Mark Morris Dance Group in action in Brussels, we were both deeply impressed by the spirit that ran through the enterprise, and Barry's personal involvement and enthusiasm made a deep impression on Katharine. Barry put Mark, the work, and the dancers first – it was as much a family as a company.

But when *Swan Lake* had the kind of success we hadn't anticipated and moved to run in the West End for months under Cameron's guidance, problems began. It was a much harder show to run than we were ready for. Cameron could help and advise both Katharine and me, but he also gave us – or our advisers – the idea that we should be a bit like him. When you went into Cameron's office, it was a big plush place with settees and awards all over the place, with lots of people there, all working for him. So, instead of working from an office at Sadler's Wells, which I had really liked, we took up a suite of offices in the heart of the West End (Trevor Nunn's old offices), very much along Cameron lines. The staff got bigger and bigger, and the enterprise got grander and grander. People were brought in to brand us, telling us how we should sell ourselves.

All of which stopped us from being what we really were: a small company doing one show at a time. We weren't creating an empire presenting several big shows round the world. In particular, we weren't making blockbuster productions that would run in big West End theatres for years at a time.

This drove Katharine and me apart in ways we'd never intended. She was doing everything she could to make the company financially viable and to keep it independent; and when it came to the West End run of *Cinderella*, which wasn't the success *Swan Lake* had been, the pressures on her were huge. For me the pressures were that, to keep the company going on that scale, I had to keep producing big box-office hits. I couldn't, for example, have imagined a *Play Without Words* in those conditions, even though that was one of my most successful pieces.

AM: *Was it you who made the break?*

MB: I did, yes. I wrote to Katharine because I needed to set down what I was thinking. I think all I said was 'I just think *The Car Man* should be our last production together.' I felt that it was time to make a clean break and start afresh. I had reached the position where I was avoiding having meetings with her. I don't need to spell out the problems; they're ancient history.

But this is the place to say that I had also been working with Disney – since 1999, I think – on the stage show of *The Little Mermaid*, and Katharine had been involved in that. For the Disney company, this was part of its trend of turning its animation features into Broadway musicals. *The Little Mermaid* had a Broadway sensibility about it, and Broadway composers involved (Alan Menken and Howard Ashman), so it seemed like a good possibility. I worked on this intermittently but seriously for two years; I still have files of stuff on it. Lez did designs and costumes. I did workshops with dancers in London; dance workshops. Twelve new songs were written. But eventually I pulled out.

AM: *Why?*

MB: It just wasn't going in a direction I felt that enabled me to do the kind of work that I do best. The book was too colloquial in its style and humour. The characters I found quite hard after a while. Disney did give me a lot of freedom. There was nothing they said that was off-putting. But they did say, 'You have to remember, this is Disney's *The Little Mermaid* you are doing, not Hans Christian Andersen's. That means using most of the songs and it means using the characters. How you put those on stage is completely up to you. But that's what you're dealing with. It's our property.' That sounded very free. But the more I looked into it, I found it more and more difficult to make it work as a concept. Sebastian the sea crab – who looks more like a lobster – I couldn't find a way of making him work . . . and that little fish called Flounder!

The final comment really is that to make a musical with a heroine who in Act One can't dance and can't walk and in Act Two can't sing is hard. You remember, she loses her voice as part of the story? But I felt sure someone would find a way of making it work brilliantly. Thomas Schumacher of Disney Theatrical wanted it to happen; he left the door open for me to come back for any other project; and he knew by then that I was always interested in the stage show of *Mary Poppins*. It was all very amicable.

As you know, the production materialized in December 2007. Francesca Zambello directed. And the choreography, I'm pleased to say, was by Stephen Mear, with whom I'd worked on *Mary Poppins*.

But, at the time, all my *Little Mermaid* work involved Katharine. First, she took it on as something that should involve AMP. Later, however, I became concerned that she was packaging the whole enterprise as more of a project for the AMP management office, whereas I really saw it as more of a freelance relationship between myself and Disney. So there was a problem there, which was solved only when – for the reasons I've just given – I pulled out of *The Little Mermaid*.

I knew that to break with Katharine – *The Little Mermaid* was only one reason of several – would take months of negotiations, and so I told her of my decision when I knew the company was booked to perform *The Car Man* for months. I knew the dancers would be employed, and I knew I would be busy on *My Fair Lady*. Katharine and Sally Greene had announced that Adventures in Motion Pictures was going to become resident at the Old Vic; I knew I was putting an end to that project too.

The whole thing was a big and painful decision for me. Adventures in Motion Pictures was the name that I (and Emma Gladstone) had created. The history of that company could possibly disappear. I didn't think I would be taking it with me. I must say Katharine's initial reaction was almost as if she knew it was going to happen: she was quite positive, quite supportive in some ways. Later negotiations were more difficult, as you might expect. But I knew the dancers and the administrative staff all had time to look for subsequent work. However, I really didn't envisage that I would ever need to create another company.

AM: *But that happened. You started a new company with a new name.*

MB: During 2001, Sadler's Wells began to talk with me about doing *Nutcracker* again. I met with Jean-Luc Choplin and Alistair Spalding. And at the same time Trevor Nunn, because I'd been working with him on *My Fair Lady* and then *South Pacific* at the National Theatre, came to me with the idea of doing a piece for the Lyttelton Theatre's Transformation season in 2002.

So now I could see a future for a new company. I said to Trevor straight away, 'Could this be a co-production between the National and my new company? Could it be the launch of this company?' The National was very happy to do that; they'd been presenting other theatre companies, like Cheek by Jowl and Théâtre de Complicité.

And I thought, 'This is great. We've actually got two productions to launch this new company with.' One taken care of by the National, and the other by Sadler's Wells and ATG (Ambassador Theatre Group). That set the tone for what we were going to do in the future, because it only needed myself and Robert Noble – Robert on a part-time basis – to oversee the productions. Robert works for Cameron Mackintosh, but had worked with Katharine and me previously at AMP, and I found I could always talk to him. He was able to organize himself so as to work part-time with me as a co-director of New Adventures. We've worked along those lines very happily ever since. What mattered to me most was that I was able to use a large number of the dancers and other staff I'd been working with at Adventures in Motion Pictures. So it became New Adventures, because it continued the work of the old company. I was desperate to hang on to the legacy of what we'd achieved in the past.

AM: *You've never had a big project with Adam Cooper since then, but you're friends again. And at the 2003 Dance Umbrella gala at Sadler's Wells, he joined James Leece, Neil Penlington, Arthur Pita, Ewan Wardrop and Richard Winsor to dance your* Spitfire *– which itself was fifteen years old that year.*

MB: We were never not friends! Yeah, he did *Spitfire*. I have offered him things along the way; I've kept the door open. But he's got his own things going on: he's moved into making his own choreography and has carved out a niche for himself in musical theatre. I would still like to create something dark and dangerous for him.

Later on, history repeated itself. At the start of 2005, I wanted Will Kemp for *Edward Scissorhands*. We had talked about his passion for this role since 1998. He'd become a company star with *Swan Lake*, *Cinderella*, *The Car Man* and *Play Without Words*, and he'd been doing other work too: all of which raised his financial expectations. So we found ourselves spending longer negotiating with him and his agent than with the rest of the *Scissorhands* cast put together. Eventually, we just had to say we couldn't afford him. As with *The Car Man*, I then became so involved with the dancers with whom I made *Scissorhands* that I can't imagine how it would have looked without them: I don't feel *The Car Man* would have felt so right with Adam instead of Alan Vincent, and I don't feel *Scissorhands* would have felt so right with Will. The show belongs to the person you make it on. Who knows what it would have become? You do get happy in the end. You move on very quickly and put all your energy into the performers that are there for you. And you think, 'Well, this is what it is now.'

AM: *Does the company have the same kind of class regime as it had during the* Swan Lake *West End run? You get teachers in to teach the company should dancers want to come? But you're not forcing them to?*

MB: Oh no, they all do it. This is a dance company. They are much more disciplined now in terms of class. The *Highland Fling* company, the *Nutcracker!* company, the *Swan Lake* company: they all do class. It comes within their working hours and it goes without saying that they attend. We offer a variety of classes within the week. Actually, there are six classes a week. Doing class has stopped being an issue. They all do it.

AM: *Did that continue during* Play Without Words, *which doesn't need so much dancing?*

MB: There I left it more up to them, because they didn't need it as much, and some of them were older. There was class every day, but certainly not all of the 'oldies' were there throughout.

AM: *Who selects the teachers?*
MB: Etta Murfitt, mainly. We talk about what kind of class each show will need. There's a lot of jumping in *Highland Fling*, for example, so we need everyone to be very fit for that show. But the dancers do want to keep being challenged as dancers, even while they're dancing roles that don't tax them that way. They want to do a class that's going to get them moving in different ways. They don't always want it to relate to the show.

AM: *How often do you watch class?*
MB: If I'm around, I'll sit there and watch them and do my notes from last night's show. I like watching class. I like to see what they can do. It reveals a lot. You think, 'Wow, they're great. I didn't know they could do that.' A good teacher will challenge them in a different way. You see how good they could be in another direction. Often you decide to cast somebody in a role you'd never have considered them for, just because of what they reveal in class.

AM: *You were talking about administrative differences between Adventures in Motion Pictures and New Adventures.*
MB: New Adventures is a much smaller concern: it's myself and Robert Noble as directors, with Scott Ambler, Etta Murfitt and Lez Brotherston as associates. (We recently added Terry Davies and Paule Constable to that list.) I have my assistant, Suzanne, who is partly paid for by the company and partly paid for by me: she works a couple of days a week. That's the company. Not a single person works for us full-time. On each show we do, we work with different partners. ATG partnered with us to do *Nutcracker!*, and the National Theatre for *Play Without Words*. *Scissorhands* we're kind of doing ourselves with two producers, Martin McCallum and Marc Platt. We did *Highland Fling* with Japanese partners. Sometimes we are the producers, sometimes we license the shows to other partners, but I retain, with Robert, the financial and artistic control of all my productions.

This means we're not paying for offices and lots of staff. The reason we took years to recoup any money on *Swan Lake* had been all that extra outlay on wages and offices in central London. Now we have an arrangement at Sadler's Wells that really goes a long way towards helping us survive. We have offices there at much reduced rent. We have the ability to do these extended seasons at Sadler's Wells.[1] We have the ability to book these shows for long seasons there. It makes money for the theatre, which enables them to do other work that would be less financially easy to do. It works for us because they give us the right length of season for London. We're not trying to be a West End show that maybe will go on a little longer if we manage it. It's a perfect situation at the moment. We're very flexible, very light on our feet in what we can do.

AM: *In the 1990s, you had become an independent company without Arts Council funding. Now you do get Arts Council support. What happened to make the change?*

MB: I think it came with touring *The Car Man*. It was difficult for us to tour such a big production without assistance, and the Arts Council is interested in taking popular modern dance to the regions. A lot of venues around Britain wanted our productions but couldn't quite afford them. So the Arts Council found a way of supporting the theatres to put us on. It couldn't support a commercial show, but it could support the theatres. And it's more or less continued that way. Until *Scissorhands* and *Dorian Gray*. Things have now changed so much that they have started to put money into the productions as well. They've become much more understanding of how to make something like this work. Their funds enable Robert then to raise private money through investors; and any profits that the production might ultimately make are put back to help make us more self-sufficient, though we will continue to need Arts Council support for our work for the foreseeable future.

You know, there was always a feeling that we were making a fortune out of *Swan Lake*, and I presume the Arts Council thought, 'Oh, it's a commercial production. They're raking it in.' But *Swan Lake* never made big money. They understand that now. So they're more understanding. We can ask them to help make shows happen. Sue Hoyle at the Arts Council was a great help that way: very willing to listen.

Now we're one of Britain's foremost touring dance companies and by far its biggest international dance export, and I'm very proud of that. But we also have our own independent status. We're not an institution like the Rambert Dance Company or Northern Ballet Theatre: we re-form for each production. Sometimes I think I'd like the official status that those

---

[1] New Adventures became resident company at Sadler's Wells in 2006. Bourne was already an Artistic Associate.

companies have. But I'm very happy that we have our independence: we don't have any outside figures controlling our policy as part of giving us an annual budget.

AM: *You said in 1998 that you made serious money only out of your musicals. Which aspect of your dance work makes money today? If any?*
MB: Well, the shows do make money now. With the original production of *The Car Man*, I reached the point where I was thinking, 'What am I doing this on? I'm not even earning a living from it, really.' Sure, Lez and I took a lower royalty to make the package work financially – and we were proud of the show – but in practice that meant I was earning less a week than the principal dancers on the show, even though my name was above the title. You know, it had begun to feel that I was working in musicals to subsidize my own dance habit. Today, with the deals that Robert does, the finances of the productions work. I can happily say that every show I have done since 2002 has recouped investors' money. I also now earn very reasonable fees and royalties for my company work as well as for the musicals.

You have to view these shows slightly differently, because other choreographers don't work in this way. The ballet company of La Scala, Milan, has approached me to do *Swan Lake*. Other ballet companies have approached me in the past: Stuttgart, the Paris Opéra, the Washington Ballet. But their approach is that I should go and see their company and then stage my production on them. I have to explain to them that it's a commercial production, with a series of royalties that have to be made on it, and of course it's usually way beyond what they can afford. That's how we finally ended up taking it to Paris in 2005–6, with our own dancers, for a multi-week season. It's not something for another company to do a few performances of during a repertory season.

So far the only other company that's presented any of my dances is the Sarasota Ballet of Florida, which is directed by Iain Webb. Iain used to work with us at AMP as ballet master; I made *Boutique* for his wife Margaret (Maggie) Barbieri's Images of Dance company in the 1990s. It was relatively easy to stage both *Boutique* and our own *Infernal Galop* for the Sarasota company; Etta Murfitt and I helped to stage them, Iain and Maggie know our style, and they went well. Iain's hoping next to stage *Highland Fling*; but, like so many of America's ballet companies, it's very hard for him to raise the money for all the new productions he'd like.

I'm always open to ideas from other companies. For example, I've just been meeting the director of the Pittsburgh Ballet, Terrence Orr, who wants to mount one of our pieces. He and Peter Boal of Pacific Northwest Ballet are both interested in acquiring *Play Without Words*; I'm afraid that I've put them both off, because it's so specifically for dancer-actors with experience of that kind of work. I am pushing him towards a more dancey piece like *Nutcracker!*, *Highland Fling*, or even *Dorian*. Then it would be a case of seeing if his company had the right kind of performers to do the work.

AM: *Ironically, in 2004–5 you became the kind of multi-project company that Katharine seems to have conceived. New Adventures was doing separate tours of* Nutcracker!, Swan Lake, Highland Fling *and* Play Without Words, *some of them simultaneous. Do all of these bring in money?*
MB: Yes, they all bring in revenue now. *Swan Lake*, for me, less than the other shows. I'm still limited in what I earn from it because the original investors are yet to be completely reimbursed.[2] This isn't a legal requirement because my old company, AMP, is in liquidation. But it involved a whole number of small-scale investors who never got their money back on that show, and so I now give part of my royalties to that fund. Because it was me they supported. I owe it to them. I give a percentage of my royalties for *Nutcracker!* and *Highland Fling* as well to pay back those people. There are too many people who were good to me, you know, to not want to do that.

AM: *Let's talk a bit more about the period of 2004–5 when you had no fewer than five different full-length shows running at the same time, each playing seven or eight shows per week to large theatres in Britain and across the world. With the possible exception of Jerome Robbins, who at one point was Mr Broadway, I know of no choreographer who had quite had this kind of exposure.*
MB: There were never five at exactly the same time. *Mary Poppins* had been running in London since late 2004, yes. At one point in late 2004, both *Nutcracker!* and *Swan Lake* were doing separate tours, and then in early 2005 we revived *Highland Fling* while *Play Without Words* was touring the States. But no more than two New Adventures shows at the same time. The main overlap happened by accident: nobody had anticipated that *Play Without Words* would have such an extended life or tour

---

[2] This was finally achieved in 2010.

so long. I never thought they'd have it at the Ahmansson in Los Angeles for eight weeks, for example; I wasn't sure it was a big enough show for that. But that's the success it had.

AM: *Even so, the feat of any one dance production managing to fill a big theatre seven or eight performances a week for months on end has very few precedents. You now have learnt how to manage it with two shows at a time. Late in 2006, your* Swan Lake *reopened in Paris while* Edward Scissorhands *started a six-month tour of the States, and you opened* Mary Poppins *in New York while it continued to run in London. Each of your big dance productions now receives hundreds of performances – something that very few ballets, let alone modern-dance works, ever achieve.*

MB: Well, we have had several years this decade when we have believed we were giving more performances per annum than any other dance company in the world except perhaps Momix, which likewise tours more troupes than one. Because each year is different, this varies. Even in our leaner years, when we're only touring one show at a time, we seem to give about 190 to 200 performances, which is the same as New York City Ballet and rather more than the Alvin Ailey American Dance Theater. In the years 2005 to 2009, *Edward Scissorhands* clocked up over five hundred performances. In 2009, we are dancing *Dorian Gray* some seventeen weeks, and *Swan Lake* for some three weeks at the year's end: the total may be about 160 performances for the whole year.[3]

This is where Robert Noble's organizational skills have been invaluable. Somehow I wasn't neglecting any of these shows either. I was actually available for all the rehearsal periods. To take the *Highland Fling* tour, for example, I was there for the whole period we rehearsed it, and I went to see it at most touring dates. I made regular visits to the revival of *Swan Lake*, even when it was up and running. I went to all the places *Play Without Words* went to, and I stayed with it for several weeks in both New York and Los Angeles. It certainly felt as if they were all going on at the same time! But actually they were so planned that I was able to give the necessary input into each one.

Of course, I have colleagues without whom these shows wouldn't get staged. Scott Ambler and Etta Murfitt were around to mount *Swan*

[3] See Appendix E on touring.

Lake, and Vicky Evans, Isabel Mortimer and others have been looking after it while it's been away on tour. As far as the other shows go, Scott's priority was *Play Without Words*: he was me when I wasn't there. And Etta's was *Highland Fling*. They had a show each, and that's how the company was divided. Fifteen people in each show.

Etta and Scott: you couldn't wish for better people to look after a show. Etta has moved on to a point where she's quite comfortable taking care of a show; she doesn't have to be in it. She enjoyed performing again in *Scissorhands*; she loves her created role as Peg Boggs. But she didn't do the entire American tour; she's got a family. She's in her forties now; Scott's five years older. He is still there on stage, with roles in most of these shows. And I'm sure there'll be other roles for them both.

AM: *Am I right, though, if I say that the name 'Adventures in Motion Pictures' was a very catchy and much-used title, whereas 'New Adventures' hasn't been used so much on publicity? By contrast, your own name is now a bigger deal.*

MB: Well, the use of my name was something that Katharine achieved in particular. She's the one who started putting my name above the titles and things. It was done mainly for *Swan Lake* – to differentiate it from other *Swan Lake*s, to stop any confusion. And now the strange thing is people use my name without us initiating that. Our current show is certainly not called 'Matthew Bourne's *Edward Scissorhands*'. Because it's not my *Edward Scissorhands*. It's too many other people's.

However, in the future we mean to push the title of New Adventures a little more than we have done previously. I know that my name seems to help with ticket sales, but it does matter that people should know we are a company with a large repertoire and a company of dancers who often work from production to production. I was in a meeting with New York's City Center Theater, one of the main dance houses there, and they didn't realize that I had my own established company of dancers. So I want to stress this, and to make sure the Arts Council realizes the importance of supporting the company – not just for myself but for these dancers. Several of these dancers have worked with me for their entire careers, for over ten years now, on a series of productions. We've grown into a real ensemble company.

(Conversations 2005–9)

13

My Fair Lady (2001),
South Pacific (2001), Mary
Poppins (2004) and Oliver! (2008)

My Fair Lady (2001)

MATTHEW BOURNE: It was Cameron Mackintosh who got me on board for the National's *My Fair Lady*, at a very early stage. He wanted it to start out at the National. A lot of good musical revivals have started life there: especially Richard Eyre's production of *Guys and Dolls* (1982) and Nick Hytner's production of *Carousel* (1992, with Kenneth MacMillan's choreography).

Cameron's original idea was to have Eyre direct *My Fair Lady*. But then Eyre left the National, and Trevor Nunn succeeded him. At one stage, Trevor had sounded me out about doing the dances for his 1998 *Oklahoma!*. I considered that seriously. I decided not to just because of other commitments (the preparation for *Swan Lake* on Broadway) and so Susan Stroman did it instead. When I saw the National *Oklahoma!*, I remember thinking, 'Oh, thank God she did it.' I find her a genius at putting together a short number, like 'The Farmer and the Cowman' or 'Everything's Up to Date in Kansas City'. She's so good at numbers. I don't think her version of the dream ballet is as good as the Agnes de Mille one in the film. But with other individual dance numbers, in a show like that, she's just brilliant.

ALASTAIR MACAULAY: *Could it be said that Susan Stroman is the nearest to an American equivalent to you at the moment? She's worked in musicals. She's now produced at least one story-based dance show,* Contact *(1999). And she's interested in direction as well as choreography.*

MB: Yes. But she belongs to a big tradition of director-choreographers in New York. There's never been a natural progression in London from choreography to direction, whereas with her it seemed only a matter of time before she would start both directing and choreographing everything she did. Yes, there are parallels between us. The biggest differences, though, are that she's never had a company and she hasn't emerged by way of making all-dance shows. But I think her *Contact* came about in a similar way to our *Play Without Words*. Lincoln Center commissioned her to do it, and she took it as a chance to try something different. The same was true with *Play Without Words* for me. Both pieces became popular, but in both cases the intention was to experiment without an eye on a commercial run.

So, when Cameron got Trevor to take up *My Fair Lady*, Trevor asked to see me. Mind you, Cameron wanted to revive *My Fair Lady*, and he had said to me all along, 'I won't do it unless you do.' Which, of course, was very flattering. So that had been an idea for years, and I really felt I'd promised him I'd do it by the time I went to see Trevor anyway. And having passed on *Oklahoma!*, I certainly knew I mustn't mess Trevor around.

AM: *But in the late 1990s, after* Oliver! *and after* Swan Lake, *you'd said that if you were to work again in musicals, you wanted to be both director and choreographer in future.*

MB: I know! And I love musicals and have wondered about staging some. But when I said that I would only consider being choreographer *and* director on any future musicals, it was because I felt that working with another director would probably compromise my ideas for staging. Trevor was different from the first, because he let me feel I would be free to explore. The whole experience felt like a true collaboration, with a complete lack of ego from everyone involved. I hadn't done a musical for a while, *My Fair Lady* felt much more of a book musical than *Show Boat* or *Oliver!*, and I needed to know how he felt about the numbers. He was very precise: 'That's yours. You do that.'

AM: *Why does* My Fair Lady *feel more of a book musical?*

MB: It's a Bernard Shaw play (*Pygmalion*), it's much more wordy than many musicals (especially in our version), and the songs all come at specific moments in the narrative and move the story forwards. Whereas with *Oliver!* there were sometimes three sentences between songs. Trevor put in a lot of work on selecting the text for *My Fair Lady*. In particular, he went to the 1938 *Pygmalion* film, for which Shaw had added some scenes, with Wendy Hiller as Eliza.

At every stage, I found Trevor to be supportive. He's so experienced with musicals, and he's perfect on the practicalities. He knew how to set up each number for me. With 'Wouldn't It Be Loverly' and 'Little Bit of Luck', for example, he'd show me the scene leading up to it; he'd say, 'OK – it starts like this.' And then he'd hand it over to me. That was just what I needed.

AM: *You've now worked with Trevor Nunn on two musicals and with Richard Eyre on one. Compare and contrast.*

MB: They're completely different, principally in that Trevor is much more on the front foot. He always appears to know exactly what he wants and is full of information. Famously, he talks a lot before you get anything done. Everyone in the business tells stories about that aspect of him. Apparently when he did 'The Farmer and the Cowman', he spent hours talking about the life of a farmer and a cowman; and then they did the whole history of the sociological situation that that was about; and then they did a workshop on the day in the life of a farmer – spread across a whole day of rehearsal. He did the same when we came to *South Pacific*. But it helped me a lot, especially on *My Fair Lady*. For example, something like 'Little Bit of Luck', I asked him to set up for me, and he did. He led right to the line where the song begins and then he just went 'Over to you.' Like that.

But Richard was much less experienced in musicals and wanted to be part of everything. Wanted to be there when the number was devised; wanted to know the story that each number was going to show; wanted to devise it together. Which was good, since for that show, *Mary Poppins*, I was co-director too: it made sense. He didn't want any divisions; he didn't want us to go into another room. Of course, sometimes we did, to work out movement. But he always wanted to have a feel of the whole. Considering that *Poppins* was a piece that hadn't been done on stage, I thought that was wise. Whereas in *My Fair Lady* you know the show works, so you can hand over a number to the choreographer. And Trevor would always have input into any number.

AM: *Some people were bothered – I wasn't – by your use of percussive dancing with dustbin lids in 'With a Little Bit of Luck'. They think it's more like* Stomp *than* My Fair Lady.

MB: *Stomp* didn't invent dancing with dustbin lids: that goes back to the music hall (as I think the makers of *Stomp* have happily acknowledged), and we were very much trying to draw from the music-hall tradition.

Likewise some people claimed to be bothered by our use of mourning costume for the Ascot scene. Actually, this production team were meticulous in their re-creation of the era in which *My Fair Lady* is set. The music department were all very conscientious about what was stylistically correct, and so was Cameron.

Lerner and Loewe set *My Fair Lady* in 1912 or 1913. Trevor decided on 1910 because he wanted to overcome the precedent of Cecil Beaton's famous black-and-white costumes for the Ascot scene. In 1910, everyone at Ascot wore mourning – it was remembered as the Black Ascot – for Edward VII, who'd recently died. In fact, that was what had given Beaton his black-and-white idea. Trevor and Anthony Ward decided to go one further, and to re-create the Black Ascot.

AM: *Which songs were you involved with?*
MB: More than you might suppose. 1: the Prologue. 2: 'Wouldn't It Be Loverly'. 3: 'With a Little Bit of Luck'. 4: 'The Rain in Spain'. 5: 'I Could Have Danced All Night'. 6: The Ascot Gavotte. 7: the Ball. 8: 'Show Me'. 9: 'Get Me to the Church on Time'. 10: 'I've Grown Accustomed to Her Face'. Some of these are just bits and pieces of individual dancing; others are big numbers. Both Doolittle's numbers, 'With a Little Bit of Luck' and 'Get Me to the Church on Time', are big: they're character numbers, supposedly show-stoppers.

Some of my involvement in other smaller numbers – the Prologue, 'Loverly', 'Rain in Spain', 'I Could Have Danced All Night' and 'Show Me' – was more along the lines of musical staging. Hence the double credit on this show. I loved working on these numbers because it was even more about story-telling; and it involved a certain amount of direction of the leading performers. I loved the 'Cabbage Queen' section of 'Loverly', the bullfight in 'Rain in Spain' and the Tube journey and suffragettes in 'Show Me'.

AM: *Is there any record of the original stage production?*
MB: I've seen film of the Hanya Holm choreography for 'Wouldn't It Be Loverly'. At least, I assume it's the Broadway choreography, because it's on one of those Ed Sullivan TV shows where the cast go into the studio and do what they've done on stage. It's maybe not the whole thing, but there are elements there. That's all. I'd never seen the show on stage, you know, and the film really isn't much help for a choreographer.

GET ME TO THE CHURCH

With Coster Mongers

Duo

Intro

Covent Garden (Show off his money – Theres Drinks ...)

Describe Dress — Bells?   Gestures   Calls him over (Costers)

Stopper   Whopper

to flower seller – gives Jamie money   Calls over pea-shellers   Kiss him on each cheek

I Gotta   for button holes

Report   Spruce up   Kiss

Grabs one woman   Other woman   Dance with women?

Dancin to dancin   Whistling

Rumpus   Onto – Travellator   No Lyrics

Covent Garden disappears   Bar comes on (or passes by)

Group   Drag me or Jail me   Group

Dennis

At First Bar – He drinks   Some bloke what able

Dennis

Lifted by others   Somestay at bar   Pick front in –   Others exit through door

Flying   Dennis   wooin   2 girls enter followed by Dennis   Group

Dennis exits the door with girls + bottle   Into Music Hall

Feather and fan

Dennis   Group   No Lyrics

92 *My Fair Lady*, Act Two, 'Get Me to the Church': notes by Bourne, describing successive phases of narrative action in Alfred Doolittle's pub crawl.

AM: *'With a Little Bit of Luck' was the first big dance item.*

MB: Trevor and I decided to build this up more than usual. In the original, it was a trio for Doolittle and two other men, with very minimal choreography. In the film, Stanley Holloway does a little bit of soft-shoe shuffle up on a table in the pub. It's all small-scale – much more realistic, say, than *Oliver!* where there's a whole street full of people dancing, but disappointing for that very reason. So we made it a major production number.

Our idea was that the number would go from the pub out onto the street, and that it would be just a lot of people falling out of the pub late at night, all singing and making a noise and a racket. And one lone woman comes out and has a go at them. That's a classic old joke really: this big noisy number is stopped by a woman who's trying to sleep. It was because we wanted noise that I saw it in terms of the Gene Kelly number from the MGM film *It's Always Fair Weather*, which I remembered they danced with dustbin lids on their feet. But in our staging they pick up other things as well.

AM: *The Ascot scene has your most original touch: you give the race-goers some equine movement, as if they've half turned into the horses they're watching.*

MB: That scene was probably my hardest assignment here. I knew *My Fair Lady* so well as a film, but in the film it's the camera that does all the movement in the Ascot scene. The people are static. The performers are all Californian *Vogue* models. And they're unemotional: that's the point of the song and its lyric. The most they do is turn their heads. So how to choreograph that on stage?

Scott Ambler, who assisted me on this show, and I came up with the idea of horsey movement – of having the people becoming the animals. Anthony Ward's set had a fence at the front and another at the back, so that gave us the idea of a pen. We imagined the race-goers as rare creatures coping with confinement. A kiss of a hand becomes a hungry horse feeding from a nosebag. Elegant men snort with pleasure and use their canes as wagging tails. Men lead women around the paddock as if they are prize creatures. The men's feet become the dainty hoofs of a dressage display. Oh yes, and there's a very bow-legged jockey! Once we'd started, the ideas came flowing. We played up the use of the canes and the binoculars. We built up a David Attenborough feel to it as well: we're showing you exotic species in confinement.

93 *My Fair Lady*, Act One, 'With a Little Bit of Luck'. Bourne's use of dustbin-lids as footwear drew on a long tradition of show entertainment.

94 *My Fair Lady*, Act One, 'The Ascot Gavotte'. Bourne overlapped the high-society scene with a study of equine behaviour.

MORE ASCOT   MENS
                                            WOMENS

1. Cane Sequence
2. Old man 'Camel' walk
3. Womans 'Lazy Cow' walk
4. Young 'Stallions' walk
5. Little old rich man with Val Cutko
6. Tail wagging cane   / Tail dragging
7. Womens hand to kiss "nosebags"
8. Men leading women on as horses on display
9. 'Sniffing' when greeting
10. Fence up at beg (½ way?)
11. 3 young colts 'padding ground' strutting + talking in paddock
12. Women - tall sticks - claw like hands
13. Men 'refuse at fence' - womens canes
14. Punting women
15. V/S stationary walking

A Intro - PART I (Extend) - Silhouette horsey mvt.
        PART II (Extend) - Social Greetings + arrivals

B 1st verse of song - where they are to audience
   2nd verse   "   - to front fence (gesture)
   3rd -   race begins and circles round to other side

C Goes into Dance break

D Trophy Giving

95 *My Fair Lady*, Act One: further Ascot notes for choreography by Bourne.

I'm probably more proud of that than any other individual number I've done in any musical.

AM: *The dance scene that worked least well for me is the ball. It just doesn't make the impact that one wants it to.*
MB: I think you're right. The staging was largely dictated by the song, 'You Did It', which is sung by Pickering and Higgins just after this scene. Jonathan Pryce quite rightly wanted the ball to tell the story that he relates in the song, with the Hungarian expert Karpathy trying to check out Eliza. But that all became very complex and drawn out.

Trevor had wanted to move 'I Could Have Danced All Night' to Act Two – he felt that it made much more sense for Eliza to sing it later, after the ball. We rehearsed the ball scene as if it were all seen through her eyes, so that it led up to her singing 'Bed, bed, I couldn't go to bed', etc. But the Lerner and Loewe estate intervened and put it back where it was originally in Act One.

When the production was new at the National, the ball costumes were also problematic. It's a designer's dream to design a ball where each dress was individual in style and colour, and Anthony Ward had given the women trains, which were historically correct. But the individuality of each dress made it very difficult to create a unified look for the scene, and the women's trains were immovable. Hooks had to be added to raise them up, but then, as the women danced, they ended up showing an unseemly amount of leg!

I liked the choreography I made in the studio! I think we all agreed at the end of the National run that we all had work to do on that scene. Some things surprise you when they get on stage – not always pleasantly. By the time we'd got to Drury Lane, Anthony had redesigned a lot of it, so that there was a colour scheme that helped.

AM: *And you were able to rechoreograph?*
MB: Well, I could do more of what we wanted to do in the first place. And whatever was there looked better because there was more unity of style and colour and it was just easier to see.

I would have liked to have gone further, I suppose. We had travelators: you know, platforms that move across the stage. At the beginning of the scene, I had people switch between travelators that were moving, so that you got a different speed because they were moving in opposite directions. There's a Fred Astaire number in *Ziegfeld Follies* – 'This Heart of Mine' – where they use travelators: lovely, because it just takes you by surprise. Suddenly someone steps onto something that you don't really see. They stop but they keep travelling: a very interesting idea. Like ice-skating, isn't it? You can hold a position and move. I'd like to explore that more.

But there was a lot of story to be told in that ballroom scene. So it's not really a dance scene as such. You've got to show how she brings off her final task, how she can pass off as a lady and win Professor Higgins's bet for him. And there's this Hungarian guy Karpathy who Professor Higgins knows and is an expert on dialects: she has to win him over. Well, he decides that she's Hungarian royalty, and so they win the bet. Also you have to have Higgins end up dancing with Eliza as well, which must mean something to the two of them at the time it happens. That part's fine – it's a dance thing. But there was a lot of dialogue too: we tried eventually to pare that down quite a lot, especially when Cameron made his usual push to cut the show's time down. We made it more of a scene that was told through movement, because you could: you didn't need all the dialogue. But because we were cutting down on the time, some of the dancing went as well. That was a shame: we could make more impact there.

AM: *Remind me what you did with 'I'm getting married in the morning'.*
MB: It was like a stag night, a pub crawl that went through several locations. It started off in the flower market, as Doolittle sings 'just a few more hours' . . . We took the 'few more hours' to mean to have a good time. And so he picks up some friends, a couple of girls, and they go in and out of pub doors, on to the next place and the next place. Again, these travelators were quite useful. The performers walked on them as if they were going somewhere, or static things like lamp-posts passed by the other way. It all had to be very carefully timed for things to come into place as the performers walked through: quite a dangerous number, setwise. And it ended up in a little music-hall type of pub – a pub that had a stage in it, with showgirls doing a riotous number.

AM: *It was a daringly long show. If you'd been the director or the producer, would you have kept it so long? Or would you have cut it elsewhere?*
MB: I found it very difficult to cut. Trevor had added a certain amount of dialogue, which made it stronger. There were new aspects that made the story much deeper. And the numbers were longer: I was encouraged to tell a story in them, to expand them, and to have dance breaks. And

on top of that, we used all of the lyrics. So the only way to cut it – if you didn't want to lose those items that had become the show's high points – was to cut the dialogue. But even that wasn't easy.

AM: *How much work did you do with Professor Higgins?*
MB: He did a bit of stuff in 'Rain in Spain', and a bit of waltzing at the ball. Jonathan Pryce, our first-cast Higgins, improvised quite a bit of 'Rain in Spain' himself, because he's a very good mover, he's very inventive with movement, and he's best left to his own devices a bit. The choreographer's task is just to shape what he does. It's better not to give him something, but to talk about ideas, let him play with them, and to give him room for variation: he doesn't like being the same all the time. But when it came to having to waltz and be in time with everyone else, he took it very seriously. The rest of the time, he finds choreography as something where his mind can't be free. I understand that: he's an actor. I'd worked with him on *Oliver!* and he'd seen some of my shows. So we had a connection. But he's not the easiest person to pin down.

AM: *A huge amount of publicity focused on the Eliza of Martine McCutcheon – another actor best known from TV, though now with a singing career – all the more when she had to cancel the last preview and then, after the first night, several weeks of performances.*
MB: She and I were born in the same hospital, on Clapton High Street! – that bonded us early on. We're both East Londoners and would giggle about a lot of the same things, especially when Martine had to explain to Trevor what a 'saveloy' is. She worked incredibly hard throughout the rehearsal period, would try anything, and was much loved by the majority of the company. She is the real thing. It's such a shame that it all ended so sadly. She wasn't really a dancer, but that actually added to the appeal of her Eliza. She, like her character, was being formed.

AM: *The later Elizas?*
MB: Probably the most accomplished was Joanna Riding. She wanted to get everything right, hand positions and everything. A real pro. But the danger was that it sometimes looked unspontaneous or not true to herself.

The Eliza I thought was the best really was Laura Michelle Kelly. Interestingly, we'd rejected her when we first did it, because they were looking for a first cover, and she was only eighteen. She had this very impressive voice. But she wasn't a dancer at all. She couldn't move, she could not be useful in the show as part of that ensemble. So she ended up going into another show. But then she came back – and now she turned out to be the most natural mover of them all.

AM: *What had changed along the line?*
MB: I don't know. Just the experience of having done major shows maybe. When she was in the character of Eliza at the ball and she was given the steps and she had the feeling of what she was doing, what she did was very feminine, very touching, very natural. She just made good choices; everything she did looked right for the character. The same carried on when we cast her as Mary Poppins: a complete natural in movement, who could pick things up really quickly and make it look good. She's a clever girl.

Trevor was just superb to work with. Because he's so experienced, he was very relaxed. That helped everybody. He and I had what he called 'a bosom experience', and so when he asked me to do *South Pacific* with him, I didn't hesitate to say yes.

South Pacific (2001)

MATTHEW BOURNE: *South Pacific* came in the wake of doing *My Fair Lady* – the same year. There was so much criticism of the National at the time for doing too many musicals, and yet Trevor decided – perversely, I thought, stubbornly – to do another big one. I really don't know why: probably because it can be a money-spinner. Which is a good reason to do it.

But the original *South Pacific* had never had a choreographer attached to it. And I presume it was put together by the performers and the original director, Joshua Logan – who directed the film as well. I have a feeling that Mary Martin may have put a lot of it together, along with a dance assistant of some kind. Which is right for the show, because all the bigger numbers that have movement in them are when Nelly Forbush (the Mary Martin role) puts on a show, and (this is mentioned in the script more than once) she is supposed to choreograph the numbers. So you assume that she's not Balanchine!

And you have to put yourself in her head. What would she do? What would she know of dance and movement? What sort of things might she want to use? We weren't trying to be amateurish, but it does have to have an amateurish edge to it, a feel of them putting this show together.

Trevor had specifically cast women who looked like the nurses on this island rather than showbizzy chorus girls. So they were all shapes and sizes and types. Very tall, skinny girls, bigger girls and . . . And the same was true of the soldiers. They were a real rough-and-tumble bunch of people. I liked that. And it was fun to make that work. I had a really good time doing it. And they were a very happy cast. But it wasn't a great choreographic show for me really – just a fun show to do.

We tried a beginning of the show that led into the opening number, 'Bloody Mary', which built up through the Olivier Theatre with soldiers doing a sort of vocal marching as they go along the beach – you've seen the sort of thing in adverts and films – where the sergeant sings something and they all sing back, repeating it, you know. As part of an exercise regime. But we went too far with it for the Rodgers and Hammerstein estate: they pointed out Richard Rodgers would never have written this kind of chord structure – that we'd taken it away from something that was Rodgers's. So we had to change some of it: which was a fair point.

Mary Poppins (2004)

ALASTAIR MACAULAY: *You opened the British production of* Mary Poppins *in 2004; it ran for over three years, and then toured Britain successfully for six months. The New York version opened in 2007, recently passed its thousandth performance, and at the time of talking is still running. After all this time of looking at the stage version, how watchable do you find the 1964 film?*
MATTHEW BOURNE: Completely.

AM: *I remember being crazy about it as a child. But about a year before the stage show opened, knowing that it was something I would review, I sat down to watch it on video. And I couldn't stand it. I remember looking at it in a state of shock and thinking, 'Oh no, I can't stand the thought of a theatre show of this.' Like every child of my generation, I worshipped Julie Andrews. But I now think that half the point of growing up is to outgrow her films.*
MB: Oh, I can't take that kind of talk. You should be ashamed of yourself. Leave this house immediately! That film's so much a part of me. But I do now see the film and the stage show as entirely separate. And I can still very happily watch the film.

AM: *There are now a great many people who say – as I do – that the stage show is better than the film. Does that make sense to you? Or is that embarrassing?*

MB: It's heresy . . . But flattering!

AM: *Cameron Mackintosh had bought the stage rights to* Mary Poppins *in the early 1990s. You were interested in being its choreographer from the time you worked on* Oliver!. *Did you also become interested in being its director?*

MB: I certainly said to Cameron, 'Look, I'd like to be involved in some capacity.' Direction was starting to interest me. But I was also aware that every prestigious British theatre director was interested in directing *Mary Poppins*, so I didn't presume to offer myself in that capacity.

AM: *The rights to* Mary Poppins *belonged to two separate empires, Disney and Cameron Mackintosh. Disney owned the rights to the songs from the film; Mackintosh had bought the stage rights to the stories from Mrs Travers. Were you the link between Disney and Mackintosh that enabled* Mary Poppins *to happen on stage?*

MB: I sometimes have liked to remember it that way! Certainly I remember the period when it seemed an impossible project to bring them together.

Actually, Thomas (Tom) Schumacher of Disney had been in business with the designer Bob Crowley for years. Bob had worked with Disney on a number of projects – such as, on Broadway, *Aida*. He and Tom had even begun talking at one point about staging *Mary Poppins* without involving Cameron. But he had worked with Cameron for a yet longer period, on such productions as *Carousel* and *The Witches of Eastwick*, and he quietly worked for quite some time to arrange the first meeting between Cameron and Tom. (In the event, the person who literally set up the first meeting was Rick Elice – best known now for writing the book of *The Jersey Boys*.) But I was around; I let both sides know I was very interested; and I'm delighted I became part of the production.

Everybody agrees the conjunction of the two empires was for the best. Cameron had always wanted to include music from the film. He'd met Mrs Travers in 1993 – she died in 1996 – and bought the rights from her. But he always discussed with her his hopes to include some of the songs from the film; he told her the show would need them.

It so happened that, in the years that followed, George Stiles and

Anthony Drewe sent him the song 'Practically Perfect'. They knew him, so they sent him this song on spec, as recorded by Claire Moore, fully orchestrated. I was played it in Cameron's office back in 1994. I wasn't sure what his plan was at that point. Cameron had already realized the stage show would need new songs. Anyway, it's characteristic of Cameron to make a show his own – to reconceive it from scratch. All this was before he'd decided on a director or a choreographer.

AM: *But not all of the film songs are in the stage show. Which ones were cut?*

MB: 'I Love to Laugh', 'Stay Awake' (a lovely song, I think), the bank song, and 'Sister Suffragette'. Everyone was very disappointed about losing 'Sister Suffragette'. (But Pamela Travers had hated Walt Disney's invention of Mrs Banks being a suffragette.)

AM: *In the event, Cameron Mackintosh asked Richard Eyre to be director, you to be co-director and choreographer, Stephen Mear to be co-choreographer. And Mackintosh told me that, because the whole production was a collaboration between him and Disney, he felt the whole show should be collaborative at every level.*

The issue has been much raised as to whether you are a director or a choreographer – some people claim you're a director but not a choreographer – and we'll return to this later. Apart from on Oliver! in 2008, Mary Poppins is the only other time you've been formally employed as director or co-director. So tell me where you felt you were involved in strict direction, as opposed to choreography. And did that take you somewhere new?

MB: I'm afraid I can't separate them that neatly. In advance, I didn't know how it would work: I was going to have to work with Richard as director, with Stephen as a choreographer, and that might have led to problems either way. But the happy thing was that Richard wanted to be part of everything and wanted us to be part of everything too, so there were no divisions. When we were making the dances, he absolutely wanted to be there and be part of the decision-making process. Quite right too: because of that, we were all the more focused on telling the story. And he would always want us there when he was making scenes because they were so music-led. So it was an unusual collaboration but a true one. All three of us contributed to the whole in a very organic way. And for me it often felt very much like doing one of my own dance shows really: I was directing and choreographing at the same time.

AM: *Were there moments when you thought, 'I'll leave this to Richard because that's what he knows about and I don't'?*

MB: Yes. Especially the bits for Mr and Mrs Banks. They felt more his area; they didn't really have any dancing to do, but they're central to the whole story.

Certainly there were times when an acting scene would be rehearsed in one place while a dance would be rehearsed downstairs, and I would think, 'Where am I supposed to be?' I hated missing out on one thing or the other. But it just worked itself out. Where it freed me was to give direction to performers without stepping on anyone's toes. Sometimes in other musicals I've felt I wanted to say something, but felt it wasn't necessarily my area. On this one, I felt, obviously, that I could get a relationship with the leading performers.

AM: *You have a particular attitude to the choreographic process with your own company. So how did you work with another choreographer? How were the dances made?*

MB: Gingerly to begin with, as you would expect. I only knew Stephen to say hello to. But he turned out to be very open. We each had particular skills that we could give the show. But we were both keen to not completely hand over any one item to each other. Some people around the production, even Richard, would assume that Stephen took charge of one number and I of another. 'Step in Time' was always referred to as 'Stephen's tap number' because he's a tap dancer; and some people assumed I did 'Jolly Holiday' because the characters have a classical side and I'm supposedly from the ballet world – which anyway we know I'm not. Well, he and I did defer to each other to a certain extent, since I don't tap and he'd never done a group number like 'Jolly Holiday' – his group numbers, hitherto, have been much more about an emphasis on ensemble, often used as a back-up for the principals. This was much more about story-telling and finding movement for the different characters. But actually we really did every number together, and we enjoyed it.

We clicked together quite quickly on 'Supercalifragilisticexpialidocious'. We decided it should be quite gestural. Well, that should have seemed more my area. You know, Stephen is Mr Showbiz, and he knows so much about steps. However, his partner is deaf, and so he knows the sign language. He taught me to do it too, and then we took that a stage further. We developed our own sign language. I think there are one or two of the original letters in the finished dance. It was something we could do together very well in front of a mirror – and it was a kind of choreography he'd occasionally done before, being gesture-based. So that was a great way of working together.

Then 'Step in Time' was a joy for me, because I've always wanted to choreograph a tap-dance number. But, unlike Stephen, I can't do the steps. Still, I guess I know enough about tap-dancing after all these decades of watching the films! I felt confident enough to say, 'Well, try this kind of thing. I don't know what the step is but . . .' Or I'd show him little clips from Eleanor Powell films and say, 'I love this step. What is that step? Can we do that?' So that felt really collaborative as well. The structure of it, and the arrangement of people within it, and some of the ideas in it, were very shared, very much a mixture.

All the numbers ended up being a mixture of the two of us. An incredible achievement really: in advance, I'd been sure we'd have to go one way or the other.

It was the same with directing the spoken scenes with Richard. I'd thought it would have to be one person's priority or the other's. But on that show it wasn't.

AM: *Did you feel, once it was finished, that it had extended you? and that you were now doing things you hadn't known you could do?*
MB: It certainly extended me in what I could learn from Stephen. I felt he had so much that I could learn in terms of delivering a kind of showbizzy kind of show-stopping number. He's got all the tricks up his sleeve. He's full of those steps, he's steeped in them, whereas I've never had them at my fingertips.

But I don't think I've learnt anything specific about putting on a show. Everyone thinks musical and dance shows are going to be so different. Yet it's still the same issues you're dealing with, always. I feel one of the most important jobs of the director is pace. And that's the same in any show. You're moving things on, you're finding ways of connecting things and connecting scenes together. You, as a director, get a lot of praise for what the brilliant actor can do without your having said very much to him or her. But the director's task is more to do with putting the production together, how it moves and the rhythm of it. And you soon know when a show hasn't been well directed, don't you? You sit there with all sorts of plodding things going on and scene changes that take for ever.

What I've learnt most from directors like Richard and Trevor is something much more general. Being a director is about never giving up. Richard and Trevor just won't accept that something's not possible, even when everyone around them is thinking, 'How are we supposed to do this?' It's a positive approach but one that requires everyone to really rethink what they're doing. I suppose I had this already, and had learnt it from previous directors, but Richard and Trevor have really exemplified it for me. And for me now that's what the director's job is. Certainly with putting on a new show like *Edward Scissorhands* or *Dorian Gray*, most of my energy is to try and make it work as a piece from beginning to end. The detail – everything in the middle within it – is something that I'm going to work on as time goes by. That's what always happens with big shows.

AM: *You say it's heresy to call the show better than the film. How is it different?*

MB: I think it's better in terms of the story it tells. It's the story of a family, told with logic. That's what everyone was happy to see in this version, and it was something people could relate to more. And Mary Poppins has more of a job to do here when she arrives than in the film. The parents in the film are a bit scatterbrained, and their kids are lovely. Mrs Banks is rather dotty and he's distracted. They don't seem to have very serious problems to deal with. We instead tried to show trouble in the marriage that parents could relate to, and we tried to make the kids rude, snobbish, and much more unruly, so that kids in the audience could relate to that and not think they were just sweet little Edwardian kids in the past. You find yourself getting more involved in it, even though you think you're watching the same story as the film. But that's not just to do with our staging – it's the way it's written as well. It's a deeper story.

AM: *Here you were up against the same issue as in your own next production,* Edward Scissorhands: *in either case, the audience comes with one specific movie in mind. I know that with* Scissorhands *there were elements you took from Johnny Depp's performance and others where you went in a different direction. With* Mary Poppins, *did you have a similar rehearsal process to take some ideas from Julie Andrews and others absolutely not?*

MB: This came up more in initial discussions than in rehearsals. We always knew we would not be re-creating the film, and we approached *Poppins* as a new book musical for the stage. We would go back to the books as much as to the film to find those characters and create that story. No one referred to the film much during rehearsals. I was the one who supposedly knew it the best – the one people always came to for information about the film! But it wasn't referred to all the time at all.

Probably many more people know the film of *Poppins* than that of *Scissorhands*, but they come because they love the piece and they want to see it done on stage. So you want to please them and surprise them. At the same time, you've got to bear in mind that there are people who have not seen the film and are coming for a new experience. You've got to tell them a story.

AM: *The whole story is a sort of inversion of* Peter Pan, *isn't it? It's all based around the nursery and flight. And what goes on outside the nursery.*
MB: Yes. Those themes keep coming back.

AM: *And that relates to* Nutcracker *too. You know, children indoors and the larger world of fantasy outside – particularly in your version.*
MB: I think Mrs Travers trained as a dancer when she was young. There's enormous allusion to movement in the books. It's one of the interesting aspects of this show – her attitude towards dancing, or what dancing meant to her.

AM: *Do you have any idea from the books what kind of dancing she had in mind? or did herself?*
MB: Not really, but there's a lot of waltzing in the books, so it seems to me. As a result, it felt like a show that needed to dance quite a lot, a show with dancing at the centre of it. And so we tried to put it in wherever possible. There's a nice kite-flying transition at one point: very brief, but balletic in its feel. That came from the books. And flying. Flying is akin to dancing, as far as she was concerned. You dance and then you take off. Even in one of the numbers that we cut, 'I Love to Laugh', there's the idea that you laugh and you lift off the ground.

You know, the park is an important place in the books. It's where things happen. And quite often the thing that happens is people start dancing. And they find themselves dancing with odd partners, like the policeman with the bird-woman. I thought that was a nice thing to get into the show.

AM: *Are there any moments you can say, 'We have taken that from the film'?*

MB: The main thing is 'Step in Time'. It feels similar because it's the same idea, though it's not a tap number in the film. All the other numbers are different. None of the numbers follow any kind of version that's in the film. I don't think people realize that when they see it.

AM: *Some people said – it didn't particularly strike me – that you've made* Mary Poppins *darker. Is that conscious on your part?*
MB: I'd like to know what people mean by darker, really. Perhaps it was the new number 'Temper, Temper' where the toys come to life. The children are put on trial for treating their toys badly. That's a darker, nightmarish idea. (We have recently, in 2009, inserted a new number here called 'Playing the Game', which has Mary Poppins involved in it but only minimal movement. I wonder which number Mrs Travers would have preferred.)

AM: *At the time of the original press night, some fuss was made that we should not bring children younger than a certain age. Is there a rule now?*
MB: What had happened when we started previewing the show in Bristol was that people would bring really young kids – babies in some cases – and every time the bank scene started, they would all start talking!

But I don't believe in those age restrictions. Kids are different at different ages. It's for parents to judge whether their kids are able to concentrate. At *Scissorhands*, we have five- or six-year-olds come, watch it very happily and quietly, and understand things about it that most adults miss. Whereas you can have twelve-year-olds who are a nightmare.

I think the age business has relaxed now. As far as I know, no child was ever barred from coming. And it was also a clever bit of publicity on Cameron's part. It wasn't saying, 'Don't bring your kids.' It was saying, 'This show is for adults as well.' I don't know how intentional it was, but Cameron's quite canny at that sort of thing.

AM: *How old are the stage children in* Mary Poppins?
MB: Well, they vary a lot. The girl's supposed to be older than the boy, so the performer tends to be about eleven. The boy's anywhere between six and eleven – even twelve, depending on how small they are. It's quite a task. They're very big roles. And the success of the evening tends to depend a lot on their abilities. If you get two bad kids, or two kids on their first show, it can kill the whole thing.

AM: *It's like casting children as Fritz and Clara in the traditional* Nutcracker. *If it's well done, you see the whole story through their eyes.*
MB: Yes. For that reason, this is a very vulnerable show.

AM: *What are the dance numbers?*
MB: There are two big ones in each half: 'Jolly Holiday' and 'Supercalifragilistic', 'Step in Time' and 'Anything Can Happen'. But there's lots of other stuff. This show was a big job, because a lot of the other numbers required staging. I'll take you through.

The prologue is 'Chim Chim Cher-ee', which brings the whole company on stage at the beginning. The rooftops. Some performers wear big top hats which look like chimneys in the silhouette. And then they sort of move with the wind. That was my idea and I really wanted that opening. I love shows where the whole company's on stage at the beginning – you know, to state something. Even though they're not completely required there at the time.

AM: *Declan Donnellan often uses this method in his productions for* Cheek by Jowl, *and of course Trevor Nunn used it in his* Nicholas Nickleby *(1980).*
MB: It states, 'Here we are. We're the people who are going to tell you the story.' And then off we go.

And having the whole company on stage talking to each other before the curtain goes up is always good for morale. It's 'How are you today?' and then you start the show. Whereas with some shows, some people arrive later because they're not called for a while, and they only ever meet each other on stage during the show.

Next we're into 'Cherry Tree Lane' (one of the new songs), which has a lot of story-telling, a lot of staging around the house, trying to make the house as busy as possible with all the characters who live there.

We spent quite a long time on 'Practically Perfect', working out how all those magic tricks were going to happen. It's not dance, but it's certainly choreography of a kind. There was a certain amount of magic stuff we had to deal with, and work out how that was going to flow and happen. It was just Mary and the children, but it took quite a while to make it look fluent. All those tricks had to look throwaway.

AM: *Some people found what you did with the statues in the park in 'Jolly Holiday' sinister – bringing them to life – though, again, none of this darkness bothered me.*

431

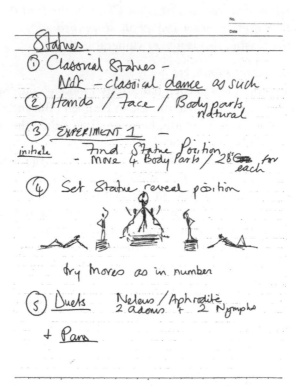

96 *Mary Poppins*, Act One, 'Jolly Holiday'. Bourne's notes for
the dancing statues.

MB: I suspect that the reason they think it's sinister is because it's not colourful. It's not what you expect to see in a musical. Interestingly, when Bob Crowley first started to design that number, he had almost psychedelic pictures of flowers, larger than life. And I liked the idea of them suddenly seeming reduced in size against very large grass and big daffodils and big butterflies. Instead we've concentrated on the statues, though the set does change colour a bit. (This changed from the Broadway production – 2006 – onwards. An enormous amount of colour was added for that.) This is very Travers, the whole business of inanimate things coming to life, particularly in a park. With Travers, a park is almost other-worldly. It's heavenly. It can turn into anything.

AM: *You went on to make topiary come to life in one of the biggest numbers in* Scissorhands. *Is that dream topiary sequence connected in your mind to these statues coming to life in 'Jolly Holiday'?*

97 *Mary Poppins*, Act One, 'Jolly Holiday', Broadway, 2007. Gavin Lee (Bert), Katherine Doherty (Jane Banks), Alexander Scheitinger (Michael Banks) and Ashley Brown (Mary Poppins), in foreground. In this number's finale, the park's classical statues and Mary adopt Bert's more vaudevillian style of movement.

MB: Well, the *Scissorhands* scene does feel like a park, and they do look like statues a bit, yes. You're not the first to bring this up. But that's just an incidental resemblance between two different stories.

In *Poppins*, the idea of statues was suggested by the Travers story of Neleus. The little boy statue has lost his father, and Mary brings him to life as a friend to the kids in the park. This statue is someone they're used to passing. They've sat beneath him many times with their books – and he's supposedly been reading, over their shoulders. That's where it came from: we expanded on that idea.

AM: *How did you take the performers into the process? How do you choreograph a big inventive number on a company of musical-comedy performers?*

MB: We began by deciding that they were all going to be of a kind, all classical statues – apart from Queen Victoria at the end. We'd wondered about making them statues from many periods really, but the decision to make them classical at once lent to their movement – gave us more ideas. So we had the Three Graces, Adonis, Hermes and Bacchus. And the Pans (who are designed, not consciously, by Bob Crowley to resemble the swans in *Swan Lake* in their lower halves): we knew they would be fun to do, being half-man, half-animal, with hoofs. We looked at the characteristics of those characters and read up on them.

And we got the performers to do research too – mainly in the studio. We had books on classical myths: Richard brought a lot of material in. So they knew who they were. Then we devised the movement from there, trying to introduce them as characters individually. Because of so many different characters, it was quite hard. I must admit I often make it hard for myself with numbers like this one: first I fill them with individual characters, then I have to find how to make it work as a single number. You soon find why, in the past, people have so often had a chorus of identical characters – that's a great deal less trouble for all concerned. You end up with dancers saying, 'I wouldn't do *that*, would I?, because my character's like *this*.' That's good, but it does drive you crazy sometimes. There are sequences where everyone has to do the same thing, and somehow you've got to find a way of making that work – of finding the same one thing that's right for everyone.

As I said earlier, several people around the production reckoned that, because this was 'classical', this number was my work. Actually, Stephen came into his own with the Pans, and with a vaudeville feel of how they would behave. He knew he had something that he could get his teeth into there.

And we devised it as we did it. Once the performers had got their characteristics, we had to plan it with the movement of scenery as well. So this is the nearest I've come in recent years to choreographing stuff on the spot as we worked through the number. Because it was difficult to plan it, to prepare it. We just had to get *these* three characters from here to there and choreograph it as it was happening. It's not my company, so I couldn't leave it up to them as much as I would with my own dancers. Instead, I actually have to do the movement. I have to show what I want. And it's good for me!

AM: *Do you get up and show a position?*
MB: Yes, I get up and dance it. As you know, I don't do that a lot. But with musicals I do it more. I feel I have to.

And some of it's quite alien to some of the dancers. They want to attack everything, to sell, to be dynamic all the time. That's their skill: they have the energy to make you go 'Wow' eight times a week. The particular feature of this number, however, is that everyone has at times to sustain a position. Something that helped was to get them holding fixed hand positions that were like statues, not like dancers. Once they'd started to get their hands right, solid, and to keep them that way when they were moving across the stage, it all worked better: they started to look like statues. Things like that we discovered along the way.

AM: *Merce Cunningham's dancers always say that one of the great tricks is to be energetic while being motionless. You may be holding one position for minutes on end but you're still dancing.*
MB: Yes, that's what we discovered. You could see the difference. I'd like to experiment more with stillness one day.

By the way, throughout rehearsals for 'Jolly Holiday', we had an ongoing gag. When anything in the show wasn't working, we'd say 'Should the Penguins come on now?' That's the bit everyone loves in the film, when Bert dances with the penguins. So whenever we felt desperate, we'd say, 'OK – penguins!'

The next number, 'A Spoonful of Sugar', was set in the kitchen. This, again, involved a number of scenic tricks: fixing the movement around collapsing tables and cupboards. After that was 'Precision and Order', the new bank number, which has choreographed bank clerks and office movement: nothing too individual here – we were more interested in their uniformity, even a mechanical quality. The next two numbers, 'A Man Has Dreams' and 'Feed the Birds', are basically songs, and we didn't make big production numbers out of them. Keep them simple: we had the next big number coming up.

AM: *This is 'Supercalifragilisticexpialidocious'. For many people, this is their favourite number.*
MB: Well, this was the hardest one to crack initially because it's so famous. Our task, here and elsewhere, was take numbers that were well known and to find new ways of using those numbers that related them back to the Travers books.

In the film, it's a horse race. Mary has just won the race and is asked at the end, 'How do you feel? There can't be a good word to describe how you feel.' And she says, 'There's a very good word to describe how I feel. It's . . .' And off she goes. And it's very brief.

We decided it's about being creative and about being inventive with words.

So it had to be another lesson for the children. I liked the idea of that. But trying to find something to do with words in a dance number was really hard. At one point, we thought of setting it in a library. It would be all about books. But that didn't seem particularly exciting, and it would involve *another* big set. I had this idea in my head of piles of books they

435

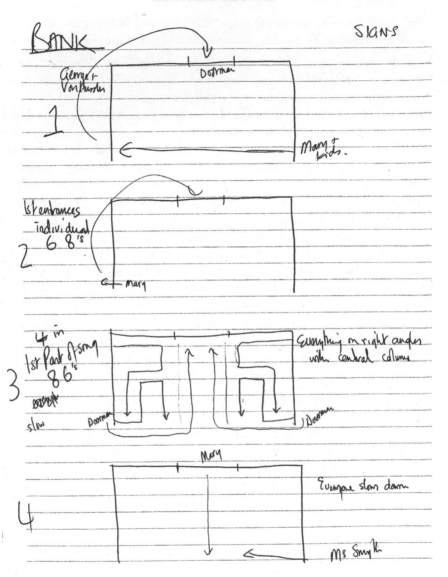

98 Mary Poppins, Act One, 'Precision and Order', Bank scene: Bourne's notes.

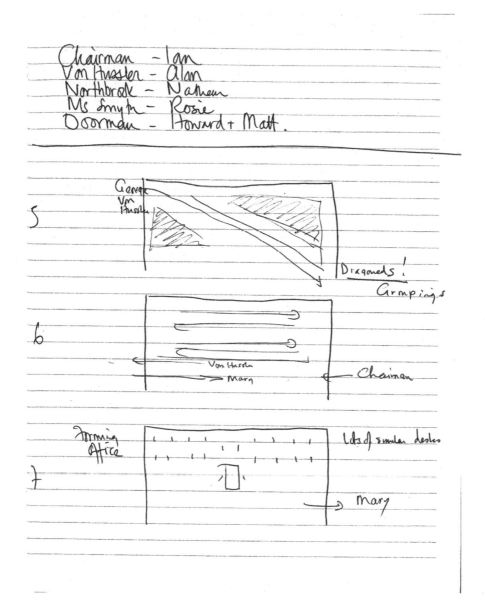

99 *Mary Poppins*, Act One, Bank scene, further notes by Bourne.

could dance across as part of the set. And then this character came to mind, Mrs Corry. Mrs Corry is a character from the Travers books. She's the world's oldest woman, she's lived for hundreds of years, she's very wise – and she sells conversations and letters and backchat. Actually, she occurs briefly in the film but in a very different way. At the very beginning, when Dick Van Dyke is busking, this Mrs Corry is standing there, a little tiny woman, with two big daughters. But the film didn't really take them anywhere. Originally, we had planned to use her as a magical character quite late in the second half who taught them a lesson. 'Anything Can Happen' was going to be her number. But now we decided to switch her to this number. She was a shop owner, she sold words and conversations. It seemed to make sense – and it came direct from the books.

Our idea was now that she takes them to a market where they meet all these people with different dialects and accents. We had a market scene (later, we reduced this; and it's not in the New York production at all) where people would speak different dialects and the kids would react: 'I don't understand what they're saying.' This brought up the whole thing of what's more important: what people say or how they say it. The answer is 'Well, what they say, I suppose.' So the lesson there is about not being snobbish about language, which the kids had been.

When people lose their voices, they need to find more words. So they go to Mrs Corry's shop, which is magical. It's where they go to buy conversations and words and letters when they run out. Mrs Corry tells the children, 'How do you think words were invented in the first place? Somebody had to make them up.'

But although I was agreeing with all this, because it all made lovely logical sense, part of me was thinking, 'I still don't really know how you do a number for this.' And it took a while. And then the idea of a sign language came up. It came not from the original number but from Stiles and Drewe having written an additional section of the number where the word was spelt out. The whole 'S-u-p-e-r . . . c-a-l-i-f . . . r-a-g-i-l . . .' was like musical notes, like singing scales almost.

AM: *Like all the things Rodgers and Hammerstein do with the word 'Oklahoma' in the title song: 'O.K.!', 'L.A.!' and so on.*
MB: Yes, except that here the fun was that they were spelling a nonsense word. Stiles and Drewe played that to me. And it formed the idea of trying to spell it out in a gestural language. As soon as I had that idea, I thought, 'That's the way we're going to go with it.' I also thought it

would be something that people in the audience would want to try and do. I was remembering how much people love any kind of language like that. 'YMCA' and all that kind of stuff! They love doing a dance that's spelling something out. And that's worked. People do want to learn it. And it came through . . . Well, I've told you about Stephen's partner being deaf.

Once we'd started with the real sign language, then we started to put in our own ideas. 'C' is 'see' – looking. Some make the shape of the letter. Some use the lower body: 'E', for example, has the foot involved as well. 'R' becomes 'Ah' – singing that note. I think that 'F' is the only one left from the real sign language. And we're not absolutely strict when the going gets fast. One of the 'I's, the one in 'G-I-L-', isn't really there: we just lean back before coming to do the 'L'! The last ones are done very quickly, and they're just done like pointing, as if we were writing them on a pad. Anyway, it's a real nonsense thing. It doesn't make complete sense even on its own terms. For example, on the second 'A', we do it like 'Eh?' – like listening for something.

AM: *What sense would it make to anybody who knew sign language?*
MB: None. None at all.

There's another aspect to it. There's quite a lot of clever use in the lyrics of other inventive words: 'Check your breath in case it's halitocious.' Which I like. I like the fact that you know what it is but it's invented. Anthony Drewe wrote some great lyrics for that. 'If you say it softly the effect can be hypnocious.' There's very little Sherman Brothers left in the lyrics, only the main 'Supercalifragilisticexpialidocious' chorus.

AM: *Does the word occur in the Travers stories?*
MB: No. The Sherman Brothers invented it for the film. They told us we got it wrong, by the way. We broke it down in the wrong way. It's supposed to be 'super-cally-fragilistic'. Laura (Laura Michelle Kelly), who created Mary Poppins, for some reason went 'super-calif-ragilistic'. [*Laughs*]

AM: *Oh, but I like that.*
MB: '-expialid-ocious'. And it's supposed to be '-expiali-docious'.

AM: *Of course!*
MB: I think Laura just perversely wanted to be a bit different. But the Shermans were not amused.

AM: *Lee Wiley pointedly sang 'It's wonderful', though Ira Gershwin had written 'S'Wonderful'. Hers is a classic recording of the song, but you see why he was annoyed.*

So, in making the gestures, how much was you and how much was Stephen Mear?

MB: We faced a mirror together with Geoff Garratt, our brilliant associate choreographer, and we just worked them out.

AM: *Just the three of you in the room?*

MB: Yes. Looked at ourselves in the mirror and got on with it. I couldn't tell you really. We just sort of did it together. But it took ages to *learn* it. Just remembering the order of the letters was slow. We had to have the letters on the floor. And the way it's done now so quickly! It was really a snail's pace to get it as a sort of rhythm. At one point, it felt like a really impossible task.

Oh, and in the film she says that you can say it backwards, and she says 'dociousaliexpisticfragicalirepus'. Which isn't it backwards really. But now Mary does actually say it backwards. (Just don't ask *me* to say it that way!)

AM: *So you came up with the gestures before you worked with the dancers?*

MB: Yes, we taught the whole company that phrase on day one. We thought we might use it in the curtain call as well, so everyone learnt it. Drove some of the actors crazy. You can imagine. But it was a fun thing to do, to get to know each other.

Then the number. Initially, we followed the ideas that were presented in the lyrics. They were the same for the early parts of the number. Then it came to the spelling-out-the-word section, which is presented as something for everyone on stage to learn. So it's done several times. Mary says it first and Bert makes up the gestures, then they teach them to everyone else. They go through it about five or six times. It builds and it gets faster. But really it is about visualizing lyrics and letters, and that's what the main criterion is. It's like a tongue-twister really: a body-twister! There's other movement in it, following other words. And there's that whole section at the end where they just dance in couples.

Before we move on, I must say that Gavin Lee, who plays Bert, was an enormous help on these numbers, and on that one in particular. He was a dream to work with and he threw out ideas all the time and was

100 *Mary Poppins*, Act One, 'Step in Time'. Sequence of three photographs featuring Bert, Mary, and the sweeps. 'If Mary chooses to dance, then she will dance very well.' Caroline Sheen (Mary), UK tour, 2008. This number features the now iconic stunt in which Bert dances right around the proscenium arch (upside down along its top). Its defiance of gravity is part of the show's elation, along with Mary's final ascent by umbrella into the 'gods' of the theatre.

so inventive. He's a tap dancer who has done lots of musicals, and he's a choreographer in his own right.

AM: *The number after that was 'Temper Temper', one of those that were new for the show.*

MB: Yes. That was a biggish number for us, with the toys coming to life. It came from another part of the Travers books. When the children lost their temper, Mary left them alone. It was her evening out. And she berated them before she left, saying, 'Temper, temper'. Then things started to happen in the room. The children's toys came to life and put the children on trial for years of maltreatment and abuse. The judge was Mr Punch! I really liked that idea. But that was a number where people – Americans mostly – say, 'Oh, it's very dark there.' We changed it to 'Playing the Game' in 2009 when we were preparing a foreign tour.

Then a reprise of 'Chim Chim Cher-ee' on the rooftop for Bert and Mary.

In Act Two, we have another new number, 'Brimstone and Treacle'. This is Miss Andrew, Mr Banks's old nanny. When she's first mentioned as 'Your nanny, Miss Andrew', there's always a little laugh in the audience – people think it's referring to Julie Andrews. It's not, of course, it's another Travers character from the books. Then 'Let's Go Fly a Kite', a song from the film that involves quite a bit of staging, and a little 'Kite Ballet' that links two scenes together.

AM: *The next big number is 'Step in Time'. Take me through that.*

MB: As I said earlier, this is closest in idea to the film. We wanted to get across a sense of danger, because of being high up, because it's on the rooftops. My question was 'How do we get the illusion of being on the rooftops?' So it's chimneys, moving chimneys. So there's a lot of chimneys that move on tracks in different directions. They can form and re-form to create different shapes, they can be all clumped in one area, they can shift along, they can be spread out across the stage, new ones can be added in the wings, and they can travel across . . . What was important was trying to travel across the rooftops. And balancing on chimney pots. And re-forming the space. In that sense, it's like the 'Get Me to the Church' number in *My Fair Lady*, because it keeps changing.

It was also obvious that we should have a tap number in this show, since we had Stephen there, and that's his forte. I can admit now that to begin with I was suspicious about whether 'Step in Time' would work as a tap number. I didn't feel it was about that, and I liked it when they used tap movement, tap rhythm, but stomped it out, so that it didn't have that clicky sound. But the tap dancers were working hard to get all their beats in. They don't really want . . .

AM: *You to mess it up?*
MB: Exactly. So I was OK about it eventually.

It became clear early on that we needed more than the original song, which is literally just a repeated phrase. You know, 'Dur dur-dur-dur, step in time, dur dur-dur-dur, step in time, dur dur-dur-dur, step in time, step in time, step in time': that's all it was really. So Styles and Drewe transformed the number in an astonishing way. It acquired light and shade rather than just being a repeated nonsense phrase. They gave it a verse, and a sort of counter-melody.

There's a section when Bert dances up and round the proscenium arch, where there's a whole sort of build-up – a chant – feel to it. And Styles and Drewe just found so much variation that was very, very helpful in putting the section together. The idea of Bert dancing on the proscenium was Bob Crowley's idea. He'd heard of it somewhere, he knew that you could do it. We then explored that and we found a video of someone doing it. It had seemed impossible to me. I just thought, 'You can't do that. It's never going to happen.' So all credit to everyone else for pushing it. And Gavin was very keen to learn. It's a really terrifying thing to do. Going up the side, dancing sideways up the wall, is OK, but when you turn right over and do the upside-down bit along the whole top of the proscenium . . . You suddenly get the oddest sensation of tapping *upwards*. Everything about tap is into the ground, but to be suspended and to be pushing upwards while tapping . . . Gavin says it's a completely different feeling. He's suspended, and he has a little bit of floor that moves along with him, which is what he taps on. So once he turns upside-down, he's not tapping *with* the force of gravity – which is what tap's generally about – but tapping *despite* the force of gravity. And it's all happening miles up. Gavin was very game for it. But sort of terrified. I remember him saying, the first time he tried it (the Prince Edward Theatre was dark at the time, and Cameron was refurbishing it, so we tried it out there), 'I think I'll come down now!' and sweating quite a lot! It's a very big theatre, that. Very high. But he and Laura were both quite fearless about all their flying and everything. They're very happy to do it. She goes incredibly high, of course, at the end of the show. I wouldn't like to do it.

AM: *Then you'd best not play Mary Poppins. It is thrilling, when he goes up and over, tapping all the way.*
MB: Yes, thank God for that idea as well. It would have been a nice number without it, but more conventional. There are some nice ideas. There's a bit where Mary stops all the sweeps, like a lollipop lady, with her umbrella. And they all pile up behind her to let the kids pass. I like that moment. And the thing about shaking a sweep's hand is good luck, and having them all join their hands together so that the whole group are joined at the elbow – so that one big hand from the whole group comes to the little boy and they all shake his hand with one handshake.

AM: *This was the dance that you were initially most distanced from. Can you say where you contributed to it?*
MB: Well, those ideas were mine. The traffic of the whole thing, the journey of the thing – I certainly helped there. Not the actual tap steps, but the arrangement of people and the constant changing of place . . . I did choreograph the 'brush swing' sequences that Bert and the sweeps do with their brushes. In that way, the number felt very collaborative. I never felt that I was taking a back seat on it. I felt as though I knew about tap: about what worked, even though I couldn't do it myself. But that's the same with most dancing I choreograph now. I can't do it myself, but that doesn't mean I don't know what I want or how I think it should look.

AM: *All this is a tribute to the kind of temperament that both you and Stephen must have.*
MB: We've both taken things from each other, I think. I saw him last night, actually, and he was saying that the work on this has really changed the way he looks at choreography. He said, 'You know, I was so much someone who did everything to the front, and it was always using formations. And what you've made me do is always question everything: "Break it up." "We're too frontal here." Or "We're too repetitive."'

AM: *And what have you taken from him?*
MB: In two points in *Scissorhands*, the swing number and Edward's solo, I used a kind of choreography that's based on tap rhythms. I said to Stephen, 'There's a bit of Mear in there somewhere. Tell me if you spot

it.' Maybe I've also taken from him the quality of not being afraid of being showbizzy at times, and going for that.

AM: *Next, 'Anything Can Happen (If You Let It)'. We're near the end of the show now, and this is the last real number. Since it is presumed by those who don't know that 'Step in Time' is Stephen's Act Two number, is it presumed by the same people that 'Anything Can Happen' is your work?*

MB: If so, then I feel I got the bum deal. I did feel that I was the person who was supposed to solve that number, and I'm not sure that, when we were preparing the original production, I knew what it was about. Part of me was trying to listen to what everyone else felt. Everyone had different views on it: from Cameron and Tom Schumacher on down. And everyone would always look at me when this number was brought up. It was like: 'What are you going to do?' And I would always hold up my hand and go: 'I don't know what this number's about.' That's the one number where there are too many cooks. As we proceeded, I felt more strongly that it should be a ballet among the stars; Richard was with me on that. But we were fighting a losing battle on that, especially with so many different characters involved in the scene. The final version, especially as realized in New York, owes a great deal to Bob Crowley, who was always so helpful in coming up with solutions along the way.

It starts off in the nursery, then Mary takes Michael and Jane on a journey to see their father at the bank, and they see the bird-woman again. But they almost take off into another place. They're in their pyjamas and she's got one in each hand. It's a little bit like *Christmas Carol* where the ghosts take Scrooge to his past, his present and his future. And that's how the number begins. You see their father, Mr Banks, at the bank. He thinks he's going to get fired, and they're present for that. He and his wife are reconciled. He's not fired.

And then we go into the main part of the number, which is in the park. It goes off into the heavens. This was the most difficult thing. It went through several versions, changed several times. At one point, we had a more literal idea of them going up into the heavens with silks coming across and them travelling across on a travelator with her umbrella: which I liked. There was a lovely central section of it, which had heavenly voices, a kind of angelic choir. That was all cut down, quite considerably.

445

AM: *She makes the park become the heavens: was that an idea in the books? Was it yours?*
MB: I think it was my idea that they were people who lit up the sky. If that came from the books, then I don't recall it. I do remember grabbing onto it, trying to make some logical sense out of it.

It had lyrics in it for all the characters you'd met throughout the evening. They're still there now; and they're all dancing round in the park, which is again a very Travers image – the policeman and cooks and all sorts of people, dancing together. But they used to have solo lines, and they used to come together in a grouping that felt very much like the end of the show. However, all the actors had problems with it. 'Why am I in this number? I don't understand why I'm here.' It was one of those times where there was constant 'I don't quite get it. Explain to us what . . .' And I couldn't often explain why. 'Well, it's just . . . It's magic.' Or 'It's what Cameron wants.' It did feel difficult. At this point in the show it needed to be the eleven o'clock number. We wanted a climax whereby Mary was being praised as the supreme heavenly being as she is in the Travers stories. One of the original ideas was a Jerry Herman-type number in praise of Mary.

AM: *Take me through the movement of 'Anything Can Happen'.*
MB: Well, we devised lots of phrases with these long poles, which were like lamp-lighting poles with little lights at the end. So the lights represented the stars, eventually. And we worked out lots of phrases in movement of something to do with flying through the sky really. Something with sweep to it.

One of the lovely images that Bob Crowley came up with was all these lamp-lighters on ladders going up to the heavens, to light the stars. We had different layers of silks, the lowest being nearest to the audience, getting higher so you had a sense of sweep going back. And there were ladders of different lengths peeking out over the top of them. But one problem was, when they leant out, there was nothing to light up. So it wasn't satisfying. And it was static as well: you stick a ladder there, they go up it and that's all . . . A lovely image, but it didn't move. So then we thought, 'Get rid of the ladders, get rid of the silks. Let's do it on the stage. Just try and turn the stage into the heavens. And trying to just do it with movement and light.' Which is what we now do.

I suppose I saw the end of the show a bit like the film. You know, I wanted the whole cast to be flying kites really at the end as a curtain call, I suppose. But I can see the nightmare that that would have been.

The major revision for New York was the addition of a giant opening Poppins umbrella, complete with parrot head, which seemed to house the heavens! This seemed beautifully poetic; and it also gave the number its 'big moment'. It comes up out of the floor. Unfortunately, no other theatre in any country has been able to afford it.

AM: *How much does Mary Poppins herself have to move?*
MB: Well, she ended up moving a lot more than I expected. I thought she would be a problem in some ways. I thought: If she's all prim and proper and very contained, does that mean that she has to restrict her movement quite a lot? Can she ever let herself go? In that sense, she's a very strange leading lady type of character. There's little bits in the film where Julie Andrews does let go a little bit. In 'Supercalifragilistic', she does this little music-hall routine. In 'Step in Time', she turns and keeps turning – and her head sort of spins. There's a close-up of a 'spotting' bit she does.

And my uncertainty was coupled with wondering how much Laura Michelle Kelly could do herself. So she started taking some tap lessons before we started. She was doing *Fiddler on the Roof* in New York, and Geoff Garratt went out there for a couple of weeks and started some stuff with her: just picking up rhythms and things. He said that she was very good and had taken to it very well. And when we started rehearsals, she was the one who really pushed us to give her more and more movement. She wanted to dance all the time. She got it into her head that singing wasn't a problem for her – she has the easiest voice, and she always sang full out. For her, finding the character was something that she had to work on. She didn't have trouble learning lines or anything. Dancing was her challenge and she really wanted to be pushed . . .

AM: *How old was she?*
MB: Twenty-three. She wanted more all the time: 'I want to do more with Gavin. I'd like to do some lifts. Can't I do a bit more here?' It was great to have someone like that. Usually lead performers are so concerned with all the other things of a principal role, the last thing they want to worry about is picking up steps. She's a very interesting girl. Her approach to work is very unusual – disjointed, in a way! You know, she'd be going over a dance step while Richard was trying to direct her in a scene or something. She wouldn't spare a moment. She didn't always

447

seem concentrated on the task at hand. But somehow it all sort of came together. And yes, she actually found that she – that Mary – could dance more and more, that she has a sense of fun about her, that she takes pleasure in showing off, that she's good at everything. If Mary chooses to dance, then she dances well.

So in 'Jolly Holiday', Mary dances with Bert. She does a soft-shoe shuffle thing; she gets lifted by the statues; she does the vaudeville bit near the end. She does everything that everyone else does in 'Supercalifragilistic'. She does all the tap – a lot of tap, quite tricky stuff – in 'Step in Time'.

Laura really did pull it off very, very well. I think it's the thing that she was the most proud of in this show. Because she'd never danced much before. Now that it's been running for over a year, the new girl we've brought in, Scarlett Strallen, is really good. She's finding the character very nicely and she's a very good dancer and she sings well. I've got nothing but praise for her. But Laura's special. She's other-worldly. She did do seventeen months with us at the beginning. That's a long time. Now she's got a recording contract and she wants to do film. But she's a stage animal. I hope she'll realize that soon.

Did I tell you about my recent meeting with Julie Andrews? I went to her evening at the National Film Theatre and she greeted me like an old friend. Which was very special for me. I didn't think she'd remember me. Then she brought up the show. She loved it, and it brought back so many memories. She thought Laura was just lovely, and when I said that she had left the show and that Cameron was not very happy about that, Julie was sympathetic. But she said, 'Well, that's what it's like for young performers now. They don't want to put in the time. There are so many temptations, and it's so easy now to do television and film. You get your head turned very quickly.' What interested me most was that she said that she'd done many solid years of musical theatre before she did her first film. She'd done music hall, she'd toured, and she'd done big shows in London. From *The Boyfriend* to *My Fair Lady* to *Camelot*, she did seven straight years of eight shows a week. Now, I must say for Laura, when she's there, she's there. She'll do the eight shows a week, and she did them for seventeen months on *Mary Poppins* straight after three months in *Fiddler on the Roof* and a whole series of shows before that. But the thing that became clear in this talk with Julie Andrews is that her theatre background had equipped her to do the large amount of dancing she does in the film *Star* and other musical films. And she said that she called constantly upon her background in theatre and music hall in these films. She'd just picked up so much stuff along the way through the work that she'd done. I'd never thought about that before.

Good news at the time of speaking is that Laura returned to *Mary Poppins* in October 2009: she joined the Broadway production. Anything can happen if you let it!

Oliver! (2008)

ALASTAIR MACAULAY: *In 2006, you told me you didn't think you'd do many more musicals. Then in 2008–9 you became co-director and choreographer for a major revival (in some respects a new production) of Oliver!.*[1]

MATTHEW BOURNE: Yes! This came up one day in January 2008 when Cameron Mackintosh brought me and Geoff (Geoffrey) Garratt into his office. Geoff was in the original cast of our 1994 *Oliver!* at the Palladium and worked with us as assistant choreographer, moving up to become resident choreographer. (I also worked with him on *South Pacific* and the many incarnations of *Mary Poppins*.) Cameron told us that *Oliver!* was coming back to the West End; that it would be at Drury Lane Theatre this time instead of the Palladium; he was linking it to *I'd Do Anything*, a new TV reality search to find people to play Nancy and Oliver; and that he'd got Rowan Atkinson lined up to play Fagin. *I'd Do Anything* would be the third TV casting-search series, following in the wake of *How Do You Solve a Problem Like Maria?* in 2006, which had brought Connie Fisher to *The Sound of Music*, and *Any Dream Will Do*, which found a new Joseph (Lee Mead) for Andrew Lloyd Webber's *Joseph and the Amazing Technicolor Dreamcoat*.

Cameron wanted me to co-direct with Rupert Goold and to work with Geoff, this time with him as Associate Choreographer, on new versions of my original 1994 choreography. Sam Mendes had said he didn't want to return to the production now, though this new version was very much based on his Palladium show. Rupert Goold had become a big name in 2006–7 with his productions of *The Tempest* and *Macbeth* starring Patrick Stewart. Geoff and I were excited straight away.

AM: *How was it different doing* Oliver! *this time?*

[1] See Chapter 7, pp. 184–9.

MB: It was marvellous to use Drury Lane Theatre, which has wonderful depth on stage. We also had more children than before. And, despite the fact that Rowan Atkinson was undoubtedly a huge draw, the success of the *I'd Do Anything* show did most of all to make this stage production a big hit. It was weekly on national television, BBC One, Saturday night, an hour-long show every week for twelve weeks, featuring songs from *Oliver!* and building up to the casting. Even though this was six months before it opened – the press night was 14 January 2009 – the production had the highest advance sales ever (fifteen million, I believe).

AM: *How much were you involved in the whole TV process and what went on behind the TV?*
MB: Odd as it might sound, we were not involved at all, even though on this production I was co-director as well as choreographer. Sometimes Cameron sought my opinion by phone, 'What do you think?', with the last three or four, but the TV producers didn't even invite Rupert, Geoff or me to go along to the studio. Like everyone else, I just watched it on TV. Graham Norton presented; Barry Humphries (billed as 'a legendary Fagin'), Denise Van Outen and John Barrowman were on the panel with Cameron. So we were simply given this young lady to work with as Nancy; and we did.

The chief judge was Andrew Lloyd Webber. He loves being on TV, but he's not a skilled performer. He tends to speak his mind; it's almost embarrassing sometimes how sincere he is. The faces he pulls when he's watching people sing: it's hilarious. People round the nation want to watch to see what his face does during the singing. The public recognizes truth, I think, and Andrew's performances have endeared him to the public in a new way.

This TV process has made the nation a bit like casting directors. Frankly, the process is the sort of thing that would happen in ordinary casting in one afternoon. You would bring in all your finest candidates with your whole team watching and listening. Each one would come in and do a song; at the end of the day, you would discuss it and decide which one you wanted. But here it's twelve hours of television over twelve weeks. People at home vote for the one they think can do the role, and the people on the panel guide them through it. Each week there is a way of 'saving' one performer. So it can be engineered that the best three performers are left at the end of the series. There's always a week, too, when the judges go off the one who looks like a dead cert, the one who's been getting the most votes every week so far. Then there's always one who gets a bit tearful, so you know his or her votes go up that week. Over the weeks the votes have to go up and down! Otherwise it's just a boring twelve weeks of the same person looking the best all the time. So it's engineered for television.

A problem with the TV show is that it has to relate to pop music. *Oliver!* isn't quite right for that. These young women have to sing all these pop songs that don't relate enough to the role of Nancy. Actually, the role of Nancy comes down to about three songs and a few lines. It's a warm personality that's wanted, that's what *Oliver!* is about. By the time the TV show has finished, you'd think it was Lady Macbeth they were casting. 'Nancy is this', 'Nancy is that', 'Nancy must be . . .' They keep changing their minds all the time.

AM: *How wide a vocal span does Nancy need to have?*
MB: You have to have the power, the big belt voice, for 'As Long as He Needs Me'. But the rest of it is more characterful and warm.

101 *Oliver!*, Act One, 'I'd Do Anything', 2008. Jodie Prenger (Nancy) and Eric Dibb-Fuller (the Artful Dodger).

But they found plenty of genuine talent there. It wasn't amateur night at all. These Nancys were all people who could be in shows although some of them were very young and inexperienced.

It came down to two girls in the end. The girl we (the public) picked was not the one that Cameron and Andrew wanted, they wanted the other one. That was a genuine public vote that Cameron and Andrew had no say in. For the last three maybe, it was out of their hands completely. They were asked who they wanted before the final public vote. But it was Jodie Prenger the public liked and she did have the right qualities for it. She's proved solid: she's done all the shows and she's a very likeable person who's also very popular. She's a very truthful performer, I find.

What's good about the programme is that it has made everyone more aware of what it takes to be in a show. All the people involved are knowledgeable theatre people, who ask the right questions: 'Does this person have the stamina to do eight shows a week?', 'Are they too young to cope with the stress of publicity?'

There's a certain uncomfortableness in the theatre industry about these newcomers being picked by TV shows. But by the time they've gone through this weekly live competition in front of millions of people, and had to sing and dance and move around the studio with other dancers, and up and down stairs and other business, they've become pretty well skilled. They've acquired toughness just by doing all that. You can't guarantee they can sustain eight shows vocally, but the panel has certainly been considering that all along.

Anything that puts theatre on prime-time television is good for all theatre. A lot of people were moaning about it, however. Kevin Spacey called it unfair publicity that helped only the producers. But that isn't so. The TV process actually makes people interested in live theatre. Even if it's only musicals on the TV show, the people who then go to see *Oliver!* may go to see other things: plays or dance.

AM: *Do you feel that the TV reality show* Strictly Come Dancing *has had the same effect of interesting the public in the hard work of dance?*
MB: Very much. I'm a big fan. It's made dance much more popular again. People watch it and they see people they know – celebrities – dancing. Now you could watch professional dancers who are always going to be great; but the pleasure of this show lies in watching an amateur gain in experience over the weeks, and in the joy and excitement they get from

actually getting it right. And I don't think anyone's made dance feel like that before. People may think it's just a big, splashy, campy, fun show, but that's not what really grabs people. I'm moved to tears often by how moved the dancers themselves are. Some of these big rugby guys are so excited when they manage to pull off a waltz! They've got tears in their eyes when they get the thumbs up from the judges, and it's genuine, it's real. It's one of the best reality TV shows because you can't lie. They're either good or they're not. You can see it, it's so obvious.

It's a great show. It has made the public want to go out not just to watch dance but to dance, to go to classes. Dance classes in general have gone up: all forms of dance. There's a real excitement about dance that's come through the television.

AM: *Back to* Oliver!. *You mentioned Drury Lane Theatre.*
MB: Nowhere else has depth like that theatre. You couldn't tour this production, at least not without reducing it crucially. At the Palladium, Anthony Ward's set had sliding buildings at the back; but now he took that idea much further. So, when the stage opens up and you see

102 *Oliver!*, Act One, 'Consider Yourself', 2008. The designer Anthony Ward's vistas at the rear half of the stage, moving on sliders, create different London environments, eventually opening out to reveal St Paul's Cathedral, far in the distance.

London and St Paul's Cathedral right at the back, you've got an enormous perspective going way back. It's spectacular.

And, as I said, we're using many more children. At the Palladium, we had twenty-four; on tour, there were just twelve. Here there are forty-eight; and on stage you find that forty-eight looks like eighty. There are additional children used from many different schools; they're all properly trained for the show, but they only participate in the early part of the production; we call them 'the coach kids'. Their big numbers are 'Food, Glorious Food' and 'Consider Yourself'. At the beginning they come on stage from everywhere, down the stairs and up through the pit. People can't believe how many kids they're seeing when it starts. So it looks like a real workhouse with the right amount of kids. The professional kids make up Fagin's gang and the children in 'Who Will Buy?'; but the extra kids are back in 'the coach' and home after 'Consider Yourself'.

That was the most exciting development. I said to Cameron, 'Nothing like this will have been seen at Drury Lane since *Cavalcade* in the thirties!' Where you feel you need to have a crowd, you really do have a crowd. At the end of 'Consider Yourself' there are almost seventy people on stage all doing the same step. It keeps building, with more and more people. Normally you would put kids up the front, but here, using the perspective of this set, we put the smallest kids right at the back. We bring Oliver on the shoulders of the gang right from the back, all through the end of the number, so that he comes right at you. It's very difficult to do that on most stages: if you want someone coming towards you, it takes maybe only ten steps. But here he seems to keep coming and coming right till the end. To be able to do that is really exciting, and I'm grateful to have a producer (Cameron) who can afford to do it: nobody can afford much these days. As a production, this is just beautiful.

Cameron was the one who understood every aspect of the piece. He had been very friendly with Lionel Bart and so sometimes he'd say, 'This week I'm putting my author's hat on.' We'd think: 'You didn't write this!' But he felt he had to represent Lionel; and he has a long history with the show. He was helpful, he treated me as an old colleague on the show and as an old friend, he was always extremely open to hear what I had to say. I would be very honest with him, I would say, 'No, I'm sorry, I don't agree with you, I think we should try this', and he'd say, 'OK, let's try it.' As a result the experience of working with him was particularly enjoyable this time for me.

Rupert Goold and I tended to tackle separate areas. I'm very proud of what we achieved, but I can't really say that I learnt from working with him in the ways that I did from working with Trevor Nunn and Richard Eyre. On the other hand, I must say what a joy it was to work again with Geoff Garratt; and I hope Rupert would agree with me when I say that the show is more Geoff's than ours. Geoff knew better than anybody the mini-detail of how the Palladium production had worked, and that was just invaluable to all of us. He's also one of the most constantly delightful and professional people in all show business. Everyone in every company loves him for making all the hard work of musical theatre fun, always while maintaining the highest standards through long rehearsal periods and endless technical runthroughs: he lifts spirits when people are down (he can be outrageously funny, indiscreet and witty) and he refocuses them when they are tired. The kids in particular adore him. One of our Dodgers on *Oliver!* asked me what my job was: 'Do you just tell Geoff what to do?' 'Well, something like that,' I said. He replied: 'Jammy!'

The usual number in *Oliver!* that gets changed a lot is 'Who Will Buy?' and yes, that got changed again. Cameron decided he wanted it to be more about buying and selling and deliveries. He wanted a more realistic approach to Bloomsbury Square and to the whole idea of the number, rather than it looking pretty and chocolate-box. So we have a Fortnum & Mason's delivery van coming in during it, with lots of parcels being delivered to houses, with maids coming out to collect things. It's much more about buying and selling now, which makes it more believable. There's still a clown figure, a street entertainer with a squeezebox. And we make quite a lot of the kids in it: schoolchildren with a schoolma'am and master.

I would say that number was very much directed by Cameron. It's a slice of life, with lots of little stories, lots of incidents, lots of charm, lots of characters, and everyone doing different things. There's no unity to it. It's a bustling place, which is quite hard to sustain on stage through a big long number. I tried to give it focus through street entertainers and children doing a country-style dance. But Cameron had strong views on what it should be like and gave clear instructions. So we ended up doing things in it that I normally wouldn't do. He said, 'It's not about dancing, this number, it's about singing.' He wanted one point where everyone just faced front and sang out – it had a very good choral arrangement – for the last ten or fifteen seconds. I said, 'Really? Do you really want that?' To me that felt old-fashioned. But I let him have what he wanted. Even then, I still put a few bits of movement within it, because I felt uncomfortable about a complete standstill.

Paule Constable has lit it wonderfully; and I'm proud that it was my idea to bring her in. She has now become an associate of New Adventures, because I think she's one of the best. And she's lovely to work with. She did *Play Without Words*, *Highland Fling* and *Dorian Gray*. Her method is to work from darkness into light, starting very dark and then feeding in what we need, whereas most lighting designers work the other way round, putting up a lot of light and then paring it down. Her method was particularly good for the Dickensian feel; it retains atmosphere better.

AM: *You worked particularly well with Rowan Atkinson. Is Fagin the biggest role to work with in the musical?*
MB: It's not a massive role – but when he appears, about half an hour into the piece, it's all about him.

We did a whole week's work with just Rowan. He turned out to be a gem and a gentleman; I loved working with him, and he was lovely with the kids. He perfectly understood there were three casts of kids, and he was so tolerant about having to repeat, repeat. He's also the only person who has ever written to me a handwritten letter the week after we opened, thanking me and saying how much he'd enjoyed it. So

103 *Oliver!*, Act One, 'Be Back Soon', 2008. Rowan Atkinson (Fagin) and Zachary Harris (as the youngest member of Fagin's gang, Nipper).

polite and so sweet. Working with him was one of the big pleasures of this production.

AM: *How much work does Oliver himself entail?*
MB: Oh, those kids are important. There are three Olivers and three Dodgers. They work very hard, they have to carry whole sections of the show. Both Oliver and Dodger need to be around ten to twelve years old, though a really good one can do it at nine. I find it really enjoyable watching those solo kids get better, and giving them personality. My favourite pairing of Oliver and Dodger from 1994 (Jon Lee and Sid Mitchell) I still know now and they've both got quite successful careers. Sometimes I hear from an Oliver or a Dodger many years on and when we meet, I don't recognize them!

AM: *How has the tone of* Oliver! *changed over the years?*
MB: In many ways it's not changed. It's not actually a terribly strong show, by contemporary musical theatre standards. In particular, it doesn't have a strong book. If you applied other modern musical theatre ideas to it, it would look terribly old-fashioned, because it doesn't set things up in the same way. And yet it's indestructible: it knows how to hit the nail on the head and it has incredible charm. Most of the dialogue – I realized this time – is from the David Lean film *Oliver Twist* (1948). I don't know how much Lionel Bart used that as his basis, but certainly the film has most of the same dialogue. Obviously it all comes out of Dickens. The British public has a particular love for *Oliver!*; you feel there's a public ownership of that piece from day one that makes it work. From the first preview, you feel the audience is saying, 'Welcome home.' It just works! People love it. And it's very nice to be part of something like that.

You've got to get the tone right, so that people watching it feel it's right for that time. People will pick you up on that quite quickly. Mind you, we do give the kids some modern gestures – hand-slapping and such – that probably wouldn't have happened in Dickens's period, but you have to judge whether you can get away with moments like that; you have to use instinct. You could, for example, try putting break-dancing into *Oliver!*, because we are trying to make the gang on stage make sense to young kids today when they come and see the show; we want them to think, 'It'd be great to be part of that gang', not 'Oh, it's something from long ago.' But if you did put that kind of street dance into the mix, people would very quickly pick you up on that. You do need to bring a modern edge to the attitude on stage; but you also need a period sense.

I've now done three London musicals: *Oliver!*, *My Fair Lady* and *Mary Poppins*, all with Cameron. I doubt I could do another. They're all quite difficult movementwise because they're all set in eras of which there's no record of any movement, you've got no film to go by. So you have to create through instinct what you think the movement might be that might work and not jar with the period. You can bring in what you know of music hall.

AM: *Any further plans for musicals?*
MB: I think in general I won't do a lot of musicals. That's not my career. I'll just do the occasional one when the idea seems really good. Mind you, I've recently been talking quite seriously about doing one.

AM: *Which?*
MB: I'm not telling. My mother gave me a firm talking-to about the first edition of this book. She said, 'You're giving too many of your future ideas away.' So on this one I'll keep mum.

(Conversations 2005–9)

14

New Productions of Earlier Work:
Nutcracker! (2002), *Swan Lake*
(2004) and *Highland Fling* (2005)

ALASTAIR MACAULAY: *Since the formation of New Adventures, you've revived three of your 'classics'. In order of your revivals:* Nutcracker! *in 2002,* Swan Lake *in 2004, and* Highland Fling *in 2005. First things first: When did the title of your* Nutcracker! *acquire an exclamation mark?*

MATTHEW BOURNE: Oh, that was back in the 1990s, after Adventures in Motion Pictures took it on as a production from Opera North. The exclamation mark was inspired by *Oliver!*

The new productions of *Nutcracker!* (2002) and *Highland Fling* (2005) were complete overhauls, with very extensive changes at every level. We've refurbished *Swan Lake*, and we've made changes; but we've kept the set and the basic shape of the story and the choreography. With *Nutcracker!* and *Highland Fling*, we had the chance to rethink them completely.

AM: *How do you get a new generation of dancers to recapture the feeling of a work that was made some ten years ago?*

MB: It's a different challenge. We begin with a movement workshop several months before and start by teaching the piece as it was when last danced. And it's at this stage that the choreography becomes much more set, adjusted, by me – this is when I'm clearest on what I most wanted all along in the detail. I become much more precise now about just how I want it to go, what the show needs, and what is in danger of being left out.

But still these dancers are encouraged to contribute new things. Ideas come up naturally. They start to suggest new story ideas, new movement,

459

new connection. Naturally, they bring themselves to it in ways that end up being very different from the original people. The shows still change a lot according to who's performing. But the basic choreography is taught. Working with the new dancers is a different process from working with the dancers who created the parts. There is a lot for the new dancers to get their teeth into and to make their own.

AM: *What differences do you see between the original casts and the casts that re-create each work?*

MB: If you look at *Highland Fling*, for example, no one performs the way Scott Ambler did in the role of James. It was very, very individually him. So for the 2005 revival, I found I wasn't thinking of Scott at all when I was watching it. It became the present generation's show.

AM: *When have you felt that you've had later casts that surpass the original casts?*

MB: Definitely in *Nutcracker!*. The level of our dancers' techniques and acting skills had risen such a vast amount between 1992 and 2002. *Highland Fling* felt like such a different show, because the cast was larger. And I loved James Leece doing James. I found I believed him more powerfully than any other James. He was feeling it for real. He went through something personal, perhaps because he's a real Scotsman called James playing a Scotsman called James. But my response is just mine. For the audience, each cast can give a very different experience; and I hear plenty from people about their devotion to casts other than James.

Nutcracker! (2002)

ALASTAIR MACAULAY: *Since you redid* Nutcracker! *first, let's start there. You had last presented your old* Nutcracker[1] *at Christmas 1994 at the old Sadler's Wells. You opened the new one at the new Sadler's Wells.*

I was one of many people who remembered the old Sadler's Wells as a dump that I loved just because I had seen so many wonderful things there. The new Sadler's Wells had a stage four times the size, a far broader proscenium arch, excellent sight lines, good seating everywhere, and spacious foyers everywhere – but for its first few seasons I and many others just couldn't love it. Your Nutcracker! *was a show that helped to make the difference: it was a hit that ran and ran, for two consecutive Christmas seasons. It also toured extensively.*

[1] See Chapter 5, pp. 96–150.

But how had you remembered or recorded your 1992–4 choreography?
MATTHEW BOURNE: We had an old video of a stage performance, the last
time it was done in the 1990s. And, I would think maybe in early 2001,
we did a couple of weeks of movement workshops with some company
members when we looked at all the old *Nutcracker!* choreography and
learnt it, changed it, got it on tape. This was about a year and a half
before we revived it on stage – something to do while we had a gap during the tour of *The Car Man*, I think – and it proved a great opportunity

104 Richard Winsor in 2002 poster design for *Nutcracker!* This image of
Winsor has been used for subsequent revivals, including that of 2011.
The jump shown here is the one performed by the men through the big
pink floral heart in the Act Two wedding adagio.

461

to reconsider the choreography. Those workshops weren't about character, they were just there to work on movement.

We often work this way now when preparing a revival. In the case of *Nutcracker!,* the dancers were so much better in terms of technique. When we looked at the old tape, some of it was cringeworthy. We were a bit shocked.

AM: *Once you'd decided to rethink* Nutcracker!, *did you think of going to a different designer?*
MB: No. I suppose I would have if Anthony Ward had decided he didn't want to do it. Lez Brotherston was keen to do it. But it was Anthony's show, and a lot of the ideas were Anthony's. We devised the characters together, you know, with Martin Duncan, back in 1992. Anthony and I had recently had a good time on *My Fair Lady*, so it was natural to turn to him now. And he really wanted to revisit it. He felt that he hadn't had the chance to get it right in 1992, because he'd done it at relatively short notice: you remember, he came in as a replacement for Howard Hodgkin. We were happy with what he did, but he'd felt it had been a rushed job.

I asked him this time to team the colours a bit so that Act Two wasn't such a riot of colour, and to connect the costumes. So he created a colour scheme that really helped when the sweets in Act Two were all brought together. The only thing that stayed one hundred per cent the same was the orphans' costumes. Everything else was different. There were strong resemblances, of course. Probably if you've hadn't seen the production since 1994, you'd think you were seeing the same thing.

AM: *The basic scenic shape of it was the same. For example, the big set-piece Busby Berkeley cake in Act Two.*
MB: Yes. The cake was now twice as big, though. And it was just a different shape really, designed for more people to go on it. It's like when you see the castle in Disneyland, California: it's tiny, compared to the one in Florida or the one in Euro Disney. Looks the same thing, but is enormously different.

The design concept for the orphanage was similar – grey, black, white, no colour – but in a different perspective. The beds go down in size, starting with the largest bed on stage right. The walls do that as well, whereas they were all equal-size before. Now we have side doors, too. Likewise the snow sequence and the ice-skating had a similar idea but with different features. I think Anthony has learnt lots about designing

105 *Nutcracker!*, 2007, Act Two. Hannah Vassallo as Clara, at the very end of the final waltz in Act Two, as the giant cake in Sweetieland (behind) is about to fade back into the orphanage.

for dance since he first did *Nutcracker!* in 1992. He's worked on ballets at Covent Garden for example. He's much more aware of what lines are going to look better on dancers and of what dancers require.

AM: *Your overall story had not changed. You'd just changed internal details.*

MB: That's right. It was very satisfying. We made more connections throughout. More connections between the orphans and the characters they were to become in the second half. We brought out aspects of the orphans' personalities that would lead to them becoming those individual Sweeties. For example, my partner Arthur Pita was Knickerbocker Glory in Act Two, smoking dangerous substances, so the orphan he plays has a little secret smoke out of the window at the back near the beginning of Act One, the way that kids do at school. And the Spanish Liquorice lady of Act Two is always slapping people's bottoms in Act

One, because that's going to be part of her dance with the Spanish men. Little things, but all part of a larger process of defining character.

106 *Nutcracker!*, Act One, The Orphanage, 2007 revival, with Scott Ambler (Dr Dross) and Etta Murfitt (Mrs Dross). This shows the new designs for 2002. Ambler, who had played Fritz in 1992–4, graduated to Dr Dross in 2002. Murfitt, Clara between 1992 and 2005, became Mrs Dross in 2007.

107 *Nutcracker!*, Act One. Scott Ambler as Dr Dross with (left) Irad Timberlake, Dominic North and (hidden) Gavin Eden; (right) Paul Smethurst, Drew McOnie and Luke Murphy as orphans.

We spent quite a bit of time making more sense of the Nutcracker character. Why does he go off with Sugar? Even if it does turn out to be a bad dream. Each Nutcracker still found it hard to act. He seemed so unsympathetic. So we put in a moment in the skating scene that closes Act One where he gets hit in the head with a giant snowball, thrown by Fritz . . . He has one of those classic film moments of being knocked out and not knowing where he is – and maybe it's like *Midsummer Night's Dream*. The first person you see after that, you fall in love with. Which he does here. The person who comes to his rescue is Sugar, and he comes to, looks at her, goes 'Wow, I'm in love!', and follows her. And forgets he was ever with Clara. We devised that to give him, the Nutcracker, his motivation. Previously he'd just felt like a villain, even if he is actually in Clara's dream/nightmare. And it isn't necessarily her dream/nightmare. Either way, it makes a big change to dramatic logic.

AM: *The fun of it is in the timing. The giant snowball bops him on the nut, and the music seems to stop. Then the big harp glissando seems to describe Sugar's rescue and – especially – the way the Nutcracker comes to (a bit concussed), and the dreamy way he just falls immediately in love with her.*

Where do the most substantial changes of choreography occur?
MB: A lot of the orphanage choreography stayed the same, though brushed up. The skating scene is extensively rechoreographed. Along the same lines. It's still very Sonja Henie.[2] We made much more of the snowfall at the end. It became much more natural. We imagined that these escaped orphans had never seen snow before. It was all about the wonder of that feeling.

AM: *The 'national' sweet dances in Act Two, most of which aren't national in your version – are they much the same as before?*
MB: All their choreography is based on what was there. Usually we learnt the old dance and then thought, 'Hmm, let's try something here.' Wherever we felt we were repeating ourselves or wherever we felt we could do better, we just did better. As before, they're integrated into the plot and connect us more clearly with the orphans we have already met.

AM: *I must say that the substance-smoking Knickerbocker Glory now belongs to your partner Arthur Pita for all time.*
MB: Remember that I did that role at Sadler's Wells in 1993. So you've just said the wrong thing.

[2] See p. 105, photo on p. 126, pp. 141–2.

108 *Nutcracker!*, Act Two, Michela Meazza as Sugar, 2007. This is from the Mirror scene to the Mirlitons music.

109 Alan Vincent as Nutcracker, Act Two, 2007. This is in Nutcracker's solo in the wedding scene.

AM: *It suits his colouring very well, and that kind of naughty languor. He told me that his favourite review described him as an 'homme fatale'.*
  In what way had the Gobstoppers altered?
MB: They're much faster. That number is quite difficult to do, very jam-packed, very tight musically. In terms of counts, it's tough. That's the point of it. The same sort of crash helmets as before; the costumes now slightly less childlike. They used to have cycling shorts;[3] now they wear black jeans.

AM: *And it's the tightness to the music that makes it get such applause straight away.*
MB: And the complete identification of the audience with these rough and ready, headbanging, naughty boys!

AM: *I would hazard that the two most thoroughly rechoreographed numbers were (a) the Waltz of the Flowers, which you make the Waltz of Fritz and all the Sweeties, and, even more, (b) the Sugar Plum adagio, which you make a bridal adagio featuring Sugar and the Nutcracker. After the Snowflakes, these are the two longest items in the score.*
MB: The Waltz of the Flowers, or Sweeties, was based on the original idea. But the old version was too repetitive. So we created lots of variations on the theme of what it was about: licking, a world of gluttony and gratification. We still use some of the original choreography in it, but we found more and more variations on it. And we cut one musical repeat just to keep the dance moving along. It's still long, but now it seems to me to move much more, and I did a much better ending. Above all, this time I think I matched the build of the music.

The old adagio was quite different. There are some similarities. But it used to be *only* Sugar and the Nutcracker as a couple, with Clara making an appearance halfway through, up above on the cake.[4] Now we bring in the Cupids and the whole company. I decided to turn it into a much more Hollywood-style, MGM-style, love number: 'We're in love', with tweetie birds, rose petals being thrown, and big hearts . . . That big Valentine heart was a new addition. A big production number.

It still starts off as a duet. Then the Cupids join it. They were Clara's helpers earlier, but here they've now been made to work for Sugar. They've been stolen away from Clara. They come on and reluctantly fire their Cupid darts into the couple. And then the company joins in. The

[3] See photo on p. 129.
[4] See photo on p. 131.

110 *Nutcracker!*, Act Two, Wedding scene (to the Sugar Plum adagio).
The two Cupids (in pyjamas) are on left and right. In the centre,
Saranne Curtin (Sugar) folds Alan Vincent (Nutcracker)'s head to her
breast, before the giant wedding cake.

boys do a very quick change – those who haven't got too much make-up on – into white trousers: skating trousers, topless, with braces.[5] And they dance with the Marshmallow girls who are all in pink. So we get a sort of pink-and-white ensemble there with the big pink heart. It's all very much about love, but in an over-the-top way that I feel matches the music. Then Clara does an emotional crossover, as a sort of sad commentary on what is happening, reminding us that the Nutcracker is her man. Despite this, the wedding of Sugar to Nutcracker still takes place. Things just keep getting worse in this nightmare. My favourite bit is where the boys all jump through an enormous heart. What more could you want as a performer? I said to the boys, 'This is your big moment. It must be what you've dreamt of doing all your life.' At the very end, the company re-enter with a sort of wedding procession.

AM: *By the Cupids, you mean the two people I call the angels, in the stripy pyjamas with the wings? I must say I didn't realize that they'd gone over to Sugar in that section. Don't they kind of look as though they're overcome with regret?*
MB: They do, but they're compelled to work for her, in a reluctant way.

5 See photo on p. 111.

The way they fire their arrows almost hoping it really will hurt, the way they throw the rose petals, as if they are dumping them in a dustbin: they're not happy.

AM: *And there's a walk they do as if to say, 'We don't want this to happen', staggering across in big misery. To me this is part of what makes your arrangement of the adagio so interesting. Yes, you catch something over-the-top and Valentiney about the music, but you also catch this tragic element too. It's the conflicting emotion – the irony – that's so remarkable. On the one hand, there are Sugar and the Nutcracker, and all the Marshmallow girls and – what should I call your chaps in white? – Nutcrackerinos, all going to glory in their Hollywood MGM exaggerated idea of romance. On the other hand, there's poor forlorn anguished Clara, whose grief is so evident, and the Cupids/angels who want things to go her way despite working for the opposition. The Cupids act as if they'd like to put the brakes on the whole Valentine marriage dream.*

I certainly don't mean that your version is the only way to choreograph this music: I'm still interested in Ivanov's original, and I revere Balanchine's. They sustain the note of radiant superhuman grandeur that must have been Marius Petipa's intention when first he planned the ballet. Ivanov's version (made when Petipa fell ill) has its beauties, but almost all its dance phrases occur two or three times in succession. Balanchine's has virtually no repetition, and it has an incomparable sense of overall architecture, especially in its use of the space. (There's a single arching grand jeté lift that crosses almost the entire stage along a diagonal, perfectly placed to the music.) But there is a note of grief in the music. Roland John Wiley wrote a famous essay, 'On Meaning in "Nutcracker"', where he proposed that the metre of the music's many descending phrases is the metre of the Russian requiem, and that Tchaikovsky was using it to transcend his mourning for his beloved and recently dead sister. And yes, there is something excessive or at any rate extreme about its sublimity. Your whole serio-comic irony catches this oxymoron in the music like no other production. It feels very much more right for the music than it did in '92–4, because we're being pulled quite powerfully in two different ways at once.

In another way, one can say your revised response to the music is now more like Mark Morris's The Hard Nut *(1991) than anyone else's. He makes that adagio a big ensemble number. He has the lead couple being supported and carried by the rest of the dancers – it's as if the whole world was carrying them.*

MB: Maybe he responded that way, as I did, because the music defeats you in terms of portraying the love of just two people.

AM: *Yes, but his version has – at this point – no irony. Yours has the whole audience going 'No-o-o-o! This is all wrong! He's not meant to be marrying her!' and sympathizing with Clara and the Cupids. So can you analyse how yours works with or against the music?*

MB: It's very emotional music, isn't it? And there's a point that always worked very well, with Clara on the cake looking down.[6] We still keep that, because it occurs at an emotional high point there in the music. I make that emotional high point a *story* element, whereas other versions don't have the story still going on. But there is the feeling of tragedy behind or within all the music's glory. It's not just there in the descending scales, it's also there in that rather unbearable tension in the music, in the way it keeps going from climax to climax. It's not pretty music, or rather it goes way beyond the prettiness that you might expect from the harp introduction. And actually it's not serene music. It's serious. You could say that it starts off very romantic, but ends up very sexual. It goes somewhere: you can't say that the end of it is the same as the beginning, not by any stretch of the imagination. If you want that to mean bigger lifts, longer balances, and bigger jumps, then that's one way to hear it. But I think it can go to other places. In 1992, I just felt a bit defeated by the enormity of it. Now I'm very happy to have found this way of matching it.

AM: *After watching umpteen productions of* Nutcracker *over the years, I realize that one of the real problems of the score – whichever way you choreograph it – is the male solo that follows this colossal adagio. (Balanchine simply cut it.) Take me through what you do with it.*

MB: It's along lines similar to those of our original production, but less throwaway than when Andrew George did it in 1992–4. He more or less ran around the stage and then did a big bump at the end with his groin; and that was it. We've added more leaps and dance moments, and I think we've tightened the dynamics considerably. Basically, though, it's about everyone wanting a piece of him, to taste him. He's the new taste in town. He's like a Pop Idol and everyone becomes his worshipping admirers. In this version, he ends with a backwards roll, a sort of banana movement through his body, and then ends up on one knee. It's

[6] See photo on p. 131.

quite a contemporary, street-dance move, and then a conventional balletic flourish. Cheeky. But it can't be anything other than throwaway
because it is throwaway. And it's over before you know it.

AM: *By contrast, the 'Sugar Plum' solo is a famous piece of music with
the celesta. And here you do quite a lot of story.*
MB: Yes, Sugar starts off with a solo, but then it turns into a quartet.
It's the most mysterious piece of music. It has a different quality to the
whole rest of the score. And under different circumstances you might
choreograph it in a different way. But I needed it for the story. If you
had another show-off solo like his there, you'd feel bloated, you'd be
weighted down by this succession of display items. And you know there's
a big coda and finale to come. So I used the mystery in the music to catch
up on the tension in the story.

The other thing to say about this revival is the astonishing success it's
had. I mean, it really amazed us. It's probably the biggest success we've
had. Even bigger than *Swan Lake* in terms of sales and instant interest.[7]

AM: *It seems so British. How has it fared abroad?*
MB: Ah, interesting, that. They love it in Japan. They love all the characters. But we did it in California, where people didn't see it as a family show.
One review had the headline 'A Disagreeable *Nutcracker*'. Generally the
reviews were split 50/50. Quite notable critics had trouble with it. I spoke
at the Dance Critics Association conference when *Play Without Words*
was in LA, and it came up in conversation with Deborah Jowitt of the
Village Voice and other critics. It had been there the previous Christmas,
and the question came up: Why did I make it so dark? And why did I turn
it into something that you couldn't bring children to? I said, 'All I can say
to you is that this is one of the biggest family hits we've had in Britain.
Parents bring their children to every show. And no one has ever had a
problem with any child. I can't see what you're saying to me.'

AM: *One of my best London friends took her children and she was
bothered that you hadn't made it dark enough.*
MB: You have strange friends! But to the Americans, *Nutcracker* is one
particular thing. And fifty per cent of the audience booked to see that
particular thing because of the title. Mark Morris's version avoids that
problem because he calls it *The Hard Nut*.

---

[7] Until the *Cinderella* revival of 2010 which became the most successful season in New
Adventures or Sadler's Wells history.

AM: *This is so strange. To me, your* Nutcracker *is mainly very bright and funny. It certainly has its pathos and its plot tension. Now that Peter Wright has ruined his originally attractive production at Covent Garden, I know only three* Nutcracker *productions that I'm happy to see again – Balanchine's* The Nutcracker, *Morris's* The Hard Nut, *and your* Nutcracker!*.*

We should talk briefly of casts. This Nutcracker! *has now been through several different casts, but I remember your saying in 2002 how delighted you were with your first cast in particular.*

MB: Well, it was wonderful to have Etta Murfitt still doing Clara ten years on, and Sara (Saranne) Curtin as Sugar – she'd been an orphan in the '92 original. And it was great to give Alan Vincent another new role as the Nutcracker. But there were a lot of revelations in the other parts. I just loved what Ewan Wardrop did as Fritz.

AM: *I thought it was the funniest, most inventive, Dickensian dance performance I'd seen in years: this selfish, demanding, greedy monster who was forever in a temper, very Wackford Squeers Junior in* Nickleby *and actually better – more detailed, more hilarious – than Harry Potter's dreadful cousin Dudley. I couldn't bear to take my eyes off him for a moment. That is to say, whenever I did take my eyes off him, I always found out he'd done something else marvellous, like the bit at the side of the orphanage party where he covers his whole face with chocolate. The way he sulks when he has to carry Sugar's and the Nutcracker's skates just makes me guffaw. And he's such a strong through-the-body dancer that he really carries the Act Two Waltz of the Sweeties much more powerfully than other Fritzes: the gestures of devouring greed have a more forceful musicality with him, and yet he's still funny.*

MB: Ewan is a unique performer. And I loved watching the detail that so many of the cast put in. In Act Two, there's a little procession when Mr and Mrs Dross, as the King and Queen of Sweetieland, walk with Sugar and her fiancé, the Nutcracker. And Emily Piercy, as the awful Queen Candy, puts in this little look over her shoulder to check out the Nutcracker's rear view, and she widens her eyes as if to say, 'Nice bum!' It happens in a moment, and it's all her own. It makes me laugh at every performance.

There have been further revivals in 2003–4 and 2007–8 at Sadler's Wells, the second one followed by another UK tour. Not much casting changed. We still had Alan Vincent as Nutcracker (as well as James

Leece and Adam Galbraith), and Michela Meazza as Sugar. We now had Kerry Biggin and Hannah Vassallo as Clara (both terrific); and some great Fritzes from Drew McOnie and Shaun Walters. Over Christmas 2003, a live recording was broadcast on BBC One: the first 'ballet' to be shown on BBC One in over twenty years. Etta Murfitt was Clara, Alan Vincent was Nutcracker, Saranne Curtin was Sugar, and Ewan Wardrop was Fritz.

Swan Lake (2004)

ALASTAIR MACAULAY: *Despite what you say of the success of* Nutcracker!, Swan Lake *is the most central to your reputation: it's the one that brought you national and international fame, and its effect on audiences is famous. How much have you changed it?*

MATTHEW BOURNE: It's the work of mine I've changed the least, both on this occasion and overall. The tenth-anniversary production had just little tightenings here and there. Some redesign. The Royal Box during the Act One Moth Ballet is scenically altered now so as to get it on and off stage with more ease. Lez had always wanted to fix that. The princesses in Act Three have different costumes.

AM: *When it opened in London in 2005, I wasn't able to see it for a week or more. I only read a very few reviews when it opened in London, but those said, 'It's not the same without Adam Cooper.' And I remember thinking, 'Well, that's irrelevant' because I'd watched it between 1996 and 2000 with about six different casts and it packed an equal punch when you saw it with Will Kemp or Simon Cooper or other Swans.*

However, when I then went to see it, I did feel something had changed. I only saw one performance, but it struck me at all levels that it was now on *the music but not* in *the music. Does that make any sense to you? Or would you defend it?*

MB: I think it's very well rehearsed in terms of steps. It's really drilled. And there are a lot of very young cast members who do as they're told. The gain is in precision and exactness. But you probably lose some individuality, some breadth, some interpretation within that.

AM: *The point of it being* on *the music rather than* in *the music is a phrase of Ashton's, by the way – he praised Fonteyn for being deeply* in *the music rather than just boringly* on *it. It's over a year since I saw that performance of your* Swan Lake. *But this point is something that occurred to me about both soloists and corps.*

MB: Well, I'm talking about the corps. It's a matter of taste, I think. Many of the reviews said it had never looked better or sharper. The principals are all a bit different and they do all bring different things to it. And they develop, and they change from night to night. Certainly when we revived it again at Sadler's Wells the next time, people had recovered from their Cooper obsession! And the production, led by Thomas Whitehead and Matthew Hart, was better received than ever before.

It depends who you get. In the winter of 2005–6, it ran very successfully in Paris, and I remember one weekend going to watch two performances. I don't want to say who the casts were, but with one cast my reaction was 'Ugh, this is all over the place. It feels edgy', and the music was being conducted in a way I've never heard it before. The tempi were all strange to me. Then I saw another performance the next day with a cast that I would call my more regular dancers: stalwarts, people who have been involved with the production for years. And the whole show seemed musical. It seemed such a relief. And suddenly it looked serious, with something to say. The previous performance had just made the show seem merely 'fun', you know, merely 'different'. I was so happy after the second show. That's how much individuals can change the whole production.

One of the recent interpreters of the Swan who especially impressed me is Jason Piper – a real creature. He does, though, take real liberties with the choreography whereas Alan Vincent, who now also plays the role, is the dancer who is most faithful to the original. Tom (Thomas) Whitehead, on loan from the Royal Ballet, was also a very fine Swan who was faithful to the choreography . . . But, interestingly, I still think there's someone out there who will come along and redefine the role again.

AM: *The only other note I made was that it seemed more obvious now that many of the dancers found it hard to play courtiers and princesses. It had got much more broad in terms of characterization and humour. I know you've said that this had been true back in 2000 – that you made* The Car Man *to give your dancers a break from the effort to be upper-class and refined.*

MB: Humour in particular can be very coarse with younger dancers, and they're just not used to doing it. They think you just pull a face and people laugh. So we give constant notes about this – in all our

111 *Swan Lake*, 2009. Dominic North (Prince) and Richard Winsor (Swan), who also re-created these roles in the 3D film in 2011.

112 *Swan Lake*, Act Two, 2009 rehearsal.
Richard Winsor (Swan) and Christopher Marney (Prince).
Whereas in the traditional *Swan Lake* it is the Prince whose
arms cradle and protect the Swan protagonist, the reverse
occurs in Bourne's production.

113 *Swan Lake*, Act Two, 2009. Swans in rehearsal.

114 *Swan Lake*, Act Three. Matthew Hart (Prince) and Saranne Curtin (Queen).

115 *Swan Lake*, Act Four, 2009. Dominic North (Prince) and Charlotte Broom (Queen) in the final scene.

116 Sadler's Wells, 2009, curtain call. Richard Winsor (Swan), Matthew Bourne, Christopher Marney (Prince).

productions, actually – as well as about the deeper process of finding the characterizations. But the problem with *Swan Lake* is that it's so well received by the audiences at every performance that the younger dancers have no feeling that they're doing anything wrong. They think: 'Look at the audiences every night. Look at the reaction. Look at the press.' Somehow this show does work for audiences at every single performance – it always gets the reaction. Yet these dancers are desperate for notes. If I'm there, they're really pleased to hear from me. They're not shut off. But there could be a mentality of 'Well, it's a hit. Why do we need to get better?' Fortunately, they get the chance to perform so much, and they learn a lot in a short space of time. After they've danced it several hundred times, they are seasoned performers.

AM: *Do you still fiddle with your own* Swan Lake *choreography?*
MB: At the time of speaking, a new revival is about to happen in 2009. This means I may have my best opportunity since the rehearsals for the 1998 Broadway production to have a re-look at the choreography, without the distraction of any other project. I want to get the tone right. I want the whole cast to approach the piece as actors as well as dancers. I aim to take out some of the humorous moments in Acts One and Three that may have gone stale or exaggerated over the years. For example, the Hungarian Princess (the one with the crop) puts her hand on the Stranger's bum in Act Three; it's almost one of the first things she does. Well, I can't bear that now. I know some diehard fans will object, but if this piece is to survive (and I want it to), it should be a living thing rather than something that is churned out every few years. I am excited about the new casts; but also – which may come as a surprise to some – I am still excited to find new things in a production that has already become something of a 'classic' in its own right. And I still think there are new discoveries to be made.

Highland Fling (2005)

ALASTAIR MACAULAY: *After you originally made* Highland Fling *in 1994 to the music and overall story of Bournonville's 1836 ballet* La Sylphide, *you told me that you now found the Bournonville original unbearably thin to look at as choreography. Since I happen to love it, and since I was the first person to show it to you on video in your first term as a student, I take this personally. Have you looked at the Bournonville recently?*

117 Poster artwork, 2005, by Hugo Glendinning (photo) and
Simon Williams (design), featuring Kerry Biggin (the Sylph) and
James Leece (James).

MATTHEW BOURNE: My main knowledge of *Sylphide*, when I made *Highland Fling*, was from watching the Peter Schaufuss production for London Festival Ballet (1979) on video. In the 1990s, I certainly came to find the choreography unsatisfying for the sylphs. Insipid. All the best choreography is for James, isn't it?

I did catch the Royal Ballet production with its first-cast couple, Alina Cojocaru and Johan Kobborg; they'd come to see our revival at Sadler's Wells just two months before. I'm afraid I still found it rather unsatisfying choreographically, or I should say stylistically. The production and in particular the sets were a disgrace. I was expecting a 'new' production, but its sets and costumes were those that had been used for the last Royal Danish Ballet production. I thought: 'What a lost opportunity!' There is so much contemporary theatrical magic (technology) that could be used to create a truly dreamlike *Sylphide* – but this was a dusty old production that reinforced all the prejudices that some people have against classical ballet. Give me a good production of *Giselle* any day! It always works. Since our *Fling* and the Royal's *Sylphide* opened so close to each other, I'm surprised more people didn't compare the two. At least, if anyone did, I didn't hear about it.

I do think *Highland Fling* is a very valid interpretation. It's got something to say. It works. I don't think it's really a particular favourite of quite a lot of dance writers, but it's still a favourite of mine. Of Lez Brotherston, too. Unfortunately, I can't get international interest in it, because it hasn't got a famous title. That's not true of Japan, where it did well. And New Zealand wants it. But in Europe and America I'm afraid the boring truth is that they want a title they know. I'm sorry, because I know that audiences really like it. It's been very successful touring round the UK. Ordinary audiences respond to it very well. They get it, even though it's steeped in dance history.

AM: *But it's also steeped in modern Glasgow and a widespread idea of Scotland today. It's like* Trainspotting.
MB: I think it's the connection of drugs and Scotland and a general idea of Romantic ballet.

AM: *So take me through what changes you made to* Highland Fling.
MB: It was redesigned. You may not remember, but the original set was very, very basic. It was made on a budget smaller than even our original *Nutcracker!*. It was a small touring production with a backdrop, some moving pieces, and flat views of cut-out trees and other objects. In

London, remember, its performance spaces were the Lilian Baylis Theatre (not Sadler's Wells next door), the Donmar Warehouse and The Place. But neither Lez Brotherston nor I wanted to go too far away from where it had come from. We wanted a larger-scale production that was right for the new Sadler's Wells and other large theatres (the Lowry in Manchester, for example), but still one that could visit smaller venues we couldn't go to with other shows. So the scenery was fuller but nothing elaborate in terms of flying the set.

We expanded the choreography for eleven dancers instead of seven. It's still the same concept: James, and the Sylph, and five other characters in Act One, who all become additional sylphs in the second half. What we've added are four further friends in the first half, who only appear at the disco in the beginning and then come back for the wedding; and they come back as sylphs in Act Two. It just gives us more to play with: above all, ten sylphs rather than six, a good number to play with. We had to be able to fill those larger stages.

The set was bigger. The backdrop, which had been just a flat before, now has layers, with a 3-D look to it. The moving pieces of scenery that become the disco toilets in the opening scene and then turn around to become the room are now a lot bigger, higher . . . And it worked extremely well. But the basic scenic concept was very similar. The company still moves the scenery and it's very manual, dancer-friendly.

AM: *When you tour Britain, what are the largest theatres you visit and what are the smallest?*
MB: The largest is probably the Edinburgh Playhouse Theatre, which takes just over three thousand people. It's too big really for some of the shows. The next largest are the Edinburgh Festival Theatre, whis is for just under two thousand, and the Lowry in Manchester, which takes just over one thousand seven hundred and has the largest stage in the UK outside of London. The smallest we go was Brighton Theatre Royal, a theatre we'd never been to before until this *Highland Fling*. Wimbledon, Norwich, Nottingham, Newcastle are all quite small. We make the sets adaptable for those venues. And *Highland Fling* is certainly more adaptable than most shows now. It's easier to do.

AM: *And what dancers did you work with?*
MB: Well, we workshopped it long before the 2005 tour, over a year before, and these workshops included people who didn't perform the show in the end: Neil Pennington and Alan Vincent. Etta and Scott, of

course, were involved, who'd been in the original. Also James Leece, who ended up being the first-cast James at Sadler's Wells; and Kerry Biggin, who played the Sylph and who now plays Kim in *Edward Scissorhands*. We had about a week, in which we looked at film of the original production, tested it out, and saw what needed changing.

Some of the people we eventually used in performance weren't in those workshops, such as Will Kemp and Noi Tolmer, who in due course came to us from Northern Ballet Theatre to be our second-cast Sylph.

Then we staged this *Highland Fling* in that busy period of 2004–5: we'd revived *Swan Lake*, we had toured *Nutcracker!* abroad, and now we were getting ready to revive *Play Without Words* for a tour. And I'd been working on *Mary Poppins* during that period too. So we split the company into two, so that we could do *Play Without Words* and *Highland Fling* at the same time. Etta Murfitt was my right-hand person on *Highland Fling*, and she and I worked on the choreography together. She had been Madge in the original, and now she looks after the show. Scott, though he was the original James and though he was involved in these workshops, wasn't involved in this production of *Highland Fling*

118 *Highland Fling*, 2005. Will Kemp (James) in the Act One urinal scene.

119 *Highland Fling*, Act Two, 2005. James Leece (James) and Kerry Biggin (the Sylph), with Ross Carpenter (a Sylph) on the left over Leece's shoulder. James has just clipped the Sylph's wings, bloodily.

120 Act Two, 2005. Kerry Biggin (the Sylph) and James Leece (James), with Adam Galbraith and Mikah Smillie (other Sylphs) lying on the floor in the foreground.

because he was busy elsewhere – partly looking after *Swan Lake*, partly touring in (and looking after) *Play Without Words*.

AM: *Where do the changes in* Highland Fling *choreography occur most?*
MB: The basic ideas and style of Act Two remained the same, but we expanded on them, and developed them. By contrast, we realized that the reel in the first half actually had too many steps. Dancers were trying to jump but not having time to be in the air. Some of it was almost impossible. So we pared it down a bit so that you could fit it to the music. And I think the reel now looks fabulous. It was also great to see better dancers doing it: people who could really jump. It was a pleasure.

People don't think sheer dancing is my thing. But I do get a lot of pleasure in working on these shows again and pushing their dance content, and pushing people to do more and go further. 'Can you try that bigger?' I do enjoy asking that. Etta and I took a lot of pride in this show. And so did the company, just because of being pushed. It came as a bit of a wake-up call: you could feel dancers react: 'Ooh, gosh, I've got to really work hard here.' Hard as dancers. Everyone did class every day. Nobody missed anything. They took it very seriously.

121 *Highland Fling*, Act Two, 2005. James Leece (James) and Kerry Biggin (the Sylph), Adam Galbraith, Ross Carpenter, Gemma Payne, Matt Flint, Lee Smikle, and Mikah Smillie (other Sylphs).

That's continued, actually, into *Edward Scissorhands*, which we went on to make during 2005. The feeling of the company now is terribly professional. There's a different type of dancer we have now, and they have to be dedicated in whatever show they're doing because they do so many shows per week for months on end. And they know much more how to look after themselves. The guys strengthen themselves for partnering and lifting. It's turned James Leece into a leading man because he can do that much lifting, partnering, jumping, that consistently.

AM: *This big dancey impulse that you like bringing out in places like the reel in* Highland Fling – *does this come principally out of your response to that music?*

MB: Yes. It comes out of the energy in music, and from a knowledge of the world it's coming from too. To do a piece that's in the Romantic ballet world, it's very easy to visualize the whole thing in dance terms. You know, sylphs are dancers. That's what they're there for. They're not characters that need motivation to dance something. The same with swans, they're there to make a dance impact. Whereas in *Nutcracker!* everybody's dancing for a reason. But swans and sylphs just *dance*. It'd be good to find another subject like that.

(Conversations 2002–9)

15

Play Without Words

2002

Idea

ALASTAIR MACAULAY: Play Without Words *has an uncanny effect. It brings to life London at the start of the Swinging Sixties, a very precise stage world indeed, but it's real and unreal at the same time. You keep showing us scenes in duplicate and triplicate, with more than one version of the same scene happening either at the same time or in succession. You've said that in* Nutcracker!, Highland Fling *and* Swan Lake *you looked for the moments of dance release, but* Play Without Words *took the other side of your talent as far as you've ever gone. In* The Car Man, *you loved the way that lots of people felt Alan Vincent didn't look like a dancer (until he danced), and now in* Play Without Words *you got your whole company moving that way. Every move was so precise, but one couldn't tell whether it was impelled by an acting decision or by a dance rhythm.*

I took a friend who'd danced with the Royal Ballet to see it. She loved it, but she honestly couldn't tell whether your performers were actors who dance or dancers who act. I imagine that's exactly what you wanted.

MATTHEW BOURNE: Does it matter? One thing I do know for sure: the piece would not work with actors who move well. The real impetus was to push further the whole notion of wordless story-telling that I had been developing with my company for some time and to use performers who had developed extraordinary talents as actors, through performing in my dance theatre work. *Play Without Words* really began as an idea back in spring '95, when we did *Highland Fling* at the Donmar Warehouse. That isn't a dance space at all: I'd seen brilliant acting there. And

487

everything in the acting there has to be very real. The audience there is on three sides, with nobody more than three rows from the stage. The intimacy was wonderful, and I knew at once I wanted to work in conditions like that again.

So I began to think of dramatic situations that would be right in a space like that. I began to think of something made up of duets – one duet after another – and it was probably then that I thought of the Joseph Losey film of *The Servant* (1963) as a starting point. But then *Swan Lake* came along, and my plans changed for several years.

As we've said, by the end of the 1990s I was known for my 'classics'. But *Play Without Words* grows out of earlier work of mine like *Deadly Serious*. It had that combination of intimacy and a scenario based on a related assortment of films.

AM: *Interestingly, in a conversation with me in 1999, you mentioned the film of* The Servant *as the basis of a possible future small-scale work. It's in the first edition of this book: 'The relationships in* The Servant *are interesting – a series of duets, with different pairings complicating it – because their relationships change all the time. It's almost like* La Ronde.'*[1]

But the actual production only came about because of the National Theatre?

MB: Early in 2002, Trevor Nunn at the National Theatre approached me. He was planning the Transformation season – which eventually was overseen by Mick Gordon and Joe Smith. Audience research had shown that the majority of the audience, at that time, in the National's Lyttelton and Olivier auditoria – its two main spaces, which bring in most of its revenue – were middle-aged or older. And his idea was to transform the Lyttelton Theatre space for the summer and to commission a series of theatre works that might bring in a younger audience. We had recently worked on both *My Fair Lady* and *South Pacific* at the National, and he asked me if I would like to contribute a 'devised' piece. I instantly said 'Do you think I could attempt a "play without words"?' – at the time more as a description than as a title.

You know, I would never have made *Play Without Words*, and I would never have commissioned that score from Terry Davies, if it had had all the pressures that my bigger shows have attached to them. With a big show, you know in advance that you have to sell a lot of tickets to

[1] First edition, p. 370.

488

survive and you have to tour it all round the country. In the event, *Play Without Words* has toured nationally and internationally, it's been a big success; but that's been a happy accident. We just needed at the time to experiment in intimate conditions.

I wanted to make a piece where it simply wasn't appropriate for anyone to say: 'He hasn't got enough *dance* ideas' or 'Where are the *steps*?' That's why it was initially billed as 'theatre' and the performers as 'actors'. When we did *Play Without Words* on tour, it depended on how each venue chose to promote it. Most of them presented it as dance. Its reputation now is certainly as a dance piece, I believe. Ironically or not, I won several 'Best Choreography' awards for it.

AM: *Basically the proscenium arch of the Lyttelton was removed, and the two levels of its auditorium were swept into a single bank of seats that led uninterruptedly down to the stage. Meanwhile up in the foyer space upstairs a new Loft space was built, for smaller plays.*
MB: Yes, but at this earlier stage of planning, the idea for the Lyttelton was more radical than it eventually proved. It was going to be theatre in the round, with audience sitting in what is usually the wings – which are very extensive there – and at the back, in banked seating. The whole plan was for yet greater intimacy. I'm still sorry that wasn't possible. Anyway, that was what led me back to the idea I'd hatched at the Donmar.

AM: *The idea based on* The Servant?
MB: That was the starting point, but actually so many other ideas came in from other British films of the 1950s and 1960s that *The Servant* soon stopped being the only source. That's how I felt, anyway. Quite a lot of people picked up on *The Servant* – I'd been mentioning it on and off since the 1990s – but I was surprised that they didn't pick up on some of the other references, which were pretty overt.

AM: *Well, the master–servant relationship in* Play Without Words *very strongly recalls* The Servant.
MB: And that whole idea of class – particularly the British class system of the late 1950s and early 1960s – was very much what interested me. It's there in *The Servant*, but once I started looking around I found it in a whole number of other films.

AM: *Such as?*
MB: At least twenty-five different films. Some of the ideas I took from the 1959 film of *Look Back in Anger* were so obvious that I was amazed

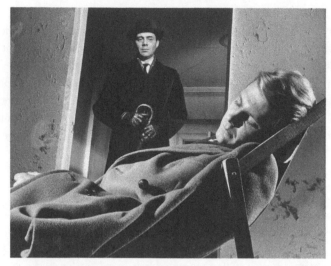

122 *The Servant* (1963). Dirk Bogarde (Barrett) and James Fox (Tony).

123 *Play Without Words*, Act One, 2002. One Prentice (Scott Ambler),
three Tonys (Richard Winsor, Ewan Wardrop and Sam Archer).
The multiplication of characters recalls Bourne's own
Town & Country (see photo on p. 69).

124 *Look Back in Anger* (1959 film). Richard Burton as Jimmy Porter.

nobody spotted them: the trumpeter in the check shirt was obviously Jimmy Porter, for heaven's sake! But nobody did. *Victim* (1961), especially, the film about a married barrister who's blackmailed for his homosexuality, and *Darling* (1965), John Schlesinger's film about the stylishness and vacuity of the sixties with Julie Christie. And the Speight character (Jimmy Porter) comes from a mix of Finney, Harris and Richard Burton, a new breed of 'working-class' actors. *Saturday Night and Sunday Morning* (1960). *This Sporting Life* (1963). *A Kind of Loving*, with Alan Bates (1962). Even *Performance* (1970), with James Fox and Mick Jagger. These suggested other character and plot ideas.

The Glenda character was a mixture of Julie Christie's character in *Darling*, Sylvia Syms's in *Victim* and Alexis Smith's in *The Sleeping Tiger*.

The Sleeping Tiger (1954) is an early Joseph Losey film, with Dirk Bogarde cast as a rather unlikely bit of rough. He's a villain, the most effete villain you'll ever see, and a psychoanalyst takes him on as a project. The analyst's wife is drawn to him. He's from another class.

125 Act Two: One Prentice (Steve Kirkham) between two Speights
(Ewan Wardrop and Eddie Nixon).

Another Losey–Pinter film I used was *Accident*. The character played
by Michael York, who gets killed in the 'accident' of the title, was very
interesting. We actually use the sound of a car crash in the piece, and I
always called that 'the *Accident* moment'. The 1968 film of Pinter's *The
Birthday Party* was quite useful, especially the two characters McCann
and Goldberg, who arrive and are so menacing in that typically Pinter-
esque way.

AM: *Other films?*
MB: Oh . . . *Girl with Greene Eyes* (1964) with Peter Finch and Rita
Tushingham. *Georgy Girl* (1966) with Lynn Redgrave. *Alfie* (1966).
Blow Up (1966). *Room at the Top* (1959). *The Leather Boys* (1964). *A
Taste of Honey* (1961). *The Entertainer* (1960). *The Loneliness of the
Long Distance Runner* (1962). And one recent film: Robert Altman's
Gosford Park (2001).

In the end, there were only three specific scenes from *The Servant*
that we used in *Play Without Words*. The duet with the tap dripping in
the background; the jazz club scene, albeit brief; and the scene where
the girlfriend comes round and changes the house by throwing cushions
around and so forth – and the servant tries to keep putting things back
as they were.

AM: *When I first had a proper meeting with Harold Pinter in 1996, it was because I'd been reviewing his plays: I'd realized that there was no living playwright whose premieres were so exciting to write about. But over lunch I mentioned that I had begun as a dance critic. And he told me that he had been through a period in the late 1940s of being a balletomane. It was Roland Petit's* Le Jeune Homme et la Mort *that had hit him hardest. Whereupon he said about his plays, 'I do think choreographically, you know, in the way I plan them.'*

MB: Wow. I love that. I guess it's all there in the very specific stage directions?

AM: *It's ironic that your company had just changed its name. Because if ever there was a dance adventure in motion pictures,* Play Without Words *was it.*

Preparation and Workshop

MATTHEW BOURNE: Because *Play Without Words* was being presented by the National Theatre, we were invited to workshop it for a week in the National Theatre Studio. This gave me the chance to start work on it in a way I had never quite tried with anything before. It really was a workshop; I wasn't sure of any of the choices I'd made at this stage, I hadn't settled on any scenario at all. We took so little into workshops. Just an idea of relationships between classes. Each company contributing to the Transformation season was asked in advance to give a single word to indicate what its piece was about, and their publicity campaign took that word. Well, our word was 'Seduction'.

ALASTAIR MACAULAY: *Which dancers were in these workshops?*
MB: Scott Ambler, Belinda Lee Chapman, Saranne Curtin, Valentina Formenti, Will Kemp, Steve Kirkham, Michela Meazza, Eddie Nixon, Emily Piercy, Alan Vincent, Ewan Wardrop and Richard Winsor.

AM: *Richard Winsor was just twenty, the youngest member of the cast. He'd danced in* The Car Man *on tour the previous year. His memory is that you told them to watch* The Servant *beforehand.*
MB: Yes, it was certainly a prime source from the beginning, but on an extensive list of films, books and plays that I gave the performers to get them into the period and style of the world we would be working in. We used a lot of acting improvisation. We began with non-verbal acting. Then we used words when they seemed appropriate. Later we took out

words to see whether the movement was saying the same thing as the words or something completely different. We tried switching dramatic situations, switching class roles. How did people from one class move differently from another? And how did they speak?

One of the exercises we tried was to learn specific movements from some of the research films.

AM: *As you know, you're not the first choreographer to have based a dance on a film. When I saw it,* Play Without Words *reminded me a good deal – happily – of a 1984 dance based on Hitchcock's* Notorious *– Ian Spink's* Further and Further into Night, *made for Second Stride. You saw that when you were still a BA student, and it was one of your models for your own Hitchcock work* Deadly Serious.[2]

MB: Yes, and I still remember the way that *Further and Further* used specific movements from *Notorious*. The way that Cary Grant takes Ingrid Bergman's scarf and ties it round her bare midriff: that was taken up very memorably in Spink's choreography and repeated as a motif.

Curiously, though, and unlike *Further and Further*, we didn't end up taking specific movements from our films. The exercise of learning moves from films was useful because it gave us a very strong period sense. I'd ask certain dancers to learn a scene, remove the dialogue, shorten it, not show it to anyone else, then show it to all of us. Then we'd talk about what was going on: what the movement said.

What emerged was that in the 1950s films – *The Sleeping Tiger*, for example – the movement expressed what the words had been saying. Whereas in the Pinter–Losey films of the early 1960s, once you took away the words, the movement was showing a whole different layer of meaning. A subtext. The way men would face each other with hands on hips; the way in *Accident* they held a very phallic cushion and threw it from one to the other during an otherwise innocuous conversation . . . Other films, too. Albert Finney and Shirley-Anne Field in *Saturday Night and Sunday Morning* on the settee, waiting for her mother to go to bed. The very strange body language in *Performance*, with Mick Jagger and James Fox, where Jagger is bouncing around Fox.

AM: *If I may take you back to* Further and Further, *I'd say the most striking point of resemblance was in the way you duplicated and triplicated roles, with three Anthonys and three Glendas, dressed identically,*

[2] See pp. xvi, 34–5, 70.

126 Three Tonys (2003): Sam Archer, Ewan Wardrop and Richard Winsor.

127 Three Glendas (2003): Saranne Curtin, Emily Piercy and Michela Meazza.

often on stage at the same time, sometimes doing the same movement or variations upon it. That had probably been the most radical feature of Spink's 1984 treatment of Notorious.

MB: *Further and Further* made a big impression on me then, so I'm sure it was there in my memory bank of ideas. Betsy Gregory, who's now artistic director of Dance Umbrella, had been in the 1985 performance of *Further and Further* that I saw at the ICA – and recently she came up and asked me about how I might have been influenced; I think she's quite possessive of her dance past, not unreasonably. And I do indeed remember her in it, and the whole feel of that work. But I wasn't consciously thinking about that in 2002; I was just thinking about all these films, and ways I could use them. I had actually used the duplicate idea before, in Act Two of *Deadly Serious*, with all those Cary Grants and Hitchcock blondes.

I'll tell you how the idea of duplication and triplication in *Play Without Words* came to me. It was during the workshop week. One day, I'd asked six men to play three servants and three masters. They worked in twos, on an idea I'd set them. *Gosford Park* had just come out here at the end of 2001. At the end of that, Helen Mirren says, 'What gift do you think a good servant has that separates them from the others? It's the gift of anticipation. And I'm a good servant. I'm better than good, I'm the best, I'm the perfect servant. I know when they'll be hungry, and the food is ready. I know when they'll be tired, and the bed is turned down.' I was very struck by that. So my exercise was: 'A servant is always one step ahead. Servants always know what their masters or mistresses want before they know. Take that into a movement idea, so that you're actually assisting them with every action . . . Play with that idea.' I watched what they came up with. As I watched them, these duos working side by side, I thought: 'Wouldn't it be more interesting to watch three couples doing this scene rather than just one?'

So that's how we came up with Steve Kirkham as the servant Prentice being one step ahead of Will Kemp as the master Anthony. When Anthony wants a drink, it's there in his hand. When he wants a newspaper, it's already on its way. Those ideas were played with in groups of two.

Once the idea of multiplication arrived, it felt like a solution. I'd been struggling to see how to use a company of twelve dancers. My story really only had three or four or five main characters. I couldn't think of a story where you could have twelve characters of equal importance. Most of them were entering into this as quite experienced performers, and they all wanted to be playing a substantial part. And the only way to have a story with more than five important characters was to multiply them. So they all felt of equal importance. I've never done any other show where everyone has been of absolutely equal importance to the piece.

You know, they say there are really only seven stories, as related in Christopher Brooker's book *The Seven Basic Plots*. And maybe you can only have so many important characters in any one piece. So this was my solution. I tried hard to make them feel of equal importance. It was a practical as well as an artistic decision.

And it felt exciting. It felt like plays where there's been two or more actors playing one role. Isn't there double-casting like this in Peter Nichols's *Passion Play*? Certainly I was thinking of the two Alan Bennetts in his play of *The Lady in the Van*. I found I could show three alternative versions of the same scene; or three successive stages of the same relationship at the same time.

AM: *Did you go straight from workshops into rehearsals?*
MB: No, there was about a month's gap.

AM: *How did you record the movement you've come up with in workshops?*
MB: Video.

AM: *Is that the most useful thing to you, apart from the dancer's memory?*
MB: Yeah, I film it myself. I make sure I get what I need to see. And I'll count as I watch it. I'll count into the speaker. So I've got my counts on the film as well. It drives me crazy listening to my voice counting for hours on end!

Scenario

ALASTAIR MACAULAY: *I'm aware that aspects of the story shouldn't be pinned down, and I understand that it kept changing right through the rehearsal period. But let's begin by establishing the main elements.*
MATTHEW BOURNE: Yes. There was a scenario.[3] It will be odd to look at that again now. Now that it's had a long life on stage, I wouldn't want to write down, 'This couple think this and this couple do that and this . . .'

AM: Play Without Words *occurs in a London house in the early sixties.*

[3] See Appendix A.

Anthony (played by Will Kemp, Ewan Wardrop and Richard Winsor), whom I, perhaps unfairly, think of as the protagonist, is at least upper middle class, and well enough off to live in what is probably at least a three-storey house (basement, ground floor, first floor, maybe more) in central London. Even though the then new Post Office Tower is part of the decor, we can tell – as the programme confirms – that this house of Anthony's is in Chelsea, near the so fashionable King's Road, as in The Servant.

He has a manservant, Prentice (played by Scott Ambler, Steve Kirkham, Eddie Nixon), who very much runs his master's life. The relationship is partly more comically absurd to watch than that in The Servant *– there's even a hint of Jeeves and Wooster about it. But it also has elements of power and control that are obviously disturbing. Nothing homosexual happens between them. Yet Prentice is the person most intimately acquainted with every aspect of Anthony, and since during the story he helps to control Anthony's heterosexual activities we can't help but feel that there is an unrealized, probably unconscious, homoerotic dimension to their relationship.*

MB: *The Servant* begins with the master interviewing the servant. When he tells his girlfriend that he's taking a manservant, she laughs and says, 'A manservant?' She's taken aback – it already seems unnecessary to her in the world of that era. But in *Play Without Words*, what's funny is how much intimacy both Anthony and Prentice take for granted.

AM: *At any rate, Anthony brings home his fiancée Glenda (played by Saranne Curtin, Michela Meazza, Emily Piercy). But Prentice is cool with her and does his bit gradually to terminate the relationship. This bit is very Pinter, because it's a dispute over territory. The drama here, as in several early Pinter plays, is about whose space this is and who's in control.*

MB: That's true. And it's why the original subtitle to the piece was 'The Housewarming', which I felt had a very Pinter-esque ring to it.

AM: *As a rival to Glenda, Prentice introduces his 'sister' Sheila, a fellow servant (played by Belinda Lee Chapman and Valentina Formenti), to Anthony. Anthony is one of a centuries-old line of upper-crust Englishmen – the line goes back at least as far back as Goldsmith's* She Stoops to Conquer (1773) *– who are flirtatiously and sexually more at ease with women from the servant class than they are with women from* *their own upper or upper middle class. Goldsmith had the good sense to find this funny: it's a kind of English disease (along with a reluctance ever to ask for directions while travelling).*

You leave it ambiguous just how much sex, if any, ever happens between Anthony and Glenda. But your eventual suggestion is that that side of the relationship doesn't work – whereas something, perhaps a lot, certainly happens between Anthony and Sheila. And Prentice acts as a discreetly unobtrusive pimp in the latter relationship. Anthony is partly related in your work to Angelo from The Car Man: *sexually inhibited with his official girlfriend Rita/Glenda, but finding some kind of release with some kind of 'forbidden' partner, Luca/Sheila.*

All this seems close to the world of The Servant. *The main non-Servant, non-Pinter ingredient you introduce is a third man, Speight (played by Eddie Nixon, Alan Vincent, Ewan Wardrop). He's partly based on the film version of Jimmy Porter in* Look Back in Anger: *he wears a check shirt, he stands on the roof and plays the trumpet. He doesn't, however, have Jimmy's particular anger. Like a number of men from other fifties/sixties films, however, he does seem largely free from the inhibitions and class-constricted correctness of Anthony and, indeed, Prentice. You suggest a whole world of people out there beyond Anthony's house, and they enter the house for a party – the housewarming of your subtitle. But of all these other figures, Speight is the one who looms the largest, especially outside the house. And when Glenda is most aware that her relationship with Anthony is failing, she suddenly has instead a one-night stand with him. Again, just how this proceeds is ambiguous.*

MB: Yes. Scenes like these came out of giving the performers experiments to do in rehearsal. I wanted to catch a whole climate beyond the stifling one in Anthony's house. To some extent, Anthony and Glenda live in a 1950s past, whereas Speight represents, or points towards, the changes taking place in the changing cultural landscape of the mid- to late sixties.

AM: *In terms of sex and class, there's nothing here that Strindberg hadn't addressed more openly and shockingly decades before in* Miss Julie *(1888). But the barriers and ironies of the class system had endured more powerfully and more subtly in Britain – especially in England – up to the 1960s than in any other country this side of India. Even now, Britain today remains the most class-conscious society in the West, but far less so than in the early 1960s. The manservant is now a very rare phenomenon indeed.*

You were scarcely out of nappies at the time The Servant *came out or at the time when* Play Without Words *is set. But your drama catches themes of inhibition and class-consciousness that still endure in Britain.*
MB: Servants certainly weren't part of the part of London I grew up in. But gradually they came to represent part of one sector of British society for me. You know, *Upstairs, Downstairs* was the famous long-running TV series of my teens. I'd already drawn on themes of class and repression in *Town & Country* and *Swan Lake.*

Don't many artists hark back to the era just before they were born or the world of their earliest memories? So many of Frederick Ashton's ballets belong to the Victorian age he hadn't known or the Edwardian era he only just knew. I really have no direct memories of the fashionable world of the early 1960s, it's true, but those films have made it part of my imagination almost ever since then.

Music and Design

ALASTAIR MACAULAY: *We've already mentioned Terry Davies's work on Bizet in the style of Schedrin in* The Car Man. *When we worked on the first edition of this book, you were disinclined to work with commissioned music. But working with Terry Davies changed your mind, and now you commissioned him to compose from scratch the score for* Play Without Words. *Since then, you've gone on to work with him on* Edward Scissorhands *and* Dorian Gray. *So tell me what it's like finding a Terry Davies.*
MATTHEW BOURNE: Well, it's fantastic to find a collaborator whom you click with and who understands what it is you're trying to do. He's such a modest guy, and, like all the people I prefer to work with, he's got no ego. But actually he's passionate about what he does. He's someone who'll keep working until it's right, you know.

AM: *Explain what you mean about ego.*
MB: He has shown astonishing willingness to work with other composers' work as well as his own. With some people in theatre, you find a self-importance, a defensiveness, a prissiness that doesn't work well with me. But Terry, like Lez Brotherston, is someone to whom if you say, 'No, that doesn't work. Let's do something else', it's never a problem.

AM: *How did you find him?*

MB: The composer Jonathan Dove was recommended to me when I was looking for someone to work on Bizet for *The Car Man*. He was unavailable, but he recommended Terry to me. Terry had written a lot of music for theatre: he'd written scores for plays at the National and elsewhere, he'd conducted and been musical supervisor on films, he'd written a musical of *Kes* – you know the Ken Loach film – and he'd written for TV (the series *Tipping The Velvet*). So his credentials already looked good. He's always been film- or theatrically minded. I don't think he just writes compositions for no reason. It's always led by the piece.

But what I've discovered about him is an astonishing stylistic versatility. Take *The Car Man*. He'd never adapted a classical score like that, and yet he did a brilliant job, using the same instrumentation as the Schedrin. Then with *Scissorhands* he showed again the same lack of ego, working with music by another composer. Whenever I've said, 'I think this track on Danny Elfman's film score is really good. Let's use it as it is', he's never had any problem with that. Some of the score sounds very Danny, and some of it is uniquely Terry's, but it's of a single piece. And yet it's worlds away from his Bizet adaptation *à la* Schedrin for *The Car Man*, the jazz score for *Play Without Words*, or his original contemporary-style score for *Dorian Gray*.

Play Without Words was only our second work together, so I didn't just say, 'Will you do it?' I said, 'I think it's got to be jazz. In the style of the early sixties. Is this something you could be interested in?' I needed to know he could do it. But he'd never attempted anything jazzy before. I was a bit worried. But he liked a new challenge – he said, 'Oh I'd love to have a go at that.' And it was his spirit that made me feel he'd be right for it, because the whole spirit of *Play Without Words* was about doing something that was new to us all.

AM: *How did you get him into the process?*

MB: By writing a theme for each of the five main characters. We knew what the characters were going to be. We didn't have much else set. Nothing was written down. There were some ideas for scenes but there was no order for the scenes. There wasn't even a rough structure really. Just this idea of seduction. Into which we meant possible seduction by power or sex or class. We knew we were going to be playing with master–servant ideas, and shifting relationships. All very vague.

So Terry wrote these themes. They became very useful. He wrote themes for Anthony, Prentice, Speight, Glenda and Sheila. For example, a saucy, trollopy theme for Sheila; a cool but slightly sensual theme for Glenda . . . These were helpful for people's characters initially. And they indicated different moods and ways of moving.

AM: *Terry has told me that these themes came to about twelve minutes of music in all, commenced while you were doing workshops, and ready when rehearsals started. He composed the rest during the five-week period of rehearsals.*

MB: It was scary! I knew there was going to be a scene in a jazz club, because there seemed to be one in every film we were looking at! So that was something for Terry to get moving on. I just tried to feed him with those things that were most obviously going to be used, and then let him react to what further ideas we came up with. Really, the more we did, the more he reacted.

AM: *How much did he take rhythm from you? or how much did you adjust your rhythm to his?*

MB: I don't remember giving him any specific clues about rhythm. He watched rehearsals, and he would pick up the mood and maybe some dynamics from that.

AM: *Did he try to catch any of your duplicate/triplicate aspect in his music?*

MB: No. He wrote for character and the main narrative line. He said he wanted the musical line to 'arc over and unite the individual details'.

AM: *Did he ever go against your specifications?*

MB: After the Bachlike section, I had asked him for a passage in one mood, but he felt it should be brighter and faster than that, for balance. And when I heard what he'd composed, I knew he was right. And the sound of his music made me devise a scene in which Anthony and Glenda do home improvements. *Play Without Words* was that kind of show, you see: everyone came up with important suggestions well into the late rehearsals, and we were able to use so many of them.

AM: *He and others have told me in particular that you set much of the Tap Duet (his name) for Anthony and Sheila before he wrote any music.*

MB: Yes, we'd reached that scene before he did, and I had ideas for how it should go, as it was one of the most memorable scenes from the film of

The Servant. As a duet it is extremely interesting, as it is the woman who is completely dominant and the more experienced of the two.

AM: *He watched what you'd developed and went away to write the music. 'It was strangely liberating,' he told me. 'I had the idea that the tap drip suggested by Matt as a scene-change sound effect could sensually power the whole piece.'*

MB: And again, once I heard what he'd written, I got excited and wanted to extend the scene. So I asked him for more music. That's why it has more repetition in the score than he originally intended. Something similar happened with the dressing/undressing scene, and with the Fireplace Duet.

AM: *The Tap Duet is danced by one Anthony and Sheila couple, then by another. Did he distinguish musically between them?*

MB: For him, there's no hard delineation between the two sections here, or in other duets where we staged successive versions. 'All edges are soft' is the way he puts it.

In general, though, we didn't rehearse for long in silence. We used music during some of the workshop phase, and particularly at one stage we used the jazz Bach music of Jacques Loussier, just playing on a loop, and Terry certainly fed off that. One of the themes he wrote before rehearsals started was along Bach–Loussier lines, and he developed that in his eventual score.

AM: *It often felt in performance as if he had fitted his music to your performers' acting, like a film composer. How did it work as the company went on dancing to it during, first, a three-week season and then, when it was revived, a long season and longer tour?*

MB: Michael Haslam was the MD (musical director) and he also played the piano. It was only a five-piece band, and he was very much in charge. He'd been in rehearsals, playing piano, throughout. Terry would often be at home composing and then would come in to watch particular episodes, but Mike would regularly be on the phone to him to say, 'Well they've changed that bit' or 'This bit needs to be a bit longer' – keeping Terry up to date with what we were doing. So Michael (Mike) was closely involved.

AM: *At the National the band was visible on stage. Did you maintain that on tour?*

MB: Yes, it's always on one side or the other.

AM: *Oh, I like that very much.*

MB: Thank you. The musicians loved it as well. To have them there was part of the whole feel of the piece. It was collaborative. But that was the process really, that we had Mike in the studio. He was the one that was there all of the time, playing piano.

And Terry did a very, very fine job with his score, as everyone has acknowledged, from Johnny Dankworth down. Since it was Dankworth who wrote the music for *The Servant* and *Darling*, no praise could be better.

AM: *Lez Brotherston has always received acclaim for his contributions to your productions, but to me* Play Without Words *is his most perfect, his most breathtaking achievement. The surreal view of London architecture, the black-and-white tiled floor, the spiral staircase (two of them), but above all the costumes were all so evocative that the show was full of moments of recognition for the audience. You didn't need to have lived through the sixties. Even if you had only a vague idea of London in that decade, these designs caught that idea so precisely. How long did Lez have to work on it?*

MB: The same time that we had. Five weeks, really. It was a superb example of how he can make the smallest budget we've ever worked with look like a million dollars. He's really very clever at that. And he has tricks up his sleeve to make it look richer. Only a little was specially made: the women's suits in particular. It was almost all stuff hired cheaply. A lot of costumes and props were from the National store. The main chair in the piece was actually the main chair from the original production of Pinter's *No Man's Land*. It's been in several productions since. That was exciting. I think we've still got it.

AM: *How much guidance do you give Lez when he's working with his ideas? How much input does he need?*

MB: I usually have one big idea that I give him. So for *Play Without Words* I said, 'The staircase is very important. You know, the servant's staircase is used a lot in the film of *The Servant* as a place where things happen or where people are on their way from upstairs to downstairs. I think we need an upstairs/downstairs feel to whatever we do. There's got to be the master's place and the servant's place. Something that signifies class as well. So take that.' And that's what he came back with: a double-stair moving structure, with one more beautiful curving staircase

128 Speight and Glenda Sex Duet, Act Two. Ewan Wardrop and
Michela Meazza, Alan Vincent and Saranne Curtin.

and a more functional staircase, which also helps create other places as well as the main house.

This is where I think Lez is so perfect to work with. He gives you a playground in which to create something. It's not all set. So it was a very creative experience for him as well, more so than any other show. We only had the basic structure and we wanted it then to become lots of things. So I'd say, 'Do you think that could become a fireplace?' Or he'd say, 'Oh look, we could have a picture in here.' So he kept adding things to it as we discovered more scenes and new ideas. He was part of the team through rehearsals as well, whereas normally the show is all designed before rehearsals begin, because it has to be made. From *Swan Lake* to *Edward Scissorhands*, the whole design – all the costumes, too – have been presented to the company on day one. Little things are added but basically it's all done. His job is then to see it through. But as a rule a show hasn't been something that he creates alongside us at the same time. Whereas he did with this one, which was nice for him. The result was brilliant.

AM: *Steve Kirkham remembers that one marvellous thing in rehearsals was that there was a dressing-up rail. It really helped. This was where he got his party character. He picked a jacket, and when he zipped it up it was too tight round the shoulders. Instead of changing it, he just went with it. It created this person whose shoulders were up by his ears and whose arms swung around a lot from the waist.*

Brotherston's costumes in general seemed to make no concession to dance convention. The women were in tight skirts and high heels. Actually, I find from talking to him that this was a clever illusion: he reminded me that the skirts were slit, and told me how carefully he'd chosen fabric that would allow for dance movement. Also he asked you carefully how much extended legwork you would be wanting from the women: 'Are they going to développé?' But none of this broke the impression that the whole piece was about the stylishness of the sixties.

MB: I remember the authentic underwear being a particular challenge to the women!

AM: *The hairdos, the lipstick shades, and the cut of the women's jackets all left a piercing impression. Lez, however, insists that he takes equal care with lipsticks and hairstyles and dress cut with every show he designs: it's just that everybody greets the sixties world of* Play Without Words *with a particular kind of recognition.*

Rehearsal

ALASTAIR MACAULAY: *Terry Davies has told me that all the music he had given you at the start of rehearsals were the themes. He and you played his demos of them to the company on the first day of rehearsal – as we've said, just twelve minutes or so of music. That was simply somewhere to start. All the rest of the music emerged during the five weeks of rehearsals.*

MATTHEW BOURNE: Yes, and it was the same for Lez. It felt such an experimental piece for us all: we were all unsure what shape it would take. But happy. Even though we were still fixing some things at the very last minute, I didn't feel the kind of stress I've known in other circumstances. (The context of an experimental festival took the pressure off, I think.) We began by working to Terry's themes – fitting the movement we'd made in workshop and refining it. And when he'd composed some more music for us, we rehearsed and made more movement to that. But sometimes his music wasn't ready for us and we found we could just carry on until it arrived.

AM: *You chose a team of dance-actors all of whom you knew before. Did they all respond equally well to the process?*

MB: Yes. They're all experienced enough to know what I like and what I was wanting from them. But they're also experienced enough with each other to explore and create things together. Several of them were young, but they were hand-picked. Richard Winsor is a very sensitive actor, and he was chosen for that reason. This was his first big break. Belinda, who was one of the maids, is unique in the way she thinks and acts; and parts of her are very close to the character. They all gelled as a team very quickly through doing it.

AM: *How early on in the process did you decide that some of them were playing more roles than one?*

MB: I decided early on, without making a big deal of it or even telling them, that one of each character would play only that character all the way through. The others all played multiple characters. In case I found myself getting into problems with story-telling, I thought it best to have some kind of continuity.

AM: *So Will Kemp[2] was only ever Anthony; Scott Ambler only played Prentice, and Alan Vincent was only Speight.*

MB: Well, mostly. Yes, Alan did play a café owner near the beginning, and Sara Curtin was only ever Glenda (apart from a little prostitute

---

[2] Later Sam Archer. Will Kemp only performed in the initial two-week season.

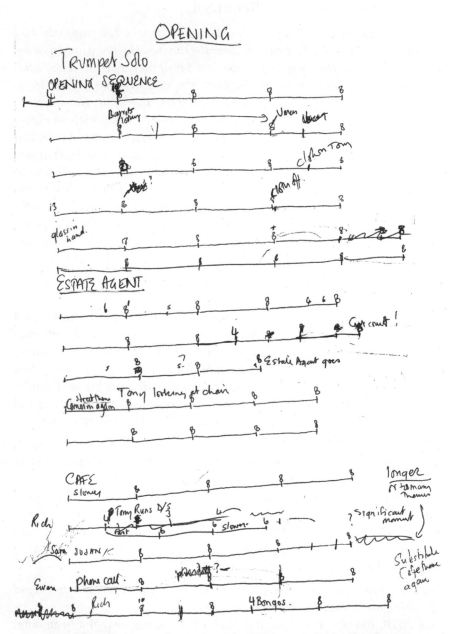

129 'Opening': notes by Bourne. The 'Trumpet Solo' is taken from *Look Back in Anger*; the Estate Agent, played by Steve Kirkham, is not a character from *The Servant*.

moment when the Prentices are passing through Soho on their way to the Salisbury pub).

AM: *This did have an anchoring effect. We knew it wasn't total dream.*

MB: And there are points within it where they're the ones of whom you think, 'Oh, I think they may be the *real* ones.' At the end of the first Anthony–Glenda scene we were talking about earlier, where the last Glenda leaves and the last Anthony's left in the house on his own, I think that's when the action becomes 'actual' rather than a fantasy or wish or whatever.

AM: *It sounds here as if you had moved way beyond letting the three different couples bring up workshop alternatives of one dramatic idea – as if you definitely shaped the material so that Couple A did one version, Couple B did another, Couple C did a third, and as if you knew at least roughly what kind of drama would be going on in each version. Am I right?*

MB: It became intentional through rehearsal. Sometimes I give the impression that everything is up for grabs. I do actually have a way of steering the cast towards what I want while making them feel that they invented it.

It's for the audience to decide who the alternative versions of the same character are. They may be fantasy moments, maybe in his mind. It's for the audience to make their minds up about that. But these two dancers are those ones you come back to. And they're the ones that stay within their original character in the party scene at the end of the first act. Everyone else becomes a different character. And they're the ones that sort of take you through the whole story. Almost.

But I didn't say that to anyone in rehearsal because I didn't want any sense that one Tony was more important than another, or one Glenda than another. I just presented it as circumstantial. That was what was happening. Sometimes – I dare say they'll probably all read this and think they've been misled! – I would sometimes say, as if I'd only thought of it on the spot, 'Oh Sara, you do this bit' and 'Emily, you do that bit.' But what I was actually doing was focusing that character through that person, without making that appear to be the case.

AM: *So there were some seven dancers who each played two or more different roles. This certainly had a terrific ambiguity for the audience. How was it for them?*

MB: Oh, they found it quite hard. Because they were trying to find a thread through it. They would come back into their main character and find they hadn't been through that character's experience all through the previous scene. Take Glenda, for example. They would often find it difficult to have to think, 'OK, although I didn't play that part in that scene, now I've had this strange relationship with this Speight character and that's moved on, but I didn't even act that bit.' So they had to keep track of where their character was at in each scene, even if that scene had been played by another performer, playing their character. Confused? It took careful work to get that right. They had to learn how to click into it.

Some of them had positively schizophrenic assignments. Ewan Wardrop looks like he's going to be the main Tony when he starts off, he starts off as Tony in the chair at the beginning, but then he becomes the bachelor in the blazer in the party, and in the second half he becomes Speight, and finally goes back to being Tony for the second part of that act. So he's changing between characters all the time. There are a couple of other roles like that. It was very testing for them to bring it off. But in performance those performers may have had more fun, because it's nice and challenging to show your versatility.

AM: *Maybe the most brilliant scene of all the multiplications comes when one Anthony is dressed by one Prentice, while another Anthony is undressed by another Prentice. At times, the two Prentices swap masters. And you turned the whole daft ritual into the beginning of a male–male tango. And then Terry Davies's music underscored all that with a jazz hint of Bach. There was so much going on, on so many different levels, we hardly had time to laugh. I can see that there were echoes here of your earlier work: the staff–servant material in* Town & Country, *the Prince–Stranger tango in* Swan Lake. *But this was so much more layered, intricate.*

MB: And a prop nightmare, I might add! You can't rely on those clothes to do the same thing at every performance. Mainly I was concerned to break it down so that it didn't look too much like a dance. But it is, of course, very musical. This was the opposite of what I'd normally try to do. The whole premise of *Play Without Words*, working from that initial Donmar idea, was to make it feel and look completely natural.

AM: *Steve Kirkham remembers that you often said at the time that actors would find it impossible to do this show: it's just too precise, and because of the dancers' experience they could make it look more seamless, so that nobody could see the strings or what was coming next.*

MB: An actor would find acting to counts impossibly restricting. A dancer is used to this. So trained dancers who are also good actors are the perfect, and only, way to cast this show. Some stuff – a lot of jazz-club material – was choreographically set, but then broken down a lot to make it look more natural. The point was not to make it less choreographed, but less dancey. I never wanted it to look at any point like a dance. I didn't want it to turn into a number – apart from the little TV dance at the start of Act Two, which is just a bit of period fun in Carnaby Street costumes.

AM: *Although you kept the ongoing line of the story going, you also kept subdividing it into three separate threads. When Anthony brings Glenda home to the Chelsea house where Prentice is in attendance, there are three Anthonys, three Glendas, three Prentices. Then Prentice produces Sheila: Anthony can do things with this servant girl he can't with Glenda. Meanwhile the controlling relationship is that between Anthony and Prentice. Sometimes the story seemed to be occurring in a hall of mirrors, sometimes it was moved into surreal fantasy, and sometimes it was as if you were pressing the rewind button to show us alternative takes. The psychological suggestions were endless. And all so damnably English.*

MB: There's a particular scene in the film of *The Servant* that gets somewhere, then stops. We took that as the basis for a duet in Act Two for Anthony and Sheila on the kitchen table. It was as if the scene in the film sets up the situation but stops, and this is what could have happened had it kept going. As we've said, this was one moment when we made much of the movement without any music: it had a momentum of its own. And yes, this is one of the scenes we played in duplicate, one after another.

AM: *One of your most amazingly dark moments occurs here. One Anthony makes love to the housemaid Sheila, while another Anthony and Sheila just watch, without expression. It's as if they're watching their own porn fantasy. It's exciting, but also dismaying.*

MB: I suppose my favourite bit of naturalistic dancing is the three couples coming back from the jazz club. They've had a sort of argument at the club about meeting Speight, Alan Vincent's character, they're in the room together, and they're all smoking and drinking, lounging

130 The 'Tap' Duet, Act Two. Belinda Lee Chapman (Sheila) and Richard Winsor (Tony). Publicity photo, 2003. The poster for the 2002 premiere featured the word 'seduction', following a request from Trevor Nunn for a single word for each contribution to the National Theatre's Transformation season. The word was dropped in 2003.

131 The 'Tap' Duet. Sam Archer (Tony) and Valentina Formenti (Sheila), in performance, 2003.

132 *The Servant* (1963). Sarah Miles (Vera) in the
equivalent scene.

about the room and making up. It's minimal in terms of story. But it's quite a long sequence. Just the movement of bodies around a room with cigarette smoke swirling around them. It definitely wouldn't have held up with one couple. But three couples doing it is mesmerizing.

AM: *Sometimes you had the three Anthonys and three Glendas moving in unison. That was an extraordinary theatrical effect in itself, because it made one very particular story about one specific set of characters feel as if it was happening in a hall of mirrors, or in parallel universes. Or – and this felt hair-raising – as if London, in fact, was full of such seemingly one-off situations.*

Another point that emerged is that we look at ordinary movement itself differently when we see it multiplied. When one Glenda takes off her jacket and hands it to the manservant, it's acting. When three Glendas do it exactly the same way, it's choreography.

MB: Thank you! I've been saying that for years, but some writers still refuse to see that sort of movement as choreography.

AM: *But the main point of this particular scene was that you were showing different versions of the same situation.*

MB: Yes, ending up with a different ending for each one. One couple go upstairs to bed, another couple are a bit more lusty and almost carry on downstairs, whereas in the third couple she decides to go home and leave him on his own. Unresolved. I like that. It felt like a new kind of dancing to me, and a new kind of story-telling.

AM: *I like it too, and it occurs to me that this multiplicity is very true to Pinter. In 1958 he wrote, 'There are no hard distinctions between what is real and what is unreal, nor between what is true and what is false. A thing is not necessarily either true or false; it can be both true and false.' In 2005 he began his Nobel Literature Lecture by quoting that.*

I've just remembered another dance based on a movie. In 1976, Lynn Seymour made a ballet – in very contemporary-dance style – of Rashomon *(based on the Kurosawa film, 1950). Rashomon shows you a story involving three people as told, successively and quite differently, by each of them. The point, as with Pinter, is that there are utterly various different versions of the same story. And that's another interpretation that arises from your choreography in* Play Without Words. *I'd forgotten Lynn Seymour's ballet until now, but I certainly thought of the Kurosawa film while watching* Play Without Words.

Another scene – very Rashomon *– where you give us three alternative versions of the same thing is when three Glendas are seduced by three Speights so variously that the scene becomes like three alternative narrations of what can only have happened once.*

In another respect, though, scenes like that seemed very unchoreographed: each time I guessed what move the performers would do next, and then they did something else.

MB: That came from treating the dancers as actors. In that respect, *Play Without Words* really was a sequel to *The Car Man* – those scenes were all studies in suspense.

Structure

ALASTAIR MACAULAY: *One of my very few reservations about* Play Without Words *is that I wanted it – like a film – in one unbroken sequence without an interval. Could it be done that way? or does a Matthew Bourne show need an interval?*

MATTHEW BOURNE: I've always enjoyed having an interval for people to have a chance to think about what they've seen . . . I find people enjoy the second halves of shows more, because they've shared something with their friends and they've all decided over a drink that they're enjoying it. And sometimes people need to be told they're enjoying it by their friends before they carry on enjoying it, you know.

And, more than that, I like a story that leads up to a question. 'What's going to happen next?' I've never really done a full-evening piece without an interval. If it had been done at the Donmar as *The Servant*, I think it would have gone straight through. But because we approached it as something wider than *The Servant*, it acquired this different structure.

AM: *In the case of* Cinderella *you had two intervals because of the nature of Prokofiev's score. But that's your only three-act show?*

MB: Yes. I really like the two-act form (usually with a prologue). A lot of Act One is used to establish character and situation, and then you build up to a kind of cliffhanger or major crisis or turning point for a character. That creates a big reason for the audience to want to come back after the interval to see what will happen next. To a certain extent you have to start again at the top of Act Two, but there is the chance to show some more character development or a passage of time or even a lighter sequence to quieten the audience down again. Then you can get into the real meat of the story and drive to your conclusion.

AM: *You know, from the mid-nineteenth century through to the 1960s, the general structure of the well-made play would be in three (or more) acts. The crisis came in the second (or penultimate) act. The first plays of John Osborne and Harold Pinter were three-acters. But it was the playwrights of the 1960s who brought in the two-act form.*

MB: And they were right. Because the second interval is a bit dreary. Generally now if you see even an old well-made three-act play by, say, Noël Coward, it's performed with only one interval.

AM: *The one exception is Kenneth MacMillan in ballet. He allied himself with the Angry Young Men, he worked with Osborne, but from 1965 to 1989 he made a series of five three-act ballets. But that's opera-house culture, where two intervals remain the norm.*

MB: It might be a good experiment to try a longish one-act one day. *Play Without Words* did give me a longing to do an experimental project of some kind, with a smaller group; and that turned out, in 2008, to be *Dorian Gray*, which has a cast of only eleven. But that had two acts!

You wrote in your *Financial Times* review that you wanted – that the audience needed – three different endings, and I liked that idea straight away. So later on we did put in three endings. (I'd already stopped reading most reviews by that point; yours was an exception. When *Edward*

Scissorhands and *Dorian Gray* were new, I managed not to read any – not even the *Scissorhands* one that my mother thought I'd really like to read.)

The different endings in *Play Without Words* are now presented to you, one after the other, as possibilities. But the show's actual ending goes back to a rerun of the first sequence. The opening sequence and the end sequence are the same, the same movement performed to the same counts, but the second time around, it's affected by what's gone on throughout the piece. So they're more emotional and/or more devious or more. . . . Things have changed. And it's exactly the same but very different, in terms of their reactions to each other and how they play it. And it's played a little bit faster as well. When we first did it, we used to end with everyone on the stairs. That ending was just made extremely quickly, just thrown on. Then we decided to end with Tony back in the chair, and the trumpet player outside, as it had begun. But it just suggests possible outcomes. It doesn't conclude it.

Performance

ALASTAIR MACAULAY: *Did you have a feeling during rehearsals that this show would have an afterlife beyond the original Transformation season?*

MATTHEW BOURNE: I suppose it had occurred to me that it could. But I wasn't confident enough to know. It was done so quickly. Everything was just thrown together. When we did the first show, nobody was sure if the idea would work. We thought the audience might be totally confused. Well, it was one of those examples of a show that only when you get an audience there do you suddenly know that it works. Because of the reaction. Not at the end but throughout. The reaction of the audience and its understanding of the piece was instant and palpable.

AM: *Were there any particular people from the sixties who came along that said, 'I know that world'?*

MB: You told me that Tom Stoppard had loved it, and I was thrilled to hear that. Of the people who came to congratulate us, the one who made me laugh most was Murray Melvin. It was as if he'd forgotten the world of the sixties altogether – he was very forward-looking – and he was quite startled when I told him that he'd been in every other film we'd been looking at, just in small roles, and that he'd been our inspiration here and there. (I was also thrilled that the piece is mentioned in John Coldstream's book about Dirk Bogarde, as an example of his continuing influence.)

When we took it to America, I got an effusive letter from Glenn Close. Philip Seymour Hoffman was fascinated by it, Liam Neeson and Kevin Kline also. I think many actors were just so impressed by the 'acting' of a dance company. It wasn't what they were expecting to see. Oh, and on opening night in Los Angeles, Kirk Douglas was there on the first night in the front row, and I was introduced to him. Several weeks later, I was back here and this admiring letter arrived from him, written to my home address in London. Wonderful.

For most of the original cast, *Play Without Words* was something they were in from those workshops in spring/summer 2002 until those performances in LA three years later. But the timescale of the original production seemed so quick. Terry once reminded me that within three months of him first composing a note for it, the show's initial run – thirty performances – was over.

(Conversations 2002–6)

16

Edward Scissorhands

2005

133 Richard Winsor and Matthew Bourne. Photoshoot for *The New Yorker*.

134 Four *Edward Scissorhands* costume images by Lez Brotherston: (a) Edward
(b) Kim Cheerleader (c) Joyce Monroe (d) Sheldon Grubb.

Idea

ALASTAIR MACAULAY: *The danceability of* Edward Scissorhands *is a puzzle to me. I straight away think, 'Scissor hands? How can those be choreographed?'*

MATTHEW BOURNE: Well, then, that is your answer. The answer is restrictions, problems, things to overcome, limitations. Those are always good to address at the outset. Because then you have to try and make them work. Often, simply because you've been addressing these problems, you will come up with something you wouldn't normally have done. When you choreograph, you can have self-imposed restrictions. With something like a duet, you say, 'You're never going to touch the ground in this duet', or 'It's all going to be on one leg.' The awful thing is simply to say 'Male–female duet, they're in love, let's go.' That really is hard. Anything that makes a dance seem a challenge, that's the hook that helps you along in the making.

When Disney approached me in 1999, to do any stage project with them, I said, off the top of my head, '*The Little Mermaid*.' Why? Because it felt like a challenge. I thought, 'This is odd. It's underwater. Surely dance can lend itself to a staging that is based in movement that suggests being underwater.' I still find that an attractive idea.

Yes, I did think Edward's hands would be very challenging. But what interested me more was Edward is a character who's silent most of the time. He would physicalize what he had seen other people doing. He learns visually. He is a mimic. That made sense – that appealed to me.

AM: *You saw the film of* Edward Scissorhands *in London when it was new in 1990. Was there any particular reason that you went to see it?*

MB: I like to go to the cinema for an experience that I can't get on TV or on video/DVD. I'm drawn to anything that has an element of fantasy about it, or has something epic about it, something that's worth seeing on the big screen. Tim Burton directed it, but I wasn't already a Tim Burton fan then: I didn't adore his *Batman* as I'm not a big comic-book superhero fan. My interest in his films started here. Just the thought of *Edward Scissorhands* sounded – as it remains – intriguing, unusual, unique. It's a mainstream film with a cultish independent-movie heart to it. I'm naturally drawn to that.

AM: *How did the story come about?*

MB: Tim Burton used to draw strange characters when he was a teenager. That's how he began: he was an artist, and originally he worked with

Disney. I think his first job was as animator on *The Fox and the Hound* (1981), which is one of the least-known Disney films. And he carried on drawing these little macabre characters. He brought out a whole book of them: characters like Oyster Boy and Toxic Girl. But they're just cartoon ideas of characters really. One of his inventions was a boy called Edward Scissorhands. The drawing actually looks very much like Tim, and I think the idea of a boy who could not touch, for fear of hurting people, was very much tied up with his own feelings of alienation as a teenager.

Then, weary of drawing cute and cuddly animals for Disney, Tim went on to direct a lot of films for other studios, such as *Pee-wee's Big Adventure* (1985), *Beetlejuice* (1988) and *Batman* (1989). The success of *Batman* was such that he was allowed to make the film he wanted to make, something that's quite rare in Hollywood, and he chose to make *Edward Scissorhands*. If he had taken the idea to the studios in other circumstances, it probably wouldn't have got made. Just as he was starting the idea, his agent arranged for him to meet Caroline Thompson – who'd written a novel at that point and a few screenplays, but hadn't done anything very well known – in the hope that they might get on well together. And Tim showed her the picture that he'd drawn. He said, 'I quite like this idea, this character.' And Caroline took it from there and developed it into the screenplay. The credits say, 'Story by Tim Burton and Caroline Thompson', and 'Screenplay by Caroline Thompson'.

AM: *Your response to* Edward Scissorhands *is very much tied up with Danny Elfman's music. At what stage was he brought in to Burton's film?*
MB: He'd worked with Tim on *Pee-wee's Big Adventure*, so maybe Tim had him in mind. But they didn't bring him in at an early stage. I know this, because Caroline once told me that one of their earliest ideas for the film was to make it a musical: she'd got lyrics that she'd written for it; and when I later mentioned this to Danny he said that was news to him. So the nature of the movie was quite fixed when he was brought in.

But for all three of them, this was a very personal project, very personal. They all feel very attached to it. And it's one of the things each of them is most proud of.

AM: *You saw it when it was new here. When did you first think of it as a dance story?*
MB: Probably around 1996, I met the composers George Stiles and Anthony Drewe, with whom I later worked on *Mary Poppins*, and they

said, 'We want to write a new show and we're looking around for ideas. Would you like to do something with us? Why don't you jot down ten ideas?' And *Edward* was the first title I put down, the first thing that came into my head. I just thought, 'Well, that would make a good musical', quite flippantly. They then got excited about pursuing that particular idea. And I realized then that it had come into my head because it felt musical anyway. It had a musical sense to it, much more than your average movie. In the film, the music is quite dominant, quite overpowering, very melodic. But also there was this element of fantasy in the strange mix of two different worlds: the Gothic world and the suburban world. George and Anthony would have liked to take the idea further.

But I realized, in the period that followed, that *Edward Scissorhands*, for me, was Danny Elfman's project. It was all to do with his music. And by that point I knew it had to be done as a dance piece. So in 1999, when I was in LA for *Cinderella*, I got the chance to meet Danny, and I put the idea to him. Just as agents had brought Tim and Caroline together, an agent now brought me – at my request – together with Danny. They asked me who I'd like to meet and I said, 'I'd like to meet Danny Elfman.' And he was there, literally the next day. He didn't know my work then, but he's seen everything since.

On that same trip to Los Angeles for *Cinderella*, I met Caroline Thompson. Alan Cumming, who was in a film that she was directing (*Buddy*), introduced us. She was already a fan of the company – she'd seen *Swan Lake* out there. And she was thrilled at the whole idea of this. She's always been the one who's the most passionate about turning *Edward* into a stage show.

Tim Burton and Caroline were both brought up in Burbank. And the characters in the film are all based on people that Caroline knew when she was growing up. Tim has spoken of the horrors of suburbia, of what goes on behind closed doors. He thinks there's a very close connection between the horror movie and suburbia.

AM: *Beautiful downtown Burbank, as they used to say on the* Rowan & Martin Laugh-In *over thirty years ago. So is Burbank implicitly where* Scissorhands *occurs?*

MB: Yes and no. In spirit, but not specifically.

Tim was the next person for me to meet. We couldn't have moved forward without his approval. He came to *Cinderella*, and enjoyed it very much and understood the kind of work it was, even though the style was quite new to him. He thought it was 'poetic'. Later that year, back in London, his agent arranged for us to meet at Soho House in London soon after that to talk about it more seriously. We weren't discussing any fixed plans. He was completely generous. He said, 'Yes, you must do this. It's not my world. You must take it and do with it as you wish.' It felt like a fellow director talking on equal terms. He was a director who had known his share of Hollywood interference and he wanted to make sure I knew he wasn't going to interfere with my conception. He said, 'If you want me there, I'll be there. If you don't, that's fine as well.'

As I said earlier, it was something I then raised with Katharine Doré as a possible project. She started the ball rolling.

AM: *So all this was in 1999. It was then that you mentioned your admiration for the film of* Edward Scissorhands *in an interview for the first edition of this book.*[1]

MB: Yes, and in a 2000 press release Katharine actually announced *Edward Scissorhands* for the next year, at the Dominion Theatre. But the rights were very complicated to negotiate, and the break-up of Adventures in Motion Pictures began. And *Edward Scissorhands* had still assumed no clear shape as a stage work.

AM: *So instead you proceeded to make* The Car Man *and* Play Without Words, *as well as working on three musicals and on revivals or new productions of three of your 'classics' – everything we've talked about in the last five chapters.*

MB: Yes, *Edward Scissorhands* happened over a period of a good many years. Caroline and I worked on various versions of the scenario, sending it backwards and forwards to each other. Danny wrote some new music for it, perhaps around 2002: some new themes and individual small sections. He really wanted to do it. He was so enthusiastic to do something on stage. He and Caroline are good friends, and we passed him each of the different versions of the scenario, so he always knew what was going on with it. Interestingly, Tim never asked to see it. So it became a project in which the people actively involved to begin with were Caroline, Danny, and me.

AM: *When Caroline Thompson and you began work on the scenario, did you both intend to make it different from the movie?*

[1] See p. 374 of original edition.

MB: We were always aware that people would be coming with the thought: 'I've never seen *Edward Scissorhands*. I don't know anything about it.' You've got to make the story work for them. For those people who know the film, we wanted to surprise them – retell the story in certain ways that would make them pay new attention. For example, since we knew topiary would turn out to be one of Edward's skills, we developed a whole topiary dream sequence, where the topiary dances with Edward and Kim. If you know the film, you're expecting topiary, but you aren't expecting the topiary to dance.

AM: *Why so long a delay before you finally put* Edward Scissorhands *on stage?*
MB: We had had the impression that, because of the work Katharine had done on the rights, it couldn't proceed without her. But in due course we realized that no deal for the rights had been signed. We met Marc Platt, a major film producer at Universal Pictures, and the producer of the stage hit *Wicked*, who became our co-producer for this show (with Martin McCallum); and he got very involved in helping us with Fox. Fox owned the film, the title, and – we found out eventually – the music. Tim and Caroline had retained the rights to the screenplay. Later, Marc Platt paid Katharine off for the work she'd put into it.

We then planned to do *Scissorhands* in 2004. But the success of *Play Without Words* kept that production going until 2005, so that there was no gap. We were able to revive *Nutcracker!*, *Swan Lake* and *Highland Fling* at various times, and *Mary Poppins* delayed it for yet another year. Only in 2005 were we able to start rehearsals for *Edward Scissorhands*.

AM: *I presume that other ideas about the story came into your mind while you were chewing it over. Like what?*
MB: I knew I wanted some of the satirical view of suburban life to resemble films by Jacques Tati.

And I got a major new Charlie Chaplin collection of DVDs. Beautiful quality. Previously I'd thought he's not hilariously funny; these have made me a big fan of his work. It's always brilliant and clever. And I feel it's utterly related to what I do in terms of visual story-telling. I've got much more interested in his bigger, more moving feature films rather than the short comic ones. These are lovely stories. Very touching stuff. And I could see they would be useful for ideas or style.

AM: *Which Chaplins do you recommend most?*

MB: *City Lights* (1931), *The Kid* (1921), *Modern Times* (1936), *The Circus* (1928).

AM: *Have you been watching any other silent movie-makers in particular?*
MB: Buster Keaton. *The General* (1926), *College* (1927).

AM: *And which Tati do you look at?*
MB: *Mon Oncle* (1958), *Monsieur Hulot's Holiday* (1953), *Playtime* (1967). I think *Playtime*'s fabulous. It's all about the modern world overtaking the old. All the historic buildings are seen as reflections – in glass doors, for example. You never actually see them. Somebody opens a door and suddenly there's the Arc de Triomphe or some beautiful old building. It's all about dealing with modernization. In *Mon Oncle*, they live in this completely futuristic house, with all this mechanical stuff for the kitchen. It's great.

But for Edward the character, I thought the stony-faced sort of silent comedians – we also looked at Harry Langdon – were really perfect. (I had read that Johnny Depp had looked at Chaplin and Keaton for his preparation too.)

AM: *Did you look at Harold Lloyd?*
MB: No. He's more of an everyman, I think, whereas the others are from another planet almost. They're like children in the way they react to things. That's what I wanted in Edward: a childlike quality. An innocent abroad.

Preparation

ALASTAIR MACAULAY: *Back in 2002, when Elfman was sending you new music, did he know any of the changes in the scenario you'd been making?*
MATTHEW BOURNE: Yes. Danny wrote a sequence of music using the scenario, near the beginning of the piece. The whole beginning. He wrote the little boy; the funeral; the trick-or-treaters . . . The whim really took him. I hadn't particularly asked him yet to write specific scenes, but he felt inspired by the clear direction and really got down to it, and wrote a whole sequence of new stuff, which he gave to me. He was really impatient for the show to happen.

Mind you, I think I panicked him on one occasion. I said to him, 'I want the end of Act One to be the equivalent of Snowflakes in *Nutcracker*. I want the music to be that varied.' The amount of musical variation within Snowflakes is what's great about it. The range of tempi is terrific. I sat there with him and said, 'Do you know it very well?' He said, 'Well, sort of. I know it a bit.' I said, 'Well, let's listen to it.' So I played it to him in his house. It was the wrong thing to do. He just went white. He asked, 'Could I do anything like this?' Well, it never happened.

AM: *The completed score incorporates his film music, but is the work otherwise of Terry Davies. What happened?*
MB: Well, after Katharine had originally announced the show in 2000, for the following years it kept falling through. During 2004, we gave specific dates for 2005 to Danny's agents, but it's my impression that they didn't take them particularly seriously. I think it was in January or February 2005 that Marc Platt and I went to New York and sat down with his agent to talk about it. They were saying, 'What are those dates again?' I said, 'Well, you've had them six months.' Then he looked down at his diary and said, 'Danny's not free then.' Basically, Danny was completely booked up with doing two films with Tim – *Charlie and the Chocolate Factory*, *Corpse Bride* – and other things as well. His agent was saying, 'He could start work in, well, looks like October.'

AM: *By which point you would have already opened the show in Plymouth. The finished score was completed by Terry Davies – your third collaboration with him. When did you start to think of asking Davies to work on Elfman's material?*
MB: Terry had always expressed an interest in being involved. He's used to working with other composers. And he's a fan of Danny's.

It would have been terrific to work with Danny as we'd hoped, and I'd love it if some other project brought us together. It was a great disappointment. To him, too: he was hurt. But what could we do? Marc and I explained very clearly that we now had agreements to rehearse and perform the work for specific dates, and that they had had the dates for many months. We just couldn't just move it, though I'm sure Danny wished we could.

But as the piece has worked out, I'm so grateful to have had someone like Terry to work with. We'd already flagged up the idea to Danny that we'd need a musical supervisor or an orchestrator. However, I discovered – not from talking to him but from a piece I read in the *New York Times* – that Danny always works with the same orchestrator for his films. This might have led to problems, especially as Danny's used to ninety-piece orchestras.

And I don't know if Danny would have been available for weeks – months – on end to work the way Terry did on *Play Without Words* and now *Edward Scissorhands*. To have a composer there with a new score, you need them there all the time. You need them to change things quickly, to have a daily involvement in it. Could Danny have committed to that? I'm not sure. Certainly I doubt he'd have been able to carry on after the opening to work on ideas for later improvements, as Terry certainly did. Things worked out well in the end.

AM: *When did you formally commission Davies?*
MB: Quite soon after that. Around April 2005. The show was due to open in Plymouth at the beginning of November, with rehearsals starting in August. The workshops started earlier, right through the summer.

AM: *And when did Lez Brotherston first draw up overall designs for the production?*
MB: He gave us his first version of the decor at the beginning of 2005. Something I really like in Lez's sets for the opening scenes is that there's an iris. Most of the beginning is all closed in. And you watch several scenes through this, and through a gauze. Which give a distant feel to those many-years-ago scenes. Then suddenly you get this big, wide opening. I look at it as when you went to the pictures, in the old days: you had the adverts, and then suddenly the screen started to get wider and you'd think, 'Ooh, it's really big, this screen.' You got all excited by that; I think the audience feels that same feeling here: 'Oh, it's enormous.' The way Lez has designed it, the perspective makes the stage suddenly feel twice its normal size. Even after that, they've almost not got the perspective until Peg comes out of her little house. She has to duck to come through the door, you know, and she seems very big beside it. So the audience has one illusion after another, which I love.

Lez also started doing costume designs early on. Stacks of them! Originally we'd thought of making one of the six families a liberal hippy family called the Rainbows, He drew up designs for all of them. But then he persuaded me that the Rainbows wouldn't work: a family that liberal would be too Edward-friendly from the first. He was right, and we decided to scrap them. I remember him throwing one whole set of designs onto the floor: 'Well, that's the end of *them*.'

AM: *Your show is set in the fifties, whereas the film's look is later.*
MB: We think the film looks eighties. But Lez just felt that he could sum up Americana much more clearly in the fifties. If you think of the

classic American family, there's a very fifties feel to it. So he lobbied to set the show literally in the fifties. But not too insistently. I let in a couple of things in it that I think are anachronistic. Those little Game Boy games one of the characters has, for example. They work fine.

A lot of periods are quite difficult for women's costumes when it comes to dance. But fifties styles always work – if you're going to do real costumes and not special dance adaptations of period dress. Fifties dresses come in at the waist with nice skirts that move well. Or they wear tight jeans.

AM: *You've started with this nice problem/challenge: 'How do I choreograph scissorhands?' I imagine you talked to Brotherston and asked 'How can I bring this off?'*
MB: This is the same as what I said, when we were talking about musicals, about directors like Trevor Nunn and Richard Eyre. You don't think that you *can't* do something. You think you *will* do it, even if you don't know how to at the time, or if you haven't got any easy answers.

Lez and I knew that we had to get the hands made early on. We had to find expert people who make these kind of things, and then we had to workshop the hands, to try things out with them. We saw what we could and couldn't do, and we experimented. To the maker, Robert Allsop, we would say what was currently not possible; and then they would go away to have additions made to make that possible.

At one point it was simply hard to keep the hands on. They would get caught up in each other, and they were heavy. Meanwhile we were asking: Can you lift at all while wearing them? Can you take any weight with your hands on the floor? Can you do delicate things with them? Pick things up?

AM: *Maximum lightness must be necessary, because otherwise the dancers playing Edward would find them intolerable weights at the end of the arms.*
MB: They still have that effect a little by the end of the show. Anything you might carry around on your hand for a whole show would have that effect. But they're light now.

AM: *Take me through just how scissors are fixed to hands.*
MB: They're almost like leather gloves as a base. A blade is attached to each finger, which articulates separately. So they're very much like fingers, even if they don't look that way from a distance. There are several

types and sizes of blades, and in one pair the blades go in the opposite direction so they look like a pair of scissors, with the positioning of the handles. And the blades are of varying lengths, but not in proportion to the length of a finger. It's odd. With each attachment of blade to finger there is a kind of mechanism: a brass section attached with a spring on it that pulls it back into place. So the blades don't just hang there. They do have something that tightens them. And when you bend a finger, there's a certain amount of pressure there. The actual blades are made of hard plastic. They're very light – and sometimes they snap, they break.

AM: *Tell me about how Davies completed the dream ballet at the end of Act One. Is the music three-four?*
MB: It's three-four, yes – I wanted a waltz – and the melody is basically the title theme at the beginning of the film. It's the music over the credits. I gave Terry the same notes I'd given to Danny. I said, 'I need a fast section in it. It needs some variation in it.' So Terry wrote the fast variation that is not in the film.

AM: *We've talked in the past of the Petipa–Tchaikovsky model for commissioning the musical detail of a score: '16 bars of this, 32 bars of that.'*
MB: Well, I wasn't as clear as that! But my guideline was that I wanted it to be like Snowflakes from *Nutcracker*. And if you listen to it now, it is quite similar. There's a section in Snowflakes which revs up and then pulls back, and there's a dreamy ending that doesn't quite go anywhere, that doesn't work to a climax. Terry's music has quite a similar structure.

AM: *You have two dancers who alternated as Edward Scissorhands: Sam Archer and Richard Winsor when it was new. On your second tour it was Matthew Malthouse and Dominic North.*
MB: I always felt that it should be equally cast and created, because I knew it was going to be a tough assignment. It would need all kinds of extra skills with hands and costume. If one Edward went injured, it wouldn't be a role you could easily have someone else go into very quickly. They would also be required for the bulk of the publicity, which can be very time-consuming.

Initially, I wanted Will Kemp for the role, and I then cast Sam as the second Edward. Will Kemp had been with us on and off for ten years: *Swan Lake, Cinderella, The Car Man, Play Without Words*, and now he was playing James in *Highland Fling*. I wanted him and Sam to

135 Sam Archer in rehearsal, Act One, 2005. Edward opens his blades
and peers through them in the bedroom scene.

play an equal number of performances however, and I don't think Will
was happy with that. But he was still on board early in 2005, when we
were doing *Play Without Words* in America. However, as I've already
touched on elsewhere, and to cut a long story short, I spent longer negotiating with him and his agents than with the entire rest of the cast. And
it just became impossible.

I'd known Sam for years. He was in *Oliver!* when he was fourteen,
and when he was at Doreen Bird College (today's Bird College) or musical theatre. I'd seen him in a student production that Geoff Garratt
directed, which was *A Slice of Saturday Night*, a sort of sixties-style
musical where he had a featured part. He's an extremely versatile performer, and incredibly inventive. I'm always looking at him to see what
he's getting up to in rehearsal, because he will just play around constantly, and then so often I'll say, 'Let's use it, it's great.' I wanted to use
him in 2002 – certainly for *Nutcracker!* and maybe for the original *Play
Without Words*, but by the time we were casting those, he was in *We
Will Rock You* in the West End, with a year's contract. In 2003 he took
over Will's role in *Play Without Words*.

AM: *Did you then realize who was going to be your other Edward?*

MB: I didn't think that I knew. A year or two earlier, I'd had Richard (Dickie) Winsor in mind for the Swan in *Swan Lake*. He trained at Central School of Ballet, and during his first year there he saw my *Swan Lake* and decided that was what he wanted to do. He was young, he'd been doing *Play Without Words* loyally for well over two years with very little dancing in it, and I felt I owed him a good dancing part. He loved *Play Without Words* and he never asked to leave, but he dances big in class. He is a big mover. I just thought, 'He's got to do some dancing, he's got to create something or get his teeth into a big dance role, or he'll be stifled.' So I tried to interest him in *Swan Lake*. When conversation came to *Edward Scissorhands*, I'm afraid I told him I didn't think he'd be right for that role. I just saw him then as big, handsome, attractive – almost too much so – as a regular guy. Since then, I've got to know him better as a person and he's very sensitive. I've always noticed he likes to bring out emotion in his style of performance. And so now, in 2005, when we were looking for another Edward, it seemed more natural to me that he would be the one.

It's ironic: Sam and Richard both joined the company at the same time, for the 2001 American tour of *The Car Man* – they auditioned together, and they both danced ensemble – and now here they are both playing Edward. They were both together in the 2003 revival of *Play Without Words*, and since then, they've both danced in *Nutcracker!*, in 2004, and have shared the role of Angelo in *The Car Man* in 2007. In late 2007 Sam went into the touring company of my *Mary Poppins* (understudying and playing Bert); and of course Richard created the role of *Dorian Gray* for me in 2008.

AM: *At the performances I attended, I noticed that whichever wasn't dancing was watching in the stalls.*

MB: Yes, they became best friends. (They were for a time known as 'The Arsors'!) And they even lined up the roles they want to do together in my repertory. They were both very keen on *The Car Man* because it's the first show they did. Sam wanted to do Angelo and Richard to do Luca. They'd decided that for themselves. Actually, in 2007, they both ended up playing Angelo!

AM: *How old were these two Edwards at the time of the show's London premiere in December 2005?*

136 Richard Winsor in rehearsal, Act One, 2005. Edward is asked to dis-arm himself and to place his 'weapons' on the ground when first meeting Peg Boggs.

MB: Richard was twenty-three, Sam twenty-four.

AM: *Meanwhile you and Caroline Thompson were still tweaking your scenario right up to the beginning of rehearsals?*
MB: Yes, we were. We were looking for more details. It was always good to come back to it after a long time, to bring a fresh eye to it really. We had such long gaps in its development. The details we kept developing were things like the names and characters of individual families, and the name of the town.

Workshops

ALASTAIR MACAULAY: *When did you begin workshops?*
MATTHEW BOURNE: In May 2005. We did six weeks of them, but not in a row. It was one week with one set of dancers, then another week with some more dancers, and so on.

AM: *Apart from dancers, who's present? You, Caroline, Terry, Lez?*
MB: Not Caroline (she lives in LA) or Terry. Lez was around a bit, working on hands and developing costume for Edward.

AM: *When you workshopped* Play Without Words, *you had only threads of ideas about the shape the show would eventually take. With* Edward Scissorhands, *you had a very definite story, even if details were yet to fall into place, and very definite leading characters, even if supporting ones might still have been subject to revision. How then did you develop characters? For example, how did you prepare the character of Edward? Did you just say, 'Look at the movie'? Or did you make the dancers look at other characters from other movies?*

MB: I had a load of notes as usual. Stuff we'd built up over time. And I started with a couple of days of game-type things.

I did one whole exercise about coming to life. Creation. First: Imagine your body coming to life through whatever means. Then: Be conscious of each part of your body. What if you suddenly woke up as a fully grown person and you didn't know how this body moved? And the guide track there was Franz Waxman music for *Bride of Frankenstein*. The whole feeling in the music is very similar. And later I got the guys to watch the Karloff films, of course.

One of our first workshop games was 'dog and owner'. Caroline felt – so did I – that Edward's like a stray dog. He'll follow you around, he wants to please, he wants to belong. And he's loyal and devoted to his master or mistress. So I got them to be dogs with owners and to see what that felt like.

I put on some music that Charlie Chaplin had written for his films. It's got a lovely, bitter-sweet quality to it: cello, violin and so forth. We used that as a background for these little experiments, these little scenes that they put together. I was telling you earlier about my new interest in Chaplin. And now I got the boys to watch Chaplin (films like *City Lights* and *The Kid*), Buster Keaton and Harry Langdon. I felt those stony-faced silent comedians would be perfect for those childlike qualities.

With Edward, Caroline had been saying, 'First you can think about him as a stray dog. Then you can think of him as a child that grows up very quickly.' In the early scenes, he's like a baby. Then he learns about things extremely fast. In the second half, he's acting quite normally, just like everyone else. He just happens to have scissorhands. He changes a lot. You may not think about it when you're watching it, but in the early scenes he needs everything done for him. He's led around and doesn't even know how to walk. But by the end he's almost a normal person in his expression and his reactions.

AM: *So from the very beginning, it's clear that nobody wants the dancers just to reproduce Johnny Depp. It's not just going to be 'The Dance of the Movie'.*

MB: No. But this was difficult, because this is the closest I've ever stayed to an original source. For any of us, it was unique in the fact that each performer was playing a role that's only ever been played by one other person. If you're playing Cinderella or if you're playing the Swan, you've got a range of choices, and you just create your own version of it. But here we were all trying to decide: 'How much of a part does the actor create?' We'd look at Johnny Depp's walk. Is that just the way Depp walks or is it something unique to Edward Scissorhands? The sort of shuffly walk that he does at the beginning: we felt that was too strong an image, associated with Edward, *not* to use that.

AM: *So where did you pointedly decide to take choices different from Johnny Depp's?*

MB: Oh, in many places. Our Edward had to move much more, to be able to dance, to do things that are just not required to do in the film. Quite often our decision was: 'Well, how far do we go in this different direction?' In the fantasy sequence without his scissorhands, we were asking, 'Does he become completely different? Or do we put little Edward-type walks in between the steps?' We decided not to put those walks into that scene because it made it comic in a way we didn't want.

Interestingly, for Edward's dance material, we looked at early Astaire: those mad Astaire solos, like 'I Won't Dance' in *Roberta* and any of those early solos where, really, he goes a bit crazy. When I brought it up, Sam and Richard initially reacted, 'Really? Fred Astaire? I just don't see it.' But I said, 'Look at this stuff, look at these solos.' And when they did, they got it. Because there is a craziness to it. It's like someone who's just discovering how to move, especially the differences between the brilliant feet and loose upper body. You know, going crazy with it and loving it.

AM: *When you're giving them all these tasks, do you stop and talk to the dancers about what the hands may symbolize?*

MB: A lot. The dancers are all asking, 'What *are* those hands?' The hands are the thing that's different. You're not playing shock-horror hands the whole time. You're playing someone who's different. Imagine him as a foreigner or an exotic person who comes to this town and is intriguing because of that. If you always played it as a piece about a boy with scissorhands, then it would just go along the same track the whole time. It would become only about being scared of hands or about getting injured.

AM: *Are the Edwards working with just their own hands at that stage? Or do they have anything attached to help them get the idea of scissorhands?*

MB: Right from the beginning, they had the scissorhands. We needed to see what they could do. The hands then went through about four stages of redesign, but the look was similar. We discovered that the hands needed to have a character of their own. They couldn't just hang there like clumsy props. They needed to tell us about how Edward was feeling. Sometimes they are the only thing that's moving; and they can tell us so much.

Another thing we discussed, which is hinted at in the screenplay, is Peg's interest in Edward. Etta Murfitt, who would be playing Peg, was present. Seemingly Peg wants to take him in because she's such a very kind person and wants to look after him. She throws a party, she makes a big deal of him being there. Possibly she's also showing off the fact that

137 Sam Archer (Edward) and Etta Murfitt (Peg Boggs) in rehearsal, Act One, 2005. Edward's first scene with Peg.

she is a generous, kind person, and that the family are too. In the film, Kevin takes Edward into his school to show him off. They all treat him like a freak in a way, without realizing it completely. But when he shows interest in their daughter, they don't like it at all. It's too close to home. That's a step too far.

After one week of workshops with just the two guys, we added the Kims, so as to start on partner work. Kim was played by Kerry Biggin and Hannah Vassallo. Kerry has done Clara in *Nutcracker!*; and, as we've mentioned, she was the Sylph in the recent staging of *Highland Fling* (and on alternate nights was part of the ensemble). She's young, and she dances young. The same goes for Hannah. (Both of them went on to play Rita in *The Car Man* in 2007.) Many of the women in my recent shows have been much more womanly. The women in *Play Without Words* are sophisticated characters, *Swan Lake* involves queens and princesses, and neither Lana nor Rita in *The Car Man* is teenage. Luckily we found two women who are perfect for the kind of freshness we need. They completely give you that spirit of a young girl.

When we brought the Kims in, the Edwards could get down to straightforward but necessarily experimental tasks, involving scissorhands, like 'Can we lift? Can we take weight? What can we do together?' Find a few lifts, a few ways of moving together. Those hands do take up an enormous amount of space if you turn with your arms outspread. It takes quite a while to get used to someone who's *that* big spatially. The Edwards were very tentative to begin with, very worried about hitting people. Later, they found so many ways of dealing with these hands, how many things you can actually do with them.

But yes, we did try some stuff out without them. The solo material, for example. After looking at the early Astaire solos, some of his madder steps, we made mad steps of our own in response, put things together, and chucked them around. Then we put the hands on. Which made us realize that if the hands weren't actively involved in the movement then it just didn't look right. The hands had to be choreographed. You had to decide what positions the fingers were in, whether they were flat or whether they were closed in or splayed.

AM: *What solos for Edward did you sketch in this period?*
MB: Four in particular, I think: his coming-to-life in the inventor's studio (*Frankenstein*), the tango-type solo he does at the start of Act Two when he's Edwardo the new celebrity hairdresser, the little one he does around

the ice sculpture, and finally the big, drunken one he does at the end at the Christmas Ball (Astaire).

AM: *You mentioned using* Bride of Frankenstein *for the end-of-creation scene, and Chaplin music for the dog exercises. What other choice of music did you make for these workshops?*
MB: Well, I also had some of the big love themes from the Chaplin film music when we were doing duets. For the Christmas party, we had a whole box set of swing music to develop the parents' social-dance movement and for his solo. And Latin. And mambo music for the barbecue.

AM: *Is this an advantage of setting it in the fifties? The swing music of that era must be more fun to choreograph than the rock music of the eighties.*
MB: Exactly. I liked the whole swing thing. And, since I'd just been working with Stephen Mear on *Poppins,* I put an element of tap-dancing into it. It's not tap that you can hear, but a lot of the steps are tap steps. And Sam Archer, interestingly, is a great tap dancer. In the workshops, he helped me develop a lot of the swing and tap material for the rest of the show – the material that's not for Edward!

AM: *After the two leading roles, who else did you involve in later workshops?*
MB: Whole groups of people. It was in workshops that we developed the idea of cars. I said to them, 'Look, this is either going to be an awful idea or it's going to be really good. Let's just try it. I've got this idea that each family has a car and that this identifies the family very clearly early on as a unit. Traffic! Let's develop some movement for going along in an invisible car with just the steering wheel. Maybe your family's got a cheap old banger that moves in a different way. Or a big sleek car . . .' It worked!

AM: *Any other exercises?*
MB: Lots. We did mambo phrases, material that might be right for the barbecue. We played around with Halloween ideas. We did one workshop on passing on a piece of gossip. Christmas carols was another: the dancers took real Christmas carols and mimed them – found a way of saying the words with gesture.

All these precise little ideas are a gift to working with a group because they're very easy for everyone to understand. If an idea is too complicated, or you're trying to get something that's too obscure, it doesn't quite connect with all the people in the studio.

AM: *So, at the end of these six weeks of workshops (late May, June, early July), how much concrete choreographic material did you have that you then could use for rehearsals?*

MB: Edward's solos were all sketched. His final duet was roughed out. And I had the phrases for the barbecue and for the swing dance. Other things, like cars, I just had as ideas, enough to make me want to take them further, but knowing that we should leave the real material until we had all the eventual dancers who would be playing the roles in all the families. It's good to give people something to create.

AM: *When you say the solos and duet were done, had you fitted them to the music?*

MB: No, we had sections of the duet, which we'd made to Danny's original music. But we hadn't put the sections together or connected them to Terry's finished version of the score at this stage.

I know now what the problems are of doing these new shows. Once they get into rehearsal, it's difficult to spend time on finding new steps, new movements, because my concern is so much to do with structure, pace and all the other issues. So the more steps you've got ready before rehearsals, the more stuff that gives you to play with. Then, in rehearsals, you can say to your dance captains, 'What was that phrase we did?' Or, 'The end bit of *that* phrase. The beginning bit of *that* phrase. What would that look like if we put them together?' That's the first time I've recorded movement on computer. It's all on there. All the workshops, divided up and labelled.

Workshops have so many advantages. They're cheaper than rehearsal, for one thing. You've got less people, you can concentrate more, you're not panicked about the structure of the piece. You're just working on ideas.

AM: *Tell me again how many orchestral players Davies does this score with.*

MB: Twelve. And there are three keyboards, which give a lot of extra sound effects and scissor sounds. Now the film has no scissor sounds in the orchestration. Ours does – not as sound effects, but as part of the music. That was a very effective element. I hadn't asked for that.

AM: *Did Terry have some kind of working score for you by the beginning of rehearsals in August?*

MB: Not really. He'd done bits and pieces. Family phrases. It wasn't finished by any means.

AM: *By what time had Lez completed most of his costume sketches?*
MB: By the time we went into rehearsal, the final ones had been done. The sketches were all there to be seen on day one of rehearsals by everyone.

Rehearsals – Act One

ALASTAIR MACAULAY: *You started formal rehearsals in August, several weeks after the last workshop. For you and the dancers, what were the main differences between workshops and the first week or two of rehearsals?*
MATTHEW BOURNE: As I've said, I'd got so much of the movement material ready in workshops that I felt very far ahead. In fact, at first I thought, 'I have to go backwards now, because all these new people don't even know who they are, what they're doing.' So they had to have the proper time to develop their characters. I couldn't on their day one just say, 'Let's talk about our characters.' They had to find them by doing a few things. So we did the car idea. They'd had all the descriptions of their characters. They needed to work with each other before we could do our usual session, the one where everyone talks about their characters.

Another early exercise was the swing dance. It took a long time for people to get the style of it, to find that way of moving. Very musical-theatre. We had the morning sessions on that. It wasn't the easiest thing to teach everyone.

AM: *You're now used to using a computer. I know that with* The Car Man *you prepared notes on each individual character before the start of rehearsals, notes that included all the possible characters and films the dancer in question might then take ideas from. Were you working this way with* Scissorhands?
MB: Yes. We knew the characters quite well before we went into it. They were all named, and all the families were given certain characteristics. So each dancer was asked to work on a much more defined character than on previous occasions. But the details could come through the dancers. It was Scott who wrote up those characters for everyone. On day one, he gave each one a file, with the whole scenario, with breakdowns of

characters, with notes on who their characters had relationships with, with references they could use or not use. Quite a lot of stuff. It was less free than *The Car Man* and almost the opposite of the freedom of *Play Without Words*. But it gave them all a bit of a head start. On day one, they also saw all the costumes they would be wearing. There was a lot to help them.

Some dancers used to come back from their fittings with *Scissorhands* with so many ideas for changes that Lez used to just laugh and say, 'We're shutting the fittings.' He laughed for half an hour when he saw Steve Kirkham in his jogging costume as George Monroe, but then he said, 'It's a good thing I'm laughing at you now, because it's great, and the audience will be laughing too.'

AM: *Does he have a team of set costume makers? The execution of his costumes always has such detail, with such good cut and line.*
MB: Yes, he always uses the same excellent team of people. Phil Reynolds does the more complex stuff: in this case, the Scissorhands costume and the topiary people. Lez can draw it, but some of it then requires an element from the maker as well. Making topiary costumes is not straightforward. How do you make them dance-friendly? How do you make topiary people able to see? So Phil Reynolds is the guy who does that kind of work.

AM: *Meanwhile, how were you keeping the Edwards and the Kims going?*
MB: Well, Kim's part of the Boggs family, so she was involved in the family stuff.

But Edward's very isolated from the group. Therefore the two Edwards were in a downstairs studio on their own, going over their material. And I'd given them new tasks to do. For example, we'd done a whole sequence of movement that was about haircutting: different ways of cutting hair. I'd say, 'Remember that phrase, I've got it here on video, look at that. Why not use some of those shapes you were making? Let's try and jump it. Let's try and move it around. See what you come up with.' They were good at being isolated from everyone: which helped with their approach to the character.

But there was one disappointment here along those lines in the swing dance. Sam does swing better than anyone else, and he helped to produce the material in the first place. His style is so right for it, so easy. I'd got so excited working with him on it, but he doesn't do it in the show. We'd had to pass the material on to everyone else.

AM: *At what point did you start to set it to music in rehearsals?*

MB: Sometimes straight away. I had all the topiary music and all the Halloween music at the beginning. But sometimes the music arrived during rehearsals, and we'd say, 'Oh, we've got this music now. Let's listen and work something out to it.'

AM: *Here's the opposite question, then. Did you ever, in rehearsals, use non-Scissorhands music?*

MB: No, we were always working on music that we had. I would tend not to work on a section until we got the music. Or part of the music at least.

Sometimes Terry wrote music that took features from the guide tracks I'd been using in workshops. The music he writes for Edward coming to life in the inventor's studio is lovely, and it takes the heartbeat drum all the way – boom, boom – from Waxman's *Bride of Frankenstein* music. The mambo section was based on some Carmen Miranda tracks I was using! – and I think you can hear an echo of that in Terry's music.

AM: *You were working with a set narrative, but still tweaking it. Did you ever find you'd have liked to alter it more than you were able?*

MB: There's a scene at the beginning that bugged me for the first season or more. I found I couldn't stage what I'd had in mind. The only reason I invented the idea of Halloween people, the trick-or-treaters, and the only reason their particular bit of music was written, was to dance. I like to have a bit of real dance early on in a show: it establishes that there will be more to come, and then you can get back to the story. My original conception really was that they'd be coming out of houses, that there'd be lots of space, and that this would be a set-piece number really. But I discovered early on in rehearsals that there would only be a little six-foot area at the front of the stage for that scene, with a front-cloth behind. The trick-or-treaters have got masks on, and they're in a precarious position at the front of that stage, and at first it just didn't deliver in the way I imagined it. They just looked tentative and cramped. Actually I never found a way around this problem – the order of scenes means that the set has to work that way – but eventually the dance did register better anyway.

AM: *When in rehearsals do you start to work with sets?*

MB: I always insist now on mock-ups of bigger pieces. We had two little houses – only the front two. We had any larger bits of scenery we needed like beds and dressing tables, and bigger props, like the barber's chair, the beanbag, things like that. Because if you don't have it in rehearsal, then it doesn't get used.

In a studio, the classic situation is that people never want to be on the sides at the front. Why? Because in a studio, that's no man's land. You're (at best) in the extreme corners of the eyes of the choreographer and his colleagues, who are sitting watching in the centre. But on stage, those front side areas are very strong. Once you get into a theatre, I always think, 'Why is no one over there? All the dancers are in the middle.'

One thing I work on endlessly is transitions. My favourite here is in Act Two, going from Kim's bedroom into the Christmas Ball with Etta and Scott coming together there and starting to dance. We bleed through, the bedroom disappears, and suddenly there's a whole group of people dancing. It's very smooth. It starts with dancing and carries on. Suddenly you're somewhere else. But this is a complicated set elsewhere for transitions. There are a lot of gauzes, which are always tricky for smooth transitions. However, the show scenically looks good, and for some people it's the best thing Lez has ever done. Cameron Mackintosh is one of them. He felt Lez had taken a step in a marvellous new direction.

AM: *One of the main things you had to fix in rehearsals was the big scenes for all the families. Complicated stuff when you've got twenty-four characters. Six groups of four. Is this the most complex ensemble you've done? There's an early scene I love in* The Car Man *when you're doing five things at once. To me, one of the big tests of a choreographer is: can he or she show three or more different things happening at the same time, in different tempi? It's amazing how few choreographers can.*
MB: The scene in Act One of *Edward Scissorhands* when we introduce the families, the 'Suburban Ballet', is certainly the most characters I've ever had to introduce at one time. They're not quite in six different tempi, but we find a range of speeds and dynamics for them. Some are in double time, some in half time, depending on who they are. They find their own character rhythm within that basic tick-tocky kind of rhythm.

It's the tick-tock of the day. Danny wrote that theme with a clock-work feel to it. The feeling is that this is a day in the life of the town. But it's not a logical hour-by-hour progress. We did think we'd do that at one point but it just would have involved too many extra things.

138 The Christmas Ball 'Swing Dance', Act Two. Etta Murfitt and Scott Ambler (Peg and Bill Boggs). The *Scissorhands* production gave several opportunities to more mature Adventures dancers, including these two longest-serving company members.

Like: 'Do we do the schoolroom? Do we do the women going shopping? Do we do men at work?' All that made it seem less interesting. So we went for the ideas that seemed fun and that helped to identify both families and individuals. I was thrilled when ninety-two-year-old Michael Kidd, the legendary choreographer, came to see the show in Los Angeles (the last performance of anything he ever attended) and complimented me on the clarity of the story-telling and the introduction of each character.

AM: *You've given the dancers notes on their families, and you've spent time collecting ideas for the families. Where do you go to for these ideas?*
MB: American sitcoms. There's one family we call the Grubbs. They're very much inspired by *All in the Family*, which is the American version of *Till Death Us Do Part*. Or *Roseanne*, the more recent TV series.

The Uptons, the mayor and his wife (Franklin and Charity) and children (Darlene and Jim), are a sort of presidential family, and they're very much based on George W. Bush and Laura and their kids. That kind of stiff, friendly, jokey, awful, everyone's-friend kind of behaviour. The daughter's very much based on the Bush daughters – grinning, naughty girls, you know.

AM: *So what material of the Bushes do you give your dancers?*
MB: Pictures, some sequences from TV . . . It's easy to get that stuff. I also asked Gareth Charlton, who is Mayor Upton, to look at *Bob Roberts* (1992), the Tim Robbins film, and *Dave* (1993), a film directed by Ivan Reitman starring Kevin Kline.

And we have the Monroe family who are the glamorous, showbizzy, high-achiever family. A bit tacky, kitschy. Joyce is a character in the film, so we took a lead from that a little bit. We decided that any son of hers would probably be a mother's boy. That's Gerald, who loves himself. And the daughter is a teen beauty queen. We based her on those awful teen beauty shows that they have in the States – often very, very young girls with frighteningly adult make-up. Horrible. She does baton twirling and that sort of thing. George, the father, is conventional, henpecked, blind when it comes to most of Joyce's behaviour.

Then there's the Evercreech family, who are dark and religious. Esmeralda Evercreech is a character from the film. But in the film she doesn't have a family. We've given her a Reverend husband, a preacher. (His first name is Judas.) There's a wonderful TV series called *Carnivàle*, an American HBO TV series with a dark preacher as one of the main

139 Michael Kidd (92, choreographer of *Seven Brides for Seven Brothers* and *The Band Wagon*), Matthew Bourne, Marc Breaux (83, original choreographer of *Mary Poppins*). Opening night of *Edward Scissorhands* in Los Angeles.

140 Act One. Vicky Evans (Charity Upton), trying to escape from
Edward's attempts to give her dog a makeover. (In Act Two she
re-enters with her pooch sporting a newly bizarre design.) Bethany
Elliott (Tiffany Covitt), Sam Plant (Sheldon Grubb), Cindy
Ciunfrini (Candy Covitt) observe.

characters. And the Burt Lancaster evangelist role in *Elmer Gantry* (1960).
The Evercreeches have got a Goth son and a self-harming daughter,
Gabriel and Marilyn-Ann. There's always a generation gap in these fam-
ilies as well – they're not straightforward. Marilyn-Ann's the ultimate
problem child. Another obvious source is *The Addams Family* (1991).
But I think we went for more real characters. And I'm quite pleased with
the way that family works. They sustain their characters really well.
They're actually not very cartoony. They never let up.

The Boggs family, the new all-American family that take in Edward,
are the hardest to do in some ways because they're mainly 'nice' people.

AM: *Any particular sources for them?*
MB: Well, there are a few early American sitcoms where everyone's very
perfect. The family in *Happy Days* is actually a good reference. There's
a great movie called *Pleasantville* (1998). They're based on the family in
that. But I wanted them – particularly Peg – to be very warm and welcoming. Not cartoony. And the son is just like every kid in America. You
know, into sports. Positive energies.

Then there's the Covitt family – who are covetous! They're the family
who want to be the Uptons. They want everything that the others have.
And they're pushy. She, Tiffany, is the desperate housewife who is a

pill-popper. She dusts everything – which is a reference to a character in Jacques Tati's *Mon Oncle*, who even dusts her husband's car as he goes out the drive. But Tiffany's husband Brad's having an affair with Joyce.

AM: *Covitts, Boggses, Evercreeches, Monroes, Uptons, Grubbs.*

MB: That's the six. There are other things that came into play too. We looked at *The Partridge Family*, an Osmond sort of family, the religious Mormon family. These were all things that people would use or not use as they chose. But we are trying to create 'all life is here' with the six families. And then within those families you have sub-groups. You have the dads, the mums, the bad kids, the good kids, the generation gap of kids versus the parents. There are the different kinds of music that the parents or the kids like. And the problems within each family. There was never an easy line of saying, 'Oh, you're all this. You're all that.' It's more complex than that. It was fun. It actually created more groups within the community.

AM: *So, after all that homework, how do you introduce this community in this scene?*

MB: First, there are the Boggses and the Monroes, then the other families, all emerging from their houses. Next we have one sequence with the kids of the town all meeting on a street corner as a group. Here we had young kids' phrases: a bit of jive. The kids of the town are meeting on the way to school.

Next we go into the cars section. Each family is in their car, driving around the town. It was hard to find something that would show how families did something together, but cars are a great way of bringing each family together, visually. So we could actually show them as families before they all start to split up as individuals.

AM: *The cars are all individual. The dancer Gareth Charlton told me that Mayor Upton's car is a 1962 Lincoln Continental four-door convertible – just like JFK's.*

MB: Yes, he obviously did his research! Then we have this mayoral rally. Keeping up with the Uptons. Up the Uptons! This brings the whole community together. There's a flag moment, and an anthem moment, and then Mayor Upton makes a speech.

Here there's a little passage we call 'Family Portraits': something that showed you how each family works together. The task I gave each family here was to make a little portrait of their family in four eights. To create something that showed you how the family worked together.

AM: *In the first edition of this book, it was amazing how often you made dance phrases that were in counts of eight. Do you still like eights?*

MB: In workshops, I'll always try to aim at phrases in eights. But once you set something to music, it's often more varied. Terry will always throw a little two or a four in somewhere. It's very rarely completely even.

AM: *In the case of these 'Family Portraits', did you tell the dancers what kind of speed the eights should go?*

MB: Yes. Then when I saw what they'd done, I changed them a bit. I didn't just leave it at that.

AM: *My sister Marian went to* Highland Fling *at Wimbledon and enjoyed it all the more because there was a Q&A afterwards, with Etta Murfitt doing the A. My sister asked, 'What is it Matthew actually does, since you contribute so much?' Etta just said, 'He's a genius. He chooses the good bits.'*

MB: That's nice. Well, people often say things like 'He chooses the best idea in the room.'

But there is more to it than that. I'm the one who sets the tasks and establishes the climate. And then I'm the one who adjusts what they come up with. The trick is to make everyone '*feel*' they have created the whole thing.

AM: *Enlarge on that, please. When you tweak material that the dancers have given you, which way are you tweaking? Are you going for a different musicality? A clearer stress on characterization?*

MB: To make it rhythmically more interesting. I'm sure I've said this about previous shows, but dancers will tend to come up with even counts and equal emphasis to everything when they're working out material themselves. I break that up.

And with some material the dancers produce, I just think, 'No. That's not clever enough. That's *not* good enough.' Or one idea is too long and too simple.

So this is what it's about. The dancers feel they've done it themselves, but actually I've done a lot with it. I've changed the rhythm, I've tightened it, I've added my own ideas, occasionally I've helped them do it all. But their sense is that they've created something. And that's really important. It's not a good process for movement to be imposed on a performer without him or her ever quite knowing where it's come from.

It's also scenes like this that contain the detail that's fun for people who come to see the show more than once. I'm always happily surprised at how much some people notice. And people have their favourite characters. In all my shows, I've found that people in the audience take a liking to subsidiary characters, and they want to watch them all the way through. I always hear, 'Oh, we've got to come back again. We missed so much. There's too many people to look at.'

AM: *It interests me that you go for different acting styles in each show. There are always elements of satiric humour, and always elements of seriousness and darkness, and in most shows there are elements of lyrical expansiveness, but the amalgam feels different each time.*

Although you're interested in realism, you've only occasionally tried for what actors call without-the-fourth-wall realism. In certain individual scenes, sure; often in The Car Man; *and in most of* Dorian Gray; *but elsewhere no. You're always very audience-conscious, and there have been times when the dancers' facial expressions and ways of looking wide-eyed out front have touched on camp. Though audience-consciousness is there in Pinter too, as it is in a great deal of spoken drama, I felt that a few of the* Play Without Words *performers in the 2003 revival, in the timing and emphasis of their eye language or the use of their mouths, were pushing the style a jot too far over the camp borderline. But that was incidental amid a powerful and imaginative work.*

In Edward Scissorhands, *your emphasis is often lighter, more cartoony, as in Burton's film. But quite a lot of the character acting on stage felt to me like mugging. I now know from talking to some of your dancers in February 2006 that they felt there was still much for them to discover in their roles, but even in December 2005 the acting style sometimes gave the opposite impression: the facial overemphasis of performers who have lost the freshness of their roles. This came and went during the show, and it's a point that I really apply only to supporting roles. But for me it was a problem.*

MB: You make a fair point here. There were young performers we were always having to caution against overdoing things. Sometimes playing a large theatre can be difficult to find the right tone in a story being told without words. Remember we are dealing with untrained actors for the most part. The aim – and the note I constantly give – is to find a truth even in the larger-than-life characters. I can only say that in more recent performances of the production, I have been very impressed by the general quality of the acting. It's definitely something to keep an eye on – in all the shows, I think.

AM: *How much do you guide the eye as where to look? Or is the main point the multiplicity of townsfolk here?*
MB: I know where I want people to look at certain moments. It's to do with emphasis and timing. In this scene, there's a lot of overlap, which is what I want. But there are moments with particular characters that I stress in a certain way so that you notice. But the main feeling here is, as you say, something larger: a day in the life, a community. It's the setting up of a world. There's a lot going on.

AM: *What happens in Edward's first meeting with Peg is a very simple form of mime, isn't it?*
MB: Yes. Edward takes a while to learn how to walk, let alone dance! This was just something that happened in the studio, just from really thinking about what the situation was. He's as scared as she is, and he cuts himself. What I like is that he just copies what she does. She puts her hands up in the air – he puts his hands up in the air. She goes 'Put those knives down' – he does the same thing.

AM: *Your first dream scene is when Edward looks at the poster of Kim as cheerleader and it became a vision of three Kims.*
MB: We had the idea – which for me worked at once – of showing her as a cheerleader with pompoms. I adored the idea that Edward would fall in love with someone with strange hands. Our co-producer Marc Platt's five-year-old son got it at once: 'The lady with the funny hands.' One of the three is Kim herself, and the other two are just clones with Kim wigs on.

The other thing I like here is that although we do cheerleader movement, it's not to cheerleader music. It's a beautiful waltz. The Kims do the odd movement of the cheerleaders, but not the rhythm. Edward doesn't really know what a cheerleader is. So in his imagination he just brings the pictures to life. The music is from her music box. She is, we reckon, about seventeen, by the way.

Then the three Kims put Edward to bed. Which is privately very funny, because all the Edwards find this the most erotic experience imaginable. They're so excited by these three girls in short skirts putting them to bed. It's a big fantasy. In rehearsals they were absolutely loving it.

And then Kim gives him a teddy bear to hold in bed. This came up in the rehearsal room and I thought, 'Well, that's very sweet. I like that.' Because he's a child, you know.

AM: *In the 'Gossip' scene after that, the style is a heightened, cartoony, kind of acting. Is it done in metric patterns?*
MB: Yes. Rhythmic acting. We've never talked about it like that, but I suppose that's what it is.

AM: *So can you now analyse anything of the nature of this acting rhythm? It's a different kind of rhythm than the one you create in* Play Without Words. *This is a more four-square kind of rhythm, isn't it? It's almost as if you're acting to a dance rhythm. The music has a dance continuity although you're doing acting motions that don't dance but have a kind of brio.*
MB: Yes. Well, this is a different sort of music. The *Play Without Words* music has a more insinuating feel to it. The more we do this scene, the more we find in it that's musical. Sometimes to find the truth in a scene you need to move away from thinking about it as a dance or even a rhythm. I usually want to try to get that back, though, because the whole thing is music-led, and it certainly does not work without that musicality. It may not be dance, but it must have a kinetic, musical sense that the audience feels and picks up on. It usually adds wit and feeling to the movement when that musical connection is strong.

What I say to everyone, and what we try to explore, is that everything you do is musical. We're never just working across the music. We're finding more and more ways of using it. The more I watch it, the more I can see how we can do that. And I keep adding things in to make it more musical. You want whatever they're doing to look – to a certain extent – natural. Yes, it's heightened, but it mustn't be fake.

AM: *I felt throughout these scenes that I was watching a greater quantity of mime, of upper-body gesticulation, than maybe in any of your previous shows. It seemed that you were coming up with your own twenty-first-century sign language as an equivalent to the mime we know from nineteenth-century ballet. And the gestures are all clear.*
MB: I think *Highland Fling*'s quite gesturey. In this case, the 'Gossip' scene is so gestural because they're doing gestural phrases about hands – about *his* hands. And yes, there's a certain larger-than-life emphasis these suburban characters have.

That whole scene ends when Joyce Monroe rings on the doorbell. And we just have that ending when just Edward's hand comes out. Caroline thought that was a bit scary. But I liked it because I think that's what they're feeling. They like the excitement of the danger of him. And it gives us a nice little button on the end of the number.

AM: *Apart from the Boggses, the first family we see on their own are the Evercreeches.*

MB: Yes. They've been very much noticed, too. The dark family. I like that aspect of the story because religion, particularly in America, is often used in a way that is destructive. And the religious fundamentalists are the first to make accusations. Shelby Williams makes Marilyn-Ann, the daughter, a very Tim Burtonesque character. She's done a brilliant job, and has been singled out by a lot of people. People really know that sort of self-harming, teenage, dark, angsty girl she's created. You know, she probably writes dramatic poetry and pulls the legs off spiders. Everyone gets her. And they love the moment in the barbecue where she wants Edward to cut her wrists. I didn't think people would spot these things, but if you happen to tune into a particular character, it's surprising how much you see. The advice that I gave everyone in this show was: 'You can make your role something that people will love to watch and will enjoy watching, however unimportant. They'll want to see your reaction to things. Your role is as good as you make it. Don't wait for me to tell you everything.' Half of them have already done that, Shelby not least.

AM: *The quartet the Evercreech family does at this point in Act One has an expressionistic early-modern-dance feeling. Were you thinking of the religious side of Martha Graham's* Appalachian Spring?

MB: Well, anything early-modern like that: Martha Graham, Doris Humphrey, Agnes de Mille even. It's all big exclamations and it's very angular. When the Evercreech family move as one, it's like a series of tableaux. And we have that cross image that I love, where the Rev. Judas is carrying his wife Esmeralda and she's the cross. Which people responded to in London, though not in Plymouth.

AM: *Do you remember how this cross came up?*

MB: I'd asked those four dancers to explore religious iconography. They had the idea of Jesus carrying the cross and then they thought, 'Wouldn't it be fun if the preacher carried his wife? As if she is the cross he has to bear?' And there's something about Rachel Morrow who plays that part. I wouldn't have thought it could be done so well, but it's a great shape she makes. She's a very angular person and the shape of her is perfect for it. She's very funny with those flexed feet and that clean position they get.

AM: *The Evercreeches' whole dynamic is quite different to all the other characters because shapes like this loom very large. It's expressionistic. But also quite brisk, urgent. Do they get significantly different music?*

141 Act One. Rachel Morrow and Matthew Malthouse (Esmeralda and Judas Evercreech). This cross image is the production's second featured moment for the Evercreech family.

MB: They have their own theme. It comes round at least three times. Near the end, it comes back when Kevin gets slashed in the face, and they come and comfort the Boggses as if to say, 'Told you so.' But it's always played on the organ. It has this little church-organ feel.

Next, the barbecue scene. Lez put him into Bermuda shorts here. There's a sign – 'Welcome Edward' – across the fence, which is sort of like in baby building-block letters. Which draws us back to referring to him as the new child of the house. There's a 'We've adopted a baby' sense.

Then he meets various people. Gloria Grubb has all her barbecue utensils in her hand, and so Edward's reaction is 'Oh! someone like me! Someone who's from my world!'

There's a nice moment in that sequence when Terry gives you the generation gap in the music. We've had quite twee barbecue fifties-type TV-theme music for the adults, now Kim and Jim come back from camp, and they have loud young people's rock music. And the movement styles change accordingly.

When he first meets Kim – the girl he knows from her picture – there's a little freeze moment. This bit of theme music comes in, briefly, just to show he recognizes her. It's not the music that accompanied his dream of her as a cheerleader, because that's not about any mutual feeling between them. Here, however, they've laid eyes on each other, and this is the melody for what will later be their duet. But her reaction isn't welcoming. She's like: 'He's just a freak. Not cool.'

Later, there's a mambo dance, which culminates in Edward doing a bit of sword-swallowing with his hands. Another party trick. It helps to make him accepted and welcomed.

AM: *The duet for Kim and Jim after the barbecue begins with quite a striking lift. Not a big lift, but it's as if she doesn't want to go there. A hint of his possible violence to women.*

MB: Yes, there's a violent, nasty side to him. That will become more apparent, but this is where we have to set it up. That's a very brief but important interlude. Like most of suburbia, these people are very different when no one else is watching!

AM: *Speak to me now of the topiary vision scene at the end of Act One. Do you think of this scene as a ballet?*

MB: Yes. I see it as a little Ashton tribute. I have a feeling he would have done this section wonderfully. This is the closest Edward comes to being a dancer – the perfect prince. He's fluent. Not awkward. And he has no scissorhands.

142 The 'Topiary Ballet', Act One. Richard Winsor (Edward, minus the hands) and Kerry Biggin (Kim).

AM: *You've often said that your work involves dream sequences. You've already had one in this show with the three Kims. But am I right in thinking that this topiary dream is the nearest you've made to one of the vision scenes that mark nineteenth-century ballet? Not least because there's a corps de ballet that becomes part of the imagery of his dream. And this topiary corps keeps changing formation around him and Kim, like the scene in* The Sleeping Beauty *where the corps of nymphs becomes the forest through which the Prince pursues the Vision of Princess Aurora, and which also separates her from him, keeping her distant from him.*

MB: Yes, that's exactly what it is. Shorter, though: just six and a half minutes.

AM: *You probably don't know the nineteenth-century ballet* Don Quixote. *It's not the favourite ballet of anyone sane. But this scene in* Edward Scissorhands *particularly recalls that, because Don Quixote is never going to get the girl but he has a transcendent wood-scene dream of her.*

MB: That's it. And you know in your heart that Edward's not going to get her, don't you? – which makes it more endearing. We've started to see the caring side of him, but here he's getting something back as well, though only in his head. It leaves you with a very clear image of an impossible love at the end of Act One.

And the corps de ballet here is of topiary figures. He's taken her to a garden of his making. It's a moving garden, but one of changing symmetries. At the end of it, she glances back at him again. A very casual glance. It doesn't give you any inkling that she would ever be interested in him. So Edward's love for her is true of so many misfits of any kind. It doesn't stop them loving the same way. I think that's very touching.

AM: *How is Kim changed in the dream?*

MB: She's not. We did go through a period when I thought, 'Well, maybe it is partly her fantasy as well.' But it didn't feel good for the story that she would be suddenly interested in him. She needed to learn about him from experience.

AM: *But are you presenting her as real-life Kim here, or are you showing her as the Kim of all Kims, the ideal Kim in his mind?*

MB: No, she's marvellous enough already. He's fallen in love with the idea of her already. I don't think he wants her to be any more wonderful.

It's an odd relationship in this act, because they don't really connect in real life. The first real contact comes early in Act Two when he offers her a haircut. She kind of wants to, but her friends – peer pressure – tell her she shouldn't. So it's not the most straightforward of love stories for the two of them who are playing it. But the audience gets what's going on.

AM: *Did the ideas for the patterns and the changing imagery of the topiary come from the dancers or from you?*

MB: From me. I felt the subject-matter allowed me to be completely classic in terms of shapes and organization. If we were to put it in ordinary dance costumes, I probably would think it was too conventional. But the images are of a topiary garden, symmetrical, with a cross shape that goes round like a wheel, with circles, and with Kim and Edward weaving in and out of the topiary. What was fun about it was that it's an ever-changing maze. Actually, while we were making the show, I went to see the latest Harry Potter film, *Harry Potter and the Goblet of Fire* (2005). There's a great sequence there where they have to go through a maze, and the walls of the maze keep changing. The hedges re-form, so they never know where they are. So that – the ever-changing topiary garden – was a nice idea to play with. And then having Kim and Edward ducking in and out of topiary shapes and then losing each other. It also made it easy for him to disappear before the end without you noticing too much and then returning with his scissorhands on. Which takes us back to where we started.

Rehearsals – Act Two

ALASTAIR MACAULAY: *In Act Two, whose idea was it to make the hair-dressing dance a tango?*

MATTHEW BOURNE: That's from the film. That's Danny Elfman. That whole musical sequence is based on the film. Everyone is very excited about this opening. He appears now with a little Errol Flynn-type moustache to show his confidence. He's Edwardo the barber. He's grown up a bit.

AM: *Is the moustache in the movie?*

MB: No. But this is the nearest he gets to being consciously swaggerish and sexy.

I was really wondering how we would show his successes as a hair-dresser, and it ended up being so simple. It's the most low-tech special effect – I mean, it's not a special effect at all! It's just a wig. Joyce lies in his salon chair, everyone makes a big gypsy blur of dance movement

143 Act Two. Michela Meazza (Joyce Monroe) and Sam Archer ('Edwardo' the
hair stylist). Etta Murfitt (Peg Boggs), Gavin Eden (Kevin Boggs), and
Rachel Morrow (Esmeralda Evercreech) observe.

around it, and it's perfectly obvious what's happening behind the blur: the dancer is changing wigs. And the audience loves it, and laughs. I was quite surprised by how simple it was to bring this off. And here as so often, the less you do, the better it works. It's silly, and the audience doesn't care. They still react to her change of wig. I love that.

AM: *Am I right that Joyce Monroe has a rumba as her seduction theme?*
MB: Yes, this is Terry's music. The rumba is one of her two themes. It comes up at the barbecue in Act One, actually. But yes, now it returns for her big seduction scene. The note I gave to Terry was Ravel's *Boléro*, actually! It just gets faster each time, but also has little pauses in it. And each time it repeats, it's faster. And it builds up.

AM: *Just as they run into her house, a beanbag falls from up above. It's just a beanbag that's part of the furniture for her house, but it falls like a huge dead weight out of nowhere, and so the audience laughs just to realize that it's not something that's fallen by accident, and that nobody was hit.*
MB: Really this beanbag-drop moment makes no sense whatsoever. But I just thought a beanbag would be fun to play with because you can change the shape of it. We had one in rehearsals. Lez wasn't entirely happy. 'Really?' he said. 'That's very seventies.' He's strict about his sense of period. But I said, 'I don't care.' Then I said, 'How on earth do we get a beanbag onto an empty stage? And it needs to be downstage.' Then I asked, 'Well, look, wouldn't it be fun if we just drop it from above?' And so it's turned into an eccentric moment that works. I think the reason the audience laughs is it's like someone pressing a button and a bed coming out. They know Joyce's character by that point. It's the equivalent of 'Now I've got you.' It's a moment everyone remembers afterwards, too.

And then Edward and Joyce go round the table and end up on the washing machine. He turns it onto maximum spin by mistake and so she finally reaches her climax on the washing machine without his help. You can get away with this because kids just think it's silly, and adults know completely what's going on. So many people love that. Perhaps because they don't expect to see it in a family show, they really scream.

Michela Meazza has been one of our leading dancers for years. I first used her in *Boutique* in 1995 when she was a student at the London Studio Centre, she's been in the original casts of *Cinderella* and *Play Without Words*, and she was the alternate Lana in the original production of *The Car Man* (and first-cast in the 2007 revival). In our 2002 *Nutcracker!* she was second-cast Sugar; in 2007–8 she was first-cast. Since 2008 she's been Lady H. in *Dorian Gray*. She's a very elegant dancer, with real glamour and sophistication on stage. But she herself is actually quite shy. Originally, she didn't see a role for herself in *Edward*, but she wanted to extend herself. So she watched the film and came to me and said, 'I know you wouldn't think of me for this part, but I'd really love to have a go at it.' I respected her enough to know that she would really make a go of it.

Steve Kirkham brilliantly plays her husband George. I see him a little bit like the husband in the stage version of *On the Town*. Did you see the recent production of that at the Coliseum? One of the women characters has a husband who's very forgiving. 'I understand,' he keeps singing. He keeps finding her in ever more compromising positions with sailors, but every time there's a little pause and he sings, 'I understand, darling.' Eventually, he cracks.

AM: *The next scene is Edward's snow sculpture, and Kim's dance. This has a beautiful beginning, as she stretches one leg and traces a semicircle on the floor –* rond de jambe à terre.
MB: She's feeling the snow on the ground. Making shapes.

AM: *In Act One of Ashton's* Cinderella, *Fairy Winter traces a whole diagonal of* ronds de jambe à terre *across the stage. The feeling is that she's spreading a film of ice as she goes.*
MB: That's it. Because if you think of ice and/or snow, you can make a shape in it with your feet. You can make a design in it in a way. I wonder if it was Fairy Winter who gave me the idea? Anyway, yes, that's what Kim's doing there.

Female solos have been quite hard for me in the past, you know. But I found it refreshing to do something for a fresh young girl, rather than a sexy, sophisticated, strong woman. Kim's innocence meant we could make something very pure and beautiful. I could get inside her head. And I get very involved in that relationship: it's very sweet and touching. The four people that play the two parts are all young and feel it in an appealing way.

And Kim's so touched that he's made this beautiful thing in her image. From then on, there starts to be a true relationship between them. She's starting to fall in love with him. I remember watching it and thinking, 'God, this little scene is so beautiful. This is the most beautiful thing

I've ever done, this little moment.' Because it's seen through a gauze as well, it feels a little removed: a moment that just happens, against the background of houses. Howard Harrison has done such a lovely job in lighting it. When it is musically good, and they dance it well, I think it's really special.

AM: *What goes on in the dancing between the two of them?*
MB: He's working away at the ice sculpture, and he dances a little solo around it. And he ends up at the top of it with the snow spraying out from his working blades. Now she comes out of the back door of the house, and she starts to sense the snow. It should feel like it's the first time she's felt snow on her skin. And he just watches her; he even hides from her a bit. She's aware of him up there. But she's just enjoying the feeling of the snow and what he's made for her. And it turns into a duet when she actually hits the position of the ice sculpture. They look at each other. He loves the fact that she likes what he's done for her. They don't actually touch each other, but they dance around each other. And he guides her through the space. It's as if he's creating her as well as the ice sculpture. He shapes her like a work of art. He makes her move.

AM: *Like a choreographer with her.*
MB: Yes. It shouldn't feel Svengali-like. But he guides her movement around the space. At the end, just by chance, they finish face to face. An eye-contact moment.

AM: *You've spoken about the swing dance that's begun by Peg and her husband at the start of the Christmas ballroom scene. It's your favourite transition, all done with dance. But can you say more about Edward's big solo in this scene?*
MB: It's a solo with an animated ensemble of people who are constantly on the move, quite a strange and interesting one. He's wearing a tux – Lez's idea, which I love. And he's tipsy.

I've never done anything like that before, where it's basically a solo but you're also animating the whole company. There's nothing worse than those solos where people are just standing around still waiting for it to finish. So the issue here was to integrate them as much as possible within it. And they all do have little moments within it with him. His solo picks up on various other characters doing little bits with him. There's a little bit with the Evercreeches. A bit of flamenco with Gerald and Chase. A bit of a tap thing with some of the women.

144 The 'Ice Sculpture Duet', Act Two. Kerry Biggin (Kim) and Sam Archer (Edward). Bourne singles this dance out as the moment of which he is proudest.

145 The Christmas Ball, Act Two. Sam Archer (Edward), not dancing,
is on the right, watching James Leece (Jim) and Kerry Biggin (Kim) leading
the Swing Dance in front of the Christmas tree.

Because it isn't just a solo, he doesn't get a solo reaction from the audience. He used to end it in a state of collapse. But now, having collapsed, he then comes up with his glass towards the audience. It gets a better reaction simply because he's asking for it. By now, however, Edward is obviously in a state of collapse, and he's an embarrassment. Dominic North, in the later casts, danced up a storm here, just by throwing himself into it and using his 'company joker' personality to great effect.

AM: *And so to the final pas de deux. Why has he run to the graveyard?*
MB: Well, that's coincidental. Part of me is aware that there's an element that doesn't make logical sense. Edward doesn't know who's buried there, he just runs. And he ends up in the graveyard. Since we have only one gravestone on our set, that of the inventor's son Edward, that's where he ends up. It's near to where the inventor lived, the house where Edward was made.

Part of me likes the fact that the story ends up where it began, and that this is the grave of the little boy we saw at the start. It's not the first time I've done something that, if you ask too many logical questions about the ending, it doesn't add up neatly. But neither do most stories. I like it theatrically and conclusionwise and storywise. It feels right to me.

I think Lez and Howard did a brilliant job of transforming that scene into a believable graveyard, turning that topiary into what could be odd tombstones with the red eyes and the way they lit them. In advance, I thought, 'How can we do this?' In the event, it looks more than OK – beautiful.

AM: *Take me through the duet and how the movement is connected to the emotion.*
MB: Well, this is something we reworked, to show more clearly how it develops in feeling. I found we were in danger of becoming repetitive with aspects of his feeling that 'Oh it can't work with these hands'. What we needed, I felt, was the initial feeling that they were in love.

It comes together when she kisses him, which is unexpected, certainly on his part. And then there's a realization that it's not a love that's allowed to be in the world. The feeling is very 'Somewhere' in *West Side Story*. Not here. Somewhere else. 'There's a place for us, somewhere a place for us.' The kiss had to lead us into something where he was excited by the possibility of love, before he could then reject the idea because of it not being able to work.

Often it's she who leads, in terms of placing his arm around her. She initiates quite a lot of movement: 'No, we can do this. We can be close.' Then there are bits where he gets overexcited and wants to hold her, but she pulls back a little bit because it's scary. He in turn realizes and pulls away from her. The duet is about them trying to work it out physically, but they can't. It's not an idea that many duets are about – the *physical* problem of being together. They don't reach a complete conclusion, because they're interrupted by Jim. The last image is her pulling his arms around her quite tightly.

But I think there's also a feeling that it isn't really going to go anywhere, and that he is going to have to leave. I don't think they've decided to run off together. I think that they've declared their love for each other and now they're going to part.

The fight that follows involves, obviously, a lot of different emotions. And Jim gets injured. And now Edward disappears. All you see are the scissors. Brilliantly done, I might say. I never see him disappear, even though I'm looking for it. I like the fact that he turns back into a pair of scissors. This, again, doesn't make logical sense, and yet I can feel it works in the audience. I can feel little kids going 'Where did . . .? What happened here? Where did he go?' Everyone's asking, 'What happened?' Did Edward magically disappear? Was he ever there in the first place? Has he managed to escape somehow? Was that what he pulled off him as he left? Is that what he's left with? A part of him? The ambiguity feels poetic.

AM: *So in this way too, your* Edward Scissorhands *is in a line of ballets that go back to* La Sylphide *and* Giselle: *it's about an impossible love, reaching a point of greatest intensity just before the final parting.*

MB: Yes. But it's she who's left, not the hero. And she's not the one who feels responsible for his demise or transformation. She knows that everyone else has done that. And it's suggested that she, as the old lady at the end, is the one person who knows that his spirit is still there somewhere. Edward is mysterious anyway, so I like an ending that doesn't give you a clear answer. He's in the snow, he's in her heart. And you get the slow curtain. Yes, the ending does feel a bit like the ending of *Giselle.*

And then the curtain call is part of the show. Edward makes it snow in the audience, literally on the audience. A sharing moment between character and audience. If you feel that snow is symbolic of him, then this is giving him to the audience. I love it. It's foam, that snow: different from the snow that's on stage, which is little bits of plastic. (Foam on stage is slippery.) Even though it's a curtain call, I think it's a bit of magic – but it's also an important part of the show: a very warm feeling. I felt the company should come on and join him. And that they should not bow, but stand there, and react to the snow, the way that Kim did earlier on: 'God, this has never happened before.' Etta Murfitt, as Peg, does this beautifully every night. And it's snowing everywhere. And then blackout.

AM: *This feeling of snow on the face relates to* Nutcracker! *– though, admittedly, the first person there to feel it is the marvellously horrid Fritz. It also relates to the feeling in Ashton's* La Fille mal gardée *when there's a lull in the storm scene, and Lise turns her face up to the blessed sky and then traces a rainbow on the horizon.*

MB: Yes. I love that. It's the child in everyone, isn't it? The other day I was sitting in the audience with Etta Murfitt and Madelaine (Maddy) Brennan, who plays Old Kim. It was the first time they hadn't been on stage in it. They'd never watched it, and they were so excited. The snow was actually coming onto them. They reacted as if they had no idea that it was going to happen. Tears were rolling down their cheeks!

Previews

ALASTAIR MACAULAY: *You previewed the show in Plymouth before bringing it to London. What did you learn?*
MATTHEW BOURNE: Not always what you might expect. Here's a small example. In the barbecue scene, someone throws a beach ball at Edward. It bursts as he catches it. In Plymouth, there was a guaranteed full-audience reaction to that moment. But when we got to London, for some reason, it was not focused as well. We had a wider stage, so I needed to focus the rest of the performers to direct the audience towards it.

Previews help to show which bits of the story still aren't clear. We worked on several versions of introducing the topiary ballet. To get his hands off, Edward has to leave the stage just when the narrative needs him to remain on stage to focus the vision that now occurs. For a while, as a result, it became unclear whose fantasy this was. This was a good example of what you learn from talking to audiences. We've now managed to get the removal of his hands down to a fine art. He's only off very briefly.

We had an accident or two in that topiary scene. Since the dancers are each dressed as a hedge, it's not always easy for them to see where they're going. One woman in the second row said, 'I suddenly had a hedge coming towards me.'

AM: *What other revisions did you make before you reached London?*
MB: In Act One, we added that bush that he suddenly is inspired to 'tope', and the unshorn dog. Seeing the bush is the moment when topiary – art – hits him as something he can do. People got the point of it at every performance: it always gets a round of applause. And then the same with the dog. When we first previewed, we only had the cut dog going across later. Now we added this shaggy one earlier, and Edward giving it a look as raw material. There's always laughter, as the audience gets his creative thought.

During previews, you've got the whole team there, still working on the show. It's a golden time and you've got to just grab it. So, in this case, our prop-maker, Mandy Burnett, was around. Within twenty-four hours of us having the idea, there the bush was, on stage, with Edward shearing it. This was a very good team.

Musically, a lot of things have been tweaked to tighten things up. There's been a lot of tightening up of scene changes. I never want one dead moment when the audience starts to think of what they might have for supper, or did they lock the front door properly.

Performance

ALASTAIR MACAULAY: *The statistics for* Edward Scissorhands's *run at Sadler's Wells are impressive. It ran for eleven weeks – the second-longest run in the history of that theatre (the longest was your* Nutcracker!, *where an eleven-week season was extended by one further week). Ninety-five thousand people came to see it. Sixty-five per cent of them were coming to Sadler's Wells for the first time.*

The show then did a fourteen-week tour around England, Scotland and Wales (106 performances in all) and then went to Korea and Japan for forty further performances. Between November 2006 and May 2007, the company did a six-month coast-to-coast tour of the United States, from San Francisco and Los Angeles to Toronto, New York (the Brooklyn Academy of Music), and Washington, DC (Kennedy Center), not to mention other cities in between: a longer tour even than the Royal Ballet ever made of North America in its heyday. By the end of that, the original company had clocked up 401 performances. Then the production toured again in 2008–9, going round Australia, several cities in Britain, a second season at Sadler's Wells (seven weeks), then Athens and Antwerp. At that tour's end, Scissorhands *had done a further 184 performances, totalling 585.*

But you made changes.

MATTHEW BOURNE: Yes, of course, there's always so much to fix. Some performers need encouraging to take their roles further. Steve Kirkham's role as George Monroe was very definitely a supporting role, but he just kept finding fresh moments because he's searching for them. We promoted him to principal after the Sadler's Wells season.

Something small but very important is the first meeting between Edward and Peg. There's so much information there, so we extended it by a couple of phrases. I felt they should almost part, and then she'll decide to take him in. First, she lets him go as a sort of tramp. Then she goes to go back in her house and has second thoughts. I wanted more hesitation there.

146 San Francisco. Sam Archer's face in the *Edward* poster.

In the bedroom scene, when Edward first sees the poster of Kim with pompoms, and then the three Kims, each with pompoms, I wanted to find a way of showing his attraction to big hands. The Edwards worked on how to get this across.

In the barbecue scene, I made a mambo sequence come more out of Joyce and Edward dancing together. He creates an 'Edward step' that everyone wants to learn, because he's the new man in town with the hip new dance.

The topiary ballet was choreographed without the costumes. I can see now that some of the shapes we were doing were cumbersome. Anything with hands up round the head makes a clump rather than a nice shape. It's mushy. So I opened out the arms away from the body, and I've taken out some of the detail. It works much better. Also I've given new movement in the air to Kim and Edward – jumps and then lifts.

AM: *That's ironic after all those years of teaching your dancers in* Swan Lake *and elsewhere to touch themselves and put their arms on their heads.*

MB: I know. But here much more balletic, much cleaner shapes were really good. So we changed the arms. The costumes already put the dancers in interesting, odd shapes, with square or circular or triangular heads, and shapes on their body. If they just stand there in a pose, it already looks really interesting.

And I reworked the last duet. We changed a couple of the lifts. Or we re-placed them, giving them more space for them to happen, so they're not up against the fences at the side of the stage. And getting more emotion into it.

AM: *Some of my problems with the show were to do with the music. I've liked Terry Davies's work on* The Car Man *and* Play Without Words *a lot, and I enjoy Danny Elfman's work on* Dangerous Housewives. *But here the sound felt overamplified – it often didn't sound like a live band – and I didn't love the instrumentation.*

MB: I would say you were in the minority on that point. One of the audience's chief delights in this piece is its music; we often hear that people find it one of the most memorable features of the show. It's true that it sometimes has sounded as if it's not live. There are boring financial reasons for this. Still, this is really not a problem for me; having worked in musical theatre a lot, I'm more used to this kind of amplification – and so are audiences. Recently I saw *Carmen* live at the Royal Opera House, and found myself so disappointed by how weak and distant the music sounded. No tingles; no thrills.

I also hope you'll see (hear) it again, because there is so much that Terry changed. It took a long time to get the conductors and players to get the right sound and tempi. It's a new score, after all. There were lots of musical details throughout the show that Terry had been wanting to do since we opened in December, or earlier. Like me, he watches the show and thinks, 'We need a little more something here', or 'A little bit more wit there.'

Another idea that I later explored is that the first thing Edward does when he's alone in Kim's room, having looked around, is to open the music box. It's a little ballerina twirling. The classic thing in a girl's jewellery box. But for Edward this is the first time he's heard music. He's scared of it initially, but then it sort of becomes something that affects him.

Do you know the *Frankenstein* where the Monster is with the blind violinist? He's on the run and he hears violin music. It leads him to this cottage. He's really affected by it. It changes his personality completely.

147 Dominic North (Edward), 2008. Final image of the show.
North was nominated for Best Male Dancer for his role
as Edward in the 2009 National Dance Awards.

He gets to the house and the man who lives there, this sort of hermit, plays the violin. He's blind so he doesn't actually see him. He brings him in as 'my friend', filling him up with some food and drink. It's a very beautiful scene really because it's someone who's accepting the monster, and not being scared by his appearance. Music soothes him. Well, I wanted to try and make this part of this scene for Edward a lot clearer. The hard thing was to make someone who knows nothing suddenly do something that feels knowing, technical. But I wanted to expand the feeling of moving to music. I got the Edwards experimenting with moving more musically through it, and we found ways of dancing it more.

AM: *There was nothing in the* Edward Scissorhands *film to prompt this. So it was a very Matthew Bourne touch. You were the child who felt that music transforms lives.*
MB: Yes. It seems like a good notion for this show. Yes. Edward has to fall in love with music, don't you think?

(Conversations 2005–9)

17

Dorian Gray
2008

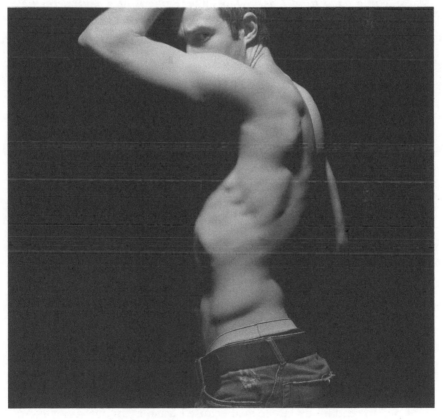

148 Richard Winsor as Dorian. Publicity material.

Idea – 1

ALASTAIR MACAULAY: *Your* Dorian Gray *is a modern-dress adaptation of Oscar Wilde's novel* The Portrait of Dorian Gray *(1890). Basil here is a photographer, and Dorian achieves fame as his new model. They also become lovers, and their relationship is partly that of artist and muse. Watching it, I thought of the many dancers you've felt inspired you, muse-fashion. Have you done pieces about the muse and the artist before?*

MATTHEW BOURNE: There's a lot of me in *Dorian*. *The Percys of Fitzrovia* had artists and models in it, but it wasn't really about one particular muse. But *Dorian* currently feels to me my most personal work.

AM: *Certainly it develops your fascination with images of beauty and desire, going back to at least* Swan Lake. *Fame isn't a central theme in* Swan Lake *but it's there.*

MB: Yes, the pressures of being a public figure are there in *Swan Lake* and yes, that's taken further in *Dorian Gray*.

AM: *Is this the first time you've handled narcissism other than in the TV film you made in 1993,* Drip – A Narcissistic Love Story?

MB: I think so. It's not a particularly attractive subject to work with. One fear we had in approaching this story was the question 'Do we have any likeable or sympathetic characters that the audience can invest in?' I tried to bring sympathy to the story, even though Dorian himself does what he does within it. And Basil is a potentially sympathetic character.

AM: *You said to me, talking about* Edward Scissorhands *in particular, that one incentive to do a new piece is to try solving a new problem for the first time. In* Edward Scissorhands *that problem was the hands. Was that part of the allure of* Dorian Gray? *to address something as unattractive as narcissism?*

MB: It was. That was the challenge of it – and the thing that put me off doing it for many years. It's always been there on the list.

AM: *Why was it on the list?*

MB: I'd loved the book from quite an early age. It was one of the first classic novels I read when I was a teenager. I always had a fascination with what it seemed to be saying. It was exciting. It was quite a comforting book to read in my late teens because I wasn't yet 'out' as a gay man and it suggested relationships between men without actually stating this was what was happening. I found that quite liberating.

AM: *You first presented* Dorian Gray *in 2008 at the Edinburgh Festival and then at Sadler's Wells. Unfortunately, I wasn't able to see it until July 2009, when it was enjoying a second run at the Wells. My first performance was a Saturday matinée, before which I found myself listening to people in the audience around me. The way they were making comparative lists of which Matthew Bourne shows each one of them had seen – 'Now you still haven't seen his* Nutcracker!, *whereas I've yet to see his* Highland Fling, *but we both loved* Swan Lake, The Car Man *and* Edward Scissorhands, *didn't we?' – reminded me of how people in the 1980s would do checklists of the Alan Ayckbourn plays they'd seen. Are you aware of this phenomenon?*

MB: Yes, I get a lot of that. People like to come to me and list the ones they've seen. It's flattering.

AM: *I remember Ayckbourn entered a dark period in the eighties when we realized each play was taking us somewhere we hadn't expected.*

MB: Could he have done that if he had not got that lead-in with the audience? I felt that way with *Dorian*.

When we first did *Swan Lake* in 1995 and toured it in 1996, we used to have regular walkouts in that show. Particularly men who, when the Swan and the Prince started dancing together, just couldn't watch. We haven't had anything like that with this. Yet *Dorian* is, by many people's standards, far more extreme in its portrayal of male relationships than *Swan Lake*. Lots of male–male duets, one after the other. We did some male–male duets in *The Car Man*, but this goes so much further.

So have things moved on in the last ten, fifteen years? There's been much more gay imagery on TV and films. Or is it just that New Adventures has an audience that will come with us and will accept more of what we do because they trust me? I don't know.

AM: *In an interview in the Sadler's Wells programme, you say: 'For most of us, the knowledge of youth, and the attraction and power that this brings you, is a fleeting thing. Dorian's tragedy is that he holds onto that power for too long. I recognized this in the novel when I first read it at the age of 19. I was at the height of my clubbing days (1979 – when disco was at its zenith) and that feeling you could have, walking into a club, as a fresh-faced youth, was probably the most powerful I have ever felt.' Let me ask you about this autobiographical point. Because, unlike most teenage clubbers who once made an impression with youthful good looks, you have progressed to other and larger kinds of power, notably over theatre audiences. So explain. Why did you feel more powerful then than now?*

MB: That was a form of power, a social power that broke down barriers of class and background. You met all sorts of people. It wasn't relevant where you came from. Maybe it was the first time I felt power?

I don't feel particularly powerful now, though I think I can make things happen if I want to, if I have got a project. I appreciate that now I am in a very privileged and unusual position in that way. For most people it's very difficult to get things off the ground. So yes, this is a form of power.

AM: *Well, if you chose to, you could try combining your current kind of power with the kind you remember having as a nineteen-year-old in clubs. You could present yourself as an intensely glamorous director-choreographer who is dressed up to the nines and lets it be known that you control the fates of all those who want to aspire in your direction. There are such figures. Instead you choose to be – or seem to those of us who know you – unspoilt. Why is that? As a teenager, collecting autographs, you were in love with fame, and you're still absolutely fascinated by theatrical and cinematic success.*

MB: I have had those times in my life where I've been the toast of the town in LA or New York. That's an exciting feeling and an exciting memory. But you don't want it to last more than a few weeks. Then you want to go back to normal. The pressure to look good all the time, to be wearing the right clothes to impress, is too much. I'm quite a casual person, really. I like to be relaxed. And that's why I surround myself with people I know.

Within the fame, you have to find the people who are genuine. Take the LA experience. I did find friends who were absolutely genuine and lasting there – Roddy McDowell was certainly one, he always kept in touch, and he would still be a friend now if he were alive – but most of your friends in those circumstances are, inevitably, of the moment. If fame of that kind goes on too long, you don't know who your friends are. This is partly what *Dorian* is about.

You remember when I met Shirley MacLaine and we spent time together in New York? Just about everyone knew her, when we walked down the street in New York. Everyone said, 'Hello!', 'Hi, Shirley!', 'You're looking great, Shirley!' She never paid for anything. Every bar we went to, every restaurant, when it came to the bill, it was 'That's fine, Miss MacLaine.' Everything was free, basically. Some days she was fine with being so well known. Other days, she'd suddenly say, 'I've gotta go! Get me a cab.' She would start to run and you would have to find her a cab really quickly and get her in it. Off the cab went and you were left there with people staring at you because you were with Shirley MacLaine and she'd gone. She loved celebrity and she hated it.

The power I felt entering clubs aged nineteen: I tried to get that feeling across to some of the people in this show. Being young, maybe they feel that way themselves? Perhaps some people don't? Looking back on that power when you don't have it any more, you realize that you had something that was attractive to people. In later life, you hope that people are attracted to you for different reasons. But the power of beauty and youth is very much a Wilde idea. A treasured thing. I do understand that.

AM: *I would say* Dorian *is your darkest piece. Is that fair?*
MB: Yes, I would say it would have to be. *Play Without Words* is quite close: it deals with dark secrets. What do people find dark these days?

One problem with a modern audience is that nothing's shocking. Some of what Wilde's novel suggested was once very scandalous. I think I was probably searching to make the story at times as uncomfortable as I could, going to places where I hadn't been to before in terms of the darkness of the characters.

AM: *What you don't address, most obviously, from the novel is the Oscar Wilde tone of flamboyant wit and elegance.*
MB: You could say it was quite bizarre to take Wilde out of Wilde, because that tone is what he's most well known for. But I think the novel is his strongest manifesto of the way he felt about ideas. It's full of great quotes, but that aspect is not the most important thing about it. If you tried to do one of the plays without the lines, it would be reduced a lot, whereas a book of themes and ideas that were important to him is something you can interpret. The dandyish nature of the characters was very much of his time. It's still there now but it comes across in other ways. In the celebrity aspect of our production, characters do have that flamboyance, but differently. Today, people are encouraged to be more real, celebrities aren't protected any more, and we see the dark, private side of them more quickly, whereas years ago they were very protected.

AM: *When you first put it on your list, were you thinking of updating it?*
MB: Yes, I thought early on that the idea of a photographer and a subject would be an interesting take on it. But I hadn't really thought much more about it than that. I never had any desire to set it in Wilde's period. I had never done a piece set today, and so that became another of the challenges and attractions. Let's try and look at today, which I suppose is more difficult than looking at the past.

The *Romeo, Romeo* Workshops

ALASTAIR MACAULAY: *In 2007 you announced plans for a week of workshops on male duets which you had named* Romeo, Romeo. *The press briefly turned this into a story that you were preparing a* Romeo, Romeo *production, so that you then had to announce that no, you had no plans for such a work, merely for this week of workshops. Those workshops then happened that summer. Sure enough, when I met you in early 2008 and asked you what was happening with* Romeo, Romeo, *you told me that you were making* Dorian Gray *instead. So was it the* Romeo, Romeo *process that brought* Dorian Gray *back to the forefront of your mind again?*
MATTHEW BOURNE: Yes. Once I'd done that *Romeo* workshop, I thought, 'We've got the basis of something here. Let's make some use of it.'

AM: *The point of the* Romeo, Romeo *workshop was always entirely male–male duets expressing romantic or sexual love?*
MB: Yes, that was the point.

AM: *And how many couples?*
MB: Three couples, six men. James Leece, Drew McOnie, Christopher Marney, Jason Piper, Aaron Sillis, Richard Winsor. Four of them – Drew, Aaron, Chris and Richard – were in the 2008 original *Dorian* production; and now, in 2009, a fifth, Jason, has replaced Aaron as Basil. (James Leece went into the West End production of *Dirty Dancing*. I'm not sure if the workshop pushed him in that direction!)

AM: *What was the process in the* Romeo, Romeo *workshops? What came up?*
MB: It began with questions on my part. Can you do male duets that you are comfortable watching both physically and emotionally? Would it end up being too lopsided with a big guy needing a little guy for lifts? Would the audience be giggling when they were watching it? I felt that

embedded in every dancer is the relationship a man has with a woman as a partner. That works: a man and a woman fit together when they dance as partners, whether they're gay or straight. You understand it and it makes physical sense. Would it make less sense with two men together? What would you have to do to change things? That's what we were exploring.

AM: *In 2005, Joan Acocella wrote in* The New Yorker: *'Thirty or forty years ago, when two men did a pas de deux – in a Jerome Robbins ballet, for example – it more or less had to be combative, or at least very butch, lest the audience get the wrong idea. Today, after gay rights and the AIDS crisis and the whole re-evaluation of gender that accompanied feminism, the male–male pas de deux may be as rich and textured as the old male–female pas de deux. (Witness the male–male duets performed by George Piper Dances, the English group, at the Joyce a year ago.)' She's right about those George Piper duets: I don't remember being very interested by the choreography, but it was quite an achievement to show two men moving in sustained close contact without ever suggesting sexual intimacy. There have been many male–female duets that didn't suggest love or sex; now this has become possible for male–male duets too.*

As for male–male duets that did suggest love or sex, these had always been rare, for the reason that people were afraid of controversy. After Clause 28 (Section 28 of the Local Government Act) legally prohibited the promotion of homosexuality in 1988 in Britain, some male–male scenes were probably against the law. No prosecutions took place, however, and the law was repealed in 2003 (in 2000 in Scotland). Both before that law and after it, I remember a number of instances of male–male partnering, and sustained male–male duets, over the past thirty years in Britain. Frederick Ashton touched on it – briefly, hintingly – in Varii Capricci *(1983) among the supporting men; I certainly remember a duet of very open affection between two men in Richard Alston's 1984* Voices and Light Footsteps *(to Monteverdi) for Ballet Rambert, and in 1988 Lloyd Newson addressed the combination of homosexuality and necrophilia in* Dead Dreams of Monochrome Men *for DV8.*

You began male–male duets and male–male partnering in your early years. There was overt male–male contact in The Infernal Galop *(1989);* Town & Country *(1991) contained one classic;* Swan Lake *contains more than one.*

MB: Certainly. Now I wanted to test it further but concentrate specifically on romantic/sexual relationships.

We tried different ways of approaching it, through stories, and in particular through classic duets that we re-created with two men rather than a man and a woman. We did some film ones. The first one we did was 'Our Love Is Here to Stay' as danced by Gene Kelly and Leslie Caron in *An American in Paris* (1951). That proved quite simple for two men, because man and woman virtually dance the same choreography and there's not much lifting in it. We did 'Dancing in the Dark', which Fred Astaire and Cyd Charisse dance in *The Band Wagon* (1953). That was more difficult to achieve: it has more partnering, it's definitely about a woman and a man, and so it didn't quite work the same way: it was a more dependent relationship, physically and emotionally.

AM: *The partnering: is the problem to do with lifts, or with a man turning a woman, or what?*
MB: The movement is characterized as male and female; the feeling is to do with a man's (Astaire's) way of idolizing a woman. What Fred does so beautifully is that he frames his partner, he shows her off. Cyd Charisse is more flamboyant with her movement and he allows that to happen, he supports her.

Once we did some improvised work, the actual issue of lifting wasn't a problem at all. The small guys were lifting the big guys and it didn't look odd. It worked.

The third duet we did – for fun, really – was our only actual *Romeo and Juliet* material. We chose the 1950s Bolshoi film (choreographed by Leonid Lavrovsky) with Ulanova, the bedroom farewell duet. Richard and Chris did this rather beautifully, and I loved that. I left them to their own devices, and they kept swapping roles, taking turns with the *Romeo and Juliet* material. By alternating some of the lifts, they made it more equal. And that absolutely started to spark off the *Romeo* duet that went into *Dorian Gray*, where Richard plays Dorian and Chris plays the dancer Cyril who is dancing the role of Romeo at Covent Garden.

On the second day, we worked from a different perspective. We took male–female film scenes. The dancers watched the scene, they listened to the dialogue, and then they interpreted the scene without the dialogue but with music. That was the first task. The next task was to take the movement of the scene and take it further into dance movement, to abstract it a little bit further. That was really interesting in terms of relationships because I didn't show the others which scenes each couple was working with. Then the others had to watch it and say who was playing the man and who was playing the woman.

We did the opening scene from Hitchcock's *Psycho* (1960), where Janet Leigh and John Gavin are discovered, post-coital, in a seedy hotel room at lunchtime. We did a sort of bedroom scene from the Visconti film *Ossessione* (1943). And – I can't believe I got them to do this! – we did the famous sex scene for Julie Christie and Donald Sutherland in Nicholas Roeg's *Don't Look Now* (1973). They did it really well, they took it terribly seriously.

AM: *When they were doing these scenes, was it an issue if they are straight or gay?*
MB: We discussed this, because there were three straight guys and three gay guys in the group. I was more concerned in the first place for the straight guys, but actually it was slightly more embarrassing, initially, for the gay guys. All six had been told what the workshop was about; they had agreed to go there; and that's why they were always one step ahead of me, adding bits of acting. The straight guys were the most confident because they knew what they were doing, it wasn't going to worry them particularly. They weren't going to get worked up through doing it, they were just doing it as an acting task. But whereas gay guys are used to dancing with women, they find that they may reveal different sides of themselves when they're dancing with members of their own sex. Straight men learn that the physical intimacy of dancing with a woman is often close to sexual intimacy with her, but for gay men it's possible that only when they are dancing with a man – especially if there is the possibility of feeling some sexual attraction for that man – do they discover how to acknowledge or use that intimacy. Eventually, whether you're straight or gay, whether you fancy your partner or not, doesn't come into it. I changed the couplings at every task, I changed around as many combinations as I could.

As the week progressed, we went into a lot of improvised tasks about men lifting each other. One lifts, the other lifts: we tried to create movement out of that. Throughout the week, we built up towards a big duet for each couple that I'd put together. I was picking them with an eye to casting by now. So that's why I put Aaron and Richard together, for example. I might not have been clear yet that I would do *Dorian*, but I knew what chemistries I wanted to showcase; and Aaron and Richard did become Basil and Dorian the next year for me. The basis of some of the movement in those duets has gone into the show.

The duets were about relationship ideas. They all had a beginning, middle and end. Very simple, really. Usually, what these men liked was the idea of a relationship with a slightly forbidden feeling to it, where they were drawn to each other despite other circumstances. The straight guys particularly identified with that because that's how they could get into being with a man, because it was something a bit secretive but they had to do it.

We developed stories that came out of personal experience. One evening, I got them all to talk about their first sexual experiences and their ideas about relationships, trying to get them all to feel we were all talking about the same thing, gay guys and straight guys. I always posed the questions: not 'How is it different for a straight guy?' but straightforward things like 'Tell us about your first time', never drawing attention to the differences but to just state things honestly.

AM: *How much were these workshop duets done in silence or to music?*
MB: I always use music. With the dances from films, we used that music. For the acting scenes from films, I found music that I thought worked. I don't like working in silence, I think it adds too much tension for the dancers, it almost makes them more comfortable doing it, and, in a way, it can get too real. But if you put on music, they feel the inner scene. I also keep the lights low. And we worked evenings. I wanted people to feel comfortable. And I was the only other person ever allowed in the room. They all knew that. 'No one else is going to come in and watch this, it's just me.' At the end of the week, we did a showing for a few people, because Sadler's Wells had given us the money to develop the project in the first place.

What the dancers gain from a workshop exploration is to get to know each other better. They become able to create better movement ideas together. To begin with, they may be as uncomfortable as any two people you could put together. But the workshop makes everybody start to talk and to explore. Though I didn't make a *Romeo and Romeo*, it all makes sense now. I see where I was heading all along.

AM: *At what point did you start to choreograph?*
MB: We had limited time and we were doing these tasks each day. I told them we were working towards a long duet for each couple and that I

would decide halfway through the week who was going to work with who. So by the time we got to the Thursday and Friday, we were well into work on each duet. And on the last day at least, the day before the showing, I worked with each couple separately for a couple of hours, restructured each duet, developing something to show. I didn't do it as strongly as I would do for a performance; I let some things pass that I probably wouldn't put in a finished work. But I did help them to structure each duet, to ask the right questions about what's involved at each moment, and to change some of the moves.

AM: *So, as you found the workshops leading to* Dorian Gray *in your mind, you realized that that show would be your most sustained study of male–male duets to date.*
MB: Yes, and that's why I probably won't stage any *Romeo and Romeo*. I feel I've explored that. There's plenty more to do with male–male partnering, of course, for me and for other choreographers.

Alan Vincent saw the show in July 2009 and was taken aback by the amount of male duets. Though he was my original Car Man and though he's danced the Swan for me, he was quite surprised by the gay nature of this story; he wasn't expecting it. If I read him correctly, he was a little put off by it. In advance, I thought that might be an issue for anyone watching it; but most people seem less taken aback than he was. Still, there are a lot of male couplings in it. One after the other!

There would have been even more if we hadn't changed the sex of Lord Henry. I think that really helps to have a woman in that role. Otherwise it would be just one long male duet.

AM: *Why did you decide to add women?*
MB: I realized that the climate on stage would seem misogynistic without women. So in particular I turned Lord Henry into Lady H.

But you know what? I remember now that at one point it was going to be all-male: something I've never actually done (contrary to popular belief!) and I thought would be interesting. I liked the idea of men playing women in a way that was serious. I remember now that that Lord Henry was going to be for Adam Cooper at one point. He nearly did the workshop in 2007, wanted to do it, but then other things came about. And he was committed to doing a piece with us the following year. So while the *Romeo* workshops prompted me to start work on *Dorian*, I began to think of Adam as Lord Henry. Adam wanted to do something and this was the piece that I was developing. I was thinking of the story in a different way then. Lord Henry was going to be a politician of some sort. But – though I certainly hope to work with Adam again one day, and though I really want to make a very dark role for him – I am actually really glad *Dorian* didn't work out that way. It would have been too one-track. I remember thinking, 'Will an all-male version come off? Will it completely work or will it be grotesque?' Once I had the idea of the sex changes within the cast, and turning Lord Henry into Lady H., that made it gel for me much more.

Misogyny was not really the reason for my other 'sex change'. In the novel, Dorian has an affair with the actress Sybil Vane, whom he eventually finds tiresome and who dies because of his rejection. It certainly feels like a false note in the novel for Dorian to fall in love with an actress. Everything prior to that leads you to believe that we have a three-way triangle with Basil, Lord Henry and Dorian. And, since I was concentrating on male–male duets, it seemed better all round to turn Sybil into Cyril.

Idea – 2

ALASTAIR MACAULAY: *One of the results of this male–male* Dorian Gray *was the Doppelgänger, whom you give us instead of the portrait in Wilde's title. When did this idea arrive?*
MATTHEW BOURNE: I was trying to find a visual – and physical – idea to represent the portrait, or the changing personality, or the Jekyll-and-Hyde nature of Dorian's life. I looked on a word search for 'doubles' and the word 'doppelgänger' came up. I thought 'doppelgänger' meant just a dead ringer until then I looked up all these myths about doppelgängers: the idea of your death following you around, your doppelgänger always walking behind you, and the point you turn round and make contact with him or her is the moment of your death, the moment when you see yourself: which we do at the end of the piece.

When I read the novel again, there was an aspect that I thought we were missing from the story. Sybil Vane's brother James goes to sea as a sailor and comes back long after his sister has committed suicide because of Dorian. James vows to search for her killer and kill him. He's always one step away from Dorian through the last few chapters of the novel; he tries to find him, and he just misses him. There's a point where he does get to him and is about to kill him, but Dorian says, 'Look at

149 Jared Hageman (DG 'The Doppelgänger') and Richard Winsor (Dorian) in rehearsal, Act Two. This scene is just before Dorian's suicide.

my face, I couldn't possibly be that person because I'm too young.' But James is not convinced and ends up chasing Dorian all around London and to the country. He's always hiding somewhere, he's always on the edge, and it makes you feel as though Dorian's death is catching up with him. Through the second half of the novel, it's a very strong theme, one I wanted to get in there.

So the Doppelgänger came through a desire to find a visual idea for the audience for the approach of death. But I was also addressing the problem of Dorian remaining beautiful. If he stays that way, how do we show what's going on inside of him? So in a way the Doppelgänger replaces him and becomes Dorian. He, the Doppelgänger, remains quite passive and pure. While Dorian shows all the emotion of how he's feeling and disintegrates in front of your eyes and becomes a crumpled figure by the end of it, the Doppelgänger is as he was. I thought that could be very helpful and would give me physical ideas.

AM: *It connects to a lot of things in your work. When you were originally talking about* The Nutcracker, *you had this idea that Clara would get abused by Dr Dross and, at the moment of abuse, she would take off out of herself into a purer world. You told me that this idea, though you never realized it in* Nutcracker!, *came out of first-person accounts of child abuse you had heard: the mind detaches itself from the present trauma and travels elsewhere. I thought of that as soon as I saw the Doppelgänger here. In* Highland Fling, *you could say that Effie and the Sylph are the opposite doubles of the same woman in James's life; in your* Swan Lake, *the Swan and the Stranger are two contrasting aspects of one figure.* Play Without Words *is full of doubles and triples.*

MB: Yes, two sides, two natures. It comes out of the search for visual imagery that will work without words.

AM: *It also connects to ideas in two best-selling series of modern fiction. In* The Amber Spyglass (2000), *the third novel of Philip Pullman's* His Dark Materials *trilogy, the heroine Lyra, passing through the world of the dead, does indeed see her own death, a doppelgänger just as you describe. And in* Harry Potter and the Half-Blood Prince (2005, *made into a film in 2009), J. K. Rowling develops the idea of a horcrux, whereby the wizard Voldemort splits his soul so as to avoid death; a particular point is made, as in your* Dorian, *that murder, as 'the supreme act of evil', rips the soul apart. Voldemort uses that soul-splitting for his own ends; your Dorian finds himself its victim.*

MB: I was also thinking of the Edgar Allan Poe story 'William Wilson', and the movie *The Double Life of Véronique* (Krzysztof Kieslowski, 1991). But once you start researching doppelgängers, you find more and more of them: it's a vast area of myth and legend that varies from country to country.

AM: *Do you think now that you were looking also for the idea of doubles when you took up* Romeo and Romeo *as a subject? Two images of the same thing?*

MB: Yes, maybe! We called the Doppelgänger 'DG': which stands for both Doppelgänger and Dorian Gray. And, oddly, a lot of the underwear was Dolce & Gabbana too. So it all worked for me in a roundabout way!

Until I thought of the Doppelgänger, the hardest aspect of the story was the issue: How do you show the change in Dorian physically without presenting a lot of distortion that would make him not beautiful? If he remains outwardly the same, how do we show his journey physically?

Then, when we first thought of the Doppelgänger, it was like an animal that follows him around, the evil grotesque version of him. But that made me realize the Doppelgänger would be the better role.

So I said to Richard, 'You should become that person, and get more distressed. Let the Doppelgänger be the passive, intense one. You should be allowed to show all the emotions of someone disintegrating before our eyes.' That led us to go further with the character and the movement.

The Doppelgänger's one of those things you're glad you found, a device that makes the whole piece more interesting. In a piece with quite a straightforward story, that added kind of interest is what you're searching for. Imagine *Play Without Words* without the triple and the double: the story might still be remarkable, but as a piece of theatre it wouldn't have been nearly so interesting without that very strong concept. I think this is the same. Some people have said, there's not a Doppelgänger in *The Portrait of Dorian Gray*. But the Doppelgänger's not a character, it's part of Dorian.

It only appears when he becomes evil. His inside changes, his personality changes, after he lets Cyril die. He allows Cyril to die in front of him; he enjoys the power. So that's when he starts to take on a different persona. Up to that point, he's just ridden his success; but now he wants to start getting rid of people that get in his way.

I don't think Dorian is an innocent at all, even at the beginning. He completely has a sense of what he's doing, and of his power. He knows how to get on. He's not at that party at the beginning just to be a waiter. He knows it's the right party to get noticed.

AM: *How do you feel Dorian Gray grows in the novel?*
MB: It's sketchy. He meets Basil at a party in the same sort of way. They're introduced by a benefactress character. He's recently out of education of some sort. He doesn't really have a job; he's going nowhere. It's the portrait that is, for him, the revelation of the power of the attraction he has for other people. He realizes it when he sees it and doesn't want to lose it.

That's where photography is quite useful in our adaptation. A photograph is a repeated image that you see everywhere. And you can take more photos and have more pictures. As with a lot of celebrities, the moment Dorian doesn't want to be photographed, this need to escape the camera becomes more of an obsession. He doesn't want to be captured, he wants to be remembered as he was, not as he is now. He feels that what's inside him is starting to show on the outside.

AM: *That connects to a feeling he has in the novel.*

MB: Yes, Basil wants to paint his portrait again. He wants Dorian to sit for him again and he wants to exhibit the portrait. That's why Dorian kills him. Basil comes and wants to see the portrait again, but it's hidden in the attic. Basil wants to exhibit it in Paris, but by this point in the novel it's changed – as far as Dorian thinks, anyway. (You can imagine that the actual portrait may not have changed.) He keeps it in his attic; and every time he goes up to see it, it's got worse, more evil-looking, so he thinks. The novel only passes through eighteen years, so there's no need to assume – as some people do – that the portrait shows an unrecognizably aged version of him. I think all the film versions take that too far. You could read it that Dorian is transferring ideas of character onto the portrait, the way people do sometimes when they look at a portrait. Is it smiling? Is it not? Someone else looking at the same portrait may see a different expression.

AM: *You imply in Act Two that Dorian infects or kills people. Death surrounds him. Does he come to want his own death?*

MB: Life starts to become less important. The fact that he can do away with people becomes part of normality for him. We know that he allows

150 'Basil Shoots Dorian', Act One. Aaron Sillis (Basil) and Richard Winsor (Dorian). There is a clear visual line with the famous poster of David Hemmings and Veruschka in Michelangelo Antonioni's film *Blow-Up* (1966).

(a)

(b)

151 (a) Photo shoot for 'Immortal' ad campaign, Act One. Richard Winsor
(Dorian). The image was actually taken by Hugo Glendinning.
(b) Jason Piper (Basil) before the 'Immortal' image taken by Basil, Act One.
In performance, 2009.

Cyril to die and we see him kill Basil. It's not too much to imagine that he kills others.

AM: *Is there any intimation of that killer instinct in him before the moment when he decides not to dial the telephone number to call aid for the dying Cyril?*
MB: That's the beginning. It's in the novel as well: he sees a way out. In the novel it's different because he doesn't allow her to die in his presence; he's just extremely cruel to her and, as soon as he leaves, she drinks poison. To himself, he justifies it by deciding he's better off without her and it's a good thing that this has happened. That's the turning point when he changes as a person: he sees a way out of this messy situation.

At the end of Act One, I try to build up a messiness for him. It's all been great, but suddenly he's got Lady H. being stroppy with him. He has to drive her around and be her escort. And he's got Basil; he needs to maintain that relationship; they're supposedly together. There are all these hangers-on in his apartment, all consuming his drinks, his drugs, his whatever. And then there's Cyril, who is one thing too many. The possibility of getting rid of him presents itself; and Dorian sees an easy way out. Everyone will assume Cyril overdosed.

AM: *Dorian's one great duet with Cyril occurs only in his head. Is that the point, that sex and love are better in fantasy?*
MB: For him, yes. That becomes more exciting. Certainly, with Cyril, fantasy was more exciting than reality, as it is in the novel with the actress, Sybil.

AM: *He doesn't have any satisfactory sex with Cyril?*
MB: Not in reality, no. Dorian doesn't have any satisfactory sex at all after that. He has to keep searching for fresh meat because sex doesn't bring him any joy.

Scenario

ALASTAIR MACAULAY: *Have you always thought about the larger issues that shape a story?*
MATTHEW BOURNE: I think so, but now I'm more and more fascinated by that. I am very interested by what works for an audience. Because we are working in a medium of non-verbal story-telling, I have to think about methods of story-telling, the different kinds of stories, and the various purposes of stories, more than if I was, say, doing a play. But

I have learnt, from the directors I've worked with, the very basics of theatre and story-telling. Trevor (Nunn), for example, is very specific about text; he wants to make sure that every word is heard. For me, that was really interesting; he would always pick people up on that. It gave a terrific sense of detail, as he made sure that every moment said what he wanted it to say, and as he kept asking how could we do that better? Very pedantic, sometimes, but also delving deeper. I think this care is part of a director's responsibility to the audience: wanting to make sure that everyone understands.

AM: *You drafted a formal scenario?*
MB: I wrote the usual scenario[1] and gave it to everyone. There's a lot of setting up of the story that I do quite enjoy. Up until the interval, there's a lot of setting up of characters. I like the slow build-up of a relationship, the very long duet between Basil and Dorian, the photo-shoot that turns into the sex and everything else that follows. You can't just jump into that. It needs the tension and some build-up. Some aspects of it were very clear. I knew we had to create what we call 'Basil's world': a world where people are judged by how they look, a world of narcissists. You don't get into the real drama until the last part of the first half. I think it's the reason why people don't decide until the end whether they know if they like the piece completely or not.

AM: *Do you pace the scenario so as to give Dorian a break at any point?*
MB: Unfortunately not. He doesn't get much of a rest!

AM: *Are there other ways – placing and pacing the duets – you structured the scenario?*
MB: Yes, I can see where the big duets are going to come along. We call the big duets for Basil and Dorian 'Basil shoots Dorian' (one kind of 'shooting') and 'Dorian shoots Basil' (another kind).

AM: *You changed Sybil to Cyril; and you made Cyril not an actor but a ballet dancer.*
MB: Dorian falls in love with Sybil, when she is speaking the words of Shakespeare, playing Juliet, and thinks she's a wonderful artist, but it's the poetry of the words. She's a wonderful actress, but when he actually meets her and gets to know her, he finds her dull: shallow and stupid, as a person. That's why he says to her, 'Without art you are nothing.' She, however, actually is in love with him. Wilde doesn't portray her as

[1] See Appendix A.

a weak character, yet she is weak: she kills herself when he deserts her. As a character, she hasn't got the strength of several other characters in the novel; she's there as a device in many ways.

For me, the parallels between Sybil and Cyril were perfect. This is one of my favourite things in the show. There's the idea of the beautiful ballet boy on stage playing Romeo with whom everyone falls in love; and there's the reality of the working dancer, for whom it's all about stretching, jockstraps, and the mirror.

AM: *The main difference between Sybil and Cyril, other than gender, is that the dancer Cyril is as much a narcissist as Dorian. Was that intentional?*
MB: It's something that came about. It's a truth, but it isn't the main aspect of the story, which is simply that Cyril isn't who he appears to be on stage. Dorian only loves him through the poetry of his movement rather than the poetry of words. Dorian falls in love with him as an image, and from that he learns about the danger of the projected image rather than the reality.

AM: *Dorian and Cyril are narcissists, but there is no shared narcissism about their relationship. When they are making love, they don't both look in the mirror as if to say, 'Doesn't this look good!' That, by contrast, does happen when Dorian has his first bedroom duet with Lady H.*
MB: In another context, I'd go further into the Cyril story and have a relationship that changes more; you could do a whole act on that. But it comes at a point in the drama where we've got to keep moving quickly and reach his death at the end of the act, since that's the turning point for Dorian. What I've had to gloss over is when they properly meet and how their relationship develops. Instead, we show it in jump cuts once they are together.

AM: *In terms of structure, what led you to decide that the death of Cyril should be the first-half closer?*
MB: Well, I've become obsessed in recent years with story-telling, in an academic way. I read both Robert McKee's book *Story* (2000) and Christopher Booker's book *The Seven Basic Plots: Why We Tell Stories* (2005). *Dorian Gray* fitted the first example of the classic stages of tragedy, which I built my scenario around. And I knew that any interval needs to come at a turning point where the audience asks what will happen next. You must give them a reason to come back after the interval.

So Cyril's death and the first appearance of the Doppelgänger seemed the perfect point for an interval. It's not an upbeat moment, however. For me, that was a little difficult at first, because I do like the audience to feel 'up'. I'm used to it now, but to begin with, in performance, it felt like a downer. The applause at the end of the act was a little uncertain. But I've realized now, through talking to people, that they're more involved than I had understood.

Certain things in the scenario I do feel a need for. One is to begin Act Two with a certain amount of humour: always. You start with action and humour to get people relaxed again, then you get back into the story in a deeper way, pare it down and give less dance, more imagery, more dramatic scenes.

I wasn't really aiming for any laughs in *Dorian*, yet instinctively I found myself providing enough to relax people. Everyone loves the *Jonathan Ross Show* sequence with the musicians, 4 Poofs and a Piano. It's a big recognition moment for the British audience: it shows the level of Dorian's celebrity. It makes complete sense: where else would celebrities be but on *The Jonathan Ross Show*? (Of course, there wasn't much recognition factor here when we showed *Dorian* in Moscow!)

AM: *Is there a duet in the piece that isn't image-obsessed?*
MB: I think not. The second duet with Basil is about Dorian's not wanting to get his picture taken, but it still relates to image. He doesn't want to be seen as he is now.

AM: *Take me through that change in Dorian.*
MB: He doesn't want the image of him tainted. He doesn't mind the original images still being there in the studio. But he seems to be fearful of new ones.

AM: *He thinks they will reveal his darker self?*
MB: Some part of him thinks that it shows now, that there's something bad inside that must be apparent outside, and he's fearful of that. He's also fearful of the competition. Those are the two things he's most concerned with. It's a vacuous life; he's got nothing to fall back on. Relationships become unimportant to him; he has too many of them. Too much has come his way.

AM: *From writing the scenario, you established that you needed a cast of eleven, and then you could prepare for casting and rehearsal?*

MB: We did have a guy in a dress in the white club scene in the 2008 production, but I've cut that this year; there didn't seem to be any point to it. Then I thought, 'A lot of the main characters in it are men, apart from Lady H., so I need to be able to cover those parts as well.' So, with a very small cast, that's how it became very male-heavy – with just three women and eight men.

AM: *Your interpretation of Dorian is as an essentially gay character who knows how to be hetero when it suits him?*
MB: I think so: basically gay, yes. As in the novel, Dorian loses interest in Basil quite quickly. Basil is in love with him, but after a while, Dorian just tolerates him.

I think he sees Lady H. as a mothering figure in some ways. She's older and she's the one he goes to in the second half when he's not happy, twice. He goes the first time when things aren't going his way; he might get some comfort from her. Then at the end, when he's murdered Basil, he runs to her; he's saying, 'I've just killed someone.' He runs to her for comfort.

AM: *We've mentioned some of the ambiguities. But do you yourself have an absolutely specific interpretation of every scene?*
MB: Yes. In my head, I know exactly where we are all the time.

AM: *Obviously, the Doppelgänger introduces all kinds of ambiguities. But you know for yourself what he means at each moment?*
MB: Yes, I do.

Preparation

ALASTAIR MACAULAY: *After the* Romeo *workshop, what happened next?*
MATTHEW BOURNE: By the end of it, I had decided that I was going to do *Dorian Gray*. I already had Richard Winsor in mind for Dorian; and soon after that I offered Aaron Sillis the part of Basil. And I got them on board too, doing their own research, helping me, getting involved, reading around the subject. I started feeding ideas out to them to start bringing material back. I also did some workshops with Richard on his own at my place in Brighton and worked on solos and on ideas of character. And we watched a lot of films together.

AM: *Can you remember what films you drew upon?*
MB: One of the most important films was *American Psycho* (2000) and also Brett Easton Ellis's novel with that name (1991). That gave us a

very similar kind of character. At the end of the novel, you're not quite sure whether he really does these things or whether it's a fantasy of his. That was very helpful to us. And it had that whole syndrome of the opposition between private and public life too; and the charming person who's very obsessed with his appearance.

We do give a suggestion that Dorian might become a serial killer, but we don't demand the audience to take that literally. There are bodies at the end, but they might not be there: they might be memories of people whose lives he's wrecked.

There's a scene where Dorian goes from partner to partner and they react badly to him physically when he picks them up. Our thought there was that he's having a lot of sex and infecting people, but again we don't insist on that interpretation. There are some things in the novel where Wilde mentions that Dorian leaves a trail of destruction behind him, ruined lives and suicides. When he walks into a room, people leave. We were trying to bring that out a little.

Antonioni's *Blow-Up* (1966) we looked at: virtually the only serious film on photography that's worth looking at. Some of the photo-shoots in that were very useful, showing the ways that photographers are provocative, so as to get feelings out of the models. We used the idea that the photographer throws things at them and makes them feel uncomfortable to get the right shot.

The best screen version of *The Portrait of Dorian Gray* is the 1976 TV version with John Gielgud as Lord Henry, Peter Firth as Dorian and Jeremy Brett as Basil. It's closest to the novel, whereas the film versions are nowhere near it with invented characters and stuff. And Gielgud's loving every second of it, you can tell!

Other novels I looked at were Brett Easton Ellis's *Glamorama* (1998), which is a contemporary version of the *Dr Jekyll and Mr Hyde* story, and Will Self's *Dorian* (2002), which updates it to the AIDS era in the 1980s, very explicitly. The idea of infection was useful to us. We didn't play on it too much, but I gave it to Richard and some other members of the company to read, to make them see the story in a contemporary way and how explicit it was, and show how far we could go. Just reading the Oscar Wilde, they're not necessarily going to think that way.

The death of Heath Ledger (January 2008, just months before we opened) went into this quite a lot, in terms of what celebrity can do to a person. He's not Dorian Gray. He was a beautiful young man but he was talented. The thing about Dorian, at least in our version, is that, as with some people who become famous just for the way they look, he finds it starts to eat him away inside after a while. You don't have your talent to hold on to, and you fear losing the beauty that made you famous: that's a very modern phenomenon. But for Heath Ledger, coming from Perth, Australia, becoming a famous person gave him access to all sorts of things. People wanted to help him and be his friend, and ended up giving him lots of stuff that eventually killed him, probably trying to be helpful. The image of the beautiful but lonely man in an apartment in the middle of New York, dying, was my thought for the end of the show: the body in the bed. And Richard Winsor does look a bit like him.

The epilogue sequence in which Lady H. arrives to find Dorian's corpse was inspired by accounts of Heath Ledger's death. (Marilyn Monroe's, too.) Who was the first person at Ledger's apartment? What did they do to him? Did they arrange him? There were a lot of phone calls. There's always a long delay with the death of anyone famous, and there's always speculation about what may have happened in those hours, and about whether an ambulance should have been called. Lady H. is the first person to arrive at Dorian's apartment and her reaction is to clean him up and wipe away the blood. That may seem touching initially – but then she brings in the photographers. She's still getting some mileage out of him even in death. That's the world we live in, where those pictures of the dead are prized. There's something so horribly sad about that – and yet you see him in the picture and he looks peaceful.

AM: *Do you look at other dances that might be connected?*
MB: Sometimes I do – we did with *Romeo, Romeo* – but not with this one in particular. However, I should mention Rudolf Nureyev here. There were quite a lot of documentaries about him around in 2007 because of Julie Kavanagh's *Nureyev* biography that year. She writes about him in the back-room clubs in New York. That was helpful to Richard: he liked the way Nureyev was in those early film clips of people trying to interview him. Nureyev would gaze at the interviewers and photographers: so superior. And the 'daisy chain' moment which we've put in the show: as I've told Julie, that's from her book.

AM: *Explain the 'daisy chain' moment.*
MB: It's one man coupling behind the other. Dorian is thinking about all these people he's encountered, he arrives at a club which is a back-room

152 Back Room, Club scene, Act Two, rehearsal. Richard Winsor (Dorian), Ashley Bain, Chloe Wilkinson, Christopher Marney, Jared Hageman, Joe Colasanti, Emily-Jane Boyle, in rehearsal. Illustrating Dorian's search for satisfaction with anonymous back-room sex, this is the male daisy-chain taken from reports of Rudolf Nureyev's later years.

orgy situation, and everyone's into him. There's a moment where he walks across, they all look at him, and he invites them in. Nureyev's need for sex with men in clubs was absolutely in my mind here: particularly the fact that he was so famous, so glamorous, and yet never seemed to find contentment in sex or love.

AM: *Once you had made the decision to stage* Dorian, *did you call in Terry Davies and Lez Brotherston straight away?*
MB: Yes. I explained to Lez what the take was going to be – the photography angle – and I told him I wanted a design that gave a smooth transition between scenes, because I was trying to do something that had quite a dreamlike quality to it – a dream that turns into a nightmare.

And Lez quickly came up with the basic set idea. As usual with him, he brilliantly captured something about the piece, which is that it can all be based around a photographer's studio and that can become many things. He suggested using a revolve, to give us the possibility of more than one type of world. So we have the white side which is the studio and then this darker world on the other side, which is more industrial. Perfect for the duality theme. Then we built up what we might have in

153 Lez Brotherston in *Dorian Gray* rehearsals.

the studio, and made it a very literal room with plugs, sockets, lamps and a CD player. And we decided to put a piano in there: we wanted music to be available, because often photographers use music to get their models in the required mood for shoots. But the fluidity of the scenes wasn't going to make it a piece of literal story-telling; we always wanted a much more surreal approach to telling the story.

The result in the theatre has been that, as people get more involved in watching, they get to know the style we've set up here, and they quickly guess where we are at any given point. I'm often thinking, 'We're on the street now, we're in this room now, we're in this club – he's just walked in.' I don't know if the audience gets every single aspect, and that's fine: it's deliberately on the surreal side.

As usual with Lez, the set takes you halfway there. From then on, the questions are: What places do we need to go to in this piece? How do we utilize what we have to create those places? What do we need to add? So Lez's set has the option to hang things on it. We had couches. And there's a bed we use quite a lot.

AM: *And at what point did you bring in Terry Davies?*
MB: Oh, very soon. Terry's an associate of the company now. He's done four shows with us – *The Car Man, Play Without Words, Edward*

596

154 *Dorian Gray*, model box by Lez Brotherston.

Scissorhands and now this. I would go to him to talk about the musical aspect of any show, even if he wasn't composing it.

I went to him and said, 'I'm doing *Dorian Gray*, I'm thinking of setting it in the present, but I don't know which way to go with it yet. Is there any particular composer that you think might work?' I was listening to all sorts of things initially. I think a contemporary piece doesn't always necessarily need contemporary music, so I was listening to some Bach; I loved the jazz versions of Bach. I thought it would be a nice mood for this, but somehow it wasn't gelling at all. I was nervous of new music (I don't know why); I thought it would be helpful to have something more familiar with this story.

One of the things that's so good about Terry is he will happily arrange another composer's music or style. He doesn't need to compose every aspect of the score from scratch or impose his own musical concept on a show. That's why he's a great person to talk to in general about what to do. In the end we thought, 'We'd better find some contemporary music we like and see if that leads anywhere.' So various ideas came into play then, musically.

I have confidence in Terry because of something he said before, about *Play Without Words*. When I said, 'I think it should be a jazz score', he said, 'I've never written jazz before.' My immediate thought was 'Oh God, I've picked the wrong person!', but he did such a great job on that. So from then on I knew he was someone who can embrace

597

different musical styles and listen. And he does his research. I know he won't write something that's the same all the way through, that people will get sick of. He serves the scene.

Actually, I know now why I was nervous of new music. I'll be fifty in 2010. I'd decided to set *Dorian* in the modern world, but at my age I had a natural fear, asking myself: 'Do I know about today? Am I the right person to comment on today?' But I think I can now answer, 'Yes', because I do know this world. I am surrounded by young people, so I get a lot from them. I know what they're into and what they're interested in. Since I wanted to avoid creating a middle-aged view of today, I listened to the members of the company and sometimes checked with them that we were going along the right lines. I was very nervous about where we would go with the music and sometimes I played some of the score to the trendier members of the cast and asked, 'What do you think of this?' And they were like: 'Mmm, cool!' and I thought, 'That's OK, then!'

I asked Aaron, for example, 'Make up a tape of music you like at the moment – the latest sounds that you think would be good for this piece. Say we're going to have a club scene in this. What do you think you would hear in this club?' As a result, certain bands came up, that sounded contemporary and had a theatricality to them and a style of music that I hadn't heard on stage before. So our opening sequence, that we call 'Basil's World', has a 'systems music' repetitious style to it. That grew out of listening to current music and finding the bits we liked. That was the contemporary side of it, but then there were other aspects to it too. I would always listen to their suggestions; I wanted it to feel right.

Once we started to get into it, it was easier than I had thought it would be. Lez Brotherston helped a lot. So much of the contemporary period feeling came from his designs: the clothes, the references on the set, the Damien Hirst references that were in the design, the skull and the dot picture above Lady H.'s bed.

Terry presented me with a piece of music and said, 'I've written this. See what you think.' That's often the way with us. Sometimes he'll write a whole piece that comes from an idea of his, or sometimes he'll write something from a guide track where I've said, 'I like the feel of this.' In this case, the piece was called 'The Portrait'. It introduces a vocal sound. We used it for a section called 'Camera Obsession'. After Dorian first gets together with Basil, he comes back into the studio, picks up a camera, and becomes obsessed with his own image in the lens, loving himself. That's when the idea of his narcissism and his two-sided nature starts to creep in. Terry thought it would be good to use a male voice in the music, and we use the Doppelgänger's voice. (By that, I mean Terry's score uses the singing voice of Jared Hageman, our first-cast Doppelgänger.) This is also the piece we use to conclude the show, leading to Dorian's death.

The Lady H. music was very surprising in every respect, the rhythmic stuff. I really liked the idea of staging scenes to a strong rhythm. But the music that's played in her home, when Dorian first meets all the suited and long-dressed high-society people who are her friends, is for piano, mandolin and guitar: a weird selection of instruments. I don't know where that came from, but I like the sound very much.

AM: *There's a scene in Act Two when the drama gets psychologically darker, with suggestions of club back-room sex and infection or multiple murder: it's staged, amazingly, to a suddenly soft and gentle piece of rock music for piano and guitar, which are joined halfway through by the vibraphone, and towards the end by a very gentle bass guitar.*

MB: Well, that scene follows another in the white club, where people are dressed in white with tattoos – which is a more straightforward club scene, where Dorian sees the Doppelgänger again and he is now the young guy in the club that everyone's looking at. But then I wanted to contrast that white club with this dark club, this back-room scene, the sex club. Like the opium den in the novel, it's low life. I said to Terry, 'Since we've used clubby kind of music for the white club, why don't we do the opposite? Do something really beautiful, so that it takes the edge off the sex.' This gives it a quality of going into his mind, so that it becomes touching. You need a moment of peace at that point to go into his character a bit, so that it's not all action. I love that moment. In my scenario, I described Dorian as wandering through 'a "dreamlike" orgy of entangled bodies, eventually allowing himself to become part of it . . . He escapes into the darkness and gives himself up to the gratification of the unknown figures who seem to devour him.' So this darkness is an escape for him. There's almost a possibility that these strangers want to eat him up, tear him to pieces. Just before it, there's a section where he's chasing people and the Doppelgänger's following him: that feels dangerous. Sirens are going off. Then he grabs one of the boys – and suddenly we go into this beautiful musical climate, almost underwater in feeling.

Basil comes to the club to look for Dorian; he's followed him there. He follows Dorian from the club, but when he approaches him he realizes he has got the wrong man: it is the Doppelgänger he has stalked.

AM: *The split-personality theme goes deeper than just Dorian and his Doppelgänger?*

MB: Yes, because there's a public/private aspect to all the personalities and characters. There's a superficial side and a truthful side, with everyone.

AM: *Is Basil a split personality?*

MB: I always feel he should be the most truthful character. He doesn't change much. He's an artist. He may at times be moody, troubled and arrogant, but he's an artist. I would say he's the least superficial person.

Rehearsals

ALASTAIR MACAULAY: *Did you know all of the eleven dancers?*

MATTHEW BOURNE: I had worked with all of them apart from Jared Hageman and Joe Walkling. Jared, our Doppelgänger, had a quality that really drew me in: really interesting. And Joe struck me as unique too, with an amazing style all of his own.

155 Act One in rehearsal: the 'Science of Beauty' scene, where Lady H. helps to create the iconic 'Dorian' image. Christopher Marney (a beauty scientist), Michela Meazza (Lady H.), Richard Winsor (Dorian), and Ashley Bain (another beauty scientist).

156 Etta Murfitt (Associate Director) and Matthew Bourne in
Dorian Gray rehearsals, 2008.

AM: *Tell me about a Matthew Bourne audition.*
MB: We tend to get lots of CVs sent to us with audition requests. So we
do big annual general auditions, to give people a chance to be seen. We'll
tell them what we've got coming up this year, and what we're looking
for. If there's nothing for them this year, we can bear them in mind too
for later.

AM: *So when you auditioned him, it wasn't necessarily with Dorian
Gray in mind?*
MB: The auditions were for a tour of *Edward Scissorhands* and *Dorian
Gray*. But I was particularly trying to find people for *Dorian*. They
needed to be people that potentially could be on the cover of a magazine.
They had to be special-looking because they had to play models: very
slim, with bodies that could belong to models. But I mostly hand-picked
from the dancers I already knew, both for their look and their ability to
create.

AM: *When did you start rehearsals?*
MB: July 2008. We had five weeks, which for me is not nearly enough
for a new piece, especially a new scenario to new music. But I had done
the workshop and I had done a further two weeks with Richard prior to
rehearsal, which took things a stage further. Even if you've already got

material made, most people have got to embrace it. That takes time. The process is always scary: skin of the teeth.

And on the Sunday after the end of the first week of rehearsals I found out that my oldest friend, Simon Carter, had died. I miss him still, of course; he'll always be a part of my life. Frankly, it was good to have rehearsals to go to because I couldn't waste an hour. And the company was great. I didn't tell them in person. I wrote to them all and told them, 'This terrible thing's happened but I'm just going to carry on.' It focused people a lot.

We had about four previews in Plymouth and then we opened in Edinburgh at the Festival in late August.

AM: *How did you make this piece musically?*
MB: Sometimes a whole piece will arrive and I will work to it. Other times, I give a lot of guidelines. I might say to Terry, 'This needs to be a lot longer, but also we need you to come in and watch because I want you to see what we're doing to be able to react to it musically, and I need something very specific at this or that point. Can you see where the idea of the scene changes here? It's not reflected enough in the music at the moment. Can you go back and make that work for us musically?' Possibly there will be some music that doesn't yet have enough drama within it and we need to add emphasis.

Terry's brilliant at this, being without ego. He will absolutely see what you want and make that work in the music. Or he'll sense something else from watching it and will say, 'I feel I need to bring a darker undertone to this sweet music, which can then build into what you next want to achieve here. So that, even if we don't notice it, we can feel it coming.' He responds to action, dance and movement in a very theatrical way in his music. He won't just say, 'Well, that's what I've written.' For that reason I get scared of working with people who are grand about their music and say, 'That's it, that's what it is.' In those cases, you have to love the music from the start to know that you're going to be OK with it. If you are working with a composer, you have to know you can work with him and change things, and that he'll get excited about that as well.

AM: *You presented your cast of eleven with the scenario, with the char-acter studies, and with your notes on the seven stages of tragedy. How useful was this for them?*
MB: The stages of tragedy were more for Richard than anyone else, because of the stages of the story for his character.

AM: *Do your performers take more from the plot or from the sugges-tions you give them for researching their characters?*
MB: You can't separate the two. They'll do a lot of research into the characters in terms of watching and reading. Through that they will make their own choices about the ideas that work for them the most. Michela Meazza found particular women that were useful to her for their attitude, in films that had nothing to do with *Dorian Gray*. Then, when reading the plot as it stands, they see how that can help them become those characters. Is there enough in the plot to achieve what you think you want to do through the research you've done for your character? The plot when we start rehearsals is always a movable feast, so the research and the beginnings of the plot give them the confidence to suggest things, because they've thought enough about the character to know how they might react in a scene.

AM: *How did you work with Richard Winsor?*
MB: He takes care of himself quite a lot. He will arrive with a lot of thoughts and will have done a lot of work and he will start performing straight away. That means I have something to work with, something I can guide. I purposely surround myself with people who are eager to bring something to the table. The bigger challenge this time was Aaron Sillis, who hadn't created a role for me before. But he really wanted to make this work and was very enthusiastic about the whole process.

AM: *How did you bring him along?*
MB: I got him to develop some movement. After seeing him do a few scenes and duets – watching how he acted – I thought, 'This is not going to work if I make this character too different from Aaron himself.' So I switched my ideas about the character to tailor it for him.

What he's very good at, because he comes from commercial dance, is bringing a mean, moody and sexy presence – but without upstaging the star (Kylie Minogue, Take That, and others). So I thought, 'Maybe we could build that up?' and I presented it to him as an idea for a char-acter – though what I was describing was the way he performed – that Basil was difficult to please and mean and moody. Not that Aaron is like that, but he looked like it when he danced. I thought we could make that character work: Basil could be on a downward spiral in terms of his work. He's not got any inspiration, nothing's exciting him any more. So when he finds something (Dorian) to inspire him, he gets excited.

Aaron's a strong character too, with his own sense of ego as well. People love him. He's a fantastic dancer, a fantastic mover. He excites people.

AM: *Unlike* Edward Scissorhands, *where the comic characters acknowledge the audience, in* Dorian Gray *there's no playing to the audience.*
MB: That's true. *Dorian* was designed as a piece without applause in the course of the action.

AM: *Even when the dancers are playing to imaginary mirrors at the front, they're not cueing responses from us?*
MB: No. That's the fourth wall, not the audience.

Maybe there's a slight connection between Dorian and the audience at the beginning of each act. He looks out. It says, 'This is my story.' Maybe there are a few other brief moments, when he's alone. It's useful because we want to go into his head: we want to connect with him. Such moments depend on the performers you choose. Richard is wary of cheesiness. In other pieces, dancers have to be cautioned about how they address the audience. With an unskilled acting cast, *Swan Lake* all looks a bit in-yer-face.

AM: *Where, in your mind, between acting and dancing does the style of the piece exist?*
MB: I wanted to say everything more through movement this time, pushing it towards dance. I certainly approached it more from a dance point of view than *Play Without Words* which was actively approached from the other direction. I always find that, if I'm not telling something about the story within a piece of movement, then I feel uncomfortable. Even within the white club sequence, there's a story about Dorian encountering the Doppelgänger, seeing someone who looks exactly like him and they do the same movements together. So we're going somewhere through that danced scene.

It all depends what your definition of dancing is. My work is deliberately on the cusp a lot of the time. I always make a decision as to how far it should go towards dance, while still hanging on to the story and the audience. It can't suddenly go somewhere that doesn't seem to be telling us anything. But it's nice to have those scenes that allow you to go for the movement more – because that makes everyone watching it completely comfortable.

AM: *Do you ever think, 'I know what I want to happen in this dance, but I have to let them discover it'?*

MB: Yes, you have to be quite clever. With some performers, you have to let them find it themselves, even though you know already where you want to go. There's no point in just imposing something they don't understand onto them. I very rarely say, 'Do this'; I usually say, 'What if . . . ?' It's a suggestion. You can tell if they get it when they grab onto it straight away as something they understand. But sometimes you get someone who persistently doesn't do what you're saying. That's because they don't get it. Then you have to stand back, because the movement has to be what's truthful to them. You help them find movement that will work for their strengths. Ultimately, that serves you better.

AM: *Most choreographers, sooner or later, start to reiterate or develop some of their older dance material. Do you ever recognize things from your earlier work?*

MB: Ideas rather than movement, I think. There is a type of movement I like and a type of movement I don't like, and obviously I am constantly pushing movement towards what I like. What I am always looking for is connection. I like logic to movement just as I like logic to stories. I like movement to make sense. It may not make sense to everyone, but there's a purpose to me about it.

AM: *If I understand your process, you choreograph the duets by drawing the movement out of those dancers and letting them create a great deal of it, but editing and highlighting and pinpointing things musically as you go along. But what occurs when you want some of that* Romeo, Romeo *material? Do you say, 'Let's go and look at the workshop DVD'?*

MB: I try to be sensitive about that. It's best to steer people towards what I want. But occasionally I said, 'I really like that bit from the workshop material. Maybe we could use a bit of that, and try and make it work?' Then I try to make it their material, let it be their starting point, especially if it's the same two dancers anyway, even if it seems like the most unlikely material. You will come up with more interesting movement that way.

Certainly the Ulanova-derived *Romeo, Romeo* duet (which fed into the Cyril duet in *Dorian*) has some unusual lifts and sequences in it, movement that would have been completely different if I had only set

157 Kenneth MacMillan's *Romeo and Juliet* (1965),
Act One, Balcony scene.

out to do a duet between Dorian and Romeo in the ballet. But I've crept
the *Romeo* movement into it rather than the other way round. There's a
very odd move early on in it: Cyril (as Romeo) turns away from Dorian
with his arm out and Dorian takes his arm in a very *Romeo and Juliet*-
type way; then Dorian lifts Cyril over his head, so he actually has a hand
on his crotch; then Dorian rolls back right over him, which is really odd;

158 The 'Romeo' duet, *Dorian Gray*, Act One, 2009 tour.
Richard Winsor (Dorian) below Dominic North (Cyril Vane).

then they turn around, Cyril's on his back and he lifts his legs. Next it's Dorian who does a very Romeo pose and lifts Cyril over his back. It's difficult to describe, I know! But my point is that there are some pretty provocative moves in there that you wouldn't find in any standard version of *Romeo and Juliet*.

What seemed good about it was that it felt as if it was partly Dorian playing Romeo and partly Cyril. They weren't just re-enacting a *Romeo and Juliet* duet. You think you're watching one thing, but then you see these provocative little moves within it that surprise you. That keeps it alive.

AM: *Only at times do the characters of* Dorian Gray *strike me pointedly as dancers dancing. Basil, interestingly, seems more of a dance-based character than Dorian. And, curiously, that works with his character.*
MB: This is not strictly true. Dorian does more dancing of the two. But Aaron, our original Basil, was not an experienced actor, yet he was a presence. So I thought we should use what he's good at, which is dancing. People loved him when he danced. So, when I wanted him to say something, I tended to throw all the movement at it. My thought was that, with him, I mustn't entirely rely upon acting. It's often the case, isn't it?, that the lead character is telling so much story all the time that you can give a lot of movement to another featured character. As a result, other characters come across in a punchier way when they do appear.

Two of my favourite things in this show are the two rhythmic duets between Dorian and Lady H. They're not really dance material at all, but the rhythm gives them wit; and everything is very carefully worked out, every step, every movement, every look. And Richard and Michela Meazza (Lady H.) are so good at the acting that you almost forget that you are watching something extremely musical. It's exciting; I like that acting-to-rhythm feel. It's unusual for me to be that specifically rhythmic without actual dance steps.

AM: *Which characters see the Doppelgänger?*
MB: To anyone but Dorian, the Doppelgänger is the new up-and-coming young thing, the new face, the young model, the new young actor. It starts right at the beginning of the second act where he's in the photo-shoot. It's a *Vanity Fair*-type put-some-celebrities-together-and-take-their-picture, Annie Leibovitz-type photo-shoot. The Doppelgänger is one of those people, in dark glasses; but Dorian's reaction is 'Who's he?' He doesn't like sharing the limelight. Lady H. ends up with this

new young model. Dorian sees him as the competition, or his younger self. You have to make your own mind up what you're seeing there. That comes from *Alfie*, actually. In the 2004 version of the film, Susan Sarandon plays the older woman that Alfie has a long-term affair with. At the end of the film, he turns up at her house and she's got someone there. He says, 'What has he got that I haven't got?' She says simply, 'He's younger.' Since she's so much older than him, that's a shock. It's a classic theme in celebrity culture, especially if you're only known for your looks. That's where the Doppelgänger becomes so useful to us in this story.

He can represent so many things. In Act One, at the party where Basil and Lady H. first spot Dorian as a waiter, the Doppelgänger is already the other waiter. His potential is there in embryo. We developed that in rehearsal; it's not in the written scenario.

One of the early ideas with the piece was of a nonentity who only becomes the image – becomes Dorian – because he was chosen to be that person. Dorian's actually not particularly noticeable for quite a long time at that party. He's just a waiter and there's this other waiter who looks very similar to him and who will become the Doppelgänger. A moment comes when the light gets turned on Dorian, in a literal way in the show, but also in the more general way that the focus is put on movie stars.

AM: *The first time I watched it I didn't realize Dorian Gray was a waiter until quite late on in the scene. I was waiting for him to make an entrance.*
MB: He's placed on the stage not very centrally, he's sideways on, and you're not supposed to notice him. He has a little moment with Lady H.

AM: *That's when you focus on him. She spots him before Basil?*
MB: To Dorian, Lady H. is the important one. If you were a waiter and a young good-looking guy at that party, she'd be the one you'd want to serve your drinks to, because she's so powerful in that world. She is the arbiter of taste.

AM: *Your whole cast is of eleven dancers, but eight of them play ensemble characters (though some of those eight also play solo roles). The ensemble get to play a good many different roles. We first see them in the gallery/photography section. Here you have dancers crossing their arms, making crosses in front of their faces or bodies. Where did that image come from?*

159 Lez Brotherston's costume designs.

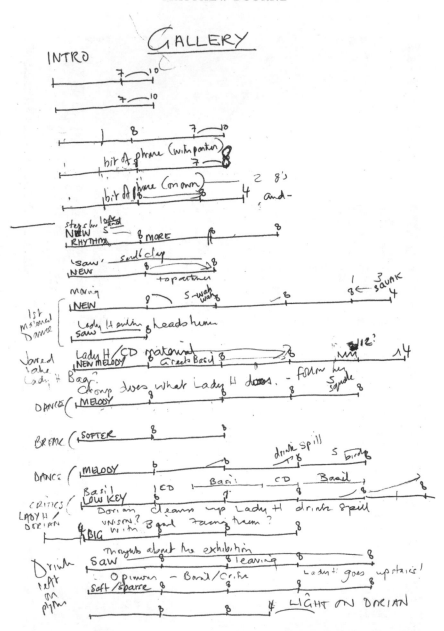

160 'Gallery', opening scene of Act One. Notes by Bourne for Basil's photographic exhibition scene.

MB: One of our first company workshops on this work was called 'I am a camera'. A central task was to create movement where your whole body became a camera. It was a mixture of what a camera can do: zooming in and out, focusing on things, editing and cutting shots, moving in and out of focus. Anything to do with the way a camera works. Can you create movement that shows us that with the body? A lot of the phrases we use in the gallery section came from that workshop. It was a very useful movement task. That crossed-arm gesture is about framing the camera view: about visualizing things and setting them up for photography.

AM: *When Lady H. takes Dorian under her wing and grooms him for stardom, her eight assistants (as they now are) prepare him in a series of rituals. How did those movements arrive?*
MB: That section is called 'The Science of Beauty'. They're like beauty scientists. It's about the process he goes through to become an icon, a figure that everyone wants to look at. Lady H. makes all the choices, since she is the judge of taste. She employs all these people, as if in a lab, to create the perfect attractive man for the world at large. We brought into this scene the physical images to which she may or may not give her

161 Act One: from the 'Lady H. at Home' scene. Richard Winsor (Dorian) with Jared Hageman, Chloe Wilkinson, Joe Walkling, Emily-Jane Boyle, Adam Maskell and Dominic North.

approval. They try out different things. He does a ballet pose, an athletic pose, and the Rodin *Thinker* pose. What are the various different types of man Dorian might be? She chooses.

AM: *It includes a ballet adagio, where he is manoeuvred by a series of partners like a ballerina.*
MB: That idea came from a longer duet we developed with Lady H. and Dorian, where she was partnering him like a man.

AM: *She's in control?*
MB: Yes, we wanted to give her that sense of power. Playing as we were with different gender roles as dancers, maybe it would be interesting to look at some traditional partnering that a man would normally do with a woman? So she promenades him round at one point. He strikes a pose; she takes his hand and partners him as a man would partner a woman in ballet. He will do what she wants and will please her because of what he gets in return, and that consists of being introduced to a whole new world and a bunch of people he's never encountered. So, through that scene with her, you see him as a vulnerable young man in a new setting, looking round this amazing apartment she has and at all these friends of hers. By the end of that sequence, he realizes that they are all drawn to him, and they all want to meet him. They all give him their cards. That giving of

162 'Lady H. at Home', Act One. Richard Winsor (Dorian) and
Michela Meazza (Lady H.), right.

the cards is all supposed to be done secretively, so each one thinks he or she is the only one who's done it. He starts off vulnerable, but by the end of all that attention, he feels really strong . . . and he's loving it.

AM: *And power is a key to how he progresses as a character. As he develops through the work, he needs to take control more and more.*

MB: This happens to everyone who achieves a certain amount of success. They believe they can do it on their own. Dorian comes to believe he doesn't need them any more. He feels he can play them rather than be played.

You always hear these crazy stories. When the Spice Girls sacked their manager, they thought they were more important than the very clever person who put them together and made them a phenomenon. But they weren't particularly talented people. It was the manager who put them together and gave them their Spice names that got people excited. I think that's true of so many famous people: the work put in by their clever managers behind the scenes goes unappreciated by the artists who have benefited from it.

AM: *And here it's most striking in how Dorian changes with Lady H.*

163 Michela Meazza as Lady H. in the scene in her bedroom, Act One. Brotherston designed this costume for the surprise revelation of her legs as she sits.

613

He's passive with her at first, allowing her to shape him, turn him, steer him. In their Act Two duet, he tries to control her; there's no moment when he will allow her to be in charge.

Another change between Acts One and Two is the increasing degree of unreality and ambiguity. You give us one fantasy duet in Act One, when Dorian/Romeo dreams of love with Cyril/Romeo. But in Act Two a great deal is uncertain.

MB: When Dorian wakes up in Act Two, as in Act One, he looks at the audience as if to say, 'This is my story, come with me.' You follow him into the madness. There's a point where you're going into his mind but some of the things there are not happening in real life. The first act is mostly what really happens. The second half gets more into what he thinks he's doing and what he thinks he's seeing. He's your unreliable narrator!

AM: *You've mentioned tasks and workshops. Take me through how you used the rehearsal period to create the show.*

MB: The first week of rehearsals was workshop. I decided we would gain plenty if I didn't try to set anything in week one, but instead just used it to explore more and to create movement. I stuck to that, though it was a bit nerve-racking: you feel you want to have something fixed! But it was very useful. I knew a lot of the material was going to be fairly intimate, and the company needed to get to know each other more. After the 'I am a camera' workshop, we move on to introduce a model – and have them relate as cameras to that. Then we did a lot of work involving the action of looking at art, reacting to it. We had half the company as models, the other half as artists arranging them like they were pieces of clay, putting groups together into shapes. It became about appreciation.

We did research about physical reactions to various drugs. Then we made up phrases of movement that were to do with these physical states. That became the basis of our white club movement.

We did a lot of quite intimate stuff in terms of the sex duets. I had to get people to move together, and I had to find a way to make that work for them without it being completely straightforward. So I came up with some ideas whereby they initially worked on their own each with an invisible partner, making love to them. They did solos based on that. Then I put them with a partner who had to relate to that solo movement but not exactly. We did a version where they didn't touch, where they were just close until they were nearly touching. Then we just went a bit further and developed it in stages, so they took it further into dance movement. But I think it's always good to start from something literal and then take it further, so that it has some truth or reality to it, even though the movement has become more abstract.

We did celebrity phrases. You announced your arrival on the red carpet by spelling out your name with body parts: literally spelling your name in the air. 'Here I am!' A physical autograph. You had a choice of what kind of celebrity you might be. You could be a celebrity who doesn't want much attention or a car-crash celebrity or a very open out-there celebrity – different types of characters. At the beginning of Act Two, they all have individual phrases that came from that idea.

Sometimes, when people aren't used to making up material, a very simple task can create nice things. Give them something too cerebral and they don't know where to begin. But tell them to spell out the letters of their name, letter by letter, using their body parts! Then tell them to find a movement to connect the letters. Then I would say 'Throw in a jump, a turn. You have to go to the floor . . .' I give them all sorts of guidelines. Eventually it becomes more and more complex, but they know completely what they've been asked to do.

AM: *Did the ensemble have to work on the sex duets?*
MB: Everyone had to work on the sex duets, including the ensemble. They all had to do it; that was part of it. Even when we did auditions, with people I didn't know, I got everyone to do sex-duet movement, because I needed to know that they were OK with that stuff. So we did a whole day's audition on that! And people really took to it; everyone took it very seriously. I needn't have worried.

AM: *What did you do in Week Two?*
MB: Week Two was the beginning of putting it all together and starting to work on sections. I had the scenario. I said to them, 'I am going to start at the beginning and work through in sequence, so you know where we're going.' On top of that, I had some duets that I had begun to work on through the workshop, so I already had some material for Dorian (Richard), Basil (Aaron) and Cyril (Chris). I could get the main duets going alongside the full company work.

The first thing we looked at was 'Basil's World', which was the photo-shoots with the models. I said to everyone, 'Pick five words that other people might use to describe you: characteristics. Beside them write the opposites of those words. So one line is who you are, and one is the other side of you, the opposite. For each word, create a movement that sums up that word. Then find a movement that connects those words, to create a phrase. So you have the way people see you and then the opposite, a phrase that changes halfway through.' Again, it was a way of finding movement that reflected their personalities, but that also had the opposite side to it. Which is part of the Dorian Gray story. We used that to come up with this model movement. On top of that we added focus, which is to do with where the camera is, which distorts it to a certain extent, changes it.

I always get each dancer to teach his or her phrase to another person, because the passing of it on always defines the phrase more. So Dancer A teaches his phrase to Dancer B, then learns Dancer B's phrase from him, then the two of them perform the same A+B double-length phrase.

There's a lot of activity at the beginning of the piece, as I always like to have. This throws a lot of ideas up, to create the world we're in: which is the world of photography, the world of the superficiality and vanity of models. But not just the vain surface, which everyone knows; instead, how competitive and stressful it is. So the scene includes a casting session where a client has to pick someone who then has to be photographed to sell his product, which is probably, in this case, a perfume. And everyone is competing to be 'the one', the person, the next new thing.

I tried to deal with one section at a time in chronological order, partly to give it continuity and partly to make sure I was making sense of it myself. I wanted to make sure we were developing in the right way. But hand in hand with working on the beginning section with everyone, I was also at work on the first big duet and Dorian's first solo (with the camera), which I had already worked on a little with Richard in Brighton.

I was also working on some material with Lady H. for her first duet with Dorian. I had her partner him like a man partnering a woman; and that led into two sections. She comes into the studio and finds him, and some of the movement went into that and some went into the section called 'Science of Beauty' where she 'creates' him as an icon. That section took probably the longest because it's very precise. It's funny: sections of pure-dance movement and phrases are often more quickly put together than something that's very exact about groupings and shapes and characters. Dressing and undressing always take a lot of time to do it precisely, to get the timing and to get it just right. That was quite a long sequence of fairly simple movement, but it had to feel right.

AM: *How far were Lez Brotherston's plans developed at this stage?*
MB: We had the set. We had the basic set and the revolve in the rehearsal room from week two. We had had the full space when we were doing the workshop in week one; then the set came into the studio when we started on the piece proper. I was quite excited about the use of the revolve and wanted to explore how it could be interesting for movement. Creating each room was really enjoyable for me. I spent hours staring at the model box! Usually in the morning when the company are doing class, I'd come in and I look at the model box and I'd move things round. So that I knew what I was going for.

All the transitions were difficult. This was one of the musical problems of the piece initially. Terry would write this music and ask, 'How long do you need for this solo or duet?' and I'd say, 'Probably two, or two and a half minutes would be all right.' But then you'd stage it and you'd find that you'd be using maybe thirty seconds of that music as a transition into the next scene. Sometimes it worked because it gave a nice fluidity, but often you wanted a bit longer. So that was something to learn: you had to make sure you had enough music for getting from one scene into another.

There were other musical things we had to take into account, such as we had musicians on stage for certain bits. We had to work out how the music would work to get them there. So we had a single percussionist playing one section, so that the band could get onto the stage to play the next section. Then there'd have to be something while they got back again.

It all had to be thought through. Did we want the set's white side or its dark side for each scene? If you wanted pieces of furniture to be set up on the other side and come round, you needed to give time for those to be put in place. If we hadn't had the set in the studio, we would never have been able to do the technical rehearsal in the theatre in the time allotted. I find this technical side quite enjoyable, but it's time-consuming.

AM: *Then weeks three, four, five?*
MB: It's impossible for me now to remember it all schematically. But I know that we moved on to the next section of the piece, 'Lady H. at Home'. Here, now she has 'created' him, Dorian almost goes back to being an innocent in a new world. It's difficult for him to begin with; but as he becomes the model, he becomes confident. At the end of that sequence, he gets his suit on, he struts up and down, and he becomes this

icon. He has the perfume sprayed on him and he feels up there and con-fident. It's difficult for him to go back down to being an innocent again. I said to Richard, 'Don't forget: that scene is the most surreal we get in Act One. In a way, it's not really happening. It's showing the audience what you have become as an image.' Then he starts to grow again, as a character, after that.

Within the Lady H. section, we see the power of youth and beauty more than anywhere else because everyone is drawn to Dorian. We use the image of the perfume, it's a smell that overtakes you. Everyone in the room – this new bunch of people that Dorian meets, Lady H.'s sophis-ticated friends – suddenly has to have him. It's like a wave that moves across them. They want him, but, because they are sophisticated, they are quite subtle about it. The perfume is a strong image because it's not physical, you have to feel it. This was the idea of it, that nobody actually touches Dorian; but they are drawn to him.

Within that section there are several scenes. It starts off in Lady H.'s bedroom where they are preparing to go out. Dorian's pouring her a drink, he has to zip up her dress, and it's all a bit uncomfortable. She's

164 'Lady H.'s Bedroom', Act One. Michela Meazza (Lady H.) and Richard Winsor (Dorian).

playing up to that, wrong-footing him, so he's not sure what to do. Then he meets the others, they all give him their business cards, and he starts to feel more confident. Everyone wants to know Dorian. Then there's a split-scene sequence where the central structure is down the centre. On the right, you get the people he's just met, in the room; on the left, you get the bedroom. Both spaces are part of her apartment. Now he finally gets somewhere with Lady H. She's powerful and he likes the sense of that power; he finds it quite exciting. They are two people who like to watch themselves when they make love. Lady H. is in control, but she's quite happy to be used. She sees it as a mutually beneficial arrangement. She's done it before. He may be another one in a long line for her, but she does have an affection for him: you see that at the very end when she kisses him on his deathbed. Once he's got somewhere with her and he's realized that everyone's interested in him, by the time he bursts back into the room, he's grown in confidence. Dorian's aware of the effect he has on people and that's his growth within that scene, to the point where everyone ends up getting close to him – the frottage sequence. Richard does it well; you believe him in each situation.

In my mind, they're all meeting at her house. She's arranged an evening to show off her new protégé to her friends, as part of which they all then go off together to the Royal Opera House, where she's got a very large box for them all.

This takes us into the next sequence: Cyril on stage, dancing Romeo at the Royal Opera House in *Romeo and Juliet*. Chris had watched various film versions of *Romeo*; he and Richard had done the Ulanova *Romeo and Juliet* duet in the workshop.

AM: *This scene leads to Dorian's first duet with Cyril. How do you show that this is Dorian's fantasy?*

MB: Well, if you've got an extremely literal mind, you think Dorian's walked out of the audience from their box onto the stage and joined in! Or maybe that he's immediately got access to meet Cyril backstage. But really the unreal nature of the duet shows that it's happening in Dorian's mind, and his acting before and after should tell you that too. We set up the idea of Lady H.'s guests all watching something on stage; then we bring Cyril on. So the audience understands that Cyril's what Dorian and the others are watching, though they are not directly looking at just him. But then spotlights go onto Dorian and Cyril; and we lose the others a bit. Dorian stands up, looking at Cyril, and starts to walk towards him as the others fade away. We've gone into Dorian's head, and then eventually we bring him back into reality, when he returns to the red seat at the Opera House with his programme – as if he's just finished watching the performance.

The first duet was some way to being done before we even started rehearsals. I wanted the second one to reflect the first but in a changed way. Because I had a lot of film of the workshop in my laptop, and because these were the same two dancers, I had a wealth of possibilities. I would often refer to the film in the rehearsal room, even just to find a phrase that I liked or a lift that I liked.

The idea of the first duet is relatively simple. You've got to see Cyril as two people, the stage persona and the real person. The movement comes out of a mixture of some of Romeo's movement from the early part of the ballet. I like playing with the idea of Dorian still being Dorian and moving around him but in a way that's not Romeo or Juliet.

Dorian's whole experience with Cyril is very much my experience of my early years of watching the Royal Ballet and trying to be friends with some of its dancers. The stage-door moment – when Dorian meets Cyril in real life – is me, isn't it? I've spent more hours than most people at stage doors.

AM: *Explain to me what it is that Cyril does wrong when he enters Dorian's loft.*
MB: He arrives, he empties his bag of dance things all over the place, he doesn't really care where it goes, he hangs his sweaty leotard up over Dorian's portrait (cardinal sin number one!), he sticks his cap on the bust of Nijinsky, he's generally stroppy and self-obsessed – but in a different way from Dorian.

AM: *When does Dorian realize that Cyril is not the man he fantasized about?*
MB: By the time Cyril's come into that scene, Dorian's already feeling that way. This is a couple of months later. That may not be obvious to the audience, but they soon pick up on the way that Cyril arrives so casually in the apartment (so he's used to going there) and on the lack of fuss Dorian or anybody else makes of him when he enters.

We're near the end of Act One. What I've set up during the act is that Dorian has three important relationships, each of which is starting to become difficult for him.

With Lady H., we show her annoyance that he ran off from her at the Opera House. When Dorian's waiting for Cyril at the stage door, she comes to find him. He's supposed to be driving her home, she's got the car keys, she gives them to him. He thinks, 'I'd better do my duty, I came with her, I've got to take her home.' She's obviously not very happy.

With Basil, Dorian's got an ongoing commitment. Basil – although he's quite a free person and accepts that Dorian has other relationships – feels he's losing him. He accepts Dorian changing but he loves him as he was. To Dorian, Basil becomes boring in a way: he's too devoted.

And there's Cyril, who's become a complete annoyance to Dorian and has become nothing but a pain for him – apart from when he sees him on stage.

Dorian wants to release himself from all three; you should feel something of that. The opportunity of ridding himself of Cyril presents itself when Cyril takes the overdose of Ecstasy by accident. Dorian didn't plan that to happen, but he witnesses Cyril's fit, deliberately does not call for help, and so lets him die. We see a change in his personality. It's a strange feeling of power and of relief. And nobody else knows, only Dorian.

AM: *The Doppelgänger arrives then . . .*
MB: Yes, that's the sign that something has changed within him. It's the beginning of the end. His personality starts to split in two directions; and the Doppelgänger starts to represent the original Dorian.

AM: *Now Act Two?*
MB: We show a series of photo-shoots and TV appearances. He's at the top, a well-known face around town. Publicly, he's adored and people love him for his simplicity. Behind the scenes, he's becoming difficult. He's competitive, and with Basil and Lady H. he's argumentative about how he wants to be viewed, not wanting to have his picture taken so much. He feels that maybe the inside is starting to show on the outside. The paparazzi are waiting for him round every corner. There's a dark scene where you see lots of flashing lights to suggest photographers hidden away. He's reached the point all celebrities eventually do – which is that you don't want your picture taken. His two-sided nature starts to reveal itself as a celebrity.

That's a very fast-moving sequence, one of those sequences that I enjoy doing where we show you a little aspect of the world we're in now. Just as we began Act One by showing Basil's world, now we show the world

165 'On the Prowl', Act Two. Dorian and his Doppelgänger: Jared Hageman (DG, left) and Richard Winsor (Dorian, right).

of celebrity: a lot of short incidents to demonstrate where Dorian's at now.

Then we go into the white-club sequence which serves to introduce the Doppelgänger again. At the club, because Dorian's probably had a bit to drink or has taken drugs, he doesn't know whether he's looking at himself or not, but he ends up sitting next to the Doppelgänger – who reflects his movement and wears the same clothes. You only notice that as he sits down. They both have the exact same detail on their vest, which is the symbol on the 'immortal' poster – a Gothic cross.

Dorian runs out of the club and goes straight to Lady H. He thinks he can be comfortable with her, but actually he's not. She's started to find him a little bit pushy. She doesn't like the arrogant way he barges in on her.

AM: *In dance terms, it's clear that he's trying to partner her here, which she doesn't like.*
MB: Yes, Dorian arrives and takes over. He tears up a picture of himself, which is her creation. He doesn't want to be her puppet any more. She knows how she wants him; he's useful as an image to her. But he wants more. He's trying to act normally but he's troubled. He attacks her quite savagely in a near-rape. That shocks her and shocks him too. It ends when she attempts to scratch his face. What stops him going any further

166 Act Two, at Lady H.'s. Lady H. fends off an attack from Dorian.
Michela Meazza and Richard Winsor.

is his fear that she may have scarred his precious face, and she knows
that his face is the most important thing to him.

When he leaves her place, we go into a sequence called 'On the Prowl'.
One of the myths of the Doppelgänger is that he goes ahead of you
to places and commits evil and embarrassing acts. It could in fact be
the person has done these things but is unaware of having done them.
Within this sequence, there are at least three moments where Dorian is
being followed by the Doppelgänger and we see a body fall out of one
of the doors – as if his double is committing acts of evil. A girl comes
towards Dorian and gets pulled away by the Doppelgänger into a dark
corner through one of the doors. The sequence ends with Dorian grabbing a boy as if he's captured a victim on the street, and this action is
promptly repeated with the Doppelgänger dragging the boy away. So
there's a series of victims with one or the other as the perpetrator. The
darker side of Dorian is revealed.

167 Dorian's loft, Act Two, with the 'bodies' of his victims. This scene is the equivalent of the eventual 'portrait in the attic' in Wilde's novel. The bodies may be interpreted as memories of victims rather than all being literally there, though this is left ambiguous.

Possibly he's killing people. But there's only one killing in the novel, Basil! More possibly, he's infecting them. He's leaving a trail of destruction behind him, by sleeping around. When we go to his home later on and see the bodies, they could be all those he's infected. We talked about this in rehearsal: though it's not a pleasant thought, everyone understood it.

In this sequence, there's a sense of him being chased and of people running away from him. There's sirens going and searchlights. It's a crazy sequence, and it leads through into the back-room sequence.

Basil has followed Dorian to the back room and can't believe the new life Dorian is leading. In Dorian's apartment, we show his collection of new art that Basil finds distasteful. Basil wants Dorian to let him take his picture again but Dorian doesn't want to be captured again in his present state. Once you've allowed one person to die, it's easier to take it one stage further. He feels he's killed, so he can do it again, and can get rid of the next person who's in his way: Basil. Ironically, he uses the camera to kill him: the thing that brought them together. It was not a planned murder: Basil just turns up. But it's clear by then that Dorian's a little 'unhinged'.

This is followed by a solo, for Dorian, based around the bloodied hand, the hand that did the deed. He feels he has disembodied hands

168 'Dorian Shoots Basil', Act Two, 2009. Dorian murders Basil:
Richard Winsor and Jason Piper, 2008. In the sex/art connection of Act One,
Basil, by 'shooting' Dorian, made him famous; in the sex/death nexus of
Act Two, Dorian, now infamous, uses Basil's camera to kill him.

coming round his body. It's a split-personality solo, about parts of your body doing something that your brain is shocked by, but the evidence is there.

As in the other moment of crisis, he runs to Lady H. again. After what happened last time, she's scared of him. He's covered in a certain amount of blood. He goes there to confess that he's killed someone. But she's got a younger guy in her room. When this person appears, Dorian sees it as the Doppelgänger, his younger self.

Now we're in Dorian's mind, not in any literal reality. As soon as he sees the Doppelgänger in her apartment, we go into a stream of consciousness in which he's back in his own apartment – where he sees the Doppelgänger again. Cyril comes back – Dorian's remembering things. He's remembering people and incidents. It's about people he has known who have gone, because of him they're not there any more. Eventually the whole room is full of these people. It's about Dorian deciding to do away with himself. It's a process of giving up.

I'm never completely sure why he kills himself in the novel. It always ends abruptly for me. To do this sequence is, I think, helpful, because it shows a series of events leading to the point at which things get so bad that he can't carry on.

At the end, he's not immortal, he's not special, he's human, he's committed a lot of bad deeds, and he needs to pay for it. Whatever's going on in his mind at that point, he's killing himself. When the Doppelgänger appears for the last time, they go to bed together. It's Dorian's decision to finish his life. What better way to show someone killing himself than doing it to his double? It connects with the portrait in the novel. The novel's final scene is between him and the portrait. He attacks it. Once he's stabbed his portrait, he's done that to himself. And the final paragraph of the book says the portrait goes back to being as it was. I don't think anything about it had ever really changed; to me, any change is what Dorian projects onto it. And I think that this is what we show with the Doppelgänger.

AM: *By what point in the five weeks' rehearsal did Terry finish the music?*
MB: Not till the very end! By the end of five weeks, we were behind with music. We'd gone ahead, working with other music. We needed the music quicker than Terry could compose it, even though he worked very long hours every day. At one point we thought, 'We can't finish this because we haven't got the music.' Well, we did, but it was very last-minute.

169 Dorian's final solo after killing Basil, Act Two. To create distortion and an uncomfortable physical violence, Dorian's legs jerk his body up off the floor. Richard Winsor (Dorian).

There were other things that fell into place late. I certainly didn't know at first how we were going to do the death of Dorian. That came about in the rehearsal room. I loved the idea of Dorian and the Doppelgänger going to bed together – it was accepting death. I hadn't even thought about it till we did it on the day, the idea of him suffocating, killing himself and the other one disappearing into the sheets. It felt so theatrical to me and it worked straight away, but it wasn't planned.

Previews, Performances, Revival

ALASTAIR MACAULAY: *Once you've rehearsed the piece, how does performance change it?*
MATTHEW BOURNE: A lot, always. Audiences tell you everything.

AM: *How were the first performances in Plymouth?*
MB: I realized that we had something different. It took me a while to realize the audience were concentrating. To me they could have all fallen asleep, for all I knew, in the first half.

And I knew there were things wrong with it. Aspects of the story were being rushed. Some of the problems I spotted then, though, I didn't fix to my satisfaction until this year.

I found it difficult to get from the point where Dorian and Cyril meet at the stage door to a point some time on in their relationship. That passage of time was hard to demonstrate until I worked out the scene where Cyril comes to Dorian's apartment and he's already got the keys, showing that he has access and has been there a lot.

AM: *At the end of each half the audience is not sure if they should applaud.*
MB: Because they're not used to it. They've not got used to clapping during the performance, so they're not clap-happy. With most of our shows, you can feel and hear how the audience is responding. Not so here. Because this show is designed to run without pauses or applause, the audience doesn't show its reaction the same way. But I've gradually come to realize that most people are very gripped.

One change I have made in 2009, to make the story of Cyril work better, is to show that he, like Dorian, is also on the make. So we show Cyril taking Dorian's card at the stage door, not being particularly interested, but then seeing Dorian's face on the billboard and doing a quick rethink. The character of Cyril is a fantastic creation of Christopher Marney's. You should hear him talk it through! As always in rehearsal, we do all these exercises where each dancer talks about his or her character. This year we had them go around in twos and talk about their characters for one minute to each other; I timed them. They have to say 'I am . . .' rather than 'My character is . . .' Then I pointed at people and I said, 'What did you find out about Cyril?' or 'What did you find about Basil?' It took them by surprise a bit, having to remember what someone else had said. Well, Cyril said, 'I'm the youngest principal ever at the Royal Ballet', and 'I've won *Dancing Times*'s "Dancer of the Month" three months in a row, it's never happened before'! He, Chris, has played the Prince in *Swan Lake* a number of times and he hits the nail on the head, for me, with that part. And I love what he does as Cyril: it's just spot on. Casting Cyril is hard, not least because we do have to believe that he's a dancer at the Royal Ballet: he's got to give off the right aura in white tights. We keep adding detail to his encounter with Dorian; I'm finding more humour.

Another 2009 change is that I've extended Richard's solo after the murder of Basil.

And last year we had no covers. This year, we've got covers and cast changes because of the longer tour. All the roles can now be done by two people. Just recently we had a matinée where Jared, who usually plays the Doppelgänger, played Dorian, and Chris, who usually plays Cyril, was Basil.

AM: *How does Lady H. work with a cast change?*
MB: There is no Lady H. save Michela. Her cover is male, when the role becomes Lord H. I wanted a woman, of course, but I felt none of the other women in the cast would have the same effect. Michela has a mature look, and the dancer who comes nearest the same quality is Ashley Bain who plays her creative director, Edward Black, in the show. He hasn't performed Lord H. yet, but we've done a run-through with him. It completely works; he does exactly the same movement as Michela's. And so it becomes an even gayer version of the story! But I didn't want a world without women originally, and I'm still happiest with a woman in that role.

AM: *Richard Winsor has carried almost all these performances in the title role. How exhausting a role is it for him?*
MB: By the end of it, he's really exhausted. Dorian's almost never off stage, he does all the club movement, and he does a lot of partnering. His duet with the Doppelgänger – the one we call 'On the Prowl' – is high-energy. The beginning is easy, but then, once he becomes featured, it doesn't let go. Richard is especially tired just now, because he's danced every performance but one. I would say it's emotionally exhausting as well.

AM: *You had Aaron Sillis as Basil last year. This year, you have Jason Piper. What's the difference between them?*
MB: Nobody knew who Aaron was until the premiere last year, and he had a big personal success with it: everyone loved him. He's a sexy guy, with a charismatic presence. He'd been doing tours with Kylie Minogue, and he knew very well the world we were showing on stage. He got nominated for a few awards for his Basil, but then he left the show to be a backing dancer for Take That.

I felt the role needed someone with a similar sort of stage charisma. Aaron had made Basil appealing as a photographer whom people were a little bit in awe of. So I went for Jason Piper, who had been a great success as the Swan in *Swan Lake* a few years earlier. He was the only other dancer I knew who had this incredible effect on audiences, really sexy and powerful. So I had to lure him out of retirement! I'm very glad he agreed.

AM: *Did Terry change the music?*
MB: A few things after the opening last year, yes, and then bigger changes this year with the second run. I had asked for some extensions; and there had also been some pieces he wasn't happy with. He now felt there were passages that need to be developed, to work better for what's happening on stage.

AM: *We've often spoken about what it's like to stage a show the second time, and you've often said that it's then, when you're coming back to a show after its first season, that 'the real choreography gets done'. But do you feel that you're making new improvements that change what you conceived originally? Or are you trying this time to bring to the surface what you always had in mind?*
MB: Both of those prove true, I find. Sometimes you're learning about it yourself; new ideas come to you that you want to get in there. Other times, you've got to try to remember how you felt originally. You think, 'I didn't quite get to that idea that I wanted; we're missing something here.'

And it distils through different casts. It becomes more specific.

(Conversations 2009)

18

Matters Arising

Priorities: Music or Story?

ALASTAIR MACAULAY: *Despite the fact that we ended our chapter on*
Edward Scissorhands *with you talking about the powerful effect of music
on your protagonist, I'd like now to observe that you are no longer
principally a music-led choreographer. In 1998–9, when we prepared
the first edition of this book, you felt you were. Up to that point, all
your work had been made in response to pre-existing scores – mainly by
Tchaikovsky (*Nutcracker, Swan Lake*), Løvenskjold (*Highland Fling*)
and Prokofiev (*Cinderella*).*

*But since 2000 you haven't been responding to ready-made music;
you've been having new music made to fit your scenarios. In* The Car
Man, *you're not just working with Schedrin's arrangement of Bizet,
you're commissioning Terry Davies to extend that score. You know the
show you want to make and you want him to find or shape the right
music to fit it. In* Edward Scissorhands, *you again are commissioning
Terry Davies to extend Danny Elfman's score, and have made much
of your story and movement before his score is brought to bear on the
action. In both* Play Without Words *and* Dorian Gray, *you go far further
in that direction. The story is largely shaped by the time Terry Davies
brings his music into play, and much of the movement is under way too.*

*So I'd like to suggest that you are now principally story-led rather
than music-led.*

MATTHEW BOURNE: You're right, and yet that's not quite how it feels.
I just don't separate the two impulses the way you're suggesting. After
all, almost all the musical choreographers we can think of have commissioned new scores, haven't they? And most of them have commissioned
new narrative scores? In those cases, they had ideas in mind before the
finished music came along. The same goes for me. But I couldn't have

begun work on *The Car Man* without loving the Bizet or, more particularly, the Schedrin: the music was part of what made it take shape in my mind as a show. And the same goes for *Edward Scissorhands*: I didn't think of it as a dance show until I realized that Danny Elfman's music was so integral to my love of the film. In both those cases, the music was still the reason for making those pieces.

In the case of *Play Without Words* and *Dorian Gray*,[1] however, yes, the process there was different. I'd got more confident. I used to be shy of working with commissioned scores, and in the 1990s I honestly couldn't imagine doing so. What's changed me is working with Terry. I've learnt how to make movement in workshops before the score is ready. But I do use music in those workshops, guide tracks, and the choice of that music ends up being important. Both with *Play Without Words* and with *Edward Scissorhands*, we've talked about examples of music used in workshops, and Terry often picked up on the music I'd chosen to experiment with. However, the piece could not have taken any finished shape until the score was part of it; until we'd reshaped the movement to the actual music. As I kept saying to the dancers in *Scissorhands*, 'Everything you do is musical, especially when you are not "dancing". Find the connection of action and sound.'

However, you're certainly not wrong about my being story-led. I feel that I just get deeper into aspects of narrative, character, emotion with every show I make. One part of me, though, really wants to get back to making something with a classical structure, as with *Swan Lake*, something that's led by music into a big sequence of dance, dance, dance. That's why the big plan for 2010 is to return to *Cinderella*.

AM: *Meanwhile, your work gets deeper into movies. As I've said before, it's ironic that your company is no longer called Adventures in Motion Pictures in the precise era when your choreography has become increasingly a series of adventures in motion pictures:* The Car Man, Play Without Words, Edward Scissorhands. *When I asked you for the films that helped to inspire* Play Without Words, *you could rattle off twenty-five without checking any notes.*

MB: Yes, but I've always been that way. Most of my references are film ones now, but the dance-history ideas are still there too. It's just that most journalists I speak to are not so aware of the dance references, so I

---

[1] *Lord of the Flies* is now Terry's third completely original score for New Adventures.

always end up talking about the film ones. I often wish I had more time to look at a wider range of choreography or even of new films. I feel I'm drawing from the same people on film I've always loved (Astaire, Hitchcock, Michael Powell, and others). And perhaps that's only right. These are lifelong loves of mine: why would it change?

A Director and/or Choreographer

ALASTAIR MACAULAY: *You're often asked the questions: To what degree are you a director? To what degree are you a choreographer? What's your latest answer?*

MATTHEW BOURNE: I am often asked this, yes. As we've said, *Play Without Words* upset some dance critics when it was reviewed by theatre critics, because they felt it was theirs to review. They insist that I'm a choreographer and therefore I should be reviewed by dance critics. The irony is that many of those people are the ones who have been telling me that I am not principally a choreographer. In New York, this became an issue to a silly extent, and quite boring in a way. But my latest answer is the same one I've been giving for several years now: I'm both.

AM: *That's literally so now. In* Mary Poppins *(2004) and* Oliver! *(2009), you're listed as co-director and as choreographer. In* Play Without Words *(2002) the credits said that the piece was 'devised by Matthew Bourne', 'directed by Matthew Bourne', and that the movement was 'devised by Matthew Bourne & the company'.*

This director/choreographer dichotomy is applied by some people in a pejorative sense. I've heard dance critics say sniffily, 'He's a director. But he's not a choreographer.'

MB: I'm certainly a choreographer. Let them make up their minds whether they like my choreography or not. Still, there are times when I feel I'm not a *proper* choreographer: you know, someone who has all the steps in his head and can just show the company what to do? I often admire the result, and I don't feel I can compete with that kind of proficiency. Perhaps that is an old-fashioned approach? On the other hand, when I work alongside directors like Trevor Nunn or Richard Eyre or Sam Mendes or Rupert Goold, I realize that I have a much more detailed and precise-feeling instinct about movement to music than they do. And in those shows I do create the movement on my own body in front of the mirror, getting up and showing the movement for the dancers.

AM: *The whole dichotomy of being* either *a choreographer* or *a director*

633

is silly. Every great choreographer has always been a director too. Isadora Duncan, Martha Graham, George Balanchine, Frederick Ashton, Anthony Tudor, Merce Cunningham, Pina Bausch weren't just people who all made steps, they made new forms of theatre that were perceived as such by many theatre-goers. The same goes today for Paul Taylor and Twyla Tharp.

The theatre critic Stark Young in the 1930s and 1940s felt that Martha Graham was absolutely among the most radical and important makers of theatre of his day. The director Peter Gill said to me in 2001 that he considered Tudor's Dark Elegies *and Ashton's* Symphonic Variations *to be among the supreme works of twentieth-century British theatre. The director William Gaskill, a long-term aficionado of Merce Cunningham, has often remarked that he always learnt from Cunningham about aspects of theatre. To my mind he's right: Cunningham's is the most extraordinary form of theatre before the public today, quite as radical as Brecht or Beckett.*

Balanchine and Ashton, like Mark Morris today, both directed opera as a second aspect of their talent. And, though movement certainly flowed inventively out of Balanchine, Ashton's usual creative method was not unlike yours: he got the dancers to contribute much of the material, and then he shaped it.

Conversely, many directors working in opera or musical theatre have a keen sense of movement or music. I can still tell you precisely on which beat of the music certain singers did which movements in some 1970s productions by the opera director John Copley (who in turn said he learnt a great deal from watching Ashton's ballets), and I can tell you just why it mattered so much. He didn't give them dance steps to do, but his feeling for stance, gesture, movement had the kind of musical eloquence that I normally associate only with choreography.

MB: I know I've got that kind of feeling for connecting movement and music, and – like an opera director, I suppose – it's what connects my music-led side to my story-led side. I agree, though, with your larger point. How can you separate choreography from direction? Anyone trying to do so is simply reducing the scope of what a choreographer does. Still, it's all labels – and I have grown to hate, but live with, the labels!

I've said to you before, at the end of our *Cinderella* chapter, that it's when I'm staging a show for the second time that the real choreography gets done. Really what I mean there is that it's the *attention* to choreography that happens more fully the second time. Perhaps it's the direction and even the 'writing' that dominate the first time. You allow your first casts a certain amount of leeway for a season or two, because they've helped to create the piece. But then you see quite precisely how you want everything to go: it's *that* arm *there* on *that* beat, and the head back *there*. Not in some clockwork musicality, but because you're connecting the drama on stage to the drama in the music and what is 'actually' coming across to an audience. There is still leeway for the individual performer, of course, but to a different degree.

AM: *When* Play Without Words *came to New York in 2005, some dance critics got bothered when you said in interview that you weren't interested in dance for dance's sake.*[2]

MB: I wish I'd expressed myself more precisely! There's a lot of dance cliché about, and I am increasingly bored and angered by ballets that shove in the same double tours en l'air and manèges of grands jetés and fouetté turns and multiple pirouettes because that's what we think a ballet audience expects to see. The problem isn't the virtuosity – I can enjoy that too – it's the feeling that the same old formulas have to be turned out again and again. What do these steps mean? In modern dance, there's a lot of pure dance without virtuosity that seems to me just as boring. I want to see dancers who look motivated and human, and I want to see choreography that's suspenseful, emotive, characterful and engaging.

---

[2] See, for example, Joan Acocella, 'Class Act', *The New Yorker*, 4 April 2005. 'Bourne comes to us rarely, but whenever he does there is a big, long fuss in the press about whether his work is dance or drama. This is ridiculous. Theatrical dance, throughout its history, has swung back and forth between story-telling and abstraction. For every Marius Petipa there was a Michel Fokine, for every Balanchine an Agnes de Mille, insisting that movement had to "mean" something. In the end, it never mattered. Narrative or abstract, some dance shows were good, and some weren't. But Bourne, for his own reasons, has revived this weary debate . . . In interviews, he has taken on these issues aggressively, casting them in terms of real life versus some other, less vital condition. Dancers, he told Jesse Green, of the *Times*, are narrow, not like him. While they were shut up in a ballet studio, he was "going out and, you know, living a bit" – seeing Fred Astaire movies and MGM musicals. As for today's concert dance, it, too, is cloistered, to the extent that it is abstract. "I can't bear it", he said to Green, "when people come forward and just do a turn in the air for no reason." He, by contrast, is a story-teller, an entertainer. One must read between the lines here. Abstract means snobbish, bad. Narrative means democratic, good.

'I don't know to what extent these statements are heartfelt. They may just be publicity. Bourne wants a big audience – he wants to be an MGM musical. So the talk about movie-deprived dancers and motivationless air turns may be his way of saying, "Come to my show. It's not one of those effete things which the nobs seem to like – it's about life." If that's what he's doing, fine. Whatever works. But if he truly thinks that dance, because it is fundamentally abstract, is inconsequential, then one has to ask why he goes on making it. And so well.'

AM: *Let me challenge you on that a little. I appreciate that you continually ask, 'What do these steps mean?' when preparing and coaching your own work, and that it's a question you apply to dance drama. The same is true for such adjectives as 'emotive' and 'characterful'. I also agree with you that there is plenty of arid pure-dance choreography around. And I don't agree with those who call dance abstract; Balanchine, Cunningham and Morris have been among those who've said dance can't be abstract anyway because it involves humans.*

But I could take you through ballets and solos by Fred Astaire you love where I don't think you or anybody could say what any individual step meant. And I don't think you mean that the steps in Balanchine's Serenade *or Ashton's* Symphonic Variations *or* Monotones *are 'characterful' or 'emotive'.*

MB: All right, let me try again to be more precise. I think I can still watch *Giselle* or *The Sleeping Beauty* for pure joy if they're done well; I still wish I saw more ballets by Balanchine; I'm still in heaven going back to see Ashton's pure-dance ballets; and in recent years several of Mark Morris's pure-dance works have made me very happy indeed. I would say that all the pieces you mention here, despite not having specific meaning in each movement, are amazingly emotive works for me. I do not see them as abstract works at all. They also have character distinct to those works. If I'm honest, I think I just tie myself in knots in some interviews, either trying to defend myself or, as Joan Acocella notes, trying to sell the show to a non-dance audience, and often say things on which I can be rightly contradicted. Plotless dance is not what I'm known for, but I get a kick out of developing the dance aspects of such shows as *Highland Fling*, and one part of me would love to try making something dancier yet. But don't be surprised if I don't get round to it. Much of my mind is concerned with story, and I don't think that's likely to change.

AM: *Everyone remarked of Alan Vincent as the Car Man that he didn't look like a dancer. Did that plant the idea in your mind of what became* Play Without Words – *that they all looked like actors?*

MB: Yes. To some extent, that's always been what I've been looking for in dancers. Adam Cooper looked less like a ballet dancer than any other man at the Royal Ballet of his day. But now it's more true than ever. I like to have a cast that looks like real people. I try to avoid the manners and affectations that some dancers exhibit. It's nice for young people to see people up on stage that they can identify with, so they can feel 'I could do that' or, more precisely, 'I can identify with that character.'

AM: *This is something you have in common with Mark Morris. His sensibility is much more dancey than yours, and he asks for a more complex musicality. But the general look of the Mark Morris dancers is natural, not as if they'd spent hours a day or years of their life in academic dance.*
MB: Yes, but they have, of course! Sometimes it looks as if you could get up there and do it with them. That's a lovely quality to have.

Music, Recording, Amplification

ALASTAIR MACAULAY: *You've used more and more amplification in recent years. On tour, you've used taped music.*
MATTHEW BOURNE: This is a very difficult area. On the Highland Fling tour in 2005, we used live music in London but not on tour. We were attacked for this by the Musicians' Union, and there was picketing outside the theatre in Glasgow. Considering how many modern-dance companies use recordings these days – and outside Britain, more and more ballet companies are too – I wondered if our lives would have been easier if we'd used a recording in London too. There wasn't any fuss when we did it to a recording in the 1990s, which in the 1990s was the only way we could afford to do it. But the expense of live music and the reactions of the MU are only part of the problem here.

I like consistency, and there can be an enormous amount of problems for dancers with live music. We have had problems with deps (deputy musicians) coming in and issues with tempi. In these circumstances, you long for the reliability of a good recording, just for the sake of the dancers.

AM: *But I've known other choreographers say that the use of taped music leads to taped performances. It creates a dead musicality. Do you find that at all?*
MB: Oh, I like live music, and most dancers do. If the music's good, that's my preference, always. Wherever we can afford it. On the American tour of *Scissorhands*, the music was live in New York, San Francisco, Los Angeles and Washington, DC. And I do appreciate the musical difference between one performance and another. That can be exciting for the dancers, especially in a long run, where they are bedded in and ready for anything.

As I said, the expense is another problem. Remember we are not funded by the Arts Council as much as the revenue-funded clients. The Arts Council is supportive to the notion that, when we tour, we sometimes use recordings. Also we have the approval of the Musicians' Union to do this too. I guess one of the points that should be raised here is that even when we do perform live, the big classics (*Swan Lake, Nutcracker!, Cinderella*, etc.) are all played with reduced orchestrations. Is this serving the music well? Our recordings, inevitably, are closer to what the composer intended with the original-sized orchestra.

This brings us into the area of amplification, because otherwise the sound isn't big enough. In those circumstances, the happy balance is a small band amplified. You end up with a bigger sound than you do at an opera house with a full band. When I go back to Covent Garden in recent years, in the audience, the sound doesn't feel big enough to me. I want more. I've become so used to hearing everything quite powerfully now.

AM: *To me, this is real heresy. I've spent decades listening to opera, ballet and concert-hall music without amplification, and I love the unassisted projection of a voice or an instrument through a theatre or a hall. The same goes for theatre: when you've heard how some actors can project in big spaces, it's dismaying to find how often whole plays in medium-sized theatres on Broadway are often amplified – and occasionally in the West End too. To me, one of the biggest problems with most big-theatre musicals is overamplification. And it's a problem to me with the sound for* Scissorhands. *I had to keep reminding myself that it was being played live – not a problem I ever felt with* The Car Man *or* Play Without Words.

MB: Heresy? I think that we have to move with the times and create an experience that can compete with any medium. Otherwise we will lose our audience. Both *The Car Man* and *Play Without Words* were amplified. You wouldn't have had the same experience otherwise.

AM: *No, you're quite right. And my problem isn't – I realize – even sheer loudness, because I have no trouble with the loud music you use in* Dorian Gray: *it was perfectly part of the stage world. But I have a problem with the volume of much film music, I have a huge problem with the overamplification of some musicals, and I have some problem with the volume at which some of your scores are played – not all.*

MB: Our sound is mixed, of course. It's not just as simple as putting a mike in front of the different seats in the band. There is someone mixing the sound and bringing it up and down and pulling it back. It's something we can afford but also something that's got a creative power to it. I was very pleased with *Highland Fling* at Sadler's Wells in 2005. This show that had never had live music in the 1990s now did have. Reduced orchestration but amplified, it had, for me, a very good sound.

I've become used to the amplification in musical theatre. I viewed *Edward Scissorhands*, because it has only twelve musicians, along the lines of a West End show. The sound had to be designed that way as these were the shows we were competing with around the world, where this sort of sound is the norm. There's a lot of keyboards and sample sounds in there. Is that why it didn't sound live to you, maybe? *The Car Man* has fifteen players: just strings and percussion. That was a score that was really worth having live, but we did do it to recordings as well. The recordings were very good, very powerful. And both the live and recorded versions were very amplified.

So my views on all this are very mixed. There are days when I just come out of the theatre and think, 'How I wish we had had the recording tonight.' Sometimes a dull conductor can actually keep the whole show on one unvarying level, with the effect that the audience don't know why they're not getting as excited as they should.

AM: *The conductor issue I certainly recognize. When Ashton's ballet* Sylvia *was revived at Covent Garden in 2004, I was one of those who were underwhelmed. Zoe Anderson of the* Independent *was able to catch a later performance when they'd changed the conductor, and she emailed me to say, 'The choreography looks twice as good now.'*
MB: I know that feeling so well. It's to do with having a conductor who has the right feeling for the music and the right understanding of the production. I am happy to say that most of our MDs are highly theatrical and strive to understand the particular production, so that you feel they're working with you. They pull back on the emotional moments, they give you time to say what you want to say, they drive the next bit. They're not just interpreting it for themselves, they're interpreting it for the show.

Unfortunately, others come in and just give their interpretation of the music. I was shocked when we presented *Swan Lake* in Paris in December 2005. Because of the conductor, one performance bore no musical resemblance to any of the versions we've ever done. Unfortunately, the dancers had grown used to it. Things that were slow had become fast, fast things had become slow. However, it had one great pay-off. The Act Three male duet was extremely slow but absolutely riveting. And both Prince–Stranger couples are making that work extremely well. It played much more like a scene than a dance. It was still danced through but it seemed so intense. So it can work sometimes, if the performers are onto it and it doesn't throw them.

Changes of Choreographic Style and Method

ALASTAIR MACAULAY: *When we worked on the first edition of this book, you had become known for your 'classics':* Nutcracker!, Highland Fling, Swan Lake, Cinderella. *They were nicknamed 'classics' because you were using the music and to a large extent the story of the full-length ballets. In this millennium, you've revived four of those. But your new works –* The Car Man, Play Without Words, Edward Scissorhands, Dorian Gray – *haven't been 'classics' at all, though each of them has been a big hit.*

MATTHEW BOURNE: Well, they are all classics, but from another medium: opera or film or fiction. I suppose when some dance critics objected to *The Car Man*, they felt I was just trying the same method. But we weren't, at any level. Though we were using *Carmen* music, we weren't trying to do the whole score at all, and the whole sound world was entirely different from the opera. And the story was completely different. So for me that was the start of a new kind of work. By the time of *Play Without Words* that was obvious. Thanks mainly to Terry Davies, I've been able to work with a composer more easily than I'd ever once have hoped.

AM: *Your choreographic method has changed. You prepare and rewrite your scenarios on your computer. You now workshop material before rehearsals. You film dance phrases and you store that on the computer.*

MB: Computer technology has made a big difference to me. Everything in one place. Research, scenarios, movement phrases, an instant Google in the rehearsal room when I need a particular image or piece of information: fantastic! When it comes to filming, I'm not as sophisticated as the Ballet Boyz, Billy Trevitt and Michael Nunn, in the way that they edit film clips together. But I have worked out how to film and then identify a clip, edit it, and then put it onto my computer, so I can just play back a phrase of movement. That's very helpful. I don't think it helps you become a better choreographer or director. But it helps you to feel you're on top of things, and you're not losing anything. That's always a great comfort.

At workshops, I always do the filming myself. I also follow around the dancer who I think has got the movement best, cleanest. I suppose I started that around the time of *The Car Man*. Another thing that happens when you're trying to make a lot of material, it's good for dancers to know they can forget it and move on. So they say, 'Oh, film it now before we forget it.' As a result, we can spread out workshops over months. In the 1990s, everything had to be done immediately prior to your first performances on stage. But with the recent revival of *Highland Fling* in 2005 we did the workshops when they fitted in between other things – about eighteen months before we eventually staged it. We saved everything on tape. Nobody needed to remember it. When we began rehearsals, it was all brought out again. That's so useful when you've got a company that's touring. You can look at a schedule and say, 'We've got two weeks spare then. Why don't we workshop *Cinderella* for a revival in eighteen months' time?' And that will be time well spent. I'm sure that most choreographers do the same thing with filming and saving material now.

But I still do my handwritten graphs, my floor patterns, and my breakdown of the score in my own counts as before, handwritten. I haven't found a way of doing that on computer yet. Occasionally I'll draw an arm position or something like that.

Politics, Sexual and Gender Issues

ALASTAIR MACAULAY: *You've mentioned 9/11 in context of the performance history of* The Car Man, *and you've referred to the Bush family as a model for characters in* Edward Scissorhands. *Otherwise we've never really talked about politics.*

MATTHEW BOURNE: Very dodgy ground. I'm not interested in talking about my political views in public. For some artists, their work is the vehicle for their politics. But not mine.

I admit that when it comes to sexual politics, I'm some kind of public figure: I'm included on these lists of influential gay men and women, certainly as far as the arts are concerned. Yet even there I'm unsure quite why. I can see that I'm some kind of good example and that my work is too; I'm not afraid of that. And I see that I'm a hero of sorts to parts of the gay community. But I'm shy of labelling my work. I don't want to tell people what it's about. I want them to feel it. Decide for themselves. As I've said, every piece I make has some gay reference. But it's not really politics. It's just giving gay people more visibility and presenting gayness in the stories as something that is part of our lives, no more, no less. It's also fun for me, it's part of my life, and I want it to be there in the work.

AM: *An occasional complaint in politicized gay circles is that you are not honest enough to be a truly gay choreographer. Discuss.*
MB: I don't know what a gay choreographer is. I mean I simply don't know what that means. Does that mean the stories I tell?

AM: *It certainly means that, when you are talking about the relationship between the Prince and the Swan in* Swan Lake, *you should be more upfront about the sexual interpretation.*
MB: But the Prince is not an upfront kind of guy! Look, I've never denied that it *can* be read as the story of the Prince's homosexual attraction to the Swan. But if you insist on only that reading, then you limit the other implications of the story. The whole story was always designed as ambiguous. It's a swan, for God's sake: it can't be *that* literal!

But there's nothing ambiguous about Angelo in *The Car Man*. His attraction to Luca is sexual, and that's real sex they have. Likewise Dorian and Basil.

I always felt that *Swan Lake*'s had a positive effect in terms of gay issues because it presents a sympathetic portrait of that character, who is a prince after all, and can't be who he wants to be.

AM: *But another complaint would be that neither the Prince nor Angelo ends up happily.*
MB: And my reply is: That's the story. The traditional *Swan Lake* doesn't end happily for a straight couple either. Nor does *Carmen* or *The Postman Always Rings Twice* or *The Servant* or *La Sylphide*.

You're deliberately talking about very diehard gay activist people who only want positive images of gay life. Fair enough: there are enough bad ones. But what you get in my work is an acceptance of gay issues and gay characters throughout the work. There are always gay characters in there, and they're presented in the richness of the way any community would be. As all characters, they vary. Whether they're happy or sad, whether they're in the forefront of the story or the background, they're there always, somewhere. There was a romantic gay liaison in *Town & Country*, and another long-term gay couple on the sidelines of *The Car Man*. I don't wish to punish gay characters for the 'sin' of their sexuality. I do need to tell good stories.

The director Michael Grandage, for one, was astounded and exhilarated that we were finding acceptance in our regional touring venues for *Dorian Gray*, which is probably my most explicitly gay production. I agree that even five or six years ago we could not have toured this piece. As I've said, we regularly used to have walkouts in the early days of my *Swan Lake*, when two men danced together in a seemingly romantic/erotic way.

AM: *Another complaint is that you're a misogynist. It's not just that you prefer choreographing for men than for women. But the women in your works are often no better than they ought to be. The Queen in* Swan Lake *and Lana in* The Car Man *are conniving, adulterous floozies.*

MB: That's just ridiculous, and is an old argument that stems from the use (and non-use) of women in *Swan Lake*. As you know, I'm especially fond of the Queen in that show as a character, and I think the Girlfriend is multifaceted too. I've created a whole range of female characters. *The Car Man* may have a gorgeous villain in Lana, but it also has a tender female character in Rita. Lady H. changes the whole world of *Dorian Gray*, and there's nothing stereotypical about the way she partners Dorian.

AM: *Yes, but it's either/or. Lana vs Rita, Clara vs Sugar. Rita is good but unsexy.*

MB: What does sexy have to do with misogyny? Rita is a sympathetic, sweet young woman. And what about Clara in the *Nutcracker!*, Cinderella, Kim in *Edward Scissorhands*? Kim is a lovely, perfect girl. She's mainly kind and thoroughly romantic and sexual.

AM: *You workshopped a* Romeo, Romeo. *But* Romeo and Juliet *was not an issue for you.*

MB: Look, you can only use your own experiences. I find it easier to identify with a love between two men really, ultimately. And, as I found from the *Romeo, Romeo* workshop and from *Dorian Gray*, I love the challenge of making male–male relationships work believably: the sheer difficulty or unusualness of it whets my interest.

AM: *You'd like to do a* My Beautiful Laundrette *ballet?*
MB: Something like that, yes. Why not? *Beautiful Thing*: what is that if not a take on *Romeo and Juliet?*

But the whole relationship between Kim and Edward in *Edward Scissorhands* I find terribly moving, as I do the love of the Pilot for Cinderella and Clara's fight for Nutcracker. I'm not uninvolved in it. I still find those stories very touching; and I love giving direction as to how they should feel in those scenes. Kim has to learn about Edward; obviously, she feels no instant attraction. She has to discover what's in him. I also love the relationship between Cinderella and the Pilot: so that I find *Cinderella* the most moving of all my works. (So really I'm contradicting myself!)

AM: *You said in the 1990s that you loved coaching the role of the Queen in* Swan Lake. *Now you're talking of coaching Kim and other heroines. I would say that many of the artists we admire – not just such homosexual ones as Ashton, but such heterosexual ones as Balanchine too – have found that their female characters release the feminine aspects of themselves. How much do you find choreography and direction have made you more aware of the feminine aspects of yourself?*
MB: Difficult question. I have always felt that relationships between same-sex couples are no different from heterosexual ones. So, when I direct female characters in romantic or sexual relationships, I call upon my own experience and the specific type of character I am creating. I don't think I am more 'aware' of feminine aspects in myself through doing this. Maybe they have always been there?

Dance Style

ALASTAIR MACAULAY: *When you choose dancers – for example, the six you selected for the* Romeo, Romeo *workshops in 2007 or the two dancers you'd never worked with before when you then made* Dorian Gray *in 2008 – you choose them for their personalities and acting, but you're looking for movement qualities you want to see. Are you able to analyse now the dance qualities you look for?*
MATTHEW BOURNE: Sometimes you only realize why you are doing what

you are doing because something shows you that you have got a certain taste in movement and in the way people move and interpret movement. But yes, I can now state some of what I'm looking for in a dancer.

Let me take Richard Winsor as an example. The reason I love his dancing is because, for me, his movement always looks natural. He has none of the affectations that can affect some dancers and that can take away the sexual appeal of a man dancing. He always looks masculine and relaxed. It's very hard to take a bad photograph of him. When he does a photo-shoot with Hugo Glendinning, for example, you find you can use virtually every shot, because of this naturalness in the way he moves. He's also a completely reliable performer, he never does a bad show. When Jane Torvill came to a *Dorian* performance, she said she loved him and that he reminded her of Christopher Dean. I asked why. She said, 'Because he's so graceful, so beautiful, but masculine, always.' And I thought, 'That's true.' Chris Dean always comes across as a man: so beautiful to watch. He never loses that quality. Misha (Baryshnikov) has always been like that as a dancer, too. Obviously the technique is incredible, but you always feel you're watching a person, a man, and nothing takes you away from that.

With some dancers and some skaters, the technique can often blur the beauty. That's why some people don't work for me in *Swan Lake* as the Swan. They get all worked up about the role's technique whereas actually I want them to feel it more.

AM: *Are there particular qualities of movement you find yourself looking for or drawing out?*
MB: I don't like overextended positions, I'm always saying, 'a bit lower in the leg'. For that reason a lot of choreography doesn't appeal to me; I find it rather freakish-looking. Since I am always looking for actors as well as dancers, I want them to look like people, not like technicians who can do something that nobody else can do. Of course, most people look at our dancers and say, 'I can't do that', but it's a question of how far you take that.

Having said that, I'm always looking for dancers who are 'big' movers and who perform with a marked sense of passion in their dancing. I am particularly interested in the fluidity of movement in the torso and shoulders, clean arms, and an abandoned, sensuous head and neck. I guess I'm not so worried about less than perfect feet or loose hips and hyperextended legs. I would much rather have a dancer who knows how to make logical and musical sense of the movement. I'm never really looking at technique; I'm looking for feeling and order and even joy in movement. But you do need a good technique to achieve this: no question about that. I often think the most telling aspect of a good dancer is how they join the movement up: the phrasing, the connections, the bits in between, so to speak.

AM: *Are there qualities of movement from dancers that you try to draw out?*
MB: There's a certain body shape which works for *Swan Lake*, which is longer limbs, longer arms. I've got to know that through doing it more. Even with the smaller guys, you are looking for proportionate bodies.

I'm always having to work on the amount they use their torso – because that's an area of the body I like. And that connects to the legs. I'm forever telling dancers to get down, to get into plié more, to be juicier with movement; and that has to do with the back and with the legs bending towards the floor. Too many people are pulled up all the time. I do see that you can need that pulled-up quality particularly in certain classical-ballet work, but I think a lot of the choreography I do should have more juice. So it means bending, arching, tipping, getting down. That's a constant note to people. And use more back, shoulders, that area of the body.

AM: *You mentioned that Alan Vincent was the most musical swan in the corps on Broadway. When you're talking about musicality in your work, what are the musical virtues that you appreciate in the dancers?*
MB: The dancers are all taught counts, but that's not what I mean. I do value precision, which is why counts initially matter, but I'm above all looking for phrasing. Most of the dancers find they forget the counts after a certain number of performances. Alan Vincent is one of those who really phrases but never departs from the main rhythmic emphasis. Adam Cooper was brilliant at this: I've never known anyone so good at playing with the music while being completely reliable in the choreography. He would speed up, slow down, catch himself up. That was because he was quite in command of his technique and what he was doing. Fiona Chadwick was the same. The two of them together were fantastic. Their musicality made it so exciting. I think Fiona could have made quite dull steps interesting by playing with the music. There are not many people like that. But it must start with a clean delivery of the choreography with a sure musical emphasis. Sometimes, though,

because of the nature of my work, the acting of the role can take over from the music. I try to get the dancers to think of the music as their script and to use it to express what they need to say as actors too. As most trained actors would be horrified to work to counts, I do quite understand the dilemma.

Criticism and Self-Criticism

ALASTAIR MACAULAY: *In recent years, you've started to talk about not reading reviews. Did this start with* The Car Man?

MATTHEW BOURNE: It started earlier. Probably around the time of the original *Cinderella*.

But you can't stay with a show and avoid every review. Sometimes people have singled out reviews for me to read. In London, when *Play Without Words* was new, yours was one of two or three reviews I read. When it reached New York, I did become aware of some of the fuss about whether it was for theatre critics or dance critics. And once a show's been doing well, it gathers a collection of press quotes anyway: that's part of the deal. I'll do interviews, and so of course I become aware of some of what's being said. When *Scissorhands* opened, I read nothing. Even when my mother singled out one that she thought would cause me no problem at all and that would interest me, I still wouldn't. It's almost a paranoia now, I suppose. I think a review's going to be something that will ruin my day. It's just too painful sometimes.

AM: *I presume you're modest enough to feel you need criticism at some stage of your shows. To whom do you go for this?*

MB: Not really to people who watch dance every other night of the week. The context is so odd for them, and not ideal for appreciating how my work might appeal to a wide audience. I surround myself with people early on who open up the forum for discussion about what the show needs, particularly early on in a run. And I will ask questions to people in the audience, and then I'll listen carefully to what they have to say. Of my colleagues I ask, 'Is there any one thing that everyone's saying? Is there a particular element that is coming across as the thing that people are not happy with?' If you've got a mix of opinions, then one person's view may be just an individual reaction.

But it's important to know the general audience and critical feeling. Also I listen carefully to every noise an audience makes in reaction. If experienced theatre people come in, the way that Sam Mendes did with

an early preview of *Cinderella*, and tell me what they are and aren't seeing, then that's invaluable too. Early on in the life of a show, I'm always
asking, 'Is this clear? Is that coming across?'

I think too that I'm very quick to criticize my own work, and all my
regular colleagues – Lez, Terry, Scott, Etta – are really good at this too.
I just will not rest until I've sorted out all the things I feel could be better. I'm almost obsessive about this. But I pride myself on being professional enough to know what can be practically achieved at any point. It's
important not to be crazy, not to try to do everything at once and drive
everyone else crazy. You need will-power, so that you can say, 'OK, I
know I'm going to do that, but it has to wait till January.'

Changing Generations of Dancers, Colleagues, Posterity, Preservation

ALASTAIR MACAULAY: *When we did the interviews for the first edition
of this book, you were taking as stars leading dancers from the Royal
Ballet – Fiona Chadwick, Adam Cooper, Lynn Seymour, Sarah Wildor.*

*But even then you were making a star out of Will Kemp, whose very
first job as a dancer was as a Big Swan in your original 1995 production
of Swan Lake. The Royal Ballet School hadn't thought he had much
hope of a major career, but thanks to you he quickly became far more
prestigious than any of his Royal Ballet School contemporaries.*

*And now your work has become the catalyst that leads some peo-
ple to dance in the first place. Or to change their kind of dance career.
Richard Winsor was training to be a ballet dancer at Central Ballet
School when he saw your Swan Lake. After that, he knew he wanted
a different career. He auditioned for your company, his first job was in
the ensemble of* The Car Man, *and now he's one of your stars, one of
the two men playing Edward Scissorhands and almost the one and only
player of Dorian Gray.*

At the end of the movie Billy Elliot, *the duckling-into-swan dance
hero grows up to go on stage as the Swan in your Swan Lake; this has
been a real-life story for several people now.*

MATTHEW BOURNE: Yes, and Richard isn't the only one of our dancers
who was turned on to dance by seeing my work. I'm very proud of that.

AM: *Back in 1991, you started to forge with Scott Ambler, Etta Murfitt
& Co. a largely collaborative creative process. But now you have*

dancers who are twenty or twenty-five years younger than yourself.
Does this collaborative process change when the dancers are of a differ-
ent generation?

MB: Do you know, it actually doesn't. The relationship is slightly different, but I still am at great pains to make them know that I'm their friend.
I want to get to know them. Not as a close friend perhaps, because the
age gap is so big. But you can be someone that they look up to. I try to
return that respect. And I try to get them to talk. It helps me to know
them as people, not just as dancers. And if you're excited by the potential of what someone can do, then the work itself becomes very exciting
to do. And these younger dancers are very open. Maybe more so than
people who were my contemporaries.

Meanwhile Etta Murfitt and Scott Ambler have become great collaborators on new work, because they understand so well how the whole
company works and how this kind of *work* works. They, and the many
other performers who have been around for some years now, are a good
example to the new company members. So you've got this mixture of the
old and the young. It works very well. I myself feel older, surrounded
by so many young people! – but the working relationships really don't
change enormously and it's always been that way, to quite an extent.
I enjoy the company of young people; I feel I have a lot to learn from
them, especially if I want my work to speak to a wide audience.

AM: *Now that you're more experienced, are you as flexible or receptive*
as you once were?

MB: Mostly, I think. I trust my instinct a lot more. I always feel the same
if I feel I've got a good idea; I'll stick with it. But I'm still as keen as I ever
was to absorb other people's ideas, whoever they are. And that's partly
why I pick the dancers I do. As you said, the credits for *Play Without*
Words say, 'Movement devised by Matthew Bourne & the company',
because there in particular I was so aware of their input. But I'm aware
of it with *Scissorhands* and *Dorian*, too: the dancers have really contributed. My fear is always people who just stand there and wait. I can't
bear that.

AM: *Building on what you said a moment ago about Scott and Etta, are*
there any others who have become part of your creative process?

MB: Lez (Brotherston) and Terry are the main collaborators, I think; and
now Paule Constable, our lighting designer. But I have dance captains,
who remember and teach material, both in new works and with revivals.

In new works, once we've developed material in workshops, they're the ones who hang on to it and then do the teaching of it when we put the show together.

Then there are people who are in charge of individual tours or revivals. For example, while *Swan Lake* did a long multi-week run in Paris, Vicky Evans was looking after that as our artistic tour director. Neil Penlington was also one of the people playing the Prince, and so he also kept an eye on it. And Isabel Mortimer and Saranne Curtin were both playing the Queen: they were both in the original 1995 production. So there are a lot of old hands who, either directly or indirectly, are looking after the show.

AM: *You've assembled and developed a whole troupe of dancers we've come to know as they've played one role after another over the years. We saw a dozen of them together in* Play Without Words. *What happens to these dancers of whom we grow so fond, when they're not in one of your productions?*

MB: The number of dancers who've played leading roles with us is now very large. And that creates problems. In 2005, I was looking at our cast for *Edward Scissorhands*. Out of a cast of twenty-nine, nineteen people have played leading roles with one or more productions of mine. So for a number of them, it's quite a step to agree to play an ensemble role in a show like this. Here, the only principal role is Edward. We do have character principals: the next rung down, you might say. That includes the dancers playing Kim (later made a principal role), Jim, Joyce, George and Bill and Peg Boggs. Everyone else is ensemble. Some people will accept this, if they're at the point in their careers where they feel they're more interested in doing new work than in playing a big role; they also know that if you do supporting roles here, they may well get a big opportunity later on.

But some of those who are a bit older just can't justify coming into a show where they're not playing a leading role. Even though everybody in *Scissorhands* has individual moments that they can make their own, there have been several dancers who feel in particular that they can't step down to that kind of supporting role – with us. They'd rather play ensemble in another show elsewhere. For them, it's a matter of pride. That's not how they put it: they look on it as 'It's time I tried something else.' But I'm always sad when this happens. I miss them. In this respect, *Play Without Words* – although great for everyone involved – was a bad show for us, because all twelve dancers were deemed to be principal per-formers, ranked equally: that's how it was negotiated with the National, and then it continued that way, throughout the history of the show, with all twelve on a principal wage. After that, I appreciate that it's difficult to go backwards. But it's lovely to see someone like Steve Kirkham, who was in my original *Swan Lake* in 1995 and who was one of those twelve *Play Without Words* principals, making such a funny, vivid job out of George Monroe in *Edward*.

AM: *You've been mentioning plans for* Cinderella *in 2010–11.*
MB: Yes, that's the big show next year. It takes me completely into pure romantic, heterosexual, female-led territory: very different from what we have been doing recently, especially from *Dorian*. It's nice to go to different extremes. I'm very much looking forward to *Cinderella* because I have a big affection for that piece; and, again, I feel it's the chance to really look at it now. It'll be a present to myself for my fiftieth birthday.

Also I'm writing a treatment for a screenplay based on *Cinderella*. BBC Films have commissioned me. I've had a few meetings recently with film companies in this country and really enjoyed it; I've felt a con-nection with the British producers that I never felt in Hollywood. In all those meetings I had years ago, I started to talk about my interests and I would feel them glaze over, apparently thinking, 'That's not very commercial.' Whereas with the UK producers, I've found myself talking about *Cinderella* as one of the ideas I've had and I've started talking about setting it during the Blitz and about Powell and Pressburger – and they get so excited! Their reaction has been: 'Yes, we absolutely want to do something like that. Something with dance in it, a mixture of dancers and actors. Let's make a Powell and Pressburger film!'
So to make a film version of that story would be exciting.

AM: *For the stage* Cinderella, *will you commission new scenery?*
MB: The original production was never made for touring. It was an unwieldy sit-down production planned for London and then resurrected in Los Angeles. Today, to make the pieces work, touring is an essential part of what we do. So Lez would need to rethink it for touring. We'd start from scratch, really.

AM: *Having seen how much you changed it when you took it to LA in 1999, I'd love London to see it. Several people I spoke to there found it a more remarkable piece than* Swan Lake, *which is not how it impressed people when it was new in London. It had acquired so much more dimension.*

MB: You know, I really thought we'd lost all record of how that revised 1999 production looked. But it turned out that Sara (Saranne) Curtin had a video that somebody made of her performance in LA, and now, thank goodness, I've got a copy of that. It was almost lost for ever.

AM: *Do you get at all interested in posterity? Do you ever want to have things notated for future generations?*

MB: I have to admit to being very interested in posterity. Why would I continue reviving my work and creating a brand about it and keeping the rep alive? Must be my love of dance history!

I always think of film as a way of preserving choreography. I know you can't get everything from that, but it's the best way I know.

AM: *You don't use a dance notator?*

MB: No. We did on the original *Cinderella*. But it's pointless with my stuff, because it keeps changing. It changes in the rehearsal room, but also with each successive revival and during the tours. The notator would have to have a full-time post. We changed so much of *Cinderella* when we redid it in 1999, for example. And some of it would be difficult to notate: there's so much involved with performance and acting.

AM: *But you're happy with a film because it preserves the performance as you want it at that time. You don't have any ambition to establish a permanent text of your works that can be done by posterity?*

MB: Not in that sense. But what I am doing at the moment with Robert Noble and New Adventures is to bring slowly back into the rep the more important big works so that they're not forgotten for long. Our 1990s stagings were never created to have long lives. The sets really weren't built for touring. Over the years, however, Robert and I have been resurrecting these productions. We plan to rebuild the scenery for *Cinderella* in 2010, for example, in such a way that it can go into storage at the end of a season or a tour until we get it out again whenever we need, just as a large ballet company would do.

AM: *Lez Brotherston feels that you take much more pleasure in reviving old works than he does. He feels so attached to the original cast that he always misses them. And his main interest is all in new work.*

MB: Well, he rarely sees the subsequent casts! Like Lez, I'm more obsessed with a new work than with an old one. Of course. But after I've seen what new, young dancers can do in creating something, then I want to stretch them with an older role. I loved seeing what the 2002 cast of *Nutcracker!* did. And I remember how much you loved Ewan Wardrop as Fritz in that – but don't forget that that role was made on Scott Ambler in 1992. I think you will agree that both were great? I loved watching what James Leece and Kerry Biggin have done with James and the Sylph in *Highland Fling*, and the latest casts of *The Car Man*, including Richard Winsor and Michela Meazza, were just sensational. Or I want to promote dancers who've been with me for years into senior roles, the way I have with Alan Vincent, Neil Penlington and Sara Curtin as the Swan, the Prince and the Queen in *Swan Lake*.

I love live performance. Every day is a fresh start and it can always be better. That's what gets me up in the morning. It's also why I may never love the process of making movies in the same way.

(Conversations 2005–9)

Appendix A

Scenarios

The Car Man, Play Without Words,
Edward Scissorhands, Dorian Gray

The Car Man (2000)

ALASTAIR MACAULAY: *According to the notes you drew up before the start of rehearsals, there's an opening sequence that runs through three parts. After sections A, B and C, you wrote, 'This whole opening sequence is a lengthy introduction to characters, place, and mood, the world our story is to be told in. It should feel like one big long number.'*

MATTHEW BOURNE: Yes. This is from the fifth draft. It's dated 20 February 2000.

'A. The Carshop/Garage (working dance).' All kinds of car work. 'Various duets, solos, trios, are intertwined throughout, ending in a brief unison section . . . Angelo walks through . . . he is obviously different from the others. There is a brief confrontation with the other mechanics, and we get the sense that he is regularly hounded.'

'B. The Shower/Locker room.' More solo, duets, trios, as the men undress, shower, dry off, dress.

'C. The Diner (outside). Early evening – midsummer . . . The diner is populated by women waiting for the men to get out of work. They are raucous, lively, playing music on the jukebox.'

AM: *This is a gender reversal of* Carmen *Act One, where the men of Seville are waiting for the female workers to come out of the cigarette factory.*

MB: Absolutely.

'Lana and Rita are serving food in pinnies. Angelo is seen in the distance, finishing his work at the gas station. There is also the local motorcycle cop, Chuck, sitting there, having his usual supper plate.' (He isn't there in the stage version.) 'Men arrive at the diner, spruced up and clean for dates/food/drink, etc. Ends in a big group dance to the juke-box music.'

Then Act One, Scene One (in and around Dino's diner). 'The high spirits of the diner are interrupted by the arrival of the drifter, Luca.' Lana is frozen; Angelo is also attracted by him.

I wanted a spotlight on Luca and Lana. What I was thinking of was the movie of *West Side Story*, and the moment when Tony and Maria first set eyes on each other.

Meanwhile other men and women are dancing, while Lana, playing coy, avoids serving Luca. Finally he 'grabs her pad, and writes his own order on it aggressively (a challenge is set)'. He dances the Habañera, which 'establishes his character – daring, cheeky, dangerous. Lana watches, we can see she likes it. (So does Angelo.) The solo ends with Lana plonking his meal down in front of him.'

Actually, Angelo isn't involved in the Habañera scene in the stage version. We needed to establish the attraction between Lana and Luca first.

Dino arrives. Luca approaches him about the job vacancy. They go into the office to talk business. 'Rita dances a solo to get Angelo's interest . . . The solo develops into a duet.' Others enter and break up the duet. Angelo gets taunted. But Luca enters and 'saves' Angelo.

AM: *That's different from what we see on stage, isn't it?*
MB: Angelo needed introducing before we saw his feeling for Luca. As it worked out, his duet with Rita actually starts with a group of townspeople chasing him. And then it shows the incomplete, unequal feelings they have for each other.

Dino emerges. Everyone clears out. Dino 'shakes Luca's hand – the job is his – Lana feigns indifference – Dino goes to the telegraph pole to retrieve the "Man Wanted" sign. As Dino tears it in two, Rita is seen looking longingly at Angelo who is looking at Luca who is looking at Lana who looks with distaste at her husband Dino.'

Now a Passage of Time sequence that I've called 'Heat'. A 'group dance about the unbearable heat – an atmosphere of sexual tension created – everyone on heat. Solos, duets, men working, stripped to the waist, two women with fans, two sunning themselves, two men having a shower, etc. No one touches the other, the lust is in the mind (perhaps some of the gestures or work tasks have a suggestive nature).'

AM: *It's amazing how body language changes in a city during a hot summer, and how much more sexual tension and sexual encounter you see in the open air.*

MB: Yes. I was especially thinking of the film *Body Heat*, and the scene there between William Hurt and Kathleen Turner. You watch them for forty-five minutes; they interact without anything happening. Then suddenly he smashes through the window and they have sex on the spot: very passionate. Then they both bathe in a bath full of ice cubes!

In *The Car Man*, this general scene leads to Act One, Scene Two. Same midday heat, but two weeks later. 'Luca is giving Angelo a boxing lesson, in their lunch hour, teaching him how to defend himself from the others.' Rita instinctively tries 'to distract Angelo from his new "best friend"'.

I was still thinking of *Body Heat* here, and both Lez Brotherston (who designed) and I wanted Rita to be 'cooling herself in front of an open fridge door'. It wasn't possible. Instead, she brings them a couple of beers. Luca takes his, but when she offers the other one to Angelo, he just doesn't notice her. Luca leads him away, which leaves her feeling deflated. Luca's in control. He's consciously trying to shake things up.

'Dino is seen in his office counting money. We see Luca taking this in.'

Lana enters, 'places a coin in the jukebox, and, to the music, dances a provocative solo, knowing she is being watched by all; of course, she is putting on this display primarily for Luca (she is prepared to make some bread, outside on the table with various pots, utensils, and dough with flour)'. (Here, with the bread, I was thinking of Jessica Lange and Jack Nicholson in their version of *The Postman Always Rings Twice*.) 'It is lunchtime at the garage, and the men have gathered, above, to watch her, clapping and stamping encouragingly . . . Chad, a young guy, helps Lana getting the things she needs from inside the diner, while she dances. He has a crush on Lana and will do anything for her. At the solo's end, she begins to prepare the dough (slowly, provocatively).'

Dino emerges, confronts Lana about her behaviour. She knows how to win him over. He leaves reluctantly after a wifely kiss on his cheek. Lunchtime is over. Lana and Luca are left alone . . . 'The boxing lesson and her dance have made him horny as hell and he suddenly pounces on her on the kitchen table – they are insatiable for each other . . .' It was always important to me that they're quite dirty with flour flying everywhere and so forth. The situation isn't planned by either – the sex is sudden and uncontrollable. And hot and sweaty.

They go off into the house, 'Luca carrying Lana'. (He doesn't carry her in the stage version.) 'The ensemble takes over in a series of steamy duets to mirror the climactic happening in the unseen bedroom.' I wanted multiplication, but diversity too. Not a traditional corps de ballet doing exactly the same as the lead couple, but the idea of a mood catching like a forest fire.

It turns to dusk. (In the theatre, the lighting makes it clear that we've shifted from midday to evening.) Dino returns, happily drunk. (I originally thought of a solo for him here – but that changed into a scene. He has to clear everyone off, and then to make a noise – knocking something over.) Lana and Luca realize he's coming. Luca escapes half-dressed out of the side window. (As we've staged it, they're still at it upstairs when they suddenly realize he's coming. All he sees through the window is Lana's top half, but because we've just seen Luca going down on her, we know what's happening out of sight.)

Various encounters occur now in another Passage of Time sequence. The scenario has a lot of dramatic detail that just doesn't happen or gets condensed – probably because of the music. And it just worked better to place less emphasis on the passing of time and to make things look quicker. In particular, to make it look as if Luca shags two people in the same night. 'We eventually arrive at another place, in wasteland somewhere away from the diner, a kind of lover's lane. A car is parked and is moving rhythmically. There is obviously some kind of sexual activity taking place inside! Eventually Luca falls out of the car, sweaty and exhausted, and tumbles to the floor. Just as we expect Lana to flop out of the other side, we see Angelo emerge . . .'

And so into Act One, Scene Three. Angelo is left alone. His 'head is spinning, he doesn't know what has happened, but he feels happy and exhilarated. (Solo.) As he leaves the stage, the dance and the feeling are taken over by Lana. (Solo – same music.) . . . They are both in love!'

That turned into a double solo to the same entr'acte music. It's my favourite bit of staging, actually: these two very different people, Lana and Angelo, in different parts of the stage, going through the same movement, the same emotion, over the same person. The scene begins and ends with a kiss: the same kiss, different people receiving it.

In Act One, Scene Four, there's a party at the diner 'to celebrate an engagement between one of the mechanics, Rocco, and his girl, Mercedes'; Dino becomes jealous and violent with Lana. He confronts her. Angelo steps in to defend her, and Dino promptly fires him. (There were

657

extra details here that I had to change in the event. It's Rita who defends Lana from Dino's confrontation, and then Angelo who finds the strength to defend Rita. Dino is so shocked to find Angelo, of all people, standing up to him, that he fires him. Everyone sees this – it spoils the party. What I was trying to set up was the eventual frame-up of Angelo – to make it look as if people might reasonably assume *he* had a motive for killing Dino.)

'Lana has had enough and wants out. As the party continues, she drags Luca away into the darkened garage, so that they can be alone. (Duet.)'

But Dino catches them. Lana grabs the nearest object and hits him over the head – injuring him badly. Luca is horrified, but Lana puts the weapon in his hand. He helps to kill Dino, but he's appalled. She's excited.

Angelo enters. Luca and Lana hide. Dino, with his dying breath, crawls towards Angelo and covers him with his blood. 'Lana, thinking on her feet, tells Luca to take and dispose of the gun and to call the police. (She has a plan.)'

There are two other areas of action here. Luca tries to make a phone call; Rita sees him with the weapon. Meanwhile Lana advances on the terrified Angelo, pretending to be shocked and to accuse him, until she knows Chuck the cop and others are coming, when she pretends to struggle and fight with Angelo, crying rape, and claiming that he murdered her husband. The crowd, remembering how Dino sacked Angelo, sees a motive for the murder. As Angelo is led away, he looks helplessly at Rita – who runs, confused, to the side of her sister Lana – and at Luca, who looks away in shame.

Act Two starts in 'an upmarket club'. I've written a note in brackets here: 'classy beatnik feel?' (It ended up being called 'Le Beat-Route'!) Lana and Luca are living the high life, spending Dino's modest fortune; they've brought some friends from Harmony (which is what we call the small town they live in). 'They are all flashily dressed (trailer trash) and a little out of place. They gamble, buy drinks for all at the bar, and dance the night away, but a moment of doubt is shown, at the end of the scene, as we see Luca remember Angelo and the fact that they sent an innocent man to prison.' This scene includes what at this stage I described as 'a cheesy Las Vegas-style cabaret lounge act' became the Martha Graham inspired act.

Fade to Scene Two, a prison. Angelo is in the country gaol. 'He is a changed man: worn down and dejected, he has obviously been beaten up.' He is hounded by a physically and sexually abusive prison warden, the sadistic Dexter. (There are overlaps with a group dance for other prisoners in the cells behind.)

AM: *It's from now on that Angelo becomes, interestingly, more and more like José in the later stages of the opera: dangerous, crazed, a potential killer.*

MB: Yes. As I've said, the Carmen/José axis in the opera turns into the Lana/Luca/Angelo triangle in *The Car Man*. But Angelo's character has no aspect of Carmen – he's entirely on the José side, and like José, he will come back from prison obsessed, a transgressor.

In prison, Rita visits Angelo. During his trial, she kept silent, partly out of anger at his rejection of her, and partly through wanting to protect her sister Lana. But now she feels guilty about that silence. She tells him her version of the facts. She believes it was Luca (not Lana) who carried out the murder. She tells Angelo of Luca's torrid affair with Lana, and she describes how she saw Luca with the weapon. (The murder is now re-enacted, in the form of a flashback, but with Luca as the aggressor and Lana looking on horrified.) She hopes to win Angelo back with this news. She wants to discredit Luca in his eyes.

But the news confuses Angelo – and enrages him. Until now, he thought Luca was his friend/lover. He starts to attack Rita, but prison guards restrain him. Rita leaves, scared and upset.

Angelo, left alone, is cornered by his admirer, Dexter. Angelo leads him on, then takes his chance. Getting him in a compromising position, he knocks him out, and disguises himself with Dexter's uniform to help him escape.

AM: *Your notes for the prison scene show a lot of multi-layering. You even thought of Luca and Angelo dancing together to show that 'they are thinking of each other'. Then a prison scene for Angelo might grow into a prisoners' dance. Next there's all the layer of re-enacted narrative as Rita tells her story to Angelo.*

MB: All of these possibilities interested me; and some remain. But the most important thing was to keep the story going. I was also going to have other women visit the prison, for example. It all got pared down.

Act Two, Scene Three is back at the club. Time has passed. There's an 'end of evening' feeling now, established by various incidental details. 'Lana and Luca's relationship is decaying. He is guilt-ridden, drinking heavily, and a mess. She is over-made-up, flirting, slightly pathetically, with any man who will pay attention. Luca is no fun any more; there is still love there, but he has changed, has become weak and troubled.

'Luca sits at a table, drinking. Lana flirts and dances with a group of men, annoying their girlfriends, trying to make Luca react. He doesn't respond . . .' Like Carmen, she's looking for the next man. But this all becomes simplified – mainly it's a duet for Lana and Luca. When she leaves, he staggers to the bar and joins 'Shirley, a fellow lush. She is beautiful but hauntingly sad and vulnerable.' This leads into a scene, where he, hallucinating, sees Dino's battered body 'come back to life as a barman'. Luca takes Shirley onto the dance floor, other couples join them, but still Luca sees Dino dancing among them.

Now back to Dino's Diner for Act Two, Scene Four. It's winter. There's a 'For Sale/Closed' sign outside. 'There is a sense that the whole community has become more violent and lusty, decaying along with Lana and Luca's relationship.' It's closing time, and Rita is getting rid of the last few people. Left alone, she has a solo, reflecting on her 'disastrous visit to Angelo'. She pulls down the shutter at the front of the diner 'and is shocked to see the word "Murderer" painted across it in blood red'.

AM: *You've kept this 'Murderer' graffiti, but you now bring it in later, and as read by someone else.*
MB: Yes.

Soon Rita comes face to face with Angelo. 'We are not sure of his motives, he seems a little unhinged. Rita humours him and tries to calm him. Angelo catches her trying to make a phone call and produces a gun from his pocket.' He puts the gun to her head and leads her to the locker room, where he'll hold her hostage. 'We fear for Rita's life.'

'Meanwhile Luca and Lana have returned with their friends from a wild car race . . .' Shades of *Rebel Without a Cause* there! (I was still working out how to get two cars packed with passengers lurching around the stage.) Eventually, everybody emerges. 'Lana is shaken to see the graffiti on the diner ("Murderer") and knows that something is up.' There's a fight contest, with Luca leading the warm-up (inspired by the Brad Pitt movie *Fight Club*). Then Angelo emerges from the crowd. 'He faces Luca as if to challenge him . . . Angelo teases Luca initially, and then, like an animal, in a savage frenzy, he beats Luca to a bloody pulp. Luca, on his knees, looks up to Angelo for mercy; they look into each other's eyes for a moment; and, as the crowd expects Angelo to finish him off with one final blow, he walks across to him, takes his bloody face in his hands, and kisses him violently on the lips and throws him to the floor. His own face now smeared with Luca's blood, Angelo turns away and laughs wildly, but his laughter soon turns to tears. He seems to regret what he has done. As Angelo turns back, Luca is pointing a gun at him, shaking. Angelo walks slowly towards him, holding his hand out for the gun. As Luca looks as if he might hand it over, a shot rings out, and Luca drops to the floor. The crowd parts, and we see the figure of Rita, smoking gun in hand. Luca is dead.'

As with every show I've done, the story itself changed as we went on working on it. Parts of this scenario occur quite differently on stage, and that's because of the rehearsal process. It isn't Rita who holds the smoking gun now! But that's the draft that I took to the first rehearsals.

Play Without Words (2002)

Various versions of the scenario exist in Matthew Bourne's notes, especially of Act One. In one, four of the five main characters had different names. Tony was still Tony (not Anthony). Glenda used to be Susan; Prentice used to be Barrett; Sheila used to be Vera; and Speight was called Porter (after Jimmy Porter, of *Look Back in Anger*). The versions do not greatly differ from each other. In one version, Act One is broken down into nineteen scenes, in another into twenty.

Some of these are minutages prepared for the composer Terry Davies, who has annotated two of them. They are perhaps the closest Bourne has come to the celebrated minutages prepared by the ballet master Marius Petipa for Pyotr Ilyich Tchaikovsky for the original productions of *The Sleeping Beauty* and *The Nutcracker*. As with those, Davies has sometimes felt free to depart from Bourne's specifications, making alternative suggestions of his own.

The first section, marked 'max 30 seconds', is called 'Porter Trumpet Solo'. '*Porter plays solo theme from the platform between the staircases.*' In one version, Bourne has added: '*Tony lies in a foetal position in The Armchair below.*' Bourne's note says, '*Music – Tony's theme.*'

On one version, Davies has written, '*Use mostly Jazz Club as source material throughout. Can revise Street material*'.

Next, the Opening Sequence, timed at '1 min 30–40 secs'. '*A sequence that introduces us to the world of the piece and the notion of more than one person playing each character.*' In one version, Bourne adds: '*Has a*

661

dreamlike/memory quality; ghosts passing through an empty house.' In the two other versions, Bourne has given a music note for Davies: '*Use the Street themes OR begin the Porter/Jazz club theme – start simple and build – could it sustain itself right through to the Jazz Club scene?*' (Davies has written, '*Or both – maybe just touch of Club rhythm.*')

Then 'Tony And Estate Agent'. In this, '*Tony is given a final viewing of his new home by his Estate Agent before the contract is signed and keys handed over. The Agent is hyperactive and eager to please.*' Bourne's timing is '40–50 secs'. Davies has jotted down, '*Jazz chords – set harmonic world.*'

Now 'Barrett and Vera in Workman's Caf'. Bourne writes, '*Barrett is found in a greasy spoon circling job applications in a newspaper. (He is joined by other Barretts and Veras and the Estate Agent. Vera looks on disinterested, eating a Mars Bar.)*' He notes '1 min'. Davies has written, '*Barrett theme over rhythm.*'

Bourne and Davies have bracketed the next four sections together. Bourne gives them a joint duration of '1 min 30 secs'. The first of them is 'Susan Arrives at New House'. In this, '*Susan arrives for a night out. Dressed only in a towel, Tony answers the door.*' (In two other versions Bourne describes him as '*a half-dressed Tony*'.) '*He leaves to finish dressing and Susan, left alone, explores the new house . . . meanwhile . . .*' Davies has noted '*romantic moment with Susan theme*' and '*orig. track starts*'.

In 'Barrett at Phone Box', '*Barrett, dragging Vera along with him, makes a phone call in answer to one of the job ads. An aggressive line forms outside the phone box, including other Barretts and Veras.*' 'Tony Answers Phone', subtitled '(part of above)', involves '*The phone rings in the house. Susan is uncertain whether to answer. As she attempts to, Tony rushes downstairs (no trousers) and nervously snatches the phone. While he is talking to Barrett, Susan teases him. He reacts like a ticklish child. An arrangement is made and he puts down the phone . . .*'

In what seems to be the original version of 'Outside Phone Box', Bourne has written, '*Porter is on his way to the Jazz Club. Barrett exits the Phone-Box and Vera follows . . .*' But in two other versions, it goes: '*A middle-aged man is propositioning Vera, as Barrett exits the Phone-Box. An altercation follows. The street is a dangerous place.*' (Davies has noted here '*start of Jazz Club theme?*')

Now 'Tony and Susan Prepare To Go Out'. This says, '*Tony finishes dressing for his night out. A triple duet to introduce us to the idea of the*

3 *Tonys and 3 Susans. All 6 leave to go to . . .*' And Bourne had added, even on his earliest draft, '*Music – jazz club theme starts to rev up here.*' In later versions he notes this section should last 45 seconds. Davies has written '*bongos enter*'.

And so to 'Jazz Club', the show's tenth section. Bourne writes: '*Small, smoky but upmarket. Two couples blow smoke from cigarettes in unison, and dance in a tight space (as a transition from the previous scene).*' (The cigarette smoke is only there in one version.) Davies has written '*main theme*' here.

'*Porter works at the club as a musician. We find him as at the start of the show, atop the highest platform, playing his trumpet, finishing off his act.*' (Only in one version is he finishing off the act.) '*The Susans and Tonys arrive*' (Davies has written '*sax solo*' here) '*and battle for space on the dance floor. They have fun in a reserved kind of way.*' (In another version, Bourne adds the note: '*Some connection between Tony and Porter? Does he follow them home?*' And he adds a music note too: '*Jazz theme at full throttle at top – dance before Tonys and Susans arrive – keep the temperature rising to a violent crescendo – something dramatic happens!*')

'*Porter appears to know Tony from the past; Tony can't place him (or pretends not to); Porter is so physically familiar that Tony gives in. Susan is appalled by his bad manners (blowing smoke in her face, being too touchy with her, knocking her drink, etc.)*' (All this detail is only in one version of the scenario. Bourne has explained that the bad manners are those displayed by the Porter/Speight character.)

'*Porter, having drunk all evening, causes a disturbance, grabbing Susan for a wild dance, which causes the Tonys and Susans to leave. Porter and the others at the Jazz Club continue to dance.*' (Again, another version of this is less detailed.)

The whole Jazz Club scene is marked '2 mins'. As it ends, in one version, Bourne says that it '*segues into . . .*' the following, which is the scene he has called 'Fireplace Duet'. '*Tony and Susan create a makeshift bed in front of the Fireplace. Their lovemaking is cool and unsatisfying. Their minds are elsewhere; they never focus on each other (Triple Duet).*' (In another version, Bourne omits the point about focus.)

'*Susan decides to go, takes her coat and leaves with the peck on the cheek.*' (A second and third version read: '*Tony eventually falls asleep on top of Susan. She releases herself, elegantly, takes her coat and leaves.*')

The first version continues: '*A frustrated Tony thinks of what might have been and curls up by the fireplace alone.*' (This line is absent from the second.)

Then: '*It is dawn. As Susan walks home alone from the house, several figures (Barrett) appear from the shadows to watch her.*' And in this (apparently earlier) version of the scenario Bourne writes here a line that – apparently later – he was to put at the end of the previous 'Outside Phone Box' scene: '*The street is a dangerous place!*' However, in (probably) later versions he elaborates about what happens as Susan walks home: '*A figure with a trumpet case – Porter – emerges from the shadows to follow her. She pauses thoughtfully, and he backtracks to his position outside Tony's house. An aggressive and menacing presence. Is it Barrett there also? Is Barrett alone? A connection with Porter?*'

Bourne also adds a music note to the later versions here: '*This is basically Susan's Theme but with a longer sustained intro to allow them to journey home. It could also be an extended journeying coda to the Jazz Club theme with a sense of menace to allow Porter to follow them.*' Bourne estimates the whole Fireplace Duet at '2–3 mins approx.'. Davies has jotted several music notes of his own, such as '*need longer and with some menace . . . rising Porter below . . .* '.

Now 'The Next Morning – Barrett Arrives'. In every version Bourne marks this as '40 secs'. '*Barrett finds the door open and a dishevelled Tony on the floor asleep, writhing around in a dream-state, remembering the night before.*' In a music note, he adds, '*Keep the above theme (Susan's) going in a very sparse way until Tony opens his eyes.*' Davies has ringed or underlined such words as '*writhing*', '*remembering*', '*dream-state*', and has written several notes in the margin: '*e.g. single-note tpt – lowish*' ('tpt' is 'trumpet'), '*don't confuse with Susan's*', and '*more direct Porter refs*'.

After this point, the versions have no notes about time-lengths.

The next scene has different titles in different versions. One Bourne simply calls 'Dance Episode (?)', and he has written '*Something to do with Porter and Trumpet (?) Other Veras? Susans?*' (Davies has written in the margin that this scene is '*self-contained*', and '*short transition*', '*up tempo*', '*Blast*', '*violent/powerful*', '*with beginning and end*'. This is in contrast to Bourne's next note, which says '*Segues into . . .* '.) Another version Bourne calls 'Porter', and his description goes: '*Porter, on the street outside Tony's House, shows us the dangerous side to his character.*'

Then 'Work Sequence'. On paper, this is quite long. Bourne has written: '*A day in the life* . . . *(Triple Duets for Tony and Barrett; Tony and Vera).*

'*Includes: Barrett and Tony*
'*(A) Being dressed in the Morning*
'*(B) General living room chores*
'*(C) Undressing for bath and bed*' Bourne has added '*(Massage?)*' in one version.

'*Vera and Tony*
'*In which Vera awkwardly goes about her chores. Tony watches* . . . *(show what he is thinking – maybe they all have an "animal" moment or there is one sequence in unison where the other Tonys break out of it and ravage Vera?*') Davies has written, '*sloppy version of work theme* . . . *Or her theme gets the Bach treatment.*'

'*(A) Bringing fresh towels into his makeshift bedroom as he is coming out of the shower. Tony feels naked in front of her.*' (That's one version, to which Bourne adds, '*Ewan [Wardrop] and Belinda*' in brackets. In another, Bourne writes '*Bringing the breakfast tray into his makeshift bedroom.*')

'*(B) Watching her tidy room – following her* . . .' (Bourne has designated that for Will Kemp and Valentina Formenti. In another version Bourne has merely written, '*Watching her tidy room (hopelessly).*')

'*(C) Passes her on stairs, she drops something, he picks up – awkwardness. (Richard Winsor and Belinda.) End this sequence with Barrett helping Tony on with his coat as Susan arrives to pick him up* . . .

'*Barrett and Vera in Kitchen.*
'*Show their difference in private.*' (In one version Bourne adds, '. . . *ends with Barrett making a phone call to Porter. (Maybe we just see trumpet case outside phone box.)*')

Next is 'Hairdressing Sequence'. (This scene was omitted from the eventual production.) '*Susan gets her hair done on the Kings Road (Dance Episode).*' In one version, Bourne – referring to individual dancers – suggests '*Sara, Emily, Michela, Alan, Ewan, Steve?? – change time.*' (Davies has written, '*self-contained, short, max/min*' in the margin.)

Now is 'The Housewarming', the episode on which Bourne has written most. In both versions of the scenario available, this is the same. '*Tony has a Housewarming for his swanky friends and business associates. The house is nowhere near finished; the guests arrive expecting something quite different. There are only boxes to sit on and nothing*

665

to eat except peanuts. Barrett treats it as if it were an Embassy Ball, almost taking over as the host. Slightly surreal atmosphere with menacing undertones. Sequence begins with . . .'

The sections that follow are all subsections of 'The Housewarming', but in one version Bourne gives them separate titles. The first is called 'Barrett preparations'. 'Barrett enjoys himself with the preparations for the Housewarming. The radio is playing an old favourite ("In a Party Mood") which speeds him around the house . . . (Vera is seen in the kitchen, biting her nails.)'

Next 'Susan Arrives'. 'He is interrupted by the arrival of the first guest, Susan. She switches off the radio and puts on a smoochy LP.' (In another version, Bourne suggests this as 'a "popular" Samba?') 'She absent-mindedly dances to it while she waits for Tony and orders Barrett around, treating him like he is there solely for her pleasure. Tony enters and Barrett pours them drinks and continues to interrupt their intimate moments, much to Susan's annoyance (the smoochy track stops). Susan and Tony argue as the first Guests arrive . . .'

Then 'The Guests Arrive'. 'The first guests arrive, a "nice" but strange couple – Maggie and Murray.' (Maggie Smith and Murray Melvin, another version explains.) 'Tony runs upstairs. Susan is in no mood to be sociable. Vera is slow and unpolished. Maggie is offered a very low box to sit on – rather awkward in her short skirt – and offered a peanut. Further guests arrive; Ruth and Michael, two enigmatic models; Laurence and James, a discreet male couple and Carol, a timid secretary who used to work for Tony's family (she has always felt that they are perfect for each other).' (Another version makes clear these people are Ruth from Pinter's The Homecoming, Michael York, Laurence Harvey, and James Villiers.) 'The guests are all incredibly mannered and elegant people: delicate, effete, tight-lipped, poised and mostly unfazed by the uncomfortable setting and situation.' (Davies's marginalia here include 'continuing samba?')

Bourne also writes extensive notes here for 'Rough Staging'. The longer version proceeds: '1) As the guests arrive, the music has changed to a cool bossa nova. Coats, bags, etc., are taken by Vera and Barrett holds court. (The music has stops and pauses within it, like tracks on an album, but all the tracks sound strangely similar to the last.) By the end of the first break all the guests are seated in various uncomfortable seats (the sound of a clock ticking is heard). The drinks trolley is taken round, etc.

'2) *Porter arrives. He is much more physically free, and makes fun of the stuffy situation. Tony re-enters, sees that it is Porter who has arrived and runs back in his room. Susan is both repelled and attracted by Porter.*

'3) *The music re-starts and the guests, egged on by Porter, start to dance in couples. Porter works his way over to where Susan is and stares her out. She pretends not to notice and, seeing Tony signalling to her at the top of the stairs, makes her way up to see him. Tony tries to make up, but Porter frog-marches him down the stairs into a game of Charades.*' (In the shorter version, Bourne writes more specifically, '*Charades – use Pinter plays or relevant films.*') '*Porter begins the game menacingly suggestive and directs his charade at Tony.*' (In the other version, Bourne adds, '*Tony is genuinely terrified of the games.*') '*During the game, Susan, whose argument with Tony continues throughout the party, starts to make her way to another room. (Powder room? Mirror?) Porter creeps out also. The game continues . . .*' (Davies's notes say, '*tight rhythmic*'.)

'4) *Revolve to find Susan and Porter in another room. She shows no sign of her attraction to him, beyond a powerful eye contact. Barrett watches in the shadows from above. Porter makes a pass or a suggestive remark. She slaps his face just as Vera comes through the swing doors. (Another Porter and Susan are seen, with Susan accepting his move?) Susan rejoins the Party. Porter and Vera have a moment. Barrett sees their attraction (Porter and Vera) and knows that he has something on both Susan and Porter.*

'5) *Revolve back to find all the others standing over Ruth and Michael. The boredom of the party has given way to lust and their sensual physicality has turned into exhibitionist lovemaking. The other guests (apart from Tony) are observing it as though it were an exhibit at an art gallery; admiringly, pointing things out, moving with the motion of their actions, etc. They all reach a climax together! Tony and Susan sit back to back, still not talking. (The music finishes, they go back to sit in their original sitting positions.) The clock ticks again . . .*' (This idea was taken from Pinter's *The Homecoming*; it was cut from the eventual production.)

Bourne's shorter version mentions here an incident omitted from the longer one: '*Musical chairs? (Use revolving staircase idea?)*'

But his longer version goes on to this: '6) *The atmosphere has turned uncomfortable. There is menace in the air. Porter bursts into the room looking a little dishevelled, as Vera re-enters from another entrance with a smile on her face. In an attempt to bring the Party to a close, Porter slowly puts a blindfold on Tony for a game of Blind Man's Buff'* (Davies has written *'darker'* in the margin here) *'– as he does so he stares at Susan – everyone else takes their opportunity to leave slowly, leaving Porter alone with Susan, and Tony idiotically moving around the room, bumping into things – something happens between Porter and Susan (a kiss) and Porter leaves – Barrett and Vera enter; Tony ends up, on his knees, feeling up the body of Vera as Barrett holds the door open for Susan. Another Barrett (Eddie) carries another Tony (Ewan) up the stairs. Another Barrett (Scott) has a fag in the Master's Chair. Another Barrett (Steve) switches out the lights . . .'* (Davies's notes here, not all legible, include, *'Hint of new Barrett theme to come – "The Future".';* *'B. clarinet? Big unison? . . .' and 'use to replace Porter phrase at end of Fireplace Duet'*) End of Act One.

For Act Two, only one version of Bourne's scenario exists, much less detailed. It begins, *'Two months later. (Some of these scenes overlap.)'*

First 'TV special 1964'. *'Dance sequence'* is all Bourne has written. Davies has jotted, *'Matt will give counts.'*

Now 'Opening Sequence': *'A version of street theme showing something about each character?'*

Next 'Barrett and Porter's Journey Through Soho'. Bourne writes: *'Tube/porn cinema or strip joint street/toilet, etc. Porter and Barrett make separate journeys to . . .'* (see the next sequence).

And so to 'The Salisbury Pub' (*'shortish'*, Davies has written, though he has also noted '1–2 min.'). *'Barrett meets up with Porter. Something passes between them . . . Are they planning something?'* (*'Furtive'* is Davies's note in the margin.)

Next 'Tony Alone/Vera alone'. *'It is a hot evening. Tony and Vera, half-dressed, are alone in separate parts of the house. Susan is calling Tony, but he is not answering . . . We see Susan exit phone box and meet the waiting Porter . . . Leads into . . .'*

'The Salisbury Pub/The Street/Cinema' comes next. Bourne's description is *'Susan's illicit meeting with Porter / Their dates are too public for a proper woman like Susan . . .'*

Then 'Tony and Vera'. Here: *'Tony goes to the kitchen to get himself a drink and finds Vera. She seduces him on the chopping block.'* This duet became known as the Tap Duet.

Now 'Porter's Squalid Flat (overlaps with above)'. *'Susan shows her passion for Porter.'*

Then 'Post-Coital'. '*Tony, Vera, Susan and Porter reflect on the above. Barrett appears to know what has been going on . . .*'

Next 'Barrett and Tony and Vera'. This says only, '*Their changing relationships.*'

Now 'Susan Outside the House'. It says simply, '*Susan watches the light in the house . . .*'

Interestingly, Bourne's most detailed account of any scene in Act Two is for the final scene: 'Susan Comes Back to the House/Montage Sequence'. He has written, '*A nightmare/dreamlike sequence. Susan has returned full of regret. She is led into the house by a very insolent Barrett, who lets her look around for herself. We expect to find Tony with Vera, but, as she pulls back the cover in Tony's bed, she finds Vera with Porter instead. Tony is in a corner, watching. She leaves for good . . . A montage sequence follows ending with a broken Tony serving a drink to Barrett, who sits in the Master's chair. Porter and Vera sleep in his bed. Susan outside at the lamp post. Another Tony crawls up the stairs . . . A strange new "family" has formed itself around Tony.*'

Edward Scissorhands (2005)

Act One

ALASTAIR MACAULAY: *I'm aware that you took years to clinch the scenario, and that you were still adjusting details in previews. Knowing your track record, I wouldn't be surprised if you went on to change the story again. But talk me through the story as it now stands on stage, without any reference to notes. Anyone who knows the film at all will see straight away that Caroline Thompson and you added a different prologue to the story.*

MATTHEW BOURNE: It starts with the projection of the words 'Once there was a boy called Edward.' And you see old Kim, this old lady. You're not sure who she is at this stage. Possibly she's a narrator, introducing you to the story.

Then you see a little boy, the original human Edward, playing with scissors in the grounds of a mansion on the hill. There's a storm brewing. Suddenly, the scissors get struck by lightning, and he's killed. His father comes out and finds his body.

AM: *It's this father whom we see in the next scene as the inventor? Trying to create a replica of the son he's lost?*

MB: It's ambiguous whether the father is already an inventor – maybe it's just the death of his son that turns him into a crazy scientist who wants to replace him.

We have a funeral moment. The father decides to make something with the scissors. They, the scissors, are the thing of his son that he still holds on to, because that's what he was holding when he died. It's the last image he has of him. He decides to remake him in, you might say, his demented grief-stricken state.

Then we have a sequence where it just says 'Many years later' on a gauze. Therefore you assume it's taken him a long time for him to find a way of making this *Frankenstein* monster.

AM: *I was relieved when I realized that 'Many years later' are the last words we see. At first I had a feeling you were going to make us read the story.*

MB: I needed to identify the little boy as 'Edward'. People who know the film would not expect to see a boy playing with scissors. I want to wrong-foot the audience, so to speak: to state, right away, that this was not the film. It all says, 'Once upon a time . . .'!

And now we have the end-of-creation scene: he's just finishing the final touches, and he brings him to life (very much like the 1930s *Frankenstein* movies).

Next we cut to Halloween night. The trick-or-treaters from the town – 'bad kids' I call them (one of them is Jim Upton) – come out for the night, dressed up in scary masks, and challenge each other to break into the scary house on the hill, and scare the crazy man that lives there. Like *Meet Me in St. Louis*, I would say. You remember how Margaret O'Brien has to go to the scary man's house? That's a dare for her, and this is for them.

AM: *They climb in through the window. At one point, Jim stands behind a mannequin, his masked face where its would be, pretending to be a doll. You weren't thinking of* Frankenstein? *Or of Act Two of the ballet* Coppélia, *where Franz climbs in the window and Dr Coppélius the doll-maker freezes, pretending to be one of his own dolls?*

MB: I know all dance critics are thinking *Coppélia* when the trick-or-treaters climb through the window. But your average audience will be thinking *Frankenstein*. On the *Newsnight* TV review, the author Ian Rankin said it was '*Frankenstein* meets *Happy Days*'. I get that.

Frankenstein is in there, like *Pinocchio*, without you having to think about it. They're influences on the original film script.

The trick-or-treat kids assume that the inventor's going to be in his studio, and they want to scare him. But what they're not expecting is Edward, whom they now come upon. They in turn are scared off, but in the course of that, the old man has a heart attack. He dies. Edward's on his own, and he runs out of the mansion he has always lived in and into the 'real' world.

Now, this is all invented for the show. It's not remotely like the film.

AM: *Is that the end of your* Edward Scissorhands *prologue?*
MB: I'm never sure where the prologue ends exactly! There are several different places it might be said to end: you could say it only includes the many-years-ago scenes. But I'd say it's really over by the next scene, when you go into the town.

Here we have a sequence called 'Suburban Ballet', which is to introduce you to all these characters and the town, which is called 'Hope Springs', and the families that live there. This is a lot of introducing to do. Six families, each with mum, dad, son and daughter.

AM: *The Tim Burton original has various individuals and some families. You decided instead to show six different versions of the same nuclear family unit: one mum, one dad, one daughter, one son. Is that to heighten the sense of some conventional Smallville?*
MB: Partly that, and partly to have enough people to make it feel as if it is a town. In the film, there are lots of other people around, but you get to meet very few characters in particular. We wanted a stronger sense of a conformist community, of separate families, and of multiple individuals. That's why they are all characterized so differently.

First, there's the Boggs family coming out of their house. Then the Monroe family next door. We show their two houses, and we show the families coming in and out of them.

AM: *The names Boggs and Monroe are from the film.*
MB: Yes. I can't say why Caroline chose them. Boggs is a downbeat name, isn't it?

Then the other families come on from different places. Episodes for separate families, for kids meeting, for everyone attending a rally for Mayor Upton. There's a lot of detail there. (A whole section with

671

'invisible' cars.) It represents 'a day in the life'. It begins at dawn and ends at dusk as everyone returns to their homes and the stage clears.

Then Edward appears. He comes through the houses, dwarfing them. I wanted the image of a big monster arriving through small houses. He should be potentially scary, like Frankenstein's monster himself, who actually has a sweet side. Do you remember the film of *Frankenstein*? When he hears music, he softens. He plays with the little girl . . . and he ends up throwing her in the lake. Because he doesn't know what to do with her. There's a sort of sweetness to him. But you don't know that. And that's the way that Edward should appear. He's presented as a monster to begin with. I love both Karloff's *Frankenstein* (1931) and, in particular, his *Bride of Frankenstein* sequel (1935).

Now we have a sequence where Edward hears someone coming, and runs away. Jim, whom we'll get to know as Kim's boyfriend, comes in with his friends. He's in the film, but there you never see his family. We made him an Upton, the mayor's son. So he's the prize catch of the community. A real jock. I'm pleased with that touch.

He and his friends are going off for a camping trip for the weekend, and he's picking Kim up. Her father, Bill, warns Jim not to lay a hand on his precious daughter. Off they go. This is the first actual reference to the film – where Kim is off on a camping trip when her mother Peg brings him home. It's an important bit of the plot, because this will be the reason why Peg puts Edward to sleep in Kim's bedroom: she's not there that weekend.

Edward comes out again, sniffs around, sees a dustbin, tries to find some food in there. A bit doglike. Dogs were going to be a big part of this at one stage. We wondered about using puppets. Edward's first meeting was going to be with the dogs of the town. Something to do with him being like a stray dog (a very important image for Caroline). But we ended up eliminating dogs. The whole style of the piece would have been very different.

Peg Boggs comes out of her house because she's heard Edward clunking around with the trash cans. His hands are rummaging inside. She goes to see who the stranger is, he turns around, she sees the blades. She's scared and runs away. She thinks he's coming at her with a knife – with knives. But he's as scared as she is, and he cuts himself.

AM: *That's like and unlike a scene near the start of the movie. There Peg is an Avon lady who is doing the rounds. No one is buying much. And then, in the wing mirror of her car, she sees the reflection of the house on the hill. Peg decides to go up to the house she's never been in to see if she can sell her Avon products. It's deserted, until she finds him up in the attic.*

MB: Yes, and there's a kind of confrontation between the two of them that's not unlike the scene we stage between them. But we bring him to town first. In the film, why is there this enormous house on a hill in the middle of town? We decided to make the house more out of town, and less castlelike.

So our way of bringing him to town is ours. When they meet, as in the film, they're both scared. But she decides to take him into her home – they're standing outside it – and look after him. He's obviously scared and alone and when she discovers that the blades are his hands, she is instantly compassionate. No questions asked.

I decided to forget the idea of her being an Avon lady. I think that would have been too camp – it's marvellous in the film ('Avon calling!'), but we couldn't have made it work usefully. Peg takes him into her house, after tending to his wounds. And he decides she's there to help him.

Then we get a little moment with the Rev. and Mrs Evercreech, the religious nuts. They set up the idea that the devil has arrived in town. They're not sure who or what he is, but their first reaction is that he's different and obviously therefore evil. The most religious family in the town is actually the worst, the first to condemn really. Which I think is often very true.

AM: *But there is no such family in the movie.*

MB: The film has one character, the woman Esmeralda Evercreech, who lives on her own and plays hymns on this little electric organ. She's the same kind of character. She has all these verses from the Bible and she spouts them to anyone who will listen. In some ways she too is an outsider in the film. I wanted her to be a pillar of the community.

That's our transition into the house. The only interior we have is Kim's bedroom, where Peg brings him now. Kim's away, so he can stay there the night. There's a sequence where Peg introduces him to her husband, Bill, and son, Kevin, and they put him to bed. They put pyjamas on him to cover his nakedness. He is an innocent, of course, and has no concept of nudity. It's an Adam-and-Eve thing. Suddenly they realize he hasn't got any clothes on, and he suddenly feels that as well. He covers himself up. It's all about little discoveries. He's observing how they move and what their lives are about, but they also make him feel different feelings as well. They impose their views on him.

The Boggses' son, Kevin, is quite excited by him – thinks Edward's very cool, something nobody else has. Mr Boggs, Bill, is shocked initially, but Peg explains that he is harmless. Then they leave him on his own in the bedroom, in his pyjamas, and turn the lights off. Here we have a big mobile above the bed that fascinates him. He gets up to explore the room. Again, none of this is in the film. He opens her music box. There's a ballerina twirling. This is the first time he's ever heard music. He loves it. (Shades of *Frankenstein* here.)

Then he sees a little doll on the table. She's got a lot of hair. He cuts a bit of her hair off – Edward the barber-to-be. (This was later changed to him imitating the ballerina in the box. One of our later casts, Dominic North, even went up on pointe.) And then he discovers his reflection in the mirror. Which he's never seen before. He thinks there's someone else there that's behind the dressing table. The only reason he knows it's him is because of his unique hands. He goes in closer, and cuts himself again by accident.

AM: *In the film, he's always cutting himself by accident. That's why he has these little scars on his face.*

MB: Yes, he hasn't quite worked out how to make the hands work himself. I think that it's a little clearer in our version that he's only recently been born. But born as a young man . . . with a very low mental age. In the film, you sense that he could have been there for a long time.

And he then notices – strangely, because they're so enormous – pictures on the wall of Kim.

AM: *In the movie, he first sees Kim in the family photos that Peg shows him when he first goes into the house. He goes through the living room, and there are photos on the mantelpiece and Peg takes him through them. 'This is my family. That's Kim, that's Kevin.'*

MB: Yes, we just took it a lot further to allow for a dance sequence. The photo of Kim is one of those classic American high-school pictures – you know, the blonde perfect cheerleader – and at once he makes a connection. So that's where our idea came from. You could argue that in our version she must be the vainest girl in the world, with all these enormous blown-up pictures of herself on her bedroom wall! Let's call it teenage narcissism.

I planned to make a fantasy sequence about her wonderfulness – like Miss Turnstiles in *On the Town*. In the scenario, we called Kim 'the perfect girl who can do everything'. So there was going to be a series of pictures on the wall of her as a scholar; her skiing; a cheerleader; a ballerina . . . But in planning the story with Caroline, and then talking it through with Lez, we felt this would hold up the story too much. We ended up going with the cheerleader idea, because it makes a link between her and Edward: Kim the cheerleader doesn't have hands; she has pompoms. He finds that attractive. And the pictures come to life in a fantasy sequence: Kim and two lookalikes – three Kims, in fact.

AM: *A female counterpart of the moment in* Nutcracker! *when Clara sees more Nutcracker heroes than one – or the moment in* Swan Lake *when the Prince sees not just one Swan but many. Or when he sees multiple versions of the Queen. Historically, this all connects to Romantic ballet, and to the moments in* La Sylphide, Giselle, La Bayadère, *and other ballets when the hero perceives the female vision he loves as one of many, as part of a larger dream world.*

MB: It's a very poetic device. The Kims put Edward to bed, giving him a teddy bear to cuddle. He ends up looking back at the single portrait of Kim on the wall. Then he looks around the room as if to say, 'I've found a home. I like it here.'

Cut to outside the house. It's the next morning. There's someone there. This section is called 'Gossip' – about the intrigue surrounding the new arrival in the Boggs household. Mr Boggs and Mr Monroe come out of their houses for their keep-fit regime. It's the weekend. People are doing sporty things. Kevin Boggs brings Edward out into the garden to play with him – and to show him how to ride a scooter. Edward's got a cap on now. Other people in the town are spying him from afar. He's the new person in town, and they are highly suspicious if not flabbergasted by what they see.

Halfway through that sequence, he notices an untidy bush outside the Boggs house. Decides to put his blades to good use and cuts a star shape. He is instinctively creative. Next, a poodle passes with the mayor's wife, Charity, and Edward is fascinated by the design possibilities. This sets up the next idea: Edward as artist.

Now comes a sequence about the whole town getting uptight about what's going on in the Boggs house. The neighbours cannot bear not knowing. You see Peg, Edward and Kevin going out shopping. Peg and

Kevin, proud to have this new creature in their house, are wanting to be 'seen' with him. And the town is desperate to find out who he is, what he's all about.

One of the observations that Tim and Caroline made is that after the initial shock, people are jealous of anything that's different. It starts as curiosity. By taking in this stray, the Boggs family have something the rest of them haven't. So the others want a piece of him. And it's his difference that's appealing. They turn him into a local hero. He gives them something: his talents and his friendship. And they feel that they've got him as well. But the moment that starts to turn sour, they will use the same reasons for falling in love with him as reasons to turn against him. The fact that he's different is the reason why they don't like him. 'He never really was one of us.'

And though he changes in his manner, he doesn't change in his feelings, his loyalties. But the others do change. And the hands, of course, are symbolic of anything. Race, sexuality, any kind of handicap or disability.

Peg invites everyone important in the town to a barbecue, which is to welcome Edward to the town. But the transition into that is a second Evercreech sequence. Until now, they've been quite mild in their response. Now they get stronger in their condemnation of the devil, the freak.

When we arrive at the barbecue, the first image is of him taking his topiary skills to new heights. He's cutting a life-size giraffe-shaped piece of topiary in the Boggs backyard. Again, the Boggses are showing off. 'Look what he can do. He's our guest.' Then he meets various people. Joyce is intrigued and excited by the danger of the blades and their extraordinary length. He meets the mayor and his wife. And then he serves the party food on his blades, like barbecue skewers. So the scene celebrates his difference both in his particular skills and then in showing what he can't do (such as the beachball-bursting moment, when he attempts to play catch with the younger kids). How he can connect and how he can't connect.

Also in that sequence, Kim, Jim, and friends return from their camping trip. They change the music, and it is loud and rocky. There's a feeling of the generation gap, and the adults leave for a quieter part of the garden at the end of this sequence. Edward notices that one of the young people is the girl he has fallen in love with in the pictures on the bedroom wall. When Peg introduces her daughter, she laughs at his awkwardness.

The townsfolk now enjoy the sun for a while. And Edward is like a child who is asked to take food around at a party to the adults. He's embarrassed by the semi-nakedness of everyone, and he's fumbling his way through the group, getting in the way. But it's also the introduction of a sort of sexuality for him. He is not sure why Joyce is so very interested in him. It's another new world to explore.

AM: *During this scene and others that followed, he reminded me of the character that Peter Sellers plays, Chauncey Gardiner, in* Being There *(1979). Especially Edward's relationship with Joyce is like the one between Sellers and Shirley MacLaine.*

MB: Yes, I've wondered whether Caroline and Tim were influenced by that. I got the Edwards to watch that film, particularly one scene with Shirley MacLaine. In both cases, the point is that the whole relationship is happening in her head. He's not really doing anything. But he says all these very simple things and they're taken as being suggestive or refreshingly wise.

AM: *By the end of that scene, is it just the Evercreeches who are alienated from him? Has everybody else accepted him?*

MB: They warm to him. Even the Evercreeches are thawing. They don't want to be not included. At one point we thought that they might change their mind in the middle and decide he was the Second Coming!

So by the end of this scene, he's been accepted and welcomed. People are eager to get to know him. And to use him.

As the barbecue ends, the family is clearing up. Edward offers to help Kim, but it's the teenage thing of being very awkward around someone that you're attracted to. He does everything wrong. Jim, her boyfriend, wants to take her off somewhere. She says she's got to stay behind and help Mother clear away. Jim gets a bit violent with her. A nasty side of his personality comes out. Edward sees this, feels protective of her, doesn't know what to do. He even doesn't quite understand that some of their physicality together may not be violent. He thinks that she's being manhandled. Jim leaves in anger. Kim is upset, and becomes aware of Edward watching her. She turns round and glances at him. The look between them gives him the idea of what he would like to be for her. He'd like to be a real boy like Jim with real hands. And he wants to take her somewhere beautiful. ('There's a Place for Us'.)

And so to a fantasy sequence where he takes her to a living topiary garden. It's a world of his art, of the things he's made. He now has normal hands and much is made in the choreography of the unusual experience of how to use those hands and to touch in a delicate and articulate way. The idea is that he's chivalrous, polite, perfect, prince-like, not himself at all really. And she's content to be with him. It's the love he'd like to have. The fantasy eventually dissolves and Jim returns to make amends with Kim. The final image sees Edward centre-stage, back with his scissorhands on, watching Jim kiss the girl he can never have.

Act Two

AM: *OK, take me through the tale of Act Two.*

MB: Edward is at the height of his fame. TV reporters are there, camera-men, important photographers. He's created a lot more topiary around the town, some of which you can see over the fences of the gardens. The stage is full of his creations. Now he's opening up Salon Edwardo in the Boggs garden for exotic hair fashions. Everyone is very excited about this opening. He's more confident; he's grown up a bit and has a moustache.

AM: *The film shows Edward cutting people's hair in the garden. Joyce having her hair cut, and, finding it very sexually exciting, is a main fea-ture there.*

MB: On stage we see the Mayoress's poodle, transformed since Act One. Edward has won over Mrs Upton. And he has a little sword-fighting moment with Kevin, who's acting as his assistant.

There's a frenzy with everyone wanting to get their hair cut. But when he offers Kim a haircut, she is touched and a connection takes place. Peer pressure makes her turn it down, but she sees him in a new light. This deflates him. But she sees what a star he's become, and that he treats her in a special way. Meanwhile everyone else is pulling him in different directions, wanting haircuts.

Joyce saves him from the crowd, kidnapping him in a sense, and runs with him into her house. It's her plan to seduce him.

AM: *This attempted-seduction scene is based on a scene in the film where she's showing him her new beauty salon. She shows him round the empty building and then starts to work on him. But because he doesn't show enough interest in her – he's just passive, unresponsive, and alarmed – she later accuses him of molesting her. She helps to turn people against him, to make him a pariah.*

MB: In our version, it's partly a farce. Edward is so polite and unknowing, whereas Joyce's intentions, to us, are all too obvious. Her husband, George, keeps bursting in on them, too, though he's too dim to get what she's up to. At the end, she reaches climax by sitting on her washing machine just as it's going into fast spin.

From this sexual moment we go into a sweet, Christmas carol-singing moment downstage. Out come the nice kids in town to sing a little carol with the Evercreeches. This takes us into the scene we call 'Christmas in Hope Springs'. Edward is excited by Christmas, but his presence has become normal to the townsfolk, who are so tied up in their present-buying that they barely notice that he is there. In one passage here, Edward is getting to know Kim better. She's got used to having him around. Noticing that everyone has deserted Edward, she tries to make conversation with him, and there's this bit of uncomfortable, shy behaviour between them. It shows they're connected but shy around each other. Jim, her boyfriend, starts to become suspicious. Edward briefly impersonates the silly, 'cool' gestures Jim does. But he still feels that he can never be what Kim wants.

What he can do, though, is create something. Something beautiful for her. An image of her. To glorify her. That's when he decides to go and create the beautiful ice sculpture, which is a memorable scene in the film.

AM: *There the spray of ice fragments from his sculpture becomes snow. And she says at one point, 'It's strange. It never snowed until he came here.'*

MB: Snow becomes an image that, for her, is about his spirit, about the beauty inside him. The snow signifies him for her from this moment onwards. And she's so touched that he's made this beautiful thing in her image. From then on, there starts to be a true relationship between them. She's starting to fall in love with him. All this develops in the short, playful dance they have now.

The moment between them is broken by Peg coming out and calling Kim back inside. Jim sees them together. But he doesn't do what you expect him to, which is to get angry. He decides to change tactics, to become Edward's new best friend, and be nice to him. He takes his new buddy back into the house.

Back in Kim's room, all the other kids are meeting there to go to the annual Christmas Ball that the town has every year. There's a little bit where the parents come in and try to be 'cool' but feel out of place. Then Jim spikes Edward's drink.

By this point, Edward is acting like a normal teenage kid. He's not acting any more as if he doesn't know what's going on. He's much more naturalistic in the way he deals with people. He's actually quite normal now. But he is not used to so much drink.

AM: *The spiking of the drinks isn't in the movie. There Jim sets him up to rob a house. It's Jim's own house, but where his father keeps something locked away that he wants. When they find out that Edward can open locks with his hands, they trick him into breaking into this house to get this equipment. He's discovered, he's put on trial, he's disgraced in front of the community.*

MB: So we had to find an equivalent that had a lot of dancing in it! I wanted something with echoes of the film *Carrie* (1976). There, the central character is a bullied girl at school and they suddenly hatch this plan to humiliate her. The school jock invites her to the prom, she's crowned Queen of the Prom, but they end up pouring a bucket of pig's blood on top of her. It's the same thing here: Jim's being nice and friendly towards Edward, but is actually setting him up. It will all turn horrible.

They go off to the party. There's the ceremonial lighting of the Christmas tree, which the mayor does each year. And a couple of the kids decide to make a big deal about Edward as the local celebrity, which upsets the Uptons. The point of this part of the story is about as many different people as possible finding that they've had enough of Edward. Other people find their suspicions are growing. And since he's drunk, he makes it all much worse. He's the embarrassing drunk at the party. Jim encourages him to dance a solo, a kind of crazy party piece, which doesn't endear him to anyone, as he ends up in a drunken heap on the floor.

Then we go into our big company swing dance. Within that, there's a bit of story-telling about Joyce and George, her husband. He wants to know what's going on with her and Edward. At the end of the number, he confronts the two of them. Joyce gets out of it by claiming that it was all on Edward's side – that he molested her. Jim has wanted this kind of trouble all along. And some other characters now turn upon Edward. Eventually, he's pushed into the Christmas tree by mistake. His hands get caught up in the wiring of the lights. It explodes. He gets caught up in the tree. Kevin, who remains his friend, goes to help him. But

Edward turns round and slashes Kevin across the face. And injures him, badly. This is where the Boggs family gets emotional, and angry: Kevin's their son. Even Kim is angry. It's her brother. She turns on Edward, but regrets it straight away and runs after him.

The Evercreeches take this as another chance to go back to the way they felt at the beginning really – that Edward is evil. They work the town up into a frenzy. This is a classic horror-movie situation: the town with torches going on a rampage to get the monster. You know: 'Kill the beast!' I resisted it for a while, but then I thought, 'Well, no, I quite like it.' It was hard to make all the characters feel the same way. They're all very different. But it's the kind of community where people get caught up in a fight or an accident. They don't want to miss out on anything. And they'll go with the flow. And it gives us an epic way of finishing with the whole town there, rather than a few characters. So they all chase after him.

He finds a place to hide. This is in the cemetery. Coincidentally, it's by the grave of the original young Edward: a touch I really like, though there's no reason why this Edward would know that. Now Kim arrives, feeling she's hurt him, wanting to show him what she feels. He can't accept that initially. She ends up kissing him. This is a big moment in the film. In the show, the kiss is just the start of the duet, which then takes the feeling further.

Eventually Jim catches up with them, and attacks them both. The rest of the town arrives now. A big fight ensues. Jim's father's trying to pull him off – Jim's trying to attack Edward but gets injured on the blades.

However, the last time that Jim comes at him, Edward doesn't fight back. He just disappears as Jim struggles with him. All that is left are the scissors. I like the unexplained feeling of 'Oh, what did happen?' Which is what all the characters feel too. Did he magically disappear? Has he managed to escape somehow? Are the scissors all that's left of him? It kind of reminds us that we are in a fairy tale or fable again. Caroline originally wanted a scene of pulling and ripping him apart. Which I found too clear-cut and a touch too horrific for our younger audience. I wanted an ending where you weren't sure what had happened completely.

AM: *In the film, they all end up back at the mansion. Kim finds him first. Then Jim comes in on his own and confronts him. Edward kills Jim, by accident but in a fight. The rest of the town catches up at the mansion*

681

gates. Out comes Kim, holding one of his hands. She says, 'He's dead. It's all over.' They all look regretful and leave. Then there's a forward sequence into the future where you see him up in the mansion, which he has made beautiful, full of topiary and ice sculptures. He lives there on his own. The snow from the ice sculptures comes out of the window and fills the town. And Kim as an old woman tells her grandchild that she thinks he's still there somewhere. Every time it snows, she knows he's still there. I've called the movie soft-centred, and I'm afraid that, to me, this clinches my point.

MB: But don't you find our version a lot more plausible? To me, that's a poetic statement she makes. But I didn't want a literal account of him being ageless and forever creative in the mansion. It makes him Peter Pan-like. And she's like Wendy in a way. I think that was conscious on Caroline's part. So I've retained the idea of old Kim from the film in a different way.

When you met her at the beginning of the show, you didn't know who she was. Now you do. She's come back to the place where he disappeared, years later. And she's still got the scissors. She puts them to her cheek. I think she's looking for a sign. And the sign is that it starts to snow. With the snow, she knows that he's still there somewhere. Very simple.

He does make one final appearance, but behind a gauze at the back. It's not a literal image. Is the image in her head? Is it a silhouette in the distance? Well, his spirit is there in the falling snow. And in her heart. Slow curtain.

Dorian Gray (2008)

Matthew Bourne's scenario, as revised during rehearsals and dated 12 August 2008

Act One

SLEEPING BEAUTY – Dorian's Loft Apartment – We hear the opening of the Overture from Tchaikovsky's *The Sleeping Beauty* (written same year as *Dorian Gray*) Slowly we see a sleeping figure in a bed stir . . . An arm reaches out and turns off the Radio alarm (Classic FM) . . . Dorian gets out of bed in Pyjama bottoms . . . Looks around his empty bedroom and stares at himself in the mirror (only other object in the room) . . . We transition into . . .

BASIL'S WORLD – Basil's Studio and Other Locations – We are introduced to the world of photography, shoots, models, castings, art, advertising (GROUP DANCE) . . . Basil as Artist, Lady H. as powerful arbiter of taste assisted by her Creative Director, Edward Black.

WHITE BOX ART GALLERY – Basil's Studio/Gallery – Opening of Basil's new Exhibition (GROUP DANCE) . . . Dorian is a waiter . . . Arty Guests soak up the exhibition and each other . . . Arrival of Lady H. causes a stir . . . Art Appreciation . . . Lady H. notices Dorian . . . we do not . . . (small moment) Lady H. and other guests are not that impressed by the direction Basil is going in . . . he knows it . . . Needs inspiration . . .

BASIL SHOOTS AND BEDS DORIAN – Studio/Gallery/Bedroom . . . Basil is deflated after lukewarm response to his exhibition . . . One of the waiters (Dorian) has remained to help clear glasses, etc. . . . . Basil notices in him something extra-ordinary for the first time . . . He turns one of the big studio lights onto him and reaches for his camera . . . An impromptu photo-shoot begins (DUET) . . . becomes more intimate, challenging and flirtatious . . . Feeling a strong animal attraction, Basil changes the musical mood and the two men end up in a makeshift bed (futon) with Basil capturing Dorian's final moment of ecstasy as a final shot . . . Basil's obsession with Dorian begins . . .

CAMERA OBSESSION – Basil's Studio – Dorian wakes up and walks from the bedroom back into the studio . . . Finds the camera . . . Dorian discovers his narcissistic nature (SOLO) . . . Watching this from a darkened corner of the studio is Lady H., who has returned to pick up her lost bag. Dorian is startled to realize he has been watched (he is only wearing underwear) . . . He is excited and shy in her presence (he knows who she is) . . . She has noticed him earlier and, before leaving, hands over her business card . . .

THE SCIENCE OF BEAUTY – Abstract World . . . Lady H. creates 'Dorian' – The Image . . . With the help of her white-coated beauty scientists (DUET and GROUP DANCE) Leads into . . .

IMMORTAL POUR HOMME – Dorian is the face of 'Immortal' – Fragrance Ad (Giant advertising billboard appears at end)
Basil dances in front of the Billboard (which has hit floor level) He has found his inspiration . . . (SOLO)

LADY H. AND DORIAN – Lady H.'s bedroom – Lady H. provocatively dresses for an evening out . . . with Dorian's help (SHORT DUET)

LADY H. AT HOME – Lady H. introduces Dorian to her high-born and influential friends and colleagues . . . He arrives with Basil. (They are now an open, well-known and very 21st-century edgy couple.) Everyone is keen to meet Dorian . . . there is something unworldly and intriguing about him that makes everyone want to know him, to connect with him, to sleep with him . . . he is special and puts people under a spell. Guests are drawn to him physically, but are subtle in their approach, fearing the others (competition) will notice . . . Everyone manages to make contact and get a business card to him! (GROUP DANCE) During the party there is a sensuous encounter between Lady H. and Dorian in her bedroom, as she prepares to go out . . . It is obvious that she has more than business on her mind and he is happy to make her believe that he is available to her (much like he is with everyone he meets). Basil sees what Lady H. is up to and storms out.

THE ROYAL OPERA HOUSE – Lady H. and her guests go to The Royal Opera House to watch a performance of the ballet *Romeo and Juliet*.

ROMEO, ROMEO – Dorian is instantly attracted to the pure, boyish beauty of Cyril Vane (the dancer playing Romeo) and imagines himself dancing with this idealized image of innocent young love . . . (DREAM BALLET!)

STAGE DOOR – Dorian waits for Cyril at the stage door after the performance. Unbeknownst to Basil or Lady H., Dorian woos Cyril and they start a secret affair . . . Time passes . . . Cyril becomes a pain . . . off stage he is a needy, messy, whiny self-obsessed ballet dancer . . . He is not the 'artist' Dorian thought he was . . .

DORIAN'S LOFT – Dorian is enjoying himself with some of the young, up-market friends he met through Lady H. and Basil, preparing to go out for the night (drink and drug activity) The problem of keeping Basil, Lady H. and Cyril secret from each other is playing on Dorian's mind and he needs a release. (SHORT GROUP DANCE)

Unexpectedly Cyril arrives, after a performance, with a massive dance bag full of smelly jocks and towels and tights, etc. He throws this stuff around, stretches and is generally obnoxious to Dorian's friends, who can't believe he would waste his time on this 'dancer' . . . Cyril has a headache and sees what he thinks are Nurofen on the table that we have seen the others taking drugs from earlier . . . We see him take them and wash it down with what he thinks is water . . . To make things worse . . . Basil arrives unexpectedly . . . Dorian bundles Cyril and his things into his bedroom . . . Basil wants to go out and have fun and joins the others' drugs-and-drink party . . . Unable to handle the tension, Dorian goes into the bedroom to find Cyril acting strangely . . . he is reacting badly to the drugs (SHORT DUET) . . . When Dorian goes back to join the others, they are too 'far gone' to notice or care about what is happening . . . Returning to the bedroom, Cyril is choking . . . cannot breathe . . . Dorian rushes to the bedside phone to call for help . . . as he picks up the receiver, he looks at the struggling Cyril and sees a way out . . . wouldn't life be easier without him? . . . he puts the receiver back down. As Cyril crawls towards him, pleading . . . he pulls the phone from its socket . . . Cyril climbs across the bed, towards Dorian and loses his fight for breath . . . (Juliet style!)

Dorian has watched him die . . .

Something about him has changed . . . he feels nothing but power and relief . . . a strange sense of enjoyment.

DG – Dorian's Doppelgänger appears . . .

A new heartless and evil Dorian has been unleashed . . .

Act Two

SLEEPING BEAUTY PART TWO – Dorian's Bedroom – Several rumpled bodies trail away from the bed . . . Dorian wakes up – switches off radio/alarm . . . Basil and Lady H. both emerge from the bed . . . Dorian is still managing to keep both parties satisfied!

CELEBRITY – Various Locations – Dorian as Celebrity! – Public Image – confident, powerful, selfish. (GROUP DANCE) The Red Carpet . . . *Jonathan Ross Show* . . . Openings . . . VIP entry to clubs and restaurants . . . *Vanity Fair* Photo-shoot . . . Ends with him leaving a club with Basil and beating up a photographer or two . . . grows to hate his own image being captured . . .

WHITE CLUB – Dorian and Basil chill out at their favourite club . . . (GROUP DANCE) Dorian becomes distressed when he sees his Doppelgänger dancing in the Club . . . seemingly more popular than him? . . . Is it him? Does he look younger than him? He feels older . . . he feels different . . . Is he watching himself? He runs out on Basil and runs to . . .

LADY H. – Lady H.'s Home – He is rough . . . cold . . . She does not appreciate being disturbed unexpectedly. He is cruel to her . . . his personality seems to snap in Jekyll and Hyde fashion . . . he attacks Lady H. sexually, becoming an animal. (DUET) Leaves her totally shocked and wondering what she has created . . .

ON THE PROWL – Streets – Darker, dangerous Private Life . . .

DOPPELGÄNGER (DG) – Mysterious figure seems to be following Dorian and committing increasingly depraved and violent acts . . . Dorian sees him only in his peripheral vision . . . (DUET) Suggestion that he might be serial killer.

BACK ROOM CLUB – **(GROUP DANCE/ORGY)** Dorian wanders through a 'dreamlike' orgy of entangled bodies, eventually allowing himself to become part of it . . . He escapes into the darkness and gives himself up to the gratification of the unknown figures who seem to devour him. Basil follows him here. Worried for him . . . His life has become too dangerous . . . Basil follows Dorian out of the club . . . but catching up with him, realizes he had followed the wrong person (Doppelgänger) Fuelled by his obsession and desperate to win him back, Basil decides to go to Dorian's loft to confront him. (SOLO)

MURDER OF BASIL – Dorian's Loft and Bathroom – Dorian recovers quickly, he acts strangely but becomes tender with Basil . . . (DUET) Dorian knows that this will work on devoted Basil . . . However, when Basil gets his camera out and wants to photograph Dorian again, Dorian becomes agitated and hides from the Camera . . . Basil thinks it's a game . . . Is the old Dorian back? They end up in Dorian's bathroom . . . Basil persists with the camera . . . But Dorian snatches it from him asks him to join him in the bathtub . . . He undresses and is pulled in by Dorian who brings the camera crashing down on his head . . . several times . . . in a frenzied bloody attack . . . Basil is dead . . .

THE STREET – Dorian runs from the apartment and passes an old broken-down poster from his Immortal campaign . . . He is now out of control . . . (SOLO)

LADY H. and DG – Lady H.'s House – Dorian bangs on her door . . . she has given up on him . . . he pushes his way in . . . She believed in him once but is now disgusted and frightened by him. (SHORT DUET) She shows some tenderness (to humour him) but a half-naked figure comes from another room . . . It is Dorian's Doppelgänger who looks him right in the eye (death foretold!) . . . Lady H. has found a younger man . . . he runs . . .

DORIAN'S DEATH – Dorian's Loft – The Loft is filled with dead bodies (victims) who interact with him at will (in his head – real or imaginary?) (GROUP DANCE) – In the bedroom Dorian confronts his other self (DG) and kills his evil double (soul) . . . Dorian has taken his own life.

EPILOGUE – Lady H. arrives . . . cleans up – arranges dead Dorian for the camera . . . Ever image-conscious . . . She kisses him on the forehead and signals for Edward Black to let the paps in to photograph Dorian, one last time! The last sound we hear is a deafening camera/flash . . .

Appendix B

Matthew Bourne's Pre-Rehearsal Notes for Leading Characters

Dorian Gray

These (incomplete) notes are given as an example of the preparation Bourne gives his dancers.

Dorian Gray

A beautiful and charismatic young man. Early twenties if not younger –

Not a preppy 'pretty-boy' but a manly and sensuous, slightly mysterious, even animalistic creature. Slightly removed from everything that happens to him. Not a victim, he loves his newfound obsession – himself! . . . And the new and dangerous pleasures that come his way.

Dorian is first seen as waiter at art party/exhibition given by Basil. Unnoticed, ordinary, until he is photographed. Basil discovers him clearing up after party . . . turns a large spotlight on him . . . Photo-shoot turns into raunchy sex . . . from studio to bedroom . . . wild, messy dance – Possibly projected live?

He begins as a blank canvas, unaware of his great attraction to people. It is only when Basil turns the camera on him, and Lady H. manipulates that image, that the attention is drawn and people start to notice him – he discovers vanity and the need to maintain the new power he has found through his youthful good looks.

Becomes a fashion/art icon – his gimmick/image? – youth, purity, innocence, desirability.

Begins by loving the camera ('makes love to the camera'). As his life becomes more depraved, cruel and evil (and as he becomes older), is afraid that this will be reflected in the images captured by the camera – will it see through to his soul? He grows to hate the camera and refuses ever to be filmed again – this leads to Basil's murder.

Original character

Dorian Gray: The story focuses on a beautiful young man and the portrait that is painted immortalising his beauty. However, for Dorian Gray, the portrait is only a reminder that his beauty will eventually fade while the portrait's beauty will last forever. Strangely though, as Dorian embarks on a life of excess, it is the portrait which reflects Dorian's cruelty and dissipation, while Dorian's beauty remains intact. Dorian becomes haunted by the corruption of the portrait, but his attempt to destroy it only unleashes his own death instead.

Reference

Rudolf Nureyev, Michael Clark
Jude Law in *Alfie, Talented Mr Ripley*
Christian Bale in *American Psycho*
Jonathan Rhys Meyers in *Velvet Goldmine*

Basil Hallward

A highly fashionable Artist and Photographer.

Late twenties – violently passionate, cultivates new sensations and experiences to help feed his work. Obsessive, impulsive, moody, masculine but sensual.

A true artist who is on the downward spiral both professionally and privately when he first meets Dorian. Dorian awakens in him a new excitement about his work and becomes his 'muse' and lover. They become a famous couple.

Two contrasting photo-shoots (Duets) between Dorian and Basil . . . one ending in sex (Dorian and Basil start an affair) . . . The other ending in murder (Dorian kills Basil) – Dorian wants the original photo-shoot of him preserved and resists a further photo-shoot with Basil – Doesn't want the corrupt and evil Dorian to be revealed and captured through the photographic images. Turns the camera on Basil and ends up smashing the camera and killing Basil.

Original character

Basil Hallward: The artist who wants Dorian to stay youthful and beautiful and act as his muse. His painting sets the story into motion, because it is such a true interpretation, not only of Dorian's appearance but of his soul: flawless and youthful at the beginning, it becomes increasingly ugly and ancient. Basil truly cares for Dorian and considers him a great friend, but while Dorian grows more corrupt and commits evil deeds, they lose touch with each other. When Basil and Dorian run into each other again many years later, Dorian reveals Basil's painting to him; Basil, shocked by the ugliness of the portrait, tries to make Dorian repent, to no avail, and he is killed by his muse.

Reference

Damien Hirst, David LaChapelle, Herb Ritts, Greg Gorman, Tom Ford
David Hemmings in *Blow-Up*

Lady H.

An influential, International art icon and benefactor.

Forty-five (looks thirty-five) – mature, sophisticated and stylish but hard and ruthless. Gets what she wants. Doesn't suffer fools . . . Always an event when she arrives anywhere.

Takes Dorian on as a project . . . Privately and professionally – Turns him into an international icon as the face of a new fragrance for men – 'IMMORTAL pour homme'.

Seduces Dorian and wears him like a trophy. They use each other.

Original character

Lord Henry Wotton: The high-society intellectual who corrupts Dorian. Though he promises Basil he will not influence Dorian, he is fascinated with Dorian's innocence and wants to have a hand in moulding it; he has long talks with him during which he exposes him to his own ideas and opinions, all the while convincing Dorian that these new feelings were inside him the whole time. He gives Dorian a book which becomes a sort of manual for how he is to live his life, leading him down a path of corruption, sin, and evil, and finds it remarkable that Dorian does not appear to age at all.

Reference

Sophia Loren in *Prêt-à-Porter*
Susan Sarandon in *Alfie*
Anne Bancroft as Mrs Robinson in *The Graduate*

Cyril Vane

A young Principal dancer with The Royal Ballet.

About twenty – Talented, immature, not intellectually challenged but devoted and really needy.

Dorian sees Cyril dance Romeo in *Romeo and Juliet* – beautiful, romantic, youthful, perfect.

But underneath Cyril is a self-obsessed ballet boy, whinging about injuries, forever stretching – tights and jocks thrown everywhere. Expects to be looked after . . . a social embarrassment.

An asthma sufferer, who uses an inhaler. Dorian eventually deprives him of this when he sees a way of getting rid of him (essentially killing him before our eyes).

Original character

Sybil Vane: The beautiful and talented actress with whom Dorian falls in love. The world of the theatre is all she has known, and when she falls in real love, she realizes the falsity of the stage, acting very poorly on the night that Dorian brings Basil and Henry to watch her. Dorian is crestfallen, and leaves her, telling her that he loved her for her beautiful talent. She kills herself the night he leaves, knowing that she can no longer live a false life when she has had real love.

Reference

Male ballet dancers! – you have all met the type!

Doppelgänger (DG) – Dorian's Double

Another performer representing Dorian's soul or conscience? He kills 'himself' at the end.

Appendix C

Touring

We are indebted to Simon Lacey for helping us to compile the statistics. Shows played for one week at each place unless noted otherwise.

Play Without Words
2002
National Theatre (world premiere 23 August 2002)
2003–4
National Theatre (first perform- ance 10 December 2003)
Norwich
Edinburgh
Milton Keynes
Newcastle
Manchester
High Wycombe
Birmingham
Woking
Bromley
Plymouth
Tokyo (5 weeks)
2005
Brooklyn (3 weeks)
Los Angeles (8 weeks)
Moscow

The Car Man (2007 revival)
Plymouth (first performance 18 June 2007)

Cardiff
Nottingham
Sadler's Wells (4 weeks)
Milton Keynes
Glasgow
Bradford
Wimbledon
Stoke-on-Trent
Newcastle
Woking
Aberdeen
Edinburgh
Manchester
Birmingham

The Car Man (original)
2000–2001
UK tour (world premiere 16 May 2000, Plymouth)
Old Vic (19 weeks)
Lisbon
Amsterdam
Tel Aviv (2 weeks)
Saint Paul, MI (2 weeks)
Los Angeles, CA (8 weeks)
Berkeley, CA

2002
Tokyo
Otsu
Osaka
Kobe

Edward Scissorhands
2005–6
Plymouth (world premiere
    14 November 2005)
Sadler's Wells (11 weeks)
Southampton
Salford
Norwich
Wimbledon
Cardiff
Birmingham
Woking
Nottingham
Glasgow
Newcastle
Wycombe
Bradford
Milton Keynes
2006
Seoul (2 weeks)
Tokyo (3 weeks)
2006–7
San Francisco, CA (5 weeks)
Los Angeles, CA (3 weeks)
Charlotte, NC
Pittsburgh, PA
Philadelphia, PA
Washington, DC
St Louis, MO (2 weeks)
Brooklyn, NY (3 weeks)
Toronto
Saint Paul, MI
Denver, CO

Seattle, WA (3 weeks) (final show
    of original company 13 May
    2006, performance 401)
2008
Sydney (3 weeks)
Brisbane
Perth
Melbourne (2 weeks)
Paris (4 weeks)
Birmingham
Manchester
Wimbledon
2008–9
Sadler's Wells (7 weeks)
Athens (2 weeks)
Antwerp (final show 22 February
    2009, performance 585)

Dorian Gray
2008
Plymouth (world premiere
    14 August 2008)
Edinburgh (2 weeks)
Sadler's Wells (2 weeks)
Norwich
Newcastle (final show of original
    company 27 September 2008,
    performance 46)
2009
Bromley
Milton Keynes
Ravenna
Parma
Bradford
Sadler's Wells (2 weeks)
Moscow
Leicester
Sheffield
Glasgow

Wimbledon
Manchester
Cardiff
High Wycombe

Birmingham
Woking (final performance
21 November 2009,
no. 155)

Choreochronicle

Professional Choreography by Matthew Bourne

Compiled by Alastair Macaulay, revising the 1995/96 AMP
choreochronicle, with the generous assistance of Scott Ambler,
Matthew Bourne, Simon Butteriss, Robert Carsen, Susie Cooper,
Richard Fairman, Simon Lacey (in particular),
Elizabeth Marshall, and Luke Rittner.

Abbreviations

A	Actors	**MS**	Musical Staging
AD	Associate Director	**N**	Note
AMP	Adventures in Motion Pictures	**NA**	New Adventures
Arr	Arranged by	**NP**	New Production
Bk	Book	**NT**	National Theatre, London
C	Costumes	**O**	Orchestration
Ch	Choreography	**ON**	Opening night (or press night)
Con	Conductor	**Pr**	Premiere
CM	Commissioned music	**Pro**	Producer
D	Dancers	**R**	Reproduced by
DA	Dance Arranger (music)	**RSC**	Royal Shakespeare Company
Dir	Directed by	**RV**	Revisions
F	Female performers	**S**	Sets
FP	First performance (including preview)	**Si**	Singers
		So	Sound
L	Lighting	**ST**	Staging (indicates that the
Ly	Lyrics	**TV**	Televised production was
M	Music by		staged largely in its original
Ma	Male performers		form)
MD	Musical director	**V**	Video design

1987

Overlap Lovers

An Intrigue in Three Parts

Dance production to recorded music

M: Igor Stravinsky: *Tango* (1953); Man Jumping; Juan de Dios Filiberto. **C:** James McCloskey with June Bourne. **L:** Ken McComiskey or David Goldsworthy. **D:** Carrollynne Antoun, Keith Brazil, Emma Gladstone, Susan Lewis, David Massingham, David Waring, Catherine White. **FP:** 15 July 1987. Bonnie Bird Theatre, Laban Centre for Movement and Dance, London. AMP.

Dedicated 'For Fred'. (Fred Astaire had died earlier that year.)

An early AMP announcement (1986–7) for this work says, 'Matthew Bourne is working on a piece, for six dancers, using the films of Alfred Hitchcock as a starting-point.' Bourne now says that any specific references to Hitchcock were removed as he made the work 'more abstract', but that they helped to give the work its sense of intrigue and sexual ambiguity.

Bourne himself later danced Waring's role, and Joachim Chandler later danced Antoun's.

In the 1987–8 season, Bourne and AMP colleagues 'directed' a number of other pieces for students at schools or youth dance centres where AMP was doing residences. Bourne has no recollection of these.

1988

Buck and Wing

Dance production to recorded music

CM: Steve Blake. **C:** Pam Downe. **Artwork:** Clive Mitchell. **L:** Tim Barwick. **D:** Emma Gladstone, Catherine White. **FP:** 22 August 1988. The ICA Theatre, London. AMP.

Dedicated 'For JM and EP'. These initials refer to Jessie Matthews and Eleanor Powell.

Spitfire

An Advertisement Divertissement

A dance to recorded music

M: Léon Minkus and Alexander Glazunov.
    1. Adage
    2. Variation I. 'String Best and Y-Front Briefs'
    3. Variation II: 'Cellular Singlet and Thermal Pant'
    4. Variation III: 'Interlock Trunks'
    5. Variation IV: 'Single Flap Access'
    6. Coda
C: Matthew Bourne. **L:** Tim Barwick. **D:** David Waring (I), Keith Brazil (II), Jo Chandler (III), Matthew Bourne (IV). **FP:** 22 August 1988. Institute of Contemporary Arts, London. AMP.

An early 1988 AMP announcement says, 'Matthew Bourne's quartet for four men takes as its starting point Perrot's famous "Pas de Quatre" and places it in the world of men's underwear advertising. Music by Glazunov and "costumes" courtesy of Marks and Spencer.'

There have been successive revisions to the third variation over the seasons.

NP: 1991. **S and new C:** David Davies. **L:** Rick Fisher. **D:** Scott Ambler (I), Ben Wright (II), Jamie Wright (III), Matthew Bourne (IV).

NP: For the Equality Stonewall Gala at the Royal Albert Hall in 1999, Bourne arranged a version for galas that featured six men but only two variations. This was performed again at the 2006 Dance Umbrella gala at Sadler's Wells. **D:** (2006) Adam Cooper, James Leece, Neil Penlington, Arthur Pita, Ewan Wardrop, Richard Winsor.

Other dancers who have danced in this work include: Theo Clinkard, David Greenall, Phil Hill, Stephen Kirkham, David Massingham. The 2006 staging is on YouTube.

1989

The Infernal Galop

A French Dance with English subtitles

A dance to recorded music

So: Anthony Cowton, arranging soundtrack with recorded sound effects.
1: 'Les Enfants du Paname'
M: 'Ça c'est Paris', sung by Mistinguett.
2: 'Fruits de mer'
M: 'La Mer', sung, with M and Ly, by Charles Trenet.
3: 'Pret-à-Porter'
M: Philippe and Fredo Boyer.
4: 'Les Grands Duets d'Amour'
M: Song, 'Hymne à l'Amour', Marguerite Monnot, sung (and Ly) by Edith Piaf.
5: 'Pistière'
M: Accordion music by Emile Prud'homme, with interjections by Médard Ferrero and Les Compagnons de la Chanson.
6: 'Le Grand Écart'
M: Jacques Offenbach, from *Orphée aux Enfers*.

S: Clive Mitchell. C: David Manners. L: Simon Corder. D: Keith Brazil, Emma Gladstone, Stephen Kirkham, Susan Lewis, Jamie Watton, Catherine White. FP: 17 August, 1989. The Place Theatre, London.

This was a Place Portfolio Commission 1989.

NP: 1992. One additional number, 'Tristesse', added – after 'Les Enfants du Paname' and before 'Fruits de Mer'. M: Additional song, sung by Tino Rossi ('Tristesse', music by Chopin, lyrics by Jean Loysel). SC: (revised) David Manners. L: Rick Fisher. D: Scott Ambler, Matthew Bourne, Ally Fitzpatrick, Andrew George, Etta Murfitt, Simon Murphy.

ST: Sarasota Ballet of Florida. R: Etta Murfitt. FP: FSU Center for Performing Arts, Sarasota, Florida 25 April 2008 sung by Django Reinhardt. M: For this production, the music for 'Pret-à-porter' was replaced by 'Nuages' by Django Reinhardt.

There are plans to revive this for NA in 2012.

Terra Firma

New one-act opera composed by Steve Martland

About 30 minutes in length. Innererkland Music Theatre. ON. Almeida Theatre, London, 16 April 1989. Mouth Opera.

Bourne describes the choreographic style, laughingly, as 'experimental'.

Mouth Opera performed *Terra Firma* as the last part of a quadruple-bill that also included *Soundtrack* by Piers Hellawell, *A-Ronne* by Luciano Berio, and *Anticredos* by Trevor Wishart. The staging of *Terra Firma* incorporated texts by Stevan Keane and video images into (in the words of *Opera* magazine) 'an indictment of Man's misuse of the Earth's natural resources'.

As You Like It

Play by William Shakespeare

Dir: John Caird. **M:** IlonaSekacz (commissioned). **SC:** Ultz. **L:** Alan Burrett. **A:** *Rosalind*: Sophie Thompson, *Celia*: Gillian Bevan, *Touchstone*: Mark Williams, *Orlando*: Jerome Flynn, *Silvius*: Alan Cumming, *Phoebe*: Cassie Stuart, *Jacques*: Hugh Ross, *Duke Senior*: Clifford Williams. **Pr:** Royal Shakespeare Theatre, Stratford-upon-Avon, 13 September 1989. Royal Shakespeare Company.

In this production, while the audience entered the theatre, the entire cast performed social dances for 10–15 minutes before the spoken beginning of the play. Phoebe danced a solo, 'in a vaguely Isadora Ducan style'.
 At the end, the entire cast performed a hoedown.
 This production transferred to the Barbican Theatre in March 1990.

Singer

Play by Peter Flannery

Dir: Terry Hands. **M:** Ilona Sekacz (commissioned). **SC:** Sanca Jurca Avci. **L:** Terry Hands. **C:** *Chorus*: Joe Melia, *Stefan*: Mick Ford, *Singer*: Antony Sher, *Mani*: Malcolm Storry. **Pr:** The Swan Theatre, Stratford-upon-Avon. 11 October 1989. Royal Shakespeare Company.

Bourne's choreography was for a brief 'play within the play'. It featured the actors Alan Cumming, Cassie Stuart and Mark Williams.
 In RSC repertory into 1990. The production transferred to The Pit, Barbican Centre, London.

Leonce and Lena

Play by George Büchner, translated by Jeremy Sams

Dir: Lindsay Posner. **M:** Stephen Warbeck (commissioned). **SC:** Julian

McGowan. **Pr:** Studio Theatre, Crucible, Sheffield, 9 November 1989. Running until 2 December 1989.

Bourne's choreography was for two actors – one male (Adam Kotz), one female – who performed as mechanical puppets.

Within the Quota

A dance to recorded music

M: Cole Porter, 'Within the Quota'. **D:** Approximately 12–15 dancers, all female dance students. **Pr:** Royal Academy of Dancing, London.

It seems likely that Bourne made this on A-level students whom he tutored at the RAD; no date has yet emerged.

1990
Children of Eden

New musical

M and Ly: Stephen Schwartz. **Bk:** John Caird. **Dir:** John Caird. **SC:** John Napier. **L:** David Hersey. **D:** Sophia Butler (formerly Susan Lewis), Anna-Jane Casey, Colin Charles, Brenda Edwards, Stephen Houghton, Vanessa Leigh-Hicks, Aaron Peth, Mitch Sebastian. **Si:** Anthony Barclay, Kevin Colson, Ruthie Henshall, Ken Page, Shezwae Powell, Frances Ruffelle. **Pr:** Prince Edward Theatre, London. **PN:** January 1991.

Greenfingers

Dance production to recorded music

M: Percy Grainger: *Country Gardens*. Elgar: *Chanson du Matin*. Grainger: *Shepherd's Hey*. **C:** Fenella Magnus. **D:** Carrollynne Antoun, Keith Brazil, Bill Eldridge, Susan Lewis, Catherine White. **FP:** Farnham-Maltings, Surrey. AMP.

This choreography was incorporated in 1991 into the 'Country' section of 'Town & Country'. It was privately dedicated to Alastair Macaulay.

1991

Town & Country

Dance production in two acts, to recorded music

Town: Louden Lots
1. 'Pomp and Circumstance'
M: Edward Elgar, arr. Paul Whiteman: *Pomp and Circumstance*.
2. 'By the Sleepy Lagoon'
M: Eric Coates: 'By the Sleepy Lagoon' (the theme tune for the BBC Radio programme *Desert Island Discs*)
3. 'Housewives' Choice'
M: Jack Strachey.
4. 'Dearest Love'
M and Ly: Noel Coward, 'Dearest Love', sung by Coward.
5. 'Brief Encounter'
M: Including Edward Elgar, *Serenade*, played by Alfred Campoli and his Salon Orchestra; Noel Coward's spoken patter from another recording; Serge Rachmaninov, arr. Matheson for *Brief Encounter*.
6. 'Music Everywhere'
M: Eric Coates.
7. 'By The Sleepy Lagoon'
M: reprise of 2.

Country (More Clingingly)
1. 'Handel in the Strand'
M: Percy Grainger.
2. 'Country Gardens'
M: Percy Grainger.
3. 'Gay but Wistful'
M: Percy Grainger.
4. 'Clog Dance'
M: J. S. Bach, arranged by Percy Grainger.
5. 'Chanson du Matin'
M: Edward Elgar.
6. 'Shallow Brown'
M: Percy Grainger (sung by John Shirley-Quirk, with chorus)
7. 'Shepherd's Hey'
M: Percy Grainger.

8. 'The Sussex Mummers' Christmas Carol'
M: Percy Grainger.
SC: Charlotte Humpston. **L:** Rick Fisher. **D:** Scott Ambler, Matthew Bourne, Ally Fitzpatrick, Etta Murfitt, Jamie Watton, Ben Wright. **FP:** Arnolfini, Bristol, March or April. AMP.

Dedicated to June and Jim Bourne.
   The production was performed in London at the Royal Court Theatre, as part of the Barclays New Stages season in June 1991.

Excerpts of the 1991 production are on YouTube.

ST: 'Dearest Love' only. **D:** Matthew Hart, Michael Nunn, Hubert Essakow. **Pr:** March 2003, Queen Elizabeth Hall, London. George Piper Dances.

ST: 'Dearest Love' only. **D:** Christopher Marney and Hendrick January. **Pr:** 26–30 August 2009. 'Hotel Follies' (**D:** Christopher Marney), Arts Theatre, London.

A Midsummer Night's Dream

Opera composed by Benjamin Britten

Words from William Shakespeare's play *A Midsummer Night's Dream*.

Dir: Robert Carsen. **SC:** Michael Levine. **A:** Puck: Emil Wolk. **Si:** *Oberon* James Bowman, *Tytania* Lillian Watson, *Bottom* Roderick Kennedy. **Pr:** Festival Theatre, Aix-en-Provence, France. Aix-en-Provence Festival production.

Bourne's choreography was largely for the boys' choir, 20–25 in number. There was also some choreography for a hoedown for the 'mechanicals', and Bourne had some involvement with the staging as a whole.

ST. This production has been revived many times in France and across Europe: at Aix in 1992, for a tour of Paris (the Opéra Comique) and seven other cities in 1994, at the Ravenna Festival and Ferrara Musica (Italy), in 1995, 1996 and 2005 at English National Opera, twice at the Opéra in Bordeaux, once at the Opéra in Strasbourg, once in Ludwigshafen (Germany), and three or more times at the Opéra de Lyon. The 1996 ENO revival included: *Puck*: Miltos Yerolemou; *Oberon*: David Daniels; *Tytania*: Lillian Watson; *Lysander*: John Graham-Hall; *Demetrius*: Christopher Booth-Jones; *Bottom*: Roderick Kennedy;

Quince: Gordon Sandison; *Flute*: Christopher Gillett; *Fairies*: Trinity Boys Choir. **Con:** Steuart Bedford. The 2005 ENO one included: *Puck*: Emil Wolk; *Oberon*: Robin Blaze; *Tytania*: Sarah Tynan; *Bottom*: Peter Rose; *Lysander*: Alfred Boe; *Hermia*: Victoria Simmonds; *Helena*: Lynda Richardson; *Demetrius*: Leigh Melrose; *Flute*: Christopher Gillett; *Quince*: Graeme Danby; *Snug*: Clive Bayley; *Starveling*: Leslie John Flanagan; *Snout*: Robert Burt; *Fairies*: Trinity Boys Choir. **Con:** Paul Daniel.

For some of these revivals, such as those for English National Opera in 1995 and 1996, Bourne's choreography was rehearsed by Catherine (White) Malone.

In April 2005 it was revived at the Gran Teatre del Liceu, Barcelona (Spain), with a cast including: *Puck*: Emil Wolk; *Oberon*: David Daniels; *Tytania*: Ofelia Sala; *Bottom*: Matthew Rose; *Flute*: Christopher Gillett; *Lysander*: Gordon Gietz; *Hermia*: Deanne Meek; *Helena*: Brigitte Hahn; *Demetrius*: William Dazeley; *Peter Quince*: Henry Waddington. **Con:** Harry Bicket. A subsequent staging occurred at the Athens Festival (Greece).

In 2009 it was revived at La Scala, Milan, with Shelby Williams staging its dances. The cast was led by the same singers as at Barcelona other than: *Tytania*: Rosemary Joshua; *Helena*: Erin Wall; *Demetrius*: David Adam Moore. *Peter Quince*: Andrew Shore; *Snug*: Graeme Danby; *Snout*: Adrian Thompson; *Starveling*: Simon Butteriss. **Con:** Andrew Davis. **ON:** 7 June 2009.

The 2005 Barcelona staging was filmed and is available in DVD format.

The Tempest

Music-theatre production

After the play by William Shakespeare. **Dir:** Nick Hedges. **M:** Various, including Noel Coward's 'Mad About the Boy', and excerpts from Paul Dukas's *The Sorcerer's Apprentice*, Richard Wagner, Harold Arlen, and recordings by Billie Holliday. **MD** (live singing by the cast): Richard Balcombe. **SC:** Brian Lee. **L:** Kevin Fitz-Simons.
A: *Prospero*: Simon Bowen; *Trinculo*: David Walliams; *Stephano*: Stuart Ash; *Caliban*: Andrew Danezi. Cast also included Sam Barriscale,

Clive Brunt, Philip Goldsworthy. All the performers, approximately 25 in number, danced. (There were 13 Ariels – a chorus.) **Pr:** 15 August 1991. Running until 24 August. The Place Theatre, London. National Youth Theatre.

There were some dance duets (for example, a tango, a sand dance and matador-and-cape duet for Stephano and Trinculo, to cha-cha music), and a big 'Hollywood fan dance'.

ST: This production was revived in 1993. National Youth Theatre.

Show Boat

Musical

M: Jerome Kern. **Lyr and Bk:** Oscar Hammerstein II. **Dir:** Ronny Danielson. **A, Si:** About 80 performers – actors, singers, dancers – in all. Some 30 members of the Malmö Balletten dance company performed most of Bourne's choreography. **Pr:** Stadsteater, Malmö, Sweden. Malmö, Stadsteater.

Bourne set dances in particular to 'Make Believe', 'Can't Help Lovin' Dat Man', 'Ol' Man River', 'After the Ballet', 'Life Upon the Wicked Stage', 'Why Do I Love You?', 'Goodbye, My Lady Love'.

ST. The production was revived the following season.

A Swedish private film exists of this production.

Watch with Mother

Dance production to recorded music

M: Voice of Joyce Grenfell, beginning of nursery-school 'Moving to Music' sketch; Percy Grainger, 'First English Waltz'; Fauré, arranged by Grainger ('Tuscan Serenade'); Grainger, 'Children's March'; J.S. Bach arr. Grainger, 'Blithe Bells'. **C:** Abby Hammond.

Bourne originally choreographed this on nine dancers in the Transitions Dance Company in autumn 1991. Three of these dancers – Saranne Curtin, Maxine Fone, Andrew George – joined AMP in 1992; Curtin also danced with NA. However – as a result of Andrew George's immediate defection to Adventures in Motion Pictures – was never performed by Transitions.

ST: In 1994, Bourne revived it for the National Youth Dance Company, rehearsing it at Roehampton Dance Institute. Pr: The Rambert School, London.

One of his dancers, Theo Clinkard, joined Adventures in Motion Pictures later that year: he was, at seventeen, the youngest-ever professional dancerto join Bourne's company.

1992

Deadly Serious

An Hysterical Double-Feature

Dance production in two acts to recorded music

First act: 'Overwrought'; Second Act: 'Rear Entry'.

M: Songs: Cole Porter's 'You Do Something To Me', sung by Marlene Dietrich. 'Stardust', sung by Ella Fitzgerald. 'Mr Wonderful', sung by Peggy Lee. Other music by: Charles Gounod (*Funeral March of a Marionette*, as used for the theme for Alfred Hitchcock's TV series); Bernard Herrmann, from the scores for *Vertigo*, *North by Northwest*, and *Psycho*; Ferde Grofé, 'Cloudburst' from his *Grand Canyon Suite*; Milos Rosza; Jean Sibelius, *Valse Triste* (Sibelius's own recording) and 'Miranda' from his incidental music for *The Tempest*; Franz Waxman, score for *Rebecca*. CM: David Manners. SC: David Manners. L: Rick Fisher. D: Scott Ambler, Matthew Bourne, Ally Fitzpatrick, Andrew George, Etta Murfitt, Simon Murphy. FP: 9 March 1992. Arnolfini, Bristol. AMP.

The 'Mr Wonderful' excerpt is on YouTube.

Nutcracker (later, Nutcracker!)

Dance production in two acts

New scenario Martin Duncan and Matthew Bourne, after an original scenario by Marius Petipa based on Alexandre Dumas *père*'s version of E.T.A. Hoffmann's *The Nutcracker and the Mouseking*. M: Pyotr Ilyich Tchaikovsky ('Mère Gigogne' was cut from Act Two). Dir: Martin Duncan. SC: Anthony Ward. L: Robert Bryan. The production, played without interval, was the second half of Opera North's centenary

705

production of Tchaikovsky's 1892 double-bill, with the opera *Yolanta* played before the interval. **FP:** 26 August 1992 King's Theatre, Edinburgh. Opera North with AMP.

D: *Dr Dross* (*King Sherbert*): Barry Atkinson; *Matron* (*Queen Candy*): Rosemary Allen; *Sugar* (*Princess Sugar*), *their daughter*: Ally Fitzpatrick; *Fritz* (*Prince Bon-Bon*), *their son*: Scott Ambler; *Clara*: Etta Murfitt; *Nutcracker*: Andrew George; *Orphans*: Teresa Barker, Saranne Curtin, Misha Downey, Maxine Fone, Friedrich Gehrig, Andrew George, Mary Herbert, Phil Hill, Susan Jellings, Rachel Krische, Jason Lewis, Simon Murphy, Anton Skrzypiciel; *Governors and wives*: Bruce Budd, David Owen Lewis, Angela Sorrigan, Gladwyn Taylor (*members of Opera North chorus*); *Cupids*: Simon Murphy, Maxine Fone; *The Doorman*: Scott Ambler; *Liquorice Allsorts*: Teresa Barker, Misha Downey, Friedrich Gehrig; *Knickerbocker Glory*: Anton Skrzypiciel; *Marshmallow Girls*: Saranne Curtin, Maxine Fone, Mary Herbert, Susan Jellings, Rachel Krische; *The Gobstoppers*: Phil Hill, Jason Lewis, Simon Murphy.
A: From Opera North chorus.

NP: This production was revived by AMP as *Nutcracker!* at Sadler's Wells Theatre in 1993 and 1994, with an interval. The credits now read: 'Devised and directed by Martin Duncan and Matthew Bourne. Choreographed by Matthew Bourne.' Slightly revised **SC:** Anthony Ward. **L:** Tina McHugh. **Arr** (reducing orchestra from 70 to 24): Rowland Lee.

D: As above, with the following main exceptions: Matthew Bourne danced an Orphan and Knickerbocker Glory. Stephen Kirkham danced an Orphan and a Gobstopper. In the 1994 revival, Saranne Curtin danced Sugar. AMP.

NP: NA at Sadler's Wells Theatre. Bourne is credited in the programme as Director and Choreographer, with Bourne and Martin Duncan listed as Original Scenario Devisers. The 1993 Rowland Lee musical arrangement is still used. **SC:** Anthony Ward. **L:** Howard Harrison.

D: *Dr Dross/King Sherbert*: Scott Ambler (James Leece); *Matron/Queen Candy*: Emily Piercy (Isabel Mortimer); *Sugar/Princess Sugar*: Saranne Curtin (Michela Meazza); *Fritz/Prince Bon-Bon*: Ewan Wardrop (Neil Penlington); *Clara*: Etta Murfitt (Valentina Formenti); *Nutcracker*:

Alan Vincent (Adam Galbraith); *The Cupids*: Valentina Formenti, Neil Penlington (Shelby Williams, Lee Smikle; Gemma Payne, Philip Willingham); *The Doorman*: Company; *Liquorice Allsorts*: Vicky Evans, Richard Winsor, Paulo Kadow (Mami Tomotani, Aaron Sillis, Simon Wakefield); *Knickerbocker Glory*: Arthur Pita (Paulo Kadow); *Marshmallow Girls*: Kerry Biggin, Belinda Lee Chapman, Vicky Evans, Sophia Hurdley, Rachel Lancaster, Michela Meazza, Gemma Payne, Emily Piercy, Mami Tomotani, Shelby Williams (five at each performance); *Gobstoppers*: Adam Galbraith, James Leece, Lee Smikle (Philip Willingham, Ross Carpenter, Simon Wakefield).

FP: 20 November 2002. NA.

N. The 2002 production was filmed for BBC TV and released in DVD form. Excerpts may be seen on YouTube.

It has been extensively toured in the UK and other countries.

The Percys of Fitzrovia

An Arty-Farce

A dance production in one act to recorded music

1. 'Still Life'
M: Madame Florence Foster Jenkins's recording of the Laughing Song from Johann Strauss's *Die Fledermaus*.
2. 'A Nest of Eels'
M: Bohislav Martinů.
3. 'Aural Pleasures'
M: Franz Liszt.
4. 'Militant Tendencies'
M: Johannes Brahms.
5. 'Hard Backs'
M: Bohuslav Martinů.
6. 'Writer's Block'
M: Tchaikovsky (Piano Concerto No. 1, arr. Percy Grainger).
7. 'The Object of Beauty'
M: Louis Ganne.
8. 'Finishing Touches'
M: Franz Ries.

9. 'Peculiar Vices'
M: Bohuslav Martinů.
10. 'The Golden Hoard'
M: Bohuslav Martinů.

SC: David Manners. **L:** Rick Fisher. **D:** Scott Ambler, Matthew Bourne, Ally Fitzpatrick, Andrew George, Etta Murfitt, Simon Murphy. **FP:** Arnolfini, Bristol. AMP.

The programme says 'The choreographer would like to thank David Manners for suggesting the idea of Fitzrovia and the performers of AMP for their many contributions to the making of "The Percys".'

The first London performance was 6 January 1993, at the Lyric Theatre, Hammersmith.

1993

Late Flowering Lust

TV film to poems by John Betjeman as set to music by Jim Parker and spoken by Nigel Hawthorne

Dir: David Hinton. Director of photography: Nick Knowland. Produced by Ecosse Films by Douglas Rae. 57 minutes. Filmed in July–August 1993. Broadcast by BBC2 on 8 May 1994. **C:** Pam Downe. Location: Bennington Lordship. **A:** Nigel Hawthorne, Richenda Carey, Jonathan Cecil. **D:** Rosie Allen, Scott Ambler, Matthew Bourne, Ally Fitzpatrick, Maxine Fone, Andrew George, Etta Murfitt, Simon Murphy. AMP.

Excerpts are available on YouTube.

Drip

A Narcissistic Love Story

Short film for TV

Dir: Frances Dickenson. **M:** Rowland Lee. **C:** David Manners. Produced by Caz Gorman. 11 minutes. Filmed: September 1993. Location: Brixton and The Criterion Brasserie, Piccadilly Circus. **D:** Rosie Allen, Scott Ambler, Matthew Bourne, Andrew George, Etta Murfitt, Simon Murphy. **Broadcast:** BBC2, 9 February 1993. AMP.

1994

Peer Gynt

Play by Henrik Ibsen, in a version by Frank McGuinness

Dir: Yukio Ninagawa. **M:** Ryudo Uzaki. **S:** Tsukasa Nakagoshi. **C:** Lily Komine. **L:** Tamotsu Harada. Co-produced by Thelma Holt, Tadao Nakana, and Duncan C. Weldon. **A:** *Peer Gynt*: Michael Sheen; *Solveig*: Catherine White; *Ase*: Paola Dionisotti; *Buttonmoulder*: Haruhiko John. 27 actors in all. **ON:** National Theatret, Oslo (Norway – Winter Olympics). Royal Shakespeare Company.

Bourne's choreography was for ensemble dances. He remembers a hoedown and a troll dance.

The Catherine White playing Solveig is not to be confused with the former AMP dancer Catherine White (now Catherine Malone).

After its initial five performances in Oslo, this production was performed at the Barbican Theatre (3–12 March), at the Palace Theatre, Manchester (17–19 March), and then at the Ginza Saison Theatre, Tokyo (Japan) (20–30 April).

Highland Fling

A Romantic Wee Ballet

Dance production in two acts

M: Hermann Løvensjold (*Silfiden*, Op. 1); Lerner and Loewe (overture to *Brigadoon*); 'Auld Lang Syne'. **SC:** Lez Brotherston. **L:** Tina McHugh.

D: *The Sylph*: Maxine Fone; *James*: Scott Ambler; *Effie*: Emily Piercy; *Madge*: Etta Murfitt; *Gurn*: Simon Murphy; *Dorty*: Rosie Allen; *Robbie*: Andrew George.
ON: Arnolfini, Bristol. 26 April 1994.

Dedication: For James [McCloskey, Bourne's first designer, who had died two weeks before the premiere]
Initially this production was to recorded music.
This production was revived in 1995 and 1997. Other, later, castings included: *The Sylph*: Jacqueline Anderson; *James*: Neil Penlington; *Madge*: Isabel Mortimer; *Gurn*: Phil Hill, Neil Penlington, Lee Boggess,

Theo Clinkard; *Dorty*: Heather Habens; *Robbie*: Mark Mitchell, Neil Penlington, Lee Boggess; *Covers/Sylphs*: Saranne Curtin, Lee Boggess, Jacqui Anderson.

NP: New Adventures. **SC:** Lez Brotherston. **L:** Paule Constable. **D:** Multiple casts are given, since all casts contributed to the creation. *The Sylph*: Kerry Biggin (Noi Tolmer); *James*: James Leece (Adam Galbraith, Will Kemp); *Effie*: Hannah Vassallo (Kerry Biggin, Mikah Smillie); *Madge*: Noi Tolmer (Gemma Payne, Mami Tomotani); *Gurn*: Ross Carpenter (Lee Smikle, Philip Willingham); *Robbie*: Adam Galbraith (Ross Carpenter, James Leece); *Dorty*: Shelby Williams (Rachel Lancaster); *Angus*: Philip Willingham (Matt Flint); *Ewan*: Ross Carpenter (Matt Flint, Lee Smikle); *Jeannie*: Gemma Payne (Mikah Smillie, Shelby Williams); *Morag*: Rachel Lancaster (Mami Tomotani, Hannah Vassallo). **ON:** 12 February 2005. Churchill Theatre, Bromley. NA.

The cast was now of eleven rather than seven.

On tour, the production used a Royal Danish Orchestra recording conducted by David Garforth. At Sadler's Wells, a live orchestra was used.

The production toured eleven cities in the UK (including two seasons at Sadler's Wells, London), and Tokyo (Japan), with a final performance on 28 August 2005.

There are excerpts of this production on YouTube.

Oliver!

Musical

M, Ly, and Bk: Lionel Bart. **Pro:** Cameron Mackintosh. **Dir:** Sam Mendes. **SC:** Anthony Ward. **L:** David Hersey. **O:** William David Brohn. **DA:** Chris Walker. **A:** (alternate casts in brackets) *Fagin*: Jonathan Pryce; *Nancy*: *Sally Dexter*; *Oliver*: James Daley (and Gregory Bradley); *Artful Dodger*: Adam Searles (and Paul Bailey). **FP:** 8 December 1994, London Palladium.

Most of Bourne's choreography was for the children (24 in each cast) and for Fagin.

This production ran until 21 February 1998, with 1,352 perform-ances. Bourne was involved in revisions to the Palladium production with three of the four later actors playing Fagin: Jim Dale, Robert Lindsay and Russ Abbott.

NP. A revised version for touring. **FP:** Theatre Royal, Plymouth. 13 August 1998. Touring UK (Manchester, Birmingham, Bradford) in 1998–99, Toronto, Canada in 1999–2000, Australia (Sydney and Melbourne) in 2002–3, Singapore in 2003, and the USA in 2003–5. Bourne was involved in revisions for this touring production.

See *Oliver!*, 2008.

1995
Watch Your Step

Musical

M and Lyr: Irving Berlin. **Dir:** John Caird. **SC:** Sue Blane (adapted around the existing set for *The Phantom of the Opera*). **A:** Henry Goodman. **D:** Rosie Allen, Scott Ambler, Matthew Bourne, Maxine Fone, Andrew George, Gareth Griffiths, Heather Habens, Phil Hill, Isabel Mortimer, Etta Murfitt. **Pr:** Her Majesty's Theatre, London. Irving Berlin Gala.

This was for a single gala performance.

Bourne recalls the choreography, especially for the title number, as being 'in the style of Vernon and Irene Castle'.

Girls were Made to Love and Kiss

M. Franz Lehár, sung by Richard Tauber. **C:** from AMP wardrobe. **D:** Etta Murfitt, Emily Piercy. **Pr:** AMP gala, Donmar Warehouse, London.

There was only one performance.

The Swan

M: Camille Saint-Saëns ('Le Cygne', sung by Richard Tauber as 'Der Schwann'). **C:** provided by Adam Cooper. **D:** Adam Cooper (then a guest dancer). **Pr:** AMP gala, Donmar.

There was only one performance.

Boutique

Dance production in one-act

M. Rossini (arr. Respighi, *La Boutique fantasque*). **SC:** Paul Edwards. **L:** Matthew Bourne.
D: *The Designer*: Kenneth Pettitt; *His Assistant*: Emma Northmore; *The Young Man*: Xavier Pont; *His Girlfriend*: Michela Meazza; *Barbie*: Cecilia Madrazo; *Ken*: Bernet Pascual; *Photographers and models*: Mirko Battuello and Amy Edwards, Juan Rodriguez and Maya Sato, Daniel Adams and Maria Rowland; *Flowerpower*: Ruriko Al, Lorena Perez, Mariana Dias, Mariah Hamid, Nozomi Saito; *Bridalwear*: *Barbie*: Cecilia Madrazo; *Ken*: Bernet Pascual. *Bridesmaids*: Nozomi Saito, Naya Sato, Gemma Matthews, Ruriko Ai; *Male models*: Mirko Battello, Bernet Pascual, Daniel Adams, Juan Rodriguez; *Pet fashions*: *Owner*: Maria Rowland; *Poodle*: Mariah Hamid; *Owner*: Mariana Diaz; *Poodle*: Jane Lawrence; *Rave Up*: The cast. *Adage*: The Cast; *Pas de deux*: Cecilia Madrazo and Xavier Pont. *Finale*: The Cast.
Pr: July 1995. Images of Dance.

This production was revived in July 1999 and 2005.

ST: Margaret Barbieri and Scott Ambler. **L** (2005): Peter Teigen.

Images of Dance, attached to London Studio Centre, is a company of graduating student dancers. Michela Meazza later joined AMP and then NA.

ST. Sarasota Ballet of Florida **R:** Margaret Barbieri. **SC:** Paul Edwards. **L:** Jim Sale.
D: *The Designer*: Jamie Carter; *The Young Man*: Logan Learned; *His Girlfriend*: Kate Honea; *Barbie*: Victoria Hulland; *Ken*: Ricardo Rhodes.
Pr: FSU Center for the Performing Arts, Sarasota, Florida. 29 January 2010.

Roald Dahl's 'Little Red Riding Hood'

TV film

Dir: Donald Sturrock. **P:** Paul Patterson. Filmed: June–July 1995. Location: Elstree Studios, TV Broadcast: 1 January 1996. **SC:** Sophie Becher.

A: *Red Riding Hood and her Grandmother*: Julie Walters; *Narrator* (*seen*): Ian Holm; *Voice of the Wolf*: Danny De Vito; *Wolf*: Peter Elliott. **D:** *Hyena*: Andrew George; *Cat*: Etta Murfitt; *She-Wolf*: Scott Ambler; *Prussian Sow*: Phil Hill; *Cow*: Emily Piercy; *Sheep*: Maxine Fone; *Pigs*: three child performers from the Sylvia Young School.

Bourne's choreography was for Julie Walters and for the dancers.
All the adult dancers were members of AMP.

Swan Lake

Full-length dance production with one interval

M: Pyotr Ilyich Tchaikovsky (arr. David Lloyd-Jones), incorporating features from both the 1877 score and its 1900 suite. **SC:** Lez Brotherston. **L:** Rick Fisher.
D: Two casts are given, since most roles were double cast in rehearsal and both casts contributed to the creation. *The Swan*: Adam Cooper (David Hughes); *The Prince*: Scott Ambler (Ben Wright); *The Queen*: Fiona Chadwick (Isabel Mortimer); *The Prince's Girlfriend*: Emily Piercy; *The Private Secretary*: Barry Atkinson; *The Young Prince*: Andrew Walkinshaw (Sid Mitchell).

Act I
Queen's escorts: William Kemp, Mark Mitchell, Simon Reglar, William Yong; *Moth Maiden*: Maxine Fone; *The Nobleman*: Phil Hill; *Butterfly Maidens*: Sarah Barron, Saranne Curtin, Heather Habens, Kirsty Tapp (Isabel Mortimer); *Evil Forest Troll*: Lee Boggess; *His Attendants*: Jacqui Anderson, Teresa Barker; *Club Owner*: Eddie Nixon; *Pop Idol*: William Kemp; *Hostesses*: Sarah Barron, Saranne Curtin; *Fan Dancer*: Heather Habens; *Barmaid*: Jacqui Anderson; *Barflies*: Teresa Barker, Stephen Kirkham; *Party Girls*: Maxine Fone, Isabel Mortimer (Kirsty Tapp); *East End Gangsters*: Mark Mitchell, Ian Wooller; *Sailors*: Greig Cooke, Simon Reglar; *Schoolboy*: Andrew Walkinshaw (Sid Mitchell).

Act II
Swans: Greig Cooke, Darren Ellis, Floyd Hendricks, Eddie Nixon, Simon Reglar, William Yong; *Cygnets*: Lee Boggess, Phil Hill, Stephen Kirkham, Quang Van; *Big Swans*: William Kemp (Colin Ross Waterston), Mark Mitchell, Pablo Pena, Ian Wooller.

Act III

Doorman: Mark Mitchell; *Press, Photographers*: Lee Boggess, Darren Ellis, Simon Reglar, Ian Wooller; *Royal Spotters*: Simon Reglar, Kirsty Tapp; *Autograph Hunters*: Stephen Kirkham, Andrew Walkinshaw (Sid Mitchell); *The German Princess*: Heather Habens; *Her Escort*: Pablo Pena; *The Spanish Princess*: Jacqui Anderson; *Her Escort*: Quang Van; *The Hungarian Princess*: Sarah Barron; *Her Escort*: William Yong; *Princess of Monaco*: Isabel Mortimer (Kirsty Tapp); *Her Escort*: Greig Cooke; *The Italian Princess*: Saranne Curtin; *Her Escort*: William Kemp; *The French Princess*: Teresa Barker; *Her Escort*: Phil Hill; *The Romanian Princess*: Maxine Fone; *Her Escort*: Floyd Hendricks; *Spanish Dancers*: Lee Boggess, Darren Ellis, Mark Mitchell, Eddie Nixon, Simon Reglar, Ian Wooller.

Act IV

Doctors and Nurses: Jacqui Anderson, Teresa Barker, Sarah Barron, Saranne Curtin, Maxine Fone, Heather Habens, Isabel Mortimer, Emily Piercy.
Pr: 9 November 1995. Sadler's Wells Theatre. AMP.

Dedicated to company dancer Simon Murphy, who had died in 1995, aged 24.

This production was extensively revived and somewhat revised. For the 1996 tour, and for performances throughout 1996 and 1997, a new orchestration for 25 players was provided by Rowland Lee. Subsequently the production has often been performed to taped music.

The six Swans were later named as Medium Swans.

A film/video/DVD of this production, featuring the first cast in almost all respects, was made in 1996. **Dir:** Peter Mumford. **Broadcast on TV:** 26 December 1996.

Touring: British tour, February–April, 1996. Piccadilly Theatre, London, September 1996–February 2007. Ahmanson Theatre, Los Angeles, 1997. Neil Simon Theatre, New York, 1998–9. Second UK tour October–December 1999. Dominion Theatre, February–March 2000. In 2000, the production visited Modena and Ferrara (Italy); Amsterdam (The Netherlands); Tel Aviv (Israel); Istanbul (Turkey); and Cologne (Germany). In 2002–3, it visited Lyon (France), Frankfurt (Germany), Tokyo and Osaka (Japan).

Excerpt (from Act II): Royal Variety Performance 1 December, 1997. This is on YouTube.

The most important subsequent additions, with AMP or NA or both, have been the following:

The Swan/Stranger: William (later Will) Kemp; Keith Roberts, Jesus Pastor, Alan Vincent, Jason Piper, Jose Tirado, Shoto Yasujiki, Thomas Whitehead, Richard Winsor, Jonathan Ollivier.
The Prince: Tom Ward, Alastair Marriott, Simon Williams, Neil Westmoreland, Matthew Hart, Neil Penlington, Christopher Marney, Dominic North, Sam Archer.
The Queen: Lynn Seymour, Marguerite Porter, Krissy Richmond, Nicola Tranah, Oxana Panchenko, Saranne Curtin, Philippa Gordon, Candice Evans, Nina Goldman, Charlotte Broom, Madelaine Brennan. Marguerite Porter, Krissy Richmond, Nicola Tranah, Oxana Panchenko, Saranne Curtin, Philippa Gordon, Candice Evans, Nina Goldman, Charlotte Broom, Madelaine Brennan. Saranne Curtin, Marguerite Porter, Krissy Roberts, Philippa Gordon, Etta Murfitt, Nicola Tranah, Oxana Panchenko, Candice Evans, Nina Goldman, Madelaine Brennan, Charlotte Broom.

NP. New Adventures, 19 November, 2004. Slight changes of **C** from Lez Brotherston.

This toured to Japan (Tokyo, Matsumoto, Osaka, Seoul) in 2005; toured the UK (September–November 2005); visited Paris (France, November 2005–January 2006). In 2006–7, it visited Sadler's Wells, London; Paris (France), Moscow (Russia), Japan and South Korea. In 2009–10, it visited Sadler's Wells, London; toured the UK; visited Japan, South Korea, Greece, Italy, and New York City Center Theater (USA).

The Rowland Lee arrangement of the music is still employed when there is live music; recordings have been used on most tours.

1997
Cinderella

Dance production in three acts

M: Sergey Prokofiev, *Cinderella*, **Arr:** Daryl Griffiths. At the end, the version of the 'Waltz of the Stars' from Prokofiev's 'Waltz Suite' was played during danced curtain calls. **O:** Daryl Griffith. Sound design: Simon King. **SC:** Lez Brotherston. **L:** Rick Fisher. Produced by Katharine Doré.

D: (multiple castings are cited to show which dancers were involved in the original creation of the role). *Cinderella*: Sarah Wildor (Saranne Curtin, Maxine Fone); *The Pilot*: Adam Cooper (Ewan Wardrop, Will Kemp); *The Angel*: Will Kemp (Arthur Pita, Adam Cooper, Theo Clinkard); *The Stepmother*: Lynn Seymour (Isabel Mortimer); *Cinderella's Father*: Barry Atkinson.

The cast also included Scott Ambler, Jacqueline Anderson, Teresa Barker, Andrew Corbett, Matthew Dalby, Darren Ellis, Vicky Evans, Valentina Formenti, Lucy Harrison, Ben Hartley, Floyd Hendricks, Phil Hill, Michela Meazza, Etta Murfitt, Neil Penlington, Emily Piercy, Colin Ross-Waterson, Tom Searle, Kirsty Tapp, Alan Vincent, Andrew Walkinshaw, Ben Wright.

FN: 26 September 1997. Piccadilly Theatre, London. AMP.

Bourne dedicated *Cinderella* 'to my late grandparents Mabel and Harry, Flora and William, who lived through the Blitz'.

Excerpts are on YouTube.

NP: AMP.

SC: Lez Brotherston. **L:** Rick Fisher. **Pr:** 30 March 1999. Ahmanson Theatre, Los Angeles. *Cinderella*: Sarah Wildor (Saranne Curtin); *The Pilot*: Adam Cooper (Ewan Wardrop, Will Kemp); *The Angel*: Will Kemp (Arthur Pita); *The Stepmother*: Isabel Mortimer (Emily Piercy); AMP.

Choreography, scenario, and designs were extensively revised, especially in Acts One and Two. Two musical items (score, end of no. 15, nos 16 and 23) were cut from Acts One and Two. At the start of Act Two, the Prelude to Act One was reprised. In Act Two, no. 24 was moved to after no. 30.

NP: New Adventures. This staging featured a new Prologue with Pathé News footage of the Blitz, some further re-ordering of Act Two dances, and a new Glenn Miller play-out ('Pennsylvania 6500') for curtain calls. **L:** Neil Austin. **So:** Paul Groothuis. *Cinderella*: Kerry Biggin (Noi Tolmer, Ashley Shaw); *The Pilot*: Sam Archer (Neil Westmoreland, Edwin Ray); *The Stepmother*: Michela Meazza (Mikah Smillie, Madelaine Brennan, Etta Murfitt); *The Angel*: Christopher Marney (Glenn Graham, Adam Maskell). The 2011 International tour included 16 performances in Moscow (where the original Bolshoi production premiered in 1946).

FP: 15 November 2010, Theatre Royal, Plymouth. **ON:** 8 December 2010, Sadler's Wells Theatre.

2000

The Car Man

An Auto-Erotic Thriller

Dance production in two acts

Dir and Ch: Matthew Bourne. **M:** Georges Bizet, arr. by Rodion Schedrin and (new) Terry Davies. **MD:** Brett Morris. **So:** Matt McKenzie. **SC:** Lez Brotherston. **L:** Chris Davey. **Pr:** Theatre Royal, Plymouth, May 2000.
D: *Luca*: Alan Vincent (Will Kemp, Ewan Wardrop); *Lana*: Saranne Curtin (Michela Meazza); *Angelo*: Will Kemp (Ewan Wardrop, Arthur Pita); *Rita*: Etta Murfitt (Emily Piercy); *Dino*: Scott Ambler; Vicky Evans, Adam Galbraith, Vicky Evans, Heather Habens, Ben Hartley, Michela Meazza, Etta Murfitt, Neil Penlington, Emily Piercy, Arthur Pita, Alan Vincent. AMP.

This production ran for 19 weeks at the Old Vic, London. It also toured in 2001 to Lisbon, Amsterdam, Tel Aviv, and the USA (St Paul, Los Angeles, Berkeley). In 2002 it toured Japan.

Taped music was used in Portugal, Amsterdam and Tel Aviv when under AMP in 2001.

NP: NA.
FP: Theatre Royal, Plymouth, 18 June 2007.
D: *Luca*: Alan Vincent (James Leece, Adam Galbraith); *Lana*: Michela Meazza (Gemma Payne, Emily Molina); *Angelo*: Richard Winsor (Sam Archer); *Rita*: Kerry Biggin (Hannah Vassallo, Shelby Williams); *Dino*: Scott Ambler.

For this production, the subtitle was dropped.

This production ran for 4 weeks at Sadler's Wells Theatre in 2007, and toured 13 other cities in the UK.

Taped music was used for some touring venues in this 2007 revival.

2001

My Fair Lady

Musical

M: Frederick Loewe. **Ly:** Alan J. Lerner. **Pr:** 6 March 2001, Lyttelton Theatre (National Theatre), London. **Pro:** Cameron Mackintosh. **Dir:** Trevor Nunn. **Choreography and Musical Staging:** Matthew Bourne. **SC:** Anthony Ward. **L:** David Hersey. **So:** Paul Groothuis. **O:** William David Brohn. **DA:** Chris Walker. **MD:** Stephen Brooker.
A: *Professor Henry Higgins*: Jonathan Pryce; *Eliza Doolittle*: Martine McCutcheon; *Alfred P. Doolittle*: Dennis Waterman; *Pickering*: Nicholas Le Prevost; *Mrs Pearce*: Patsy Rowlands; *Mrs Higgins*: Caroline Blakiston.
FP: 5/6 March 2001. **ON:** 15 March, 2001. NT.

There were 132 performances at the Olivier Theatre.

ST: Theatre Royal Drury Lane. **FP:** 21 July 2001. **ON:** 24 July 2001, running until 30 August 2003. The production also did extensive national (2005–6) and international (2007–8) touring.

Later interpreters of Henry Higgins in this production included Alex Jennings, Anthony Andrews, Christopher Casenove, and Harry Burton. Later interpreters of Eliza included Joanna Riding, Laura Michelle Kelly, Lisa O'Hare.

Later interpreters of Mrs Higgins (on USA Tour) included Sally-Anne Howes (who had been the second actress to play Eliza in *My Fair Lady* on Broadway) and Marni Nixon (who had sung Eliza's songs for Audrey Hepburn in the film)

South Pacific

Musical

M: Richard Rodgers. **Ly and Bk:** Oscar Hammerstein II. **Original O:** Robert Russell Bennett. **Pr:** 3 December 2001, Olivier Theatre (National Theatre), London. **Dir:** Trevor Nunn. **New O:** William David Brohn. **S:** John Napier. **C:** Elise Napier and John Napier. **Ch and MS:** Matthew Bourne. **SC:** Anthony Ward. **L:** David Hersey. **So:** Paul Groothuis. **O:** William David Brohn. **MD:** Stephen Brooker.

A: *Nellie Forbush*: Lauren Kennedy; *Emile de Becque*: Philip Quast; *Bloody Mary*: Sheila Francisco; *Lt Joe Cable*: Edward Baker-Duly; *Luther Billis*: Nick Holder; *Captain George Brackett*: John Shrapnel.
FP: 30 November 2001. ON: 12 December 2001.

There were 163 performances at the Olivier Theatre.

2002

Play Without Words

Production in two acts, devised and directed by Matthew Bourne

Ch: Matthew Bourne and the company. **CM:** Terry Davies. **SC:** Lez Brotherston. **L:** Paule Constable. **MD:** Michael Haslam. **So:** Christopher Shutt.
D: *Anthony*: Will Kemp, Ewan Wardrop, Richard Winsor; *Glenda*: Saranne Curtin, Michela Meazza, Emily Piercy; *Prentice*: Scott Ambler, Steve Kirkham, Eddie Nixon; *Sheila*: Belinda Lee Chapman, Valentina Formenti; *Speight*: Alan Vincent, Ewan Wardrop, Eddie Nixon.
FP: Lyttelton Theatre (National Theatre), 20 August 2002. **ON:** 23 August 2002. A National Theatre and New Adventures co-production.

The original 2002 production had 30 performances. The 2003 revival had 54 at the Lyttelton Theatre. The UK tour (2004) had 70 performances. The foreign tour included Tokyo (70 performances) in 2004, and the USA (Brooklyn and Los Angeles, 81 performances) and Moscow (8 performances) in 2005.
   Excerpts are on YouTube.

2004

Mary Poppins

New Musical

Author of the original 'Mary Poppins' stories: P. L. Travers. Co-created by Cameron Mackintosh.

Pr: A Disney and Cameron Mackintosh presentation, produced for Disney Theatrical Prods by Thomas Schumacher. **Bk:** Julian Fellowes.

Original film M: Richard M. Sherman and Ly: Robert B. Sherman. CM and DA: George Stiles. New Ly: Anthony Drewe. Dir: Richard Eyre. Co-dir and Ch: Matthew Bourne. Co-Ch: Stephen Mear. O: William David Brohn. SC: Bob Crowley. L: Howard Harrison. Si: Andrew Bruce. MS: David Caddick. MD: Nick Davies.

A: *Mary Poppins*: Laura Michelle Kelly; *Bert*: Gavin Lee; *Mr Banks*: David Haig; *Mrs Banks*: Linzi Hateley; *Jane Banks*: Charlotte Spencer (Nicola Bowman, Carrie Fletcher, Poppy Lee Friar, Faye Spittlehouse); *Michael Banks*: Harry Stott (Jake Caterall, Perry Millward, Ben Watton); *Mrs Brill*: Jenny Galloway; *Admiral Boom* and *Bank Chairman*: Ian Burford; *Bird Woman*: Julia Sutton; *Miss Andrew* and *Queen Victoria*: Rosemary Ashe; *Valentine*: Nathan Taylor; *Robertson Ay*: Gerard Carey. FP: Bristol Hippodrome, 12 September 2004, running to 2 November. Prince Edward Theatre, London: FP: 2 December 2004. ON: 15 December 2004.

The production ran at the Prince Edward Theatre to 12 January 2008. It also toured the UK (Plymouth, Birmingham, Edinburgh) in June–December 2008.

Notable replacements included Scarlett Strallen and Lisa O'Hare as Mary Poppins and Gavin Creel as Bert.

On 17 March 2005, Julie Andrews (Mary Poppins in the film) visited the show as a guest. She joined the cast on stage during curtain calls, and gave a speech recalling her own memories from making the film and praising the cast for their new interpretation.

NP: New Amsterdam Theatre, New York. FP: 14 October 2006. ON: 16 November 2006. This production featured revised designs, especially with full colour for 'Jolly Holiday'.
A: *Mary Poppins*: Ashley Brown; *Bert*: Gavin Lee; *Mr Banks*: Daniel H. Jenkins; *Mrs Banks*: Rebecca Luker; *Jane Banks*: Katherine Doherty, Kathryn Faughnan, Delaney Moro (alternating); *Michael Banks*: Matthew Gumley, Henry Hodges, Alexander Scheitinger (alternating); *Mrs Brill*: Jane Carr; *Bird Woman*: Cass Morgan; *Miss Andrew, Queen Victoria, Miss Smythe*: Ruth Gottschall; *Robertson Ay*: Mark Price; *Admiral Boom, Bank Chairman*: Michael McCarty.

Notable later interpreters of Mary Poppins included Scarlett Strallen and Laura Michelle Kelly. Later Berts included Adam Fiorentino and Christian Borle.

This production celebrated 1,000 performances on 9 April 2009. It has also toured extensively in the USA.

Excerpts are on YouTube.

ST: The production has also been staged in The Hague (The Netherlands) and Melbourne (Australia). Other productions – in Stockholm (Sweden), Helsinki (Finland), Copenhagen (Denmark), Budapest (Hungary), Brno (Czech Republic) – were made without direction or choreography by Bourne.

2005

Edward Scissorhands

Dance production in two acts

Dir and Ch: Matthew Bourne. **Original story and motion picture director:** Tim Burton. **Original screenplay, story and co-adaptation:** Caroline Thompson. **CM:** Terry Davies, based in part on original motion-picture score by Danny Elfman. **SC:** Lez Brotherston. **L:** Howard Harrison. **So:** Paul Groothuis.

D: Two casts are given both because they alternated and because each contributed to the roles' creation in rehearsal. *Edward*: Sam Archer (Richard Winsor); *Kim Boggs*: Kerry Biggin (Hannah Vassallo); *James 'Jim' Upton*: James Leece (Adam Galbraith); *Peg Boggs*: Etta Murfitt (Madelaine Brennan); *Bill Boggs*: Scott Ambler (Andrew Corbett); *Joyce Monroe*: Michela Meazza (Mikah Smillie); *George Monroe*: Steve Kirkham (Andrew Corbett); *Kevin Boggs*: Gavin Eden (Drew McOnie); *Bunny Monroe*: Sophia Hurdley (Mikah Smillie); *Gerald Monroe*: Shaun Walters (Drew McOnie); *Charity Upton*: Heather Habens (Mikah Smillie); *Mayor Franklin Upton*: Gareth Charlton (Adam Galbraith); *Darlene Upton*: Gemma Payne (Mami Tomotani); *Esmeralda Evercreech*: Rachel Morrow (Rachel Lancaster); *Rev Judas Evercreech*: Matthew Malthouse (Ross Carpenter); *Marilyn-Ann Evercreech*: Shelby Williams (Rachel Lancaster); *Gabriel Evercreech*: Ross Carpenter (Philip Willingham); *Tiffany Covitt*: Madelaine Brennan (Mikah Smillie); *Brad Covitt*: Jake Samuels (James Leece); *Candy Covitt*: Hannah Vassallo (Rachel Lancaster/Kerry Biggin); *Chase Covitt*: Philip Willingham (Drew McOnie); *Gloria Grubb*: Mami Tomotani (Rachel Lancaster); *Manny Grubb*: Adam Galbraith (Andrew Corbett);

Sandra Grubb: Dena Lague (Sophia Hurdley); *Sheldon Grubb*: Lee Smikle (Drew McOnie); *The Inventor*: Adam Galbraith (Andrew Corbett): *Little Edward*: Gavin Eden (Drew McOnie); *Old Kim*: Madelaine Brennan (Mikah Smillie); *Cheerleaders*: Hannah Vassallo, Madelaine Brennan (Kerry Biggin, Mikah Smillie/Rachel Lancaster); *TV Reporters*: Andrew Corbett (Steve Kirkham) and Madelaine Brennan (Mikah Smillie); *Photographer*: Adam Galbraith (Andrew Corbett).
FP: Theatre Royal, Plymouth, 14 November 2005. New Adventures.

Bourne's dedication: 'For Mum. You always made me feel special, but it was you who were the special one.' June Bourne died in 2006.

This production ran at Sadler's Wells for 11 weeks in 2005–6, toured to 13 other cities and Japan in 2006, and in 2006–7 did a six-month 12-city tour of the USA and Canada. In 2008–9, it toured Australia (Sydney, Brisbane, Perth, Melbourne), Paris, the UK (Manchester, Wimbledon, and 7 weeks at Sadler's Wells), Athens and Antwerp. The final performance on 22 February 2009, was its 585th performance.

For the 2008–9 tour, Matthew Malthouse and Dominic North alternated as Edward, while Noi Tolmer (replacing Hannah Vassallo) became one of the interpreters of the role of Kim.

Excerpts are on You Tube.

2008

Dorian Gray

Dance production in two acts

Based on novel *The Portrait of Dorian Gray* by Oscar Wilde. **Dir and C:** Matthew Bourne. **CM:** Terry Davies. **SC:** Lez Brotherston. **L:** Paule Constable. **V:** Mark Grimmer. **So:** Paul Groothuis.

D: *Dorian Gray*: Richard Winsor; *Lady H.*: Michela Meazza; *Basil*: Aaron Sillis; *Cyril Vane*: Christopher Marney; *Doppelgänger*: Jared Hageman; *Edward Black*: Ashley Bain; *Other roles*: Drew McOnie, Ebony Molina, Joe Walkling, Shaun Walters, Chloe Wilkinson.
FP: Theatre Royal, Plymouth 14 August 2008 (previews). **ON:** Edinburgh Festival, King's Theatre, August 2008, as part of the Edinburgh International Festival. New Adventures.

Dedicated: 'For Simon Carter (1960–2008). With love and thanks for 37 years of friendship and laughter. MB.'

There were no alternate casts until 2009, when Jared Hageman (*Dorian*), Dominic North (*Cyril Vane*), Christopher Marney (*Basil*), Adam Maskell (*Doppelgänger*), and Joe Colasanti (*Edward Black*) alternated with the original interpreters. Jason Piper replaced Aaron Sillis as Basil for this tour.

The production enjoyed greater box-office success than any previous production in the history of the Edinburgh International Festival.

In 2008, this production toured three other cities in Britain, including Sadler's Wells Theatre, London. In 2009, its tour included Italy (Ravenna and Parma), Moscow, and 13 cities in the UK, including a return to Sadler's Wells.

Excerpts are on YouTube.

Oliver!

Musical

See 1994 production. **NP: P:** Cameron Mackintosh; **Dir:** Rupert Goold. **Co-Dir:** Matthew Bourne. **Ch:** Matthew Bourne. **Co-Ch:** Geoff Garrett. **SC:** Anthony Ward; **L:** Paule Constable. **So:** Paul Groothuis. **O:** William David Brohn. **DA:** Chris Walker. **MD:** Graham Hurman.
A: *Fagin:* Rowan Atkinson; *Nancy:* Jodie Prenger (Tamsin Carroll); *Bill Sikes:* Burn Gorman; *Oliver:* Harry Stott (Laurence Jeffcoate, Gwion Wyn Jones); *Artful Dodger:* Ross McCormack; *Mr Brownlow:* Julian Glover; *Mr Sowerberry, Mr Grimwig:* Julian Bleach; *Mrs Sowerberry:* Louise Gold; *Mr Bumble:* Julius D'Silva; *Widow Corney:* Wendy Ferguson.

FP: Theatre Royal, Drury Lane, 13 December 2008. **ON:** 14 January 2009.

As in 1994, Bourne's choreography was for Fagin and the children; the children were now increased in number. The production is running at the time of this book going to press.

Notable subsequent Fagins have included Russ Abbott, Omid Djalili, Griff Rhys Jones.

Excerpts are on YouTube.

2011

Lord of the Flies

Based on novel *Lord of the Flies* by William Golding. **Dir and C:** Matthew Bourne. **CM:** Terry Davies. **SC:** Lez Brotherston. **L:** Chris Davey. **So:** Paul Groothuis. **AD:** Scott Ambler
D: Adam Galbraith, Danny Reubens, Dominic North, Jack Jones, Luke Murphy, Philip Jack Gardner, Sam Plant, Tim Bartlett.
FP: Theatre Royal, Glasgow. 2 March 2011. New Adventures.

Index